P9-DGU-255

The Purposeful Argument:
A Practical Guide

Second Edition

Harry R. Phillips

Patricia Bostian

Central Piedmont Community College

All Illustrations by iStockphoto.com/A-digit

CENGAGE

Australia • Brazil • Mexico • Singapore • United Kingdom • United States

CENGAGE

The Purposeful Argument:
   A Practical Guide
Second Edition
Harry Phillips, Patricia Bostian
Product Director: Monica Eckman

Product Manager: Kate Derrick

Senior Content Developer: Leslie Taggart

Development Editor: Stephanie Pelkowski
   Carpenter

Managing Developer: Megan Garvey

Product Assistant: Cailin Barrett-Bressack

Media Developer: Janine Tangney

Marketing Brand Manager: Lydia LeStar

Senior Content Project Manager:
   Aimee Chevrette Bear

Art Director: Hannah Wellman

Manufacturing Planner: Betsy Donaghey

Rights Acquisition Specialist: Ann Hoffman

Production Service: Q2A/Bill Smith

Text Designer: Shawn Girsberger

Cover Designer: Wing Ngan

Cover Image: © ZUMA Press, Inc. / Alamy

Compositor: Q2A/Bill Smith

For product information and technology assistance, contact us at
Cengage Customer & Sales Support, 1-800-354-9706

For permission to use material from this text or product,
submit all requests online at **www.cengage.com/permissions**.
Further permissions questions can be emailed to
permissionrequest@cengage.com.

Library of Congress Control Number:

Student Edition

ISBN-13: 978-1-285-43805-4

ISBN-10: 1-285-43805-1

Cengage
20 Channel Center Street
Boston, MA 02210
USA

Cengage Learning is a leading provider of customized learning solutions
with office locations around the globe, including Singapore, the United
Kingdom, Australia, Mexico, Brazil and Japan. Locate your local office at
international.cengage.com/region.

Cengage Learning products are represented in Canada by
Nelson Education, Ltd.

To learn more about Cengage platforms and services, register or access
your online learning solution, or purchase materials for your course, visit
www.cengage.com.

Instructors: Please visit **login.cengage.com** and log in to access instructor-
specific resources.

Printed at CLDPC, USA, 08-18

BRIEF CONTENTS

Preface   xv

PART 1   How to Approach Argument in Real Life   1

 1   Argue with a Purpose   2

 2   Explore an Issue That Matters to You   21

PART 2   How to Establish Context Through Research   51

 3   Develop a Research Plan   52

 4   Evaluate and Engage with Your Sources   80

 5   Read Critically and Avoid Fallacies   110

 6   Work Fairly with the Opposition   136

PART 3   How to Plan, Structure, and Deliver an Argument   155

 7   Explore an Issue   156

 8   Consider Toulmin-Based Argument   187

 9   Consider Middle Ground Argument, Rogerian Argument, and Argument Based on a Microhistory   205

 10   Build Arguments   239

 11   Support an Argument with Fact (*Logos*), Credibility (*Ethos*), and Emotion (*Pathos*)   271

PART 4   How to Take Ownership of Your Argument: A Style Guide   293

 12   Enhance Your Argument with Visuals and Humor   294

 13   Develop and Edit Argument Structure and Style   319

PART 5   An Anthology of Arguments   353

PART 6   MLA and APA Documentation Systems   621

 Glossary   660

 Index   665

Preface   xv

PART 1   How to Approach Argument in Real Life   1
1   Argue with a Purpose   2
2   Explore an Issue That Matters to You   21

PART 2   How to Establish Context Through Research   51
3   Develop a Research Plan   52
4   Evaluate and Engage with Your Sources   80
5   Read Critically and Avoid Fallacies   110
6   Work Fairly with the Opposition   136

PART 3   How to Plan, Structure, and Deliver an Argument   155
7   Explore an Issue   156
8   Consider Toulmin-Based Argument   187
9   Consider Middle Ground Argument, Rogerian Argument, and Argument Based on a Microhistory   202
10   Build Arguments   239
11   Support an Argument with Fact (Logos), Credibility (Ethos), and Emotion (Pathos)   271

PART 4   How to Take Ownership of Your Argument: A Style Guide   293
12   Enhance Your Argument with Visuals and Humor   294
13   Develop and Edit Argument Structure and Style   319

PART 5   An Anthology of Arguments   353

PART 6   MLA and APA Documentation Systems   621
Glossary   666
Index   665

Discover Causes or Consequences   164

Present Comparisons   168

Propose a Solution   170

    Section A: Exploring the Problem   171

    Section B: Different Types of Exploration   173

    Section C: Exploring Implementation   178

Evaluate Your Claim   181

Write an Exploratory Essay   183

    Sample Exploratory Essay   184

© iStockphoto.com/A-digit

8 Consider Toulmin-Based Argument   187

Construct an Argument to Fit Your Purpose   189

Terms of Toulmin-Based Argument   189

    Claim   191

    Reasons   191

    Support   191

    Warrant   192

    Backing   192

    Rebuttal   192

    Qualifiers   193

Map a Toulmin-Based Argument   194

Student-Authored Toulmin-Based Argument   198

9 Consider Middle Ground Argument, Rogerian Argument, and Argument Based on a Microhistory   205

Middle Ground Argument   207

    Make a Middle-Ground Position Practical   207

    Recognize Where Middle Ground Arguments Are Possible   208

    Map a Middle Ground Argument   209

Student-Authored Middle Ground Argument   214

Rogerian Argument   217

    Listen Closely to the Opposition   217

    Identify Common Ground   219

    Map a Rogerian Argument   221

Sample Rogerian Argument   224

Argument Based on a Microhistory   226

    Focus on the Local and Specific   226

TABLE OF CONTENTS

Preface   xv

PART 1   How to Approach Argument in Real Life   1

1   Argue with a Purpose   2

What Argument Is and What Argument Is Not   3
Excerpt from "The Price of Admission," by Thomas Frank   4

Recognize Where Argument Is Appropriate in Real Life   6

Argue about Issues That Matter to You   7

Establish Local Context via the Research Process   10
Determine Your Audience   10
Establish Local Context for Your Issue   11
Connect Local and Global Contexts   13

Recognize Why Arguments Break Down   15
Arguments Break Down When They Do Not Persuade an Audience   15
Arguments Break Down When There Is a Lack of Balance in the Support   15
Arguments Break Down When the Audience Is Poorly Defined   15
Arguments Break Down When They Contain Fallacies   16
Arguments Break Down When They Do Not Fairly Represent Opposing Views   16

Match Argument with Purpose   16
Toulmin-Based Argument   17
Middle Ground Argument   17
Rogerian Argument   18
Argument Based on a Microhistory   19

2   Explore an Issue that Matters to You   21

Determine What Matters to You and Why   23

School/Academic   23

Workplace   24

Family/Household   24

Neighborhood   25

Social/Cultural   25

Consumer   25

Concerned Citizen   26

Choose an Issue within a Topic   27

Pre-Think about Your Issue   29

Brainstorming   29

Freewriting   30

Mapping   30

Move from Boring to Interesting   30

Define and Target Your Audience   32

Stake, Defend, and Justify Your Claim   34

Develop a Claim, Reasons, and Qualifiers   34

Argue with a Purpose   36

Vary the Types of Support You Bring to an Argument   37

Support Based on Fact   37

Support Based on Your Character   37

Support Based on the Emotions of an Audience   38

Working with a Target Audience: Two Examples   38

Argue at the Right Moment   46

Getting Started   47

© iStockphoto.com/A-digit

PART 2   How to Establish Context Through Research   51

3   Develop a Research Plan   52

Use Reference Works, Encyclopedias, and Topic Overviews Profitably   54

Read an Overview of Your Topic   54

Gather Search Terms   56

Use Search Engines to Find Internet Sources on the Surface Web and on the Deep Web   57

Search the Surface Web   57

Search the Deep Web   59

Perform Keyword Queries   61

Find News Sites and Use RSS Feeds to Receive Updates   62

Find and Use Databases in Libraries   64

Find and Use Primary Sources   68
  Find and Use Government Sources   70
  Find and Use Multimedia Sources   72

Find Books   75
  Find Books in Libraries   75
  Find Books on the Internet   77

4   Evaluate and Engage with Your Sources   80

Take Notes, Read Critically, and Evaluate Internet Sites   81
  Critically Read Material on the Internet   82
  Evaluate Internet Sites   83

Take Notes, Read Critically, and Evaluate Articles   84
  Read Articles Critically   85
  Reading Strategies for Longer Articles   86
  Evaluate Articles   90

Take Notes and Read Books Critically   90

Take Notes and Evaluate Primary Sources   91

Introduce and Comment on Sources   92

Quote and Cite Quotations   95
  Quoting Material Quoted in the Original Source   98
  Alter Quoted Material   99

Summarize and Cite Summaries   100

Paraphrase and Cite Paraphrases   101

Avoid Plagiarism   105

Documentation: Works Cited Page   107

5   Read Critically and Avoid Fallacies   110

Define Fallacies   111

Identify and Avoid Fallacies   112

Avoid Fallacies of Choice   114
  Blanket Statement   115
  False Dilemma, Either–Or, and Misuse of Occam's Razor   116
  Slippery Slope   117

Avoid Fallacies of Support   119

    Circular Argument   119

    Hasty Generalization and Jumping to Conclusions   120

    Faulty Causality: Post Hoc, Ergo Propter Hoc   *120*

    Non Sequitur, Red Herring, and False Clue   *121*

    Straw Man Argument or Argument Built on a False Fact or Claim   122

Avoid Fallacies of Emotion   124

    Ad Hominem   124

    Testimonials and False Authority   125

    Bandwagon   126

    Ad Misericordiam   126

    Scare Tactics   126

Avoid Fallacies of Inconsistency   128

    Moral Equivalence   129

    Material Equivalence   129

    Definitional Equivalence   129

    Inconsistent Treatment (from Dogmatism, Prejudice, and Bias)   130

    Equivocation   130

    False Analogy   131

6   Work Fairly with the Opposition   136

Why the Opposition Matters   138

Resist Easy Generalizations   139

Listen to Local Voices   140

Summarize Other Voices Fairly   141

Value Expertise over Advocacy   145

Avoid Bias When You Summarize   146

Find Points of Overlap   148

    Identify Common Ground with the Opposition   148

Respond to Other Views   151

PART 3   How to Plan, Structure, and Deliver an Argument   155

7   Explore an Issue   156

Use Definitions   158

    Seven Types of Definition   160

Make Room for Local Histories   227

Work with Primary Materials   229

Subjects and Materials for Microhistories   230

Map an Argument Based on a Microhistory   231

Sample Argument Based on a Microhistory   233

10   Build Arguments   239

How a Claim Functions   241

Claim: The Center of Your Argument   241

Connect Claim with Purpose   243

Five Kinds of Claims   244

Claim of Fact   244

Claim of Definition   246

Problem-Based Claims   248

Claim of Evaluation   249

Claim of Cause   251

Use Reasons to Support Your Claim   252

Build Body Paragraphs around Reasons   255

Use Qualifiers to Make Your Argument Believable   257

Justify Your Claim with a Warrant   259

Use Your Audience to Construct a Warrant   260

Know What Your Audience Values   260

Let a Warrant Bridge Claim and Support   261

Use Backing to Support a Warrant   263

Let Your Audience Determine the Extent of Backing   264

Make Backing Specific   265

Respond to Audience Reservations to Make a Warrant Believable   267

11   Support an Argument with Fact (*Logos*), Credibility (*Ethos*), And Emotion (*Pathos*)   271

Field-Specific Support   272

Find Support for the Physical Sciences   273

Find Support for Education, History, and Social and Behavioral Sciences   274

Find Sources for the Humanities and the Arts   275

Use All Three General Kinds of Support   276

Use Support Based on Facts and Research (*Logos*)   277

Facts and Opinions   277

© iStockphoto.com/A-digit

Statistics   279
Scholarly Articles   283

Use Support to Create Credibility (*Ethos*)   284

Use Support to Create Emotion (*Pathos*)   287
Anecdotes   288
Photographs   289

PART 4   How to Take Ownership of Your Argument: A Style Guide   293

12   Enhance Your Argument With Visuals and Humor   194

What Are Visual Arguments?   295

Understanding and Using Visual Arguments   297
Reading Photographs and Illustrations   302
Using Photographs and Illustrations in Your Argument   305
Reading Graphs and Charts   306
Using and Creating Graphs in Your Argument   308
Reading Advertisements   310
PowerPoint Presentations   311

Uses for Humor in Argument   312
Strategies for Using Humor   313
Using Humor in Your Arguments   316

13   Develop and Edit Argument Structure and Style   319

Consider Your Argument's Claim   320
Introduce Your Claim   320
State Your Claim   323
Position Your Claim   326

Introduce Your Opposition   329
The Opposing View Is Incorrect   330
The Opposing View Is Correct, but ...   330

Create Strong Introductions   331
Anecdote   332
Misdirection   332
Conflict   333
Suspense   334
A Seeming Impossibility   335

Write Memorable Conclusions   336
  Broadening Out   336
  Opposition   337
  Circling Back   338

Edit and Organize Your Argument's Support   339
  Edit Support   339
  Organize Your Support   342
  Three Organization Samples of Body Paragraphs   343

Supply a Strong Title   347

Participate Effectively in a Peer Review Session   348
  Your Role as a Reviewer   350
  Your Role as a Reviewee   350

© iStockphoto.com/A-digit

PART 5   An Anthology of Arguments   353

Intersections   Contemporary Issues and Arguments   354

School and Academic Community   354
  Karoun Demirjian, *What is the Price of Plagiarism?*   354
  Gad Saad, *I'll Have Large Fries, a Hamburger, a Diet Coke, and an MBA. Hold the Pickles*   357
  Douglas B. Reeves, *Remaking the Grade, From A to D*   360
  Michael J. Seiden, *For-Profit Colleges Deserve Some Respect*   364
  Anna Lappé, *Cafeteria Consciousness*   367
  Jeffrey J. Williams, *Are Students the New Indentured Servants?*   372

Workplace Community   380
  Gar Alperovitz and Keane Bhatt, *Employee-Owned Businesses Ignored by Mainstream Media*   380
  David L. Hudson Jr., *Site Unseen: Schools, Bosses Barred from Eyeing Students',
    Workers' Social Media*   383
  Jan Edwards and Molly Morgan, *Abolish Corporate Personhood (Thinking Politically)*   386
  Rinaldo Brutoco and Sam Yau, *The Current Business Paradigm is Toxic to Business
    and Society. Here's How We Change It.*   393
  Ken MacQueen, with Martin Patriquin and John Intini, *Dealing with the Stressed: Workplace Stress
    Costs the Economy More Than $30 Billion a Year, and Yet Nobody Knows What It Is or How to Deal
    with It*   404
  Rich Meneghello, *Solutions at Work: When Love Enters the Workplace*   410
  Danny Postel, *I'm Not Dangerous*   413
  Denise Venable, *Women Do Not Earn Less than Men Due to Gender Discrimination*   415

Family and Household Community   418
  Mary Eberstadt, *Eminem is Right: The Primal Scream of Teenage Music*   418
  Sue Ferguson, *Leaving the Doors Open*   424
  Jewel, *Street Life is No Life for Children*   427

Environment News Service, *North America: Ecological Breakup*   431

Richard Louv, *Introduction from Last Child in the Woods: Saving Our Children From Nature-Deficit Disorder*   432

Gregory A. Pence, *Reproductive Cloning Would Strengthen the American Family*   435

Mugambi Jouet, *Why Gay Marriage Is So Controversial in America*   442

Dahr Jamail, *A Morally Bankrupt Military: When Soldiers and Their Families Become Expendable*   445

Neighborhood Community   451

Leo W. Banks, *Under Siege*   451

Isabelle Nastasia and Manissa McCleave Maharawal, *Why Race Matters After Sandy*   457

Leyla Kokmen, *Environmental Justice for All*   460

Tim Guest, *Crime in Virtual Worlds Is Impacting Real Life*   466

Philip Mattera, *Greenwashing Remains a Challenge to the Green Building Community*   472

Tracie McMillan, *Jicama in the 'Hood*   477

Eleanor Novek, *You Wouldn't Fit Here*   483

James Q. Wilson, *Bowling with Others*   489

Social/Cultural Community   496

Christian Science Monitor Editorial Board, *The Potential in Hillary Clinton's Campaign for Women*   496

Daniel J. Solove, *Why "Security" Keeps Winning Out Over Privacy*   498

Leadership Conference on Civil Rights Education Fund, *Wrong Then, Wrong Now: Racial Profiling Before & After September 11, 2001*   501

Doug Walp, *The Importance of Political Awareness in America*   506

Michael N. Nagler, *The Cassandra Syndrome*   508

Valerie White, *A Humanist Looks at Polyamory*   510

Jeff Yang, *Killer Reflection*   515

Consumer Community   520

Judith Simmer Brown, *A Buddhist Perspective on Consumerism*   520

David Ebel, *Telemarketers Should Be Censored*   524

Ray Fisman, *It's Like eBay Meets Match.com: Does Peer-to-Peer Lending Work?*   527

Dinyar Godrej, *The Ad Industry Pins Us Down*   530

Mark Boyle, *Buy Nothing Day 2012 Is Approaching. Could You Stop Spending for One Day?*   535

Andy Kroll, *How the McEconomy Bombed the American Worker: The Hollowing Out of the Middle Class*   538

Oliver Broudy, *The Practical Ethicist: "The Way We Eat" Author Pete Singer Explains the Advantage of Wingless Chickens, How Humans Discriminate Against Animals, and the Downside of Buying Locally Grown Food*   542

Dali L. Yang, *Outsourcing Compromises the Safety and Quality of Products*   548

Concerned Citizen Community   555

Harry Binswanger, *The United States Should Adopt Open Immigration*   555

James L. Dickerson, *Climate Change Could Cause Disease Resurgence*   560

Tom Engelhardt, *Is America Hooked on War?*   564

Chris Hedges, *Corporate Media Obituary of Occupy Premature*   569

David Kelley, *Private Charity Should Replace Welfare*   573

Paul Roberts, *Over a Barrel*   579

Matthew Rothschild, *Nationalize the Banks*   583

Alexander Keyssar, *Voter Repression Returns: Voting Rights and Partisan Practices*   587

Classic American Arguments   592

Susan B. Anthony, *On Women's Right to Vote*   592

Mary Antin, *Have We Any Right to Regulate Immigration?*   593

Alexander Hamilton, *The Federalist No. 6*   598

Thomas Jefferson, *The Unanimous Declaration of the Thirteen United States of America*   603

H. L. Mencken, *The Penalty of Death*   606

Judith Sargent Murray, *On the Equality of the Sexes*   609

Leo Szilard and Cosigners, *A Petition to the President of the United States*   612

Sojourner Truth, *Ain't I a Woman?*   614

Booker T. Washington, *Atlanta Compromise Address*   616

PART 6   MLA and APA Documentation Systems   621

APPENDIX A   MLA Documentation and the List of Works Cited   622

APPENDIX B   APA Documentation and the Reference List   643

Glossary   660

Index   665

- Part Four, "How to Take Ownership of Your Argument: A Style Guide," now includes a guide for obtaining peer reviews of one's writing.
- Twelve new essays in the anthology, Part Five, demonstrate how contemporary writers build arguments in response to specific issues affecting the seven communities addressed in *The Purposeful Argument*: school, the workplace, family, neighborhood, social-cultural, consumer, and concerned citizen.
- Part Six, MLA and APA Documentation Systems, now contains a complete APA student essay to accompany the annotated MLA student essay.

Key Features

- Writers are encouraged to argue in response to issues in their everyday and academic environments—school, the workplace, family, neighborhood, social-cultural, consumer, and concerned citizen—and thus learn how argument can become an essential negotiating skill in their lives. This book emphasizes local and intellectual issues throughout and provides a methodology for connecting the local with global trends. Importantly, this allows writers to build a strong understanding of an issue by generating broad context.
- Argument structure is presented in practical, how-to ways, complete with exercises, charts, and real-life examples. Ways to organize an argument—Toulmin-based, Rogerian, Middle Ground, and Microhistory options—are fully defined and demonstrated.
- Simplified text format and page layout improve upon conventional argument textbook design by making information direct and accessible.
- Checklists throughout *The Purposeful Argument* provide support for writers as they craft their own arguments.
- Annotated examples of effective arguments illustrate strengths and weaknesses.
- "Your Turn" exercises consist of questions and prompts so that writers can apply argument structure to arguments they are building. "Internet Activity" prompts direct writers to online investigations that connect to the research process.
- "Tips" panels typically are clues for ways of thinking about a feature of argument during the planning process.
- Key terms are bolded throughout the text. A Glossary related to practical argument provides an alphabetized reference for these and other terms found in *The Purposeful Argument*. A term is defined with regard to its function and placement in an argument.

PREFACE

Purpose

Since our department first offered a course in argumentative writing in 1998, teachers at our community college have expressed frustration with the range of textbooks available for the course. This second edition of *The Purposeful Argument* continues to respond to this concern. Our textbook—aimed at freshman writers at two- and four-year colleges—delivers the essentials of argumentative writing in accessible, student-friendly language. The textbook allows writers to recognize where argument fits in their lives and how it can be a practical response both to the issues in everyday life and to academic and intellectual problems encountered in the classroom. In this way, the text meets student writers on their own terms, in their own lives, and demands that they determine what they argue about. Changes to this new edition reflect the suggestions of our students and those of veteran teachers of argument, who are sensitive to what makes a textbook genuinely useful.

The philosophical center of *The Purposeful Argument* rests with John Dewey's notion that public education can best serve a democratic culture when it connects classroom with community and by thinking of the classroom as a laboratory for intelligent democratic activity. Building on this idea, those who argue competently can become the lifeblood of local action and change. Put another way, a nation, state, or community that does not engage purposefully in regular discussion and informed argument cannot fulfill itself.

Accessibility is central to the purpose of this project, and this second edition includes a streamlining of many features of the textbook. From many students' perspectives, some current argument texts are dense and filled with examples apart from their worlds. In response to these concerns, *The Purposeful Argument* relies less on discussion via traditional academic language to get across a concept and more on cogent definition, explicit example, and practical exercises that guide student writers through the process of assembling an argument. Examples of student, local, and professional writing are in many cases annotated and color-coded so as to identify elements of argument structure.

From another perspective, *The Purposeful Argument* puts in place the groundwork for student writers to create possibilities for themselves in a culture that demands more and more from its citizens. When so much of what we encounter has to do with the lure of consumption, and when so much of our national discourse is riveted to economic conditions, job security, and terror and intervention, it can be tough for freshman writers to think of themselves as agents capable of meaningful change. But at its core, *The Purposeful Argument* argues this very position. In its purest moment, this guide enables student writers to establish rhetorical places for themselves that ideally can reinvigorate our democracy via responsible citizenship. Because communication is less local in advanced industrial nations, this project invites a return to a more traditional form of democratic participation with its attention to local engagement. And local engagement can begin with a writer's commitment to the idea that the private responsibility to argue is essential to the public good.

With this emphasis on local engagement, we have noticed stronger, more focused arguments in the past several years. In general, when students are encouraged to honor and respond to issues that matter to them, their investment becomes evident and the writing, purposeful. This kind of ownership, we believe, results from an approach that steers writers into issues originating in the larger worlds of political, economic, and social issues as well as into their own worlds and concerns. With some students, this means arguing on issues that are solidly academic and intellectual in nature; with others, it means tackling issues of immediate concern in everyday life. Thus, compelling writing has emerged on issues as varied as the U. S. Supreme Court's ruling on corporate personhood, student loan requirements, China's behavior at the climate change conference in Copenhagen, favoritism in the workplace, recent health care reform and its implications for students, social networking and employment, religious values and curriculum design in Texas, and American consumers' role in the mining of "conflict minerals" in the Republic of the Congo.

A central focus of *The Purposeful Argument* is our intention to write to our specific audience—first-year writers—and this means delivering the fundamentals of argument to many nontraditional students, to nonnative speakers of English, to parents, to students who work one or more jobs, often in excess of the traditional work week, and to students who may or may not have experience with conceptual material and its application in their academic careers. This book is structured to accommodate our students and the diverse life experience they bring to our classrooms. Following are features of *The Purposeful Argument* that, in our view, distinguish it from the many excellent argument textbooks currently on the market—textbooks that may, however, fall outside the lines of accessibility and usefulness to many college students.

Organization and Chapter Flow

Part One of this guide attends to how effective arguments work. Chapter 1 introduces readers to essential features of argument and their interrelatedness. The chapter's sections move students into thinking about argument as a practical response to both everyday and academic issues and briefly introduce them to the types of argument found in the book. In Chapter 2, the crucial need to separate issue from topic is treated early. As a way to recognize issues and where they arise, this chapter identifies communities we belong to and some issues within these communities. The chapter offers numerous prompts and strategies for exploring an issue, such as prewriting activities that help students make a topic they might initially see as "boring" interesting to them and their readers. Audience focus, emphasized throughout the chapters, is introduced here, and students are presented with practical ways to determine appropriate audiences for their arguments. Arguing at the right time and establishing credibility fill out this chapter.

Part Two begins with the essential work of building clear context for an issue, the focus of Chapter 3. It is here that students are introduced to sources and how to access and use them. We choose to bring in the research process earlier rather than later because building a knowledge base often can enlarge the way we think about an issue, and this can influence what a writer claims and the way an argument is structured. Chapter 4 is geared toward the important work of using resources and how to read and evaluate them critically. As well, this chapter is a primer for working responsibly with borrowed material and ideas. Learning how to recognize and avoid fallacies is the center of Chapter 5. This chapter organizes fallacies—common in advertising and politics—into categories of choice, support, emotion, and inconsistency. Chapter 6 is devoted to the opposition, why it matters, how to work responsibly with it, and finding points of overlap. This chapter, we feel, adds to conventional approaches to opposing points of view.

Part Three treats the how-to of argument building. Chapter 7 helps students develop their argument strategies based on definitions, causes or consequences, comparisons, solution proposals, and evaluations, concluding with a rubric for preparing an exploratory essay. Discussion of Toulmin-based argument makes up Chapter 8. Chapter 9 introduces Rogerian argument, in addition to two less traditional approaches to argument in American classrooms: Middle Ground and Microhistory. We are enthusiastic about students learning to argue from a middle-ground perspective, as this approach insists on a close knowledge of audience and opposition. The middle-ground approach has, in the past few years, been popular among writers looking to escape either–or thinking and instead craft practical positions on complex issues. We are equally enthusiastic about a fourth kind of argument discussed in this chapter—an argument based on a microhistory—where writers work with primary documents and then forge a position apart from conventional understanding of the period in which these documents originate. Chapter 10 is about building arguments. It is example-rich and orients writers to the building blocks of argument—claims, reasons, qualifiers, support, the warrant, backing, and audience reservations. We view this chapter as one writers will use frequently during the drafting process. We elaborate in Chapter 11 on how to use support effectively, and this involves establishing writer credibility, specific appeals to audience, and a rubric for evaluating support brought to an argument.

Part Five is centered in the ideal of ownership, that is, in ways writers can make arguments distinctly their own. Chapter 12 is a discussion of tactics—visual argument and humor, among others—that let writers vary their approaches to an audience. And Chapter 13 is devoted to writing style and editing. While material in this final chapter is typically relegated to textbooks designed for earlier writing courses, we present this material in the context of argument writing as what we feel are necessary refreshers.

All chapters in Parts One through Four begin with a narrative that describes a real-life issue and conclude with a "Keeping It Local" exercise, pointing out that argument is a practical way to negotiate purposefully issues in everyday and academic life.

Part Five is an anthology of arguments written by everyday people who have stakes in local issues and by professional writers whose commentary on a given issue can provide a larger critical frame. Arguments are followed by questions tied to argument structure, audience, comprehension, and ways to connect concerns in the local community with the broader geopolitical culture. Another level of questions prompts students to acknowledge issues in their own lives that are the same or similar to issues found in the readings.

Part Six is devoted to MLA and APA documentation systems. For each system, guidelines and examples are provided. The important work of documenting carefully material borrowed from other writers and sources is addressed in this section.

New Features

- New examples illustrate each of the four types of argument *The Purposeful Argument* covers. These argument types are now spread over two chapters, with Chapter 8 devoted to Toulmin-based argument and Chapter 9 focused on Middle Ground argument, Rogerian argument, and argument based on a Microhistory.
- New assignments in Keeping It Local boxes at the end of each chapter prompt students to try out the chapter's strategies on an issue relevant to their own communities.
- New checklists throughout consolidate for students the key features of particular kinds of argumentative writing and research.
- Research is now consolidated in Part Two, making it easier for instructors to assign whenever they prefer.

Teaching and Learning Aids

The supplements listed here accompany *The Purposeful Argument*. They have been created with the diverse needs of today's students and instructors in mind.

- MindTap for *The Purposeful Argument*, 2/e, is a personalized, fully online digital learning platform of authoritative Cengage Learning content, assignments, and services that engages your students with interactivity while also offering you choice in the configuration of coursework and enhancement of the curriculum via complimentary web apps known as MindApps. MindTap is well beyond an ebook, a homework solution or digital supplement, a resource center website, a course delivery platform or a Learning Management System. It is the first in a new category—the Personal Learning Experience.

- The instructor's manual provides course-specific organization tools and classroom strategies, including sample syllabi, designs for mapping the course, assignment flow, ways to utilize the book, suggestions for teaching the course online, and ways to best use electronic resources. The center of the guide is a series of rubrics and exercises that can be adapted to an instructor's work with each chapter.

In sum, *The Purposeful Argument* is a student-centered approach to argument. It is a guide that lets students determine how they can use argument in life and equips them with a concrete, how-to approach. It lets instructors play to their strengths by letting writers work with their strengths—their investment in issues that matter to them in daily and classroom life. From the beginning, the text presents argument in ways that can empower and enable writers to publicly validate what most concerns them.

The Purposeful Argument is designed to complement and not overwhelm. The language of *The Purposeful Argument* is friendly and direct. Short, concise paragraphs are the rule; paragraphs are followed immediately by real-life examples, checklists, charts, rubrics, exercises, and sample student writings.

Competent, informed argument is as important today in American life as it was during other crucial periods in our history. It was and is a way to be heard and, when conditions permit, to be granted a seat at the discussion table. While public memory has shaped the way we view extraordinary moments in our past—indigenous peoples' fate at the hands of colonizers and an aggressive government, debates over sacred and secular ideals, arguments for political independence, the rhetoric of abolition and women's rights movements, the voice of labor, and the Civil Rights Movement—it is crucial to remember that, in addition to the arguments of accomplished writers, activists, and orators associated with these moments, a turbulence of voices was audible. These were the sounds of everyday people moving the culture forward. Without their contributions, the figures we celebrate now would be footnotes only. The voice of the individual *does* matter. If we choose not to speak up, others will make decisions for us.

ACKNOWLEDGMENTS

We are grateful to many individuals for their help creating this edition. Development Editor Stephanie Pelkowski Carpenter has shown Olympian patience with this current edition. She's also offered dozens of insightful suggestions regarding changes and new features. Her grasp of the project's vision from the beginning has guided the revision process. We are grateful in no small way for her professionalism.

Margaret Leslie, Senior Product Manager, deserves special recognition for her continued encouragement and good cheer and her ability to steer the project in very positive directions. Leslie Taggart, Senior Content Developer, Lydia LeStar, Brand Manager, and Aimee Bear, Senior Content Project Manager have our gratitude for their expert guidance throughout the process. Cailin Barrett-Bressack, Editorial Assistant, also provided timely and useful assistance.

The astute reviewers for this second edition helped us to identify ways to reach first-year writing students more effectively. We are grateful for their advice and ideas:

James Allen
College of DuPage

Karen Golightly
Christian Brothers University

Marsha Anderson
Wharton County Jr. College

Nate Gordon
Kishwaukee College

Lynnette Beers-McCormick
Santiago Canyon College

Lauren Hahn
DePaul University

Laura Black
Volunteer State Community
  College

Betty Hart
The University of Southern
  Indiana

Mary Chen
Tacoma Community College

Erik Juergensmeyer
Fort Lewis College

Kathleen Doherty
Middlesex Community College

Lindsay Lewan
Arapahoe Community College

Cassie Falke
East Texas Baptist University

Theodore Matula
University of San Francisco

Mandy McDougal
Volunteer State CC

Gary Montano
Tarrant County College

Elizabeth Oldfield
Southeastern Community
   College

M. Whitney Olsen
Arizona State University

Amy Ratto Park
University of Montana

Deborah Ruth
Owensboro Community and
   Technical College

Dan Sullivan
Davenport University

Robert Williams
Grossmont College

We also wish to thank members of the Advisory Review Board and the more than 65 reviewers and focus group participants who contributed steadily to the first edition. Their thoughtful feedback allowed us to refine and improve a range of chapter-specific features of this textbook.

Susan Achziger
Community College of Aurora

Kara Alexander
Baylor University

Steve Anderson
Normandale Community College

Sonja Andrus
Collin College

Joseph Antinarella
Tidewater Community College

Brad Beachy
Butler Community College

Evelyn Beck
Piedmont Technical College

Jeff Birkenstein
Saint Martin's University

Carol Bledsoe
Florida Gulf Coast University

David Bockoven
Linn-Benton Community College

Ashley Bourne
J Sargeant Reynolds Community
   College

Michael Boyd
Illinois Central College

Marty Brooks
John Tyler Community College

Shanti Bruce
Nova Southeastern University

JoAnn Buck
Guilford Technical Community
   College

Carol Burnell
Clackamas Community College

Anthony Cavaluzzi
Adirondack Community College

Mary Chen-Johnson
Tacoma Community College

Scott Clements
Keiser College, Melbourne
   Campus

Jennifer Courtney
University of North Carolina at
   Charlotte

Susan Davis
Arizona State University

James Decker
Illinois Central College

Tamra DiBenedetto
Riverside Community College

Connie Duke
Keiser University

Keri Dutkiewicz
Davenport University

Sarah M. Eichelman
Walters State Community College

Gareth Euridge
Tallahassee Community College

Jane Focht-Hansen
San Antonio College

MacGregor Frank
Guilford Technical Community
  College

Richard Gilbert
Benedictine University of Illinois

Nate Gordon
Kishwaukee College

Virginia Grant
Gaston College

Valerie Grey
Portland Community College

Annette Hale
Motlow State Community College
  (McMinnville Center)

Pamela Herring
Southwest Texas Junior College

Cheryl Huff
Germanna Community College

Sue Hum
University of Texas at San
  Antonio

Rachel Key
Grayson County College

Jill Lahnstein
Cape Fear Community College

Charlotte Laughlin
McLennan Community College

Gordon Lee
Lee College

Michael Lueker
Our Lady of the Lake University

Anna Maheshwari
Schoolcraft College

Jodie Marion
Mt Hood Community College

Sarah Markgraf
Bergen Community College

Melinda McBee
Grayson County College

Randall McClure
Florida Gulf Coast University

Jeanne McDonald
Waubonsee Community College

Jim McKeown
McLennan Community College

Richard Middleton-Kaplan
Harper College

Gary Montano
Tarrant County College

Jennifer Mooney
Wharton County Junior College

Vicki Moulson
College of the Albemarle

Andrea Muldoon
University of Wisconsin-Stout

Mary Huyck Mulka
Minnesota State University
  Moorhead

Lana Myers
Lone Star College

Marguerite Newcomb
University of Texas–San Antonio

Troy Nordman
Butler Community College

Eden Pearson
Des Moines Area Community
  College

Jason Pickavance
Salt Lake Community College

Paula Porter
Keiser University

Jeff Pruchnic
Wayne State University

Esther Quantrill
Blinn College

Maria Ramos
J. Sargeant Reynolds Community
  College

Arthur Rankin
Louisiana State University at
  Alexandria

Simone Rieck
Lone Star College

Jeffrey Roessner
Mercyhurst College

Ron Ross
Portland Community College

Jennifer Rosti
Roanoke College

Karin Russell
Keiser University

Debbie Ruth
Owensboro Community &
  Technical College

Jamie Sadler
Richmond Community College

John Schaffer
Blinn College

Dixie Shaw-Tillmon
The University of Texas at San
  Antonio

Suba Subbarao
Oakland Community College

Daniel Sullivan
Davenport University

Susan Swanson
Owensboro Community and
  Technical College

Paul Van Heuklom
Lincoln Land Community College

Angie Williams-Chehmani
Davenport University

Will Zhang
Des Moines Area Community
  College

Traci Zimmerman
James Madison University

Harry Phillips would like to thank Aron Keesbury, formerly acquisitions editor at Thomson Publishing and now with National Geographic Learning, for his steady encouragement and insightful feedback during the early stages of this project.

Patricia K. Bostian would like to thank her wonderful family for their generous support, particularly her husband Brad for his many wonderful textbook ideas, and her children Wyndham and Rhiannon for allowing her to talk about her ideas with them.

Finally, we want to acknowledge the steady interest our students have shown in argumentative writing over the last 15 years. In truth, it was their authentic interest in the course and their recognition that argument could serve them in daily life that fueled original interest in this project. As teachers, the course inspired us to regularly refine our approaches and, mostly, to listen closely to student writers who sensed, perhaps for the first time, that their private concerns could influence public thinking and decision making. In particular, we are grateful to Linda Gonzalez, Blaine Schmidt, and Ben Szany, among other students, for their willingness to contribute arguments to this textbook.

Harry R. Phillips

Patricia Bostian

PART ONE

How to Approach Argument in Real Life

CHAPTER 1 Argue With a Purpose

CHAPTER 2 Explore an Issue
that Matters to You

All Illustrations by iStockphoto.com/A-digit

CHAPTER 1

Argue With a Purpose

This text introduces you to argument and how to use it in response to everyday issues—at school, in the workplace, at home, in your neighborhood, with people who matter to you, in the swirl of community politics, and on a national or global scale. You will be able to use the tools in the following chapters to build practical arguments that make your voice clear and direct on issues in which you have a stake. Skills in argument will help you in your life as a student, a member of the local labor force, a consumer, a concerned citizen, and perhaps a parent and homeowner; in fact, argument can help you address all of the many issues associated with life in these communities.

This chapter is an overview of the nature and purpose of argument. Later chapters address the apparatus of argument—how to craft a claim, build support, work with the opposition, and build other structural elements. Think about argument as a set of tools that lets you negotiate your world with clarity and purpose. The skills you take away from this text, and the work required to complete a class in argument, can transfer to the real world. You may simply be responding to short-term assignments, but in doing so, you will learn to build sound arguments—a skill that will be useful long after your final class project is turned in.

In the sections that follow, you'll get a sense of what argument is and what argument is not, and you'll learn how to:

- Recognize where argument is appropriate in real life.
- Argue about issues that matter to you.
- Establish local context for an issue through the research process.
- Recognize why arguments break down.
- Match argument with purpose.

What Argument Is and What Argument Is Not

You are arguing when you claim a point of view on an issue, defend your claim with different kinds of support, and respond fairly to those with differing points of view. Argument is useful when you want to persuade others (decision-makers, fellow classmates, coworkers, a community agency or organization, a special interest group, elected representatives, business leaders, or an individual) to take seriously your point of view; when you want to find out more about something that matters to you; and when you want to establish areas of common interest among different positions. With nearly all arguments, it is essential to establish a clear context for your issue and to have a target audience.

Argument is not about putting yourself in uncomfortable, win–lose, either–or situations. It is not about fighting or trying to shame someone who holds a different point of view. Some people associate argument with anger, raised voices, and emotional outbursts. But when these people behave in competitive, angry, and overly emotional ways, communication is often sealed off and the people involved become alienated from one another. This is not the aim of argument. Argument creates a space where we can listen to each other.

The following essay by Thomas Frank is excerpted from "The Price of Admission." The full essay appears in the June 2012 issue of *Harper's*, a magazine that began publication in 1850 and today treats a wide range of issues in literature, politics, culture, finance, and the arts. In the essay, Frank includes a claim, various levels of support, and efforts to build his credibility as one taking a position on the issue of college tuition. Missing from the excerpt, but present in the longer essay, are attention to the opposition, reasons that support the claim, and a warrant, that is, attention to the values that motivate the writer to argue on this issue. The essay is accompanied by an editorial cartoon by R.J. Matson (see Figure 1.1).

Excerpt from "The Price of Admission"

by Thomas Frank

Figure 1.1 Editorial cartoon by R.J. Matson

Massive indebtedness changes a person, maybe even more than a college education does, and it's reasonable to suspect that the politicos who have allowed the tuition disaster to take its course know this. To saddle young people with enormous, inescapable debt — total student debt is now more than one trillion dollars — is ultimately to transform them into profit-maximizing machines. I mean, working as a schoolteacher or an editorial assistant at a publishing house isn't going to help you chip away at that forty grand you owe. You can't get out of it by bankruptcy, either. And our political leaders, lost in a fantasy of punitive individualism, certainly won't propose the bailout measures they could take to rescue the young from the crushing burden.

What will happen to the young debtors instead is that they will become *Homo economicus*, whether or not they studied that noble creature. David Graeber, the anthropologist who wrote the soon-to-be-classic *Debt: The First 5,000 Years*, likens the process to a horror movie, in which the zombies or the vampires attack the humans as a kind of recruitment policy. "They turn you into one of them," as Graeber told me.

Actually, they do worse than that. Graeber relates the story of a woman he met who got a Ph.D. from Columbia University, but whose $80,000 debt load put an academic career off-limits, since adjuncts earn close to nothing. Instead, the woman wound up working as an escort for Wall Street types. "Here's someone who ought to be a professor," Graeber explains, "doing sexual services for the guys who lent her the money."

The story hit home for me, because I, too, wanted to be a professor once. I remember the waves of enlightenment that washed over me in my first few years in college, the ecstasy of finally beginning to understand what moved human affairs this way or that, the exciting sense of a generation arriving at a shared sensibility. Oh, I might have gone on doing that kind of work forever, whether or not it made me rich, if journalism had not intervened.

It's hard to find that kind of ecstasy among the current crop of college graduates. The sensibility shared by their generation seems to revolve around student debt, which has been clamped onto them like some sort of interest-bearing iron maiden. They've been screwed — that's what their moment of enlightenment has taught them.

As for my own cohort, or at least the members of it who struggled through and made it to one of the coveted positions in the knowledge factory, the new generational feeling seems to be one of disgust. Our enthusiasm for learning, which we trumpeted to the world, merely led the nation's children into debt bondage. Consider the remarks of Nicholas Mirzoeff, a professor of media at New York University, who sums up the diminishing returns of the profession on his blog: "I used to say that in academia one at least did very little harm. Now I feel like a pimp for loan sharks."

Analyze this Reading

1. What is the writer's claim, the position the writer takes in response to the issue of student debt?
2. Identify examples the writer uses to support his claim.
3. How does the writer establish his credibility; that is, how does he build trust with readers regarding his competence to take a stand on this issue?

Respond to this Reading

1. The writer contends that political leaders won't make the effort to bail out today's college students from debt. Do you favor a legislative bailout? Explain, and if you don't favor such a bailout, what claim would you make to address the student debt problem?
2. What is your relationship to education and debt? What examples would you use to demonstrate this relationship?
3. If you were to argue on this issue, at what target audience would you aim? Would your audience be officials at your college, your state legislators, your peers, or the members of your community? Explain.

Recognize Where Argument Is Appropriate in Real Life

You'll get to know this guide as a student in a class, one class among many that you need to complete as you move toward your degree, but there is another, equally important way to think about your work with argument—the set of skills you'll acquire and take with you when class is over. Make these skills serve what matters to you, in and beyond the classroom. Whether it's a small group of coworkers, the author of a scholarly article, your local parent–teacher organization, the editor of an online magazine, a car mechanic, or the billing agency for your cell phone or broadband service, you'll have a better chance of being taken seriously when you support your point of view with credible information delivered through a variety of logical, ethical, and emotional appeals.

Vital issues in our lives occur both in the academic world and in the swirl of everyday life. When you have a clear point of view (a claim) about the quality of cafeteria food at your child's school and then justify your claim with effective support, thereby establishing your credibility as a concerned parent, your audience will listen. Similarly, if a teacher in one of your classes asks you to claim a position on the status of immigration reform in your state and you respond by drafting a claim based on thorough research, your argument is likely to fare well when it is evaluated. This is especially true when you come across as well informed and sensitive to those who might differ from you. And if conditions at work start to resemble positions that were recently outsourced, you're more likely to get the attention of your boss or coworkers when you present a balanced, fair-minded argument that takes into account those who view the issue differently.

In your life as a student, are there issues that involve tuition, lodging, the accessibility of your teachers, course policies, conflicts with your job, and loan opportunities? Are there also intellectual issues in your life as a student that you are asked to respond to, such as genetically engineered food, climate change, and representative government as practiced in our country? And outside the classroom, if your street lacks adequate storm-water facilities, if earlier public-school start times are proposed by the school board and you know that this will affect your family's schedule, or if a family member has a contrary idea about what makes a sensible budget, a well-crafted argument allows you to move away from emotional arguments (a trap for many) and into the realm of reason, common sense, and community. An emotional argument, on the other hand, lacks the support of a rational approach to an issue and puts in jeopardy your credibility with your target audience. The exact change you want is never a guaranteed outcome of a good argument, but at the very least you will have made your voice audible before an audience that matters to you.

From another perspective, you affect and diversify the particular community you address with an argument. A well-organized argument gets you a seat at the discussion table, whether in the classroom or before your city council. This means that your position on an issue can matter in the local decision-making process (see Figure 1.2). If we say nothing, others will speak for us or make assumptions about us that may conflict with who we are and what we value.

Argue About Issues That Matter to You

Argue about what matters to you as a student and in everyday life. Some people associate argument with dry, abstract issues that may or may not directly affect their lives, but this is an attitude to stay away from. Good writing, and similarly, good argument, spring from the same place—from the effort of everyday people struggling to define and solve problems. A good argument will touch the reader in many ways: logically, because you provide real-life support for your point of view; emotionally, because you touch on something that the reader cares about; and ethically, because you establish your credibility as an informed community member whom your audience can trust.

One way to think about argument is as a practical tool for the regular challenges we face. For example, would it be helpful to know how to present your

Auremar/Shutterstock.com

Figure 1.2 Speaking up in response to issues that matter to us is the heart of argument. In this photo, the figure speaking is responding to a workplace issue and delivering her ideas to coworkers.

point of view to city and county politicians when repairs on your street are neglected while streets in other areas are taken care of much sooner? Might it be helpful to compose an argument in the form of a letter to a son, daughter, parent, or in-law regarding an important family matter? Do you have an idea about how certain parts of your job can be improved, and would a logical, well-researched proposal directed to a supervisor be a reasonable first step? Do parking problems and a smoking ban at school disturb you, and do you want to find out more about these issues and formulate a claim that is reinforced by careful research? If you answer "yes" to these or similar everyday issues, then this guide can be useful as a way to represent yourself with integrity.

Let's look, for example, at the issue that begins this chapter and one that nearly all college students contend with these days—increasing tuition rates. Some of us may be compelled to argue on this issue because we're forced to work more hours during the week to pay for this semester's tuition, forced to take out loans that mean years of debt after college, and disturbed that our college seems to endorse lending practices that unfairly burden students heading into the world after graduation. A carefully arranged argument gives us the chance to claim a strong position on tuition rates, conduct research on the nature and history of the problem, listen to other points of view, and then propose a way to address the problem reasonably. After choosing to argue on this issue, a reasonable first step would be to establish context and determine your target audience, tasks discussed in the next section.

Another way to think about argument is as a practical tool for the intellectual and academic work you are asked to complete as a student. The steps in developing a good argument are the same, whether you are writing for a class assignment or about an issue in daily life. In both contexts you will need to evolve a precise point of view and then defend it. Successful arguments about the origins of our national debt, same-sex marriage, interpreting constitutional amendments, health-care policy, and the federal government's relationship with the banking industry are built on the same foundations as arguments responding to the everyday issues of life.

In fact, one measure of good arguments on issues like these is their ability to connect local and global contexts. So much of what comes to us through mainstream news—issues in the fields of medicine, technology, health care, and geopolitics, for example—has its origins beyond our immediate lives and communities. You can of course apply the tools of argument to these issues, and with good success, but argument on these issues can and should be connected to local contexts, too. The list below is a small sampling of large issues that have local impact.

Standardized testing
Gun laws
Video cameras and public schools
Promotion practices in the nursing
   profession

Bullying in schools and in the
   workplace
Choice and public schools
Benefits for same-sex partners
Taser guns in public schools

Immigration reform and local business

Cell phone use while driving

High school dropout rates

Local job outsourcing

The elderly and nursing home care

Eminent domain and home owners

Fossil fuels

Local road repairs

Campaign Finance Reform

Returning veterans and health care

Health care and non-native speakers

Payday lending

Big box construction and local business

Living wage proposals

Probation and oversight

Local transit

Crowded classrooms

Sex offenders in the community

Climate change

Photo-ID voting requirements

Locally grown food

Energy rate hikes

Teen crime and sentencing

Medicare and Social Security

In today's world, we all face multiple demands as we move through our day. Combine this busyness with the sheer scale of many of the issues we face—the economic recession, global warming, health care, security, terror, and military intervention—and it can be tough to believe that articulating our point of view on an issue is worth the effort or makes any difference. But it *can* make a difference, and building a good argument is a way to exercise some control over your life and establish your influence in the community. When your well-planned argument articulates your view on an issue in a thorough and compelling manner, you can generate confidence in yourself and respect from your audience. A sound argument does not, of course, guarantee that your issue will be resolved or that substantial change will result, but you can define for yourself exactly where you stand. For a democracy to remain healthy, it must function in large part by individuals responding to the forces that global environments put in our way.

Well-crafted argument is a way to represent yourself publicly with dignity and in an informed, fair, and open-minded way. Learn these skills now, and you'll have them forever.

your turn 1a ▸ GET STARTED Acknowledge Issues That Matter to You

Make a list of issues that concern you today. Include issues in your personal life, your workplace, your school, your church, a group you belong to, your neighborhood, and your town or city. As you make your list, consider also national and global issues that affect your life, such as conflicts in other countries, environmental concerns, or fuel costs. As a way to narrow your focus to issues most important to you, respond to the following questions.

1. Identify a major issue in your life or a position a teacher asks you to take in response to an academic issue.
2. When did this issue begin, and why does it continue to be a problem?
3. Identify a second issue that concerns you. If in question 1 you identified an academic issue, identify a more personal issue here.
4. When did this issue begin, and why does it continue to be a problem?

Establish Local Context via the Research Process

The important work of establishing local context for an issue involves aiming your argument at an appropriate audience, conducting research so as to generate a history for your issue, and when possible, connecting your local issue to broader, even global, conditions. These essential features of building local context are described in the following section.

Determine Your Audience

Recognize a practical audience for your argument; that is, direct your argument to those you most want to inform and persuade. Once you identify your audience, make a close study of them. An audience can be as small as one person, especially appropriate for an argument in a letter format, or your audience can be as large as your community or a block of undecided voters in a statewide election. Other audiences can include the following:

- Your class or certain members of a class
- Members of your church or parents in your neighborhood or school district
- The local school board, city council, county commission, or state legislators
- Family members, friends, or a partner
- A teacher or school administrator
- A supervisor at work or coworkers
- Readers of a zine, blog, listserv, special interest newsletter, or your local or school newspaper

Your audience may or may not agree with your point of view. In addition, an audience may not be as fully aware of the issue as you are, and in these cases you'll need to inform readers in order to get your claim across. Your job is to persuade an audience to think seriously about your point of view, and this means that you must know what your readers value. It's vital that you listen closely and get a sense of *why* they feel the way they do. What is it about their histories and values that make them see the issue differently from you? While you may deviate from your audience on a given issue, your argument will be much stronger and more concrete if you take the time to listen charitably—that is, without judgment and with an open mind—as you attempt to understand their viewpoints.

With regard to the tuition issue, one practical approach might be to target your city or town council and ask members to approve a resolution that you and other students have drawn up calling for a moratorium on tuition hikes.

Your argument will become more persuasive as you find overlapping points of view with your audience. Determine what you have in common with your audience—what values, beliefs, expectations, and fears you share. Move away from oppositional thinking, the "I'm right/you're wrong" approach. In the real world, when you work to identify common ground, you're more likely to get others to listen to you and move toward consensus.

> **your turn 1b** ▶ **GET STARTED Identify a Target Audience**
>
> Begin thinking about a practical audience for an argument by responding to the following questions.
>
> 1. Who might be interested in hearing what you have to say about the issues in your life today? Why?
> 2. Is there a specific person or group who could benefit from your perspective, affect an issue, or resolve it or modify it in some way? Explain.
> 3. How will you learn more about this target audience?
> 4. What tempting assumptions about this audience may prove inaccurate?

Establish Local Context for Your Issue

No man is an island! When English poet John Donne delivered this idea in a 1624 meditation, he claimed that, while isolation may be a part of living, we are all connected to the continent, to a community. We do not live separately from our communities, although sometimes it may feel as if we're living on their margins. The point is that when you decide to claim a position on an issue that matters to you, gather plenty of information so that you're fully aware of the **context**, the past and present, of your issue. An issue materializes in the swirl of local events and occurs because folks disagree—about its cause, what should be done about it, the terms that define it, whether or not it actually exists, and/or how it should be evaluated. So if you feel hemmed in by an issue, find out through research what others think and how they're responding.

You have many ways to find out where your issue originates. For an issue occurring at work, look into what created it. You may already know the answer, but asking fellow workers their understanding of the issue can fill in gaps. You may also want to gather information about your employer's past to get a sense of how the issue evolved. If you work in a large industry, you can read up on the deeper roots of this issue and how it is handled elsewhere in the state, country, or world. If your English teacher requires that you develop an argument in response to a character's behavior in a short story or poem, or if your history teacher asks you to evaluate the term *American exceptionalism*, plan to gather online and print sources as a way to inform yourself of the context in which your issue occurs and what scholars have to say about it.

When you argue in response to an issue on local or neighborhood politics, access the archives of your local newspaper and study the history of your issue. Newspapers often are available for free via online databases. For issues involving a family member and a health problem, for example, there are a number of databases available that house articles and essays on health-care issues, and your school may subscribe to these databases. Building local context can also involve interviews with knowledgeable professionals or those who have been invested in the issue over time. You also design and administer a survey that will add to your information base.

Returning to the tuition issue, this problem has a significant and well-documented local and national history. Scores of students, faculty, and social justice activists have responded to regular tuition hikes since they began. From the perspective of your school's administration, funding priorities may prevent immediate action, but during an interview you may learn a great deal from a school official who defends the hikes but is sympathetic with your desire to succeed with your education. And often you can count on there being a knowledgeable reporter in local media who can provide a larger frame for this issue as well as links to factual information. These are resources that can help you build local context for this issue.

Creating this kind of context does two important things for your final argument: It lets you argue with a strong sense of local history, and it sends a direct message to your readers that you've done your homework, that you've thought deeply about your issue, and most importantly, that you should be taken seriously.

Figure 1.3 Protestors respond to tuition hikes and other issues important to their local context.

internet activity 1a **Exploring**

Conduct an informal Internet search to look for general background information on an issue, perhaps one that you identified in the Your Turn 1a activity. Begin by accessing the online archives of your local newspaper; continue by using the academic databases your school provides and other online sites that your teacher recommends. Answer the following questions:

1. Has your search produced answers to some of your questions? Explain.
2. What kind of additional information do you want to gather?
3. As you begin to gather information, is your perspective changing; that is, does learning more about your issue let you see the issue in different and perhaps broader terms? Explain.

Connect Local and Global Contexts

When you write specifically about a local issue, like tuition hikes, plan to connect the issue with a context beyond your community. This makes a positive impression on readers because it shows that you're able to frame your issue in broad terms. It reveals that through your research you recognize that your issue is influenced by trends in regional, national, or global cultures. This will also allow your audience to think more critically about the issue, and it will likely make your argument more persuasive.

For example, escalating tuition rates in this country, Canada, and England, among other countries, reflect economic realities and corporate decision-making outside our communities (see Figure 1.4). When you argue about having to pay more for your education, you must bring to your argument a broad context for tuition hikes so as to orient readers to the origins of this issue. Similarly, when the outsourcing of certain jobs—like those in manufacturing, web design, accounting, and customer support—affects the local economy, trace this outsourcing to the global economic climate in order to form a larger picture for your

Jeff Parker/Caglecartoons.com

Figure 1.4 Editorial cartoon by Jeff Parker

Figure 1.5 Connecting a local issue to a broader context can be powerful.

audience. In addition, issues associated with food in local markets—the conditions in which it's produced and harvested, transportation, health concerns, pricing, and availability of certain items—typically lead to issues in another part of the country or world. Standardized testing, according to some researchers, can be traced to the presence of a business model in many of our public schools; learning about this aspect of the issue—and about the values and motives for this kind of testing—can fill in important background for this arguable issue. If you are motivated to write on local environmental matters like air and water quality, you'll want to read up on the influence of local development and regional energy production to get a sense of what causes these problems.

Whether the local issue that concerns you is in the area of health care, education, politics, work, family, or a retail industry, there likely are larger, often global, forces shaping the issue. When it's a trend you can trace beyond our national borders, we might use the term **glocal** to connect local and global contexts. When you look at what sustains us—air, water, food, transportation, education, and electronic communication—it won't be difficult to connect local issues with broader contexts. And when you look at what we desire materially—dwellings, cars, fashion, and so on—and begin examining American consumer culture, you should be able to make some revealing connections that will enlighten readers and move your argument along.

The key to connecting local and global contexts is found both in your own good sense of how things work and in your ability to research thoroughly in order to familiarize yourself with the history surrounding an issue. Your research process is vital to the success of your argument.

your turn 1c   GET STARTED Connect the Local and Global

Answer the following questions to get a sense of how local issues can have global effects.

1. Identify a single *glocal* issue that concerns you, and describe its local effects.
2. How do these effects have an impact on your life and the lives of others?
3. In general terms, explain how economic and political ripples from a global or national issue may spread and affect the lives of others across your region, state, and community.

Recognize Why Arguments Break Down

Arguments can succeed when a writer has something to say, knows to whom it should be said, and knows how to present supporting information in persuasive ways. But arguments can also fail, especially when the essential steps needed to build good arguments are not given thorough treatment. Following are some of the major reasons why arguments don't succeed.

Arguments Break Down When They Do Not Persuade an Audience

Sometimes writers summarize and explain rather than argue. This can occur when a discernable issue is not separated from the larger topic. For example, by deciding you want to write on problems in your workplace, you've identified a good *topic* but not an arguable *issue*. There are numerous issues under this big topic—hiring practices, the politics of promotion, compensation, environmental impact, benefits, working within a hierarchy, discrimination, communication, and so forth—and it is vital that you choose a single issue on which to argue. When you fail to narrow and instead stay with the big topic, your writing lapses into summary and general statements, and this is death to persuasive writing. By focusing on the big topic, problems in your workplace, you'd be treating important issues only superficially. Each of these sub-issues is worthy of a full argument. Narrow your topic to a single issue that affects you, and you will be able to dig deeply and avoid spreading out generally.

Arguments Break Down When There Is a Lack of Balance in the Support

By loading body paragraphs with facts and logical appeals only, your argument will lack a cooperative, humanizing feel. The idea is to place ethical appeals (in which you establish your credibility through personal experience and the testimony of experts) and emotional appeals (in which you touch readers with emotionally charged examples) in balance with logical support. When you tilt too much in the direction on one kind of appeal, readers lose interest. After all, we're complex beings, and we want to be convinced in a variety of ways. Experts tell us that logical appeals should dominate in most arguments, comprising some 60–70 percent of an argument's support. When you focus your arguments in this way, you earn the opportunity to address your readers ethically and emotionally. They must know that you've done your research and that you write from experience; then, you can broaden your argument with different types of appeals.

Arguments Break Down When the Audience Is Poorly Defined

Nearly 2,500 years ago, Aristotle explained that a target audience is essential to competent argument. Early in the writing process, you should decide precisely whom you want to persuade. This will allow you to focus closely on

 tip 1a

Embrace the Glocal!
Remember that you are a local resident *and* a global citizen. Things are so interconnected today that it's hard to define ourselves and the conditions we live in without recognizing forces—economic, political, and environmental—that originate beyond our communities.

an audience whose values you understand. Knowing these values lets you build a bridge to the audience, which is necessary if you are to persuade them. This is what warrant and backing are about. You can design a good argument when you know what an audience expects, what touches it, and what kinds of appeals are likely to be effective. For example, if you want to argue for a moratorium on tuition hikes in your school or in all public colleges in your state, consider your target audience. To rally immediate support, your audience might be students, but to work toward real change, your target audience might be state lawmakers who have the decision-making capacity to enact legislation.

Arguments Break Down When They Contain Fallacies

Fallacies, often found in an argument's claims and reasons, weaken an argument because there are mistakes in logic and can involve unfair treatment of others. Fallacies are common in the many advertisements we take in every day. For example, ads for a certain brand of car, clothing, food, or medication, may promise that if we purchase the product, prestige, attractiveness, taste satisfaction, and health will be ours. These ads contain fallacies because the promise cannot be kept. In an argument, fallacies are statements that mislead due to poor or deceptive reasoning. For example, if you claim that third parties are the only way to restore true democracy to our political system, you have committed a fallacy based on a hasty generalization. Some readers of your argument may agree that third parties are needed to restore democracy, but some may claim that campaign finance reform, term limits, and citizen activism are also needed. The hasty generalization backs you into a corner.

Arguments Break Down When They Do Not Fairly Represent Opposing Views

The rebuttals and differing views you bring to your argument should not be brief and superficial: They should attend to what the opposition claims, how it supports a position, and what it values. This easily can require several full paragraphs in an arguments. When you respond to a rebuttal after having treated the other side fairly, you are in a position to thoroughly counter or build on another view. When full treatment of another view is neglected, however, writers tend to profile and stereotype, and this can offend perceptive members of an audience.

Match Argument with Purpose

After you decide what you want to accomplish with an argument, you can choose the kind of argument that fits your purpose. This guide helps you choose from four kinds of argument, all of which are treated in detail in Chapter 8, "Consider Toulmin-Based Argument" and Chapter 9, "Consider Middle Ground and Rogerian Argument, and Argument based on Microhistory."

Figure 1.6 Four Kinds of Arguments

For example, an issue that received a lot of attention in North Carolina a few years ago concerned the attorney general's recommendation that children of illegal immigrants be barred from pursuing degrees in the state's community colleges, a recommendation that the president of the community college system chose to follow. The issue generated much discussion across the state based on the news media's regular attention to it. A writer's decision to argue in response to this issue would require choosing the kind of argument practical to the arguer's goals with a specific target audience.

The following paragraphs describe how different kinds of arguments might be applied to the issue of barring children of illegal immigrants from attending the state's community colleges. These paragraphs provide an overview of four kinds of arguments (see Figure 1.6). Think about how these approaches to argument can fit with issues you plan to address in argument.

Toulmin-Based Argument

Using a Toulmin-based approach, a writer would focus closely on his audience—in this case, the State Board of Community Colleges—and what it values. He knows that individuals on this board are committed to workforce training, economic development, and service to local communities. With this in mind, the writer can develop convincing support by using many examples of children of illegal immigrants succeeding in community colleges and going on to hold good jobs and contribute to their communities. Examples can include statistics, scholars analyzing the community college as a resource for the children of illegal immigrants, and firsthand student accounts. This varied support will honor values held by the board. Additionally, the writer can elaborate on why training, business, and service are important to the state's quality of life. And because the board is charged with carrying out the policies of the state's community colleges, the writer could craft a problem-based claim and ask that the board permit children of illegal immigrants to pursue degrees. Rebuttals brought to the argument would focus on the opposition's concerns with legality and citizenship. Central statements in the argument, such as the claim and reasons, would include qualifiers that keep writers away from making absolute, and unrealistic, points.

Middle Ground Argument

A middle ground argument on this issue would view the "for" and "against" positions as extreme and argue instead for a practical position in the middle.

Each extreme position would be analyzed in terms of why it fails to offer a practical perspective. Based on the reasons listed previously, those who favor barring children of illegal immigrants from seeking degrees could be analyzed as extreme because this position fails to note the many contributions immigrants make to their communities, the taxes they pay, the contributions they make to the workforce, and the long delays they endure with regard to immigrant legislation. Those on the other side of this issue could be considered impractical because they lump all immigrants together and thus do not take into account the very different experiences of the various immigrant groups living in the United States. For example, the immigrant group getting the most attention today is from Mexico, and its experience in American culture is in some ways quite different from that of groups from various Asian, Caribbean, and Latin American countries. Over-generalizing about diverse groups plays to a limited understanding of the varying immigrant experiences in the United States, and arguments built on such over-generalization can be considered impractical for this reason.

Several middle-ground positions are possible with this issue, and each has been argued over the course of the debate. One such position argues that the "for" and "against" reasoning described previously ignores the reason that many immigrants move to the United States—jobs—and that until local businesses enter the debate (because of their practice of hiring illegal workers), nothing will change. Another position argues that this issue should be moved into the courts and that in the meantime community colleges should remain open-door institutions, admitting all who apply regardless of citizenship status. While those holding these positions may consider them moderate and middle ground, each position must be proven to be a practical and logical choice between two extreme positions.

Rogerian Argument

In a Rogerian argument, the writer would aim to create a space for positive back-and-forth discussion between his view and one or more different views. To do this, the writer would need to present other views with respect and accuracy, emphasizing the values embedded in these views. Having established this respectful tone, the writer is now in a position to introduce his view by looking for areas where values on all sides overlap. This is the common ground that makes Rogerian argument a practical choice when parties are far apart on an issue.

If the writer opposes barring immigrant students from attending community college, he would pay close attention to the opposition and focus on its values and reasons for supporting the regulation. The writer notices strong emphasis on values of citizenship, employment, education, and rights. While the writer may differ in how these values can be extended to the children of illegal immigrants, he shares with the opposition a deep commitment to these values and their importance in community life. This is the common ground that the writer would hope to create. On the surface, the views are far apart, but underneath the sides share strongly held values. There is of course no guarantee that the writer of this argument and his opposition will now or in the future see eye to eye on this controversial issue, but the writer has made the effort to listen to and honor the opposition. Because an audience may acknowledge his objectivity and sense of fair play, he is in a position to earn some measure of credibility, a necessary condition to the success of any argument that seeks to create common ground.

Argument Based on a Microhistory

An argument based on a microhistory can be a practical approach to this issue because an arguer could provide specific history relevant to the recommendation to bar children of illegal immigrants from community colleges and then offer a claim. This kind of argument could be used to look closely at one feature of this issue—for example, the reaction of a student, parent, teacher, or concerned citizen. Studying the response of a prospective community-college student affected by the recommendation could bring in from the margins of this issue a voice that media and the general public do not hear, an aim of the microhistory. Primary materials needed to prepare such a microhistory could include interviews with the prospective student or something the student has written. The center of the microhistory would be the ways in which the student's life will be affected by having the opportunity to attend college withdrawn and how this student's experience reveals something about our culture and what it values. Additionally, the arguer will need to provide context for the student's experience, and this must include an overview of this issue in the state, region, and country. Having provided extensive information about the student and the history of the issue, the arguer is then in a position to offer a claim that an audience may view as credible based on the arguer's extensive research. Arguments based on microhistory focus an argument in the commonplace and everyday, perspectives that many mainstream and conventional approaches to history often neglect.

Reflect and Apply

Directions: The following questions ask you to step back and reflect on the concepts delivered in this chapter. You should think about the questions that conclude each chapter and apply them to your own writing. We encourage you to think about how the various pieces of an argument fit together and why they're all necessary.

1. In your own words describe what an effective argument does. Include in your description how you think about argument now contrasted with how you thought about argument before reading this chapter.

2. Early sections of this chapter encourage you to use skills associated with argument both inside and outside the classroom. Explain how these skills would be of value in everyday life.

3. Clarify why a target audience is essential to a good argument. Include in your response what an argument would look like with a vague or unspecified audience.

4. Define the term *context*. Describe its place in an argument in terms of your credibility as arguer.

5. Identify the reasons why arguments break down. Which of these reasons will you need to pay close attention to so that your arguments don't break down?

CHAPTER 2

Explore an Issue That Matters to You

Seven weeks into the semester, you're between worried and anxious about next week's midterm exam in your online "Early American Literature" class. At a coffee shop on campus, you run into a pal you met in a class last year, and the two of you begin talking. A minute into your conversation, you confess your anxiety about the exam and suddenly realize that you're both in the same class and that your friend is also worried about the exam. You share the concern that the instructor does not participate regularly on the discussion board, takes too long to answer email messages, and sometimes does not respond to messages at all. He has made it clear from the beginning that he'll respond to messages "time permitting." The first two units in the course include much tough reading, and there have been times when you wanted honest and prompt feedback, especially as to your comprehension of the challenging readings. The instructor has informed the class that the exam will include a section on analyzing passages, and this makes you even more anxious. The two of you gather yourselves and decide to meet for a study session over the weekend.

All illustrations by iStockphoto.com/A-digit

COMMUNITY	
School-Academic	**TOPIC:** Life in the Online Classroom
Workplace	**ISSUE:** Teacher–Student Interaction
Family-Household	**AUDIENCE:** Director of Distance Learning
Neighborhood	
Social-Cultural	**CLAIM:** Clear standards for teachers' commitment to interacting regularly with students should be stated in the introductions to online English courses.
Consumer	
Concerned Citizen	

An argument is a practical response to a pressing question, problem, or concern that generates differing points of view, such as the issue described above. An argument works best when you are invested in an issue, like online instructor response time, and when you feel that what you want to achieve is being hampered. For example, if you feel you're being paid unfairly at work in comparison with other workers of similar experience and seniority, you have an arguable issue. Or, if you feel strongly about stem cell research, about credit card marketing campaigns targeted at you and other college students, about accusations of racial profiling by local law enforcement, about the quality of food at your child's school, or about red light cameras at traffic intersections in your community, you can construct an effective argument that fully represents your point of view, your claim, on such an issue. But first you must assess current issues in your life and determine those that genuinely matter to you. This is the vital first step in the argument process. This chapter guides you through the process of choosing issues for argument.

In Chapter 2 you will develop a research plan to:

- Recognize yourself as a member of many communities.
- Identify topics associated with each community.
- Respond to issues within topics that you feel strongly about and may want to argue on.
- Aim your argument at a specific audience.
- Deliver your argument at a time when it is most likely to be taken seriously.
- Troubleshoot your issue by responding to practical prompts as a way to get started with an argument.

Determine What Matters to You and Why

All of us belong to many different communities—school, workplace, family neighborhood, social–cultural, consumer, and concerned citizen—and our individual worlds are defined, at least in part, by the issues we encounter in each of our communities. Some of these issues are the results of external forces acting on our lives (a directive from a supervisor at work, a public ordinance that permits one kind of gathering but not another, an assignment from a teacher) while other kinds of issues are of our own choosing (who we vote for in an election, our decision to become active in response to a community or national issue, decisions we make about parenting). And the issues you choose to write about, whether you argue for something to change or simply want your audience to reflect on your point of view, should originate with what is most important to you. Your arguments become compelling to readers when you write in an informed way about something that deeply concerns you. So, while you will learn how to build arguments in structured, logical ways, *what* you argue on should begin with issues that stir your emotions and that motivate you to speak out, as in the case of the mother speaking in Figure 2.1. Consider the communities you belong to and some, but not all, of the topics that can affect each community.

A **community** is a group of individuals that share common experiences, interests, needs, and expectations. Students in your classes, the general college community, people you work with, your neighbors, and citizens with a stake in local politics are examples of communities. Review the following communities and some of the issues associated with each community.

School/Academic

As a member of your academic community, what issues affect your goals of acquiring knowledge, learning new skills, and earning a degree so that you can move on to the next phase of your life? Consider below some of the topics that affect your life as a student.

AP Photo/The Laramie Boomerang, Barbara J. Perenic

Figure 2.1 Compelling arguments become possible when individuals argue about what matters most to them. In this photo, a mother speaks to a group of University of Wyoming students about her son, and seven other students, who were killed in a car crash caused by a drunk driver, the man to her right in the yellow shirt.

Costs	Curriculum design	Campus safety
Degree requirements	Life in the online	Transportation
Life in the real-time	classroom	Tuition
classroom	Issues in your field of	Blogging
Teacher attitudes	study	Fairness
Time management	Personal responsibility	Plagiarism
Free speech	Academic integrity	Grade inflation
Diversity and tolerance	Privacy and	Extra credit
Student services	surveillance	

Workplace

At many points during our working lives, we face conditions that affect our motivation, engagement, and sense of fair play. Other times the workplace offers opportunities that are welcome challenges. What are your conditions at work? By what are you challenged? Consider the following list of topics as a way to identify issues that most matter to you.

Job expectations	Dispute resolution	Privacy and
Balancing work and life	Training	surveillance
Bureaucracy and red	Bullying and	Advancement
tape	harassment	Discrimination
Pay scale	Corporate social	Leadership
Benefits	responsibility	Favoritism
Commuting and	Daily conditions	Job security
telecommuting	Stress	Rankism
Cubicle culture	Downsizing and	Team building
Organizing and	layoffs	Office politics
negotiation	Unions	

Family/Household

This community refers both to a traditional family unit—parents (or parent) and children—and to any group of individuals sharing a home and its responsibilities. Issues can spring from relationships within and across generations, from economic and purchasing concerns, and from household maintenance arrangements, among many others.

Toy safety	Home owners	Product safety
Financial planning	associations	Neighbors
Landscaping	Food safety	Parenting
and grounds	Diet/food	Same-sex marriage
maintenance	consumption	Pet care
Children and online	Health care planning	Senior care
safety	Home improvement	Wills and trusts
Home buying and	Furniture and	
mortgages	appliances	

Neighborhood

Neighborhoods are distinct geographical areas. Some neighborhoods comprise a three- or four-block square within a city or urban area. Other neighborhoods comprise only a single block or even a single complex of dwellings. People living in a neighborhood frequently are affected by residential and commercial development, by local government decisions, and by activities such as local parades or events, school closings, or rezoning.

Street improvement	Storm drains	Property alterations
Rezoning ordinances	Sidewalks	and additions
Graffiti	Economic development	Safety
Erosion	and housing	Gangs
Yard maintenance	Water and sewage	Noise
Neighbors with special	Waste collection	Traffic
needs	Parking	Crime
The digital divide		

Social/Cultural

Some communities link us to people we'll never meet, yet we share with them features that are central to our self-concept. Based on your religious, sexual, and political preferences, are there issues before you? And based on the racial or ethnic group you identify with, the virtual environments you spend time in, or the friendships and loyalties you keep, are there concerns that might motivate you to argue?

Profiling and	Relationships	Friendship
stereotyping	Local government and	Loyalty
Sex and sexuality	the individual	Gender
Public space	Racial and ethnic	Education
Political preference	identity	Economics
Virtual environments	Training and	Religion
Class status	opportunity	

Consumer

We live in a consumer-oriented society, one in which advertisements from competing companies and producers rain down on us every day. We regularly make decisions about what we eat and wear, how we transport ourselves, how we stay warm, what we purchase for our children, and how we entertain ourselves. Are there issues important to you as a consumer that fall under these and other topics?

Prescription drugs	Electronics and	Utilities/energy
Local lending	communication	Food consumption
practices	Consumer fraud	Insurance
Identity theft	Shopping at home	Investing
Telemarketing	Landlord/tenant	Credit
Home repairs	relations	Advertising
Transportation	Demographic profiling	

Concerned Citizen

While much of our focus concerns the local and the personal, many of us—as concerned citizens living in a democratic culture—naturally pay attention to politics, economic trends, and social concerns that extend beyond our communities; in other words, we pay attention to what we can term the *glocal* environment. Arguments deriving from some of the topics below, and many more, are vital to our commitment to democratic life, because democracy means speaking up about what matters to us; if we don't speak up about our issues, we may be left out of the conversation completely. What issues come to mind when you investigate some of the broad topics below?

Environment	Electronic voting	Animal research
Agricultural practices	Private corporations	Alternative energy
National security and	and the public	Individual rights and
surveillance	interest	counterterrorism
Substances and	Public schools	Scarcity and abundance
regulation	Immigration reform	Globalization
Prisons	Science/technology	Ballot access
Health care reform	and ethics	Military action
Class division	High school graduation	Digital access/privacy
Phone culture	rates	Homelessness
Genetically modified	Information	Air and water quality
foods	distribution	Climate change
Professional behavior	Criminal justice	Censorship

Communities and topics listed above should get you thinking about what matters to you at this point in your life. These lists are not intended to be comprehensive; rather, they are intended to help you identify issues in the various communities to which you belong, especially issues that motivate you to argue.

 tip 2a

Listen to Your Emotions

As you note issues in your life, pay close attention to your emotional responses. Are there some issues that make your heart beat faster? This is often where good arguments are born. While this guide will steer you through logical approaches to practical arguments, it is often these emotional and intuitive moments that signal the beginning of a strong argument.

your turn 2a ➤ **GET STARTED Focus on Communities**

For each community above, identify two or three topics that concern you, and then answer the following questions.

1. What issues within these broad topics most concern you?
2. Overall, what two or three issues matter to you most? Why?

Choose an Issue within a Topic

The categories listed previously help you identify the communities to which you belong and the important issues in your life—not that you necessarily need reminders of what's most pressing for you. Nevertheless, completing the "Your Turn 2a" exercise should get you thinking about what motivates you to argue, and it will likely affirm your sense that life is quite complex and varied these days. This section asks you to begin the argument process by narrowing your focus to a single, arguable issue.

An argument will fail if its focus is too broad. For this reason, it is essential that you distinguish between a topic and an issue. A **topic** is a category—such as local politics, transportation, neighborhood security, race relations, or family planning—that contains numerous issues. Topics are places from which issues and arguments are derived. In contrast, an issue is a specific problem or dispute that remains unsettled and requires a point of view and sometimes a decision. It always occurs within a larger topic and within a precise context, or set of conditions.

Monashee Frantz/Jupiterimages

Figure 2.2 This writer is gathering information from a print source for a single issue. Narrowing your focus to a specific issue, rather than writing generally about a topic, lets you write about a precise set of conditions and thus appeal to an audience more directly.

A good argument results from a process of narrowing from a broad topic to a specific, arguable issue. For example, as a concerned citizen, if you state that you want to argue about America's military presence in the Middle East, you'd be taking on a big topic, one that might require book-length treatment with chapters devoted to separate issues. This topic actually includes dozens of issues, and your job as arguer would be to narrow your focus and choose one specific issue. Instead of spreading out and writing generally about America's military presence in this region, choose a single issue and write very specifically about it. Any argument you build will be more effective when you focus on a single issue. This will give your argument depth and precision, features difficult to include when writing about a big topic in a relatively short argument.

The topic of our military presence in Middle Eastern countries includes, among many others, the following specific issues: the cost of wars; the wars' effects on economic growth; the spike in oil prices, the wars' effects on ethnic populations in Iraq, Afghanistan, and other countries; the decision to begin a preemptive war; concerns about weapons of mass destruction, diplomacy, reconstruction and humanitarian efforts; democracy and governance in these

☛ **tip 2b**

Narrow to a Single Issue

To make sure you are focused on an issue and not a topic, make a list of the reasons you intend to use to support your argument. Do some reasons seem substantial enough to become full arguments in themselves? If yes, consider refocusing on one of these issues.

Immigration Reform
• Border security • Citizenship • U.S. Intervention • Local business • Guest worker programs • Worker verification systems • Effects on citizen workforce • Workplace enforcement • Green cards

Office Politics
• Communication • Honesty • Taking credit • Rankism • Relationships • Trust • Dispute resolution • Fair treatment

Diet/Food Consumption
• Who grows it? • Working conditions • Pay scale • Transportation and greenhouse gases • Processing and packaging • Genetically engineered food • USDA standards • Obesity and advertising • Advertising and customer perception • Environmental impact, biodiversity loss, and excessive pesticide use • Global trends and local effects • Regulating imports

Life in the Classroom
• Disruptions and tardiness • Plagiarism • Assignments • Teacher performance • Course organization • Teacher availability • Relevance of course • Attendance policy

countries; the U.S. Constitution and the War Powers Resolution; returning veterans and their treatment; and the duration of the wars. Choosing one of these issues will make building your argument more manageable and more realistic.

The following section provides four topics, each from a different community, along with some of the many issues found within each topic. As outlined, immigration reform, office politics, diet/food consumption, and life in the classroom are broad topics containing many issues; if you're compelled to write within one of these categories, narrowing your focus to a single issue can result in a powerful, focused argument. Again, the issues identified for each topic are but a small sampling of the many issues related to each.

The work you do at this point—narrowing your focus to a single, arguable issue—can be the most important effort you make as you pull together an argument. Focus on a community, narrow your broad topic down to a single issue, probe the issue fully, and then determine where you stand and what you want to accomplish.

Pre-Think about Your Issue

Whether your topic has been assigned or self-selected, your argument will be much more successful if you are able to find an approach that is grounded in your own interests. It often happens that a topic is assigned and may not be one you wish to argue. As you work on your argument, at any stage before and after collecting your research, you should take some time to pre-think. Pre-thinking is a low-stakes process of thinking and writing about your issue. There is no right or wrong way to go about pre-thinking; its function is to give you time to reflect on your argument as it comes together. All pre-thinking methods do not work for all people. Some writers find freewriting provides them with the most ideas; some look at a blank page and freeze. Some love lists; others hate outlines. Find a process or method that works for you, but do spend time pre-thinking. During this process you may find an angle to your argument you had not expected, or you may be able to anticipate potential problems to avoid. The purpose of reflective thinking/writing at different points along the argument process is to allow you to see what you know so far versus what you still need to know, to question your assumptions, and to better explore your understanding of the audience.

There are some standard methods of pre-thinking that may already be familiar to you: brainstorming, mapping (or clustering), and freewriting. These are covered in this section, along with a more nontraditional method, "moving from boring to interesting."

Brainstorming

Brainstorming is one of the easiest prewriting techniques to use. Although you can brainstorm by yourself, it works best with several people. By yourself, you list as many topics that you can think of that relate to your topic, not bothering with connections, continuity, or practicality. The increased effectiveness of this technique when used with a group is apparent. As one person thinks of an idea, it prompts another person to think of another one, and a true storm of ideas can occur. Here is an example of a brainstorming session about an argument on wastewater assigned in an Urban Studies course.

• gray water	• chemicals	• cooking
• pollution	• household cleaners	• doll-making
• groundwater runoff	• white water rafting	• gardening

As you can tell, some terms likely inspired others (chemicals—household cleaners) and others are less obviously connected (pollution). Once a list is generated, you can begin seeing if there are any individual terms that may be a starting point for more brainstorming or a more focused argument topic. You may also find that there are terms that can be grouped together to make for a focused topic.

Freewriting

Freewriting is a technique made popular by Peter Elbow in his 1973 *Writing Without Teachers*. This technique shuts off the inner censor and frees you to write down all of your thoughts about a topic—random or focused. What do you know about your topic so far? What do you find interesting or boring about the topic? Can you find a personal connection to the topic? Some people time themselves or set a page limit, which forces them to produce material. When you have reached your time or page goal, you will no longer be faced with a blank page, and you may even have some ideas among the free-wheeling thoughts that could help you get started. An example passage of freewriting (on the same topic used for the brainstorm above) may look like this:

What can I say about wastewater? I don't think I have ever even thought about where the water from my toilet or sink goes. I have heard that some people use the water from their showers in their gardens. Is this even safe in a vegetable garden? But how safe is our water anyway? In a history course I learned that water from factories used to be directed into the rivers that people drank from. And people fuss about fluoride in their drinking water?

As the writer looks over the passage, she may find the idea of gray water a good starting point. Maybe the safety issue could lead to another round of freewriting to think more about those ideas.

Mapping

Mapping, also known as *clustering*, is a more focused form of brainstorming in which the writer consciously attempts to make connections between terms. In Figure 2.3, the term to be mapped is in the center circle, and the circles radiating from the center follow subterms.

Move from Boring to Interesting

One of America's best-loved authors, Ray Bradbury, loved to write and enjoyed his writing career immensely. The author of dozens of science fiction stories, Bradbury talked about the worst essay he ever wrote—a piece magazine editors asked him to write about life on other planets. Although he loved science fiction, he wasn't really interested in the assignment. Bradbury forged ahead and tinkered endlessly with the piece. He researched the topic to death and wound up producing a dead piece of writing. It took several editors to bring the article back to life. Bradbury, best known for his science fiction stories about life on other planets, was embarrassed. Bradbury's advice, and ours, is to write about what you are interested in, a topic that means something to you.

Angry at your city council for refusing to do anything about the graffiti problem near your child's school? Write a letter. See a problem at work? Send a memo. Have an assignment that seems boring? Find your own angle into the topic. Become engaged, and your writing will be engaging as well.

Writing about real-life situations rarely leads to boring arguments, but trying to write about an instructor-assigned topic can. How can you take a boring topic and find an interesting way to write about it? We call our method for addressing this problem "moving from boring to interesting."

This method can be applied to any topic. Let's say that in your Urban Studies course, you are assigned the topic of wastewater treatment plants, perhaps not the most exciting of topics. Can you really find something interesting to say about treating wastewater? Try this: list all the things you are interested in; it doesn't matter if they appear to have nothing to do with clean water.

Now try to make a connection between each of these topics and the one assigned: wastewater treatment plants.

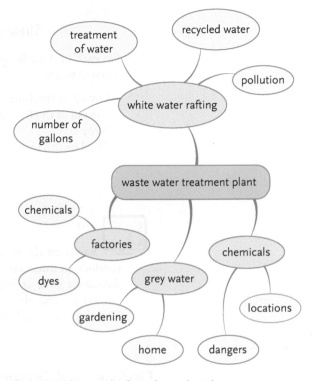

Figure 2.3 An example of mapping or clustering

- Where does the water come from for the new artificial white water rafting course in town? How is it treated?
- Cooking grease going down the drains—how does it get cleaned out of the water?
- How did the old process of draining dyes from nineteenth-century fabric manufacturers into rivers change the way water is treated today?
- Can gray water be used safely for gardens?

your turn 2b ▶ **GET STARTED** Use Boring to Interesting Strategies

For each of the following topics, make a connection to a topic that is of interest to you:

• Circadian rhythms
• The fall of the Roman Empire
• *Moby Dick*
• Rural health care

internet activity 2a **Exploring**

Based on the issues of concern you identified in "Your Turn 2a," conduct an informal Internet search for each issue. Use the academic databases your college provides, the online sites your teacher recommends, and the recommended websites described in Chapter 3, "Develop a Research Plan."

Define and Target Your Audience

A **target audience** is the group or individual at whom your argument is aimed; you want them to accept or at least acknowledge your position on an issue. Your audience initially may be opposed to your position, undecided about it, or lean toward accepting it. You may want audience members to take immediate action, to reflect on your argument, or to rethink their own points of view.

Aristotle, a founding father of what we know today as argument, encouraged his students to know their audiences before delivering arguments. As you choose issues on which to argue, make sure you know the people you plan to address. Are they inclined at first to accept or reject your claim? What are the ages and occupations of your audience? Are most people in your audience wealthy,

Figure 2.4 When you make an argument, choose your audience carefully and work to understand that audience as fully as possible.

Jetta Productions/Iconica/Getty Images

struggling financially, male, female? Use the following exercise to understand your audience. The work you do to understand your audience and its values will make it easier to craft a practical claim and find the best support to produce a solid, persuasive argument.

your turn 2c ▶ GET STARTED Define Your Audience

Your argument must be aimed at a specific target audience. To ensure that you're focused on a specific audience, answer the following questions about an issue and its relationship to your audience. Remember that you will argue before an audience that is as invested as you are in the issue at hand.

1. Who is the group or individual you want to persuade? List the reasons you want to target this audience. Be careful to avoid arguing to a general or neutral audience. Remember that you are writing to individuals with whom you may share certain values, goals, and expectations.
2. What are the physical characteristics, or demographics, of your audience? Consider these criteria as you make this determination: occupation, family size, age, gender, marital status, political leaning, religion, race or ethnicity, education, income, and geographic location.
3. Does your audience already have a position on your issue? Is your audience undecided about your issue? Is it likely to accept or reject your claim? Or does your audience occupy an extreme position? Explain.
4. What are the biases and limitations of your audience?

your turn 2d ▶ GET STARTED Reach Your Audience

Answer the following questions to identify the most practical ways to build an argument that is effective for your audience.

1. What sources will you use to establish full context for your issue? How will you research your issue so that you have a sense of how important the issue is to your audience? See Chapter 3, "Develop a Research Plan," for a guide to researching issues.
2. What kind of language makes your audience comfortable? Is it formal and academic, is it the language of political debate, is it the language of mainstream media, or is it informal language? Whatever language makes your audience comfortable, plan to use it in your argument.
3. How will you demonstrate respect for your audience?
4. Can you find common ground with your audience based on what audience members' values, experiences, loyalties, and likely emotional responses are? Explain.

5. Because establishing credibility with an audience is so important, what values and beliefs do you share with your audience?

6. What precisely do you want to accomplish with your audience? Do you want your audience members to question your issue, to learn more about it, to convert to your point of view, or simply to examine their current thinking on the issue?

7. To what extent will you need to inform your audience so that it can accept your argument? Based on what you know about your audience members, what can you assume they already know versus what they need to know in order to accept, but not necessarily agree with, your claim?

8. What will your audience permit you to claim; that is, what are the practical limits of your ability to persuade this particular audience? What is the range of perspectives audience members will accept regarding your issue? To determine the answers to these questions, you will need to know, at least generally, the beliefs and attitudes your audience holds on your issue. Guard against assuming that others share your views and values to keep you from "preaching to the choir," that is, addressing those who feel as you do about an issue.

Stake, Defend, and Justify Your Claim

Fully supporting your claim—your point of view on an issue—is vital to building a successful argument. And before you bring in specific information to defend your claim, it's essential that you use reasons in support of a claim. Many body paragraphs in effective arguments begin with reasons and then bring in specific support. Qualifiers, as noted in the second example below, make your claims and reasons more realistic and more practical.

Develop a Claim, Reasons, and Qualifiers

A claim is the most important part of your argument. Claims use precise language to let your audience know your point of view. For example, writing on the issue of bullying at your child's school requires orienting the reader right away to your point of view. Your claim organizes and centers an argument. Choose the kind of claim you want to use as the basis for your argument.

Working with Claims, Reasons, and Qualifiers: Three Examples

Each of the following three examples contains a sample claim and an explanation of that claim. Attention is also paid to the necessary elements of reasons and qualifiers, which are used to support the claim.

Claim: "Bullying at my child's school continues because school administrators refuse to thoroughly respond to this problem."

Discussion: The arguer has centered her argument in a clear claim that indicates cause and effect. The rest of the argument will be devoted to proving the accuracy of this claim. She'll need to be sure that readers understand the nature of school bullying and its effects, by defining the term *bullying* in specific language. The writer will also need to provide reasons that directly support her claim, and this will mean digging into the reasons administrators are failing to address the problem.

Figure 2.5 Defending a claim thoroughly with reasons and support is essential to a successful argument, especially when you have the attention of an audience. In this photo, the arguer is defending his claim to others who are also concerned about the issue.

Ted Soqui/Corbis

Claim: "Most people in our state favor giving tax breaks to new companies able to produce alternative energies, but many of our elected representatives seem to be working against this kind of incentive."

Discussion: The arguer can use this claim of fact to articulate the priorities that separate voters and representatives based on the factual information he brings in. He must prove that his claim is factual by bringing in support—examples, studies, testimony from experts, and so forth. Staying with this issue but centering his position around a claim of value, the claim might look like this: "It is unfair that the representatives we voted for are working against our calls to produce more alternative energy in the state." The word "unfair" makes this claim one of value; he has judged his representatives for overlooking popular interest. In the rest of the argument, the writer must prove precisely how the situation is unfair. Note the qualifiers "most," "many," and "seem" in the writer's claim. While the writer believes that numerous representatives have differing agendas on this issue, he avoids claiming that *all* representatives differ from *most* people. Qualifiers make claims more believable.

Claim: "Start times for local high schools should be moved back one hour."

Discussion: A few years ago, a parent made a compelling argument about the issue of start times for local high school students. Reasons were something like this: The parent was motivated because her kids had to get up early and were not at their best during the school day, and early start times and rescheduling transportation caused problems at home for everyone. She used a problem-based claim because she wanted something to change.

Choose the kind of claim that works best for what you want to accomplish in your argument. Choose the kind of claim that will put you in the best position to persuade your audience. Chapter 10, "Build Arguments," discusses claims and how they can serve your purpose in an argument.

Argue with a Purpose

Make the claim in your argument match the intensity of your purpose by asking yourself what, exactly, you want to accomplish. When you land on an issue that matters to you, you're in a position to argue with a purpose and strength. From there, you must ensure that everything you bring to your argument relates to your purpose.

Do you want readers to understand your issue more clearly and in terms that differ from its mainstream representation? Do you want to argue that something should change? Do you want to redefine a term or terms that in your view need clarification? Do you want to argue what causes an issue? Or do you want to respond to an issue through the lens of your own strong values or beliefs? Answering these questions will let you narrow your focus and choose the kind of claim that matches your purpose, thus letting you argue more persuasively. The kinds of claims described in Chapter 10, "Build Arguments"— fact, definition, evaluation, cause, and problem-based—give you the chance to build an argument around the kind of claim that best matches your purpose.

If extra-educational problems at school (for example, lack of parking, financial aid services, or academic advisors) interfere with the deeply held belief that your education will afford you opportunities for future success, then you have a purpose and a center to an argument. The reasons, varied support, and attention to the opposition you bring to such an argument will anchor your purpose and provide readers the concrete evidence needed to defend your claim.

your turn 2e ▶ **GET STARTED Identify Your Purpose**

Focus on two current issues in your life, one academic and one personal, and answer the following questions.

1. What would be your purpose in building an argument for each issue?
2. What is the claim you want to make for each issue?
3. What reasons come to mind as you reflect on each issue?
4. Can you bring to your argument personal experience with each issue? Explain.

Vary the Types of Support You Bring to an Argument

Our understanding of how support functions in an argument begins with the work of Aristotle, a Greek philosopher who used the terms *logos*, *ethos*, and *pathos* to categorize the ways in which an audience can be persuaded to accept a claim. Aristotle knew that the impression the arguer makes on an audience often can determine whether an argument will be taken to heart; he theorized that a conscientious audience wants to be assured that you appeal to it in three essential ways—through practical evidence grounded in reason (*logos*), through your good character (*ethos*), and through emotional appeals that touch the audience's values (*pathos*). While a sound argument is typically a blend of these appeals, good writers often devote 60 to 70 percent of their support to rational appeals. Use all three kinds of appeals in order to build the credibility of your argument and make it more believable. Following is an overview of these three kinds of support, all of which are covered in more depth in Chapter 3, "Develop a Research Plan."

Support Based on Fact

Factual support, or *logos*, includes verifiable information gathered from your research and experience. Arguing before your local school board for or against end-of-grade testing, for example, you'll want to do much of your persuading with facts, statistics, a range of documents, and other kinds of rational evidence. Documented reports from other school districts, for instance, are a kind of rational appeal. They can be studied and evaluated as part of the problem you're attempting to solve.

Support Based on Your Character

This kind of support, which Aristotle termed *ethos*, establishes your credibility. It is your job to present yourself as knowledgeable and, just as important, honest and fair-minded. Doing this thoroughly can build trust with your audience, essential to a successful argument. On the other hand, if your audience senses that you have an unstated motive or that you're not representing other views fairly, then trust is usually impossible. To earn credibility with your audience, be informed, make smart use of your own

Gary Conner/PhotoEdit

Figure 2.6 This arguer is building a research base for an argument by drawing on the work of experts. By presenting his research in a fair, open-minded way, he can build trust with an audience, vital to any competent argument.

experience, bring in the testimony of experts, respect readers by making your
language accessible, and reveal your motives. Bring in your child's experience
with end-of-grade testing, for example, to provide an insider's perspective on
testing issues. Balance your personal viewpoint by bringing in the findings of
bipartisan and independent professionals who have studied your issue.

Support Based on the Emotions of an Audience

Using emotional appeals, or *pathos*, is effective when you know what your
audience members value and the emotions that may sway them to accept your
claim. Examples from your life or from the lives of others in your community are especially useful. When you let readers identify with an emotionally
engaging example, you create a positive connection. If your neighbor believes
that end-of-grade testing narrows what's taught and does not encourage
intellectual curiosity, you can bring that perspective into your argument as
a way to touch other parents who agree with the neighbor's perspective. This
kind of appeal can also build a sense of community between you and your
readers, adding to the momentum of an argument.

your turn 2f ▶ **PRACTICE Vary Your Support**

Practice working with support for a claim by answering the following
questions, based on an issue you are considering for argument:

1. What kinds of facts can you offer?
2. How can you establish your credibility on the issue so that your audience will trust you?
3. Identify emotional connections you can create between your audience
   members and yourself that will allow readers to identify with your issue.

Working with a Target Audience: Two Examples

When you are motivated to argue on an issue, aim your argument at an
audience willing to listen, rethink the issue, and perhaps act on your claim.
Targeting the right audience can determine the success or failure of an argument. Review the following sample issues and arguers' efforts to target
appropriate audiences.

EXAMPLE 1

Develop a Claim and Target an Audience

The explanations in this first example walk you through the process
of determining a practical claim and audience for the issue of teacher
workload. As you can see, there are important choices an arguer must
make before the drafting process can begin.

TOPIC: Working Conditions

ISSUE: Workload

AUDIENCE: Readers of local newspaper

CLAIM: Current teacher workloads at our college limit the quality of education that students receive.

COMMUNITY:	Workplace
TOPIC:	Working conditions
ISSUES:	Salary
	Job description
	Interview and hiring protocol
	Benefits
	Workload
	Professional development opportunities
	Union representation
	Equal opportunity employment
	Dispute resolution policies
AUDIENCE:	State community college system officials
	College board of trustees
	State legislature
	College president
	Student body
	Coworkers
	Local government
	Readers of local newspaper
CLAIM:	Current teacher workloads at our college limit the quality of education that students receive.

Much thought has gone into this claim. Because it reveals an important issue in the lives of the arguers and because their purpose is to persuade, careful planning is needed when determining an appropriate audience. Review the following planning process regarding claim and audience for this "workload" issue.

Why this issue?

The workplace, a community nearly all of us belong to, is full of arguable issues. For example, we are authors of this text on purposeful argument, and we are workers in a labor force. As teachers we have issues, among them a deep concern about the number of classes we are required to teach each term. We feel that this issue of workload affects our job performance, our professionalism, and importantly, our ability to serve students. We plan to aim our argument at a specific audience and to prove our claim with specific kinds of support.

Why this audience?

This argument will target readers of our local newspaper and thus will appear both in print and online formats. We chose this audience because its members' tax dollars in part support our publicly funded college, because members of our community expect quality services, because individual readers of the argument (and perhaps their family members) have attended our college, and because the integrity of the local workforce is dependent on the graduates of our college and their training. We feel that other audiences may view our issue from different perspectives and may be less likely to be swayed by our claim.

Why this claim?

We will work with a claim of cause because our intention is to inform readers how teacher workload compromises our ability to meet students' expectations, the mission of the college, and the school's service to the community. We are not calling for immediate action; rather, the purpose of the argument is to let readers know in specific terms about the issue and to suggest that they reflect on it. As a first step in acting on this issue, we hope to generate interest and awareness. A follow-up argument would be aimed at a different audience, one with decision-making power, and may require a problem-based claim in which we argue for a reduced workload. But for now our goal is to raise awareness of this workload issue. (For descriptions of kinds of claims, see Chapter 8, "Consider Toulmin-Based Argument," and Chapter 9, "Consider Middle Ground and Rogerian Argument, and Argument Based on Microhistory.")

We assume that many of our audience members know the services our college provides, but that many may not be aware of teacher workload and how it affects delivery of the expected services. Accordingly, the support we bring to the argument, especially specific examples drawn from our experiences, will be vital to fully informing our audience. Because the college has served the community for many years, we can expect some immediate "permission" from our audience to argue our claim, but based on our research, we also know that there has been some persistent grumbling in the past two election cycles over bond proposals that, if passed, would earmark money to the college, and we will need to fully acknowledge and respond to this concern in one of our rebuttals.

EXAMPLE 2

Map an Argument for a Target Audience

> **TOPIC:** The Online Classroom
>
> **ISSUE:** Teacher–student interaction
>
> **AUDIENCE:** Director of Distance Learning
>
> **CLAIM:** Clear standards for teachers' regular interaction with students should be stated in the introductions to online English courses.

When you settle on a claim and a target audience, it can be helpful to rough out most of an argument. This example presents a preview of a Toulmin-based argument, typically the most common kind of argument used in academic writing. (Toulmin-based and other kinds of arguments are discussed in Chapter 8, "Consider Toulmin-Based Argument," and Chapter 9, "Consider Middle Ground and Rogerian Argument, and Argument Based on Microhistory.") The example picks up on the issue that opens this chapter. This will give you a sense of how the parts of an argument work together. All parts of an argument are fully discussed in chapters that follow.

COMMUNITY:	School/Academic
TOPIC:	The online classroom
ISSUES:	Course navigation
	Clarity of course objectives and expectations
	Online courses and ADA requirements
	Teacher–student interaction
	Grading policies

	Teacher feedback
	Accessibility of course materials
	Course technologies
	Student support services
AUDIENCE:	Teacher
	Department chair
	Other online students
	College dean
	Readers of your local newspaper
	Director of distance learning
	College president
CLAIM:	Clear standards for teachers' regular interaction with students should be stated in the introductions to online English courses.

Why this issue?

Of the many issues that fall under the topic of the online classroom, teacher–student interaction is the most compelling in the online course experience of this writer. Writing about distance learning in general is much too broad, and a writer is sensible to choose a single issue that can be argued in depth. Other issues listed may be of concern, but for this writer they are not as pressing as the need for clear guidelines regarding the interaction with and availability of instructors of online courses.

Why this audience?

The writer plans to aim this argument at her college's director of distance learning in the form of a substantial letter. While there are other possible targets for this argument, the director of distance learning may be the most practical choice because the director is invested in the integrity of the college's distance learning program and capable of acting on the writer's concern for regular interaction with her online teachers. Other audience choices are not as directly tied to online course concerns. Additional practical reasons to target this audience may include the director's ability to suggest options that address the writer's concern, such as disseminating to teachers online course templates that model effective student interaction; designing workshops for teachers; and producing comprehensive student opinion surveys where students' concerns about contact with teachers can be documented.

Because the director is the most important person associated with online instruction at this school, the writer can assume the director knows the importance of student–teacher interaction in online environments. Additionally, the director likely has training in current theoretical approaches to distance learning and thus is in a position to hear the arguer's concern. Writing to a department chair, dean, or college president would add another administrative layer and probably would require considerable explanation of the claim.

As the audience for this argument likely shares the writer's goal of supporting student success in online courses, the director of distance learning may find reasonable a claim for establishing clear standards; in addition, these changes are well within the director's decision-making limits. This kind of "permission" from an audience is essential.

Research

The writer would be wise to research the goals of the college's distance learning program and its commitment to students. This information should be available on the college's website and in the print catalog. However, a quick review of several institutions that offer online programs shows that the schools' websites offer little information about teacher–student interaction standards for online courses. The University of Illinois's online catalog, for example, describes the kinds of lectures that may be offered by its online faculty but suggests that students contact faculty for specifics about how the courses will be managed. And many community colleges in the state offer no information about expectations for student–teacher interaction in online courses.

Why this claim?

The writer is clear in her claim that she wants her audience to respond to this argument by way of direct action. In this case, the writer strongly implies that she wants the director to respond to her point of view and take action that will result in improved interaction with her online teachers. This kind of claim, where a writer is arguing for something to change, is a problem-based claim.

Other possible claims

The five kinds of claims available to a writer arguing on a particular issue are discussed in Chapter 10, "Build Arguments." The following types of claims represent those a writer might consider specifically when arguing the issue of student–teacher interaction in the online classroom.

- Teaching effectively in the online classroom includes interacting regularly with students. (This is a **claim of definition**, where the writer will center an argument by defining a key word or term and then provide reasons for the definition. In this example, the writer would define the phrase "teaching effectively in the online classroom.")

- Regular interaction with teachers is essential for success in online courses. (In this example, the writer would use a **claim of fact** and prove in the argument that it is a fact that succeeding in online courses requires regular interaction with teachers.)
- The absence of clear standards regarding student–teacher interaction in online classes is unfair to students. (A **claim of evaluation** involves the writer making a judgment or evaluation. In this example, the writer will be responsible for proving that it is unfair to students when they enroll in online courses that are missing clear standards for student–teacher interaction.)
- Regular student–teacher interaction in online courses will often result in better grades and better understanding of course content. (A **claim of cause** argues that one thing causes another. In this example the writer would argue that regular interaction in the online classroom can lead to better student grades and a better grasp of course content.)

When you are fully motivated to argue a point of view on an issue important to you and are realistic in the audience you target, you can begin building your argument. Continuing with the issue of student–teacher interaction in the online classroom, this is how the writer might outline the remainder of her argument before beginning work on a first draft.

Warrant/Justification   This term is discussed fully in Chapter 8, "Consider Toulmin-Based Argument," and refers to a deeply held value, belief, or principle you share with your audience. To make a successful argument, your audience must, in a sense, grant you permission to make your argument based on a shared value, such as the belief that students should succeed in online courses. In this argument, a successful warrant might be: "Student success in online classes means that students will complete their educations and the college will fulfill its mission to educate students."

Reasons   Reasons, similar to topic sentences, are used to support your claim. They are followed by more specific kinds of support. Here are reasons this writer might use in building her argument:

- Specific turnaround times for responses to email messages and graded assignments will guarantee feedback for my questions and performance on my assignments.
- Regular teacher participation on the class discussion board means that all members of a class benefit from the teacher guiding us through challenging parts of the course.
- Trust and teamwork in a class are more likely to develop when the teacher is prompt with feedback.
- Teachers can and should model practical ways to interact online.

Support   Specific kinds of support the writer can bring to these reasons fall into logical, ethical, and emotional categories (discussed in more depth in Chapter 11, "Support an Argument with Fact (Logos), Credibility (Ethos), and

Emotion (Pathos)." This writer certainly can rely on personal experiences in online classes, refer to experts in the field of distance learning and the experience of other students, and use examples that will appeal to readers' emotions.

Backing and Reservations   Backing is the support you bring for your warrant. In this argument, examples of student success will provide effective backing that, overall, the college does fulfill its mission. A reservation is a statement that cautions readers that the warrant does not apply in certain circumstances. For example, a reservation in this argument might be: "But if online students do not have the chance to evaluate teachers' abilities to interact with students during a course, then standards may not be effective."

Rebuttals and Differing Views   A writer brings rebuttals and differing views to an argument to acknowledge and respond to other points of view on an issue. Some objections to this writer's claim might include the following: online courses are more time consuming than real-time courses for teachers and thus there is limited time to interact with students; many online teachers feel that students should use online resources instead of depending on teacher feedback; and teacher–student interaction in online courses is not part of a teacher's annual review and therefore is not considered, by many teachers, to be important. The writer must answer, or counter, each rebuttal. Differing views on this issue may not argue directly against this writer's claim but may approach the issue from different perspectives. The writer may choose to build on and extend these views or to demonstrate their shortcomings.

Qualifiers   Qualifiers make an argument more practical because they involve words and terms like "in most cases" or "often" that replace words like "only" and "always." For example, would the second reason given above— "Regular teacher participation on the class discussion board means that all members of a class benefit from teacher guidance through challenging parts of the course"—be more believable if a qualifier were added and read, "Regular teacher participation on the class discussion board means that *many* members of a class would benefit from teacher guidance through challenging parts of the course"? Qualifiers should be used throughout an argument and are discussed in Chapter 10, "Build Arguments."

your turn 2g ▸ PRACTICE Map an Argument

Based on the overview of the argument process this chapter provides, identify a pressing issue in your life and perform the following tasks:

1. Write a first draft of a claim.
2. Identify the values you share with your audience.
3. Draft reasons and outline support for your claim.
4. Establish backing to address audience reservations.
5. Identify opposing viewpoints and rebuttals.
6. Use qualifiers to make your claim and reasons practical.

Argue at the Right Moment

The essential work you must do in planning an argument—determine an issue important to you, identify a practical target audience for your argument, and map your argument—requires another vital consideration: arguing at the right time. This means delivering an argument at a time when it is most likely to be heard and responded to. As a perceptive arguer, take advantage of current local and intellectual interest in an issue to energetically deliver an argument, something the individuals in Figure 2.7 are prepared to do.

An argument can be effective when you deliver it at the right time, what in classical rhetoric is known as *kairos*, or timeliness. This means having a strong understanding of your audience and how ready it is for your claim. It also means having a sense of the issue's urgency. For example, if your audience is your colleagues—your fellow students—when might be the best time to argue about the issue of increased campus parking fees? You may decide that early in the semester is best—a time when registration, textbook fees, and parking fees are fresh in the minds of other students *and* a time before projects are due or major exams are looming.

If, on the other hand, your aim is to inform readers of your local newspaper (via a substantial letter to the editor) that home foreclosure rates are increasing in your community due to predatory lending practices, you may determine that the best time to make your argument is when local media are reporting on this issue and when community interest is high. Likewise, an argument on the issue of air quality will have more currency during the run-up to an important policy decision on toxic emissions than after such a decision.

When you sense that the time is right to deliver an argument, take full advantage of the momentum surrounding your issue. This is good timing. Delivering an argument before an audience is ready for it or when an issue's urgency has passed can render the argument, and your efforts, ineffective. So how can you determine the right time to make your argument? Determine how an issue is affecting an audience. For example, if you're concerned about how wounded troops returning from Iraq and Afghanistan are being treated, and you know that local and national news media are reporting on this issue, you may decide to target your state's U.S. senators as your audience and let them know that legislation should be proposed based on this current problem. You can also keep your focus closer to home and target veterans' groups and area veterans' affairs hospitals. Deliver your argument when public exposure and interest in an issue

Gerry Boughan/Shutterstock.com

Figure 2.7 Deliver an argument to an audience when there is genuine and immediate interest in an issue. In this political rally, individuals are responding with genuine interest to the issue of health care reform.

have created an opening for change so as to ensure that your argument has currency and that your voice will be part of the conversation.

What might be the best times to argue the sample issues discussed previously? The writer who claims the need for clear standards of interaction with her online teachers may choose to deliver the argument toward the end of the academic term, a time when she will have established her credibility with her audience as a serious student wanting more from her online course and also a time when the director of distance learning may take seriously the need to implement new policies for the next term. Concerning our goal of raising local awareness of the workload issue at our college, we plan to deliver the argument to our local newspaper in October, approximately a month before voters decide on a bond proposal that would direct money to our school. We also note local and national media reporting on the trend of more students electing to complete their first two years of study at two-year and community colleges, as tuition cost in those institutions is substantially lower than at four-year colleges. With both issues, arguing at appropriate times will be crucial to attracting the immediate interest of an audience.

> **your turn 2h** ▶ **GET STARTED Argue at the Right Moment**
>
> Answer the following questions about your claim or one of your claims. Is it a good time to argue your claim with this particular audience? If not, how can you either adjust your claim so that it is timely or target a different audience that you determine is the right one to hear your claim right now?
>
> 1. Are you arguing at a time when your audience is aware of and invested in your issue? Explain.
> 2. Are you confident in your claim and prepared to defend it? Explain.
> 3. Describe the ways your audience can benefit from reflecting on or acting on your claim.
> 4. Are conditions such that your audience is willing to tolerate differing views on your issue? If yes, describe how you will take advantage of this time in an informed way in your argument.

Getting Started

After you decide on an issue, target an audience, map your argument, and decide on the right time to deliver your argument, use the following prompts to get started. These prompts are designed to move you deeper into your feelings about an issue and help you determine whom you want to persuade, what you want to change, and how accepting your claim can benefit the audience you're targeting. Answering these prompts can give you insight into the direction an argument should take.

 tip 2c

Read the Signs!
To determine if an argument will carry weight with an audience, make a list of the indications, or signs, that the time is right to craft and deliver your argument. This list can include conversations you participate in and overhear, articles in the local media, and references to the issue that you find in blogs, magazines, and websites.

your turn 2i ▶ GET STARTED **With an Argument**

Complete the following sentences as a way of getting started with an argument.

1. What topics *not* included in the earlier section "Determine What Matters to You and Why" might you be interested in addressing?
2. Thinking in terms of both your personal life and your academic life, what issues concern you the most?
3. What are the two or three most pressing issues for you both inside and outside the classroom?
4. What is the single issue on which you are most motivated to argue? Explain.
5. In response to question 4, what makes you sure that you are taking on a manageable issue and not a broad topic?
6. In addition to your own position on this single issue, briefly describe other points of view.

your turn 2j ▶ GET STARTED **Target the Right Audience**

With regard to the issue you have identified as motivating for you, describe your target audience by answering the following questions.

1. What are the two or three most practical target audiences for this argument?
2. How do you want your audience to respond after taking in your argument?
3. Based on how you want your audience to respond, what is the most practical target audience for your argument?
4. What is it about the demographics of your target audience that suggests it is a practical choice?
5. What are the values and beliefs you share with your target audience?
6. In practical, everyday terms, why do you want to persuade this target audience?

your turn 2k ▶ GET STARTED **Draft the Right Claim**

Respond to the following questions as a way to determine whether a claim is appropriate for your argument.

1. By accepting your claim, how will your target audience benefit?
2. Of the five kinds of claims described under "Example #2: Map an Argument for a Target Audience," what kind of claim is most appropriate for your audience? Explain.

your turn 2 GET STARTED **Research an Issue**

As a way to begin your research process, respond to the following questions.

1. So as to fully inform an audience about your issue, what sources will you consult first?
2. Based on the issue you plan to argue on, why will it be necessary to gather compelling evidence to defend your claim and reasons?
3. Are there particular biases and limitations that could get in the way of your target audience accepting your claim? If yes, what are they?
4. What opposing points of view do you feel should be included? How will you respond to them?
5. Why is now a practical time to argue on your issue? Explain why your target audience will have a natural interest in this issue.

Reflect and Apply

Answer the questions that follow to ensure that the argument you plan to build is a practical response to an issue that matters to you.

1. Explain why the issue you're working with is important to you now. Why is it more important than other issues in your life?
2. Discuss how you'll focus on a single issue in an argument and thus avoid the kind of general writing that results from a focus that is too broad.
3. Who is your target audience? What are its values? What research will you pursue to better understand this audience?
4. Discuss how the parts of an argument mentioned in Example #2— warrant/justification, reasons, support, backing and reservations, rebuttals, and qualifiers—will be treated in the argument you plan to build.
5. Of the types of claims discussed in this chapter, which one seems the most practical for the issue you're addressing? Explain.
6. Defend the timeliness of your argument; that is, explain why now is a practical time to build and deliver it. Refer to successful arguments, in either public or private life, that have been delivered at the right moment.

KEEPING IT LOCAL

POWERFUL, compelling arguments often begin in very private, personal moments with issues that present a struggle for you. Pay close attention to these moments. Writing an argument gives you a structure to dignify what you're feeling and to influence an audience. Choosing to write on issues that matter to you can clarify how argument fits into your life and how sound arguments can serve your short- and long-term goals. When you make your point of view on an issue known, you also contribute to democratic life in your specific and broader communities.

The writer who argued about the need for better interaction with her online instructor forged a clear, purposeful claim and wanted immediate action taken in response. After all, in practical terms, she won't be a student at her college much longer, and she's speaking up with the hope that she will not run into this problem in another online course. The anxiety she felt about her upcoming exam and her desire to be prepared for it made the problem she had with her instructor an issue that mattered to her. The issue evolved from a community (school) in which she invested much time and money. Because she wanted her issue to be addressed with action, her argument moved beyond the status of class assignment and into real life. This is how argument can be a practical skill for everyday living. The writer targeted her argument at the director of distance learning at her college, an official who could be motivated to act in response to the issue. In this case, arguer and audience overlap in their concerns for effective student–teacher interaction, prompt delivery of services, and higher education as an essential step in meeting career goals. Furthermore, delivering her argument at the right time—during her college career and during a course in which teacher response time needs to improve—also makes her argument practical. This student wasn't getting what she needed from her online instructor and did something about it. Mapping her argument carefully, she supported a strong claim and aimed the argument at an audience likely to take it seriously. Her efforts are proof that argument can serve what matters to us.

● – – – – – – – – – – – – ●

In the last few weeks or months, what is the most compelling argument you've encountered? From what community in the arguer's life did it spring? What got your attention and what made it compelling? Describe how an issue in your own life can match the intensity and purpose of the argument you identify.

PART TWO

How to Establish Context through Research

CHAPTER 3 Develop a Research Plan

CHAPTER 4 Evaluate and Engage with Your Sources

CHAPTER 5 Read Critically and Avoid Fallacies

CHAPTER 6 Work Fairly with the Opposition

All Illustrations by iStockphoto.com/A-digit

Develop a
Research Plan

You always arrive a few minutes early to your office to check your personal email at your desk. Then, about midmorning, when your colleagues are taking a smoke break, you log on to the Internet to check the scores for last night's baseball games. When things get a little slow after lunch, you sometimes play a couple of hands of solitaire on the computer. At your yearly evaluation, you are surprised to receive not only poor comments but also a reprimand that you are wasting company time by misusing your computer. How did your boss know what you were doing at your desk? Electronic surveillance. Can your company watch what you are doing on your computer? Is it legal for the company to "spy" on you? You head back to the computer, the one at home, and begin researching employee monitoring. You're surprised at what you find.

COMMUNITY

School-Academic

Workplace

Family-Household

Neighborhood

Social-Cultural

Consumer

Concerned Citizen

TOPIC: Computer Usage

ISSUE: Privacy and Computer Use

AUDIENCE: Business Ethics Professor

CLAIM: Workplace electronic monitoring practices should be revealed to employees through company policies.

Research is the backbone of much of the writing you will do in school and in the workplace, and there are many ways to conduct research—via print sources, the Internet, interviews, and so on. These sources have to be integrated with your own ideas to create a researched essay or report that follows a certain format appropriate either for your academic classes or for your workplace. The whole process can become overwhelming, particularly with the additional burden of avoiding plagiarism.

In Chapter 1, "Argue with a Purpose," you learned how argument can work for you, its purpose, and some argumentative strategies. You discovered the process of choosing an issue to argue in Chapter 2, "Explore an Issue that Matters to You." The focus of this chapter is on introducing the various types of resources available and how to find them. Chapter 4, "Evaluate and Engage with Your Sources," will focus on how to evaluate and read the various types of resources and how to incorporate and cite information from those sources into your writing. "Appendix A: MLA Documentation and the Works Cited Page" and "Appendix B: APA Documentation and the References Page" cover how to create a works cited page for your researched report or essay in MLA and APA format.

Throughout Chapters 3 and 4 you will follow the progress of Hal, a college student who is writing a researched argument on computer surveillance of employees for his Business Ethics course. Whether you have two weeks or two months, the strategies in these chapters should help you tackle any project.

Once you have your issue in mind, and at any other stage of the argument–writing process when you need more information, it is time for serious research. The types and number of sources available are seemingly endless. Google, the most popular Internet search engine, searches billions of pages of information. Many libraries now subscribe to thousands of newspapers, journals, and magazines through databases. These databases also offer reference and scholarly books that can be read online. Large libraries house thousands of books and other print media. If you plan on finding any needles in this enormous information haystack, you will need a research plan. Begin with setting up a basic library of reference tools that can answer questions and provide facts.

In Chapter 3 you will develop a research plan to:

- Use reference works, encyclopedias, and topic overviews profitably.
- Gather search terms.
- Use search engines to find Internet sources on the surface web and on the deep web.
- Perform keyword queries.
- Find new sites and use RSS feeds to receive updates.
- Find and use databases in libraries.
- Find and use primary, government, and multimedia sources.
- Find books.

Use Reference Works, Encyclopedias, and Topic Overviews Profitably

Although they are not considered acceptable sources to include in college-level arguments, reference works and encyclopedias are extremely useful for fact checking and providing issue context. Many of these sources, such as the *CIA World Factbook*, the *Infoplease Almanac*, dictionaries, and encyclopedias, are available on the Internet or through public and college libraries. Find them and bookmark them so that they are literally at your fingertips when you need them. Infoplease (http://www.infoplease.com) provides quick facts through a world atlas and almanac, the *Columbia Encyclopedia, Brewer's Dictionary of Phrase and Fable*, information on U.S. politics, world rulers, and much more.

Here is a good list of sites to bookmark:

- The CIA's *The World Factbook*: https://www.cia.gov/library/publications/the-world-factbook
- RefDesk.com, which has links to reference sources covering medicine, people, weather, government, and public records, among many other subjects: http://www.refdesk.com
- The U.S. Census Bureau's Quick Facts: http://quickfacts.census.gov/qfd/index.html

Read an Overview of Your Topic

What do you know about your topic? Often you will be familiar with topics assigned in class: the Battle of Appomattox; the id, ego, and superego; teenage suicide; *The Scarlet Letter*; Russian propaganda posters. Familiarity, though, is not enough of a foundation for a written argument. Too many writers skip making themselves familiar with their topic and rush to gather sources.

At the beginning of your research, find an overview article, brochure, or reference work about your topic. This is the one time in the research process to find an encyclopedia article. Encyclopedias are a great, yet often misused, resource for writers. Even though you may not use material from an overview or general reference work or encyclopedia in an academic argument, these sources are invaluable for two things: (1) providing an understanding of the background and context of your issue and (2) offering a list of search terms. Encyclopedias offer background information in a brief outline, listing key people and events involved in the issue and providing a list of search terms that will be of great value when you begin your more sophisticated searches. Your library will have at least one encyclopedia, usually electronic, and often more than one. Encyclopedias can be found on the Internet as well.

The most frequently used Internet encyclopedia is Wikipedia. This resource accepts contributions from anyone who cares to write on a topic. While scholars are working to produce stronger and more research-driven articles, Internet encyclopedia articles have their fair share of errors. They are still excellent sources for compiling search terms, bibliographies, and links to other sites. Some of these articles are well written and supported with sources; others are not. You must use some caution and some common sense to avoid information that is misleading and erroneous. Looking at articles on your issue in more than one encyclopedia will provide you with even more information to get you started. You may not cite from any encyclopedia, print or online, in academic writing.

To return to our example, Hal was interested in an overview of electronic surveillance of employees in the workplace, so he began a search with *Funk & Wagnall's New World Encyclopedia*. He tried several search terms, including *electronic surveillance* and *email privacy*, but had no luck. He then tried *Wikipedia* and found a lengthy article on surveillance that included privacy issues and links to legal resources. An article on email privacy netted him even better results. One of the valuable terms he gathered was the Electronic Communications Privacy Act and a link to the legal case of *Smyth v. Pillsbury*, in which "a reasonable expectation of privacy" was not found to extend to emails sent from company computers. This helped Hal to understand what has been done on the issue so far.

Other overviews can be found by simply typing some of the following words, along with your topic, into an Internet search engine:

- Overview
- Context
- Background
- History
- Introduction

Hal tried the word "overview" along with "Internet privacy" and retrieved a Congressional Report that provided an overview and the most current legislation on the issue.

☛ **tip 3a**

List Search Terms and Vocabulary

As you conduct your research, keep track of words and phrases that apply to your issue. When you conduct searches on search engines and in databases, having a list of search terms will make your searching more effective.

Gather Search Terms

To find information more efficiently, keep a thorough list of search terms. Once established, a list of search terms can be plugged into as many search engines as you care to use. Be as concise with your terms as you can, but be prepared to broaden your terms if you are not receiving any hits.

Hal came away from his overview reading with a number of search terms that he found:

- Internet privacy
- e-Government Act
- Email tracking
- Employee privacy
- Electronic surveillance
- Electronic communication
- Employee privacy rights
- Email privacy

As Hal reads, he will add more terms to his list.

Notice that some of these terms seem very close to each other, and some are actually synonyms. It is important to think of all the ways a topic may come up so that you are not cutting off avenues of research because your selected search term does not match the one used by the creators of the search engine. For example, if you are searching for statistics about car buying trends, you should use both the terms *car* and *automobile*. The more terms you use, the less likely you are to miss potentially useful sources.

Background Research

- ☐ 1. Check reference sources for basic facts.
- ☐ 2. Consult encyclopedia or reference book overviews for context, search terms, and links to articles.
- ☐ 3. Develop list of search terms.

internet activity 3a Read Encyclopedia Articles or Other Overviews on Your Issue

Find at least two introductions to your issue, and answer the following questions about each:

1. What is the background of your issue?
2. Who is involved?
3. What are some of the search terms you can use when conducting further research?
4. How do the articles compare with each other? Are there any incidents of personal opinion or bias in the articles? Do the articles seem objective and fact oriented?

Use Search Engines to Find Internet Sources on the Surface Web and on the Deep Web

Armed with a better understanding of the history of electronic privacy, Hal prepares to conduct an Internet search. This process will take place many times throughout the research and writing process, as new information is needed or new ideas elicit new searches. Many people content themselves with visiting their favorite search engine and using whatever sources appear on the first page of hits. This may be fine if you are looking for football scores (though there are better ways to find even that information), but if you are looking for sources suitable for academic writing, you'll need to dig further.

Not all search engines produce the same search results. Most people are familiar with Google, Ask.com, and Yahoo!, but there are many more search engines available that do different things. Even if you are happy with Google, you are probably not using all of the powerful research tools it has to offer. We will learn some of its features throughout this chapter.

Search the Surface Web

You are likely already familiar with **search engines,** vehicles for finding material on the World Wide Web. What you may not know is that search engines are not all the same. Type in the same query at each of the engines listed below, for example, and you will get different results from each. The way they each search, collect, and rank hits is different.

Some consistently useful search engines include:

- Google   http://www.google.com
- Yahoo!   http://search.yahoo.com
- Ask.com   http://www.ask.com
- Bing   http://www.bing.com

A considerable list of search engines is also available through Mohawk Valley Community College at http://mvcc.libguides.com.

Hal used the same search term ("electronic privacy" + work) in four different search engines: Ask.com, Bing, Yahoo!, and Google (see Figure 3.1). You can see that the search results and their organization are very different from one site to the next. In addition, three search engines offer additional search terms to use and one doesn't. Find a search engine that retrieves results in a method that makes sense to you.

Hal began a new search on Google using the phrase "workplace privacy" (see Figure 3.2). The sites highlighted in purple are the ones Hal visited. Notice that the ending of the URL (the website's address) for these three sites is ".org." This indicates that the site is maintained by an organization, although the rules for determining "organizational" status seem to be flexible. By visiting the Privacy Rights Clearinghouse, the Electronic Privacy Information Center, and the American Civil Liberties Union, Hal was able to come away with several views of the issue of workplace privacy.

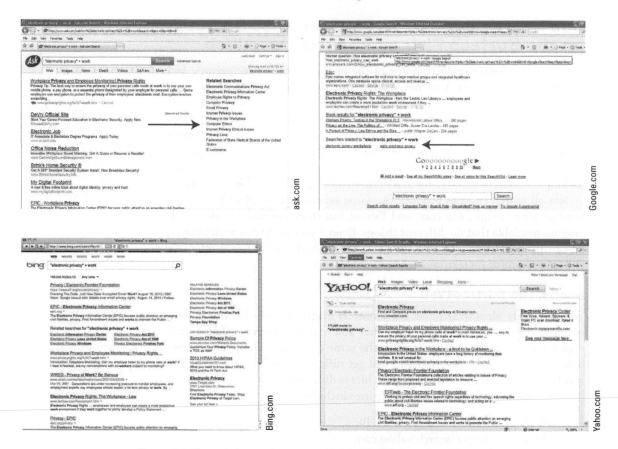

ask.com

Google.com

Bing.com

Yahoo.com

Figure 3.1 The same keyword search conducted with different search engines

Google.com

Figure 3.2 Google search screen

Other than .org domains, a URL can end with the following extensions:

- .com   a commercial site
- .edu   an educational site, such as a school or university
- .gov   a government site, for example the Library of Congress or the White House
- .int   not so common, but refers to an international site
- .mil   extension used by U.S. military organizations such as the Army or Navy
- .net   used as a generic extension for many types of sites
- .org   used by an organization

internet activity 3b Compare Search Engines

Select several search engines and conduct a quick basic search to see what hits are returned and how they are organized. Which search engine appeals the most to you based on page layout, number of hits, and organization?

Search the Deep Web

The search engines listed above will search the surface web, but did you know that there is more to the Internet than what Google and Yahoo! can find? There are thousands of sources that cannot be easily accessed by general-purpose search engines. This information is called the "deep web," or sometimes the "invisible web." Some studies indicate that what we can generally access on the Web is only 1/500th of what is out there. Some of this information is password or firewall protected, but much of it is just in formats that do not make it easy for the search engines to find. Many databases housing scholarly or scientific information are available in the deep web, and there are search engines and database sites developed to access much of it.

- LibrarySpot.com (http://libraryspot.com): Particularly useful are the site's link to scholarly journals that can be accessed online and its link to museum sites. The World Digital Library, for example, offers thousands of images from many countries.
- Infomine (http://infomine.ucr.edu): This site indexes scholarly Internet resource collections arranged by subject.
- Academic Info (http://www.academicinfo.net/subject-guides): This site has a wonderful directory of subject guides that offer links to resources. The link to Afghanistan News and Media, for example, offers links to Afghan newspapers, documentaries, and materials from the State Department.

- Scirus (http://scirus.com): According to the Scirus home page, the search engine finds "not only journal content but also scientists' homepages, courseware, pre-print server material, patents and institutional repository and website information."
- Librarians' Internet Index (http://www.ipl.org): This search site is organized by subject. The government subject link has 34 additional subtopics that can be browsed. It is a real gold mine for finding quality material. The Internet Public Library (IPL) has recently merged with the Librarian's Internet Index (LII) resulting in IPL2.
- Find Articles (http://findarticles.com): This site contains articles from many journals, but not all of the articles are free. You can always retrieve abstracts of the articles, however, which can help you determine if the article is one you may want to request through your library's interlibrary loan service.
- Intute (http://intute.ac.uk): According to the website, "Intute is a free online service providing access to the very best web resources for education and research." Sources are organized into four broad categories: science and technology, arts and humanities, social sciences, and life and health sciences.

Other search engines to use are Complete Planet, http://completeplanet.com and Surfwax, http://surfwax.com. Try them all to see what you can find on your issue. As you can probably tell, research is not a one-stop activity. The broader you cast your net, the more likely you will find sources that are reputable and pertinent to your issue.

Keep this template (and all the other publication information templates typed in red in this chapter) available as you collect sources. Not all information will be available on every website; record what is available. You may want to be careful about sites that do not have authors that you can find out more about.

 tip 3b

Using a Bibliography File

Always collect publication information for an electronic source. If you do not have this information when you write your report, you will not be able to use the source. And trying to relocate an Internet source can be exceedingly frustrating and time consuming.

A bibliography file is a great way to keep your sources organized. You may not have a use for a particular article once you've completed your assessment, but you may change your thesis at a later date, and a previously useless article may now be useful.

Source Information: Template

Author, if one is listed: _____

Title of the specific web page: _____

Website that hosts the page: _____

Date it was posted: _____

Date you accessed it: _____

Note that if you find a source that is actually an article from an online periodical, you will need to gather the complete periodical publication information in addition to the site information.

internet activity 3c **Explore the Deep Web**

The deep web is a great place to explore. Take your time playing with the search engines and databases, and mark the ones that include material on your issue for future searches.

Perform Keyword Queries

Now that you are familiar with some of the available search engines and database sites that will look for information on the Web, you should read the following instructions on basing keyword queries on the vocabulary lists you created during your basic fact and encyclopedia reading so that your searches will be more effective and efficient. Remember when Hal typed in the query "electronic privacy" + work? He was using a **search string** to tell the search tool what he was looking for. You can use Boolean search operators (*not, and,* and *or*) between your search terms to tell the search engine exactly what to look for. Boolean logic can be tweaked endlessly, whereas using + and – signs will only add or subtract terms from your search. The following chart lists the basic kinds of search strings you can use and what they mean.

Search String	What You Are Asking For
electronic privacy	Pages that have both the words *electronic* AND *privacy* somewhere on the page
"electronic privacy"	Pages that have both words next to each other
"electronic privacy" AND work	Pages that have both words next to each other AND include the word *work* somewhere on the page
"electronic privacy" + work	Same as above
"electronic privacy" NOT surveillance	Pages that have both words next to each other and do NOT include the word *surveillance*
"electronic privacy" – work	Same as above
"electronic privacy" 2010...2014	Pages that have both words next to each other AND only pages that have material between the date range of 2010 and 2014
site: .edu	Pages from educational websites only

You will need to gather the following publication information for articles found on the databases. Record all available information—not every site will have all the elements listed.

Source Information: Article from Website (Basic)

Author of article: _____

Title of article: _____

Title of periodical: _____

Publication information of periodical: _____

And then,

Author(s) of web page: _____

Title of web page: _____

Title of website: _____

Date originally posted: _____

Date you accessed the site: _____

MLA no longer requires the URL, but recording it is helpful in finding the site again.

 internet activity 3d Perform Internet and Internet Database Searches

Using one of the search engines or database sites listed previously, find three Internet sources pertaining to your topic. Use the advanced search feature for your search engine, or use the search strings above to limit your results to .edu domains for the past three months only.

Find News Sites and Use RSS Feeds to Receive Updates

Hal also decides to take advantage of the archives that newspapers and other news sources provide. Although the issue of privacy in the workplace is a longstanding one, the constant development of communication technology makes this issue particularly current. News search engines are a good place to search for information about current issues. The following is a good beginning list:

- CNN   http://www.cnn.com
- CBS News   http://www.cbsnews.com
- ABC News   http://abcnews.go.com
- Google News   http://news.google.com
- Reuters   http://www.reuters.com

- BBC News   http://news.bbc.co.uk
- The Associated Press   http://www.ap.org
- *The Wall Street Journal*   http://online.wsj.com/home-page
- *The New York Times*   http://nytimes.com
- National Public Radio   http://www.npr.org
- *Slate Magazine*   http://www.slate.com
- Topix   http://www.topix.net (news aggregator that can bundle the news for your ZIP code)
- Yahoo! and Google also search for news and have searchable news archives

Play with the various sites to learn how the news is organized on each site and to use their search functions. When you find a news article you like, collect the following publication information for later use:

Source Information: Article from News Site

Author(s) of article: _____

Title of article: _____

Title of journal, newspaper, magazine, or web page: _____

Original publication date: _____

Title of website: _____

Date you accessed the site: _____

MLA no longer requires the URL, but recording it is helpful in finding the site again.

 internet activity 3e **Perform a News Search**

Visit two of the news search sites listed previously and find information on the same stories. How is the material treated differently by the different news sites? Which appeals the most to you based on design and organization? Which seem to have the most links to your issue?

If you find sites that consistently provide you with information you find useful on your issue, subscribe to the RSS feed at that site and you can receive updates on your issue as news becomes available. Many websites now offer RSS feeds to their readers. You will often find one of the two icons shown in Figure 3.3 on a site, which you can click on to subscribe to a feed. Sometimes you will see the RSS in a box.

©Soland/Dreamstime.com

Tamilsma/Dreamstime.com

Figure 3.3 Look for one of these two icons to subscribe to a feed.

Subscribing to a feed can be a big time saver if you are following a changing story or if you are tracking several sites and don't want to have to keep visiting over and over to see if new information has been posted.

An **RSS feed** delivers updates on your issue to you, either through a reader that you can access online, to your email account as alerts, or to a mobile unit, such as your phone. These feeds are free to subscribe to, and so are most **newsreaders,** also known as "aggregators," which are needed to read the feeds as they come to you. Different newsreaders work differently, so you'll have to play around to see which may work best for you. Yahoo! offers links to many of the most popular newsreaders on its directory.

With newsreaders, you can control how often you receive updates: hourly, as they happen, or weekly. With a good search query, you can sit back and let the computer do some of the leg work for you.

 tip 3c

Use RSS Feeds

Other sources you can use to gather information about your topic are RSS feeds to newsgroups, discussion boards, and blogs.

Find and Use Databases in Libraries

Databases that you access through your library (EBSCOhost, MasterFILE Premier, ERIC, etc.) are collections of articles from various publications gathered in one place to make research easier. Instead of subscribing to hundreds of journals for which they have little physical space, libraries now subscribe to databases so that journals can be searched electronically. Some databases are field specific. For example, ERIC is a clearinghouse of education sources. There are databases specifically for newspaper articles, for business sources, for medical articles, and so on. Most of the time, though, a general database like EBSCOhost will work for you.

Searching a database is not so different from searching the Internet. You have choices such as date ranges, publications, and document type that can make your searching more efficient. Most libraries offer connections to their databases that you can reach from your home computer. Hal accessed EBSCOhost through his library's remote connection. When you use databases on the deep web, some of the search screens will look a lot like the ones described here;

OPPOSING VIEWPOINTS
IN CONTEXT

All   Viewpoints   Academic Journals   Primary Sources   M

A

| Home | Browse Issues | Maps | Resources |

Advanced Search

Find

Search for [workplace privacy] in [Keyword ▾]

[And ▾] [ ] in [Document Title ▾]

[And ▾] [ ] in [Publication Title ▾]

⊕ Add row   ⬛ Delete row

[Search]

Limit To

☑ Full Text Documents
☐ Peer Reviewed Journals

Limit By

Publication Date

From [January ▾] [1 ▾] [2010 ▾] To [December ▾] [21 ▾] [2012 ▾]

Document Type

A B C D E F G H I J K L M N O P Q R S T U V W X Y Z

| Abstract | Article |
| Advertisement | |

Cengage Learning

Figure 3.4 Opposing Viewpoints advanced search screen.

others, though, will have their own idiosyncrasies for searching. Most database sites have tutorials that will walk you through the search process, and the results will be worth it—lots of articles you can use in academic writing.

Hal narrowed his date range to two years and selected the Full Text check box so that the results generated by his search would include available full-length articles only (see Figure 3.4). This step is necessary unless you have time to request through interlibrary loan articles that are not available in the database. Most professors will not allow you to cite from article abstracts alone; you must have access to the full-text article.

Documents accessed through a computer database such as EBSCOhost will appear in one of two formats: PDF or HTML. A **PDF document** requires that you have Adobe Acrobat Reader on your computer. If you do not, you can download Adobe Acrobat Reader free from the Adobe website.

An article in PDF format is simply a photocopy of the original article—page breaks, images, and so forth are maintained, and reading the article is no different than it would be if you were turning pages in a print journal. The publication information is usually found at the top or bottom of the journal pages (see Figure 3.6). When you cite from an article you accessed in PDF format, you can refer to specific page numbers as they appear, just as you normally would with a print document.

An **HTML document** appears as a continuous page, generally with no page breaks or images. The publication information you will need appears

☛ **tip 3d**

Verify Citations

Before you end your database search session, verify that you have all of the article's publication information. Some databases will also help you generate a complete citation (see arrow in Figure 3.7).

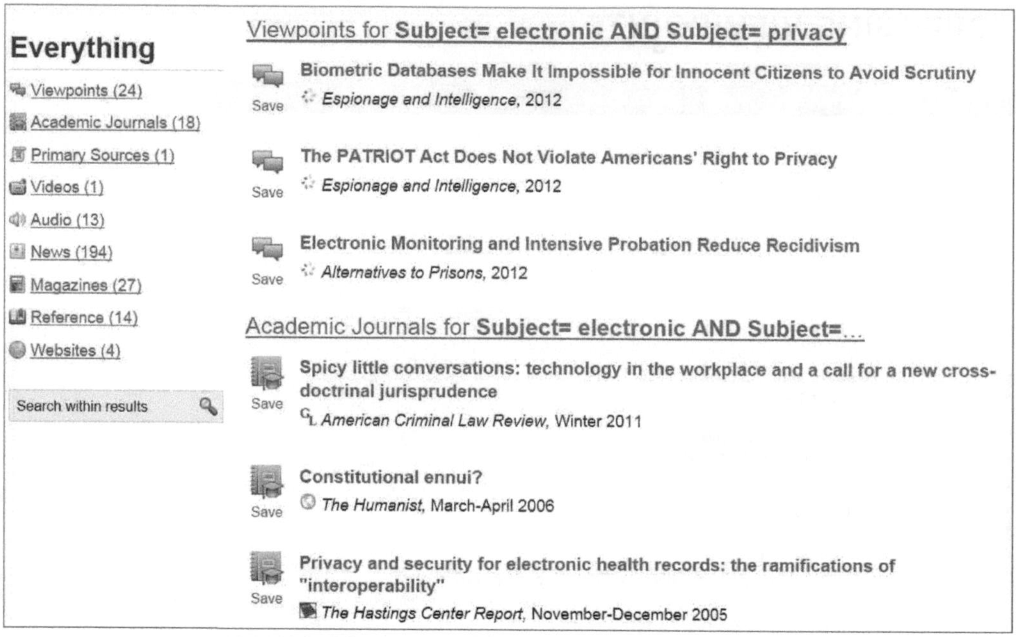

Everything

Viewpoints (24)
Academic Journals (18)
Primary Sources (1)
Videos (1)
Audio (13)
News (194)
Magazines (27)
Reference (14)
Websites (4)

Search within results

Viewpoints for **Subject= electronic AND Subject= privacy**

Save **Biometric Databases Make It Impossible for Innocent Citizens to Avoid Scrutiny**
Espionage and Intelligence, 2012

Save **The PATRIOT Act Does Not Violate Americans' Right to Privacy**
Espionage and Intelligence, 2012

Save **Electronic Monitoring and Intensive Probation Reduce Recidivism**
Alternatives to Prisons, 2012

Academic Journals for **Subject= electronic AND Subject=**...

Save **Spicy little conversations: technology in the workplace and a call for a new cross-doctrinal jurisprudence**
American Criminal Law Review, Winter 2011

Save **Constitutional ennui?**
The Humanist, March-April 2006

Save **Privacy and security for electronic health records: the ramifications of "interoperability"**
The Hastings Center Report, November-December 2005

Cengage Learning

Figure 3.5 Opposing Viewpoints Database search results

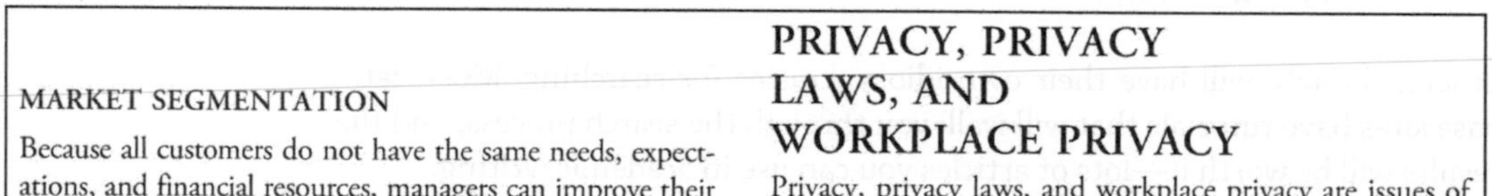

MARKET SEGMENTATION

Because all customers do not have the same needs, expectations, and financial resources, managers can improve their pricing strategies by segmenting markets. Successful segmentation comes about when managers determine what motivates particular markets and what differences exist in the market when taken as a whole. For example, some customers may be motivated largely by price, while others are motivated by functionality and utility. The idea behind segmentation is to divide a large group into a set of smaller groups that share significant characteristics such as age, income, geographic location, lifestyle, and so on. By dividing a market into two or more segments, a company can devise a pricing scheme that will appeal to the motivations of each of the different market segments or it can decide to target only particular segments of the market that best correspond to its products or services and their prices.

Managers can use market segmentation strategically to price products or services in order to attain company objectives. Companies can set prices differently for different segments based on factors such as location, time of sale, quantity of sale, product design, and a number of others, depending on the way companies divide up the

PRIVACY, PRIVACY LAWS, AND WORKPLACE PRIVACY

Privacy, privacy laws, and workplace privacy are issues of major concern to individuals and organizations in the modern world. Privacy violation and encroachment have become a norm as a result of the surveillance capabilities of the new and emerging electronic gadgets and information technology (IT) systems. This trend has prompted many countries to pass laws that govern the handling and collection of personal information of individuals and organizations with the use of electronic instruments.

WHAT IS PRIVACY?

What constitutes an encroachment to an individual's or an organization's rights to privacy? In legal terms, privacy simply refers to the accepted standards of related rights that safeguard human dignity. Definitions of privacy vary according to the environment, the participating interests, and the contextual limits. In many countries, the concept of data protection is included in the definition of privacy to achieve an interpretation that views privacy in terms of boundaries to an individual's personal information or an organization's data.

Cengage Learning

Figure 3.6 Page from a journal article in PDF format

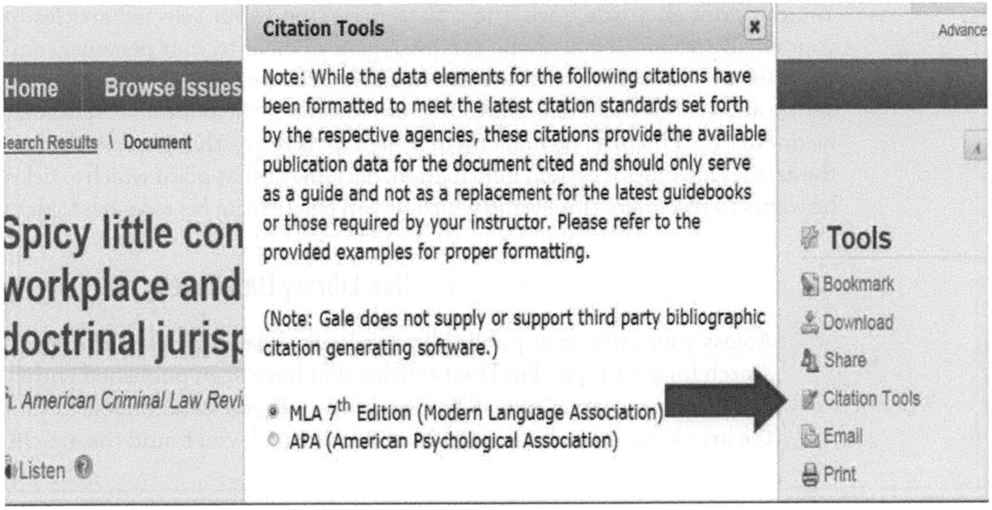

Figure 3.7 Some databases help you generate a complete citation

either at the beginning of the article or at the very end of the article. You cannot refer your readers to specific page numbers when you cite from an article in HTML format, as HTML documents do not contain page numbers. A reader would, however, be able to easily perform a search of the original article for cited material.

The publication information you need to gather for a journal, a magazine, or a newspaper article is as follows:

Journal	Magazine	Newspaper
Author(s)	Author(s)	Author(s)
Title of article	Title of article	Title of article
Title of journal	Title of magazine	Title of newspaper
Volume and issue numbers	Publication date (month/week + date/year)	Publication date (day, month, and year)
Year of publication (sometimes includes season—e.g., Fall)	Page numbers of article (if available)	Page numbers of article (if available)
Page numbers of article (if available)	Title of database	Title of database
Title of database	Date database accessed	Date database accessed
Date database accessed		

You can print an article, save it to a flash drive, send your selected articles to your email account (if you are on campus), or save them to your personal computer (if you are working from a remote location). Because Hal has the option of saving any articles that look interesting and reviewing them more closely later, he doesn't read them as he finds them. When he is ready, though, he will skim the articles looking for certain information, deciding at that point which articles he wants to read more closely and which he can delete from his research folder.

> **your turn 3a**   **GET STARTED** Use Library Databases
>
> Access your campus or public library's journal databases and conduct a search for your topic. Find two articles that have been published within the past two years. Copy all information that you would need to find the article again, including the database in which you found the article.

Find and Use Primary Sources

Using primary sources can help you get closer to the heart of an issue. Whether your argument is concerned with historical issues or current ones, whether you are arguing in the classroom or in the community, asking questions that can be answered by interviews, surveys, court transcripts, letters, photographs, raw statistics, or congressional hearings will put you in closer contact with the real people behind the issue. It is easy to fall into the trap of looking for the "truth" of an issue, looking only for hard facts to support your rational argument, when, in fact, there is rarely only one truth involved in any issue. People are rarely factual, nor do they usually operate on strictly rational lines of thought. Real people are motivated by a variety of reasons, which are not always based on the relevant facts of an issue. Determining the facts that are relevant to your issue is without a doubt extremely important. However, it is how these facts are interpreted by the stakeholders, the real people involved in your issue, that will determine how successful your argument ultimately will be.

We've already covered some of the many sources to choose from when you are researching your issue. Will newspaper or journal articles answer your research questions, or do you need to conduct interviews or gather statistics? **Secondary sources** are those that analyze or explain some aspect of your topic. A magazine article evaluating the dangers of factory emissions would be a secondary source. **Primary sources** are original documents or information gathered from firsthand research—yours or someone else's. An interview with a resident of a neighborhood affected by factory emissions would be a primary source.

Primary Sources
- Historical newspapers
- Public records
- Government documents

- Interviews
- Surveys
- Statistics
- Historical documents
- Diaries
- Letters
- Advertisements
- Maps
- Documentaries
- Archives

Secondary Sources
- Most articles from current newspapers
- Articles from magazines and scholarly journals
- Books

There are several excellent websites that offer tips and strategies for conducting primary research and for evaluating the sources once you have found them. One of the most useful sites is Patrick Rael's *Reading, Writing, and Researching for History: A Guide for College Students* at Bowdoin College (http://www.bowdoin.edu/writing-guides). Some of the general issues in evaluating primary sources are determining the purpose of a document, evaluating its validity or accuracy, and determining what was important to the author of the source, especially in the case of diaries or letters.

The U.S. Library of Congress has an amazing website that offers links to hundreds of sites housing primary sources in every area from literature to history to sociology (http://www.loc.gov/index.html). Here you can explore photographs, diaries, videos, links to statistics, interviews, maps, and so on.

Here are more sites that may help in your search for primary sources:

- U.S. Census Bureau—Data tables and maps presenting census data, plus materials to help use census information (http://www.census.gov).
- Survey Research—The Writing Center at Colorado State University presents this guide to conducting survey research and reporting on results (http://writing.colostate.edu/guides/research/survey/index.cfm).
- Public Agenda Online—Polling data on a wide array of topics and issues (http://www.publicagenda.org).
- National Criminal Justice Reference Service—Data, reports, and links from the Department of Justice on topics related to criminology and corrections (http://www.ncjrs.gov).
- National Opinion Research Center—This center at the University of Chicago indexes studies on a wide variety of topics from aging to energy consumption to substance abuse (http://www.norc.uchicago.edu).

- Pew Global Attitudes Project—This ambitious project from the Pew Research Center presents the results of more than 90,000 interviews in 50 countries (http://pewglobal.org).
- Population Reference Bureau—Articles, datasheets, and lesson plans on topics related to the study of population (http://www.prb.org).
- FedStats—A single point of access for statistics maintained by U.S. government agencies (http://www.fedstats.gov).
- First Measured Century—This companion website to a three-hour PBS special with Ben Wattenberg presents information on social trends in the twentieth century (http://www.pbs.org/fmc/index.htm).
- Institute for Social Research—Results of research studies done at this center at the University of Michigan. Topics range from attitudes toward cell phones, to why some women don't enter careers in math and science, to how wealth influences people's experiences in their last year of life (http://www.isr.umich.edu).
- U.S. Vital Record Information—Allows you to access certain public records (http://www.vitalrec.com).

 tip 3e

Primary Source Citations

There so many types of primary sources that it is often difficult to determine what publication information you need to gather. Part VI, "MLA and APA Documentation Systems," of this text covers quite a few primary sources you are mostly likely to come across in your research.

Your college or university library may also have special collections of primary sources, particularly those related to the school, its surroundings, and famous people in the area.

internet activity 3f **Find Primary Sources**

Visit a number of the sites for primary sources listed previously, and play with the search features to find sources relating to your issue. What kinds of material do your selected sites search? Historical? Literary? Legal? Business? Medical? What sites best meet your needs for your issue?

Hal decides to use several primary documents in his research project: (1) laws governing employees' rights to privacy; (2) a survey of employers completed by the American Management Association; and (3) interviews with both employees and supervisors at his company. He found several transcripts of court cases at the Electronic Frontier Foundation and one at Find Law, which covered the 2003 ruling against a Nationwide Insurance employee's complaint about invasion of his workplace privacy.

Find and Use Government Sources

These days it is very easy to find government-printed brochures and guides, copies of Senate and House reports, and bills. Don't be intimidated by the format of these documents. Most are searchable for keywords even though they can be tricky to cite. You can search for particular documents by title on any search engine, but visit the following sites to browse and conduct deeper searches.

- USA Government (http://www.usa.gov) is the U.S. Government's official website with access to consumer brochures, information on taxes, family care, and Internet security, among dozens of other categories. You can also find historical documents, statistics, maps, and links to various government agency libraries, including the Pentagon's.
- At the Library of Congress, Thomas (http://thomas.loc.gov) offers links to bills, the Congressional Record, treaties, and other government research.
- The Catalog of U.S. Government Publications (http://catalog.gpo.gov) provides access to and information about government publications. Many of the documents are online, but the search features are not easy to use. You'll need to follow its search tips for the best results.
- The White House website (http://www.whitehouse.gov) offers links to many primary sources as well.
- The U.S. National Archives website (http://www.archives.gov) houses 70 years worth of government documents including naturalization and war records.

Gathering publication information for government publications can be difficult. These documents are often written without a clear indication of author, title, publisher, or copyright date. Look for available clues, and give as much information as possible, including the URL and date accessed. In general, cite what you can find, in the order listed here. Not all government sources will have all of these items.

Source Information: Government Document

Name of government: _____

Name of agency: _____

Document title (underlined or italicized): _____

If applicable, number and session of Congress; type and number of publication: _____

Title of publication: _____

Name of editor or compiler of publication (first, middle initial, last):

_____

City of publication, publisher, date of publication: _____

Pertinent page numbers (if available): _____

Title of online collection (underlined or italicized): _____

Date of posting or most recent update (if available): _____

Name of project or reference database (underlined or italicized): _____

Name of sponsoring institution (e.g., Lib. of Congress): _____

Date of access and electronic address: _____

internet activity 3g Find Government Sources

Using the sites given above, perform keyword searches for government sources relating to your issue.

Find and Use Multimedia Sources

From audio transcripts of Barack Obama's inauguration speech, to videos of protestors in Iran, to podcast lectures of a professor at Stanford, to blogs of newspaper columnists, to the latest images of Mars craters, there is a host of valuable resources online that goes beyond print. Millions of viewers use YouTube to find serious lectures, music, and film clips, along with silly videos and instructional videos. Websites such as NPR and PBS have archives of video, and as of this printing, PBS is offering full-length episodes of some of its programs. Many libraries also subscribe to full-series PBS programs. The Library of Congress's (LOC) American Memory Project (http://memory. loc.gov/ammem/index.html) houses audio and video interviews with former slaves, documentary footage of Thomas Edison at work, and many other marvels of early film and recording technology.

The U.S. National Archives (http://www.archives.gov) just launched its own YouTube channel. Movies Found Online (http://www.makeuseof.com/ dir/moviesfoundonline) offers access to free public-domain documentaries as does Truveo (http://www.truveo.com). Of course, news services such as BBC and CNN have live news feeds featuring breaking news around the world. FreeDocumentaries.org offers full viewing documentaries.

You will need to gather the following publication information for videos found on the Internet covering topics from slavery to animal activism.

Source Information: Video Clip

Author's last name, first name OR corporate/institutional author name, if available: _____

Title of document or file: _____

Document date OR date of last revision: _____

Medium (e.g., online video clip): _____

Title of larger website in which clip is located: _____

Name of hosting library or agency (if appropriate): _____

Access date: _____

URL: _____

In Chapter 12, "Enhance Your Argument with Visuals and Humor," you will learn about the power that visual images can add to your argument.

There are many repositories of photographs, drawings, artwork, and maps on the Internet. Be sure to document your images properly (see the discussion in Chapter 12 and Appendices A and B). Some wonderful sources of images are:

- Digital History (http://www.digitalhistory.uh.edu). A link to images is provided.
- Image searches at Google (http://images.google.com) and Yahoo! (http://images.search.yahoo.com). Try them both as they offer different advanced search options based on color, size, date, and so on.
- The Smithsonian Institute (http://photo2.si.edu).
- National Geographic Photography (http://photography.nationalgeographic.com).
- The New York Public Library Digital Gallery (http://digitalgallery.nypl.org/nypldigital/index.cfm).
- Pulitzer Prize winners for photography (http://www.pulitzer.org/bycat).

You will need to gather the following publication information for an image:

Source Information: Image

Artist name: _____

Title of the work: _____

Date it was created: _____

For artworks, include

Dimensions of the work: _____

Repository, museum, or owner: _____

City or country of origin: _____

Podcasts of all sorts are gaining space on the Internet. Podcast Alley (http://www.podcastalley.com) and the Podcast Bunker (http://www.podcastbunker.com) can help you find podcasts on dozens of topics from the arts, to politics, to the news, which you can download to your iPod or listen to on your computer. Some of the most reputable podcasts are those that come from syndicated shows such as *Face the Nation* and the news sites. You can subscribe to many podcast feeds as well. You can also perform a keyword search with your search engine as follows: inurl:podcast "your keyword." Hal tried this search with the keywords "workplace privacy" and found several podcasts covering the workplace privacy debates in California.

You will need to gather the following publication information for a podcast:

> ### Source Information: Podcast
> Name of author, host, or producer (if available): _____
> Title of podcast: _____
> Date of podcast: _____
> Podcast series: _____
> Title of podcast show (if different from title of podcast): _____
> Title of larger site (if available): _____
> Date of download: _____

Blogs are online journals that focus on any topic imaginable. Many news columnists have blogs affiliated with their news sites. For example, the *New York Times* has blogs covering Afghanistan, Pakistan, and Iraq reportage; the arts scene; business mergers and acquisitions; medical science; the latest technological trends; and photographic, visual, and multimedia reporting (http://www.nytimes.com/interactive/blogs/directory.html).

Although many blogs are useful and entertaining, you will need to be careful about what blog information you use in your argument. Do you care what the man on the street in Anchorage thinks about the cost of college tuition? You might, but whether you want to cite information from his blog will be determined by the scope of your argument.

You will need to gather the following publication information for a blog entry:

> ### Source Information: Blog Entry
> Author: _____
> Title of the entry: _____
> Title of the blog: _____
> Name of the blog host: _____
> Date: _____

internet activity 3h Find Multimedia Sources

Find images that will support your issue. Find audio and video links of speeches, press conferences, or breaking news. Finally, find a blog that discusses your issue. How reputable do these sources feel?

In Chapter 4, "Evaluate and Engage with Your Sources," you will learn how to evaluate Web content, but for now, base your response on how the host site is organized, how neutral the coverage of events are, how the words are or the speech is presented, or how the tone of the blog feels. Would you use these sources in your argument? Why or why not?

Find Books

It may seem odd that books are listed last in this chapter. It's not that we don't think books are important; it's just that, for most issues, your readers are look-ing for the most current, up-to-date information. It can take years from con-ception to printing to make a book available. An issue can change a lot in a few years. For very current issues, books may not be the way to go. For issues that have a history or that will always be on the table (child care, human and animal rights, some environmental issues, etc.), older books can still be useful in establishing a context or background for the reader. In this section, we will cover how to find books in brick-and-mortar libraries and in virtual libraries.

Find Books in Libraries

Most libraries have similar catalogs. You can search for books by title, author, or subject. Hal's next step is to look for books in his school's library. He will perform the same search in his local public library as well. Hal is looking for books that are fairly current.

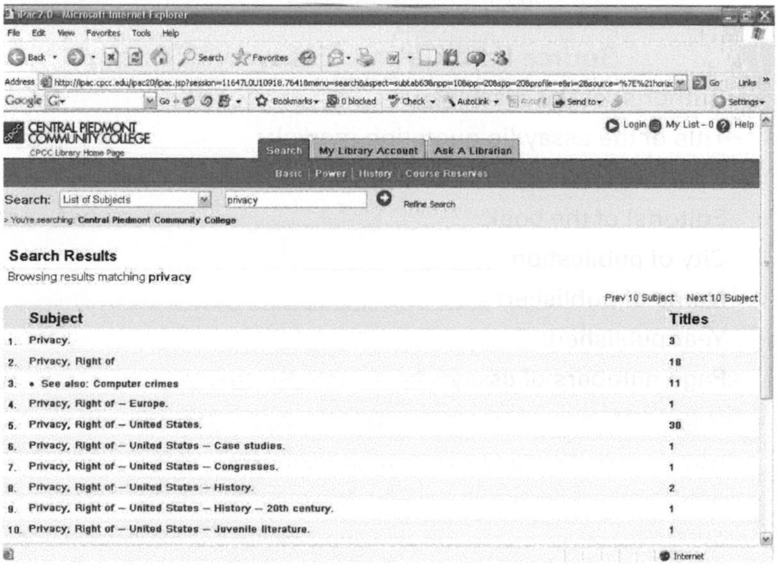

Figure 3.8 Library catalog search results

Hal decides to search by subject and types his search term "workplace privacy" into the library catalogue. This term doesn't yield any results, so he tries the more general term "privacy" (see Figure 3.8). His library has 18 titles on the subject of the right of privacy, not so many that he needs to narrow his search further. He clicks on the subject "Privacy, Right of" and scans the titles for books that meet his criteria of being predominantly about privacy in the workplace and specifically about emails and Internet usage.

Hal finds a couple of sources, and depending on how much material he feels is useful in each one, he either photocopies the useful pages or checks out the book to review later.

You will need to gather the following publication information for books:

Source Information: Book

Author(s) or editor(s): _____

Title of the book (in italics): _____

City of publication: _____

Name of publisher: _____

Year published: _____

If you are using an essay from a book, collect the following publication information:

Source Information: Essay from Book

Author(s) of the essay: _____

Title of the essay (in quotation marks): _____

Title of the book (in italics): _____

Editor(s) of the book: _____

City of publication: _____

Name of publisher: _____

Year published: _____

Page numbers of essay: _____

---

your turn 3b GET STARTED **Find Books in Libraries**

Find two books on your topic. Make sure that they have been published within the past five years. Copy all information that you would need to find the book again, including the call number, which indicates where on the shelves to find the book.

Find Books on the Internet

Even large colleges may have limited library space. Students can find ebooks in the library catalog and have access to many databases with more current information that is frequently updated. The number of books available electronically is growing rapidly, which is great for libraries with space limitations. Library resources such as the Opposing Viewpoints Database allow readers to access chapters and essays from hundreds of titles covering every issue imaginable.

The Opposing Viewpoints Database houses a collection of articles, book chapters, and other types of documents organized by subject. The title is a bit misleading: The articles are wide ranging, not just pro-subject and con-subject. Your professors are not looking for you to find material supporting only your side and the opposing side; this structure implies that there are only two sides to each issue, which, of course, is nowhere near reality for most argumentative issues.

your turn 3c GET STARTED **Find Books in the Opposing Viewpoints Database**

Access your library's Opposing Viewpoints Database or any other database available to you to find books or book essays on your issue. Find as many viewpoints as possible.

Most libraries require a library card to access their **ebooks.** Ebooks are just like print books, except they can be searched and read online. Many times, you cannot copy from them, though, and must take notes manually.

Books can also be found on the Internet, the majority of these titles being out of copyright. Project Gutenberg (http://www.gutenberg.org/wiki/Main_Page) and ManyBooks.net (http://manybooks.net) offer thousands of books that can be downloaded or read online. The Internet Sacred Text Archive (http://www.sacred-texts.com) houses full-text books on every religion imaginable. For more recent scholarship, though, you can read significant chunks of some current titles at Google Books.

Research can seem daunting. There are so many resources available to us that this wealth of riches can seem more of a curse, and it is tempting to rely on Google and the first few hits that match our search terms. But take the extra time to go beyond the first page of search engine hits or Wikipedia entries. By searching for types of sources that you may not normally consider, such as blogs, documentaries, or news feeds, you will open your research up to paths that will provide you with many rewards.

Reflect and Apply

1. In what ways can you use encyclopedias and basic reference sources to help orient you to your issue and its parameters, vocabulary, and viewpoints?

2. Much of Chapter 3 is devoted to finding sources through Internet searches. How are you using primary sources to gain insight into different facets of your issue? What sources are you using to find secondary material that is academically acceptable?

3. How are you using your school's research databases? Are there databases that seem to be consistently useful in researching your issue?

4. How will you manage your materials as you find them? What organizational system are you using to efficiently track your notes from print sources?

5. How are you keeping track of bibliographic information as you find it? How are you managing image, video, and audio sources along with their publication information so you can access it all readily?

KEEPING IT LOCAL

Playing a game of solitaire on your computer during work?
Surfing the Net while answering voicemail?
Sending personal emails from your office?

ALL OF THESE activities can be monitored by your boss and can get you fired. Whether you work in a small local company or a sprawling national or even global firm, you need to know your rights as an employee. Not asking can get you in trouble. But performing better on your job requires work on your part as well, work that includes knowing where to look for answers. Knowing how to develop a research plan and how to find the sources you need to answer questions about your privacy rights and anything else that pertains to your employment is crucial to your job success. Books, journals, Internet sites, and libraries all have valuable information, if you know where and how to look for it.

Research is at the heart of your argument. Your credibility and support rest on the thoroughness of your research strategies. Unlike some college skills, research is one skill that you will use in every part of your life: at school, at work, and even while addressing the needs of your community. What research sources will work for your needs? Can you use multimedia sources to help you address a problem at work? Will newspapers provide the support you need to solve a neighborhood dispute?

CHAPTER 4

Evaluate and Engage with Your Sources

This morning you sat down to read the newspaper while you ate breakfast. An article in the financial section about employees' rights caught your attention. The author of the article made some claims that didn't seem accurate to you. Later in the day, you tried to find sources that supported the author's claim but couldn't find anything. One database search uncovered several studies that seemed promising. As you began reading, however, you realized that one study used so much jargon that you couldn't understand it at all. Another report was 50 pages long. Although the title looked promising, you just didn't have time to read the entire report. Frustrated, you gave up.

TOPIC: Computer Usage

ISSUE: Privacy and Computer Use

AUDIENCE: Business Ethics Professor

CLAIM: Workplace electronic monitoring practices should be revealed to employees through company policies.

Chapter 3, "Develop a Research Plan," focused on introducing the various types of resources available to you and on how to find them. Chapter 4 will focus on how to evaluate and read the various types of resources. You will also learn how to incorporate information from those sources into your writing and how to cite them appropriately. For full information on creating a works cited page for your researched report or essay in MLA and APA formats, see Part VI, "MLA and APA Documentation Systems."

As you find materials, you will need to evaluate their accuracy and their usefulness for your argument.

In Chapter 4 you will learn to:

- Take notes, read critically, and evaluate Internet sites, articles, and books critically.
- Take notes and evaluate primary sources.
- Introduce sources and engage with them.
- Quote and cite quotations.
- Summarize and cite summaries.
- Paraphrase and cite paraphrases.
- Avoid plagiarism.

Take Notes, Read Critically, and Evaluate Internet Sites

In Chapter 3, "Develop a Research Plan," we followed Hal's research strategies as he found a wealth of information on electronic privacy in the workplace on the Internet. Finding material, though, is only the beginning. Now he must evaluate the sources and determine what he needs to use in his argument. Internet sources are easy to find but not always as easy to evaluate as print sources.

Hal's method of note-taking for Internet sources is a good one. He pastes the information he finds useful into a document he saves as "Workplace Privacy Notes." Hal is careful to keep track of information he copies verbatim so that he does not accidentally plagiarize it. His favorite method is to leave all verbatim sources in a different font color so that he does not forget that the material is not his original wording. He will keep all of the research he gathers from electronic sources in a folder he saves on his computer. He will also keep a folder for print sources that he photocopies and for newspaper clippings, brochures, and so on.

There are also online services that allow you to save links to web pages. Some of these tools even allow you to clip, highlight, and write comments on your clippings, gathering them all in one spot. There are many online organizational tools that can help you keep track of your research, for example, Zotero.org.

As he gathers electronic sources, Hal makes sure to comment on *why* he saved this material and *how* he thinks he may use it. Of course, how and why may change over the course of his research, but always determining the reason for keeping a source will keep him from gathering material that will not be of any use. Hal also remembers to copy any publication information that he will need later to document the sources he uses in his paper. As of the 7th edition, MLA documentation no longer requires the inclusion of a URL in a citation, but you should keep this information so that you can find the site again if necessary.

Critically Read Material on the Internet

Narrowing his search still left Hal with thousands of results, but the first one he looked at, "E-Mail Privacy in the Workplace," seemed promising. Now he had to decide not only if the information provided on the site was useful but also if it was **credible**. We all know that, along with the wonderfully useful information on the Web, there is also a lot of garbage. Reading critically will help you sort through it all. The first step Hal took when he accessed the site was to determine its credibility.

Seriousguy/Dreamstime.com

Figure 4.1 Critically reading content on the Internet is the first step you can take when determining credibility.

Hal asked himself a few questions about the article "E-Mail Privacy in the Workplace." The first step Hal took was to determine who sponsored the web page. By clicking on the "About" link, he found that the authors of the site are concerned with providing accurate information to those working in the security industry. They provide only articles that are well-researched so that decisions based on their material would meet current security laws. Hal felt that this site, although not geared toward employees of companies, had solid, trustworthy information about employees' rights to email privacy, so he marked the site for further reference.

When you are accessing unfamiliar websites, it is best to evaluate them using a series of questions like the ones below. Taking this precaution will ensure that you have credible material to use in your argument.

Evaluate Internet Sites

The following checklist provides some important questions you should ask about Internet sources before you use them.

Internet Evaluation Checklist

☐ **Author of Page/Site**

Who is the author of the page or source? Can you contact them or is there an "About Us" tab with author details? Is the author credible? Have they published other material on the topic or are they considered experts in their field?

☐ **Extreme Bias**

Chapter 5, "Read Critically and Avoid Fallacies," will discuss bias further, but ask if the bias exhibited in the web source exceeds what you feel comfortable with. In other words, is there evidence of racism, sexism, or extreme political or religious views?

☐ **Up to Date**

When was the site or source last updated? Are there links to the latest publications or sites?

☐ **Navigation**

Do all links to other sites work? Do images and files open quickly? Are there any dead links or dead ends in the site itself?

 internet activity 4a **Evaluate Internet Sites**

Using the Internet Evaluation Checklist, evaluate one of the sources you found for Internet Activity 3d. Is it a credible source? Why or why not?

Take Notes, Read Critically, and Evaluate Articles

The Computer Age has made research worlds easier than it was even 20 years ago. Along with the advantages of researching and writing with computers are some disadvantages that can cause headaches. There are still many sources, particularly older ones, that are not accessible either through library databases or on the Internet. Let's address journal articles that you have accessed in print (paper) journals on the library shelves that you cannot find online or in your library's databases.

The better way to take notes is to photocopy the article you want, making sure that all the needed publication information is printed somewhere on the photocopied pages, and to write your notes directly on the article itself. Highlight those passages that you think are useful, writing notes in the margins about how to use this material or making note of questions you need to ask, words to look up, or other sources to gather. Keep these photocopies in a folder so that they will be available when you are ready to write the report.

So that's easy enough. You'd think, then, that taking notes on articles you have downloaded to your own computer would be even easier. After all, there is no retyping to do—you can use your computer's cut-and-paste function to copy material from the original article to your own document.

But there are several errors that writers can make during this process, some of them costly. To avoid errors while taking notes on computer documents, follow the steps in the following Careful Note-Taking Checklist.

◗ Careful Note-Taking Checklist

☐ Have you made sure to differentiate your own ideas from the ideas you have borrowed? When pasting material from the original source, remember to highlight this material in some way to indicate to yourself later that this material is not based on your own ideas or words. Some people, like Hal, type all their original ideas in a different color or font to separate them from the information borrowed from an article. Forgetting to give credit to borrowed material, whether intentionally or accidentally, will be viewed as **plagiarism**, cheating by using the work of others as your own. (See the tips for avoiding plagiarism at the end of this chapter.)

☐ Have you commented on your sources? Writers frequently paste information into their own document and then later have no idea what this information means or why they saved it. Always make comments on the copied material, discussing what its function will be in the argument and why it is important. For example, will it support your own claims or provide an illustration of an opposing viewpoint?

☐ Have you included documentation for all sources? Another costly error is neglecting to include documentation for where you retrieved the material. A simple note in parentheses as to the origin of the source will save you time tracking down a source later, and sometimes saves you from having to leave out a source because you cannot document it.

Read Articles Critically

Articles, whether accessed through an online database or elsewhere, are originally published in academic journals, magazines, or newspapers. Understanding the differences between the sources can help you better understand the articles they contain. Although magazines and journals share similarities, a journal differs from a magazine in several ways. Both types of periodicals can be directed toward a particular audience. For example, the 2012 issue of *IUP Journal of Chemistry* includes the article "Arsenic Removal from Potable Water Using Copolymer Resin-III Derived From P-Cresol." The article's abstract offers the following:

Copolymer was synthesized by condensation of p-Cresol (p-C) and Adipamide (A) with Formaldehyde (F) in the presence of 2M HCl as catalyst with 4:1:5 molar ratios of reacting monomers. Water is the most important constituent of our body. Thus, its quality should be good and perfect because it directly affects our health. Water pollution due to arsenic leaching is one of the biggest problems all over the world. Ion-exchange studies of this purified copolymer resin were carried out for As^{3+} ions. 'A' proved to be a selective chelating ion-exchange copolymer for certain metals. Chelating ion exchange properties of this copolymer were studied for As^{3+} ions. Batch equilibrium method was employed to study the selectivity of metal ion uptake involving the measurements of the distribution of a given metal ion between the polymer sample and a solution containing the metal ion. The study was carried out over a wide pH range and in media of various ionic strengths. The copolymer showed a higher selectivity for As^{3+} ions.

Compare the language from the technical journal to that used in a magazine aimed at the general reader in the article about arsenic in the drinking water, "Textile Dyeing Industry an Environmental Hazard," in the magazine *Natural Science*.

> *Color is the main attraction of any fabric. No matter how excellent its constitution, if unsuitably colored it is bound to be a failure as a commercial fabric. Manufacture and use of synthetic dyes for fabric dyeing has therefore become a massive industry today [. . .] Synthetic dyes have provided a wide range of colorfast, bright hues. However their toxic nature has become a cause of grave concern to environmentalists. Use of synthetic dyes has an adverse effect on all forms of life.*

Rita Kant. "Textile Dyeing Industry an Environmental Hazard," Natural Science, Vol. 4, No. 1, 22–26 (2012).

You can easily see the difference—the *IUP Journal of Chemistry* article is more technical, using **jargon**, language that is used in a specific field and may be unfamiliar to those outside the field. Besides the language difference, journal articles are written by scholars or industry experts. The journals themselves are often peer reviewed, which means the articles are reviewed by other experts in the field before they are printed. Journals are also usually sponsored by a university or organization.

Magazines, on the other hand, are written for the everyday reader. Even someone with little familiarity with the topic of drinking water contamination would be able to read and understand the magazine article published in *Natural Science*. Less technical in nature, magazine articles are often written by freelance writers with little experience in the area about which they are writing. Your project may include information from both journal and magazine articles, depending on the assignment's requirements.

Finally, newspapers are usually produced daily. Those with online versions often provide updates during the day. They feature articles on crime and politics, along with human interest stories. Editorials and opinion pieces express the views of individuals, whereas the news stories themselves are mainly reportage of events.

None of these three types of periodicals are free of bias. **Bias** refers to the particular viewpoint or slant that an author or a publication leans toward. Bias is neither good nor bad, as readers can choose to read a publication or not depending on their own interests, beliefs, and values. A good researcher/writer understands that biases exist and is careful to select sources that are not bigoted, misleading, or downright false.

Reading Strategies for Longer Articles

A few reading strategies will make your time spent reading longer articles both more efficient and successful. At this stage, you are trying to quickly determine if an article is useful to you. Use the following questions to aid you in making that determination.

Initial Assessment Checklist

- ☐ Is there an **abstract**? An abstract is a brief overview of the author's argument, usually outlining the article's thesis and main points of support. Reading the abstract is no substitute for reading the full article, but the abstract will tell you at a glance if the article fits your needs.
- ☐ If no abstract exists, can you determine what the author's argument is? Although critical articles are longer than essays you may write, there still should be a clear beginning (with a thesis statement within the first one to three paragraphs), a body with supporting ideas, and a conclusion. Read the introduction and the conclusion for the main idea—in a critical article, the author's argument should be in one if not both places.

☐ Scan the article subheadings and any graphics (tables, charts, etc.). Being aware of how the author has organized the material into sections can help you both navigate and understand the article more easily. Tables and other graphic organizers can also help you understand the article's material.

☐ Is there a bibliography or footnotes? Although you should not necessarily reject an article that does not have a works cited page or a bibliography of further reading, the appearance of one is a bonus, as it gives additional avenues of research.

☐ Look up all words that keep you from understanding the article. Most journals are trade or field specific. They are not written for the general reader but for those already in the field; the vocabulary, therefore, can be a stumbling block. The language and vocabulary of a scholarly article may be unfamiliar to you, but the writing should not be so dense that you cannot read it at all. If you cannot comfortably read *most* of an article, then reject it in favor of an article that is easier to comprehend.

That may look like a lot of steps to take before you actually read an article, but following them will save you a great deal of time. After assessing your article, you will be able to determine if it is right for your purposes instead of reading 20 pages only to come to the same conclusion.

Using the Initial Assessment Checklist, the first step Hal takes when he is ready to review his journal articles is to look for an abstract. The article on email privacy does not have an abstract, so Hal continues to the second step and reads the introductory paragraphs and conclusion. At the end of the second paragraph, he finds the article's claim: "This article examines the employer/employee workplace privacy relationship, identifies the existing federal and state law governing workplace privacy, and discusses the rapidly developing monitoring software market."

Hal's next step is to scan the article subheadings and any graphics (tables, charts, etc.). At the end of the article is a list of references and a brief biography of the author, including contact information. The inclusion of references and author contact information is reassuring to Hal as is the easy-to-read format and language of the article. This one is a keeper. Hal decides that this article is worth reading and adds its publication information to his bibliography file.

But where do you find the elements to help you assess a journal article? Pages 87–88 include examples of these elements—Abstract, Key Words, Conclusion, and Works Cited—from an article in a humanities journal. The annotations in the margins identify key parts.

The Carnivalesque in Nathaniel Hawthorne's *The Scarlet Letter*

by Hossein Pirnajmuddin and Omid Amani

ABSTRACT: This study sets to examine the applicability of Bakhtin's theory of the carnivalesque to Nathaniel Hawthorne's *The Scarlet Letter*.

Abstracts are useful for identifying the central claim of the author's argument and often provide an explanation of how the claim is going to be supported. They can also set the context for the claim.

Along with the abstract, some journals require a list of keywords. Pay attention to these keywords as they not only help you grasp the scope of the article, but can help you when you are performing your own searches.

The canonical novel of the American literature published in the middle of the nineteenth century portrays the genesis of the American Puritan culture, while the polyphonic nature of the novel, it is argued, exposes the rifts of and the grotesqueness of this culture.

Key Words: Nathaniel Hawthorne, *The Scarlet Letter*, Bakhtin, Carnivalesque, Polyphony, Heteroglossia, Grotesque

Conclusion

The conclusion of most arguments in the humanities often restates the initial claim.

Nathaniel Hawthorne's *The Scarlet Letter* deftly addresses the Puritan culture of the seventeenth-century America as, to use Bakhtin's terms, a "monological culture." Hawthorne's novel is, among other things, the fact that laughter and the spirit of carnival cannot be totally repressed even in the most ideological and monological cultures. Although the writer apparently creates a Romantic grotesque, that is, one of dark, gloomy monstrosities, to intimate the distorted nature of the society he portrays, the implication is that the Bakhtinian conception of the grotesque, one associated with "light" (Bakhtin, *Rabelais and His World* 41), with the carnivalesque, capable of subverting the rule of 'darkness,' 'decrowning' it, is in the background too.

Works Cited

A works cited, references, or bibliography can provide additional sources, and depending on the format of the source, even links to other materials that can help you write your argument.

Adamson, Joseph. "Guardian of the 'Inmost Me': Hawthorne and Shame." *Scenes of Shame: Psychoanalysis, Shame, and Writing.* Eds. Joseph Adamson and Hilary Clark. New York: State U of New York P, 1999. 53–82.

Arac, Jonathan. "Hawthorne and the Aesthetics of American Romance." *The Cambridge History of The American Novel.* Eds. Leonard Cassuto and Clare Virginia Eby and Benjamin Reiss. Cambridge: Cambridge UP, 2011. 135–150.

your turn 4a ▶ **Conduct an Initial Assessment of Your Articles**

Using the Initial Assessment checklist, find a source and determine if it is right for your argument. Which of the steps helped you make a decision?

The next set of questions will help you make sense of articles you have determined will be useful. You need to be able to find the author's main argument(s) and the examples being used to support the argument(s). You should also be able to determine the article's strengths and weaknesses. Use these steps to find the main ideas and examples.

Reading Checklist

☐ Look for the main idea. If the thesis cannot be found on the first page, write the main idea at the top of your photocopied or saved article for easy reference. (If you do find the thesis on the first page, simply highlight it.)

☐ What evidence is the author offering to support his or her argument(s)? If an article is very long, there may be subsections, titled or not, that indicate movement from one example (or argument, if the author has more than one) to another. Look for these. Skim quickly, reading only the first and last sentences of each paragraph as you look for ideas and arguments. When you find something particularly useful, read the entire paragraph to make sure you are not reading anything out of context.

☐ Make notes throughout. Highlighting a passage is great, but if there are no comments made next to the passage, chances are good that, when you are ready to write your paper, you may not remember what struck you as important when you highlighted it.

☐ What are the article's strengths and weaknesses? Skim through several articles, reading the bibliographies and noting which sources are mentioned frequently. These are the sources you should definitely read. They will serve as touchstones by which to gauge the arguments of the articles you've selected. This is not to say that all of your articles need to agree with your touchstone articles. However, the touchstone articles will give you some idea of the general trends of thought concerning a topic, and they will allow you to judge if your selected article is too far off base to be reasonably considered.

☐ Come to a conclusion about the author's arguments. Do you agree or disagree? Do you see how the article can be used in any part of your own essay? Do you agree wholeheartedly and therefore can use the article as support for your own thesis? Do you disagree and want to use the article as an argument you wish to rebut (destroy)? Is the author's idea useful but limited? Maybe the author doesn't take an idea as far as you would like to take it?

your turn 4b ▶ **Read the Articles You've Selected**

Using the Reading Checklist, skim quickly through the article you evaluated from Your Turn 4a, or if that article did not work, select a new one. What is the author's claim? What support is provided by the article? What are the article's strengths and weaknesses? What is your final opinion of the article? Is it one you can use effectively in your argument? Why or why not?

Evaluate Articles

Before you add information from that article to your argument, make sure that you have determined that it is credible. Is your source actually an essay from a college student? A graduate student may have written a solid researched argument on homelessness, but your professor is undoubtedly looking for material that is more expert in scope. Research the author of the article, whether it is in a magazine, a website, or a scholarly journal. Answer the following questions before using any article:

Article Credibility Checklist

☐ Who is the author? Conduct a quick Internet search to determine if the author has published anything else on the topic. With whom is the author affiliated (an academic institution, or an industrial or business institution, for example)? Is there any scandal surrounding the author's integrity that may throw suspicion on his or her work?

☐ What is the reputation of the venue (periodical or site) in which the article is published?

☐ How current or reputable is the information cited in the article? A bibliography is not always necessary, particularly if original research is being conducted, but it helps to see what sources the author uses to support his or her argument.

Take Notes and Read Books Critically

So now, like Hal, you've completed your review of the library's catalog and you've got a long list of books you think may be useful in your research project. You gather them and set them all out on a table in front of you. Now what? Well, what you shouldn't do is take them all home with you. Do a cursory inspection of their tables of contents and their indexes; read a bit of the authors' prefaces or introductions. Make sure that you are not aggravating your tennis elbow unnecessarily by lugging 15 pounds of books to your car. Select books that seem promising. Are there any chapters or essays specifically on your topic, or at least near enough? Do your search terms appear in the index? Is the book's age appropriate? For some projects, older books may be fine, but for others more current material is preferable. Once you've made your selection, save yourself a great deal of time by using the FLOI method, discussed next.

The **FLOI method** will help you investigate books in a consistent manner and will save you time.

First: Read the author's introduction or preface. Read the first chapter looking for a thesis or a main argument.

Last: Read the final chapter to find out the author's conclusion and to make sure it is summarizing what you thought was going to be proven.

Outside: Look at those materials that are outside the text. The table of contents and the index will direct you to supporting examples and illustrations of the book's thesis. The dust jacket can be very helpful, providing a brief overview of the author's intent. Skim through any maps, appendices, glossaries, tables, or charts.

Inside: At this point, you can take one of two steps. If you have plenty of time, or the book appears to warrant it, you can read the entire book. Most of the time, however, it will suffice for you to skim the text carefully, looking for words and phrases that pop out—you'll notice that the things that catch your attention are the good examples, things that are interesting to you that you can use in your report.

> **your turn 4c** ▶ **GET STARTED Use the FLOI Method to Skim a Book**
>
> Use one of the books you found for Your Turn 3b, and skim it using the FLOI method.
>
> 1. First: Skim the preface and any other introductory material, and record the author's claim or main point.
> 2. Last: Read the last chapter. How does the author conclude the argument? Are you surprised by the conclusion? Is it what you thought it would be based on the preface?
> 3. Outside: Skim through the table of contents and the index. List any of your search terms or additional topics of interest that are covered. Flip through the book looking for graphs, charts, or illustrations. Are they clear and easy to understand? Do they offer any insights into your topic?
> 4. Inside: Does the book warrant your time reading it, will skimming suffice, or is the book not a good match for your subject?

Take Notes and Evaluate Primary Sources

Hal gathered a large number of primary sources, including interviews, documentaries, acts, and laws. Before he uses any of them, he asks himself a series of questions to determine who produced the source, why, for what audience, and under what circumstances.

Primary Sources Checklist

☐ Who created the source and why? Was it created through a spur-of-the-moment act, a routine transaction, or a thoughtful, deliberate process?

☐ Did the recorder have firsthand knowledge of the event? Or did the recorder report what others saw and heard?

☐ Was the recorder a neutral party, or did the creator have opinions or interests that might have influenced what was recorded?

☐ Did the recorder produce the source for personal use, for one or more individuals, or for a large audience?

☐ Was the source meant to be public or private?

☐ Did the recorder wish to inform or persuade others? (Check the words in the source. The words may tell you whether the recorder was trying to be objective or persuasive.)

☐ Did the recorder have reasons to be honest or dishonest?

☐ Was the information recorded during the event, immediately after the event, or after some lapse of time? How large a lapse of time?

Source: Questions for Analyzing Primary Sources, Library of Congress http://lcweb2.loc.gov/learn/lessons/psources/studqsts.html

internet activity 4b **Evaluate Primary Sources**

Select one primary source you gathered in Internet Activity 3f. Answer the eight questions above about your source to determine its credibility.

Introduce and Comment on Sources

One of the more difficult aspects of writing any sort of research report is smoothly incorporating your own ideas on a subject with ideas you've gathered from other sources, such as newspaper articles, books, a television documentary, or a web page. It's very important to be clear about what material in your report is yours and what comes from an outside source. You must make sure that any ideas you use, whether you are quoting a source verbatim or paraphrasing, are attributed to their original author.

Three steps should be followed when using source material, either quoted or paraphrased:

1. Introduce the source, also known as *source attribution*.
2. Provide the source.
3. Cite the source.

It is often best to introduce the author of your source material, especially if you are paraphrasing and likely to confuse source material with your own original ideas. The phrases used to introduce sources are called **attributive phrases or statements**. An attributive statement tells the reader who is being cited. It may indicate the author's name and credentials, the title of the source, and/or any helpful background information. Here are some examples of attributive words:

accepts	considers	explains	rejects	acknowledges
affirms	argues	asserts	contradicts	adds
contrasts	criticizes	declares	interprets	shows
defends	lists	states	believes	denies
maintains	stresses	cautions	describes	outlines
suggests	claims	disagrees	points out	supports
compares	discusses	praises	concludes	emphasizes
proposes	verifies	confirms	enumerates	confutes

The first time you introduce a source, you should provide the first and last name of the author you are citing. It is also helpful to give the author's credentials.

> David Solomon, the leading critic of Ira Levin's novels, argues . . .

> In *Rosemary's Offspring*, David Solomon's recent book of essays on Levin's novels, he explains . . .

In subsequent references to the author, you may just use the last name.

> Solomon defends . . .

If there is no author, you should introduce the source by a title.

> According to the USDA website, nutrition . .

> The article in the *New York Times*, "Fowl Play on Chicken Farms," states . . .

Never include website addresses within the text of the paper; these will appear in the works cited page.

your turn 4d ▸ PRACTICE Introduce Sources

Select three passages from this excerpt from "Notification, an Important Safeguard against the Improper Use of Surveillance" by F. Boehm and P. de Hert. Introduce the sources properly, using the list of attributive words or other words or phrases.

1. Introduction

The surveillance of individuals and the resulting collection of information are regarded by the security community as an effective tool to locate terrorists and other criminals. In addition to the establishment of crime-fighting databases, the travel behaviour of citizens is recorded, and telecommunication and internet data are required to be retained for possible use in investigations. Databases and information systems containing such data exist at both national and EU levels. Personal data are increasingly collected, analyzed and interlinked. This article examines the importance of the right of citizens to be informed that their data has been collected, or that they have been the subject of surveillance, by reference to current laws. It first provides a brief overview of the increasing surveillance measures at EU level, then analyzes the current notification requirements existing in the EU, and discusses the right of notification in the framework of the Council of Europe and the case-law of the ECtHR. With the proposed changes to EU data protection law in mind, an overview of potential future regulation in this field is then essayed.

2. Increased surveillance at EU level

Before discussing existing and potential notification rules, a brief impression of the current databases and systems of surveillance within the EU is instructive. Post 9/11 policy concepts, such as proposed in the Hague and the Stockholm programme led to an increase of systems developed to control various parts of our daily life. Surveillance thereby takes place at different levels: On the initiative of the EU, Member States implement the data retention directive to reinforce their police and secret service activities. At EU-level, so called anti-terrorism measures are increasingly often initiated: travellers are comprehensively checked when they enter EU territory and EU databases and information systems serving multiple purposes are installed to collect and analyze information (see further, Boehm 2012). In addition to databases serving police purposes (the Europol Information System) (EIS), the Schengen Information System (SIS) and the Customs Information System (CIS), databases initially installed to facilitate border control such as the Visa Information System (VIS) and Eurodac are increasingly used for surveillance purposes. In fact, almost all existing databases have multiple functionalities. The SIS for instance is a database in the framework of law enforcement and immigration control and collects data of third state and EU nationals. The CIS serves customs control purposes but also contains personal data of individuals suspected of illicit trafficking activities. The VIS serves the purpose of the exchange of visa data and entails information of third state nationals who apply for a visa

*to enter the EU. Plans to give law enforcement access to the VIS
are under consideration. Eurodac stores fingerprint data of asylum
seekers and should prevent that asylum seekers make multiple asylum applications in different Member States of the EU. The EIS and
Eurojust's database entail data of criminals, but also of suspects, victims and witnesses. Frontex is the EU's border agency and collects
data of third state nationals trying to pass the external borders.*

*The rise of techniques and databases developed in recent years
touches therefore on different aspects of the daily life of citizens. Not
only traditional criminals are targeted by such measurers, but also
individuals not suspected of having committed a crime. A shift towards
the preventive entry of citizens in databases serving police but also
other purposes can be observed. The rights of individuals affected by
such measures do not always keep up with this fast developing field of
different surveillance techniques (Van Brakel & De Hert 2011).*

Source: Boehm, F., and P. de Hert. "Notification, an Important Safeguard against the
Improper Use of Surveillance - Finally Recognized in Case Law and EU Law." *European
Journal of Law and Technology* 3.3 (2012).

Quote and Cite Quotations

When you use an author's exact words in your own writing, you are **quoting**.
There are certain rules to follow to properly introduce, quote, and cite the
material you take directly from a source.

First, you want to use direct quotes very sparingly—it is almost always
better to put original material into your own words (see paraphrasing below).
Occasionally, though, a quote is the way to go. Save quotations for those times
when there is no better way to say things, or for when you are citing laws,
definitions, or comments that are best quoted in full to avoid confusion or
misrepresentation.

Let's use the following excerpt from an Internet source as an example.
The highlighted text is what Hal wants to use in his paper on privacy in the
workplace.

Employee Monitoring: Is There Privacy in the Workplace?

*Employers want to be sure their employees are doing a good job,
but employees don't want their every sneeze or trip to the water
cooler logged. That's the essential conflict of workplace monitoring.*

*A 2007 survey by the American Management Association and the
ePolicy Institute found that two-thirds of employers monitor their
employees' web site visits in order to prevent inappropriate surfing.
And 65% use software to block connections to web sites deemed*

off limits for employees. This is a 27% increase since 2001 when the survey was first conducted.

Source: "Fact Sheet 7: Workplace Privacy." Privacy Rights Clearinghouse. January 2013. Retrieved February 25, 2013, from http://www.privacyrights.org/fs/fs7-work.htm

The paragraph that includes the desired material has survey results for employer monitoring. Hal wants to use just the first item and decides to quote it directly. Here is that highlighted information included in a paragraph as a direct quote.

DIRECT QUOTE[1]

In 2007, the American Management Association and the ePolicy Institute conducted a survey on the use of monitoring practices of employers. The survey found that "two-thirds of employers monitor their employees' web site visits in order to prevent inappropriate surfing" ("Fact Sheet 7"). These results seem extremely high and indicate the widespread use of monitoring software used in the workplace.

Hal does not have an author to introduce. Notice how he instead introduces the quote by indicating that a survey was conducted by the American Management Association and the ePolicy Institute. He leads into the quote with the attributive "the survey found." Then he begins his quote with the words "two-thirds" and ends where the original sentence ends. Note that the quotation marks only surround the quoted material, not the citation information in parentheses (highlighted).

After the quote, Hal comments on the information, helping the reader to understand the importance of the quoted material to his argument. Never just drop a quote into a paragraph without any explanation. Provide commentary that explains the cited material. Does it provide an illustration of a point you've made? Does the quote represent confirmation of or disagreement with a point you've made?

When you use an outside source, either as a direct quotation or as a paraphrase, you need to provide readers with information that tells them the origin of that source. This is done both internally and in a reference list at the end of the paper. This reference list is usually called a **works cited page** and includes only those sources you have actually used in your report. To cite the quote Hal used from the Internet source above, he will have to put in parentheses at the end of the quoted material where that information can be found. This information should be the same as it appears on the works cited page. A longer title may be abbreviated as Hal has done here. See the following sample works cited page; the source in question is highlighted.

---

[1] These examples are in MLA format; both an MLA and an APA formatting guide is found in Part VI, "MLA and APA Documentation Systems," of this text.

Works Cited

18 USC Chapter 119—Wire and Electronic Communications Interception and Interception of Oral Communications. Legal Information Institute. 2013. Web. 25 Feb. 2013.

"Fact Sheet 7: Workplace Privacy." Privacy Rights Clearinghouse. January 2013. Web. 25 Feb. 2013.

Lazar, Wendi S., and Lauren E. Schwartzreich. "Limitations to Workplace Privacy: Electronic Investigations and Monitoring." *Computer & Internet Lawyer* 29.1 (2012): 1–16. *Business Source Complete.* Web. 26 Feb. 2013.

Taylor, Raymond E. "A Cross-Cultural View Towards the Ethical Dimensions of Electronic Monitoring of Employees: Does Gender Make a Difference?" *International Business & Economics Research Journal* 11.5 (2012): 529–534. *Business Source Complete.* Web. 26 Feb. 2013.

In the citation, then, Hal should include as much information as the reader needs to be directed to the source on the works cited page:

> The survey found that "two-thirds of employers monitor their employees' web site visits in order to prevent inappropriate surfing" ("Fact Sheet 7").

Because this source does not have an author, it is alphabetized on the works cited page by the first word of its title: Fact. When you provide article titles in parentheses, as done here, you may shorten lengthy titles to the first few words.

There is no page number included in our example because the source is from a website. If there are page numbers (from a book, print copy of a periodical, or from a document in PDF format), then the page number(s) from which the cited material comes is included; for example, (Lazar and Schwartzreich 9).

Notice that the quotation mark ends after the last word in the quote. The citation is considered part of the sentence, and the period comes after the parentheses.

The excerpt in Figure 4.2 is from the third item on Hal's works cited page (the Lazar and Schwartzreich article) and includes page numbers.

If authors are introduced in the attribution, their names do not need to be repeated in the parenthetical citation; only the page numbers are necessary, if there are any.

> In a study of workplace privacy conducted by Wendi S. Lazar and Lauren E. Schwartzreich, the authors found that the courts must be able to "balance a business's need to protect data and proprietary information against individual rights and freedoms" (9).

Hal introduced the authors in the preceding example, so he only included the page number of the quoted material in the parenthetical citation. Notice, too, that the authors' first and last names in the body of the paragraph are in the normal order—reverse the order of the first author's name only in the works cited page for alphabetization purposes.

Privacy

false light invasion of privacy (*e.g.*, for online misrepresentations about employees, such as statements made by managers on social networking sites like LinkedIn),[115] intrusion of seclusion,[116] or tort claims arising out of workplace cyberstalking.[117] It may also be possible to bring a tortious interference with contract claim against an employer that requires an employee to authorize employer access to a social networking site profile by claiming that this act violates a service agreement or that doing so violates public policy concerns.[118]

International Trends in Workplace Privacy Protections

Unlike the United States, many countries have had strong privacy policies in place since World War II, in both the public and private workplace. In fact, in many countries such as Chile, France, and Mexico, the right to privacy in regard to emails in the workplace is an unwaivable right.[119] In most European Union (EU) countries this was a direct reaction to the holocaust and widespread civilian collusion with the Nazi regime.[120] In certain Asian countries and in parts of South America, data privacy and other individual privacy rights in the workplace are protected by statute and in some countries they are constitutional rights.[121] In the global workplace, however, all of these countries, much like the United States, share an increased sense of urgency in dealing with the technological revolution in the workplace and its resulting lack of employee privacy.

Specifically, in many European countries, monitoring, gaining access to employees' computers, and video surveillance are void *ab initio* or circumscribed by statute.[122] In 2007, the European Court of Human Rights held, under Article 8 of the European Convention on Human Rights, that employee email messages are protected communications.[123] More recently, the EU released a plan to revise European data protection rules based on the Commission's position that an individual's ability to control his or her information, have access to the information, and modify or delete the information are "essential rights that have to be guaranteed in today's digital world."[124] Increasingly, individual EU nations are poised to enact more stringent privacy laws. For instance, Finland recently introduced a statute expanding employee privacy rights,[125] and Sweden is expected to follow suit.[126] Within the last year, Germany (a country that instituted strong data privacy and anti-monitoring laws after the holocaust) also approved a draft law amending its Federal Data Protection Act, which prohibits employers from disciplining employees for their private online activities, to provide even broader protections.[127]

Even outside the EU, other countries continue this trend toward protecting employee privacy rights. In the Middle East, the Israeli National Labour Court issued a decision in February 2011 that severely limits the extent to which employers can monitor their employees' emails. According to the opinion, employers must now create an understandable policy for employee use of communications systems at the workplace. This policy must be clearly communicated to all employees, and must be written into their contracts.[128]

Conclusion

The changing forms of technology and their vast access to information will undoubtedly continue to dictate operational realities and expectations of privacy in the workplace. The challenge for courts is that they must continuously monitor these changes and balance a business's need to protect data and proprietary information against individual rights and freedoms. In the wake of *City of Ontario v. Quon*, and facing the risk of sacrificing overbroad constitutional rights, courts may consider the societal role of the particular electronic communication at issue and refrain from issuing rulings based solely on the language of a standardized privacy policy. In *Quon*, the Supreme Court recognized the increasing importance of technology in workers' lives, noting that "[c]ell phone and text message communications are so pervasive that some persons may consider them to be essential means or necessary instruments for self-expression, even self identification."[129] As the Court explained, the more pervasive and essential or necessary an electronic tool becomes for an individual's self-expression or identification, the "[stronger] the case for an expectation of privacy."[130] As new technologies become the norm of everyday life and employees' private lives intertwine with their work lives, the law will have to respond with safeguards that prevent employers from abusing and interfering with their employees' everyday communications and recognize that workplace privacy is a value worth protecting.

Notes

1. Social media sites are "a popular distribution outlet for users looking to share their experiences and interests on the Web," which "host substantial amounts of user-contributed materials (*e.g.*, photographs, videos, and textual content) for a wide variety of real-world events of different type and scale." Hila Becker, Mor Naaman, & Luis Gravano, "Learning Similarity Metrics for Event Identification in Social Media," Proceedings of the third ACM international conference on Web search and data mining, WSDM '10, 291-300. This umbrella term encompasses social networking sites such as Facebook, LinkedIn and MySpace, and microblogging information networks, such as Twitter. *See* Lisa Thomas, Comment," Social Networking in

The Clute Institute

Figure 4.2 Source material from a PDF article including page number

> A study of workplace privacy found that the courts must be able to "balance a business's need to protect data and proprietary information against individual rights and freedoms" (Lazar and Schwartzreich 9).

In this second example, Hal needs to include the authors' names in the parenthetical citation because they do not appear in the introduction to the quote.

Quoting Material Quoted in the Original Source

Occasionally you will want to quote material that your source itself is quoting (see Figure 4.3).

In this excerpt from the Schatt article, an item is quoted from a source in which the author was quoting another source. To use quoted material, you do not need to track down the original source. (Note that in the parenthetical documentation in Figure 4.3 there is an author's last name, year, and page. The article's authors are using APA style, which is covered in full in Part

Motivation is the foundation for human achievement. A psychological construct, "motivation is considered both a catalyst for learning and an outcome of learning" (Hurley, 1993, p. 17). Without motivation little can be achieved, but with the appropriate inspiration, substantial growth may occur. A study by Cattel, Barton, and Dielman (1972) noted that nearly 25% of student achievement might be attributed to motivational elements. Asmus (1994) suggested that estimates of student achievement that were due to motivation ranged from 11 to 27 percent in the literature. Experienced educators may believe that this percentage is even higher yet.

"Achievement Motivation and the Adolescent Musician: A Synthesis of the Literature." Research & Issues in Music Education 9.1 (Sept 2011).

Figure 4.3 Quoted material in original source

VI. In MLA, you would use the author's last name and a page number, with no comma separating them.) You need only indicate that the material you are using is a quote from another source:

> *There are several definitions of motivation that have to do with learning and music: "Motivation is considered both a catalyst for learning and an outcome for learning" (Hurley qtd. in Schatt 4).*

"Qtd." is the abbreviation for "quoted." The use of it here indicates to the reader that, although the quoted material appeared in the Schatt article, this author got that information from Hurley.

Alter Quoted Material

Here is an example of quoting a quote, where the original material was altered slightly to fit the sentence into which it is to be inserted.

> The court explained: "If [an employee] had left a key to his house on the front desk at [his workplace], one could not reasonably argue that he was giving consent to whoever found the key, to use it to enter his house and rummage through his belongings. ..."

In the original material that Lazar and Schwartzreich cited, the material in the brackets [ ] was in the plural form—"employees" and "their workplaces." The authors needed these terms to be in the singular form to fit the rest of their paragraph. It is acceptable to alter quoted material so that it fits grammatically with your sentence as long as you indicate changes by using the brackets. If you remove material, you would use an ellipsis where words are missing.

your turn 4e PRACTICE **Quote a Source**

Use the first page of Wendi Lazar and Lauren Schwartzreich's "Limitations to Workplace Privacy: Electronic Investigations and Monitoring" to write a paragraph on workplace privacy. Incorporate two quotations from the article in your paragraph, making sure (1) to introduce the quote, (2) to quote the original using quotation marks, and (3) to include a parenthetical citation. The passage below is from page 1 of the article.

As cell phones, the Internet, and social media continue to define personal and professional communication, federal and state laws are redefining and, in many ways, broadening the concept of workplace privacy. For years, employers in the private sector paid little attention to concerns over workplace privacy, as few laws prevented employers from monitoring employees and employees had greater control over their personal communications. As technology developed, however, employers quickly obtained resources to conduct sophisticated searches of employees' or prospective employees' backgrounds, to monitor employees in and outside the workplace, and to track and access employees' Internet usage. Most recently, employers have begun to demand access to employees' personal communications through third-party service providers, such as wireless cell phone providers and social networking sites.

Over the last decade, courts and legislatures have responded to these developments by applying existing laws in ways that protect employees' privacy rights and enacting new laws to provide a remedial effect. Nevertheless, private sector employees continue to face many challenges to their workplace privacy.

Source: Lazar, Wendi S., and Lauren E. Schwartzreich. "Limitations To Workplace Privacy: Electronic Investigations And Monitoring." *Computer & Internet Lawyer* 29.1 (2012): 1–16. *Business Source Complete.* Web. 26 Feb. 2013.

Summarize and Cite Summaries

Sometimes you will want to summarize the contents of an article, its main ideas or arguments. In summarizing, you do not need to explain secondary ideas, details, or tangents. It sounds easy, but it takes skill to summarize effectively. Follow these guidelines when you need to summarize the contents of a source.

Summary Checklist

- ☐ Provide the title of the source and the author, if available.
- ☐ In your own words, explain the source's thesis (i.e., claim or main idea) in one sentence.
- ☐ Make sure that you are not using any phrases from the original; if you decide to use a phrase, maybe a special term the author has created, put that phrase in quotation marks.
- ☐ Answer as many of these questions as are relevant: who, what, where, when, how, and why.

☐ Do not include any opinions or first-person commentary.

☐ Do not include details or examples.

You will introduce your summary as you would any other source, by author or title.

Paraphrase and Cite Paraphrases

It is tempting to use only quotations in your writing as it is easier to avoid plagiarizing. After all, you only have to put quotation marks around the borrowed material and put any additional information in the parenthetical citation and you're finished. But a collection of quotes does not make a research paper. You are being asked to incorporate your research with your own ideas, and this involves reading and digesting your sources and connecting ideas into a cohesive argument. This can best be accomplished with paraphrasing: putting source material into your own words. Let's look back at Hal's source on employee monitoring again.

Employee Monitoring: Is There Privacy in the Workplace?

Employers want to be sure their employees are doing a good job, but employees don't want their every sneeze or trip to the water cooler logged. That's the essential conflict of workplace monitoring.

A 2007 survey by the American Management Association and the ePolicy Institute found that two-thirds of employers monitor their employees' web site visits in order to prevent inappropriate surfing. And 65% use software to block connections to web sites deemed off limits for employees. This is a 27% increase since 2001 when the survey was first conducted. Employers are concerned about employees visiting adult sites with sexual content, as well as games, social networking, entertainment, shopping and auctions, sports, and external blogs. Of the 43% of companies that monitor e-mail, nearly three-fourths use technology to automatically monitor e-mail. And 28% of employers have fired workers for e-mail misuse.

Here was how Hal quoted material from that source:

In 2007, the American Management Association and the ePolicy Institute conducted a survey on the use of monitoring practices of employers. The survey found that "two-thirds of employers monitor their employees' web site visits in order to prevent inappropriate surfing" ("Fact Sheet 7"). These results seem extremely high and indicate the widespread use of monitoring software used in the workplace.

Taylor, Raymond E. "A Cross-Cultural View Towards the Ethical Dimensions of Electronic Monitoring of Employees: Does Gender Make a Difference?" *International Business & Economics Research Journal*, May 2012.

Hal also could have incorporated the same material by putting it into his own words, as shown in the following example.

> In 2007, a survey was conducted by the American Management Association on the use of monitoring practices of employers. The survey found that a large percentage of employers, 66%, keep a watch on how often and where employees go online ("Fact Sheet 7"). These results seem extremely high and indicate the widespread use of monitoring software used in the workplace.

This is called **paraphrasing**. As you can see, the paraphrase is very different from the wording of the original, yet it conveys the same meaning. You can still tell the difference between Hal's words and the words of the source. Even though Hal may put the survey information in his own words, the ideas have been borrowed from a source—they are not his—and he must provide a citation to that source material in the same way as if it were quoted.

Hal avoids plagiarism by carefully paraphrasing material from the article "A Cross-Cultural View Towards the Ethical Dimensions of Electronic Monitoring of Employees: Does Gender Make a Difference?" published in the May 2012 issue of *International Business & Economics Research Journal*. Hal's first task was to decide what parts of this article he could use as source material. He came up with three items he wanted to use:

1. A summary of the author's argument
2. A paraphrase of the criticisms of electronic monitoring
3. A quote from one of the author's research questions

After Hal reads "A Cross-Cultural View," he decides he wants to offer a summary of the main points of the article. For our purposes, a passage from the article's introduction is provided here, in which the author states the purpose of his article:

> *In developing partnerships between Chinese and foreign companies, it is important to be sensitive to the mindsets of both parties, especially when merging organizational policies. With this in mind, this article presents the results of a study examining the attitudes of Taiwanese and American study participants regarding the ethics of electronically monitoring employees. (page 529)*

Hal's summary of the article may appear in his paper in this way:

> "A Cross-Cultural View" offers a good overview of some of the issues involved in electronic monitoring in the workplace in Taiwan. Raymond E. Taylor feels that to establish sound partnerships with Taiwanese businesses, the different attitudes of the Taiwanese and Americans need to be examined. To understand ...

> Business executives have always monitored their employees' behavior. Electronic monitoring may be especially useful in training and improving productivity (Blylinsky, 1991, and Laabs, 1992). However, critics of electronic monitoring suggest that the more obtrusive forms of electronic monitoring can lead to elevated levels of stress, decreased job satisfaction and quality of work, decreased levels of customer service and poor quality (Kallman, 1993). Electronic monitoring, by imposing excess control over employees' behavior, can alienate employees and develop a feeling of working in a modern "sweatshop" (Kidwell and Bennett, 1994). Employers have the legal right to electronically monitor their employees (Kelly, 2001). The question is not whether or not employers can electronically monitor their employees, but rather "how should it be done?"

The Clute Institute

Figure 4.4 Passage from "A Cross-Cultural View"

Notice that Hal summarizes the article's main ideas, or at least those that are relevant to his essay (the ethics of electronic monitoring). Use only what you need from a source. Too often writers include information that is not needed, cluttering a paper and diluting its strength with unneeded material. Also note that Hal did not cite any page numbers. This is because he is not citing anything specific from the article; he is only summarizing the article's contents. He does, however, mention the authors' names and the title of the article.

Next, Hal is interested in the passage in Figure 4.4. The article offers many criticisms of electronic monitoring, and he is interested in discussing a few of these. In doing so, he must be careful to put the material in his own words and not to include any phrasing that too closely resembles the authors' words.

Original Source

Hal's first attempt at paraphrasing the passage did not go well:

> Electronic monitoring by imposing excess control over employees' behavior, can alienate employees and develop a feeling of working in a modern "sweatshop" (Kidwell and Bennett, 1994).

PARAPHRASE

> Kidwell and Bennett argue that imposing excess control as a means to monitor employees' behavior makes people feel they are working in a modern sweatshop (qtd. in Taylor 539).

You can see that many of the phrases of Hal's paragraph come directly from the passage. Even though Hal has indicated that the material came from an article and even cited the authors' names and page number, he is indicating that he has put all of the material into his own words when in fact he has not done so. This is an example of plagiarism.

Plagiarism is, of course, using materials produced by someone else as if they are yours. This includes a range of infractions extending from the accidental omission of a citation to passing off an entire essay as your own. In this case, Hal has used much of the authors' wording and indicates by his lack of quotation marks that the material is in his own words.

SECOND ATTEMPT AT PARAPHRASING

Kidwell and Bennett argue that the use of electronic monitoring is detrimental to employees' morale and creates an unhealthy environment where their every action is monitored to make sure they are constantly working (qtd. in Taylor 539).

The concept of the sweatshop, a place where employees are closely watched to make sure they meet their work quotas, is still there, but it is now in Hal's own words.

Sometimes it is just easier to quote, and as suggested earlier this is often the case when citing policies and laws: these materials usually need to be presented in their original form. The author of this article provides two research questions, and Hal wants to include one of them. A direct quote would be appropriate here as well.

ORIGINAL SOURCE

Does "giving notice" versus "secretly monitoring" make a significant difference in the ethical dimension of electronic monitoring?

Notice that in this example there are quotation marks around certain words. When Hal cites this research question, he needs to turn those double quotation marks into single quotation marks to indicate a quote within a quote.

HAL'S USE OF THE SOURCE

Taylor provides two research questions for his study. The first one, "Does 'giving notice' versus 'secretly monitoring' make a significant difference in the ethical dimension of electronic monitoring?" (530). The importance of determining the ethics of monitoring employees' computers and cell phones hinges on whether they know such monitoring is going on.

Hal does a few important things here.

1. He introduces his quote; it is not just dropped in via parachute to land where it will. He sets up the quote for the reader.
2. He begins and ends his quotation with quotation marks. The marks indicate that everything inside of them comes directly from an outside source. Note that the quotation marks end after the quote, not after the parenthetical citation.

3. Hal takes into account the fact that, in the original, the phrases *giving notice* and *secretly monitoring* were in quotation marks. Hal follows the rule for reducing the quotation marks to 'single' quotes and using "double" quotes around the entire quotation.

4. After Hal ends his quote, he comments on why the material is important.

Following these techniques when summarizing, paraphrasing, or quoting will save you a lot of grief and help you avoid charges of plagiarism.

Avoid Plagiarism

The definition of plagiarism is using the work of others as if it were your own without proper attribution. To most readers (instructors, bosses, etc.), there is no difference between accidentally forgetting to cite a passage and deliberately presenting outside material as your own. How to avoid a failing grade (or a job dismissal)? Avoid plagiarism by following these guidelines.

Avoiding Plagiarism Checklist

☐ Cite all outside material whether you have quoted it or paraphrased it.

☐ Introduce source material and comment on it afterward so the reader is clear which ideas are yours and which came from the source.

☐ When pasting material from a source into your paper, make sure to mark it in some way (e.g., by using boldface type, by using a different font color or size, by highlighting) so that you will remember that the words are not yours. Then go through your document thoroughly to make sure you have cited all the highlighted material correctly.

☐ Always include the source publication information in your bibliography file or on your photocopies. If you do not have author or publication information when you are ready to use the source, you cannot use it.

your turn 4f ▶ PRACTICE **Paraphrase Properly**

Read the following article on some of the costs of delaying comprehensive immigration reform legislation, an issue in 2008, when the essay was first published, and for today's U.S. Congress as well. Write a paragraph about immigration reform and include paraphrasing of two passages from the article by following the tips to avoid plagiarism and citing them correctly.

I'm Not Dangerous

By DANNY POSTEL

The past six months have seen three of the largest workplace immigration raids in U.S. history. In May [2008], the rural Iowa town of Postville was convulsed when 900 Immigration and Customs Enforcement (ICE) agents stormed a kosher meatpacking plant and arrested 389 workers. In August, ICE agents descended on an electrical equipment factory near Laurel, Mississippi, detaining nearly 600 workers. And in October, the scene was repeated in Greenville, South Carolina, where 330 workers were swept up at a chicken-processing plant.

The humanitarian costs of the raids, according to a statement issued by the U.S. Conference of Catholic Bishops Committee on Migration, were "immeasurable and unacceptable in a civilized society." Children were separated from their parents for days. Those arrested were not immediately afforded the rights of due process. And local communities were, in the words of John C. Wester, bishop of Salt Lake City and chairman of the Committee on Migration, "disrupted and dislocated." These raids, he said, "strike immigrant communities unexpectedly, leaving the affected immigrant families to cope in the aftermath. Husbands are separated from their wives, and children are separated from their parents. Many families never recover; others never reunite."

The bishop called on the Department of Homeland Security, of which ICE is an agency, on President George W. Bush, and on then-candidates John McCain and Barack Obama to "reexamine the use of worksite enforcement raids" as an immigration-enforcement tool. He noted that immigrants "who are working to survive and support their families should not be treated like criminals."

Having visited Laurel after the ICE crackdown, I must report that is exactly how the workers there have been treated and made to feel. The majority of the immigrant workers caught up in the raid were taken immediately to a holding facility in Louisiana. ICE released a number of women, some of them pregnant, on "humanitarian" grounds. But many of them were shackled with ankle bands equipped with electronic monitoring devices. Several expressed their humiliation and shame—not to speak of their physical discomfort—at having been branded this way. For days, one of them told me, she avoided going out in public or to the grocery store. "It makes me look like a criminal, like a dangerous person," she lamented. "I'm not dangerous."

This woman told me she had come to the United States out of sheer desperation. She said she was unable to feed her children in her home village in Mexico. Now, with deportation imminent and no means to pay her bills, she and her coworkers were facing a further harrowing fate.

Immigration raids, even large, media-covered ones, are selective and symbolic in nature. They are orchestrated to send a political message that the government is willing and able to enforce the law. But why penalize the least among us—hardworking people who earn very little and endure some of the harshest conditions in the American workplace? The Postville and Laurel plants both have long histories of taking advantage of their workers. Iowa's attorney general recently filed charges against the Postville meatpacking plant for more than nine thousand labor violations. In July, religious and labor leaders joined more than a thousand marchers in the town to show solidarity with those seized in the ICE raid.

Indeed, religious communities have been playing a pivotal role in the aftermath of these raids. Catholic parishes have been safe havens for families scrambling to feed their children amid the turmoil. Immaculate Conception Church in Laurel and Sacred Heart Catholic Church in Hattiesburg worked virtually round-the-clock to feed and provide for the affected families.

To remedy what the U.S. bishops call "the failure of a seriously flawed immigration system," they "urge our elected and appointed officials to turn away from enforcement-only methods and direct their energy toward the adoption of comprehensive immigration reform legislation." That is now up to the new administration and to Congress.

Documentation: Works Cited Page

One of the most tedious aspects of writing research reports of any type is the documentation. You must supply publication information for every source you use in your report. This information must appear in a standardized format or style sheet dictated by your company or instructor.

- In the humanities (fine arts, literature, and history), the most common format is MLA—the Modern Language Association.
- Fields such as sociology, anthropology, education, psychology, and business often require writers to document sources in APA—the American Psychological Association.
- The Council of Science Editors' manual (CSE) is used for the natural sciences, such as biology and geology.

All of these style guides are similar in *what* information you should provide for a source, but they vary in *how* that information is presented. For example, see how a book is cited for MLA, APA, and CSE side by side:

MLA	APA	CSE
Collins, Harry. *Basics of Welding.* New York: Anchor Books, 2005. Print.	Collins, H. (2005). *Basics of welding.* New York: Anchor Books.	1. Collins, Harry. (2005). *Basics of welding.* New York: Anchor Books; p. 532

The complete guides to MLA and APA can be found on the Internet at a variety of sources. If you do not have access to the manuals themselves, a very reliable Internet source for both is The Online Writing Lab at Purdue University:

(MLA) http://owl.english.purdue.edu/owl/resource/747/01/

(APA) http://owl.english.purdue.edu/owl/resource/560/01/

In Part VI, "MLA and APA Documentation Systems," we will cover how to cite sources in both MLA and APA format, how to use the hanging indent function, and the strengths and weaknesses of citation-generating software.

your turn 4g ▶ Integrate a Source

Once you have found the information you want to use, follow Hal's example and (1) introduce your sources. Explain to the reader why you have selected this source. Why this author? Then (2) paraphrase the source, putting it entirely in your own words. Your argument should not be a string of quotations. Quotations should be used sparingly. And finally (3), comment on the source. Do you agree with the author's points? Is this a source you disagree with? Do you have more to say on the subject or point the author raises?

Reflect and Apply

1. As you are collecting your sources, how are you evaluating them for unacceptable biases?

2. How are you maximizing your time as you determine which sources are the most useful for you? As you read through your sources, how are you taking notes that pull from material at the beginning, middle, and ends of them in order to avoid using material out of context?

3. How are you determining the value of any primary sources you are finding on your issue?

4. When you use research material, in what ways are you making sure the reader knows why you are using that particular source at that particular time?

5. How are you guaranteeing that all source material in your argument is properly paraphrased and cited, eliminating accidental plagiarism?

KEEPING IT LOCAL

THE WORLD IS SHRINKING, or expanding, depending on how you view the changes in technology. We have access, even in small towns, to vast amounts of published research from all over the world. We can access blogs written by experts in every field imaginable. We can also access blogs written by anyone who wants to write one on any subject, whether they are an expert or not. We can read articles published by highly credible sources in distinguished journals. We can also learn that those same experts are guilty of plagiarism, making all their work suspect. It is important, now more than ever, to use the Internet wisely to learn as much as we can about the authors of any material we plan on using to support our arguments. Embrace all that the world of technology offers, but do so with great caution.

Approach the sources you have selected for your argument by assessing their usefulness. How many sources are still useful after your initial assessment? Do you need to find more sources that fit your argument better? Take the remaining sources and assess their credibility. Do you feel the articles are credible once you have assessed them? Finally, read the sources, making sure you have identified the authors' claims and all supporting and opposing views. Answer these questions: Who is the author? What is the claim? What are the supporting views? What are the opposing or alternate views addressed?

CHAPTER 5

Read Critically and Avoid Fallacies

Once again, you receive an email request from your boss to donate to a large national charity. Because of recent misappropriation of the charity's funds in particular and the downturn in the economy in general, the charity is receiving fewer donations. It's not that you have anything against the charitable organization, and you recognize that it does great work. You feel pressured, however, to give to an organization that you have not chosen. Your boss has sent several emails encouraging donation, emails that ask employees not to leave children without proper meals or winter clothing. You don't want to be the only bad guy, so you write a check.

Later, you are approached by a coworker to buy Christmas wrapping paper as a fundraiser for her son's fourth-grade fieldtrip. If enough money isn't raised, the children won't be able to go, and then they won't be able to compete for future opportunities with the kids at the more affluent schools because they won't have the same background experiences. Again, you reach for your checkbook.

All Illustrations by iStockphoto.com/A-digit

COMMUNITY

School–Academic

Workplace

Family–Household

Neighborhood

Social–Cultural

Consumer

Concerned Citizen

TOPIC: Workplace

ISSUE: Peer/Employee Pressure

AUDIENCE: Fellow Employees

CLAIM: Employees should be free from solicitations for donations or purchases in the workplace.

It is difficult to sort through the arguments that seem logical on the surface or that stir your emotions. Which arguments or causes are valid, and which are meant only to part you from your money? Which arguments contain fallacies to get you to do things you don't want to do? In Chapter 5 you will learn how to identify the four major categories of fallacies in the arguments of others and learn to eliminate each type of fallacy from your own arguments.

In Chapter 5 you will learn to:

- Define fallacies.
- Identify and avoid:
  - Fallacies of choice.
  - Fallacies of support.
  - Fallacies of emotion.
  - Fallacies of inconsistency.

Define Fallacies

Very often when we are listening to a speaker's argument or reading an argument in a magazine or newspaper, it is easy to get caught up in the speaker's excitement and overlook the fallacies in his argument. **Fallacies** are errors in an argument, whether accidental or deliberate, that serve to draw attention away from the problems in the argument's claim or support. They can be the result of a poor understanding of the subject, or they can be deliberate manipulations of the argument to misdirect readers. The difficulty with fallacies is that they are often hard to spot, in your own writing and in the writing of others.

ryccio/Getty Images

Figure 5.1 Information overload can make us feel that we are always a step behind.

Detecting fallacies in arguments is a component of reading well. How well do you know how to read? "I can read just fine," you say. But there is a type of reading that many struggle with—critical reading. **Critical reading** is a more active form of engaging with a text, be it a newspaper article, a politician's speech, or a note from your son's teacher. For example, what is really being said in that politician's speech? You are hearing her words, but are you really listening to what she is saying? The two actions are not the same thing. The best-sounding arguments can fall to pieces when examined closely by a reader who is actively responding to them, rather than passively receiving them.

We are bombarded daily with an overwhelming amount of information. We must sort through emails; phone messages; and newspapers and news programs, which now have 24-hour-a-day updates. You can even subscribe to sites so that updated news on certain topics can be emailed to your computer or sent to your phone. Then there are all of the other sources of information you encounter: reading for your courses; updates to the Operations and Procedures Manual at work; and the buzz about the latest movies, television shows, music, and fashion trends. Miss one day's information due to a cold, and you feel you have fallen behind a week. This anxious feeling is called **information overload**—the sense that you are always one step (if not more) behind.

Spotting fallacies can be difficult, but it is not impossible. The more tools you have at hand, the easier your job of cracking someone's argument will be. In Chapter 4, "Evaluate and Engage with Your Sources," you learned that there are some methods that will help you get to the heart of any argument, whether the argument is presented in print (such as a book, an article, or an Internet posting) or orally (such as a speech or an advertisement). In this chapter, you will learn to demand of authors that they convince you that their claims and support are valid. By learning to identify fallacies in the arguments of others, you will also learn how to avoid using them in your own arguments. Let's tackle the most common forms of fallacies.

Identify and Avoid Fallacies

Many arguments can sound good until you begin to follow them closely. All of a sudden, those high-flying words seem to be saying very little. You begin to suspect that the writer is trying to hoodwink you. And you may be right.

Dishonest arguers often use fallacies to direct the reader's attention away from the real issues or to hide their real purposes. Just as frequently, though, inexperienced writers use fallacies because they don't know any better. Fallacies are errors in a writer's argument—not errors in fact, but errors in reasoning.

In a recent class, a student writer argued, "I think we should stop spending so much money on the space program because people are starving here on Earth." Other students disagreed, but they were not sure what to say to counter the argument. One traditional way of arguing is to learn to recognize specific fallacies and then see if the argument you disagree with contains one of these errors in logic. Is this an *ad hominem* or an *ad misericordiam*? Is the argument a *post hoc* fallacy, a *com hoc* fallacy, or maybe a *tu quoque* fallacy? One thing is certain: if you take this route, you may be studying fallacies *ad nauseum.*

The good news is there is a far easier way. All fallacies boil down to four categories. There is overlap between types, and you could argue that a fallacy can fall into more than one category, but in general the four categories are as follows:

1. Fallacies of choice
2. Fallacies of support
3. Fallacies of emotion
4. Fallacies of inconsistency

In the argument against the space program, the fallacy happens to be a false choice, an either–or argument that tries to force you into supporting either feeding the hungry or exploring space. This is a smart move. Of those two choices, what ethical person would ever choose space exploration over feeding people who are starving? But there is also inconsistency. The arguer is assuming that there is only enough government money to do one of two things: (1) feed the hungry or (2) explore space. But, of course, that same arguer drives over roads paid for by government money, lives in a country defended by a military, and will someday retire and receive Social Security benefits from the government. In fact, there are lots of programs she doesn't propose to sacrifice in order to feed the hungry, so why should she pick on the space program? She is being inconsistent. The problem is that she is not directly articulating the inconsistency. Some fallacies are obvious, but most require you to dig a little deeper into the arguer's assumptions. Luckily, you don't need to know the name of each fallacy in order to find the inconsistency.

Keep in mind that even a fallacious argument can be right—just as a stopped clock is right twice a day. We shouldn't just accept fallacious arguments any more than we should tell time by a stopped clock. In each case, further investigation is warranted. How else might it be? Maybe the clock is working after all, and we just looked at it wrong. Or maybe we can fix it; it might just need a new battery. And maybe it's telling the right time, even though it won't be in just one minute from now. The goal is not understanding all of the types of fallacies but learning how to recognize when someone is being inconsistent. Every time you want to test the strength of an argument, look closely at what it is saying and what it assumes.

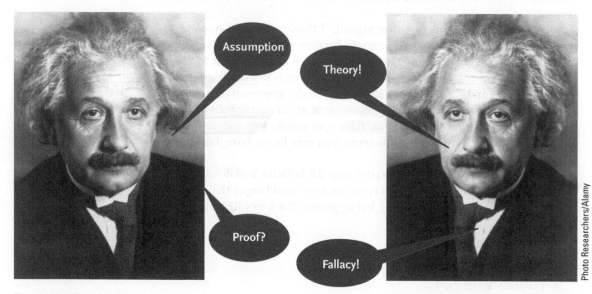

Figure 5.2 Albert Einstein

Photo Researchers/Alamy

Before we go any further, let's discuss bias. Say you're writing a paper with the following claim: the study of extrasensory perception (ESP) deserves equal funding with stem cell research. One obvious assumption (warrant) the claim makes is that ESP is real. Another is that it is worth studying. It is impossible to write any argument without some fallacies, especially bias, since we are all biased. The very fact that we are making a certain claim and dismissing alternatives to that claim is evidence of our bias toward our own claim. We also tend to give short shrift to competing evidence and make leaps of logic that may not be warranted.

The heart of critical thinking is asking, "How else might it be?" Looking for fallacies involves a search for answers to that same question. If I use a blanket statement and say, "Everyone is born with paranormal powers," I am dismissing the possibility that some people are born without any extra-mental powers, that they can't read minds, tell the future, or move objects simply with the power of thought. The first category of fallacies involves making bad or unwarranted choices about what to believe.

Avoid Fallacies of Choice

Fallacies of choice ask you to make the wrong choice by limiting your view of what the future holds or what the choices are. They put things into simplistic terms that don't allow for positive alternatives. They tell you that only the choice they want is possible or worth-while. You will see how this overlaps with scare tactics and other emotional fallacies.

Blanket Statement

Blanket statements use the language of absoluteness. They use words like *all, always, never, no, every,* and *none.* They are fallacies as soon as someone can think of an exception. If someone claims that all dogs have tails, you could go home and chase your dog around with a pair of scissors, trying to prove that person wrong. (See Figure 5.3.)

Some people take the sixth commandment to mean that a person should never kill. But, of course, people kill to live by eating plants and animals. And people kill to defend themselves, or to serve their country in times of war, or to mete out punish-

Yann Arthus-Bertrand/Documentary Value/Corbis

Figure 5.3 The Schipperke is a tailless dog

ment for murder. To say that we should never kill is a blanket statement. If you believe that killing is sometimes okay, then you have found an exception and turned the blanket statement into a fallacy. Some examples of blanket statements include:

- Cell phone use in the classroom is *always* inappropriate.
- The *only way* to understand the increasing high school dropout rate is to study the lack of student motivation.

Both of these claims use unqualified terms (*always, only way*) that can easily be rebutted. Of course there are times when it is appropriate to use a cell phone in the classroom—calling security, for example. Students drop out of school for many reasons, not just lack of motivation. Avoid absolutes. Blanket statements hinge on the following terms and terms like them. Be careful to qualify these **absolute terms** in your own writing. Also note that plural nouns can imply absolutism (for example, using the word *students,* implies "all students"). You can modify these terms using the qualifiers in Chapter 10, "Build Arguments."

Absolute Terms			
all	no	none	100 percent
every	always	never	must
has to	can't	won't	only

False Dilemma, Either–Or, and Misuse of Occam's Razor

False dilemma/either–or thinking suggests that only one thing can happen—either A or B. As in the sample claim that the space program can exist only at the expense of the poor, arguers who make this type of mistake state that there are only two choices in the argument.

> So much of the food I eat, the fuel I expend, and the clothing I wear work against the idea of sustainable living. Why should I even bother to try?

This student's claim suggests that there are only two choices available to the speaker. He can either (a) live a lifestyle that is completely geared to sustainable living, from food to fuel, or (b) not even try to make any efforts at sustainability. A critical reader will ask, "Does it have to be either–or?" This author has created a false choice, a dilemma that is not really there. A person may not be capable of living in a totally green way, but most people agree that anything done to help the planet is a good thing.

Occam's razor is a philosophical point of view that argues that the simplest solution is usually the correct one. If it walks like a duck, looks like a duck, and quacks like a duck, chances are very good it is a duck. Most of the time, using Occam's razor to cut through far-fetched and overly complex theories is the way to go. But this chase for simplicity can be misused.

The following story is an example of public officials finally breaking out of fallacious false choice/either–or thinking. For many years, suicidal people had been leaping to their deaths from the Golden Gate Bridge, yet nothing had been done to stop it. Partly the inaction was born from a desire to maintain the landmark beauty of the structure by not cluttering its profile with high fencing. Partly the inaction stemmed from the fallacy of thinking that any suicide prevented at the bridge would simply take place elsewhere. There were, the doubters argued, only two choices: either keep letting people kill themselves and leave the bridge unchanged, or force depressed people to kill themselves elsewhere by marring the beauty of the bridge with new barriers. In this view, nothing could be done about suicides, because anybody who wanted to kill themselves enough to jump off a bridge would simply find another way to do it. Either people wanted to keep living or they didn't, in which case there was nothing anyone could do to stop them. Because it was impossible to prevent all suicides, the decision was made to prevent none. Any other choice, such as the plan recently adopted, was considered impossible.

In fact, suicide is often preventable, and it's also an act of opportunity. No sane person would hand a suicidal individual a loaded gun. Why? Because it would be giving the person an opportunity. Because it could *change the person's behavior*. Therefore, it stands to reason that removing opportunities for suicide might also change behavior. At last, bridge officials decided to break free from their loop of fallacious thinking by adding nets below the bridge's surface. This solution prevents suicides at the bridge, while damaging the bridge's landmark profile very little. As a result of breaking through the either–or thinking, a solution that considered both sides of the argument was reached.

Slippery Slope

A **slippery slope (or staircase)** argument is one of the easiest fallacies to recognize. You will often hear people say that, if we let one thing happen, then that will cause some other thing to happen, which in turn will lead to something bad, which then will cause chaos. If we take that first step, then we will fall all the way down the slippery slope to chaos or evil, as illustrated by Figures 5.4 and 5.5.

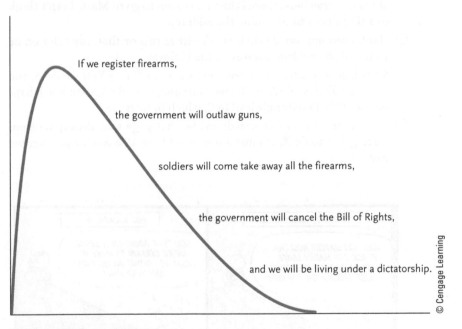

If we register firearms,

the government will outlaw guns,

soldiers will come take away all the firearms,

the government will cancel the Bill of Rights,

and we will be living under a dictatorship.

© Cengage Learning

Figure 5.4 A slippery slope argument

But events do not always follow the predicted slope. For example, in contrast with common gun-control arguments, some societies have taken away guns without becoming dictatorships, or they took them away for a while and ended up giving them back later on. A good history lesson often reveals that the "slippery slope" in an argument is actually an unlikely series of events. A better description for most such cause–effect chains might be a "staircase" because we usually can move up the slope and down the slope. Sometimes it is a slippery staircase, but it's rarely inevitable that if we take the first step, we will slide all the way down.

internet activity 5a

Use the Opposing Viewpoints database or another available database to find arguments about gun control. Read through these arguments and see if you can find slippery slope fallacies. What makes them fallacious? Where do they start, and where do they end?

Signs that you may be reading or writing fallacies of choice include:

☐ Support for extreme positions: we *must* do something (e.g., bomb, invade, kill, torture, outlaw, silence, close a factory, fire an employee, censor objectionable material).

☐ The language of certainty: all, every, 100 percent, never, none, each, always, everywhere, there is just no reason to go to Mars, I can't think of a single benefit of joining the military.

☐ Hard, even impossible choices: it's either this or that, my solution or your hellish problem, my way or the highway.

☐ Surprising conditionals: if we don't do X, we'll face Y; if we do A, the sky will fall; if we do A, we'll reach nirvana; if we do A, then B will happen, and B will naturally lead to C, which in turn . . .

☐ Support for a decision already made: that page was already written; we're going to do X, it's just a matter of how; one way or another we have to . . .

Figure 5.5 This cartoon uses the slippery slope fallacy to make its point

your turn **5a** ➤ **PRACTICE Identify Fallacies of Choice**

Here is a paragraph from the paper on ESP. See if you can spot the types of fallacies. Match the numbered fallacies with the correct box below.

The study of extrasensory perception (ESP) deserves equal funding with stem cell research. ❶ We can recognize this fact, or we can continue to waste the opportunities such funding represents. ❷ No medical treatment comes without a price in terms of research funding. ❸ It's hard to think of treatments that didn't involve some government-funded research; therefore, it's safe to assume there aren't any. ❹ If we continue ignoring this potentially valuable source of knowledge, we can expect to begin ignoring other valuable types of innovation, and after that, what's next? Like any species, human beings survive and prosper by constantly learning and adapting to a changing environment. Without ESP funding, we may well face extinction.

Which numbered sentence in the paragraph best represents each type of fallacy? Fill in each box with a different number.

☐ Blanket Statement   ☐ False Dilemma/Either–Or
☐ Misuse of Occam's Razor   ☐ Slippery Slope

Avoid Fallacies of Support

Fallacies of support involve making connections and conclusions that aren't warranted. If Michelle had two ducks and someone gave her two more ducks, no one would suggest that she now had five ducks. Yet this often is exactly what people do with the logic of their arguments. They support their claim with their claim. They jump to conclusions based on very little evidence. They make superstitious connections between events, build arguments on falsehoods, and support their claims with facts that aren't even relevant.

Circular Argument

A **circular argument** is simply one that ends up relying on its own claim for support. In this way, it seems to chase its own tail. A person who doesn't agree will tend to see the arguer as trapped in her own logic. The arguer is caught in the circle of her own prior beliefs. For example, she may assume that God exists and is all-powerful. Anything less than God's full existence would violate her assumption of God's full existence. That's the circle. (See Figure 5.6.) Other arguers might believe in other, equally powerful beings. Do they all have to exist? Only to someone trapped in that particular circle of logic.

> We need to drill more for oil. Why? Because gas prices are high. Why? Because we need more oil than we have available to us. Why? Because we haven't drilled enough oil wells.

This kind of argument ignores all other possibilities, such as conservation, alternative energy sources, or simply letting shortages raise prices to the point that we only use the oil that is absolutely necessary, a kind of conservation that would be enforced by the marketplace laws of supply and demand. The argument also ignores any balancing of costs and harm from more oil drilling and simply treats it as a good thing that we may or may not do, instead of a complex thing that may do as much harm as good, for example, by continuing global warming.

Courtesy of the author

Figure 5.6 A circular argument that uses its claim as its support

Hasty Generalization and Jumping to Conclusions

The fallacy of **hasty generalization** involves taking a single case and generalizing from it. Your friend takes a ride in a vintage automobile from the 1930s and the axle breaks, causing an accident that breaks your friend's leg. Now, you refuse to ride in anything older than last year's model. Or your grandmother smoked cigarettes and lived to be 90. Therefore, smoking must be harmless and all this talk about lung cancer and early deaths is just a scare tactic.

Faulty Causality: *Post Hoc, Ergo Propter Hoc*

Post hoc, ergo propter hoc: This Latin phrase sounds complicated, but it's really simple, and it represents a fundamental process in animal thought. The entire phrase can be translated as "After this, therefore because of this." When two events happen one after the other, we naturally tend to think the first event caused the other event. We kick the sleepy copy machine, it starts working, and we assume it was our kick that did the trick. In fact, maybe it had just then finished its warm-up cycle. This is how superstitions get started. A baseball player forgets to change his underwear, and he pitches a no-hitter. Well, no way is he changing that underwear. No, he's going to wear the same pair every time he pitches until the magic finally wears off.

> Parents should not have to vaccinate their children because vaccinations cause autism.

A classic case of *post hoc* fallacy presents itself in arguments that claim vaccinations cause autism. We don't yet know what causes autism, but we do know that it exists. A certain percentage of children will be diagnosed with autism at a young age. If virtually all young children are given, for example, the MMR (mumps, measles, and rubella) vaccine, it is certain that, soon after, some of those children will develop autism. If none of the children are vaccinated, it is equally certain that, soon after, some of those children will develop autism. After all, the MMR vaccine is given to children at 12 to 15 months of age. Autism is usually diagnosed around three years of age. Therefore, MMR almost always comes before a diagnosis of autism, making it is easy for parents to assume a causal connection, even if there isn't one.

The fallacy comes into play when parents assume that the vaccine caused the autism, even though they would never assume that the lack of a vaccine would cause autism, though the evidence is the same in both cases. That is the inconsistency at the heart of the *post hoc* fallacy: just because one thing happened after the other doesn't mean the first thing caused the second thing. The MMR vaccine comes before autism, but often so does potty training. Could potty training be the cause of autism? Could baby formula? The fact is, we don't know what causes autism. It might be a genetic disorder. It could be caused by hormones while the fetus is in the womb. It could be a result of exposure to common household materials or chemicals. The fact is, we don't know.

Many errors in arguments come from making mistakes in causality. You may believe that a chain of events exists where it doesn't. You may believe that one event is caused by another. You may believe that only one cause is responsible when there may be a combination of causes leading to an effect.

Fallacies in causality are not easy to spot. Keep your eyes open, and do some investigating on your own about claims of causality that seem too easy or are not well supported.

> Some people have claimed that the city council's decision to again postpone its discussion of homelessness is only increasing the number of homeless in our community.

Here, it cannot be proven that the city council's inaction has anything to do with the increase in homelessness. More research would need to be done.

Non Sequitur, Red Herring, and False Clue

Authors of murder mysteries are famous for planting false clues, otherwise known as red herrings. They force the detective and the reader to follow a scent that doesn't lead anywhere or leads to the wrong conclusion. A false clue in a murder mystery is simply one that doesn't support our attempt to identify the real killer. But false clues appear in all kinds of arguments. So do statements that don't follow what came before, that are out of order, or that might sound good but don't actually relate.

In Latin, *non sequitur* means "it does not follow." Often, an arguer will write or say something that doesn't seem to belong, that suddenly shifts the focus or the argument, or that makes a conclusion that doesn't seem justified from the evidence that has been presented.

Some of these *non sequiturs* are accidental. A writer might suddenly change the subject or make a point that comes from out of the blue. Or the writer might even force in a point that doesn't belong, simply because he likes it. This is known as "shoe-horning," after the old metal scoops that people used to use to guide their feet into tight leather shoes. Another term for a person's pet interest is a "hobby-horse," and a person with a pet argument "has an axe to grind."

If a writer's claim is that diet can help to prevent diabetes, discussion of issues not related to diet or diabetes may seem like *non sequiturs*. Discussion of illness prevention in general could be risky, in that it could seem like it's off topic. Or it might simply be an example of broadening out the claim to include other kinds of disease prevention besides diet or diabetes prevention. In the following passage, however, the writer goes way off the track.

> Diet can help prevent type 2 diabetes. A new study published in *Diabetes Care* compared the glycemic control (blood sugar levels) of patients on traditional American Diabetes Association diets with a low-fat vegan diet. Patients on the vegan diet did roughly twice as well in reducing their glycemic index. This goes to show that the Texas beef producers were wrong for suing Oprah Winfrey for her 1996 anti-beef comments. When it was pointed out that cows were being fed to other cows, Oprah said, "It has just stopped me cold from eating another burger!"

Sentence 4 came out of left field, didn't it? The writer shifted suddenly from discussion of diabetes prevention to a lawsuit concerning a statement by a celebrity.

Some *non sequiturs* represent conscious efforts on the part of the arguer. The intent might be to change an unpleasant subject. A politician who is unpopular for her handling of a state's economy might take a strong interest in creating harsher penalties for child molesters. A skeptic of global warming might bring up the subject of government conspiracies in hopes that an audience upset about the possibility of too much government control might forget all about potential harm from changes in the climate.

Straw Man Argument or Argument Built on a False Fact or Claim

Straw man arguments are those that are based on incorrect information, whether the intention is to deliberately misrepresent an opponent's claims or because the facts that are being used are plainly incorrect. For example, someone might claim "One piece of the solution to homelessness in our community is more affordable housing." You would be committing a straw man fallacy if you said "My opponent says that we can end homelessness just by building cheap apartments." The misrepresentation of that position makes it easy to dismiss.

Signs that you may be reading or writing fallacies of support include:

☐ Making the same point in two places in a chain of reasoning: the economy is bad because the housing market fell, which happened because wages were not rising fast enough for people to afford the higher prices, which resulted from a weakening economy.

☐ Support based on a single case, anecdotal evidence, or making too much out of a few cases: back in 1979 . . . , reports of similar occurrences indicate . . . , this incident shows that . . .

☐ The language of time or events happening after each other: then, after, when, preceded by, I'll never get a flu shot—my aunt and uncle got a flu vaccine and then they came right down with the flu.

☐ Sudden or unexplained shifts in topic.

☐ Unquestioned assumptions: everything hinges on . . . , the key is that . . .

☐ Statements that put words in someone else's mouth instead of quoting them in context.

your turn 5b ➤ **PRACTICE Identify Fallacies of Support**

Here is a paragraph from the paper on ESP. See if you can spot the types of fallacies. Match the numbered fallacies with the correct box below.

❶ Whenever researchers take ESP seriously, they document many more cases, which shows that the first step toward unlocking paranormal powers is simply to look for them. ❷ In one case, the paranormal researcher herself began reporting the ability to move objects without touching them, showing that if she, a trained, hardened scientist can do it, anyone can. ❸ According to that researcher, Dr. Ruth Bandylegs, ESP could even lead to an increase in religious faith and consequently better our world in that way too. ❹ However, paranormal powers are not taken seriously by most scientists, most likely due to their bias toward traditional science. In traditional science, the emphasis is placed on the known laws of physics, but ESP must work based on physical laws that are unknown. Otherwise, traditional science would have taken it seriously by now, and those laws would be recognized. ❺ Since paranormal research has been shown to increase both incidents of ESP and also its importance in religious faith, an increase in funding is definitely warranted.

Which numbered sentence in the paragraph best represents each type of fallacy? Fill in each box with a different number.

☐   Circular Argument

☐   Hasty Generalization/Jumping to Conclusions

☐   Straw Man Argument

☐   Faulty Causality/*Post Hoc*

☐   *Non Sequitur*/Red Herring

Avoid Fallacies of Emotion

Appeals based on emotion are those that evoke sentiment, fear, desire, and so on. But wait a minute, we said in earlier chapters that emotional appeals are a good thing. Can they also be fallacies? Well, not in theory, but in practice they can be. Whenever we rely too much on any one kind of support, we can run into trouble because we are giving it more weight than another kind of support and, therefore, being unbalanced. Many people would claim that in the end, everything we believe comes down to emotion. Perhaps this is true; even when an argument is based on scientific evidence, at some point we accept that evidence because we like it. In other words, we accept it not because it fits the definition of good scientific evidence, but because it's a definition that we like. Fallacies of emotion are a problem because they completely replace evidence with feelings. They play on the heart strings and the fears of the audience. They name-call, they poison your view of things, they make you feel left out, and they use famous people to vouch for things they know very little about.

Ad Hominem

Ad hominem simply means "to the person." It is the fallacy of arguing based on the arguer's personality or character, credibility, or authority. It's the opposite of shooting the messenger because you don't like the message. Here, you shoot the message because you don't like the messenger.

> We cannot believe she will follow through on her plans to funnel more money toward charities. Can we trust a former alcoholic?

The inconsistency of *ad hominem* fallacies is that we dismiss arguments from people we dislike but accept the same arguments from people we admire. Another way to say it is that, when we do like the arguer or when we do not have an emotional response one way or the other, we generally judge an argument as good or bad on its own merits. To be consistent then, when we don't like the arguer, we should still judge the argument on its own merits.

Testimonials and False Authority

The opinions of people with authority can provide valuable support to an argument, but only if the **testimonials** come from true experts in the relevant subject area. Otherwise, the arguer is guilty of using **false authority**.

Consider this the flip side of an *ad hominem* attack. Here, instead of attacking the messenger instead of the argument, we embrace the argument because we like the messenger. This often means giving someone unwarranted credibility. If Einstein said that whales should wear velvet waistcoats to hit home runs, should we believe it? We love Einstein, and he was a genius. But what did he know about baseball, or marine biology, or fashion design?

A well-known commercial for diabetes supplies presents Wilford Brimley as someone you can trust to give you good advice on buying these needed supplies. Wilford Brimley is a famous character actor, so what does he know about medicine or medical supplies? It turns out that he has diabetes, and so he is an expert in using the supplies. He is an expert consumer, someone who other consumers of diabetes supplies might want to listen to. A close look reveals that Brimley is not a false authority. Michael Jordan does commercials for men's underwear. Well, he is a man, so we can assume that he does wear men's underwear. Testimonials like these don't represent a fallacy. However, they still should be balanced against the bias that comes from the "expert" being paid to represent a product.

Vice President Al Gore and U.S. Senator James Inhofe are both famous for their views on global warming. Gore has spent decades calling for action, and he even won the Nobel Peace Prize for his work. Inhofe has long been a denier who has called global warming the "greatest hoax ever perpetrated on the American people." What are their grounds for authority? Senator Inhofe has a bachelor's degree in economics and has worked in business and insurance. Gore got a bachelor's degree in government and has also studied law, divinity, journalism, and English. Neither is a climate scientist. If they have any authority at all, it has come from studying the work of those scientists who do the actual research and who are the actual experts.

In some cases, the fact that a person is an anti-authority actually makes the case stronger. President Ronald Reagan famously opposed funding for AIDS research, thinking that AIDS patients were responsible for having the disease. After he left office, he made a television commercial pleading for Americans to give money for AIDS research. He said, "You see, sometimes old dogs can learn new tricks."

Sometimes, even a true authority can be used in a fallacious way. Email and the Internet are often used to spread stories or warnings on the basis of fraudulent information or testimony. In one such case, the Apollo moon landings were argued to be a hoax staged by NASA. One piece of "evidence" offered was a statement by Stephen Hawking that humans could not survive a trip through the Van Allen radiation belt. Stephen Hawking is a renowned physicist, so he could be trusted as an authority on this issue. The problem is he never made such a statement.

Bandwagon

A **bandwagon fallacy** means that since everybody believes it, I should too. This is the fallacy of following popular tastes, or accepting a claim simply because other people do.

There is a clichéd response to this fallacy that clearly shows the inconsistency: "If everyone jumped off a bridge, would you do it?" This type of fallacy involves people basing an argument on the popularity of the claim or proposal, rather than its merits. "Everybody is getting tattoos, so you should get a tattoo" is an example of a bandwagon argument. But if everyone says "Hey, I really like that Hitler—he really has some good ideas," is it then okay to jump on the Hitler bandwagon and accept those Nazi arguments? Of course not, because to be consistent, we need to consider every argument on its merits, rather than accepting the ones we like and denying the ones we don't.

> There must be something to that Kennedy assassination conspiracy, or why would so many people believe it?

There is power and peril in group thinking. The power is that we can rely on other people to get there ahead of us, to discover things we don't have time or resources to discover. Other people blaze the trail. We just follow along. That's also the peril. If the trail they blaze leads to a cliff, then we can find ourselves in big trouble, believing things that don't make sense, or that are even harmful. In the case of the John F. Kennedy assassination, so many different kinds of people have raised questions about the lone gunman theory that it feels like "Where there's smoke, there's fire." All those theories with all those points of evidence can't be wrong—can they? The fact that many people believe something is not, by itself, evidence.

Ad Misericordiam

Ad Misericordiam is an appeal to pity. Users of this fallacy are trying to win support for their argument by manipulating the audience's feelings of guilt or pity. As instructors, we are frequently on the receiving end of this type of fallacy: "Please let me take the exam. My dog died, I lost my job, and I think I have the flu. Please don't make me fail school as well!"

Governments often use gut emotions like fear, revenge, or pity to motivate their citizens in time of war. This poster from World War I show the extent to which our government used images portraying Germans as barbarians, animals, and rapists terrorizing innocent women and children. Did our government do the same after 9/11 in the war with Al Qaeda?

Scare Tactics

When all else fails, frighten your audience. Fear is a powerful emotion. Fear of homosexuality, fear of Islam, fear of MRSA, fear of other races: humans have a long history of acting poorly when they are afraid. Scare tactics capitalize on poor economies, war, and any other controversial issue to persuade their audiences to act or not act in a way that is beneficial to the arguer.

A common advertising technique is the use of scare tactics in order to sell products or encourage people to vote or act in a certain way. (See Figure 5.7.) Either the audience acts in the desired way, or it will suffer some terrible fate. Don't buy our brand of teeth whitener? Your dates will draw back in horror when they see your gray teeth. Use our competitor's vacuum cleaner? It actually manufactures toxic dust that will quickly fill your rooms to the depth of your ankles. Scare tactics always work to create this kind of either–or choice.

Sometimes, there is good reason to be scared. The stock market in 2008 lost almost 50 percent of its value. Investors are now gun shy, and it looks like the very worst time to invest in stocks. Even in this case, reacting purely out of fear represents fallacious thinking. Bad times can often bring opportunities. Many successful businesses are started in a down economy when everyone else is retrenching. Companies often cut their advertising budget when sales drop, but that's the most important time to advertise. The most successful companies—Dell, Coca Cola, McDonald's—advertise no matter what their sales look like. Success in business often means not letting fear influence decision making. Buying stocks when times are terrible might just mean getting a bargain.

Figure 5.7 Posters from World War II encourage the viewer to feel a strong bond against the enemy

The opposite is also true. In 1996, Alan Greenspan, chairman of the Federal Reserve Board, referred to people's excitement over rising stock prices as "irrational exuberance." The lack of fear was sure to precede a crash. Just four years later, Internet and technology stocks crashed.

The best way to avoid being taken in by scare tactics is simply not to react. It's best to react when a bus is flying toward you down a hilly street. When there is no immediate danger and someone argues that there is, that's a good time to pause, and do nothing except examine the situation more closely.

Signs that you may be reading or writing fallacies of emotion include:

- ☐ Discussion of someone's background or life, or of aspects unrelated to their argument
- ☐ Reasoning based on what the crowd is doing: mention of high or increasing popularity; discussion of how new something is
- ☐ Off-topic testimonials: for example, a baseball player used as support for a type of plant fertilizer; celebrities touted for their opinion, not their expert judgment
- ☐ Emotionally charged language: worry, hope, fear, desire; that would be a disaster; such a thing should worry any sane person

your turn 5c ➤ **PRACTICE Identify Fallacies of Emotion**

Here is a paragraph from the paper on ESP. See if you can spot the types of fallacies. Match the numbered fallacies with the correct box below.

> *If it led to breakthroughs in the practice of ESP, a full-fledged research program could help us tackle some of the world's biggest problems.* ❶ *Right now, countless children in the Third World are going to bed without their supper; millions of thinking, feeling animals are being mistreated in factory farms; and far too many women are suffering the torments of oppression and domestic abuse.* ❷ *In a world with so many problems, we simply can't afford to neglect any possible avenue for solutions, and we do so at our own peril.* ❸ *We also can't afford to miss the boat, as France, Belgium, and Botswana have each set up their own state-of-the-art government-funded research facilities.* ❹ *No less than the Royal Prince of England has called for similar efforts in his own country.* ❺ *It seems clear that anyone who would refuse to explore such promising opportunities for advancement just isn't thinking straight.*

Which numbered sentence in the paragraph best represents each type of fallacy? Fill in each box with a different number.

☐ *Ad hominem* or other inappropriate negative personal argument

☐ Testimonials, false authority, or other positive personal argument

☐ Bandwagon

☐ *Ad misericordiam*

☐ Scare tactics

Avoid Fallacies of Inconsistency

All fallacies boil down to an inconsistency, but some arguments are blatantly inconsistent. One obvious but all too common kind of inconsistency is a **double standard**. Someone might say, "I like Chairman Gripspike because he is vocal and really speaks out for what he believes, but Chairwoman Leadpocket sure got on my nerves; she was so pushy and opinionated." A common complaint women leaders make is that, when men assert themselves, they are considered strong and capable, but when women assert themselves, they are considered difficult to work with. Anyone with a strong enough bias will use this kind of inconsistency, often without realizing they are doing so. To a white racist, a white criminal is simply a bad egg, an exception, but a black criminal is one more bit of evidence to show that black people are thugs. A black racist might see a wealthy black business person as a hero to be admired and emulated, while seeing a wealthy white business person as a typical selfish oppressor who only looks out for himself.

Sometimes instead of treating similar things inconsistently, people will treat different things as if they are the same. This is a fallacy of false consistency, or false equivalence, treating things as the same when they really aren't the same.

Moral Equivalence

In this fallacy, two very unequal things are balanced against each other *morally,* as if they are equally bad or good. Your boss catches you leaving the office with a company pen on the same day she fired your coworker for embezzling thousands of dollars from the company advertising account. She confronts you and says you are just as guilty as your coworker and need to be fired. Technically, stealing is stealing, but are these two acts really morally equivalent?

Material Equivalence

Here, two very unequal things are equated, or balanced against each other as if they are *materially* equivalent. If an apple a day keeps the doctor away, does it matter if the apple is a red one or a green one? An apple is an apple, right? Well . . .

Sweet gum trees give off gases that, when mixed with automobile emissions, can contribute to ozone pollution. Trees also take in carbon dioxide and give off oxygen. Someone might say that these two things balance out, that the material effects of a tree cancel out so completely that cutting down trees will neither help nor harm the environment. President Reagan was famous for his statement that trees pollute more than cars, so we shouldn't complain or worry when they are cut down. In reality, trees suck in carbon dioxide, a principal greenhouse gas responsible for global warming, and they also give off oxygen. Until we actually weigh trees' beneficial effects against their harmful effects, we don't really know if the material evidence is equal. And it turns out, trees do far more good than harm, so we should not cut them down.

Definitional Equivalence

In *definitional* equivalence, two things are defined as being the same, whether they are or not. Often, before we can tell if two things are morally equivalent or have equivalent material effects, we first have to know what the things are. Do they even belong to the same category? The abortion debate centers around the definition of personhood. Is a fertilized egg a human life? Is a fetus a person? The U.S. Constitution defines a citizen as someone born or naturalized in the United States. What does science say? What do the courts say?

Life is so diverse that scientists can't agree on a single definition of what a species is, so more recently they have begun using a combination of definitions. These kinds of arguments sound pretty esoteric, but in fact they can matter in the real world. Suppose a population of foxes is threatened by a home builder's development activity. If it represents a separate species, it could be protected under the Endangered Species Act. If it is defined as simply a subgroup of a common fox species, it might be exempted from any protection. A developer could lose big money, and people might not be able to buy homes where they'd like, or a species might disappear from the earth. A definition, then, can seal the fate of an animal.

Inconsistent Treatment (from Dogmatism, Prejudice, and Bias)

Often this fallacy shows itself in the way an arguer supports a claim. Arguers look for facts to help their side of the argument but ignore facts that work against their side.

One infamous case of inconsistent treatment involved voting laws. Various poll taxes were levied and literacy tests adopted to make it harder for black Americans in Southern states to vote. Many black citizens in the early twentieth century were poor and so could not pay the tax, or they would have had trouble answering detailed written questions about the U.S. Constitution. They were effectively disenfranchised when they went to the polls to cast their vote. Poor and illiterate white citizens were often waved through or given easier questions to answer.

Even strictly equal treatment can be considered unequal when the audience is unwittingly biased and looks for treatment that favors their own point of view. The issue of media bias is a good example. During any election cycle, watch the letters to the editor. Democrats write to complain of bad pictures and negative stories about their Democratic candidates, while Republicans write to complain about similar treatment of the candidates they favor. Truly unbiased studies that could find true cases of bias are rarely done. When they are done, they are often attacked for using biased criteria to measure bias. For instance, next time there is an election, gather an equal number of friends from different political sides (say, Democrat, Republican, and Independent). Set some criteria that you can all agree are unbiased (number of minutes spent on a story about a candidate or issue, number of words, pictures with a smiling or frowning candidate), and start counting to see if your own impression of bias holds true.

Equivocation

Good thinking requires us to look at various sides of an issue and consider contradictory evidence. Or we might consider various sides because we are trying to explore a subject, or even come to a compromise. In that case, it would be okay to consider contradictions without resolving them.

In a traditional persuasive argument, however, it is considered a fallacy to make contradictory claims. People call it "arguing out of both sides of your mouth." A cliché line of attack in a courtroom is to catch a witness making two opposite statements and then to ask the witness, "So which is it, Mr. Knucklepump, were you lying then, or are you lying now?" Equivocation occurs in a context, and that context is crucial. For example, equivocation undercuts an argument because, if the arguer can't even agree with her own argument, why should we agree with her? But in a more exploratory situation, equivocation can actually help to build trust with an audience, to establish a spirit of going forward together in order to find enough evidence to form a conclusion.

Equivocation often happens because we keep arguing a claim we like, regardless of the support. If one reason fails, we try another, and so we set one reason against another. The war in Iraq could be considered representative of this type of equivocation. It was first presented as a means of defending the world against weapons of mass destruction. Later it was declared to be about fighting terrorism by Al Qaeda. When resistance by Saddam Hussein's armies collapsed, a banner was raised that said "Mission Accomplished." Later, the U.S. Government claimed that a premature end to the Iraq war would be disastrous. This example of equivocation shows how the seeds of doubt in an argument can be sown. That is why they are considered fallacious.

False Analogy

An analogy is a comparison between two things or a claim that two situations are similar. A good analogy can help people think about things in a new way by pointing out parallels. A **false analogy** occurs, however, if an arguer says the situations are comparable but they really aren't.

Arguers use many analogies to support a position, and often those analogies don't hold up because the situations are more different than they are alike. In other words, analogies do not always present fallacies; often an analogy does hold up, and the situations are alike in some essential way. The Bush administration argued that we could help a defeated Iraq become a democracy because after defeating Japan and Germany in World War II, the U.S. helped them become democracies. It is a judgment call whether or not that is a worthwhile or a false analogy. One strike against the argument may be that both Japan and Germany were homogenous societies, whereas Iraq is divided into several ethnic and religious groups, making a transition to a working democracy difficult if not impossible.

All fallacies boil down to an inconsistency of one kind or another. We're almost always inconsistent when we argue, because we have our own point of view. We have values and beliefs. We want to believe certain things, and we want to support those beliefs. Intentionally or unintentionally, these factors sometimes leads us to argue inconsistently, favoring our view of things.

Even though fallacies are to some extent inevitable, they are a matter of degree. We can be as fair as possible, including and weighing other views along with our own. We can be somewhat fair, acknowledging other claims, or we can purposely try to manipulate our audience by ignoring evidence that supports another side of things.

Signs that you may be reading or writing fallacies of inconsistency include:

☐ Unbalanced discussions: 90 percent of the support falls on one side of an argument.

☐ Undeservedly balanced discussions: 50 percent of the support falls on each side of an argument (33 percent with three sides), with no real justification.

☐ Language of contradiction: but, however, on the other hand, still, while at the same time.

☐ Language of equivalence: this is like, just as, in the same way that, similarly.

☐ Comparisons that don't sound right: being a president is a lot like being a restaurant owner.

your turn 5d ▸ **PRACTICE Identify Fallacies of Inconsistency**

Here is a paragraph from the paper on ESP. See if you can spot the types of fallacies. Match the numbered fallacies with the correct box below.

❶ *Perhaps those who dismiss paranormal research are thinking straight; maybe they just don't know the facts.* ❷ *They might not realize that not funding ESP is essentially the same as using Jewish prisoners in dangerous medical experiments.* ❸ *It's just as unethical, too.* ❹ *Perhaps they don't know that, just as the hard sciences have their flagship institution, the Massachusetts Institute of Technology (MIT), paranormal research also has had its flagship in the Institute for Parapsychology at Duke University, an equally prestigious institution, albeit that the university broke ties with the Institute in 1965, when its founder retired.* ❺ *The advancements of the paranormal sciences should receive exactly the same funding as the natural sciences; nay, they should in fact receive more, to make up for the funding inequities of the past. If we do these things, we will likely ensure a better future for our children, and isn't that what it's all about?*

Which numbered sentence in the paragraph best represents each type of fallacy? Fill in each box with a different number.

☐ False analogy: Moral equivalence

☐ False analogy: Material equivalence

☐ False analogy: Definitional equivalence

☐ Equivocation

☐ Inconsistent treatment (from dogmatism, prejudice, or bias)

To be able to identify fallacious strategies in the arguments of others is a great asset to being a stronger reader and thinker. To be able to avoid these same fallacious strategies in your own arguments makes you a stronger writer.

your turn 5e ▸ **PRACTICE Identify Four Types of Fallacies**

In the following passage, try to spot the fallacies from all four groups:

- Fallacies of choice
- Fallacies of support
- Fallacies of emotion
- Fallacies of inconsistency

> We should get rid of our current male president and put a woman in the White House. Every bad thing that has happened in this country has happened under a male president. We had slavery, the Civil War, the Great Depression, Pearl Harbor, and the defeat in Vietnam all under male presidents. Therefore, a woman president could only do a better job. There is nowhere to go but up.
>
> Furthermore, little girls all over this country have grown up with no presidential role model. The damage of this injustice has been devastating to the psyche. We might as well have shackled these girls and tied them to a ball and chain. There is no doubt that this lack of inspiration has held women back.
>
> One perennial problem that traditionally faces this country has been budget deficits, yet this is an area a woman president is uniquely qualified to handle. For centuries, women have successfully managed home finances, keeping a budget, spending their limited incomes wisely to keep their families fed and clothed. A woman would bring that same kind of efficient money management to the White House.
>
> Women have run countries before. Margaret Thatcher was widely considered to be an excellent prime minister of the United Kingdom. That proves that women in general can lead and lead well. Men, on the other hand, are worthless as leaders. Consider recent history. We elected Richard Nixon, and we lost the Vietnam War. We elected Jimmy Carter, and we had an oil crisis. We elected Ronald Reagan, and the stock market crashed. We elected Bill Clinton, and the White House was used for sleazy activities. If we keep electing male presidents, the country will keep falling. If the country keeps sliding into corruption and moral decay, we may soon find ourselves a mini-power instead of a superpower. We could end up last among nations. And keep in mind that Hillary Clinton would have beaten John McCain in a head-to-head match-up.
>
> It may be true that the gender of a candidate has no bearing on how effective a leader he or she may be. On the other hand, the famous musician Gidget Snotbrackler has said that we need now more than ever to "Go pink." For the sake of our little girls, can we afford not to?

Reflect and Apply

1. As you read your sources, what steps are you taking to evaluate them for fallacious information?

2. As you write your argument, what are you doing to ensure that you are not including fallacies? Do you have a way to identify these fallacies as you review your argument?

3. If you are using emotional support, how are you preventing your images or anecdotes from becoming fallacies of emotion?

4. As you include material from multiple points of view in your argument, how are you avoiding fallacies of inconsistency?

5. What is the harm in selecting sources only because they support your own views, or because they espouse views that are easy to dismiss? Which type of fallacy is involved in doing so?

KEEPING IT LOCAL

You like your coworkers and want to get along with them all, but you don't like feeling pressured to participate in every fundraiser that comes along; you would like to be able to pick the fundraisers that seem to support the most important causes or that are selling products in which you are truly interested. The same holds true for donations. Many charitable causes are legitimate and do a lot of good work. But again, you don't want to have to donate to causes that you have not selected.

The biggest obstacle to taking a stand is that so many of the arguments your coworkers give seem so persuasive. "If we don't raise enough money, the Tigers bowling team will be disbanded and these children will never learn to work as a team." "How can you look at the faces of these poor hungry people and not contribute to hunger relief?" "Everyone else has already placed an order for doughnuts." These are fallacies—each and every one of them. Ask questions, dig deeper, and find out more before you pull out your wallet. Maybe you will be perceived as heartless, or maybe you will be seen as the department hero.

●━ ━ ━ ━ ━ ━ ━ ━ ━ ━ ━ ━ ●

Detecting fallacies in the wide variety of sources you read, view, or listen to can be difficult. But actively asking questions about each source and each claim can keep you from passively accepting illogical or manipulative arguments. Look for fallacies of choice, of support, of emotion, and of inconsistency in the sources you are using in your argument. Secondarily, can you turn your critical focus on your own writing and detect any fallacies in your own writing? Doing so will make you a stronger reader, writer, and thinker.

CHAPTER 6

Work Fairly with the Opposition

For the past few months, you have been aware of a neighbor whose health and well-being seem to be suffering. From others in the neighborhood, you learn that the neighbor, John, lost his job and health insurance earlier this year and has complained about not being able to afford his medical bills and that this has discouraged him from visiting his doctor as often as he needs to. Additionally, family members are unable to stop by regularly, and it is increasingly difficult for John to visit friends because the closest bus stop is nearly a half mile away. John is a proud man, and while he appreciates the efforts of you and others on your block to check up on him, he wants more control over his life and his health. John's monthly unemployment check, modest as it is, puts him on the outside of a health care system on which he has become dependent. Your frustration with John's situation increases as you realize, uncomfortably, that family and neighbors are not enough to supply John with what he needs, and your thoughts, like the thoughts of many associated with folks in John's circumstances, turn to our health care system and how it might better serve John. And among your very first thoughts is the awareness that we are sharply divided about whether to continue to keep the health care system as it is, reform it, or change it entirely.

COMMUNITY

School-Academic

Workplace

Family-Household

Neighborhood

Social-Cultural

Consumer

Concerned Citizen

TOPIC: Health Care

ISSUE: Universal Health Care

AUDIENCE: State and Federal Representatives

CLAIM: Universal health care should be a right guaranteed to all American citizens.

We build arguments to articulate positions on issues that matter to us, like the one described above, and knowing who disagrees with us and why is vital to the success of any argument. This chapter is devoted to strategies useful in responding to those who argue positions different from your own. When you conduct your research thoroughly and understand what motivates an opposing argument and how this argument is supported, you are in a position to interact with respect and fair-mindedness. This will earn you credibility with an audience.

When we plan and deliver an argument, we're nearly always in conversation with others. It's important to remember that those opposed to a claim we make are equally invested in the issue at hand—but from different perspectives. Treat the opposition respectfully and as fellow members of the community tied to your issue. Acknowledge the values that motivate an opponent. Send the message to your audience *and* your opponents that you can accurately identify and summarize positions other than your own. In an argument, it is your job to remain critical and fair-minded at the same time. This chapter offers guidelines for working with the **opposition**, guidelines that will be helpful when you construct various kinds of argument—Toulmin-based, Middle Ground, Rogerian, and the Microhistory—all of which are discussed in Chapter 8, "Consider Toulmin-Based Argument," and Chapter 9, "Consider Middle Ground, Rogerian Argument, and Argument based on Microhistory."

In this chapter, we discuss why the opposition matters in an argument; additionally, you will learn how to:

- Resist easy generalizations about an opponent.
- Listen to local and scholarly voices on an issue.
- Summarize other voices fairly.
- Avoid bias when you summarize.
- Find points of overlap.
- Respond to other views.

Why the Opposition Matters

Opposing points of view on an issue matter. Like you, your opponents are part of a conversation on an area of life important to them. In most cases, you'll learn more about an issue when you study the opposition. For example, based on how an opponent supports a position, you can:

- Acquire new context.
- Learn to see the issue from another perspective.
- Recognize the values that motivate an opponent.
- Familiarize yourself with a body of specific support different from yours.
- Recognize what you have in common with your opponents.

Suppose you plan to argue on free universal health care for Americans, both a national and a local issue. Based on your experience with your neighbor, you feel compelled to encourage your state's senators and representatives in Washington, D.C., to move beyond the Patient Protection and Affordable Care Act, commonly referred to as "Obamacare," and to support free universal health care. From your research, you know that the issue is complex in terms of its many well-supported positions. For example, various opponents claim that universal health care would undermine the insurance industry, that higher taxes would result, that the government bureaucracy would mean long delays for patients in need,

Troy House/Corbis

Figure 6.1 Paying close attention to points of view that differ from your own builds credibility with an audience.

that consumers would no longer be able to shop for their best health care values when government replaces free-market competition among providers, and that health care standards may erode with a single provider. These differing positions matter. If your view on free universal health care is to be taken seriously by your audience, you must negotiate your way through these different views. As you do so, you'll learn about the strengths and weaknesses of arguments competing for the attention of your audience. This can make all the difference to an audience—your willingness to study the opposition thoroughly and to present it in both fair and critical terms.

---

your turn 6a ▶ **GET STARTED Size up the Opposition**

Based on an issue you're working with, respond to the following questions and prompts:

1. On what issue do you plan to argue?
2. What motivates you to argue on this issue?
3. Based on your general awareness of this issue, identify two or three positions different from your position.

Resist Easy Generalizations

Oversimplifying an opponent's position weakens your argument. Different positions on an issue endure because they are built on solid foundations that appeal to people. Your task in an argument is to resist **easy generalizations** of other views and instead summarize them in dignified, respectful terms. This means reading the other position closely so that you can identify and put into your own words its claim, warrant, reasons, and support. This method will get you away from generalizing another position in just a sentence or two. Plan to devote a substantial paragraph to each differing view you bring to an argument.

In your background reading, you likely note a persistent opposing claim arguing against universal health care for Americans. Principal reasons supporting this claim include problems in other countries where universal health care is provided: long waits in doctors' offices, frequent cancellations of appointments, and the pain that patients often must endure while waiting for health care services. This opposing argument brings in effective support, including data that reveal the number of Canadians (Canada's universal health care system is often suggested as a model for an American system) who have died or suffered heart attacks while waiting for health care services. Other data suggest that an alarming number of Canadians perform their own medical and dental procedures instead of waiting. Additionally, examples of the suffering of some individuals make for compelling support. This view also holds that universal health care in Canada is unfair to many everyday people.

The argument is thoughtful and well structured. Your aim in working with this opposing view, or rebuttal, is to summarize it accurately. Doing so will set a respectful tone of fairness.

 internet activity 6a **Exploring**

Conduct an informal Internet search, and identify two or three differing positions on your issue. For each opposing view that you might include in your argument, answer the following questions.

1. What, exactly, does each differing position claim?
2. What reasons support each differing claim?
3. What effective support—such as particularly compelling facts and data, personal examples, and research from experts—does each differing position use to support its claim?
4. What makes these other positions valid and arguable? Is your perspective on your issue getting broader based on familiarity with these other views? Explain.

Listen to Local Voices

Before beginning your formal research into scholarly sources on an issue, there are many ways to get a sense of why an issue is important to people in your community and your peers in the classroom. Conversations with colleagues, friends, and family are one way. Another is your local media. Many online sources, like news sites, information sites, and opinion blogs, can provide useful glosses of an issue. Your local and regional newspapers can also be helpful, and most online editions of newspapers contain a search feature that allows you to read past articles and thus get a sense of the history of an issue in your area. Refer to Chapter 4, "Evaluate and Engage with Your Sources," for specific information on gathering online sources.

Listen closely to **local voices**. This will allow you to craft an argument that becomes part of a local conversation on an issue that means something to you and your neighbors, coworkers, or classmates. Whether you take in differing perspectives on an issue over coffee with friends, in conversation with coworkers, during a class discussion, at the dinner table, from your local news, or by interacting on Facebook or a favorite blog, open yourself to the range of attitudes on an issue. Familiarizing yourself with this local knowledge will make your argument more focused and immediate; it will also let you appeal to your audience with specific information.

As we know, the issue of health care in our country can elicit strong points of view. If you happen to be in conversation with a health care professional—a nurse, doctor, or emergency medical technician—you may run across the view that a universal health care system might limit earning power, as government-assigned fees would be less than what market value is now and that this would in turn reduce the number of trained professionals entering the health care field. Additionally, many argue that burnout would occur when the government overloads doctors with patients. Another conversation might avail you of the financial hardships a family endures because of rising costs and that free health care is necessary. Still another conversation puts you in touch with the view that free health care would eliminate the advantages of a

Stan HONDA/AFP/GettyImages

Figure 6.2 Take advantage of informal, local moments as a first step in familiarizing yourself with the opposition.

competitive, free-market system, a system that many feel is responsible for innovation and efficiency in the medical field. Listening with an open mind and heart to these and other views can sensitize you to others and their investment in the issue. Your fair acknowledgement of their views in your argument will make positive impressions on your readers.

your turn 6b   **GET STARTED** Listen to Local Voices

Answer the following questions as a way of acknowledging local views on an issue you plan to argue.

1. What individuals in my community are most deeply invested in this issue?
2. What, in their personal and professional lives, motivates them to speak out?
3. What reasons do they give for their positions on the issue?
4. What solutions do they propose?
5. After listening to others invested in my issue, what do I know about this issue now that I did not know before?

 tip 6a

Access Local Voices
Your local newspaper may have a search engine that allows you to search past articles and issues. Find the link to this search engine on your newspaper's home page, and then type in keywords connected to your issue.

Summarize Other Voices Fairly

To earn the trust of your audience, it is important that you treat your opponents fairly, and this means withholding judgment of opponents' views when you introduce them in your argument. Your evaluation of differing views can

bobbieo/Bobbie Osborne/iStockphoto.com

Figure 6.3 To a target audience, fairness is often measured by how an arguer treats those holding opposing views. It is essential that the arguer makes the effort to summarize the other side fairly.

and should occur *after* you summarize them in a neutral tone. In many cases, those holding other views are just as determined as you are to be heard and to influence local thinking. Review the following examples of writers' treatments of differing positions and the analysis that follows each summary.

Summary #1: By Linda Gonzalez

This writer is responding to the issue of illegal immigrants in the United States having driver's licenses and claims that immigrants should be allowed to obtain licenses under certain conditions. In the paragraphs that follow, the writer summarizes a view opposing her claim.

Another point of view is the one held passionately by opponents of giving driver's licenses to illegal immigrants. These opponents argue that driving is a privilege and not a right. For instance, Republican Sue Myrick of Charlotte, North Carolina, says, "Our feeling is that a driver's license is a privilege for citizens and legal aliens and it shouldn't be something given to somebody who broke the law" (qtd. in Funk and Whitacre 2). Backers of Myrick agree by saying that issuing driver's licenses to undocumented people would attract more illegal immigrants to the country and it would then be easy for terrorists to come to the United States. Considering driving as a privilege, many politicians are completely against a plan that would allow illegal immigrants to obtain a driver's license. They believe that because people who have entered the country illegally have broken the immigration laws, they should not be allowed to receive any kind of benefits in this country. Moreover, a driver's license allows a person to be able to work, drive, and open a bank account; all these things make life easier for undocumented people in this country. One opponent argues that, "one legitimate kind of ID leads to more, leads to more, leads to more, and pretty soon, they've got an entire identity established" (Johnson 2). He also adds that having a legal document can give the idea of citizenship.

Additionally, the government is taking stricter ways to keep the nation safe. One effective way is to not issue driver's licenses to illegal aliens so they cannot enter federal buildings, board airplanes, or use it as identification to give the impression of being legal. An illustration of this in their favor is that 8 of the 19 men in the terrorist attacks on September 11, 2001, got licenses in Virginia after presenting a simple notarized form saying they were state residents (Johnson).

Another example of illegal immigrants threatening the nation's safety is that there are drug dealers and criminals looking for easy ways to get licenses. "Driver's licenses are as close as we get to a national ID," says John Keely of the Center for Immigration Studies, a group in Washington that advocates limited immigration. "While the overwhelming majority of immigrants don't pose a national security threat," [Johnson said], "I don't think issuing driver's licenses to them affords protection to Americans, but hurts the efforts to shore up national security" (3). Authorities against a plan to provide driver's licenses to illegal immigrants do not take into consideration that undocumented people are not going to go away just because they do not have driver's licenses and that they will drive with or without it. Certainly, the arguments in favor of and against issuing driver's licenses to noncitizens are so strong that it is difficult to imagine an alternative position.

Discussion

This is a fair-minded summary of a position different from the writer's. The writer maintains a respectful, neutral tone in reference to her opponents. The writer identifies the opponent's claim of driver's licenses being a privilege of citizenship in the second sentence. Views of Myrick, Johnson, and Keely appear without judgment. The writer briefly disagrees with her opponents in the next-to-last sentence of the final paragraph, and her final sentence hints that her claim and support will occur later in the argument. The summary avoids brief, superficial treatment of opponents, and the writer is in no rush to dismiss them. This summary appears in a middle ground argument, as the last sentence suggests, where the writer will offer a practical position between what she views as two extreme positions. See Chapter 9, "Consider Middle Ground and Rogerian Argument, and Argument based on Microhistory," for a full treatment of middle ground argument.

Summary #2: By Brittney Lambert

This writer is responding to the issue of whether students on college campuses should be allowed to carry concealed weapons. She claims that students should be granted this right. She begins her paragraph by identifying a view opposed to hers.

One argument against the right to carry concealed weapons on campus is that students' protection and safety should be left to the police. This is because police have gone through four to five months' worth of training, but citizens who carry licensed concealed weapons have only gone through about a day of training. First of all, adults with concealed handgun licenses can protect themselves in most "unsecured places" already; they just lose that right when they step on campus. Secondly, police officers cannot be everywhere all of the time. In a study by the U.S. Secret Service, 37 school shootings were researched. Of the 37 school shootings, "over half of the attacks were resolved/ended before law enforcement responded to the scene. In these cases the attacker was stopped by faculty or fellow students, decided to stop shooting on his own, or killed himself. The study found that only 3 of the 37 school shootings researched involved shots being fired by law enforcement officers" ("Answers" par. 1).

Discussion

Although the writer has written an otherwise strong argument, there is room for improvement in her coverage of the opponent's position. This summary is not as strong as it could be because only the first two sentences of the paragraph address the opponent's position. The opponent's claim is clear, that campus safety is the responsibility of the police, but only one reason is given, that campus police have undergone training. The student's argument could have been stronger if she had included support for the opponent's claim-quotations, facts, or specific examples. Sometimes when an arguer glosses over an opponent's claim, it can strike an audience as unfairly brief, especially when the remainder of the paragraph is devoted to countering the opponent. By devoting only two sentences to another view, the writer might appear dismissive and unwilling to treat the opponent fairly. With some adjustments, this essay could become a strong, Toulmin-based argument, a kind of argument discussed in Chapter 8, "Consider Toulmin-Based Argument."

Summary #3: By James Guzman

In the following summary, the writer focuses on health care and whether it should remain privatized or change to a system with free services to all Americans. He argues a middle-ground position and claims that the answer to the health care question is to reform the present system. Prior to the paragraph below, the writer summarized the view of those opposed to free health care. He is now summarizing what he considers to be a second extreme position on health care.

On the other side are those who believe that our country should provide universal health care to all American citizens. The 46 million uninsured citizens are a disgrace on our country that is thought of as the land of opportunity for all. It's their opinion that this number alone is reason enough to warrant universal health care. It is hard to brag about equal opportunity when there are a huge number of low-income families that do not have a doctor or receive the necessary medical attention to maintain their health. Every other wealthy country has found it unacceptable to have portions of the populations uninsured and have implemented universal health care. Of all things that the government provides, health is surely up there with education and police protection in importance. It is true that this huge number of uninsured is alarming, but is it really *society's* responsibility to take care of those who choose not to buy health insurance? If a person truly is a hard-working citizen, we have tax credits designed specifically for those who buy their own health care. This argument could be easily interpreted as class envy. If this is another weapon in class warfare, then it would no doubt turn out to be another wealth-transfer system designed to punish the successful.

Discussion

This summary has both strengths and weaknesses. The first half of the summary identifies a claim and then refers to very clear reasons that support this claim. Brief support is included in the form of "46 million uninsured citizens" and "every other wealthy country." Yet this support would be even more compelling and trustworthy if documentation as to where the writer gathered this information were given. Proper documentation, examples, quotations, and other specific support for this opposing view would strengthen the summary and move the writer closer to earning credibility with his audience.

In your own arguments, include the strengths and avoid the weaknesses in the preceding summaries. Each of these writers crafted strongly worded claims and reasons and brought plenty of effective support to his or her argument, but only the writer of the first summary was fair and thorough in her treatment of an opposing view.

your turn 6c ▶ **GET STARTED** Evaluate Summaries of Differing Positions

Based on your treatments of opponents in an argument you are building, answer the following questions.

1. What does each opposing position claim? What reasons and support for opposing positions do you include in your summaries?
2. Do you document in parentheses the source of quoted and summarized material?
3. Is your audience likely to believe that you achieve a tone of fair play and mutual respect in your summaries of other positions? Explain.
4. In your view, would those holding the differing positions you summarize approve of these summaries? Would they feel they've been treated fairly and with respect? Explain.

Value Expertise over Advocacy

Make every effort to include opponents who support their claims with clear reasons and thorough support. In addition to local sources, bring to your argument opposing visews found in scholarly journals and periodicals gathered from academic databases and from search engines that allow access to scholarly and professional material. Avoid sources that are purely ideological, overly emotional, brief, and general. Referencing an advocate for or against universal health care, for example, who argues on primarily emotional grounds will weaken your argument. Your audience will have difficulty taking such an advocate seriously, and this will reflect on your willingness to treat

☞ **tip 6b**

Search Thoroughly to Avoid Shallow Summaries

Many of us tend to default to mainstream search engines as a way to begin researching an issue. Avoid this habit! Instead, consult the academic search engines and databases to which your school subscribes, some of which are devoted specifically to particular fields, such as medicine, the environment, education, government, business, and specific academic disciplines like English, history, and computer science. See Chapter 4, "Evaluate and Engage with Your Sources," for additional sources housing scholarly material.

the opposition fairly. On the other hand, when you refer to an opposing view that is full of effective support and grounded in strong values, your argument becomes more credible and, importantly, challenges you to make your argument equally compelling in view of a well-informed opposition.

For example, during a prewriting activity in class you choose to share with your group a neighbor's complaint that universal health care is merely "welfare for the uninsured" and "rewards the lazy." The neighbor appears to offer no support for these claims. This is the kind of opposing view to avoid in an argument. Without substantial support, such claims become fallacies only. See Chapter 5, "Read Critically and Avoid Fallacies," for a full discussion of fallacies and how to avoid them in your writing.

internet activity 6b Connecting

Working with the online materials you gather for an argument, answer the following questions.

1. What specific research will you bring to your argument? How does this research go beyond mere advocacy along ideological grounds for a position and use facts and credible information as support?
2. While another position may include emotional appeals, is the position centered in primarily rational support? Explain.
3. Are the opposing views you bring to your argument found in reputable publications that include current facts and statistics? What are these publications?

Avoid Bias When You Summarize

Summarize positions of your opponents accurately, in your own words, and without a hint of judgment or evaluation. Your summaries should be so accurate that opponents approve of them. Consider the following paragraphs and the two summaries: one brief, inaccurate, and full of **biased language,** and the other accurate and objective. The paragraphs are from the article "Universal Healthcare's Dirty Little Secrets," by Michael Tanner and Michael Cannon, well-informed opponents of universal health care.

> Simply saying that people have health insurance is meaningless. Many countries provide universal insurance but deny critical procedures to patients who need them. Britain's Department of Health reported in 2006 that at any given time, nearly 900,000 Britons are waiting for admission to National Health Service hospitals, and shortages force the cancellation of more than 50,000 operations each year. In Sweden, the wait for heart surgery can be as long as 25 weeks, and the average wait for hip replacement surgery is more than a year. Many of these

individuals suffer chronic pain, and judging by the numbers, some will probably die awaiting treatment. In a 2005 ruling of the Canadian Supreme Court, Chief Justice Beverly McLachlin wrote that "access to a waiting list is not access to healthcare."

Everyone agrees that far too many Americans lack health insurance. But covering the uninsured comes about as a byproduct of getting other things right. The real danger is that our national obsession with universal coverage will lead us to neglect reforms—such as enacting a standard health insurance deduction, expanding health savings accounts and deregulating insurance markets—that could truly expand coverage, improve quality and make care more affordable.

Summary #1

Michael Tanner and Michael Cannon, both from the Cato Institute, argue the same tired conservative position we have heard for years. They provide only negative evidence from countries with free health care and want us to think that many people die before getting treatment because delays are so long. They view a competitive, free-market approach as better than guaranteeing that everyone receives health care.

Discussion

This brief summary is biased and inaccurate. Using words like "tired," "conservative," and "negative" establishes a narrow, judgmental tone. The summary ignores the factual support the writers bring to their argument. It also ignores the writers' call for specific reforms and their attention to those Americans who are now underserved. In general, the summary is not effective because it misleads and includes biased language.

Summary #2

Michael Tanner, Director of Health and Welfare Studies at the Cato Institute, and Michael Cannon, Director of Health Policy Studies at the Cato Institute, provide substantial data to argue against universal health care. They refer to other countries with established universal health care systems—Great Britain, Sweden, and Canada—and claim that large numbers of citizens have to suffer through long delays for hospital service and for operations. In Sweden, for example, the authors claim that some patients will die while waiting for heart surgery and hip replacement. Tanner and Cannon agree with their opponents that "far too many Americans lack health insurance" (par. 3), but they feel that reforming our present system is a more practical approach to this issue. Specifically, they want to see a deduction built into health insurance policies, an emphasis on health savings plans, and expanded deregulation of the health insurance industry.

Universal Healthcares Dirty Little Secrets, by Michael Tanner and Michael Cannon

tip 6c

Peer Edit Summaries
As a check against offering biased summaries, ask a peer to evaluate your summaries of differing views on the issue you're working with. Pay close attention to these peer responses, as they can point out biased language that can block fair representation of other views.

Discussion

This is a fair-minded, objective summary of an opposing viewpoint. The opposition's claim (first sentence), selected support (sentences two and three), and warrant (sentence four) are noted. The summary is free from biased language.

your turn 6d   ▶ GET STARTED Avoid Bias

Based on your research of opposing views on an issue you're working with, answer the following questions.

1. Have you avoided judgmental or emotionally loaded language in your summary that could mislead an audience? Explain. What words might you replace to assure your audience that your summary is accurate and fair?

2. Are your summaries mostly in your words with only occasional quotations? Would your opponents agree with your summary of their positions, and would you feel confident presenting your summaries to your opponents? Explain.

3. When quoting or paraphrasing an opponent, do you document in parentheses appropriate page or paragraph numbers?

Find Points of Overlap

Although you may differ with your opponents, there likely are points in your argument where you overlap and share certain concerns and values. For example, you favor free universal health care and others oppose it, but in closely studying other views you'll probably observe that some of your values and the values of opposing views are quite similar. Often the best place to find shared values is at the level of the warrant in an argument, that is, the moral grounding on which an argument is based. For example, all players in the free health care debate may agree that:

• Quality health care should be available to those in need.
• Delivery of health care should be timely.
• Health care services should be run efficiently.

These shared values make rational communication possible and create a positive bridge between you and others at the discussion table. This bridge becomes possible because of your willingness to take in without judgment the views of others.

Identify Common Ground with the Opposition

The following issues are controversial because they elicit strong and often emotional responses. On the surface, it may seem that finding **common**

Figure 6.4 Acknowledging shared concerns and values is a strength in an argument.

ground would be impossible. But when you dig beneath attitudes and proposed solutions to our most controversial problems, you may uncover core beliefs, values, and principles that reveal some common ground. To make these revelations possible, be diligent in your research process and keep an open mind to those who differ from you.

Example #1

Issue   Should water be publicly held or privately owned?

Description   This is a full-fledged issue in several western states and in numerous countries. Proponents of classifying water as a privately held commodity argue that, although water is a basic need, access to it should not be a legally guaranteed right. This side also reasons that private companies are better at protecting water than the government, that innovation in the water industry springs from privately owned water companies, and that competition among companies can drive down the price of water for the consumer. On the other side, those who favor public ownership of water claim that water is too essential for survival to let it be distributed by companies. This side also argues that the government is needed to ensure that water resources are conserved, that water remains safe, and that it is not subject to changes in an economic market, as this can work against its availability to consumers.

Common Ground   Shared values among opposing sides on this issue may include the recognition that, in recent decades, many water sources have diminished and become tainted and that efforts to purify our water are essential, that apparatus for distributing water be efficient, and that any realistic assessment of our future must include water availability.

Example #2

Issue Does homeschooling threaten American democracy?

Description Many critics of homeschooling claim that homeschooled students may succeed as students but not as citizens. They reason that homeschoolers are trained to be more concerned about themselves than their communities, that they are subjected to educational agendas grounded in religious or ideological beliefs, and that the social isolation in which homeschooled students learn steers them away from civic involvement. On the other hand, many proponents of this movement argue that homeschooled students in fact make better citizens than students educated in public schools. As studies emerge following the first generation of homeschooled students in recent American history, these supporters note that homeschoolers contribute to democratic culture in greater percentages than graduates of public schools in the following areas: support of political parties, membership in civic organizations, voting, speaking out on public issues, and community service work.

Common Ground Opponents in this issue may overlap in their belief that children deserve an education that prepares them for active citizenship and that this includes participation in civic and political activity.

 tip 6d

Recognize Shared Values

Like yours, an opponent's public position on an issue and his or her problem-solving apparatus rest atop a set of values and core beliefs. This is where you can look to find common ground when none is immediately evident. Sometimes the opposition will spell out in direct language his or her values and beliefs; at other times, these values are implied or stated only indirectly. When researching other positions, remember to read carefully for the values that underlie a position.

Example #3

Issue Is it fair to make birth records unavailable to adopted children?

Description States vary in the laws that prohibit, limit, and allow access to the birth records of adopted children. Many claim that it is unfair to prohibit access to records on grounds that medical information of birth parents can reveal conditions that may affect adopted children and future generations. Another argument on banning access involves the regret and sense of loss that some women later feel after giving up their children for adoption, often at a young age. Others feel that laws protecting the privacy of biological parents should be honored, especially with regard to women who chose to give up their children with the understanding that confidentiality would be assured. Additionally, this side argues that the privacy of the adopted family would be compromised were adopted children given access to birth records.

Common Ground Both sides on this issue have in common deep concern for the welfare of adopted children. This value alone can make communication possible when differing views are treated respectfully. Building on this shared value, this issue can reveal the importance of precisely crafted claims, those that avoid all-or-nothing approaches. For example, given that both sides want the best for adopted children, qualifiers can be built into claims that allow for access to birth records under certain conditions based on the needs of birth and adopted parents.

your turn 6e   GET STARTED **Find Common Ground**

Based on your understanding of views different from yours on an issue, answer the following questions.

1. What values and principles do you share with your opponents?
2. What reaction can you anticipate from your audience based on the shared values and common ground you establish with your opponents? How will audience reaction help your argument?

Respond to Other Views

This chapter is devoted to opposing points of view on an issue and how to present them fairly. But you should also plan to respond to differing views, and in general there are three approaches. First, based on your careful evaluation of another position, you may find yourself in disagreement with it, and your argument will be stronger if you spell out precisely why you disagree. Second, you may agree with another position, and this means that you should state why you agree. This view may not directly oppose your position, but it may approach your issue from a different perspective and bring in different reasons and support. Explaining the grounds on which you agree will add momentum to your argument. And third, you may choose to work with another view that you both agree and disagree with.

Whether you disagree, agree, or agree only in part with another view, it is essential that you respond immediately after summarizing the different view. This can occur in the same paragraph with your summary of another view or in the paragraph immediately following the summary.

Use the prompts in your turn 6f, 6g, and 6h to practice disagreeing, agreeing, and both agreeing and disagreeing with other views.

your turn 6f   PRACTICE **Disagreeing with Another View**

To respond to a view you disagree with, answer the following questions. This will put you in a position to explain in specific terms the basis of your disagreement.

1. What are the limitations of this view; that is, what does it fail to acknowledge about the issue at hand and how do these omissions affect its credibility?
2. Does this view include overly general statements that do not stand up to close investigation? If yes, what research will you bring in to reveal the weaknesses in these statements?
3. Does this opposing view include the elements of good argument? For example, is support effective and free from fallacies, and does it include fair treatment of the opposition?

4. Is sufficient context part of this opposing view, and is the presentation of this context fair and objective?

---

your turn 6g   **PRACTICE Agreeing with Another View**

To respond to a view you agree with, answer the following questions.

1. Are there values in this view with which you overlap? If yes, what are they, and why are these values appropriate in an argument on the issue at hand?
2. How does research validate this view?
3. What makes this view a practical approach to this issue? In your answer, identify how readers can benefit in practical ways by reflecting on this view.
4. In what ways does this view move beyond popular, less-informed responses to this issue?

---

your turn 6h   **PRACTICE Agree and Disagree at the Same Time**

To respond to a view you both agree and disagree with, answer the following questions.

1. On what specific points do you agree with this view?
2. What keeps you from fully accepting this view?
3. How, precisely, does your view improve on, or add to, this view?
4. To what extent will you recommend this view to your readers?

Reflect and Apply

1. Based on an argument you plan to build, what opposing views will you include and how, specifically, will you be thorough and fair in presenting them?
2. What sources will you draw from as you gather research for your argument? Explain why an audience would consider them credible.
3. What common ground are you finding with other views in your argument? How will you make use of this common ground?
4. Your turn 6f, 6g, and 6h list ways of responding to other views in an argument. How will you respond to each differing view you bring to your present argument?

KEEPING IT LOCAL

As DISCUSSED IN CHAPTER 1, "Argue with a Purpose," and Chapter 2, "Explore an Issue that Matters to You," an issue exists because people have different points of view on something that affects them. Views different from yours need to be acknowledged. After all, if you want a seat at the discussion table in your community and in the classroom, it's essential that you acknowledge and validate others at the table. When you bring in differing views on an issue and do so with accuracy and a sense of fair play, you strengthen your argument and move yourself closer to winning the respect of an audience.

Returning to the matter that begins this chapter—a writer's concern with her elderly neighbor—you should now see why it's important to make plenty of room for the opposition in an argument; additionally, the exercises in the chapter provide you with a methodology for proceeding with others in a thorough, fair-minded way. The writer recognized that rallying those on her block to look in on John would not be enough. At this point, she began looking at her issue in broader, systemic terms, a choice that led her to advocate for free health care. The student who prepared this argument still looks in on John. The debate over free versus private health care systems continues. But because this student crafted an argument responding to a neighbor's circumstances and took in a range of other perspectives, she earned the right to be heard. A solid argument does not ensure change, but it does let us speak up on issues that matter to us and puts us in touch with others equally invested in local and, in this case, national issues.

● – – – – – – – – – – – ●

Based on the argument you're working with now, how will you make sure that your treatment of opposing views is fair and thorough? And if your issue affects the local community, how will you identify various positions that respond to the issue? Your answers to these questions will be the foundation for a major piece of your argument. Keep in mind as well that your treatment of the opposition can build your credibility with your target audience.

PART THREE

How to Plan, Structure, and Deliver an Argument

CHAPTER 7   Explore an Issue

CHAPTER 8   Consider Toulmin-Based Argument

CHAPTER 9   Consider Middle Ground and Rogerian Argument, and Argument based on Microhistory

CHAPTER 10 Build Arguments

CHAPTER 11 Support an Argument with Fact (*Logos*), Credibility (*Ethos*), and Emotion (*Pathos*)

All Illustrations by iStockphoto.com/A-digit

Explore An Issue

As you stand in line to order a soda at a local fast-food restaurant, you notice a young mother with three children taking their food to a table. The trays Mom is juggling are piled with burgers and fries, even though healthier kids' meals are offered by the restaurant. You're puzzled. If healthy options are offered, why hasn't this mother taken advantage of them? You begin to think that maybe the mother just doesn't know any better. By offering healthy choices for children, fast-food restaurants are doing their part. But is there more that can be done?

You think about the family while you develop ideas for a nutrition course paper and wonder what your claim should be. Should you argue the causes of childhood obesity or the effects of children eating a fast-food diet? Should you work to discover the problems underlying childhood obesity and offer a solution? Along the way you will need to define terms and evaluate any solutions you propose. How can you use similar situations, maybe involving food served in school cafeterias, to compare with food served in fast-food restaurants?

COMMUNITY	TOPIC: Food Consumption
School-Academic	ISSUE: Fast Food and Health
Workplace	AUDIENCE: Fast-Food Restaurant Owners
Family-Household	
Neighborhood	CLAIM: Fast-food restaurants should move beyond just offering healthy foods to encouraging children to eat healthier.
Social-Cultural	
Consumer	
Concerned Citizen	

There are many argumentative writing tasks you may be asked to perform in your college writing career. In a business course, you may be assigned an evaluative essay that asks you to determine the feasibility of a new project. In a political science course, you may be asked to compare the governmental systems of two countries. Most frequently, you will be asked to argue a position. In Chapter 8, "Consider Toulmin-Based Argument," and Chapter 9, "Consider Middle Ground Argument, Rogerian Argument, and Argument based on a Microhistory," you will learn about formal types of argument (e.g., Toulmin, Rogerian). Here we will discuss the practicalities of presenting definitions, evaluations, causes and consequences, comparisons, and solution proposals.

Chapter 7 is designed to help you explore your issue from different angles, further solidifying your claim so that the argument's organizational structure becomes clear.

In this chapter you will work toward solidifying your claim as you:

- Develop an argument strategy based on:
  - Definitions.
  - Causes or consequences.
  - Comparisons.
  - Solution proposals.
  - Evaluations.
- Write an exploratory essay.

Figure 7.1 Images like the above may inspire you to explore the issue of childhood obesity.

Use Definitions

Use a **definition** when an argument may benefit from an in-depth discussion of the terms involved. Throughout your college career (and very frequently in your professional career as well), you will be asked to define terms. Maybe you are developing a brochure for your clients and want your services to be clear. You would define each one. Maybe you are debating the outcome of a battle in a history course. Who won? That depends on the definition of *winning* that you use. Sometimes you will need to define terms within a paper in conjunction with other types of support; other times the definition will be the point of the paper.

Defining terms can be a useful way to begin your argument. But please do not begin every essay with "According to Webster's Dictionary … " Supply a definition only under these circumstances:

- Your definition of a term is very different from that normally provided.
- There is a controversy surrounding the definition of the term, and it is important for your audience either to know about this controversy or to understand why you have settled on the definition you are using.

- Your term may have a multitude of meanings, and you need to clarify how you are using the term.
- Your term is often misunderstood.

For example, Brandon is working on an argument for his political science course. He is interested in the debate surrounding genetically modified foods, or biotech foods that are derived from genetically modified crops or organisms (GMOs). Brandon wants to argue that GMOs are safe, but will need to define some terms, particularly *GMO*, in order to specify how he is going to be using the terms. Here is his claim and two supports that provide two different definitions: one from the FDA and another from an anthropologist. These are then presented as an introduction and two body paragraphs.

CLAIM:	GMO foods are safe because they meet the standard of being substantially equivalent to their natural counterparts.
SUPPORT ONE:	The FDA's definition of *substantial equivalence*.
SUPPORT TWO:	The anthropologist's definition of *natural foods*.

The term *GMO foods* refers to foods that are made from genetically modified organisms. Specifically, this means organisms modified through the use of genetic engineering, or intentional manipulation of the organism's genetic material, its genes, or its DNA. Organizations that regulate food health worldwide use the concept of substantial equivalence to determine whether or not GMO foods are safe. If the modified food is substantially equivalent to its natural counterpart, it can be considered safe. Piet Schenkelaars, a biotech consultant, explains that the original definition of the term *substantial equivalence*, created in 1993 by the Organization for Economic Co-operation and Development, was that the GMO food in question "demonstrates the same characteristics and composition as the conventional food."

Some studies have found that genetically modified foods have more or less of certain important nutrients, therefore calling into question the idea that these foods are substantially equivalent. The whole usefulness of this safety standard depends on how we define the term *substantial*. Does it make a substantial difference if we eat soybean products that contain more lectin but less choline? The FDA specifically looks for substances that are new to the food and for different levels of allergens, nutrients, and toxins.

It may help to define *substantial equivalence* by comparison. There will always be differences between GMO foods and their natural counterparts. However, how great are these differences compared to the differences between other kinds of foods and their natural counterparts? After all, most of the foods we eat were genetically modified using traditional mutation and breeding techniques. One study even showed that these other differences were greater than those found in GMO soy. The study by Cheng, et al., was titled "Effect of Transgenes on Global Gene Expression in Soybean is within the Natural Range of Variation of Conventional Cultivars." If we accept some differences between the foods we eat and their natural counterparts, why should differences in GMO foods be especially worrisome?

Another issue is the context behind the definition of the term *natural foods*. No two varieties of conventional foods share the "same characteristics and composition," yet we readily accept these differences. In addition, virtually all of the foods we eat are very different than the original wild varieties. An anthropologist might define *natural foods* as those that human beings evolved to eat or those that were cultivated long ago. In prehistory and throughout our agricultural history, humans have selected and bred the plants that we preferred. Through this process of human intervention, the original ears of the teosinte plant have been transformed from the size of a slender finger to the foot-long ears of corn we know today. According to *Corn: Origin, History, Technology, and Production*, corn (officially "maize") allowed civilizations like the Mayans and Aztecs to flourish and is currently one of the most important food crops in the world (Smith). Which variety—conventional maize or the original teosinte—should be used as the "natural counterpart" for comparing with GMO maize to see if it is substantially equivalent? Are GMO strains natural counterparts of the foods we eat today, which have been created through techniques like mutation and selective breeding? Or should the GMO foods be compared with the original wild varieties that human beings evolved to eat, but which most of us have never seen, let alone eaten? These questions should be a part of any discussion of GMO food safety or the issue of substantial equivalence.

Works Cited

Cheng, K. C., et al. "Effect of Transgenes on Global Gene Expression in Soybean Is Within the Natural Range of Variation of Conventional Cultivars." *Journal of Agricultural and Food Chemistry* 56.9 (May 2008): 3057–67.

Schenkelaars, Piet. "Rethinking Substantial Equivalence." *Nature Biotechnology* 20.119 (2002): n.pag. Web. 19 Jan. 2013.

Smith, C. Wayne, Javier Betran, and E. C. A. Runge, Eds. *Corn: Origin, History, Technology, and Production*. Hoboken: Wiley, 2004.

Discussion: Notice that there are two definitions included in Brandon's supporting material: the definition of *GMO* and the definition of *natural foods*. Both definitions support the larger question of how to define *food safety*. His argument will undoubtedly include more terms to be defined because his audience will need to understand these terms in order to agree with his claim that GMOs are safe. In his argument, he will need to support each of these definitions with research.

Seven Types of Definition

There are many definition strategies that you can use in your academic writing. They may be combined as needed. An overview of seven of the types (Scientific, Metaphoric, Example, Riddle, Functional, Ironic, and Negation) follows.

Define with Science (Descriptive, Factual)

In this type of definition, whether the subject is scientific or not, you are answering questions such as, "How big?" "What color?" and "How old?" You are describing the subject systematically. Usually, you are describing those characteristics that make the subject what it is—a mammal, a poem, a weapon, a disease.

Bees are insects with six legs and two pairs of wings. Bees vary in size from roughly four millimeters to well over four centimeters in length, and weigh anywhere from ....

your turn 7a **Define with Science**

Define an issue that you are working on in terms of science. What are its component parts? Describe it accurately.

Define with Metaphor (Comparison)

Metaphors are not just useful in poetry and fiction. Metaphors provide a new way of looking at a subject and comparing it with other things. You may use metaphors and similes, and you might also include analogies and list synonyms for your subject term. Metaphorical definitions are very common. The following examples explain how metaphors can be used to define terms:

- A new diet, technology, or government program might be referred to as "a panacea." The real Panacea was a Greek goddess of healing. Now any time something seems like a cure-all, it will invariably be called a panacea.

- To convey that something is a burden, you might call it an "albatross." Here the reference is to the bird (an albatross) that was tied around a sailor's neck as a punishment in a poem by Samuel Taylor Coleridge.

- If you are defining something as a "red herring," you would be saying that it is irrelevant and out of place, like an actual red herring would be.

- An "anchor tenant" is a retail business that, like the anchor on a ship, provides stability for a shopping center or a mall. It consistently draws in customers who may or may not also shop in the smaller satellite stores. A store would be defined as a satellite if it is peripheral to the anchor tenant the way a satellite orbits the periphery of the earth.

> **your turn 7b ▶ Metaphorical Definitions**
>
> Metaphorical definitions can be very effective in introductions. Write an introduction in which you define your term using a metaphor. What does this metaphor add to your introduction?

Define by Example

With this method, the writer provides examples that exemplify members of the category being defined. What are some examples of great athletes, poor drivers, early mammals? By describing the features of the individuals in the group, you will be defining the group as well.

A great writer is someone like William Chaucer, Jane Austen, or Theodore Geisel, better known as Dr. Seuss.

> **your turn 7c ▶ Define by Example**
>
> Use examples to define your issue. Why are these examples good representations of the category into which your issue falls?

Define with a Riddle

Riddles work well in introductions. The definition is given, but the reader has to guess what is being defined.

If we allow these people to be integrated into the military, they will cause great harm to morale and discipline. They will cause dissension in the ranks and destroy unit cohesion. If unit cohesion goes, so will military readiness. If we lose military readiness, the defense of our country will be at risk. Our very survival is at stake. We must keep these people separate.

Who are we talking about? Homosexuals? No. Women, then? No. This is a great example of misdirection. Keep going back in time to the first people the military tried to keep from integrating. Of course, the remainder of the argument can use any of the other definition methods to expand upon the answer to the riddle.

> **your turn 7d ▶ Define with a Riddle**
>
> Write an introduction that poses your issue as a riddle. If you can mislead your reader, all the better. How is a riddle an effective strategy for introducing your issue?

Define by Function

When you are looking at your subject's function, you are explaining what it can (or cannot) do. The function of the space program is what? The function of a sphygmomanometer is what? The function of war is what? The essay then discusses these functions.

Functional definitions define things by what they do. To some people, a religion becomes different from a philosophy when it plays a psychological or sociological role. The social and legal definition of *family* was once biological, but that is now giving way to a functional definition.

- A family is a group of people who act as a family, with the bonds of family, or the behaviors or living arrangements of a family.
- A vegan is someone who doesn't eat any animal products.
- Functional definitions also help to classify things. Illicit drugs are classified according to their harmful effects on people. Whenever the government finds that people are using a substance to significantly alter their mood, no matter how natural that substance is, some officials will invariably call for that substance to be defined as a drug and outlawed. (The more harmful the substance, the higher its classification, with "A" indicating the most dangerous class of drugs.)

> **your turn 7e   Define by Function**
>
> Define your issue in terms of its functions. Identify at least three functions related to your issue. Which may be the most important function and why?

Define with Irony

In an ironic definition, you are arguing that something is not necessarily what it seems, or you are arguing that it is something other than it seems, usually the least likely possibility. You are using ironic definition when, for example, you define a forest fire as the bringer of life. This statement seems counterintuitive, going against reason; after all, so much is destroyed in a forest fire. However, there are many important benefits that come from the destruction. One benefit is that the high temperatures of a fire allow certain pine cones to release their seeds.

> **your turn 7f   Define with Irony**
>
> Irony is related to tone, so you do not want to push your irony to the point of sarcasm and put off your argument. Again, an introduction is a good place to provide an ironic definition. Write an introduction that defines your term in an ironic way.

Define by Negation

When you define a subject by what it isn't, you are setting up an interesting essay. For example, you could define *education* as NOT merely recall. You can use negation with description, example, function, and so forth. Philosophers say that you cannot define anything by using only negatives, but in fact, negative definitions are often quite useful.

- A virgin is a person who has not yet had sex.
- Parallel lines are a pair of lines on a plane that do not meet or cross.
- Candidate A is nothing like Abraham Lincoln. (Political candidates are often defined by negatives—i.e., they lack a certain quality, such as integrity, or they lack a qualification, such as military experience.)
- A manx is a certain breed of cat that originated on the Isle of Man, but it is also a cat without a tail.

your turn 7g   Define by Negation

Sometimes it is easier to define your issue by what it is not, particularly if you are trying to highlight how your issue is lacking or approached differently in a different culture or situation. For example, you may define *democracy* by describing a country where democracy is not the standard way of life. Take a moment to define your issue in terms of what it is not.

Discover Causes or Consequences

A thorough examination of the causes or consequences of your argument (both good and bad) can help you select the best evidence to support your claim. What good would come if your argument is accepted? What bad? What might happen if your argument is not accepted? **Consequences (or effects)** look to the future; **causes** look back at the past. Together they create a chain of evidence that can be very convincing (as shown in Figure 7.2).

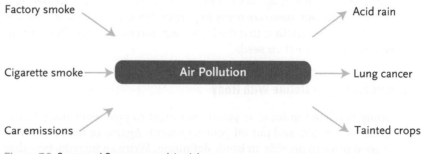

Figure 7.2 Cause and Consequence (simple)

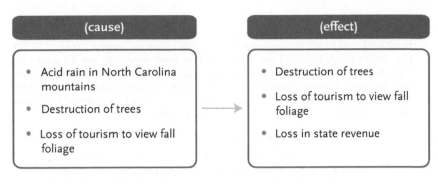

Figure 7.3 Cause and Effect (complex)

Are you interested in arguing based on causes or consequences (effects)? If you need to explain how something came about, you are arguing causes. Do you want to argue what the outcomes of a particular event will be? Then you're interested in presenting evidence of effects. But it's not as simple as it appears. In the example posed in Figure 7.2, we can see that a few of the causes of air pollution are on the left and some of the effects of air pollution are on the right. Air pollution is an issue that can be approached using both cause and effect. The effects themselves can go on to be causes of future events (as shown in Figure 7.3).

> **Claim:** Several factors are responsible for the acid rain destroying North Carolina's mountain trees.
>
> **Causes:** Factory smoke and car emissions cause acid rain.
>
> **Claim:** Acid rain in the North Carolina Mountains results in the loss of state revenue.
>
> **Consequences:** The destruction of trees will discourage tourists from visiting the mountains in North Carolina to view the fall foliage.

As you can see, each effect in turn becomes the cause of something else. And each one of these effects could be argued as being caused by factors other than the ones selected. Cause and/or consequence support can be useful, but very tricky. How far back do you need to research before you feel comfortable that you have reached the earliest cause? How far do you need to project into the future to feel confident that you have anticipated all reasonable consequences? Can you differentiate between primary causes and secondary causes?

A **primary cause** is the one that immediately precedes the effect. It can be very difficult to determine the primary cause of an event. As a humorous example of causal narrative, review this student example:

 tip 7a

Difference between *Affect* and *Effect*

One is a noun:
The effect of cutting back on welfare payments is that single mothers have to pay more for childcare.
One is a verb:
This affects their budgets adversely.

> This morning I broke my arm. This is how it happened. Last night my husband and I had an argument. Because I was so angry, I forgot to set the alarm clock before I went to bed. The next morning we all woke up late, so we were rushing around. As I went to leave, I realized I could not find my glasses. Figuring it was too late to search for them, I rushed out of the door and, to my dismay, stepped on the skateboard my son had left on the front steps. I fell and broke my arm.

The scenario may be silly, but an analysis of cause is not. Can we determine the primary cause of the student's broken arm? Was it the fight with her husband? Not wearing her glasses? The skateboard being in the wrong place? Actually, we could say that the primary cause of the injury was the contact of the cement steps with her arm bone! It is the one cause about which there can be no dispute. Concrete usually wins out over unprotected bone.

But what about secondary, sometimes called "peripheral," causes of the accident? **Secondary causes** are contributing factors. The list of factors contributing to the broken arm is quite long: an unset alarm clock, missing glasses, a misplaced skateboard. How far and wide should the net be cast when exploring secondary causes? It depends. Here are a couple of examples. The first is real, the second hypothetical.

> **Claim:** The rubella outbreak in the mid 1960s resulted in closed-captioning television.
> **Causes:** 1963–65 Rubella outbreak ⟶ high numbers of deaf children ⟶ as these children grew, they demanded closed-captioned TV.

Discussion: The link between the cause and effect could leave many scratching their heads. According to an April 1982 *New York Times* article, between 1963 and 1965 eight thousand pregnant mothers became infected by the rubella virus and gave birth to deaf children. As these children became adults in the early 1980s, they (along with other hearing-impaired individuals) demanded equal access to television programming. Closed captioning was developed in 1980 and spread quickly through the industry. At first, the claim—that the rubella outbreak led to the development of a technology that allowed deaf people to access television programming—seems unlikely. Yet, through a presentation of contributing factors, the connection is clear. Links such as these must be established with a chronology of events connecting the cause to the effect.

This next example involves a hypothetical plane crash. Note the different claims that are put forth by different participants in the scenario. The participants are

- Attorneys for crash victim's families
- Attorneys for the airline
- Attorneys for the Fancy School of Aviation Mechanics (FSAM)

Claim One (made by attorneys for crash victims' families): A stress fracture (*effect*) in the plane's wing was the result of poor inspections by the airline (*cause*).

Support: The inspectors were poorly qualified.

Claim Two (made by attorneys for the airline): The stress fracture was missed (*effect*) because the inspectors were poorly trained by FSAM (*cause*), an accredited school from which we have been hiring inspectors for years.

Support: Inspectors are trained by FSAM, not the airline.

Claim Three (made by attorneys for FSAM): A lack of funding (*cause*) has led to the loss of quality instructors (*effect*).

Support: FSAM's president embezzled millions of dollars affecting the school's budget.

Discussion: Plane crashes are always investigated, but not always for strictly humanitarian reasons. The primary cause of a crash can often be determined fairly quickly: a wing fell off, a bomb was detonated, the controls jammed, the pilot ignored the air traffic controller. The secondary causes, however, are often messier, and uncovering them is often a more protracted task. To determine the reason, blame has to be assessed. Who is at fault, and therefore, who must pay the cost of lost lives, cleanup, and so on?

How far back can we go to find contributing factors of a plane crash? Would it be unreasonable for the airline's attorneys to argue that the cause of the crash was the embezzlement of millions of dollars of school funds by the FSAM president? Follow the flowchart in Figure 7.4 to see how such a chain of evidence could evolve.

Claim Four (made by the attorneys of the families): Because the airline hired the inspectors, the airline is responsible for the plane crash (*cause*).

Consequence: The airline must pay restitution to the victims' families (*effect*).

Discussion: Obviously it is in the airline's best interests to argue that the cause of the plane crash originated elsewhere. After all, if the airline is held liable for the crash, all sorts of consequences could arise, including loss of revenue due to loss in reputation and millions of dollars lost in insurance claims. The immediate, primary cause of the plane crash may have been the wing falling off of the plane, but the secondary causes are more important in this argument. Most important in determining cause is to find the right one for the effect. Too often, arguments are based on flimsy cause–effect relationships, resulting in arguments that are not persuasive.

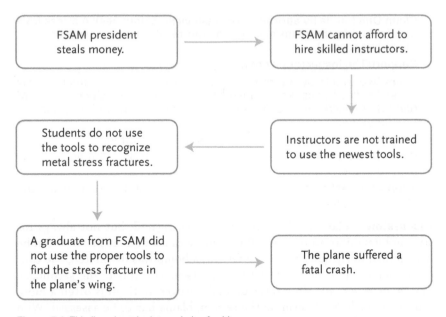

Figure 7.4 This flowchart depicts a chain of evidence.

How far in both directions (toward causes and toward consequences) do you need to go to be comfortable in supporting your claim?

your turn 7h   Explore Causes and Effects

Cast your claim in terms of causes. What is the primary cause of your claim? What are at least two secondary causes? Which of these causes would be most persuasive to your audience? What about effects? List at least three effects of your claim. Are they positive? Negative?

Present Comparisons

Comparisons can be very useful for establishing precedence and examining how similar situations have been handled. Perhaps your claim is one that is often lumped in with other topics. You may want to argue that compared with the other topics, your claim is significantly different and should be examined separately. Or you may be arguing that your claim is similar to other claims made and should be addressed in the same way.

Claim: Stop signs need to be installed at the intersection of Beadle and Poppin Streets, which is surrounded by a shopping center and a large neighborhood.

> **Support:** The intersection of East and West Streets, similarly situated between a neighborhood and a shopping center, has benefited from traffic signs.

Discussion: It can be useful to compare the intersection to another one in town that has the same shopping center/neighborhood configuration. Why does location B have a light, but location A does not? What is similar about the locations? What is different? Are the differences significant enough to allow B to have a light, but not A?

> **Claim:** The intersection of Beadle and Poppin Streets is being denied a traffic signal because it is in a lower income section of town.
>
> **Support One:** Of the requests for any improvements (roads, sidewalks, lights, etc.) in upscale Mayfair neighborhood, 80 percent are being granted; yet only 10 percent of requests from lower income Saxony neighborhood are being granted.

Discussion: What if there is no closely related situation? Then you should look for a situation that has similar characteristics. This type of comparison is larger in scope than an obvious comparison, such as one intersection and another, but it is helpful in shoring up your argument.

You can look for historically similar situations as well. This is called **precedence** and is one of the tools used by lawyers and judges in evaluating court cases. What past cases (in this town or in other towns) have been similar to this one? How were they handled? Knowing how previous problems were solved may be useful in arguing how the new problem can be solved. (See "Propose a Solution" in the section that follows.)

For example, a similar case of seeming discrimination was handled in Atlanta by the establishment of a citizen's group, which investigated all requests and routed them on to the correct departments after the investigations were complete. This group was composed of individuals from all areas of the city and therefore less likely to discriminate or show favoritism. Can such a solution be effective in Saxony? You may argue that it could.

One of the most frustrating experiences you can have in doing research is not finding anything on your particular subject. You know your issue is important, but you are just not finding any support that relates directly to it. Let's look at the issue of including extreme sports in the Olympic Games. We'll narrow the issue even further to target the inclusion of skateboarding. You have spent hours online and in the library but have found nothing really useful on skateboarding and the Olympics. Perhaps you need to do some historical research.

Maybe you can answer the question, "When were women first allowed to compete in the Olympics?" or the question "Why were women not considered athletic competitors in the first place?" Another question to research is "How did an obscure sport like curling become part of the Olympics?" Based on the answers to these questions, you may be able to argue by **analogy.** An analogy is a type of comparison. What about the history of curling is similar to the history of skateboarding? Can the same arguments for including one sport be extended to including the other? How can the answers to questions about including women and curling in the Olympics relate to including skateboarding, an activity that some people do not even consider a sport?

your turn 7i ▸ Look for Comparisons

In support of your claim, what can you use for comparison? How are the two situations similar? How are they different? Are there enough similarities that your audience would agree to entertain the comparison you are making?

Propose a Solution

As you continue to develop your argument, it may be useful to think in terms of problems and solutions. There are 13 exploratory steps that we suggest you consider in proposing a solution to a problem. You may find that you need to look at all 13 steps for your issue, or you may need to examine only a few. For example, you may already know the problem, such as when an instructor has assigned you a particular issue to research. Your goal may then be to find support for your claim, Section B. Or maybe you have a great solution but are not sure how to implement it; Section C would be the most useful for you. The chart below offers an overview of the 13-step problem–solution exploration process.

Section A: Exploring the Problem	1. Preparation and Persistence 2. Understanding the Problem 3. Ethical Considerations
Section B: Conducting Different Types of Exploration	4. Historical Exploration 5. Process Exploration 6. Creative Exploration 7. Critical Thinking Exploration 8. Metaphorical and Analogical Exploration
Section C: Exploring Implementation	9. Selecting Solutions 10. Implementing Solutions 11. Communicating Solutions 12. Evaluating Solutions 13. Future and System Considerations

These steps need not be followed in order, but by considering all of them, you will develop a clearer idea of what your argument is actually about, and you will know how to creatively find ideas and solutions that may elude you otherwise. As you skim over the list, you can see that it can lead you to ideas you had not considered, or that it may help you in solving a problem or implementing a solution (Section C). You may find that you are reinventing the wheel because you have not looked at how a particular problem has been solved historically (Section B). What has been done before and why did it not work? Or maybe you have to consider the ethical nature of a problem in determining fair and equitable solutions (Section A).

At the heart of this process is creative thinking. Ask yourself the question, "How can I approach my topic in a more creative way?" A wonderful book about creative thinking is Robert and Michèle Root-Bernstein's *Sparks of Genius* (Boston: Houghton Mifflin, 1999). The authors researched ways that creative people in varying fields and disciplines came up with ideas. They found, for instance, that a physicist might get

Figure 7.5 Using the science behind obesity and nutrition can help identify a process solution.

ideas by listening to a Bach concerto. A sculptor might discover a new technique by meditating. An engineer might find a solution to a problem while rowing a sea kayak in a storm. Creative thinking refuses to shut out possibilities and embraces ideas that can be found in all avenues of life. The most creative people do not close the door to ideas; instead, they find them in unexpected areas.

Our 13 items reflect many of the ideas that the Root-Bernsteins developed in their research. These steps are meant to be practical tools you can use to come up with ideas that strengthen your arguments. Let's follow the progress of a student, Lise, as she works through all 13 steps to develop a solution to the persistent problem of unhealthy fast-food meals and their link to childhood obesity.

Section A: Exploring the Problem

The steps in this section are very basic. What exactly is the problem at hand? Very often, problems can be challenging to solve because the exact cause is not clear; it can be difficult to find the causes of the problem, who it affects, and who is responsible for it. Moving through these steps can help you address these initial considerations.

1. Preparation and Persistence

What do you need to solve the problem? What are the necessary resources? Do you have enough assistance and persistence? Do you have the time, money, strength, and faith to continue toward a solution? Thomas Edison said that "Genius is one percent inspiration, ninety-nine percent perspiration." It is easy to be inspired, but it takes hard work to complete a task. What do you need to complete your task?

- Do you need to talk to people in relevant fields?
- Do you need research help from librarians?
- Do you need to start all over from scratch?

Lise's issue is one that she is arguing in her college health course, so the possibility of getting a high grade contributes to her motivation to find a solution. However, because she is studying to be a dietician, her motivation is professional and personal as well. Issues such as fast food and childhood obesity relate directly to her chosen career. In addition, she genuinely wants to help people eat better. A strong database of medical articles is available to her, making research easy. Lise's college's health program is linked to the local hospital which means she has access to faculty at the hospital as well. She envisions interviews with doctors at the hospital along with traditional library research.

2. Understanding the Problem

What exactly is the problem? Identify it. Define it. Define it scientifically; descriptively; metaphorically; by example; define the solution without naming it; define the problem by its function; ironically; by its negation; using elaboration; using evaluation.

- What exactly is the problem?
- Is it made up of several smaller problems?
- For whom is it a problem? For whom is it not a problem?
- What caused the problem?

Answering this set of questions will ensure that you are arguing about the real problem. In the student sample below, the problem is not the quality of the product, but the public's perception of the cost.

What does Lise really know about the problem of childhood obesity? Lise's reading so far indicates that there are both controllable reasons (e.g., diet and exercise) and uncontrollable reasons (e.g., genetics) for childhood obesity. Which of the controllable reasons are the biggest culprits for weight gain in children?

- Fast-food diets
- School lunches
- Lack of exercise at school and at home
- Too many unhealthy snacks

Lise will have to decide which problem to tackle. After witnessing the family ordering burgers and fries at the fast-food restaurant (as discussed in this chapter's first pages), she is leaning toward writing about the problem of fast-food diets.

3. Ethical Considerations

What are the rights and wrongs of solving your problem? In other words, how will solving your problem be right and wrong, and for whom?

- Should this problem even be solved?
- What will solving it do to the people involved?
- What will solving or not solving the problem do to the main purpose or core business of the problem-solver?
- What happens if the problem is not addressed or solved?

Solutions require us to expend resources, and they also affect future decisions and operations. Is solving the problem worth the costs, and to whom? Always consider the main purpose of the problem-solver. At our college, our main purpose is to serve students and our community. We consider our decisions ethical if they're good for students and good for our community.

But issues of right and wrong are often complicated. For instance, my purpose is to make a good living for my family. If the state of North Carolina raises instructors' salaries, where will the money come from? Higher taxes on other families who are already struggling with the economic downturn? Ethics can be a cloudy area.

> Lise is convinced that it is extremely important to solve the problem of unhealthy fast-food products being targeted at children. She feels restaurants have a moral obligation to improve their nutritional options for children and to provide encouragement and education through marketing programs or brochures. If the problem is not solved, those families who—by lack of better nutritional options or lack of education—frequently eat fast food will be raising an unhealthy generation of children who will develop health problems that will strain our medical system.

your turn 7j ▶ Explore the Problem

For Steps 1–3 above, explore your own issue, following Lise's example.

Section B: Different Types of Exploration

Now that you know what the problem is, where can you look for solutions?

4. Historical Exploration

Historical exploration answers the question, "How have similar problems been solved in the past?" Past cases and examples generate solutions. There is no sense in always starting from scratch. If we know how similar problems have been solved in the past, we may be able to adapt those solutions to fit our current needs. Looking to the past is often a very productive step toward a solution. Always start here.

- What have been some of the historical solutions to the problem?
- Why have they failed?
- Did they fail because the solution was a poor one or because it was not implemented correctly?
- Can an historical solution be used and improved upon with some newly available modifications?

Of course there have always been overweight children, but studies show that the number of children considered overweight in this country is increasing at an alarming rate. In the past, most childhood weight gain was due to overeating and lack of exercise. The solution was considered simple: eat less and exercise more. Today, though, the childhood obesity problem is complicated by families eating out more, by the increased availability of cheap fast-food options marketed to children, and by skyrocketing food prices that encourage parents to buy cheaper, usually less healthy, foods. If families are having to cut back and are going to be eating out frequently, then one solution is to make sure fast-food restaurants have healthier options and that families know how to choose nutritious foods.

5. Process Exploration

How does the problem work? How do possible solutions work? When we explore processes, we are looking at how things work in order to generate solutions. Areas of exploration can be laws, policies, rules, or psychological and scientific theories. For example, advertisers market their products to younger people, even though older folks buy more products. The reason? They know that the older we are, the less likely we are to change brands, and that getting consumers to change brands is one main purpose for advertisements. Advertisements, then, target the audience that is most likely to be responsive. The idea is that if we know how things work, we can use known processes, theories, tendencies, and behaviors to help craft solutions.

Some processes are informal and more likely to change; they aren't written in stone. Whenever a new president comes into office or a new manager comes into a business, the staff has to figure out what the new person likes, dislikes, tolerates, expects, and so forth. These changing processes may depend on the new leader's personality, but the effect they have on people's lives is every bit as real as the law of gravity or criminal statutes.

- What processes are at work in relation to our problem?
- What are the existing theories in this field or area of activity?
- Which sciences are involved, and what do the experts tell us about our problem?
- What are some predictable behaviors surrounding our problem and its possible solutions?

How did fast-food restaurants begin serving such bad foods to children? When did kids' meals become popular? Lise suspects that fast-food advertising during Saturday morning cartoons began the craze for kids' meals and the toys they contain. By including toys that relate to popular movies, the restaurants and the kids' meals become even more attractive to children. Who makes the choices at the local level about what restaurants serve? For example, McDonalds has locations all around the world, and different foods are served in different places. To some extent, local decisions must determine which products are sold in each location; Lise needs to learn the processes that governs who makes these decisions.

6. Creative Exploration

This process allows you to explore and answer questions such as, "How else might the situation be?" and "What could we add to it or put in its place?" As important as it is to research historical solutions to similar problems, it is also important to use creative free-range thinking. For this step, ignore processes, past examples, and assumptions. If you could wave a wand to come up with any solution you like, what would that solution be? Then, once you've imagined the solution, no matter how far-fetched it is, work backwards to see how you might get there. Freeing yourself from logical thinking can often have amazing results. Perhaps you had a good idea all along, but your fears of looking foolish prevented you from committing the idea as a solution. Through creative exploration, you may discover that the idea may actually work! Here are some examples of creative problem-solving:

- When the Japanese invaded Okinawa, in 1607, the locals were forbidden to carry weapons, so they developed a form of open-hand combat called karate.

- According to legend, Irish step-dancing came about because dancing was outlawed but people wanted to dance anyway. They held their arms still and moved only their legs, which allowed them to dance behind stone walls without appearing to be dancing at all.

- When parents are desperate, they find creative ways to motivate their children to get good grades. Some of them even pay their children money for grades.

People have a long history of coming up with creative solutions to difficult problems. Climb out of the box for solutions. Read books or articles about topics that seem different from yours in order to see how other problems have been solved. For example, if your company has tried unsuccessfully to motivate employees with bonuses, try reading trade journals in other fields to see how different kinds of businesses motivate their employees.

Creativity shows up in the restaurant business frequently. "Thinking outside the bun" led to the creation of tortilla wraps. The focus on low-carb eating resulted in the introduction of ethnic cuisines, such as lettuce wraps.

In the best of all possible worlds, children would be able to eat hamburgers and French fries that would actually be healthy for them. Fast-food restaurants are missing an opportunity to think outside the box about what healthy eating means. If a father insists on feeding his children a steady diet of burgers, then the burgers should at least be healthy. There are dozens of vegetarian versions of burgers that kids love. Potatoes are not inherently unhealthy, but frying is, so the fries could be baked instead. Apples can be served instead of apple pie; low-fat yogurt with granola can be served instead of full-fat yogurt with candy sprinkles. Problems that seem impossible at first can often be addressed with a little creative thinking.

7. Critical Thinking Exploration

How else might the situation be? What could we take away from the problem or from each possible solution? Question your basic assumptions to generate solutions.

- Do you even need to solve the problem?
- Are the rules governing the problem mandatory?
- Did past solutions work for the reasons you thought they worked?

At a local pizza shop, customers who pay with plastic have a long wait-time. In order to process credit card transactions, the cashier has to ring up the order at the register, swipe the card, walk across the store and around a shelving unit, wait to gather the receipt once it prints, come back, and only then complete the transaction. The manager's explanation of the problem was, "Our credit card machine runs through the computer, which is across the store." Hasn't she considered moving the systems closer together? A little critical thinking could make credit card processing more efficient.

It often pays to ask, "What if the accepted 'truth' is not actually true?" What if there really is no gravity? What if we don't have to die? What if the earth *isn't* round? The weird people who ask these odd questions end up discovering new things. In fact, our latest theory of gravity (Einstein's) is being questioned and may soon be replaced with a new theory. In fact, science may find a solution to the dying process in your lifetime. In fact, the earth is bulgy, not round.

Is fast food really the problem? Isn't lack of exercise just as important a factor in childhood obesity? The assumption is that children are getting too many "bad" calories from burgers and chicken fingers, but do we know that is true? Perhaps the number of times a week a family stops at Burger Barn is a bigger factor than what is actually consumed. Lise asks questions that seem obvious but need to be addressed. She also needs to examine the products that popular fast-food chains actually offer children. Have the restaurants tried to provide healthy options in the past? Were these attempts profitable? What could they do to increase the profitability of healthy options?

8. Metaphorical or Analogical Exploration

Metaphorical thinking asks us to see the connections and similarities between seemingly different things. Analogies involve seeing similarities between seemingly different situations. It can be helpful to think more creatively about your issue. For example, Lise was having difficulties untangling all the threads of her issue to determine which one to present as her claim. She could concentrate on fast-food advertising, the types of kids' meals restaurants serve, the types of families that eat in fast-food restaurants frequently, and the cost of the food. Until the image of a tree with branches came to her, Lise couldn't see that her argument had one "trunk" and that the different areas of her argument could be organized into "branches." Her metaphorical thinking yielded an organizational format that she couldn't see before: one main problem with smaller problems branching off from the main trunk.

- What is the problem like?
- What are possible solutions like?
- Can a metaphor be created?
- Is an analogy better?

Example of Metaphor:

Let's say I sell used cars and I'd like to double my sales. I can cast about in my mind to answer the question, "What else doubles?" and come up with the answer, "Bread dough." "How?" "Yeast." "What's the yeast in sales?" "Energy, charisma, good looks, manipulation, reciprocity, value, compassion—whatever is needed." One of these ideas might prove to be an important part of the solution, no matter what an expert consultant might say. My car lot might well need sprucing up. Or my cars might not seem to have much value. Or my staff might smell bad. Textbook solutions (historical and scientific) are wonderfully important in many cases, but in this case the metaphor might be useful because thinking of my sales as bread dough sent me looking for the "yeast" that might be missing.

Example of Analogy:

I had a problem keeping all of the leaves and debris out of my pool. I live in the country, surrounded by nature's abundance, and a lot of stuff gets in the pool. It is almost an everyday affair to keep it cleaned. I could clean it myself, but doing so would take up immense amounts of my time and energy. While I was watching a show about animals whose teeth and bodies are cleaned by other animals, I thought of my pool-cleaning problem. In order to clean themselves, the animals would expend energy and time, just as I would do if I cleaned my own pool. They would have the impossible task of growing new appendages, just as I would have the impossible task of creating more time. I decided to invest in an automatic pool cleaner—just as the animals have "automatic" teeth and body cleaners.

If a solution has been found to a problem that is similar to yours, perhaps you can apply or adapt that solution.

What object, issue, or situation does the problem of childhood obesity resemble? The more Lise read, the more the issue seemed to branch off into other issues. Before long, her issue had become as tangled as tree branches. The metaphor of a tree worked for Lise. She could see the different types of problems (poor nutrition, lack of family time, the low cost of fast food) as branches of a tree (fast food). Chopping the tree down is not an option, but leaving it alone only allows it to continue growing wildly in any direction it chooses. Lise started to think about ways that the branches could be pruned and shaped so as the tree continues to grow, the branches (the issues) will be directed. How can specific foods offered by fast-food restaurants be modified to become healthier?

> **your turn 7k**   **Look for Creative Answers**
>
> For Steps 4–8 above, explore your own issue, following the student models of Lise.

Section C: Exploring Implementation

Maybe your problem is not coming up with solutions, but identifying which potential solution would be the best choice. Or maybe you have settled on a solution but don't know whom to address in your claim or how to implement your solution.

9. Selecting Solutions

Which proposed solution should be chosen? Often, a given problem will have several potential solutions. Deciding which one to choose is difficult. If it's your problem, you have to satisfy yourself, right? What if it satisfies you but makes your family mad? Or your boss? Or what if you can't afford it?

- Which is the best solution?
- Which is the simplest solution?
- Which solution best fits your goals?
- Which solution is the most ethical?
- Which solution is the cheapest?
- How will you decide which solution to propose?

As Lise continued her research, she saw solutions that companies in other industries had used, and she began thinking of how to apply those solutions to the problem of fast-food meals for children. But which of these solutions should be present in her argument? Some solutions would be expensive because they would involve introducing new products, and passing this cost on to the consumer would drive lower-income parents to search out cheaper types of fast food. Some solutions would involve developing clear nutritional guidelines for kids' meals. Some of the less expensive solutions might not offer the same degree of success. Cost and effectiveness were the two variables that Lise decided to use as her guide in crafting solutions that would please both fast-food restaurants and families.

10. Implementing Solutions

How can the solution best be implemented?

- What resources will the solution entail?
- What process should we put in place?
- Will it involve monitoring and enforcement?
- Who should do the implementing?

I went to a discount store the other day and encountered a problem. When I asked the cashier to ring up six bags of dirt, she told me I needed to go outside and make sure it was there. I said it was probably there and asked her to go ahead and ring it up. She was very nice but refused to let me pay for the dirt until I had gone personally to verify that it was in stock. I looked at the long line behind me and left the store. The store had a problem: How could they make their products convenient to buy? In other words, how could they save their customers time and money? The first solution they tried didn't work in my case: they wanted employees to remember what the store had in stock and not ring-up anything else. This solution relied too much on training employees to remember which products were in stock.

The next time I purchased dirt at the discount store, a new solution was in place. The manager had checked the stock and covered the bar codes on the scan sheets to show items not in stock. That way no one could ring up something they didn't have. The second solution was easier to implement, a lot cheaper than training, and a lot more reliable than a busy clerk's memory. They solution had been possible all along, they just hadn't identified it.

Lise comes to realize that fast food causes big problems for children struggling to maintain a healthy weight. When children eat a steady diet of fast food, they do not thrive physically. Issues contributing to the problem were food cost and fast-food convenience. Lise decides that issues of time and money are not as easily addressed as food quality. Since restaurants can be required to provide nutritional information for the foods they sell, then surely they can be required to provide nutritious food for children. School lunch programs have become healthier by providing options that do appeal to children; fast-food restaurants can do the same.

11. Communicating Solutions

Very often, solutions are devised at the very top of an organization, and the steps required to implement the solution are communicated quite efficiently throughout the organization. Unfortunately, the reason for those steps often does not filter down, diminishing the effectiveness of the solution. How, then, can the solution best be communicated?

> Lise's argument has to be presented as a researched paper to a college professor. However, if she were working for a particular restaurant desiring to provide healthier foods, she would probably have several choices in how to communicate her findings to her boss. Here are two of her choices:
>
> • A formal report may be the best choice in response to a request by the boss for a study of the issue
>
> • A memo may be appropriate if she is the one bringing up the topic with her boss and wants to do so informally

12. Evaluating Solutions

How can the effectiveness of the solution be evaluated? Was it really the best solution? Although it is most often thought of as occurring after a solution is implemented, evaluation is actually part of every step: before, during, and after implementation. At each of these stages, the key to good evaluation is to understand the real values we need to measure the results against.

> To determine whether a solution is effective, Lise will have to implement it and develop a tool to evaluate its effectiveness. What would such a tool look like? To whom should she propose her solution and how might it be implemented? Lise's research led her to believe that in addition to submitting her argument to her professor, she could pitch her problem–solution argument at the fast-food restaurant in her neighborhood, a locally owned eatery. She develops a new policy to encourage children to lose weight and get fit using a "fat-to-fit" program that will result in increased sales. She now has a narrower perspective on the issue, and this narrows the type of research she needs to do. A narrow angle can really benefit an argument by allowing the writer to focus on specifics.

13. Future and System Considerations

Now that we've solved the problem and evaluated the effectiveness of the chosen solution, what is the next step?

- Should we consider the process closed? Or has our solution created another problem to solve?
- Has the solution eliminated our argument's reason for being?
- Has it changed the nature of our core business?
- What are the unintended consequences of the chosen solution?
- How has the solution changed the internal or external organizational system?

A positive example of evaluation of a solution is provided by the G.I. Bill. After World War II, huge numbers of young men came back from the war and enrolled in college using money from the G.I. Bill. That gave them the skills they needed to compete for good-paying jobs. In turn, that boosted our economy, which in turn helped people make more money and buy houses and pay more in taxes, so that the government had even more money to give the next generation of soldiers to go to college. It helped the whole system.

> After using the problem-solving process to evaluate her topic, Lise now has a claim that she can research and a solution she can propose. She may even be able to evaluate the solution if it is implemented in her community. If successful, a change in a small local restaurant may spark interest in the larger chains, prompting them to implement similar changes. Lise is ready to tackle her research in earnest, and her argument will be more effective and focused, using specifics instead of abstractions.

your turn 7l ➤ **Implement Your Solutions**

For Steps 9–13 above, explore your own issue, following the student models of Lise.

Evaluate Your Claim

An **evaluation** should be used when you are attempting to persuade your audience that one thing is better (more efficient, more feasible, etc.) than another. As long as you clearly explain your evaluation criteria, evidence that provides an evaluation of your problem and solution can be important in persuading your audience. When presenting your evaluation, you will sometimes be asked to offer a single solution or to offer several solutions and indicate which is best based on the indicated criteria. For example, in a humanities course, you may be asked to which category, genre, or movement a work of art, a text, or a piece of music belongs.

> The Problem: *Madonna and Child with Angels and St. Jerome* by the Italian artist Parmigianino (see Figure 7.6), is an example of what style of art?
> The Solution: *Madonna and Child with Angels and St. Jerome* is an example of Mannerist art because ...
> The Criteria: ... it exhibits the following characteristics of Mannerism:
>
> • Elongated figures and forms
> • Garish color combinations
> • Exaggerated body positions
>
> Parmigianino's painting is an example of Mannerist art because it exhibits all three characteristics of that art style.

Madonna with the Long Neck, 1534–40 (oil on canvas), Parmigianino (Francesco Mazzola) (1503–40)/Galleria degli Uffizi, Florence, Italy/Alinari/The Bridgeman Art Library

Figure 7.6 Parmigianino, *Madonna and Child with Angels and St. Jerome*

In an evaluation, you will:

- Select the criteria or characteristics that you will use to evaluate your subject.
- Discuss your selection of criteria.
- Present an evaluation of your subject based on that criteria.

your turn 7m ▸ **Evaluate Your Solution**

From your exploration of your issue from the 13-step problem–solution perspective, evaluate the solution you decided upon. Make sure to select the criteria you will use, and evaluate the solution based on those criteria. Alternatively, develop three solutions and use your criteria to determine which solution best fits the problem.

Write an Exploratory Essay

An exploratory essay is a useful way to examine both a) what you know about your topic so far, and b) what directions you may still need to pursue before putting your argument together.

What do you know about your issue? An exploratory essay usually is undertaken after you have completed some research on the issue, maybe after you have worked through some of the prewriting methods or the problem-solving items. Don't narrow your research too soon. At the beginning, read enough on the subject to be conversant with the players involved, about the problems and different points of view. You can then sift through your materials and decide what parts of the issue you are now comfortable with. What you do know may include:

- Historical or cultural background on the issue.
- The players involved in the issue.
- What claims you may want to make.

Once you have seen what you do know, it is time to examine what elements about your issue that are confusing or that require further research. As you tackle what you do know, you may often find more questions that need to be answered.

What you don't know may include:

- Support for your claims.
- Where to look for materials such as statistics, interviews, articles, and so on.
- Possible solutions.

Your essay should present the reader with a clear idea of what your questions are, what you have learned so far, and what you still need to do to complete your argument.

▧ Exploratory Essay Checklist

Have you included the following elements in your exploratory essay?

- ☐ Claim
- ☐ Background that includes context and all those involved
- ☐ What you know so far (research and common knowledge)
- ☐ What you still need to research
- ☐ Types of support you will need (see Chapter 11, "Support an Argument with Fact (Logos), Credibility (Ethos), and Emotion (Pathos)")

Sample Exploratory Essay

Below is Lise's exploratory essay, along with her instructor's comments.

Lise Holt

Health 232

Professor Smith

4 September 2013

Exploratory Essay

What is the specific claim to be made? What organizational strategy would best be employed?

Fast-food restaurants have been around for quite a while now. They have not traditionally been known for their healthy foods; they are popular for their ability to get hungry, busy people in and out fast. Can't the two goals, health and speed, be combined? In particular, can't healthy foods and a healthy eating program be combined to help families eat healthier? I am arguing that fast-food restaurants should add nutrition-education programs, using their websites and brochures, to explain their healthier kids' menus. My primary strategy will be to offer a solution with a fat-to-fit program at Mama Maya's Italian Eatery in town. The program will be both healthy and cost effective.

Who are the players involved in this issue?

Who is involved in the issue? Families with children who eat at fast-food restaurants are the focus of my claim; they would be the beneficiaries of any educational programs and the improvements that restaurants make to their kids' menus. The restaurant owners themselves are the second interested parties. Their motivation is keeping businesses. How would they be motivated to change their menus? Are they receiving any complaints now? If not, what would be their motivation to offer education and new menu selections?

By selecting a topic that generates personal interest, Lise will be able to begin forming opinions about the issue and selecting research that is more focused on her particular claim.

I became interested in this topic when I was standing in line at Mama Maya's ordering dinner. It occurred to me after seeing several parents ordering food for their children that they were ignoring the healthier options on the menu. In my health class, we are currently debating the issue of obesity in children and I immediately thought of the kids at the restaurant.

What is there still to be done? Lise has now identified a claim that will help her direct her research and gather appropriate support.

My next step will be to research the argued causes of childhood obesity. I will also need to find out why some restaurants have begun offering healthier options for kids and others haven't. Finally, I will develop a fat-to-fit program to accompany Mama Maya's menu.

your turn 7m ▶ **Write an Exploratory Essay**

Address these items in an exploratory essay about a topic you are researching.

- What is the historical or cultural background to the issue?
- Who are the players involved in the issue?
- What tentative claims do you want to make?

Include what you do not know that needs more research. What you don't know may include:

- Support for your claims.
- Where to look for materials (statistics, interviews, articles, etc.).
- Possible solutions.

Reflect and Apply

1. As you explore your issue, you will need to make some choices about how to arrange your argument. Explain your decision to use one of the following organizational strategies: define, compare, evaluate, or evaluate causes and effects. Why did you select your organizational strategy? How would your argument be different if you selected a different strategy?

2. Once you have identified which sections of the exploration process you need to apply to your issue, work through them carefully. Explain what these processes add to your thinking about your issue. What solutions do these processes suggest?

3. Your exploratory essay is an opportunity to take a step back from your issue and consider what you have discovered and what more needs to be done. How are you articulating your ideas to your reader in your exploratory essay? Are there any questions that your reader may still have after they read your exploratory essay? How would you answer those questions?

KEEPING IT LOCAL

IN EVERY TOWN there is at least one popular local restaurant that everyone flocks to after football games, soccer practice, even church on Sunday. For as diverse a culture as we have in the United States, the offerings of these restaurants are surprisingly similar. Most menus will include hot dogs, hamburgers, fried fish or shrimp, chili, ice cream or shakes, and cakes and pies. Even those eateries that offer veggie plates usually fry their okra or boil their field peas with fat back. If we want our children to eat better, we cannot rely on fast-food restaurants to magically begin putting healthier foods on the menus. By using different argument strategies, we can compare restaurants' offerings in parts of the country where people are considered healthier with those in parts of the country where people are not so healthy. We can define what healthy food choices mean to us and outline processes to meet these definitional goals. We can campaign against bad food choices based on their effects on our children's lifestyles and health. By examining the restaurant issue, or any other issue important to us, through multiple lenses, we can discover powerful methods of developing solutions to seemingly insurmountable problems.

● – – – – – – – – – – – – – – ●

What issue is important to you? Start the exploration process by asking yourself the questions in the "Propose a Solution" section. Where are these questions taking you? Sometimes you may find that these questions are opening avenues that you had not considered. Are you ready to go down those avenues and learn something new?

CHAPTER 8

Consider Toulmin-Based Argument

During a class activity, a student spoke intently about the political climate at our community college. He was born in the United States, and his native language is English. His parents moved to the United States from another country 25 years ago, bringing his two sisters—who were very young at the time—with them, so that he and his siblings could enjoy more opportunities and the promise of better lives. Ever since he can remember, his parents have contributed to the civic and religious life of our community. Both hold full-time jobs, and his mother has been promoted several times at work. This student has earned top grades, and his sisters plan to attend the same college in the next few years. But last spring, just after the end of the semester, our state—North Carolina—became the first in the country to recommend that children (who do not have lawful immigration status) of illegal immigrants be barred from attending community college. While the student will complete his degree next semester, he worries about his sisters not being able to attend community college, which will mean that college will be delayed for them. He reveals that he is caught in a swirl of emotions and is not sure what to do. Motivated by concern for his sisters and others in the community who had planned to take advantage of the reasonable tuition and convenience of the local community college, he wants to make his point of view known on this important issue.

The student decides to contact two instructors at the school and ask if they would be interested in supporting him. Together, the three decide to aim an argument at the State Board of Community Colleges, an organization in a position to ensure that the community college system continues its original open-door policy.

All Illustrations by iStockphoto.com/A-digit

COMMUNITY

School-Academic
Workplace
Family-Household
Neighborhood
Social-Cultural
Consumer
Concerned Citizen

TOPIC: Children of Illegal Immigrants in the Community College System

ISSUE: Admission Policy for Children of Illegal Immigrants

AUDIENCE: State Board of Community Colleges

CLAIM: Children of illegal immigrants should be allowed to attend community colleges.

This chapter introduces you to Toulmin-based argument and the ways this structure can serve your purpose as you argue an issue that matters to you. As discussed in Chapter 2, "Explore an Issue that Matters to You," an argument should be a practical response to an issue, especially when you have a good sense of your audience, what it values, and why this issue is important to this audience. In the example that opens this chapter, the writers have made a practical decision to target the State Board of Community Colleges as the audience for their Toulmin-based argument.

You should construct an argument so that all its pieces serve your purpose. If your purpose is to convince an audience of the rightness of your own claim, as opposed to differing claims on an issue, then working with a Toulmin-based approach can serve your purpose. As you'll see in Chapter 9, "Consider Middle Ground Argument, Rogerian Argument, and Argument Based on a Microhistory," there are other argument structures that may be appropriate for your purpose. For example, if your intention is to argue for a practical position between two extreme positions, then a middle-ground strategy can serve your purpose. But if your purpose is to create productive dialogue and common ground on a testy issue with an individual or group whose perspective differs sharply from your own, then a Rogerian approach is practical. And if your purpose is to examine closely a largely forgotten individual, place, or event from the past, then an argument based on a microhistory can work for you.

In this chapter, you will learn how to:

- Structure a Toulmin-based argument to fit your purpose.
- Apply the features of Toulmin-based argument to an issue.
- Map a Toulmin-based argument.

Construct an Argument to Fit Your Purpose

Once you've decided what you want to accomplish with a Toulmin-based argument, make sure you (as discussed in Chapter 2, "Explore an Issue That Matters to You"):

- Deliver your argument at a time when your audience is invested in the issue at hand.
- Center your argument in what is practical and possible.
- Know what your audience values.
- Let your audience know what it has to gain from your argument.
- Earn credibility early in the argument by establishing your knowledge of the issue and by defining your relationship to your audience.

For example, the narrative that opens this chapter addresses an issue getting a lot of attention in our state these days. The issue originates with the attorney general's recommendation that children of illegal immigrants be barred from pursuing degrees in the state's community colleges, a recommendation that the president of the community college system has chosen to follow. Because this student attends a community college and because his coauthors teach at the same college, writers of this argument have firsthand knowledge of this issue, and this may establish their credibility with their audience. The issue is generating much discussion across the state based on the news media's regular attention to it. Thus, the argument will be delivered at a decisive moment in the state's struggle with the immigrant presence in schools and other publicly funded institutions. The writers' decision to use a Toulmin-based approach is practical for their purpose—to convince their audience that "children of illegal immigrants should be allowed to attend community colleges." Consider how an argument centered in this issue might take shape using a Toulmin-based approach.

Terms of Toulmin-Based Argument

Contemporary British philosopher Stephen Toulmin has shaped the way we think about argument today. Where classical argument is centered in a three-part structure called a syllogism (major premise, minor premise, and conclusion), Toulmin renames these terms, adds three additional terms to the model, and moves argument from an exercise in logic to a practical scheme geared toward audience acceptance. Toulmin's six terms can be used as a checklist for writing effective arguments when your purpose is to persuade an audience of the rightness of your position. Those terms, defined in the following section, are *claim, support, warrant, backing, rebuttal,* and *qualifier*.

When you build an argument based on the Toulmin model, it's helpful to think of each term as a question that you must answer. With regard to the term *claim*, the question you must answer is, "What is my point?" or "What am I trying to prove?" For the term *support*, the question is, "How will I prove

Ozgurcankaya/E+/Getty Images

Figure 8.1 Close attention to audience and what it values is the hallmark of a Toulmin-based argument. The need to convince an audience of the rightness of a claim depends in large part on the range of support, or evidence, the arguer brings to an argument.

my point?" For the term *warrant*, the questions are, "Will my audience believe me based on values we share?" and "How can I justify my claim?" For the term *backing*, be prepared to answer the question, "What additional support for my warrant will I need in order to persuade my audience?" The term *rebuttal* requires that you ask, "What points of view different from mine should I bring to an argument?" And for the term *qualifier*, you must ask, "How can I modify the language in my argument, especially with reference to my claim and reasons, to make an argument more acceptable?"

But we must add a seventh and vital term to the Toulmin model, and this term is *reasons*. A reason falls between a claim and the specific support you bring to an argument. A reason supports a claim, and in turn, a reason requires support to make it believable. For example, focusing on the issue of children of illegal immigrants being barred from attending community colleges, if you claim that children of illegal immigrants should be allowed to enroll, you will need to provide reasons in support of this claim. One reason the coauthors can address beyond moral or financial arguments is that a skilled workforce is better for the state's economy. This reason requires specific support. So, while the term *reasons* is not among the terms usually used to develop a traditional six-part Toulmin argument, this seventh term is important, especially when you use a Toulmin approach to build a practical response to an issue affecting you.

Claim

A **claim** organizes your argument. It is the single statement to which every-thing else in an argument connects. It focuses your audience on what you want to achieve. It's the point you want to make. For example, a few years ago, a student new to her city made this claim in her first argument: "Links to websites that promote dangerous, antigay propaganda should not be posted on official community websites." Her online search for gay organizations at one point led her to a site stating that same-sex relationships were mor-ally wrong and that counseling was available for those struggling with their sexual identity. The fact that a link to the site appeared on the Chamber of Commerce website motivated her to argue.

Key Questions:
What is my point? What am I trying to prove?

Reasons

Reasons are direct support for your claim. Reasons often function as topic sentences, which you studied in earlier writing courses: they many times begin paragraphs and announce a paragraph's main idea or focus. As a way to begin working with reasons in an argument, think about immediately following a claim with the word *because*. Thus, the claim "Links to websites that promote dangerous, antigay propaganda should not be posted on official community websites" was supported with these reasons:

Key Question:
What comes after *because*?

- Because sites that promote "recovery" from homosexuality are just as harmful as explicitly hateful sites, such as "godhatesfags.com," a site promoting lies and cruelty
- Because not only is the information from such "recovery" sites harmful, it is also inaccurate
- Because the dangers of antigay propaganda are vast, the most visible occurring in antigay battery and assault

Support

Bring in specific **support** to defend your reasons. As we will see in Chapter 11, "Support an Argument with Fact (Logos), Credibility (Ethos), and Emotion (Pathos)," support can be logical (e.g., facts, statistics, data), ethical (e.g., scholarly articles, credible publications, examples from your own and oth-ers' experiences), or emotional (e.g., examples and startling information that can cause an audience to react emotionally). Vary the support you use, but remember that logical support is proof to an audience that you've done your research and that you're prepared to defend your claim on rational grounds. In most arguments, your goal is to have your audience accept your claim, and the thoroughness of supporting evidence is often what sways an audience. Consider the support this writer brings to her argument.

Key Question:
How will I prove my point?

- Logical support includes numerous examples drawn from antigay web-sites; the FBI's *Uniform Crime Report*, which reveals the annual number of hate crimes based on victims' sexual orientation; and an academic study focused on gay teens and suicide.

- Ethical support includes quoted and paraphrased commentary on homosexuality from the American Psychiatric Association and the dean of the Georgetown University Medical Center, along with examples—from the writer's experience and those of her friends—of antigay violence, including slurs, bullying, beatings, and property damage.
- Emotional support includes reference to Matthew Wayne Shepard, a gay man beaten and left for dead in Wyoming (an example that opens the argument) and personal examples of her experience with those in her new community who offer "love and guidance" as "solutions" to her sexual orientation.

Warrant

Key Questions:
Will my audience believe me based on values we share? How can I justify my claim?

Use a **warrant** to identify the values and beliefs you share with an audience. The warrant grants you permission to address your audience with your argument because you share at least some moral principles. A warrant justifies a claim; as a writer, you must make clear to your audience that the moral principle in your warrant justifies your claim. This is the warrant the writer used to argue against antigay websites: "I do not want any person to suffer the harm and injustice that so many GLBT (gay, lesbian, bisexual, transgender) persons suffer on a daily basis." This writer connects warrant and claim. The principle in her warrant—not wanting people to suffer harm and injustice—justifies her claim of not wanting her local Chamber of Commerce, a publicly funded organization, to support an antigay website.

Backing

Key Question:
What additional support for my warrant will I need in order to persuade my audience?

Backing supports a warrant. Bring in backing when you sense that an audience will need additional convincing of your warrant. In support of the warrant that centers on the need to avoid harm and injustice, the writer explains why sexual orientation should not be cause for discrimination. She brings in compelling examples from individuals who have suffered harm and injustice as well as examples from individuals who live in communities where sexual orientation is not an issue.

Rebuttal

Key Question:
What points of view different from mine should I bring to my argument?

A **rebuttal** argues against a claim. It presents a different or opposing point of view on your issue. It is helpful to anticipate objections to an argument for several reasons. First, when you summarize a differing view fairly, you become credible to your audience—because you can be trusted to describe without bias another view. Second, countering a rebuttal to your claim gives you the chance to demonstrate to an audience that your claim (or solution) is more practical than the one proposed by the opposition. A rebuttal needs to be countered, with an eye toward why an audience might consider a position different from yours. In the issue we're working with, the writer brings in two rebuttals. One claims that choosing a gay lifestyle is abnormal and unhealthy. The second argues that homosexuality is "wrong, immoral, and dangerous" and should be corrected. The writer counters both rebuttals by claiming that sexual orientation is not about choice; rather, she explains, sexuality is a "precognitive aspect of personality developed even before language skills." Additionally, she counters both rebuttals by referring to the American Psychiatric Association and the scientific view that homosexuality is not a psychiatric illness and that the only disorder in this context has to do with not accepting one's sexuality.

Qualifiers

The great strength of Toulmin's system is its focus on audience. A claim is your position on an issue, a position that must be delivered to an audience open to hearing it. The support you bring to an argument will be of three kinds—logical, ethical, and emotional—and each kind should appeal to your audience in a practical way. Your warrant ties you to your audience based on shared or similar values, beliefs, and feelings. Backing allows you to elaborate on your warrant in order to appeal more specifically to your audience's value system. A rebuttal (or rebuttals) in an argument lets you anticipate audience objections to your claim, objections that you can then counter. **Qualifiers** prevent you from making absolute statements because they involve words such as *often, typically,* and *in most cases* (instead of words like *always, only,* and *for certain*). Collectively, wise application of these qualifying terms centers an argument in practical—rather than idealistic, unrealistic—appeals.

As you can see, Toulmin-based argument is about arguing before an audience that is invested in your issue and therefore willing to listen to what you have to say. This kind of argument is also about each part of an argument supporting another part—a warrant that supports a claim, backing that supports a warrant, specific support that strengthens reasons, and reasons that support a claim. The seven strands of a Toulmin argument are knit together to form a single garment, a single argument. Each part serves the next with no room for filler. With reference to any single strand, a question helpful in building a Toulmin argument can be, "How does this part of my argument move my audience closer to accepting my claim?"

Key Question:
How can I modify the language in an argument, especially with reference to my claim and reasons, to make an argument more believable?

> **your turn 8a** ▶ **GET STARTED A Toulmin-Based Argument**
>
> Answer the following questions as a way to begin working with the Toulmin model.
>
> 1. What issue will you argue on? Why is it important to you? What might you claim?
> 2. What reasons can support your claim?
> 3. What support will you use to prove your reasons? Specifically, what kinds of logical, ethical, and emotional appeals will you use with your audience?

4. What values and beliefs connect you to your audience? Explain how you will build on this connection during your argument.
5. Describe the rebuttals you'll bring to your argument. How will you counter these differing views?
6. In addition to your claim, would other statements in your argument benefit from the addition of qualifiers? If yes, what are the statements, and what qualifiers will you use?
7. Bring to class an example of a Toulmin-based argument. Find this argument in an online or print newspaper or magazine.

Map a Toulmin-Based Argument

Below are outlines for two arguments that use the Toulmin system. Figure 8.2 on page 197 provides a visual reminder of the way Toulmin argument works. Note that the term *reasons* is given separate treatment and lies between *claim* and *support*.

COMMUNITY

School-Academic

Workplace

Family-Household

Neighborhood

Social-Cultural

Consumer

Concerned Citizen

TOPIC: Food Consumption

ISSUE: Traditional vs. Fair Trade Bananas

AUDIENCE: Church Social Action Group

CLAIM: Consumers should buy organic, fair trade bananas because of the high humanitarian and environmental cost of marketing traditional bananas.

Reasons

• Most workers on traditional banana plantations labor under unsafe conditions.
• Low wages prevent the majority of workers from improving their living conditions.
• The absence of child labor laws means that children, many of whom are more susceptible to dangerous pesticides than adults, are often made to work on these plantations.
• Workers who do manage to organize and strike for better conditions often are threatened with violence if they do not return to work.

- Many banana producers blatantly violate environmental laws.
- Local ecosystems can suffer due to the intensive use of pesticide and antifungal chemicals.

Support

- Logical support includes facts, figures, statistics, and commentary that describe the banana trade and conditions for workers, as well as definitions for the terms *organic bananas* and *fair trade practices*.
- Ethical support can include scholarly articles and research drawn from credible online and print sources that focus on conditions of banana production and marketing. It can also include personal examples that motivate readers to buy fair trade bananas.
- Emotional support can focus on your decision to switch to organic, fair trade bananas; descriptions of working conditions; and examples drawn from the experience of workers, families, and children associated with traditional banana production.

Warrant

The fair treatment of workers and good stewardship of the environment are important for the global economy.

Backing

Support for this warrant can include examples of the increasing number of importers that will buy bananas only from companies that guarantee worker rights and environmental standards. It can also include the commentary of economists who view fair trade as essential to the global economy.

Rebuttals

The following rebuttals will need to be countered.

- Major banana exporters argue that they comply with the "Social Accountability 8000" labor and human rights standard.
- Major exporters also claim 100 percent compliance with the Rainforest Alliance's "Banana Certification Program," designed to protect workers from excessive exposure to pesticides and to protect the environment from pollution and deforestation, among other requirements.

Qualifiers

Note that in the first reason, the qualifier *most* is used, and that in the second reason the phrase *the majority of* functions as a qualifier. The third reason includes the qualifiers *many* and *often*; the fourth reason also uses the qualifier *often*; and the final reason uses the qualifier *can*.

COMMUNITY
School-Academic
Workplace
Family-Household
Neighborhood
Social-Cultural
Consumer
Concerned Citizen

TOPIC: Relationships

ISSUE: Online Dating Sites and Advertising Practices

AUDIENCE: Members of My Writing Class

CLAIM: Some high-profile online dating companies use extreme and unfounded claims to attract clients.

Reasons

- Some companies, though they do not openly deny access to gays and lesbians, nevertheless deny options for people seeking same-sex matches.
- Other companies seem to require a religious preference and will not pursue matches for clients falling outside this invisible guideline.
- As a way to lure clients, a number of companies create false profiles representing potential matches; then, after the prospective client pays the joining fee, the enticing profiles disappear.

Support

- Logical support can include factual information from online dating companies, such as questionnaires, application materials, and promotional language and images; statistics drawn from scholarly articles; and surveys conducted by reliable sources and by you.
- Ethical support can include personal experience with online dating; the experience of others with online dating; the use of credible, agenda-free research on online dating companies; and proper documentation of your research, including quoting and paraphrasing.
- Emotional support can include brief, powerful anecdotes drawn from your experience with online dating; the testimony of others with regard to online dating; and examples drawn from your research that appeal to your audience's values and emotions.

Warrant

What I want to stress most is that no one should become a client of companies that discriminate.

Figure 8.2 The Toulmin model of argument

Backing

- Everyone deserves to be happy and find special love, regardless of faith, sexual orientation, or race.
- These companies need to reevaluate their policies and realize that today gay couples raise families and in most cases experience no ill will from their communities.

Rebuttals

- If these complaints about online dating companies are taken seriously, it can lead to overregulation of a successful industry, and this will damage profits.
- Many companies have successful histories matching their clients.

Qualifiers

Note the qualifiers used in the claim and reasons above. Do they make these statements more believable than if they were left out? Note also the absence of qualifiers in the warrant and backing. Are these statements acceptable as they are, or would they benefit from qualifying language?

PRACTICE **Map a Toulmin-Based Argument**

Map a Toulmin-based argument for each of the following five issues. Specifically, in response to each issue, draft a claim, two reasons that support this claim, two or three specific examples supporting each reason, and a warrant along with backing for the warrant. Then identify one or two rebuttals you might encounter.

1. The term *food dumping* refers to the practice of industrialized countries providing free food to developing countries. Some critics claim that this practice hurts rather than helps, because the injection of free product into local markets causes small farmers in developing countries to go out of business and thus fall further into poverty.

2. Promotions and higher pay at your job are based strictly on seniority. In your view, your job performance exceeds the performance of some coworkers with more seniority.

3. Because of increasing development in your community, air and water quality have declined. Laws are in place to monitor and respond to these declines, but local officials claim that hiring an adequate number of trained inspectors will raise local taxes.

4. Pharmaceutical companies defend targeting their research at markets that will generate profitable returns. Returns from drugs for Alzheimer's, male enhancement, and cancer, for example, allow research to continue. Some argue that pharmaceutical companies are without social conscience for neglecting the many devastating tropical diseases that affect poor people.

5. The prevailing attitude of many local school board members is that the history of slavery, especially as it concerns the treatment of the enslaved, is an inappropriate subject for public school students.

 tip 8a

Use Visualization with Toulmin-Based Argument
Visualize yourself as an attorney defending an unpopular client. Know that your case must be painstakingly researched, that you must answer the opposing attorney's claims, and that you must use varied appeals to sway the jury.

Student-Authored Toulmin-Based Argument

In the following example, a student is using a Toulmin-based approach to advocate for a school voucher system in his community. As a home-schooled student, the writer is intent on proving the advantages of an education apart from public schools. His audience includes members of his writing class, especially those who defend public schools and regard home-schooling as ideological and prescriptive. Strengths of this argument are the writer's application of the Toulmin approach, his effective research, and his inventiveness to offer and defend an original idea.

Ben Szany
ENG 112-04
Professor Phillips
March 18, 2013

Vouching for Our School System?

Our public school system is our country's biggest and most inefficient monopoly, yet it keeps demanding more and more money.—Phyllis Schlafly

A monopoly is defined as exclusive control of a product or service ("monopoly" Def. 1). Public schools may not possess *exclusive* control of education in Charlotte, but for low-income families there are no real alternatives. Private schools cost several thousand dollars a year per child. Home-schooling is very difficult to nearly impossible in single-parent households or in situations where both parents must work. The problem would be lessened if the public schools provided a good education. However, in 2011, only 72.2% of Charlotte-Mecklenberg high school students earned a diploma (Chesser par. 4). How can we give families more options for their children's education? By giving parents vouchers for education, we can create an opportunity for parents to send their children to the private school of their choice. The Charlotte Mecklenburg School system and local government must allocate vouchers—which can be exchanged at public schools, private schools, and home-schools—to parents.

In a school voucher system, the money follows the student. A month before school enrollment opens, families would receive a voucher for every school-aged child in their family. Each student could only redeem a voucher in his or her name. Vouchers could not be stockpiled, saved from year to year, or reused. When the time came to enroll in school, the student could redeem the voucher for a given amount of money at any qualified private school and receive a credit toward the cost of enrollment. At a public school, the cost of enrollment after a voucher would always be $0, just as the cost of enrollment in public school is currently $0. If used toward a private school, the voucher's value would vary based upon income of the family. Poorer families or children with disabilities would receive vouchers worth more than vouchers for children of the middle or upper classes. This would make private school significantly more affordable for lower-income families. For those parents who home-school, the vouchers would have a value dependent upon the income of the family. Home-schooling families would turn in the vouchers when filing their taxes; the money would be given in the form of a tax refund. The amount would be worth 15% of the voucher's value at a private school. If the voucher was worth $1,600 because of the family's income level, they would receive $240 if they home-schooled. This money could be spent on school books, supplies, computers, or other educational items.

All families, regardless of income, can benefit from a school voucher program. Lower-income parents gain access to a wider range of educational

Although the title does suggest the subject of the argument, opening with a question often is not effective. An assertive title, one that hints at a writer's claim, is a good strategy.

The quotation orients the reader as to what will follow and sets a decisive emotional tone.

A qualifier, such as *some* or *many*, in front of *parents* would make the writer's assertion more believable.

The final two sentences of the first paragraph are the writer's warrant and claim. The warrant is grounded in values of "opportunity" and "choice."

The paragraph opens with a reason that directly supports the writer's claim.

options. Often these parents are forced to leave their children in failing or low-performing schools. As Harvard University Professor Paul E. Peterson explains, "I would say the results on parent satisfaction are overwhelmingly conclusive. If parents are given a choice, they're very happy. They're much happier with their private schools" ("The Case for Vouchers"). A school voucher program would greatly aid these parents, who are desperate to give their children the educational opportunity to succeed. Wealthier families' tax dollars would continue to fund the public school system as they do now, and they too would receive educational savings from the vouchers if they choose to enroll their children in private schools or home-school, although these savings would be modest at best. Thus, the vouchers do not ignore the needs of the poor nor do they swindle the wealthy; they are fair to both.

This clearly worded reason links directly to the writer's claim and announces the purpose of the paragraph.

Making private schools and home-schools more affordable offers another advantage to parents; it forces the public school system to become more competitive. Currently in Charlotte, the public schools have something of a monopoly, especially regarding the education of children from lower-income families. By providing the opportunity for these parents to more easily remove their children from the public school system, we level the educational playing field. The Charlotte Mecklenburg school system will have no alternative but to improve performance in schools that consistently score below average. If they do not, children will leave the failing schools in favor of local private schools. This has already happened in Milwaukee, a voucher-using city that is comparable to Charlotte in both population and ethnic diversity. After 11 years of the voucher program, a study conducted by Harvard's Caroline Hoxby showed increased scores from children who used the vouchers to enroll in private school *and* from the children in local public schools. Public school test results jumped by 8.1% in math, 13.8% in science, and 8% in language (Stossel 135–136). The number of private schools in Milwaukee had increased to meet the demand of parents who opted out of the public schools (Koch 15). "The public schools," wrote John Stossel, host of ABC's *20/20*, "didn't want to lose their students to voucher schools, so they tried harder. They did a better job" (136). There is no reason why a school voucher program in Charlotte would not provide a similar improvement in results.

In terms of its persuasiveness, this is the most effective paragraph in the argument—because the writer documents his idea about vouchers with factual information, which is vital to readers who are undecided about an issue.

The final sentence makes a dangerous guarantee, a problem that would be avoided by the use of a qualifying phrase to replace "There is no reason."

There is some concern that a school voucher program would greatly weaken Charlotte's public school system. Sandra Feldman, president of the American Federation of Teachers, stated, "[School vouchers mean]: Give up on public education in America; stop investing in it, siphon off as much funding as you can" (qtd. in Koch 5). A school voucher system would lessen the public school's monopoly on education, but it would not mean abandoning the public school system. The Charlotte Mecklenburg school system would still be expected to teach a majority of local students. Presently, public schools are responsible for the education of 90% of American children. With a universal school voucher program, that number is estimated to drop to 60 or 70% (Hood par 9). Despite this shift, Charlotte schools would be able to spend more money per pupil than without a voucher system. How is this possible?

This opposing view and the opposing view in the next paragraph need fuller treatment so that (1) readers understand what drives Feldman's comment and (2) so that the writer demonstrates a willingness to work with the opposition fairly.

In Milwaukee, the average cost per voucher is $4,894 (Koch 11). That figure is several thousand dollars less than the $7,155 that Charlotte schools spend per pupil (Roberts 29). In other words, if the Charlotte school system would spend $7,155 to educate a child for one year, and that child instead uses a $4,894 voucher to go to a private school, the public school system nets $2,261 per voucher, which can then be spent on other students. "What's more," said Virginia Governor Tim Kaine, "for every few hundred students who accept vouchers, the district saves itself the expense—tens of millions of dollars—of building a new school to accommodate rising enrollment" (Hinkle par 9). It isn't just theory. In 2001, Scott Greenberger, a staff writer at the *Boston Globe*, wrote that, "In Milwaukee, which has the nation's oldest and largest voucher program, even voucher opponents now acknowledge that no public school has been decimated by a loss of money or pupils. Furthermore, many public school principals and teachers here say the voucher program has pushed them to improve" (par 7). A school voucher program would not signal abandonment of the public school system but a desire within the community to improve the educational system as a whole.

Opponents of a Charlotte Mecklenburg school voucher system claim that such a program would be unconstitutional because many private schools have religious affiliations. Elliot Mincberg, of People for the American Way, argues, "Voucher programs that include sectarian schools grossly violate the constitutional separation of church and state" (qtd. in Koch 16). However, children are not ever required to use the voucher at a religious private school. Only their parents can decide where they go to school. In other words, if a parent does not want their child in a religiously oriented setting, there is nothing that can force their child into such a school. The decision is entirely up to the family. It must also be noted that public funds often support students in religious schools. Students receiving federal grants are free to attend sectarian universities such as Brigham Young University (Mormon) or Notre Dame (Roman Catholic) (Koch 9). Federal child care funds can be used by parents to send their toddlers to religiously affiliated day care centers. Finally, the Wisconsin Supreme Court ruled that Milwaukee's school voucher program was well within the bounds of both the state constitution and the U.S. Constitution (Koch 7). A voucher system that permits enrollment in religious schools does not violate the rights of any citizen, and the decision to send a student to such a school can only be made by that student's parents.

The Charlotte Mecklenburg school system holds a monopoly on education in Mecklenburg County. Breaking this stranglehold with a school voucher program would give parents more educational options and force the public and private schools to compete. This healthy competition would provide a better and more fruitful learning experience to students currently stuck in the public school system.

This conclusion can be stronger. Ideas in the writer's claim and warrant are repeated, but some attention here and earlier in the argument is needed to address why this competition would be "better and more fruitful" for students. Backing for the writer's warrant would be effective.

Works Cited

Chesser, John. "The Highs and Lows of High School Graduation Rates." *UNC Charlotte Urban Institute*. 24 Aug. 2011. 17 Mar. 2013. Web.

Greenberger, Scott S. "Voucher Lessons Learned." *Boston Globe*. (2001). *NewsBank*. 8 Mar. 2013. Web.

Hinkle, A. Barton. "The Governor Makes a Pretty Good Case for School Vouchers." *Richmond Times—Dispatch*. (2006). *NewsBank*. 15 Mar. 2013. Web.

Hood, John. (2007). "Spend a Lot to Teach a Little." *The (NC) Laurinburg Exchange*. *NewsBank*. 16 Mar. 2013. Web.

Koch, Kathy. "School Vouchers." *CQ Researcher* 9.13 (1999): 281-304. *CQ Researcher Online*. *CQ Press*. 16 Mar. 2013. Web.

"monopoly." *Dictionary.com Unabridged (v 1.1)*. Random House, Inc. 16 Mar. 2013. Web.

"The Case for Vouchers." *Frontline*. PBS. UNC-TV, Research Triangle Park, 23 May 2000. Television.

Roberts, Cheryl and McCracken, Lee. *Charlotte's Education System: Measuring Up?* (2004). Charlottechamber.com. 8 Mar. 2013. Web.

Stossel, John. *Myths, Lies, and Downright Stupidity: Get Out the Shovel— Why Everything You Know Is Wrong*. New York: Hyperion, 2006. Print.

Reflect and Apply

Answer the following questions as a way to review the purpose of a Toulmin-based argument.

1. Based on the argument you're presently building, why is or isn't a Toulmin-based argument appropriate to your purpose?

2. Map a Toulmin-based argument based on an issue you're struggling with in daily life. Where would you place the rebuttal and how would you respond to it?

3. Stephen Toulmin believed that argument should have a practical function and that an effective argument could be modeled, in part, on sound courtroom practice. Given a Toulmin-based argument you intend to build and with a courtroom setting in mind, how will you balance the support you bring to your argument; that is, will you balance evenly logical, ethical, and emotional support, or will you emphasize some kinds of support more than others? Explain.

KEEPING IT LOCAL

THE COMPELLING NARRATIVE that begins this chapter responds to a local and personal issue with a Toulmin-based argument. It is the kind of argument the writers consider most practical when they want to prove the rightness of their position and when they want action taken in response to their claim. The student bringing this issue to the table is motivated by deep concern for his siblings, by his parents' efforts to create opportunities for their children, and by others in his community who happen to be children of illegal immigrants. Had this writer elected not to respond to the state's recommendation to bar children of illegal immigrants from attending community colleges, then the public debate over this issue would be missing the informed position of a stakeholder in this important controversy. When we fail to speak up on an issue that matters to us, we let others make decisions for us, and this means that our position on an issue may be left out of the conversation. And because the writers want immediate action taken on this issue, they aimed their argument at the State Board of Community Colleges, an audience in a position to act. They are careful to identify values they and board members share and then build their arguments based on these values. Toulmin-based argument gives these writers, and us, a way to respond to important personal issues. This kind of argument and the kinds of argument discussed in Chapter 9, "Consider Middle Ground Argument, Rogerian Argument, and Argument Based on a Microhistory," are created using practical skills that can be deployed before audiences we want to influence and inform. Learn these skills and you'll be in a position to represent yourself with integrity and with a sense for what is practical on issues that matter to you.

● - - - - - - - - - - - - ●

As you work through your argument, consider the following questions: At what audience will you aim your Toulmin-based argument? How did you narrow to this audience?

A common complaint about arguments is that they're too theoretical and not practical enough. What, exactly, will make your Toulmin-based argument practical?

Consider Middle Ground Argument, Rogerian Argument, and Argument Based on a Microhistory

A couple of your coworkers were recently detained by police for remaining in the lobby of the local utility offices after being told to leave. After a good conversation with your coworkers, you understand the issue and why they were willing to be arrested. You learn that your local utility is actually a monopoly across the state and that it recently announced plans to ask a state regulatory agency for permission to request regular rate hikes. You also learn that the utility is stuck on a model of generating nearly all its electricity from coal, nuclear, and natural gas, and that this means continued dirty air, economic risk, and hydraulic fracturing. You were vaguely aware of these issues in the past, but you now view them as threats to the local quality of life. Further research informs you that the utility is backing a law that would effectively reduce the opportunities for public comment on proposed rate hikes and that it wants ratepayers to finance construction of new nuclear plants— whether or not these plants reach completion.

You decide that the state Utilities Commission is the most practical audience for your argument because it is the organization with the power to regulate the powerful utility. More specifically, the commission can approve, reject, or call for modifications on the utility's policies and activities. This choice of audience seems practical because the Utilities Commission is charged with being on the look-out for any economic hardship that the utility might cause citizens of your state. The stated values of the Utilities Commission must overlap considerably with the values of ratepayers like you who may suffer from rate hikes and other utilities-related issues.

COMMUNITY

School-Academic

Workplace

Family-Household

Neighborhood

Social-Cultural

Consumer

Concerned Citizen

TOPIC: Utility Company's Proposed Rate Hikes and Other Potential Dangers

ISSUE: Regulation of utility company

AUDIENCE: State Utilities Commission

CLAIM: The Utilities Commission should announce a moratorium on requests from the utilities for rate hikes and changes to public hearing requirements.

The chapter introduces you to three approaches to argument: Middle Ground, Rogerian, and Argument Based on a Microhistory.

Each of these approaches is uniquely different from Toulmin-Based Argument, the focus of Chapter 8, "Consider Toulmin-Based Argument." Collectively, the four kinds of argument provide you with options when you approach a given issue.

To distinguish in a general way among these approaches, it can be helpful to think about audience. In a Toulmin-based approach, the idea is to persuade an audience of the rightness of your position by using convincing support and effective handling of the opposition, much like the arguments created by competent trial attorneys. A middle-ground approach allows you to offer an audience a reasonable middle position between two relatively extreme positions. A Rogerian approach challenges the arguer to demonstrate common ground among sharply divergent positions on an issue; Rev. Martin Luther King, Jr. takes up this challenge in "Letter From Birmingham Jail" (excerpted in sections that follow). Finally, an Argument Based on a Microhistory lets you step into the shoes of a historian as you work with primary sources: in this kind of argument, you are making sense of the past in a new way, one that can let an audience view a particular event, for example, from different perspectives. Let the approach you choose to work with complement your goals with your audience.

In this chapter, you will be introduced to three approaches to argument:

- Middle Ground Argument
- Rogerian Argument
- Argument Based on a Microhistory

Middle Ground Argument

A **middle ground argument** argues a moderate, practical claim between two extreme positions (see Figure 9.2, p. 212). Middle ground arguments often are used with political, business, religious, and even personal issues and can provide a practical position when two sides of an issue are far apart. When aimed at an appropriate target audience, the middle-ground approach offers a practical, more moderate alternative to two more extreme positions. When an audience is uncertain, unaware, undecided, or silent on an issue, arguing for a practical middle position—or what you *perceive* to be a middle position—can be an effective strategy.

Make a Middle-Ground Position Practical

Importantly, a middle-position approach is used when you believe your solution to be between two extreme positions, but you still must *prove* that your middle-ground position is practical. Do this by discussing why the other positions are extreme and by providing your audience with persuasive reasons and support for your position. As with a Toulmin approach, you will include a claim, reasons, support, warrant, backing, and qualifiers. But compared with the Toulmin approach, middle ground argument requires much more attention to the opposition, or the two extreme positions you argue against. In Toulmin argument, attention to the opposition is called "rebuttals."

A sensible approach to middle ground arguing is first to introduce an issue and explain why a middle position is appropriate at this time. This introduction can then be followed by substantial and accurate summaries of each extreme position, with

© Kablonk/SuperStock

Figure 9.1 Middle Ground argument means arguing for a position between two extreme positions. This photo reveals a thoughtful third party who may be ready to argue for a more practical solution to an issue.

special emphasis on what makes each position impractical. These summaries first should be accurate and objective; second, each summary must be followed by your evaluation of each position, in which you identify the shortcomings of each view. The remainder of your argument should prove why your position is more practical than the two positions you have identified as extreme. In contrast with the Toulmin structure, you will devote up to half of your argument to the opposition before you get to your own position. (See Chapter 6, "Work Fairly with the Opposition," for tips on presenting the opposition fairly.)

your turn 9a ▸ PRACTICE **Recognize When a Middle-Ground Approach Is Practical**

Respond to the following questions as a way to begin thinking about how a middle-ground approach can offer practical choices on tough local and global issues.

1. Identify three issues—a personal issue, a community issue, and a global issue—that are polarizing or that set two clear positions against one another. For each issue, describe the two positions.
2. Focusing on one of these issues, does each group seem extreme or impractical in its position? Why?
3. What middle-ground position can you offer? Why would your position be more practical than either of the other positions?

Recognize Where Middle Ground Arguments Are Possible

Consider the following three issues, the two extreme positions for each, and then the claims that argue for middle-ground solutions. With each issue, the two extreme positions are far apart; this can open the door to a more practical middle position.

Issue #1: "Brain drain" of health care workers from poor to rich countries

- Extreme Position A: Doctors and nurses from poor countries have the right to pursue opportunities in rich countries.
- Extreme Position B: Doctors and nurses from poor countries have an obligation to serve people from their home countries.
- Middle-Ground Position: Groups such as Human Rights Watch should recommend that doctors and nurses from poor countries serve people in their native countries for a minimum five-year period.

Issue #2: Flying the Confederate flag in our community's public cemeteries

- Extreme Position A: The Confederate flag should be flown daily as a way to honor our ancestors who died during the Civil War.
- Extreme Position B: The Confederate flag should not be flown at all because it symbolizes a way of life that kept many of our ancestors oppressed.
- Middle-Ground Position: The Confederate flag should be flown on national holidays only.

Issue #3: Reducing carbon emissions in our state

- Extreme Position A: The best way to reduce carbon emissions in our state is to make a complete switch to alternative fuels in the next 10 years.
- Extreme Position B: Because laws are now in place to protect our air and water quality, we simply need to hire more inspectors and regulators.
- Middle-Ground Position: The governor needs to appoint a committee that allows consumers to work with public policy experts and energy companies in order to create a realistic plan to lower carbon emissions.

Let's say that the arguer targets students in her nursing classes as an audience for the "brain drain" issue. For the Confederate flag issue, the arguer aims at readers of the local newspaper. And for the carbon emissions issue, the governor is the target audience. Because there are strong views on all of these issues, it will be vital that arguers offer middle-ground positions that appear reasonable and well thought out. But remember that the audience might not agree with the arguer's opinion that the middle position offers a compromise or that it presents the middle ground between two extreme positions. Your best chance at having your middle position accepted is to know what your audience values and then craft appropriate appeals based on these values. Because writers of middle-ground positions regard other positions as extreme, they will need to specify why the extreme positions are less practical than the proposed middle position. Furthermore, while the writer's middle-ground position differs from the other positions, the writer must nevertheless respect the differing views and acknowledge points of overlap. It may be that underneath the differences all groups want a similar outcome, but the methods each extreme position advocates are less practical than your approach. In general, you will need to earn credibility from your audience by appearing fair-minded in your summaries and critical in your evaluations. Use Your Turn 9c as a guide to setting up middle ground arguments.

Map a Middle Ground Argument

An outline for a middle ground argument addressing the contentious issue of extra credit work and whether it should be allowed in college classes appears in the following section. To many students and teachers, extra credit is an important issue because it touches one's sense of fairness. In fact, the following positions, labeled "extreme" by many, may not seem extreme to readers of the college newspaper, the writer's intended audience. If the middle-ground position is to be convincing, it surely must acknowledge—and, when possible, honor—the range of school newspaper readers and their values. This will be challenging work for this writer because research demonstrates that most students favor the chance at extra credit work, especially when their grades are low or some of their required work is missing. The support this writer uses with his reasons must be compelling and reveal the practicality of his position.

EXTREME POSITION #1:	No! It's unethical.
CLAIM:	Extra credit work rewards students for being irresponsible; therefore, it is unethical.

Reasons

- Extra credit work rewards students for failing to learn course content, as reflected in poor exam scores.
- Final course grades should reflect performance only and not be based on extra credit work.
- Extra credit usually is not available in the real world, especially in the workplace.
- Extra credit opportunities are unfair to responsible students.

EXTREME POSITION #2:	Yes! It's practical.
CLAIM:	With so much pressure on students to complete a college degree and transition into the workplace these days, teachers should allow extra credit opportunities.

Reasons

- Extra credit gives students a second chance.
- Denying extra credit can be a roadblock to success.
- Demands of family and job get in the way of preparing for class.
- Extra credit rewards effort.

MIDDLE-GROUND POSITION:	Yes, extra credit work should be allowed, but only when it leads to deeper knowledge of the content area.
CLAIM:	Extra credit should be allowed for students who want to pursue a question or problem that falls outside requirements of a course but within the content area.

Reasons

- Extra credit assignments can be designed to create deeper familiarity with course content.
- Extra credit is one way to encourage research and critical-thinking skills.
- This kind of extra credit is a way to reward genuine effort beyond what is expected.
- Establishing and maintaining a single standard for extra credit work is one way to keep grading policies consistent and without exception.

COMMUNITY

School-Academic

Workplace

Family-Household

Neighborhood

Social-Cultural

Consumer

Concerned Citizen

TOPIC: Grading Policies

ISSUE: Extra Credit

AUDIENCE: Readers of School Newspaper

CLAIM: Extra credit should be allowed for students who want to pursue a question or problem that falls outside requirements of a course but within the content area.

Based on the middle-ground position this writer will defend, Position #1 is considered extreme because it shuts the door on the possible benefits of extra credit work. It makes a dangerous assumption that extra credit work encourages irresponsible behavior. It does not allow for the chance that some students may want to pursue deeper work with a topic. It ignores the conditions for extra credit that some teachers set, such as limits on how extra credit can affect a final grade or that all required coursework must be completed before extra credit assignments can be pursued. This position also assumes that students seeking extra credit did not put forth effort in a class. Finally, it neglects to consider circumstances such as illness and family duties, which can get in the way of a student's preparation for exams and assignments.

Position #2 assumes that students need second chances in order to succeed. The argument assumes that teachers—not students or the circumstances of students' lives—can be roadblocks to student success. Implicit in the reasons for this claim is the attitude that students are naturally under duress and unable to keep up with requirements of their courses.

With these extreme positions summarized for the audience, the writer must now aggressively support his claim and prove that his middle position is more practical. The writer is a teacher who has struggled during his career with the idea of extra credit. For the past five years, he has settled on the position defended below. Claim and reasons were noted in the previous section under "Middle-Ground Position."

Support

Support will be drawn primarily from the writer's experience with extra credit work over a 20-year teaching career. References to published scholarly research addressing extra credit in the college classroom also will be included.

Warrant

Providing opportunities for students to pursue a problem or topic connected to course content rewards intellectual curiosity.

Backing

- Intellectual curiosity is important because it complements critical-thinking skills, a core competency at our college.
- Intellectual curiosity is important because it respects a student's interest in a course and the questions that follow from this interest.

Qualifiers

The claim does not make extra credit work available to all students under unspecified conditions; instead, it limits extra credit work to students who want the chance to pursue a question or topic not covered in class. Reason number one includes the qualifier *can*; reason number two includes the qualifier *one way* (as opposed to *the only way*); reason number three includes the qualifier *a way*, and reason four includes the qualifier *one way*.

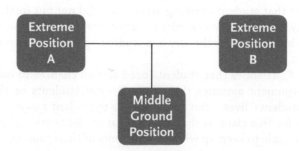

Figure 9.2 The middle ground model

your turn 9b **PRACTICE Middle-Ground Thinking**

Based on the following descriptions of six different issues, along with the two extreme positions noted for each, write a claim for each issue that offers a middle position. Below each claim you offer, list two or three reasons that support your claim.

1. Executive compensation—salaries and bonuses paid to executives in American companies—has come under fire recently. Some argue that a top executive in a company should not be allowed to earn more than 25 times what the lowest paid employee in the company earns. Others believe that attractive compensation packages are needed to attract top talent and should not be regulated.

2. Plagiarism occurs in our schools and colleges at alarming rates. One possible response is to institute a campus-wide honor code that mandates a single standard: expulsion. Another view claims that a more practical approach would be for writing classes to provide more comprehensive attention to the issue of plagiarism and how to avoid it.

3. Undocumented workers in the United States are the subject of a long-standing debate. The center of this debate is whether or not penalties should be levied on employers hiring undocumented workers. Several political action groups have formed to protest the hiring of undocumented workers, arguing that these jobs should belong to American workers and that penalties should be levied on employers. Another side claims that most American workers don't want these low-paying jobs and that employers are left with little choice other than to hire undocumented workers.

4. *Digital divide* is a term that refers to the gap between people who have access to the Internet and people who do not. Some people believe that Americans whose annual income falls below the poverty line should be given inexpensive laptops and access to the Internet. Others hold that the this provision is unnecessary because Internet technology has become available to almost everyone through schools, libraries, and a range of social programs.

5. The local newspaper's recent series of stories on poultry processing plants revealed horrific worker conditions that have resulted in many chronic injuries. Some concerned parties advocate for union representation for workers; others argue that laws are already in place to protect workers and that hiring more inspectors to enforce these laws is the solution.

6. Tipping in local restaurants, a concern for servers whose income depends on tips, generates two extreme positions: first, that a mandatory 15 percent tip should be noted on restaurant menus; or second, that tipping should be at the discretion of customers, who presumably base the tip amount on the professionalism of the server.

tip 9a

Identify Local Models of Middle-Ground Positions

In many ways, we are trained to look to leaders beyond our immediate communities for practical solutions to pressing issues. But this need not be our first line of inquiry. Identify practical middle-ground positions offered to address local issues. These solutions might be offered by friends, fellow students, coworkers, or family; they might also be found in the local newspaper, on your favorite blogs, or on social networking sites. What makes the middle-ground positions more practical than the extreme positions?

your turn 9c ▸ GET STARTED **Set Up a Middle Ground Argument**

Answer the following questions to set up a middle ground argument.

1. Identify the issue you plan to address and describe the specific context you bring to your argument. How far back in time will you need to go to reveal the roots of this issue? What are these roots?
2. Why, exactly, is this issue deserving of our attention now? What specific present conditions make this issue important?
3. What does each extreme position claim? What is the history of each group with regard to this issue? Why is each group so deeply invested in its position?
4. How does each group justify its position? What is the warrant for each group's claim? What support does each group use?
5. What values and beliefs do you share with each group?
6. What are the limitations and potential damages you see with each position?
7. What is your claim on this issue? Why is it more practical than other positions?
8. What reasons will you use to support your claim? What major examples, statistics, and personal experiences will you use as part of your support?
9. What does your audience have to gain by accepting your position? How will the community benefit?

Student-Authored Middle Ground Argument

Illegal immigrants, mostly Hispanics, are employed extensively in the community in the construction, landscaping, and food and beverage industries. The writer of the following argument is responding to the issue of whether illegal immigrants should be eligible for driver's licenses. This issue has been a matter of public concern for several years and is reported on regularly by local media. The writer perceives the need for a more practical approach, so she has chosen to write a middle ground argument, one that (in her view) offers a practical middle position between two positions that the author considers extreme. The writer's purpose is to generate awareness of the importance of driving privileges for illegal immigrants in the community. Her audience is her writing class, most of whom are U.S. citizens. The first paragraph introduces the issue, the next two paragraphs present the two extreme positions, and the fourth paragraph presents the writer's claim. The remaining paragraphs, not included here, support the claim with reasons and plenty of support. Also not shown here is the Works Cited.

Linda Gonzalez

English 112

Professor Phillips

19 November 2013

Driving to a Reasonable Solution

Millions of illegal immigrants live in the United States. Most of them drive to work every day without a driver's license. Before 9/11, illegal immigrants in North Carolina could get a driver's license if they presented a foreign legal document to the Department of Motor Vehicles (DMV). Some of the documents accepted at the time were passports, birth certificates, voting cards, and driver's licenses from applicants' countries of origin. Then, the DMV stopped accepting foreign documents and asked for a document issued by the US Government. Originally the W-7 form was among the US-issued documents that could be used to obtain driver's licenses. The W-7 form, used in order to apply for an Individual Taxpayer Identification Number, used to be provided to people regardless of their migratory status by the Internal Revenue Service. According to DMV commissioner George Tatum, 25,957 undocumented people applied for a W-7 in 2004, fewer than the 41,977 applicants in 2003 (Funk and Whitacre 2). Today, Maryland is one of the states that still issues driver's licenses without asking applicants to prove their migratory status. Some state authorities want to adopt a plan to issue driver's licenses to undocumented immigrants while others are totally against it.

Those in favor of providing driver's licenses to illegal immigrants think the roads would be safer because driver's licenses would bring people out of the shadows and allow them to obtain insurance. The proponents of this solution would issue driver's licenses that distinguish illegal immigrants from U.S. citizens by noting the driver's migratory status. This driver's license would be strictly for driving purposes (i.e., it would not allow the holder to board airplanes or enter federal buildings). John Madden, a New York planning consultant, supports the plan and says, "Most illegal immigrants drive without driver's licenses anyway. You might as well make them legal drivers" (qtd. in Crawley 2). In every U.S. State, one must pass a written test and a driving test in order to get a driver's license. Because illegal immigrants would need to read the driver's handbook in order to pass these tests, allowing illegal immigrants to get driver's licenses would make them more aware of the rules of the road and thus make them safer drivers. Immigrants also would be able to get insurance at the same rates as other drivers. According to New York's State Department of Insurance, expanded license access would reduce the premium cost associated with uninsured motorist coverage by 34%, which would save New York drivers $120 million each year (Crawley 3). Additionally, people would get out of the shadows. Jack Schuler, a reverend of Our Lady of Guadalupe Catholic Church in Cool Valley, California, says, "It is a matter of accepting that illegal immigrants are here; it is a reality, and they are an integral part of the state" (Johnson 1). He claims that not only do these people exist, but that they are simply trying to make a living and that others cannot pretend they do not exist. What they fail to see is that illegal immigrants would not want to have a driver's license showing their immigration status. They fear being deported; therefore, many would prefer to remain without a license than risk police finding out that they are in the country illegally.

Another point of view is held passionately by opponents of giving driver's licenses to illegal immigrants. They argue that driving is a privilege, not a right. For instance, Republican Sue Myrick of Charlotte, North Carolina, says, "Our feeling is that driver's license is a privilege for citizens and legal aliens, and it shouldn't be something given to somebody who broke the law" (qtd. in Funk and Whitacre 2). Backers of Myrick agree, claiming that issuing driver's licenses to undocumented people would attract more illegal immigrants and make it easier for terrorists to come into the United States. Considering driving as a privilege, many politicians are completely against a plan that would allow illegal immigrants to obtain driver's licenses. They believe that because people who have entered the country illegally have broken the immigration laws, they should not be allowed to receive any kind of benefits in this country. Moreover, driver's licenses allow people to work, drive, and open bank accounts, thus making life in this country much easier for undocumented people. According to Johnson, "One legitimate kind of ID leads to more, leads to more, leads to more, and pretty soon, they've got an entire identity established" (2). Johnson adds that having a legal document can give others the impression that a person has citizenship. Additionally, the government is seeking stricter means to keep the nation safe from terrorists; one effective way to do so is to deny driver's licenses to illegal aliens, thus preventing them from entering federal buildings, boarding airplanes, and using the licenses as identification to give the impression of being in the country legally. Most readers will consider it relevant that 8 of the 19 men in the terrorist attacks on September 11 got licenses in Virginia after presenting a simple notarized form saying they were state residents (Johnson 2 par 11). Another example of illegal immigrants threatening the nation's safety is that there are drug dealers and criminals looking for easy ways to get licenses. "Driver's licenses are as close as we get to a national ID," says John Keely of the Center for Immigration Studies, a group in Washington that advocates limited immigration. "While the overwhelming majority of immigrants don't pose a national security threat, I don't think issuing driver's licenses to them affords protection to Americans, but hurts the efforts to shore up national security" (Johnson 3). Authorities against the plan to provide driver's licenses for illegal immigrants do not take into consideration that undocumented people are not going to go away just because they do not have driver's licenses and that they will drive with or without licenses. Certainly, the arguments in favor of and against issuing driver's licenses to illegal immigrants are so strong that it is difficult to imagine an alternative position.

However, there is another position, one held just as passionately by its proponents as those just described. I agree with many people who think that driver's licenses should be given to illegal immigrants. If that cannot be accomplished, then at least licenses already obtained by people without legal status who have no major traffic violations should be renewable. Individuals who hold this point of view say that issuing driver's licenses to illegal immigrants would help the police do their job better. In addition, they believe allowing immigrants to get driver's licenses would help the economy because then this population will be paying taxes; in addition, this plan would lower the use of false documents.

Rogerian Argument

Rogerian argument is a way to establish **common ground** between a position you hold and positions that one or more other parties hold on an issue. It is a kind of argument built on fair, compassionate presentation of differing views, and it highlights the strengths of each, along with points of overlap with your view.

Listen Closely to the Opposition

Rogerian argument is centered in good listening and in close, respectful consideration of points of view different from your own. It is an argument strategy adapted from the work of psychologist Carl Rogers, who was interested in factors that help or hinder good communication. He theorized that good communication requires that each position on an issue is fully acknowledged—without judgment. Rogers believed that a careful, empathic listener can clarify differing positions and create space for productive interaction. This approach to an issue asks that a writer listen and respond with charity in order to create common ground based on shared values and a shared sense of purpose. Rogers believed that, although on the surface of a contentious issue the sides may seem far apart, on a deeper level warring sides may in fact

Figure 9.3 Taking in fully another view and then presenting it fairly is at the center of the Rogerian approach.

Bruce Ayres/Stone/Getty Images

share some values and beliefs. However, before such commonalities can be identified, we must first take the time to cool our emotions and really listen to each other.

For example, when Martin Luther King, Jr. reaches out to white clergymen in his famous "Letter from Birmingham Jail," he refers to his audience—the same clergymen who helped put him in jail—as "men of genuine good will," and as "Christian and Jewish brothers." In addition, throughout the letter he emphasizes their common faith and adherence to religious principles. In this letter, King responds to a moment of intense racial and political separation by studying with compassion the values of his opposition, who vigorously oppose the nonviolent demonstrations supported by King and the Southern Christian Leadership Conference. He identifies a desire on both sides for negotiation, but he also embraces the need for a "constructive, nonviolent tension which is necessary for growth."

Over the years, many students have claimed that Rogerian argument is a practical approach to controversial issues, especially in the workplace and in local politics where compromise is essential. They reason that when things need to move forward—for example, a company's projects, production, and sales; decisions affecting local schools; help for the increasing number of homeless people; crime prevention in the community—it becomes essential to listen closely to individuals deeply invested in their positions. While resolution of every issue cannot be guaranteed, many businesses practice Rogerian methods, simply because when a positive dialogue is created production and efficiency improve. Dispute-resolution programs used by large community organizations, such as local post offices and city governments, value Rogerian strategy because it emphasizes listening and mutual respect, allowing disputing parties to better understand each other. And when understanding and respect are built, better communication often follows.

Writers of a Rogerian argument are similar to mediators, people who facilitate settlements among two or more disputing parties. In a closed mediation, a mediator often asks each party to restate the other party's position; in this way a sense of understanding and trust can begin to develop. Sometimes a resolution of the issue can result; almost always, parties understand each other better. Your job as a writer is to adapt this process of close listening to a written argument as you respectfully and accurately present positions that differ from yours. Usually during the second half of a Rogerian argument the writer steps out of the mediator role and brings in his or her claim and support for an issue, creating common ground with other views.

Rogerian strategy replaces rebuttal of opposing views with efforts to understand them. Because the foundation of Rogerian argument is an accurate, bias-free description of an opposing view, make sure you restate accurately for readers other positions on issues you address. Strategies for fairly negotiating with the opposition are discussed in Chapter 6, "Work Fairly with the Opposition."

In brief, Rogerian argument requires the arguer to see an issue from other points of view, emphasizing points of overlap, or common ground, among differing positions. (See Figure 9.4 for a representation of Rogerian argument.) A successful Rogerian argument allows your audience to judge for itself whether or not your claim is practical. And along the way you do much to earn credibility with an audience through your compassionate and accurate restatement of opposing views.

Identify Common Ground

The following two issues recently were addressed successfully with a Rogerian approach. Note the common ground that each writer creates.

Issue #1: Living at home while attending college

This writer fully acknowledges her parents' position that, because she has completed high school, living at home is no longer an option. Her parents content that they can no longer afford for her to live at home, that they plan to downsize to a smaller home, and that she should take on the responsibility of paying for things herself. The writer honors her parents' position by describing it fairly and without judgment. She offers these reasons for wanting to remain at home: she will be able to devote more time to her courses and earn her degree sooner, she won't have to work a second and possibly third job to cover costs of living on her own, and she will be there to help with chores around the house. But before delivering her reasons, the writer first creates common ground with her parents by identifying certain shared values and beliefs tied to this issue. For example, both parties value the importance of a college degree, professional competence, financial independence, and the ability to provide for one's family.

In this example, the writer's audience (her parents) is also her opposition. To earn credibility with this audience, the writer completes the two essential steps in Rogerian writing: she describes without bias her opponent's position and locates common ground. Rogerian strategy is more about reaching into opponents' camps and representing their views fairly; it is less about achieving a desired outcome. Rogerian argument extends the olive branch of peace and fair play.

Issue #2: Homelessness in the community

With the recent downturn in the economy, the number of homeless people in the community—including children who attend local public schools—is increasing. Area shelters provide beds for less than 25 percent of the homeless population, and it is uncertain when new shelters will be available. At a recent county commission meeting, a coalition of local organizations working with homeless people rolled out a 10-year plan to end homelessness in the area. The plan was unanimously approved by commissioners, but more than a year later, no funding has been approved. Last week your teacher invited the volunteer coordinator from the city's largest shelter, along with an expert on affordable housing, to speak to your class, motivating you to act. You want to argue that funding the 10-year plan is the community's best hope for addressing the homelessness crisis. Based on what you learned during the presentations, you know that your opposition is not a single individual or a single group but an attitude that is held by many local citizens who would rather not deal with the issue because it is uncomfortable and without a clear solution. Additionally, many people in this silent majority believe that homeless people do not make the same kind of effort as those who work hard to pay for their homes and that the homeless are gaming a system that will allow them to get by without assuming the responsibilities of citizenship.

You choose as your audience members of your communications class, and you plan to deliver your argument as a speech due in this class in a few weeks. You choose a Rogerian approach because you know that if the 10-year plan has any chance of being funded those on opposite sides of this issue must begin listening to each other. You identify and honor values of citizenship that you share with those reluctant to fund the plan: making positive contributions to the community, paying taxes, sustaining employment, and renting or owning a home. These points of overlap become clear when you converse with your opposition. You are now in a position to build on the common ground you have created by paying close attention to another perspective on homelessness. Because you have established this common ground and validated your opposition, you can argue your claim without rebutting.

Furthermore, you now have a chance to provide some education on the issue of homelessness. You recognize that many citizens opposed to funding the 10-year plan may not have a clear sense of the causes of homelessness, such as mental illness, physical disability, job loss, natural disasters, divorce or break up, and a full range of unforeseen events that throw an individual off balance. By listening closely to your opposition, you have earned the chance to deliver your argument on homelessness. Whether your claim is accepted is another matter, but you have put your best foot forward by building your argument on a foundation of shared values and beliefs.

The issues discussed above—one personal and the other local and national—involve parties that at first are far apart and aggressive defending their positions. Toulmin-based arguments might produce rhetorical victories, but a Toulmin approach would miss the common ground of the disputing parties. Similarly, a middle-ground approach would miss chances to work with shared values and instead emphasize the failures of the opposition on these important issues. Rogerian argument, however, can bring sides closer together. Its aim is to identify values that the disputing parties share. In turn, these shared values can make clear for all sides a common ground, where strategies for resolving issues can be discussed openly and without fear of judgment.

> **your turn** 9d ➤ **PRACTICE Rogerian Thinking**
>
> For each of the following issues, provide your claim and one or two claims made by differing points of view; then identify common ground. Plan to research issues with which you are not familiar.
>
> 1. Campaign finance reform in your state: This movement seeks to limit the amount of monetary contributions that can be made by individuals and groups to the campaigns of political candidates.
> 2. Affordable housing and homelessness: The term *affordable housing* refers to housing that does not exceed 30 percent of the household or family income. The term is often used in the discussion of homelessness in the United States.
> 3. Stem cell research focuses on scientists' ability to reproduce cells from living organisms. Some argue that this kind of research has important medical and reproductive benefits for humans; others feel it unfairly manipulates human life and that it can be used for cloning.
> 4. Course evaluation and instructor performance surveys are common in U.S. colleges. They are often used as a performance measure during an instructor's annual review.

Map a Rogerian Argument

The earlier examples about living at home and homelessness, both rooted locally, suggest ways to build arguments based on Rogerian strategy. The key to the success of this kind of argument is your ability to understand and honor differing views. The following section presents a fuller treatment of another local issue, this one related to the workplace. The writer is frustrated with a pay scale based on seniority; her supervisor is the audience for her argument.

Supervisor's View

CLAIM: Increases in salary should remain tied to the seniority system.

Reasons

- The seniority system has been in place for many years and has been proven to help with employee morale.
- A clear standard for pay raises supports consistency and prevents favoritism.
- Our company values employee loyalty and years of service, and the seniority system is a way to reward employees who share these values.
- Many of our senior employees are hard working and productive.

SUPPORT:	Because the supervisor has been at the company for many years, she can attest that few complaints have been filed with regard to the seniority system, loyal and productive employees, or the company owners' commitment to fair treatment.
WARRANT:	The seniority system is effective because it maintains an ethical standard that employees are aware of from the beginning of their employment.

Backing

- Consistency and fair play are important in the workplace.
- A predictable reward system can mean fewer complaints from employees and greater worker satisfaction.

Writer's View

COMMUNITY
School-Academic
Workplace
Family-Household
Neighborhood
Social-Cultural
Consumer
Concerned Citizen

TOPIC: Compensation
ISSUE: Pay Scale and Seniority
AUDIENCE: Supervisor
CLAIM: Our company should award salary increases based on production and efficiency.

Reasons

- Efficient, productive employees can generate more profit for this company.
- Regular effort and productivity should be rewarded with regular salary increases.
- Pay raises based on productivity can elevate morale and foster loyalty to the company.

SUPPORT:	Much of this writer's support should be drawn from her experience as a productive, hard-working employee. Examples can reveal her contributions to company expectations and beyond. Additionally, research drawn from professional and academic journals can reinforce her pay-based-on-productivity request. Personal

	examples can also speak to the writer's ability to maintain good work habits while pursuing her college degree.
WARRANT:	Ethical standards should be maintained in the workplace.

Backing

- Consistency and fair play are important in the workplace.
- A fair, predictable reward system can lead to increased worker satisfaction.

COMMON GROUND:	Listening closely to her supervisor, the writer is able to pin down common values and goals. They include shared concerns for employee morale, avoidance of favoritism, company loyalty, and hard work and productivity. In the summary of her supervisor's position, the writer can validate these concerns and then build on them as she delivers her argument. Often, common ground among disputing parties is established at the level of the warrant, and this should be clear in the mapping of this argument. Ethical standards, consistency, a sense of fair play, and predictable rewards are common values the writer shares with her supervisor.

Note that the writer avoids at every turn rebutting her supervisor. From her experience with this company, it likely would be easy to rebut with plenty of specific examples. But she has chosen a Rogerian approach to this sticky problem, and this means making her best effort to demonstrate that she understands and honors her supervisor's reasons and values. In practical terms, a Toulmin-based approach might have produced a solid argument, but it could have left the writer out in the cold in terms of getting her supervisor to acknowledge her position on salary increases. When your audience is your

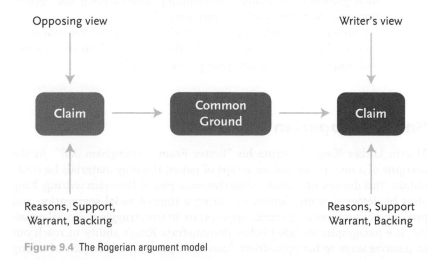

Figure 9.4 The Rogerian argument model

☛ tip 9b

**Acknowledge
and Validate the
Opposition**

Put yourself in the frame
of mind to build a Rogerian
argument by recalling a time
in your life when others put
you first and listened closely
and without judgment to your
opinion on a given issue.
What might have motivated
these individuals? What
might motivate you to behave
this way with an opponent?

opposition, as is frequently the case in Rogerian writing, make the effort to dignify the other view, honor its strengths, and point out shared values; this can indicate that you are less interested in dueling and more interested in a serious, mutually respectful conversation.

your turn 9e ➤ GET STARTED **A Rogerian Argument**

In introducing an issue, what historical context will you provide? What specific information will you use to orient readers to the issue? Answers to these and the following questions will help you start your Rogerian approach.

1. When sides are far apart, a Rogerian approach often works best. Are you working with an issue that is sufficiently controversial to generate distinctly different sides? Explain.

2. What is the claim, what is the warrant, and what are the main reasons for each view on this issue? What beliefs and values do each of the parties hold?

3. What measures will you take to avoid judging or rebutting your opposition? How will you establish and maintain a neutral, objective, fair-minded attitude toward each opposing view and those who hold it?

4. Would each party with a stake in this issue be comfortable with how you present its position? Explain.

5. How will you maintain a neutral tone toward other parties? Explain how your tone calms rather than ignites emotions.

6. What is your claim? Describe your warrant. What are the main reasons and kinds of support you bring to your position?

7. What specific values and beliefs do you share with each party? What values does your audience hold regarding this issue? Establish common ground by describing overlapping values among the opposition, your audience, and your own view.

8. Is your audience likely to accept your claim based both on your accurate, fair-minded presentation of other views and on the reasons and support you build into your position? Explain.

Sample Rogerian Argument

Martin Luther King, Jr. wrote his "Letter From Birmingham Jail" in the margins of a newspaper and on scraps of paper, the only materials he could obtain. This document contains effective examples of Rogerian writing. King aims his letter at white clergymen during a time of racial segregation and profound differences over tactics appropriate in the struggle for racial equality. The paragraphs included below demonstrate King's ability to reach out in positive ways to his opposition. These few paragraphs are part of a long letter to the very clergy who recommended his incarceration: remember that a Rogerian approach is often practical when opposing parties are deeply divided. Note below how the writer finds common ground and uses it to both respect his opposition and deliver his ideas.

PARAGRAPHS FROM "LETTER FROM BIRMINGHAM JAIL"

By Martin Luther King, Jr.

MY DEAR FELLOW CLERGYMEN:

[Paragraph #1] While confined here in the Birmingham City Jail, I came across your recent statement calling my present activities "unwise and untimely." Seldom do I pause to answer criticism of my work and ideas. If I sought to answer all the criticisms that cross my desk, my secretaries would have little time for anything other than such correspondence in the course of the day, and I would have no time for constructive work. But since I feel that you are men of genuine goodwill and that your criticisms are sincerely set forth, I want to try to answer your statements in what I hope will be patient and reasonable terms.

[Paragraph #3] But more basically, I am in Birmingham because injustice is here. Just as the prophets of the eighth century B.C. left their villages and carried their "thus saith the Lord" far beyond the boundaries of their home towns, and just as the Apostle Paul left his village of Tarsus and carried the gospel of Jesus Christ to the far corners of the Greco-Roman world, so am I compelled to carry the gospel of freedom far beyond my own hometown. Like Paul, I must constantly respond to the Macedonian call for aid.

[From Paragraph #31] But though I was initially disappointed at being categorized as an extremist, as I continued to think about the matter I gradually gained a measure of satisfaction from the label. Was not Jesus an extremist for love: "Love your enemies, bless them that curse you, do good to them that hate you, and pray for them which despitefully use you, and persecute you." Was not Amos an extremist for justice: "Let justice roll down like waters and righteousness like an ever-flowing stream." Was not Paul an extremist for the Christian gospel: "I bear in my body the marks of the Lord Jesus." Was not Martin Luther an extremist: "Here I stand; I cannot do otherwise, so help me God." And John Bunyan: "I will stay in jail to the end of my days before I make a butchery of my conscience." And Abraham Lincoln: "This nation cannot survive half slave and half free." And Thomas Jefferson: "We hold these truths to be self-evident, that all men are created equal . . ." So the question is not whether we will be extremists, but what kind of extremists we will be. Will we be extremists for hate or for love? Will we be extremists for the preservation of injustice or for the extension of justice? In that dramatic scene on Calvary's hill three men were crucified. We must never forget that all three were crucified for the same crime—the crime of extremism. Two were extremists for immorality, and thus fell below their environment. The other, Jesus Christ, was an extremist for love, truth and goodness, and thereby rose above his environment. Perhaps the South, the nation and the world are in dire need of creative extremists.

[Final paragraph] I hope this letter finds you strong in the faith. I also hope that circumstances will soon make it possible for me to meet each of you, not as an integrationist or a civil rights leader but as a fellow clergyman and a Christian brother. Let us all hope that the dark clouds of racial prejudice will soon pass away and the deep fog of misunderstanding will be lifted from our fear-drenched communities, and in some not too distant tomorrow the radiant stars of love and brotherhood will shine over our great nation with all their scintillating beauty.

Argument Based on a Microhistory

An argument based on a **microhistory** allows you to comment on a particular part of our past, especially if what you have to say differs from the conventional understanding of a person, event, or place you are studying.

Focus on the Local and Specific

Microhistory is a relatively recent approach in the field of history. Traditionally, history sought to record the accomplishments of a few individuals in positions of power, sometimes called "the history of great men." Or traditional history was focused on military and political histories of a country or culture. Social histories focus on emerging social movements and what caused these movements, and they can include economic, legal, and labor histories. Common to these traditional approaches to history is the attention they give large social and political institutions, group behavior, and, in general, central and mainstream features of a society.

In contrast, a microhistory narrows the scope, focusing on:

- A person, a certain event, or a particular place.
- The margins or fringes of a certain culture or society, the ordinary people and events that typically are considered unimportant and that often are left out of larger histories.
- Precise, or "thick," description of the everyday details of an individual's life, a place, or an event.
- Primary documents and materials created by or connected to an individual, an event, or a place.
- Connecting the microhistory to the larger culture as a way to reveal trends, forces, pressures, and expectations acting on an individual or place.
- Filling gaps created by broadly focused histories so as to acknowledge and honor common people *and* to reveal the effects of economic and political forces on the common people.

Building this kind of argument requires that you work as a historian and then use the microhistory that you prepare in order to deliver an argument. Writing an argument based on a microhistory means that you will:

- Introduce to your audience the subject of your microhistory and the light you hope to shed on its significance.
- Explain your interest in your subject and the questions you hope to answer by compiling your microhistory.
- Provide extensive context for the individual, event, or place you will study. This means accessing as much primary source material as you can—court and public records, diaries and journals, letters and correspondence, articles and information drawn from local newspapers, newsletters, special-interest publications, maps, and in general any materials that clarify the daily realities of your subject.
- Draw conclusions for your audience that reveal how a close study of the individual, place, or event reveals something about the larger culture. This will mean background reading in secondary documents to get a sense of what the culture values and how its rules and regulations affected the lives of everyday people.
- Deliver at or near the end of your argument a claim based on your microhistory.
- Give voice to the questions and uncertainties that remain for you at the end of your argument.

Make Room for Local Histories

Delivering an argument based on a microhistory can be a powerful experience for a writer. It is a chance to collect and analyze primary historical material and then argue a claim based on that analysis. The ideas you bring to the conclusion of your argument as you make sense of the historical information can bring to light some of the challenges everyday people weathered during an earlier time, challenges that often are missing in broader histories. Your research and the conclusions you draw can add to our "public memory" of a certain time and place, and this is no small contribution.

But what role can argument play in a microhistory? Based on the primary materials you're working with and the sense you make of them, you are in a position to make a claim that argues against the generally accepted understanding of a particular time and place in history. For example, if you choose to dig into that box of letters your great-grandmother wrote three generations ago, you may find information that contradicts our general notion of women's roles during your great-grandmother's time. Suppose you learn that your great-grandmother was active in civic life, spoke up at town meetings, and wanted women to be allowed to enter the fields of law, medicine, and finance. You learn that in some letters she wrote to a friend about religion and spirituality, marriage, and food and diet. At the end of your work with these primary documents, you know that your great-grandmother's life differs from our culture's general understanding of women's civic and intellectual lives during your great-grandmother's time. Based on your work with the letters, you are in a position to make a claim that argues against the limited understanding of women's lives three generations ago.

Two additional examples might help clarify the value of forging an argument based on a microhistory. Recently, a student and passionate baseball fan crafted a compelling argument focused on the integration of Major League Baseball in 1947. Mainstream history represents this event as a victory in American race relations, with much of the credit going to an executive with the Brooklyn Dodgers, the team that penciled Jackie Robinson into its starting lineup. The student moved outside this perspective by reading the columns of an African American sportswriter for the black-owned *The People's Voice*, a weekly newspaper published from 1942 to 1947. In these columns, the student uncovered a new perspective, one that told a very different history than the formerly accepted "history." The sportswriter revealed that integrating Major League Baseball was not completely positive: as a result of the integration, the Negro Leagues were dead a few years later, leaving the players and employees for these teams out of work. Having studied this primary material, the student was motivated to claim that integrating Major League Baseball in 1947 was a partial victory only. He supported his claim with evidence from the sportswriter's columns. The opposing point of view in this argument is the more general and common history of baseball's integration.

The second example involves a writer's work with a historical monument erected in 1929 next to what is now a college campus. The monument commemorates a reunion of Civil War veterans and reads as follows:

> GLORIA VICTIS
> IN COMMEMORATION OF THE 39TH ANNUAL REUNION OF THE UNITED CONFEDERATE VETERANS AT CHARLOTTE, NORTH CAROLINA, JUNE 4–7, 1929.
> A STATE AND CITY'S TRIBUTE OF LOVE; IN GRATEFUL RECOGNITION OF THE SERVICES OF THE CONFEDERATE SOLDIERS WHOSE HEROISM IN WAR AND FIDELITY IN PEACE HAVE NEVER BEEEN SURPASSED.
> ACCEPTING THE ARBITRAMENT OF WAR, THEY PRESERVED THE ANGLO-SAXON CIVILIZATION OF THE SOUTH AND BECAME MASTER BUILDERS IN A RE-UNITED COUNTRY.
> VERITAS VINCIT

Language on the monument motivated the student to research events associated with the reunion—a large parade, social activities, reports and editorials in the local newspaper, and so forth—and it motivated the student to understand how ideas grounded in racial inequality could be memorialized. Interestingly, in her research, this writer also learned much about African American political life in the community in 1929, and this information allowed her to think about the monument in much broader terms. She argued that the marker must be contextualized to include differing ideas in the community regarding notions of "civilization" and a "reunited country." Specifically, editorials in the community's black newspaper and references to sermons delivered by African American ministers provided a much different history for the monument, one not grounded in "tribute" and "love."

Work with Primary Materials

A first step in preparing a microhistory is locating **primary materials.** Local and college libraries often hold special collections and archived material. This material can include letters, various other kinds of correspondence, court and legal records, diaries, journals, bills of sale, and business records. Local museums, churches, and historical societies are also depositories for this kind of primary material. Communities always keep records of their past in one way or another, and sometimes this information is kept by families and individuals. It may be that members of your immediate or extended family are keeping such records and that some of those records may inspire you to prepare a microhistory and offer a claim based on what you learn. Think of yourself as an archaeologist uncovering neglected artifacts at the site of a dig. Your job is to describe and make sense of your findings.

There are many excellent, book-length microhistories. All are built on very specific information that reveals more complete pictures of a culture. Subjects of microhistories have been far ranging and include people, products, places, and facts that fall outside the scope of mainstream history: the natural ice industry in nineteenth-century North America; the final Civil War

Hank Frentz/Shutterstock.com

Figure 9.5 Primary documents, like this collection of old photographs, and their interpretation are the center of arguments based on a microhistory. The ways in which these documents argue against common and more general treatments of a historical period can reveal the complexity of our past and steer us away from damaging stereotypes.

battle at Gettysburg in 1863; cadavers; the cockroach; and products including Spam, sugar, coffee, coal, and cotton. Sometimes microhistories consider community institutions whose histories have been overlooked, such as local businesses, social service organizations, hospitals, schools, and government-related agencies. Of course a microhistory that you prepare for an assignment will be shorter than book length, but the narrative you piece together and the conclusions you draw can be just as compelling as longer projects.

Subjects and Materials for Microhistories

Subjects practical for arguments based on microhistories can include but are not limited to the following.

Individuals

- A family member or relative
- A member of your community whose life experience is not part of public knowledge
- A local employee, official, coach, clergy, teacher, neighbor, or police officer
- Any other person, living or dead

Events

- An event that affected your family, such as a marriage, a divorce, a hiring or firing, a birth or death, a dispute, or a relocation
- An event in your community, such as a business closing and the resulting loss of jobs, a celebration, a battle, or a natural disaster

Places

- Neighborhood
- Natural area
- Home
- Factory, warehouse, place of employment
- School
- Church
- Government building

Sources

Primary materials to consider when preparing a microhistory can include:

- Letters
- Journals
- Diaries
- Family histories
- Business records

- Court documents
- Legal documents
- Photographs
- Church records
- Newspapers and newsletters
- Sermons
- City and community histories
- Oral histories

Map an Argument Based on a Microhistory

Following is an outline for an argument based on a microhistory. Note that the structure of this kind of argument differs from Toulmin-based, middle ground, and Rogerian arguments.

COMMUNITY
School-Academic
Workplace
Family-Household
Neighborhood
Social-Cultural
Consumer
Concerned Citizen

TOPIC: Justice

ISSUE: Murder of a Female Slave

AUDIENCE: Members of Writing Class

CLAIM: Evidence like this court transcript suggests that in some areas of the slave South justice was applied across the color line.

Support

- Primary documents: Transcript of 1839 Iredell County, North Carolina Superior Court decision. The transcript recounts the trial of a slaveholder who, with "malice aforethought," murdered his female slave. The transcript is lengthy and full of details about owner–slave relations.
- Secondary documents: Scholarly books and articles about justice regarding slaveholders and slaves.

What the Microhistory Reveals about the Culture

The court records document the court's decision to execute the white slaveholder for murdering his slave. This decision in many ways reveals that some communities delivered justice when and where it was due, regardless of color and status.

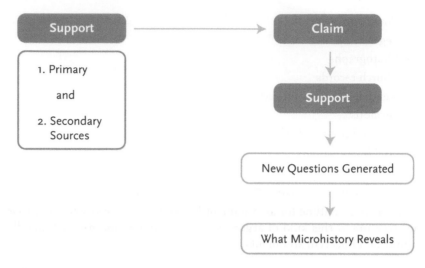

Figure 9.6 The Microhistory model

Claim

Evidence like this court transcript suggests that in some areas of the slave South justice was applied across the color line.

New Questions Generated from the Microhistory

Based on work with these primary documents, findings can move readers away from thinking about justice in the slave South in common and stereo-typical ways. New questions might focus on how justice was carried out in a particular community or on a particular plantation, how this kind of information can be incorporated into public school curricula, and what factors from the local culture influenced this court decision.

 tip 9c

Think of Microhistory as Archaeological Work

Writing a microhistory means working outside the mainstream. Your work will involve digging into mostly unrecognized corners of our past and bringing to light a person, place, or event. Your job is to uncover, dust off, and interpret the primary materials you identify and review.

your turn 9f ▸ GET STARTED Set Up an Argument Based on a Microhistory

1. What is the subject of your microhistory? What motivates you to study this subject?
2. What do you hope to learn from this project?
3. What primary source materials will you use as you prepare your microhistory? Where will you find these materials?
4. What secondary sources will you use to establish cultural context, or background, for your subject?
5. What does the larger culture's history seem to value about the time period you are examining? For example, were there acceptable and unacceptable kinds of behavior and attitudes during this time, and does your microhistory contradict these ideas?

6. What does your subject reveal about the culture? For example, if your subject is an individual, how does he or she fit into or not fit into the norms and expectations of the culture? If your subject is an event or place, what does it tell you about how the larger culture functions, about behavior the larger culture approves or disapproves of, about behavior the larger culture encourages or discourages?

7. Based on this close study of your subject and its time period, do you now think differently about this period? Explain.

8. Based on your microhistory, what will you claim?

9. What additional questions do you have about your subject and the time period of your microhistory?

10. How can your argument based on a microhistory make us think more realistically about the period, individual, event, or place that it addresses?

The questions in Your Turn 9f are challenging, and because you have made a careful study of your primary documents, you can answer them in order to prepare a sound argument. While the other approaches to argument that are discussed in this chapter—MIDDLE GROUND and Rogerian—devote much attention to support for the claim, an argument based on a microhistory requires that you devote most of your project to support. Bring your claim in at or near the end of an argument based on microhistory, after you establish credibility with readers based on your work with primary source material. A warrant and backing are addressed when you discuss how your subject reveals something new about the culture and what we can learn from your subject today.

The microhistory you prepare will be original and unique to you. While this project likely will be submitted as a class assignment, the work you do and the insights you generate will help fill gaps in our culture's collective memory and widen the window to our past. Furthermore, because your subject in all probability has been left out of conventional histories, you bring in from the margins of a culture an additional perspective that can help us better understand our past and our present.

Sample Argument Based on a Microhistory

In the following microhistory, what this New York City writer considers is the integration of Major League Baseball. The writer's primary material is an extensive archive of columns written by area sportswriters. The writer's claim, appearing in the argument's conclusion, is that while Jackie Robinson and Branch Rickey should be honored as the player and executive who broke the barricades preventing Black ballplayers from entering the Major Leagues, the real heroes of this civil rights victory are the sportswriters because they did the hard work of building support for integration over many years. The idea for the microhistory originated in columns found in family scrapbooks. The writer then accessed research libraries, including the Schomburg Center for Research in Black Culture, which houses many columns written during the run-up to April 15, 1947, the date when Jackie Robinson was penciled into the starting lineup of the Brooklyn Dodgers. The writer's careful research allows him to argue against our limited public memory of this seminal historical event; that is, the research allows the writer to focus attention on the heroic work of these sportswriters, figures all but lost in our overly generalized understanding of Major League Baseball's integration. The first paragraph introduces the writer's project, and the other paragraphs focus on primary materials.

Baseball, Integration, And Militant Rhetoric:
The Pioneering Work Of New York City Sportswriters

Jackie Robinson and Branch Rickey are American heroes, and everybody who knows even a little about baseball respects them. They are heroes because they had the courage to cross the color line and integrate our national game. They should always be heroes. But if we want to really understand why Black ballplayers were finally allowed to compete alongside whites, it is essential that we honor the work of sportswriters who fought over many years to convince readers of the moral rightness of integrating the game.

As a nation, we focus our eyes on April 15, 1947, the day when Robinson started at first base for the Brooklyn Dodgers. A 2013 movie, *42*, was made and many books have been written about this day and about Robinson's career, about the regular taunting from opposing players and hostile fans and about his incredible determination and strength to keep going. I probably would have walked away and hoped to take some of my dignity with me.

Making all this possible were mostly Black sportswriters like Joe Bostic, Dan Burley, and Romeo Daugherty, who toiled for Black-owned dailies and weeklies. Perhaps the greatest praise should be heaped on a white sportswriter, Lester Rodney, who began campaigning for integration of baseball in 1936 as sports editor for the *Daily Worker*, the newspaper of the Communist Party. If we want to know about the difficult work of creating social change, we must study the historical columns of these brave sportswriters.

Joe Bostic was sports editor from 1942 to 1945 for the militant *The People's Voice*, a Black-owned newspaper published in Harlem. Bostic often called out the white baseball establishment for its racist practices. He also questioned the presumed superiority of white players and whether or not integration would mean a step up for Black players. In a July 11, 1942 column, he writes, "We're not convinced that the baseball played in the organized leagues necessarily represents the best caliber of ball played per se, and therefore, the Negro players would not be moving into faster company than that in which they were already playing" (Reisler 85). One has to wonder how Bostic flipping the "superiority" mindset might have influenced readers. Bostic also knew that while integration might be a social victory, it would also be a financial defeat for the Negro Leagues, a predominately Black-owned industry.

In what some view as the most aggressive challenge to Major League Baseball's segregationist policy, Bostic arranged a tryout at the Dodgers' spring training camp in April of 1945 for two Negro League players, Terris McDuffie and Showboat Thomas. Bostic appeared at the camp uninvited and knew that he'd cause trouble. He was challenging Dodgers' President Branch Rickey to make practical his contention that he favored integrating the game. Rickey was furious and never spoke to Bostic again. The players were not signed. Bostic wrote about the tryout, embarrassed Rickey, and added a few more soldiers to the march against segregation.

After reading all of Bostic's baseball columns, I am convinced that he should be in the Baseball Hall of Fame for his efforts. Mostly I see him as a man ahead of his time. He knew that the game would be integrated, especially after Commissioner Landis died, but he wanted the world to know that the Negro Leagues were successful in their own right and that Black players were unlikely to find "faster company" in white leagues. He also exposed Branch Rickey, a powerhouse in the baseball establishment, for wanting to integrate the game on his terms only. For me, Bostic's militancy distinguished the Negro Leagues and, ultimately, contributed to the work of integrating the game.

Lester Rodney is not exactly a household name, but it should be. Rodney was sports editor for the *Daily Worker* from 1936 to 1958 and spent much of his first decade with the paper working aggressively to promote the integration of baseball. Rodney believed that a Communist critique of a capitalist system could occur on sports pages as well as anywhere, and that these pages were good places to appeal to workers. Rodney was different from most Communist Party hard-liners in that he believed that workers' passion for their teams was genuine and not something manufactured by the system. On a personal level, Rodney describes his drive for integration this way: "I was in it because I wanted the damn ban to end, to bring elementary democracy to the game I loved and to see the banned players get their chance to show they belonged" (qtd. in Tygiel x). Rodney's many columns on the issue spurred the *Daily Worker* to conduct petition drives in which more than one million people signed in support of the integration of baseball. Rodney and writers at some Black papers regularly shared information in a concerted drive to build momentum.

Rodney did not hold back in his criticism of American racism. Of April 15, 1947, he writes: "It's hard this Opening Day to write straight baseball and not stop to mention the wonderful fact of Jackie Robinson. You tell yourself it shouldn't be especially wonderful in America, no more wonderful for instance than Negro soldiers being with us on the way overseas through submarine infested waters in 1943" (qtd. in Silber 98).

Sometimes Rodney's columns issued challenges. For example, in an interview Rodney recalls a conversation he had with the great Negro Leagues pitcher Satchel Paige in 1937 in which Paige had suggested that the winner of that year's Major League World Series play an all-star team of Negro League players:

So I say to him, "What makes you so sure you'll win?" And he replies, "We've been playing teams of major league all-stars after the regular season in California for four years and they haven't beaten me yet. . . . Must be just a few men who don't want us to play Big League ball. The players are okay and the crowds are with us. Just let them take a vote of the fans whether they want us in the game. I've been all over the country and I know it would be one hundred to one in favor of such a game (qtd. in Silber 62).

Like Joe Bostic, Rodney used various strategies to push the integration movement forward. He is a hero, more than deserving of a prominent place in our public history.

Works Cited

Bostic, Joe. "In Re Negroes in Big Leagues." *Black Writers, Black Baseball: An Anthology of Articles from Black Sportswriters Who Covered the Negro Leagues.* Ed. Jim Reisler. Jefferson: McFarland, 2007. 84–86. Print.

Silber, Irwin. *Press Box Red: The Story of Lester Rodney, the Communist Who Helped Break the Color Line in American Sports.* Philadelphia: Temple UP, 2003. Print.

Reflect and Apply

Answer the following questions as a way to determine the kind of argument practical to your purpose.

1. Identify a few issues in your personal or public life that seem especially appropriate for middle-ground approaches. If you were to argue on these issues, how would you reconcile their extreme positions with more practical claims?

2. How does the approach to the opposition in Rogerian argument differ from the approach to the opposition in Toulmin-based argument? Reflecting on issues in your life as a student, worker, consumer, and concerned citizen, explain why some issues are appropriate for a Rogerian approach.

3. Regarding your family or your community, what part of history do you want to know more about? Why? What primary documents available to you could lead you into a deeper understanding of an earlier time period?

KEEPING IT LOCAL

THE NARRATIVE that opens this chapter—a writer's burgeoning awareness of how a big utility impacts citizens' daily lives and the writer's task of crafting a Middle Ground argument in response—provides a strong lesson in audience awareness. Because the writer aimed at the state Utilities Commission, and not the utility, the general public, or elected officials, the writer could emphasize the commission's dual role to both protect ratepayers and ensure that the utility brings in sufficient profit to continue operating. Had the writer aimed the argument at the utility, then a Toulmin-based approach would have been appropriate because of the writer's concern for ratepayers. Or, had the writer aimed the argument at the Chamber of Commerce, a group representing the interests of local businesses, then a Rogerian approach may have been practical because of business owners' sensitivity to the utility as a business not only providing an essential service but also vulnerable to economic risk. In a middle-ground approach, the writer identified the two extreme positions as (1) the utility's request for regular rate hikes in the midst of a tough economic cycle, and (2) some ratepayers' demands that the utility reduce rates and cross over to renewable energy sources in the next few years. The writer's claim: "The Utilities Commission should rule that yearly rate hikes are unacceptable and mandate an energy portfolio standard that includes increasing percentages of renewable energy sources."

It's important, always, to decide early in your writing process whom you want to influence and inform on an issue. Knowing what an audience values—profit, public service, or both—makes it easier to choose the best approach to your argument. Your choice of approach begins with a sense of your local community: who holds the reins of power, who looks out for everyday people, and where openings for change can be found.

● – – – – – – – – – – – – – ●

When our opinions on an issue differ with others' opinions, we tend to think in "I'm right, and you're wrong" terms. In many ways, that is how we have been trained to think. In everyday life you have choices about your thought process in situations where you differ with others on an issue that's important to you. How will you remind yourself that these choices exist?

Now identify the single most difficult issue in your life, the one you'd most like to avoid. Now that you have learned four ways to approach an issue, which approach to argument would you choose for this tough issue? What would you claim?

CHAPTER 10

Build Arguments

The current assignment in your argument class asks you to argue on an issue that affects the local environment. Your teacher advises the class that extensive research will be essential to forge a persuasive argument because environmental issues are usually evaluated in terms of the factual evidence supplied by each side. A brief conversation with your neighbor, who opposes the construction of a nearby coal-burning plant, compels you to do some preliminary research, and the issue motivates you to argue a position. The two sides are clear: for and against. Each side supports its position with scientific studies, personal testimony, and a lot of economic data and projections.

To date, opponents of the plant have been unsuccessful in their efforts to halt construction, even though protests and public hearings have received substantial media coverage. On the other side, the private utility provider building the plant argues that jobs created by the new plant are essential to the local economy and that improved technology will limit emissions of coal dust into the air.

With the plant's construction already underway, you decide that your argument must generate local awareness of the health risks the plant poses to your community. With its extensive circulation, the local newspaper seems to be a practical place to present your argument, especially because twice a week, the paper provides space for editorials that address local issues.

All Illustrations by iStockphoto.com/A-digit

COMMUNITY

School-Academic

Workplace

Family-Household

Neighborhood

Social-Cultural

Consumer

Concerned Citizen

TOPIC: Air Quality

ISSUE: Construction of Local Coal-Burning Facility

AUDIENCE: Readers of Local Newspaper

CLAIM: Concerned citizens in our community should be aware that completion of a coal-burning plant will create health risks for the next 50 years.

A powerful local issue like this one calls for a practical response. When an argument contains a clear center that an audience recognizes as thoughtful, direct, and fully supported, it presents such a response. In Chapters 8, "Consider Toulmin-Based Argument," and 9, "Consider Middle Ground Argument, Rogerian Argument, and Argument Based on a Microhistory," you learned about kinds of argument, that is, approaches to an issue that can serve your purpose. But any of the four kinds of argument treated in these chapters require some or all of the following parts: claim, reasons, support, qualifier, warrant, backing, and reservations. This chapter teaches you how to use each of these parts to build your argument and in this way fleshes out the four kinds of argument discussed in Chapters 8 and 9.

At this point, it may be helpful to think about a complete argument as having two major parts. (See Figure 10.1.) Part one is built around a claim, its support, and the qualifiers that make your argument realistic. Part two is built around a warrant, backing, and reservations, elements that justify your claim. With both parts of an argument, pay close attention to your audience and let your argumentative strategies appeal both to your audience's values and to your audience's reservations.

In this chapter you will learn how to:

- Understand the function of a claim.
- Choose the kind of claim appropriate to your purpose.
- Recognize the function of reasons.
- Use qualifiers to make your claim believable.
- Use your knowledge of your audience to build a warrant.
- Use backing to support a warrant.
- Address audience reservations to make your warrant believable.

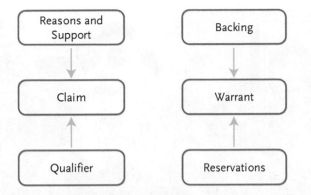

Figure 10.1 The two major parts of a complete argument

How a Claim Functions

The following sections explain why a claim must be the center of an argument. It is the single statement that your readers, including your teacher, refer back to in order to stay focused on your purpose and position in an argument. Unlike a thesis that explains, summarizes, or confesses, a claim is a type of thesis that argues. It identifies an issue, takes a position, and addresses those who hold differing views.

Claim: The Center of Your Argument

A **claim** is the center of an argument and is a kind of thesis. It is your position on an issue, the idea or belief that motivates you to argue. From the perspective of you, the arguer, a claim answers the following questions:

- Where do I stand on this issue?
- What point of view do I want my audience to accept at the end of my argument?
- What is my purpose in delivering this argument?

A claim is also a position you are prepared to defend with reasons and support. The effectiveness of a claim always depends on your ability to convince an audience of its truthfulness. A claim is the single statement that members of your audience, including your teacher, regularly revisit in order to confirm that you remain focused on your claim.

An audience may agree with a claim, it may agree in part with a claim, or it may be skeptical of a claim and require substantial convincing. In all cases, careful study of your audience will put you in a position to craft a claim practical to your purpose. As you begin building an argument, it will be helpful to review the Chapter 2 section titled "Define and Target Your Audience" (page 32) regarding the importance of aiming an argument at an appropriate audience.

Figure 10.2 In this photo a New York University student is addressing the media during a student-led protest. The setting and her expression reveal three elements of a successful claim: the arguer knows where she stands on the issue at hand, she knows what she wants her audience to accept, and her purpose is clear.

From the perspective of an audience, a claim should answer these questions:

☐ Where does the arguer stand on this issue?
☐ What is the arguer trying to prove?
☐ What are we being asked to accept or consider?

A claim is often most effective when placed at the beginning of an argument, in your introduction or in an early paragraph. But depending on your purpose, sometimes a claim is effective at or near the end of an argument, especially when it is important for you to first fully inform an audience about an issue. Consider the issue below and how the writer builds a focused, clearly worded claim that is aimed at a specific audience.

COMMUNITY

School-Academic
Workplace
Family-Household
Neighborhood
Social-Cultural
Consumer
Concerned Citizen

TOPIC: Discrimination in the Health Care Field

ISSUE: Promotion Practices

AUDIENCE: Director of Hospital Services

CLAIM: Competent, qualified nurses of color in our hospital are often passed over for better-paying positions.

In response to this issue of promotion practices at a local hospital, the arguer has chosen a claim of fact (defined in Table 10.1) as the center of her argument. She makes clear her position, or what she wants her audience to accept, and implies that she wants her claim acknowledged as objective fact in the hospital where she works. In terms of audience, the arguer makes it clear where she stands, and she implies that she intends to prove that this kind of discrimination exists. Then she must sway her audience using convincing support. The arguer plans to target the individual who oversees promotions and disputes as the audience. The arguer's purpose is to make this person aware of her claim of fact. Later arguments on this issue may require different kinds of claims, such as a claim of cause or a problem-based claim, especially if the arguer intends to argue for something to change. This claim is strong because it is direct and because it targets an appropriate audience.

Connect Claim with Purpose

Choose a claim based on what you want to accomplish with an audience. If your aim is to rally an audience to action based on your solution to a current problem, then a problem-based claim would be appropriate. When you determine that confusing or ambiguous language characterizes an issue, you can isolate a key term or word and offer a precise meaning in a claim of definition. If you are motivated to argue an issue on moral grounds, choose a claim of evaluation in which you can center your argument in the particular moral principle in question. When you prove that something is factual that is not regarded as factual by everyone in your audience, a claim of fact forms the foundation of the argument. And when you are compelled to reveal the history of an issue and thus to connect the past with the present, a claim of cause can be effective. Use Table 10.1 to determine the kind of claim that best fits your goals with your audience.

All three kinds of support—logical, ethical, and emotional—can be used effectively in any type of argument. The category "Primary Support," in Table 10.1, identifies the *essential* support required in each kind of claim.

> **your turn 10a** ▶ **GET STARTED Determine Your Purpose before Writing a Claim**
>
> Answer the following questions to determine the kind of claim that fits your purpose in an argument. Use Table 10.1 as a guide.
>
> 1. On what single issue are you motivated to argue?
> 2. What is the audience for your argument? Why, exactly, is this audience a practical target?
> 3. What do you want to accomplish with this argument?

Five Kinds of Claims

Practical arguments require clearly worded claims directed at specific audiences. When your goals with your audience are clear, choose the kind of claim that matches your purpose. Kinds of claims are discussed in the following sections.

Table 10.1 Finding an Appropriate Claim

Purpose of Argument is to . . .	Appropriate Kind of Claim	Essential Support
Prove something as true Prove that something happened	Fact	Logical facts examples credible research
Define Clarify Identify characteristics	Definition	Logical and Ethical facts personal examples credible research
Prove a problem exists Prove a problem needs attention Offer a solution Rally audience to action	Problem-Based	Logical, Ethical, and Emotional facts credible research personal examples emotional example
Make a judgment Prove relevance of a principle	Evaluation	Logical and Ethical personal examples credible research facts
Establish cause and effect Identify relationships Position an issue in history	Cause–Effect	Logical facts credible research

Claim of Fact

A **claim of fact** argues that something is a fact—an event or series of events, a trend, an attitude, or a part of history—that may not be considered a fact by everyone. When you argue a claim of fact, you argue that something is truthful and can be proven objectively in the real world. Your responsibility in this kind of claim is to bring enough support to make your claim believable. Review the following examples of claims of fact.

- Although many local businesses claim to be green, problems with air, water, and waste continue and, in some cases, have gotten worse.
- Despite the complaints of many students about online courses, I gain a lot from these courses: I interact more effectively with my teachers than in the classroom, I get more thorough feedback, and members of my group are more responsible.
- Bailing out big banks helps the banks but not everyday Americans.

In each of these claims, arguers have claimed as facts events that others might dispute. If these claims are to appear truthful to target audiences, arguers must bring in convincing support in the form of powerful reasons, personal examples, and credible research.

your turn 10b   PRACTICE **Writing Claims of Fact**

Write a claim of fact in response to each of the following issues.

1. The United States' military spending is the highest in the world.
2. You and several classmates are confused about an essay assignment.
3. Production of renewable energy is now mandatory in many states.
4. Multinational corporations should be held responsible for poor working conditions in the farms and factories these corporations own.
5. Sentencing juveniles as adults enrages many people across your state.

your turn 10c   GET STARTED **Claims of Fact**

Use the following questions to begin work with a claim of fact.

☐ What kind of logical support will you use with your claim? Specifically, what facts, data, and statistics from your research will help support your claim? What examples from real life will you bring in as part of your support?

☐ To gain credibility with your audience, you will need to draw on the work of experts and professionals. Who are these experts, and what makes them credible? Are you careful to avoid using personal beliefs and speculation as part of your logical support?

☐ What, exactly, is the context you provide for your audience on your issue? What is the specific history of your issue? What are the key terms you define as you orient your audience to your issue?

☐ As part of the context you use for your audience, describe the time-line, or chronology, you provide for your issue. What are the important events along your timeline?

☐ What does your audience have to gain by accepting your claim of fact?

☐ What are the strongest lines of support you will use in your argument? Will you place them early in the argument?

☐ What, precisely, are you claiming is or is not a fact?

☐ In addition to your claim, where in your argument will you use qualifiers? How will these qualifiers make your claim more believable?

Additionally, answer the following questions to test the validity of your claim of fact.

☐ Are there clear points of view different from the claim of fact you may work with, and thus does your claim of fact respond to an issue that can be considered legitimate and arguable? Might some people question whether your claim is factual?

☐ Are you prepared to prove your claim with specific information?

If you answer "yes" to these questions, then your claim of fact may be interpreted as valid by an audience.

Claim of Definition

A **claim of definition** defines a word or term that is central to an issue. This kind of claim typically offers a definition that is different from popular understanding or different from a definition associated with a particular point of view or agenda.

Sometimes issues occur because people have different meanings for key words or terms. For example, the word *patriotic* to one person may mean supporting American military presence in Iraq and Afghanistan, but to another person this term may mean opposing our presence in these countries. A claim that offers a precise definition for each key term, a definition that is fully supported with convincing evidence, can be the center of an effective argument and can clarify and bring broader meaning to a confusing or controversial term. Consider the following examples of claims of definition.

- Group work in my online classes has not been about higher education.
- So much of the food I eat, the fuel I expend, and the clothing I wear works against the idea of sustainable living.
- A curriculum based on workforce training alone ignores the ideals of American citizenship.

Popular terms in the above examples—*higher education*, *sustainable living*, and *American citizenship*—need to be defined. In the first example, the arguer will need to demonstrate how group work in online classes does not fit with the definition of the term *higher education*. In the second sample claim, the arguer has outlined an argument in a way that can define the term *sustainable living* in terms of food, fuel, and clothing. And in the third example, the arguer will need to identify and discuss the ideals implied by the term *American citizenship*. These terms do not mean the same to everyone, and the arguer's task is to bring in convincing support to argue for more precise definitions.

Because easy-to-remember terms and slogans are everywhere in mainstream media, it is important to know who is using them and for what purposes. Often, slogans convey one impression but hide agendas that tilt toward one side of a political or economic spectrum. Slogans like "family values," "change," "health care for all," and "survival of the fittest," to name just a few, are often used to reduce complex issues to catchy, simplified language. The power of an argument grounded in a claim of definition is that it can move beyond this kind of oversimplification by acknowledging the complexity of an issue.

> **your turn** 10d **PRACTICE** Writing Claims of Definition

Write a claim of definition in response to the use of italicized terms in the following statements. Remember that these popular terms have multiple meanings in our culture. Write claims that offer your definitions of the terms.

1. Those who argue for gay marriage are only being *politically correct*.
2. The *Race to the Top* program has presented a fair and equitable approach to improving public education in the United States.
3. An *economic bailout* is the only practical way to restore confidence in our banking system.
4. *Free trade* benefits everyone because it lets other countries do business more easily with the United States.
5. In view of last week's protests, the *sexual misconduct* policy at our college needs to be revised.

> **your turn** 10e **GET STARTED** Claims of Definition

Determine whether a claim of definition is appropriate for your purpose by answering the following questions.

☐ What is the word or term you intend to define? Who is your audience?

☐ What context will you bring in to establish this word or term as controversial? What research will you reference in order to establish the word's different meanings, the various agendas these meanings serve, and that the word's meaning is being disputed?

☐ What populations are being affected by this word's various meanings?

☐ How will you argue against popular and dictionary definitions of this word?

☐ Because your job is to replace vague meanings of a word with a precise definition, explain how you will bring in and discuss clear characteristics, examples, and synonyms for the word.

☐ How will you clarify the specific conditions your definition must meet in order to be accepted by your audience?

☐ Does your definition include discussion of what the word or term *is not* as well as what it *is*? Explain.

These kinds of claims should identify a popular and controversial word or term. The support that follows your claim should offer specific explanations for the definition you support. Your ability to defend your definition with compelling support will determine the success of an argument based on a claim of definition.

Problem-Based Claims

Problem-based claims propose solutions to issues. They address issues with answers, with specific suggestions, and with a practical sense for what will work in a given context. This kind of claim responds to a problem with a solution. Sometimes called a "proposal claim" or a "policy claim," the problem-based claim must include a plan to solve a problem, and this plan must be defended by the arguer with plentiful support. Problem-based claims often include words and phrases like "must," "should," and "would benefit from." Review the following problem-based claims, and note how each one offers a specific solution to a problem.

- The state's Public Utilities Commission should hold public hearings across the state in response to an energy company's request for a permit to build another coal-burning power plant.
- To serve all our residents, the community's suicide prevention center must agree to work with the general population, not just teenagers.
- Students at my school would benefit from completing a service learning requirement in order to graduate.

The problems that these claims address—that citizens are concerned about the effects of a coal-burning power plant, that not everyone considering suicide has access to a potentially life-saving resource, and that an education is not complete without some connection to the local community—are met with solutions. The arguer now must follow through on a claim with a set of practical reasons and specific support to make a solution realistic and believable.

your turn 10f PRACTICE Writing Problem-Based Claims

Write a problem-based claim in response to each of the following issues.

1. A growing debate across the country is whether water should be a publicly owned or privately held resource.
2. The Department of Homeland Security, so important after the 9/11 attacks, has faded from public view.
3. End-of-grade testing in public schools has some parents crying, "Unfair!"
4. Some states' decision to reject federal money for Medicare services will plunge many older people into poverty.
5. Many subscribers to social networking sites have mixed feelings about these sites owning materials that subscribers post.

your turn 10g GET STARTED Problem-Based Claims

Based on the issue you're working with now, answer the following questions to begin work on a problem-based claim.

☐ What specific context will you bring in to prove that the problem exists and needs attention

☐ Is your audience in a position to act on your claim? Is it clear what you're asking your audience to do?

☐ Explain how well you know your audience and why you feel you can engage this audience with emotional examples that inspire action. What does your audience value, and what will motivate your audience to act on your claim?

☐ What are the compelling reasons and logical support you will use to prove that your claim is practical? Describe the research you will use to support your plan. What are your strategies to argue for the advantages of your claim and to show how it is more practical than what is in place now?

☐ How will you respond to rebuttals that assert that there is too much uncertainty about your claim because it involves a new approach to the problem?

Do your claims propose solutions to problems? Will your audience take your claim seriously because it offers a practical answer to a local problem? It is especially important with this kind of claim to understand when and where an issue began, its history, and why it continues to be unresolved.

Claim of Evaluation

A **claim of evaluation** centers on a judgment you make. It argues that something is practical or impractical, ethical or unethical, fair or unfair, healthy or unhealthy, worth our time or not worth our time, detrimental or beneficial, and so on.

Because an audience naturally will ask how you can make such a judgment, an argument centered in a claim of evaluation insists that you identify the standards and guidelines used to make your judgment. In other words, you must state the reasons you believe that something is good or bad, right or wrong, fair or unfair, safe or unsafe. Then you must support these reasons with examples, the testimony of experts, and appeals to the values of your audience. Review the following examples of claims of evaluation.

- A single-payer, government-funded health care system is a bad idea for most Americans.
- The lyrics in most hip-hop songs are more socially relevant than the lyrics of 1960s rock songs.

- Lifting the ban on fracking in our state would create unsafe conditions we're not prepared to tolerate.
- The best way to address the problem of increasing traffic congestion is to vote in favor of an increased transit sales tax.

In the first example, the arguer must spell out what is bad about a single-payer approach to health care. With the second claim, the increased social relevance of hip-hop songs must be demonstrated. In the third claim, the term *unsafe* must be broken down into categories that can be supported with specific information. And in the fourth claim, it must be clear why voting for an increased transit sales tax is better than other ways of guarding against future traffic congestion. With all four examples, the effectiveness of each argument depends completely on the arguer's ability to defend an evaluation.

your turn 10h PRACTICE **Writing Claims of Evaluation**

Write a claim of evaluation for each of the following issues.

1. Arranged marriages, practiced in some Asian and African cultures, involve a marriage arranged by people other than the bride and groom.
2. Civil disobedience, the decision to break the law as a way to engage in political protest, has a long history in the United States.
3. Job outsourcing, as many Americans know, can have profound effects on the local economy.
4. A carbon tax aims to penalize those who pollute the environment with excessive carbon emissions.
5. Supporters of a Voting Rights Act claim that the Act will eliminate voter fraud at the polls.

your turn 10i GET STARTED **Claims of Evaluation**

Respond to the following questions to get started on a claim of evaluation.

☐ Based on how you want your audience to react to your evaluation, what values do you share with your audience?

☐ What specific context will you bring to your argument?

☐ Given that your claim is grounded in a value or values you hold, are you prepared to support your claim with credible research and evidence grounded in logic and reason? Describe your research and evidence.

- [ ] What are the standards and guidelines you use to make your evaluation? Describe how you will justify these standards based on the examples you will use.
- [ ] Regarding your claim and the standards you use, what rebuttals do you anticipate? How will you counter these rebuttals?
- [ ] Will you compare your evaluation with other, similar claims, and will you contrast your evaluation with other, differing claims? In other words, how will you position yourself as part of an ongoing conversation on your issue?
- [ ] What emotional examples will you use to inspire and motivate your audience?

Claim of Cause

A **claim of cause** argues that one thing or event sets in motion a chain of events. This kind of claim requires the arguer to recognize connections between events, determine a reasonable cause for events, and demonstrate factual relationships between one event and its effects.

A claim of cause can be a powerful choice as the basis for an argument because you will identify for your audience a pattern of connected events. In most cases, a claim of cause works best when you bring in relevant factual information or when you make realistic comparisons to similar cause–effect patterns. Review the following claims of cause.

- Evidence of global warming has caused widespread local activism across the country, as many Americans now try to limit their use of various energy sources.
- My boss is inconsistent in his comments about customer complaints, and this is causing the company to lose clients.
- The city council's decision to again postpone discussion of homelessness is only increasing the number of homeless in our community.

In each of these examples, the arguer claims that one event is causing another event or chain of events. To convince a target audience of these claims, specific relationships that a certain event has generated must be demonstrated with factual information and/or with realistic comparisons to other cause–effect patterns. A successful argument based on a claim of cause can lead to a later argument centered in a problem-based claim, where you can offer a solution to the problem at hand.

your turn 10j **PRACTICE** Writing Claims of Cause

With attention to the italicized words, write a claim of cause that responds to each of the following issues .

1. *Grade inflation*, a cause for concern among students and local employers, seems to continue from one semester to the next.
2. *Recent federal laws that permit new kinds of surveillance and interrogation* are necessary if we want to ensure national security.
3. *Stress in the workplace*, a problem for everyone I know, cannot be discussed during my annual review.
4. *Children and online safety* is now a national topic of debate.
5. The issue of *undocumented workers* never seems to be addressed in our community.

your turn 10k **GET STARTED** Get Started: Claims of Cause

Answer the following questions to get started with a claim of cause.

☐ What, exactly, is the cause–effect relationship you are claiming?

☐ Because you will argue that one event has caused other events, it is vital that you bring in adequate history for your issue. What is the history of your issue? What are the specific conditions that your audience needs to know in order to establish the cause–effect connections that your argument requires? How far back in time must you go in order to convince your audience?

☐ What are the factual examples you'll bring in to make your cause–effect connections believable?

☐ Based on your research, do others argue for causes different from yours? Describe these other claims. Why is your claim more practical?

☐ Should your audience agree with your claim of cause, how will it benefit?

☐ What values do you and your audience share, and what appeals will you make based on these values?

 **tip 10a**

Know What You Want to Accomplish with an Audience

Many arguments are written to solve problems, and thus problem-based claims are common. But if your aim is to demonstrate that something is unfair or unsafe, then a claim of evaluation is appropriate. Or if you want to reveal that one event causes another, that something is factual, or that clarification is needed for a word or term, then claims of cause, fact, and definition become practical. The key to choosing a practical claim is to identify an audience that is invested in your issue and then create a claim that audience is willing to accept.

Use Reasons to Support Your Claim

Reasons give your claim direction and make it believable. They organize an argument into manageable parts. Plan to devote one or more paragraphs in support of each reason you bring to an argument. Position a reason at the beginning of a body paragraph and follow it with specific support, such as examples from your experience, facts and statistics drawn from your research, and the commentary of experts. Without reasons to direct your audience, an argument lacks structure and becomes only a collection of information.

Use reasons that are immediately relevant to your claim. As you begin to think through your claim, you may jot down some eight to ten reasons that seem appropriate to your argument. But be critical when deciding on the reasons you choose to support. It may be that three or four reasons stand out from the rest based on the support you know you can bring to each reason. Choose reasons that are likely to appeal to the values of your target audience.

Reasons are essential in an argument because they:

Michael Doolittle/Alamy

Figure 10.3 Similar to this photo in which the speaker is explaining one part of an idea or position he is defending, reasons organize and provide direction for an argument. They link to an argument's claim and alert the reader that specific support will follow.

- Defend your claim.
- Announce the focus of each paragraph in an argument.
- Frame the specific support you bring to an argument.

Review the following issue and the reasons the writer brings to the argument. Note that some reasons are more practical than others based on the specific targeted audience.

COMMUNITY	
School-Academic	**TOPIC:** Degree Requirements
Workplace	**ISSUE:** Service Learning
Family-Household	**AUDIENCE:** Teachers at My College
Neighborhood	**CLAIM:** Students at my college may benefit from completing a service learning requirement in order to graduate.
Social-Cultural	
Consumer	
Concerned Citizen	

REASONS CONSIDERED

- Personal enjoyment
- **Become aware of local service agencies**
- Vary course options
- **Experience serving a population**
- Find a career direction
- Get leadership training
- Become more compassionate
- **Connect classroom and community**
- Volunteer opportunity
- **Works with any subject area**

REASONS FINALIZED

- By fulfilling a service learning requirement, students would become aware of service agencies in the community and why they are important.
- Students would gain hands-on experience serving a specific population in the community.
- Students would be in a position to make connections between what's learned in the classroom and what they learn in a community agency.
- Service learning is appropriate for any subject area.

These reasons answer the question, "Why is my claim important?" They also structure this argument into manageable parts. With a focus on awareness, experience, and connections, each reason is distinct from others and implies that specific support will follow. The arguer's target audience—the school faculty—may pay close attention to these reasons based on their values as educators and whether they feel service learning is appropriate. Faculty unfamiliar with service learning may benefit from the specific support the arguer uses. Of the original ten reasons generated during a prewriting session, four are chosen based on the arguer's knowledge of the audience.

your turn 10 ▶ **PRACTICE Writing Reasons**

Complete the following sentences to determine the soundness of reasons you plan to use in an argument.

1. My claim is important because . . .
2. I want to use this reason in my argument because . . .
3. This reason should appeal to my audience because . . .
4. Each reason connects directly to my claim because it . . .
5. I plan to delete some reasons from my argument because they . . .
6. Some of the information I plan to bring in to support this reason includes . . .

Build Body Paragraphs around Reasons

The reasons you bring to an argument must be supported, and it is this specific support that forms the bulk of body paragraphs. The vital question you must ask when building a body paragraph is, "Will the support I bring in justify my reason?" As always, knowing your audience and its values will determine the specific support you use. Full discussion of support is covered in Chapter 11, "Support an Argument with Fact (Logos), Credibility (Ethos), and Emotion (Pathos)." For your claim and reasons to be taken seriously, you must use support that an audience finds credible and current. The body paragraphs in the following section are taken from arguments written in recent argument classes. Carefully read the discussion sections that evaluate how reasons and support and defend claims.

COMMUNITY

School-Academic

Workplace

Family-Household

Neighborhood

Social-Cultural

Consumer

Concerned Citizen

TOPIC: Transportation

ISSUE: Red Light Cameras at Major Intersections

AUDIENCE: Readers of the Local Newspaper

PROBLEM-BASED CLAIM: The use of red light traffic cameras should be discontinued on our streets.

Sample Body Paragraph

Red Light Cameras—Pursuing Profit without Process or Purpose

When first considered, red light traffic cameras seem benign. After all, the stated purpose of the cameras is to improve safety on Charlotte streets. *However, red light traffic cameras are a serious concern because they are owned and operated by private companies that are motivated by profit rather than justice.* In July 2003, *The Charlotte Observer* reported that red light traffic cameras extracted $7.4 million over a five-year period from the taxpayers driving in Charlotte. Of that, $3 million went to the city—and nearly $4.5 million went to the private contractor (Whitacre 1A). The American Civil Liberties Union explains that "many red-light camera systems have been installed under contracts that deliver a cut of ticket revenue to the contractor [as in Charlotte]. That creates an obvious incentive to contractors to 'game' the system in order to increase revenue and, in turn, generates public cynicism and suspicion" (Steinhardt 1). Ron Arnone, an employee of Sherman Way and Woodman, a red light traffic camera company in Los Angeles, bluntly states, "I never heard them talk about safety. It was all about finding good locations to make these people [the owners] a lot of money" (qtd. in Goldstein 1). An illustration of this comes from John Irving of Bethesda, Maryland. He was ticketed for running a red light so he went back and timed the yellow light. John found that the camera-patrolled intersection had a yellow light set to 2.7 seconds, while every other yellow light on that stretch of road was 4 seconds ("Tale of the 3-Second Yellow Light" 1). Obviously, the contractor or the government gained by shortening the yellow light as that one traffic camera netted $1 million in 14 months.

The third sentence in the previous body paragraph, the italicized sentence, is a reason. It directly supports the writer's claim that red light traffic cameras should be discontinued. This reason is followed by specific support, both from experts and from people affected by red light cameras. The reason also announces the focus of the paragraph and is followed immediately by logical, ethical, and emotional support.

COMMUNITY	
School-Academic	**TOPIC:** Energy Dependence
Workplace	**ISSUE:** Wind power as a viable alternative to oil and coal
Family-Household	**AUDIENCE:** Leaders of the Local Construction Industry
Neighborhood	**PROBLEM-BASED CLAIM:** America needs a plan, and the Pickens Plan will benefit our country because the fuels are ready now, it will keep money in our country, and it is environmentally friendly.
Social-Cultural	
Consumer	
Concerned Citizen	

Sample Body Paragraph

Pickens Has the Plan for the Future

First, the fuels for this plan are ready now. Throughout the world today there are over 14 million cars on the road fueled by compressed natural gas (CNG) and liquefied natural gas (LNG), and only a handful of them are in the US ("Natural Gas and Propane" 1). There is currently only one CNG-powered car made in the US, the Honda Civic GX. Toyota will be introducing its CNG-powered Camry in November to compete ("Toyota Decides" 2). The technology and the fuel are ready and used throughout the world today, and we are behind the power curve. The Midwest of the United States has the greatest wind energy potential in the world and is what some call the "Saudi Arabia of wind power." Pickens is currently in the process of building the largest wind farm in the world. Once built, it will produce 4,000 megawatts of energy, the equivalent output of four large coal-burning plants combined, and will double our country's wind production ("Pickens Building World's Largest Wind Farm"). The largest solar plant in North America will be finished soon in Nevada. Once finished, it will provide 15 megawatts of energy, 30% of the consumption of the neighboring Air Force base where 12,000 people work and 7,215 people live ("Air Force Embraces" par 8). As you can see the potential is there for development of these resources, we just need leadership with the ambition to lead the way.

The reason (i.e., the italicized first sentence) announces to readers that fuels needed to replace oil are available and should be used in the United States. This reason supports the claim that the Pickens Plan is needed and that it will benefit our country in terms of our dependence on foreign oil. The writer supports this reason by referencing the potential of planned wind and solar operations. The writer's reason links claim with support.

The various kinds of support needed to make reasons credible and demonstrated in the preceding examples are covered in Chapter 11, "Support an Argument with Fact (Logos), Credibility (Ethos), and Emotion (Pathos)."

Use Qualifiers to Make Your Argument Believable

A **qualifier** can make a claim or reason more believable to an audience. It limits a claim or reason to what is reasonable or possible within a given context or set of conditions. Simply put, it can be wise to change words and phrases like those in the left column (in the following table) to qualifiers in the right column.

tip 10b

Make Sure You Can Defend Reasons
Draft your reasons carefully; make sure you can follow them with logical, ethical, and emotional support. Make a list of reasons you may use in an upcoming argument. Are some grounded primarily in emotion? Are some grounded in stereotypes and hearsay? Delete these from your list and focus on reasons that you are prepared to support.

always never absolutely only in all cases	*change to*	usually probably possibly in many cases generally most likely may or might can with few exceptions sometimes

AP Photo/Reed Saxon

Figure 10.4 Qualifiers are crucial to making a claim or reason believable because they move the arguer away from absolute statements and toward qualified statements that speak to certain conditions. In this photo, a seventh-grade student addresses an audience at a school board meeting, a meeting in which the board announced that more than 400 out-of-district students would be removed from a local school and forced to enroll at other schools.

Qualifiers keep you from making absolute statements and broad generalizations, a habit that can make your argument vulnerable to criticism from the opposition. If you claim, for example, that Macintosh computers are by far the most practical choice for students today, some members of your audience may reject your argument based on the cost of a Mac. A revised, more realistic claim would include a qualifier: "For students who can afford them, Macintosh computers are practical choices." This limits the range of your claim and makes it more likely to be accepted by your audience.

With most issues, steer clear of generalizations and statements that claim certainty. Narrow a claim to what your audience is most likely to accept. When your claim is too broad and you promise too much to an audience, you leave yourself vulnerable to attack.

your turn 10m ▶ PRACTICE Writing Qualifiers

Explain why the following claims may not be believable to an audience. Rewrite each claim using an appropriate qualifier.

1. There must be a law that prohibits credit card companies from marketing to college students.
2. Texting in the classroom is always inappropriate.
3. Homeschooling is never a substitute for a local public school with high academic standards.

4. The only way to understand the increasing high school dropout rate is to study the lack of student motivation.
5. Homelessness in our community can be solved with more affordable housing.
6. The boom in green building means that we are reducing the effects of global warming.
7. Low voter turnout in our last local election obviously means that most of us are not interested in the issues that affect our daily lives.
8. Employers have every right to monitor employees' online behavior.
9. It is now clear that success in professional sports is due to steroid use.
10. Because it's so convenient, researching online is more practical than hunting for print sources in a library.

Justify Your Claim with a Warrant

Arguments succeed because they persuade audiences. A claim, the center of an argument, can be convincing to an audience when it is followed by reasons and plenty of support. But a claim requires another line of support—a justification, or warrant—to be successful. A **warrant** justifies a claim, it bridges a claim and its support, and it identifies a value, principle, belief, regulation, or law that an audience finds important. Without a warrant, an argument is rudderless, steering in no particular direction and aimed at no particular audience. In fields like medicine, law, and the sciences, warrants often take the form of justifying evidence in an argument. But for our purpose—constructing practical arguments that address everyday issues—warrants based primarily on values are most appropriate.

In the narrative that opens this chapter, the writer has targeted an audience that may be practical for his argument—readers of the local newspaper—because it is the writer's intention to generate local awareness of health risks from a proposed coal-burning plant. Having drafted a claim and gathered support, the writer then must articulate in a warrant common ground that he and his audience share. The writer instinctively may know what this common ground is, but it is his responsibility to put into words precisely the values he shares with an audience. The writer must also include support for his warrant—backing—should he sense that an audience may need proof that his warrant is practical for and relevant to the argument he plans to deliver. Additionally, when a writer anticipates an audience having some difficulty accepting a warrant, he should acknowledge these audience reservations. Just as including a qualifier can make a claim or reason more believable, including possible audience reservations in a warrant can make that warrant more believable—and more practical.

 tip 10c

Peer Edit a Claim and Its Reasons
For an argument in progress, ask a few writers to evaluate your claim and reasons. Ask writers to base their evaluations on whether your claim and reasons are realistic and practical and whether you should add or refine qualifiers. See Chapter 13, "Develop and Edit Argument Structure and Style," for more tips on peer review.

Figure 10.5 Connecting with an audience, especially where audience and arguer are far apart on an issue, means identifying a value or belief that differing sides have in common. Building a warrant on a shared value is a way to make this connection.

Use Your Audience to Construct a Warrant

Think of a warrant as permission from an audience to deliver an argument. If an audience finds your warrant acceptable, it likely will grant you permission to argue. But if an audience rejects a warrant—that is, if it does not share in some way the values, principles, or beliefs you include in a warrant—then permission will not be granted and the remainder of your argument will be regarded as unwarranted. As discussed in Chapter 2, "Explore an Issue that Matters to You," targeting a specific audience and its values is an essential early step in building a practical argument.

A warrant answers the following questions:

☐ What values, beliefs, and principles do I share with my audience?
☐ Why would an audience grant me permission to deliver an argument?
☐ How can I justify my claim and support?

Know What Your Audience Values

Consider the following issues and the claims and warrants that respond to each issue. Note that each argument is aimed at a specific audience. Remember that, in relation to an issue, a target audience will expect you to appeal to its values, beliefs, and principles. Hence, knowing an audience well is an important first step in having an argument accepted.

When you feel that textbook prices at your college are too high and are motivated to speak out on this issue, study your audience carefully. For example, targeting other students via your student newspaper means that you should know what most students value in relation to this issue. This likely includes values of wanting to pursue an education, the importance of a good career, the need to budget money carefully, and a commitment to balance work, family, and school responsibilities. Your warrant should reflect these values and might read like this: "As students with full lives, it's important that we be allowed to pursue our academic and career goals without the inconvenience of overpriced textbooks." Such a warrant identifies and honors audience values and grants you permission to make your argument.

Working with this same issue of textbook prices, suppose you target a different audience—readers of your local newspaper. The values of this audience are in some ways different from those of students at your college. Members of this audience include local employers, alumni of your college, and taxpayers whose money supports the college. Values may include training a local workforce and keeping the college in line with its mission of providing affordable education to local residents. With these values in mind, your warrant might read like this: "Affordable workforce training is essential to our economic future." Because you have acknowledged and plan to honor these values, you are in a position to deliver an argument to this audience.

Should you choose to direct your argument on textbook prices to another audience, this time the president of your college, another set of values would need to be acknowledged. In relation to this issue, the president values the need to maintain a budget, produce trained graduates, and continue her commitment to serving the community. With this in mind, you might craft a warrant like this: "Our college can better serve the community by offering discounts on textbook prices." The message you send to this audience honors its beliefs and professional commitments. That you have taken the time to study your audience puts you in a position to argue in a focused, purposeful way, a way that lets you address your audience from a practical perspective.

> **your turn 10n** GET STARTED **Determine What Your Audience Values**
>
> Based on the issue you're working with now, determine what your audience values by answering the following questions.
> - ☐ Why is this audience invested in this issue?
> - ☐ What is the history of this audience's connection with this issue?
> - ☐ What values, principles, and beliefs motivate this audience to care about this issue?

Let a Warrant Bridge Claim and Support

A warrant should be a bridge between your claim and support. (See Figure 10.6.) It justifies your position on an issue. With many arguments, it may seem that a warrant will be instinctively understood by an audience, especially an audience you know well, but we strongly urge you to spell out in specific terms warrants in your arguments. As you gain experience building arguments, you may choose to leave a warrant unsaid based on your knowledge of an audience. But at this point, consider it essential to make your warrant a clear, strong statement.

Recently a student writer chose to argue on the issue of the local high school dropout rate and to deliver this argument during a parent–teachers' association meeting. As a prospective teacher and parent, the writer crafted a warrant that identified the value for student success and higher-performing schools she shared with the parents and teachers in her audience. In a nutshell, her argument looked like this:

CLAIM:	Systemic changes in the way our school system is structured are needed to lower the high school dropout rate.
SUPPORT:	Research that featured reasons, examples, data, statistics, and the opinions of experts as to how systemic changes can reduce the dropout rate were included. Attention to principals having more control, a longer school day and year, the need for more courses, and a teacher reward system based on performance were addressed.
WARRANT:	Student success and higher-performing schools are essential to the future good health of our community.

The warrant in this example bridges claim and support. The change the writer wants to see is supported with reasons and examples and then justified by shared values. Identifying these shared values in her warrant means that her audience may be willing to grant the writer permission to deliver her argument. Without shared values and common ground, this audience would be less likely to permit such an argument.

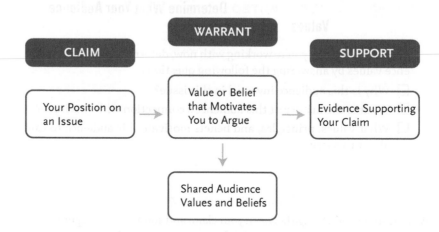

Figure 10.6 A warrant bridges claim and support

your turn 10o ▶ PRACTICE **Bridging Claim and Support**

Write a warrant for each of the following examples. Build each warrant based on values, beliefs, and principles the writer may share with the audience.

1. Issue: Requiring Extra Materials for a Class
    Audience: Your College Faculty Senate

Claim: Teachers should not require students to purchase materials for a class beyond a digital or print textbook.

Support: Reasons may include that requiring additional materials causes economic hardship for students and that additional materials should be made available through online sources. Specific support may include examples of how students are inconvenienced by having to spend more on a class, such as impact on individual and family budgets.

Warrant: _____

2. Issue: Road Repair in My Neighborhood
    Audience: County Commission
    Claim: Road repair in my community is based on economic status.

    Support: Reasons may include that wealthier neighborhoods are prioritized above poorer neighborhoods and that wealthier neighborhoods have more political influence. Specific support may include examples of longstanding problems with roads in poor neighborhoods and the fact that road problems are addressed more promptly in wealthier neighborhoods.

    Warrant: _____

3. Issue: Legalizing Prostitution in Our State
    Audience: Members of Introductory Ethics Class
    Claim: Legalizing prostitution will reduce sex crimes in our state.

    Support: Reasons may include that legalizing prostitution may reduce sex trafficking crimes in our state, may reduce rape and sexual assault, and may improve public health. Specific support can include extensive data drawn from academic studies, from state crime reports, and from health care professionals in the community.

    Warrant: _____

Use Backing to Support a Warrant

An analogy may be helpful to begin work with another building block of practical argument—**backing**. The analogy: support is to a claim as backing is to a warrant. To be convinced of a writer's claim, an audience requires specific support. Similarly, to be convinced of a writer's warrant, an audience requires a similar kind of support, and this is called *backing*.

Backing answers the following questions:

☐ Why do you believe your warrant is credible?
☐ What specific support can you bring to your warrant?
☐ How will backing your warrant make your argument more convincing?

Let Your Audience Determine the Extent of Backing

Close knowledge of your audience should determine how much backing you bring to a warrant. You may feel that an audience generally is in line with the values stated in your warrant, and this means that backing may be limited to a few facts or examples. However, when an audience may not completely share the values in your warrant, or when an audience may question the relevance of your warrant to the issue at hand, more extensive backing (i.e., more support for your warrant) may be required.

Consider the following arguments and the extent of backing needed to move an audience closer to accepting the writer's claims.

ISSUE:	Supporting the Microcredit Movement
AUDIENCE:	Members of Your Writing Class
CLAIM:	Microcredit is proving to be an ineffective response to poverty in developing countries.
SUPPORT:	Reasons may include that in many cases microcredit loans are not used for entrepreneurial purposes, as intended, but for everyday needs such as food and health care; that this kind of lending traps borrowers in a cycle of borrowing without measurable improvement to earned income; and that repayment officials are often aggressive and threatening. Specific support can be drawn from the increasing number of academic studies and from professional reporting on this issue.
WARRANT:	Institutional and individual lenders should stop wasting their money on microcredit and instead encourage mid-size companies to relocate to developing countries and provide jobs to those who are now impoverished.
BACKING:	Examples of companies building factories and production centers in poor countries and providing jobs are plentiful. Equally effective support for this warrant can include beliefs that compassion for poor people should be grounded in financial common sense and not in fostering economic dependency, and that job security can reduce the need to borrow.
	The target audience for this argument, members of a writing class, may or may not be familiar with the microcredit movement, and the writer's aim is to generate awareness *and* deliver a judgment on this issue. Appropriately, the writer crafts what is both a claim of fact ("is proving to be") and a claim of evaluation ("an ineffective response"). Sometimes kinds of claims overlap, as in this case. Backing for this warrant is effective because the writer emphasizes values of efficiency and avoiding waste, values that this audience more than likely shares with the writer, especially during a period of economic recession.

ISSUE:	Banning Social Networking Sites at Work
AUDIENCE:	Your Employer
CLAIM:	Occasional use of social networking sites should be allowed in the company.
SUPPORT:	Reasons may include that a sense of trust is established between employer and employee when occasional social networking is permitted; that productivity is not affected; and that company security is not compromised. Specific support can include numerous personal examples that demonstrate company loyalty, reference to performance reviews, and professional and academic studies supporting your claim.
WARRANT:	Responsible use of social networking sites is good for the company.
BACKING:	Several studies show that employee retention improved and that security systems were not breached when social networking was allowed. Additionally, many employees at your and other companies claim that the chance to spend 15 to 20 minutes during a work day on Facebook or MySpace makes for a more comfortable work environment, and some argue that allowing social networking can sometimes create new business contacts.

Because the audience targeted for this argument is the writer's employer, it is important that the writer provide plenty of backing for a warrant that the employer may question. The writer is wise to identify the good of the company as a shared value, but because the employer predictably may not be convinced that spending time away from work while social networking is good for company business, substantial backing should be included in this argument. The writer has chosen to balance academic studies with personal examples from his and others' experience on the job. Improved retention may suggest employee job satisfaction to the employer, and an unhampered security system may relieve concerns about system safety. Examples of new business contacts made possible from social networking may allow the employer to move closer to accepting the writer's claim.

In each of the preceding examples, the writers' target audiences are likely to need some convincing before these arguments are accepted. The backing the writers bring to their warrants validates the values and beliefs on which each argument is built. Without this backing, writers limit an argument's audience appeal.

Make Backing Specific

Backing is most effective when it is specific. Like the support you use with a claim, you should use reasons, facts, examples, statistics, data, and the research of experts to back up a warrant.

Regarding the issue of microcredit and social networking on the job, specific kinds of backing are noted. Note that audiences for these arguments may require substantial backing to make the warrant acceptable. As we know, arguments fail if warrants are not accepted by audiences, and writers of these two arguments must back up warrants with plenty of specific support.

Let's return to the earlier argument where a writer addresses the high school dropout rate, and let's consider effective backing for the warrant, "Student success and higher-performing schools are essential to the future good health of our community." Values embedded in this warrant include concern for student success, higher-performing schools, and the community's economic future. But unlike the audiences targeted for the microcredit and social networking arguments, this audience may need less convincing at the level of the warrant. The writer may know that an audience of parents and teachers, for the most part, share these values; thus, the amount of backing needed for this warrant may be less than what is needed for warrants in the other two arguments, where audiences may require more convincing.

> **your turn** 10p **PRACTICE Building in Backing to Support a Warrant**

Note the following issues, claims, and warrants. What kind of backing is practical for each warrant? Note that categories in number 4 are blank. Complete this part of the practice based on the argument you are currently building.

1. Issue: Tuition for International Students at Your College
   Audience: College Administration
   Claim: Tuition for international students should be reduced from five times what in-state residents pay to twice what residents pay.
   Warrant: International students should be allowed to pursue college degrees without taking on an unreasonable financial hardship.
   Backing: _____

2. Issue: Online Privacy
   Audience: Friends and Classmates
   Claim: Google and Facebook are invading my privacy.
   Warrant: We should be protected from private companies with large data warehouses that can search our private lives.
   Backing: _____

3. Issue: Arranged Marriages
   Audience: Members of Sociology Class
   Claim: Arranged marriages are a realistic alternative to "love" marriages.
   Warrant: Most successful marriages are built on trust and responsibility.
   Backing: _____

4. Issue: _____
   Audience: _____
   Claim: _____
   Warrant: _____
   Backing: _____

Respond to Audience Reservations to Make a Warrant Believable

Acknowledge in an argument objections an audience may have with your warrant. This move can earn you credibility with an audience because it presents you as thorough and fair-minded. Audience objections to a warrant are called **reservations.** An audience may reserve its full acceptance of a warrant because there may be circumstances in which the warrant is not convincing or morally acceptable.

Responding to audience reservations answers the following questions:

☐ What objections does my audience have about my warrant?

☐ What limits or qualifications can I use to support my warrant and thus make it more acceptable to my audience?

AP Photo/K.M.Chaudary

Figure 10.7 Audience reservations should be responded to in ways that acknowledge an audience's objections to the warrant that are based on moral grounds. In this photo, two Pakistani students address the media at Lahore Airport in Pakistan after being deported from England on unsupported allegations of terrorist activity.

In the earlier argument about microcredit, some members of the writer's audience may take issue with the notion that supporting the microcredit movement is wasteful and thus have reservations about the writer's warrant. Specifically, some members of the audience may believe that helping poor people through low-interest loans to be morally sound behavior. Reservations to the warrant that supporting the microcredit movement is wasteful and inefficient might be stated in the following sentences.

- Supporting microcredit in developing countries, especially via loans made by individuals, provides an economic option where others do not exist.
- Microcredit is a way to aid individuals directly without having to encounter formal institutions or governments.

In the earlier argument about social networking on the job, the writer's audience (i.e., the employer) may not completely accept the warrant that responsible use of social networking sites is good for the company. The employer may have reservations about the validity of this warrant, and you should acknowledge similar reservations in your argument. The audience's reservations in this argument might look like this:

- In some companies, employees have been known to spend too much time on social networking sites.
- Some employers are concerned that employee performance will suffer when there is no policy for social networking.

When you include audience reservations in an argument, you demonstrate respect for your audience and confidence in yourself. An audience may accept a warrant only in part, and it is important to validate these reservations. As noted earlier in this chapter, construct a warrant so that the values you share with your audience are clear. Acknowledging the audience's sense of a warrant's limits can make an argument more practical. (Additionally, see Chapter 6, "Work Fairly with the Opposition," for working with the opposition.)

 **tip 10d**

Interview Your Audience

Think of yourself as a journalist and interview your audience to determine its reservations about your warrant. Depending on your audience, the interview can occur in-person during a conversation or through careful research. Record the values your audience holds. Think through the reservations this audience may have based on your warrant.

your turn 10q   GET STARTED Acknowledge Audience Reservations to a Warrant

Answer the following questions based on an argument you plan to build.

1. What might prevent my audience from fully accepting my warrant? That is, are there certain conditions in which exceptions to my warrant are valid?
2. Will your argument be strong enough to accommodate your audience's reservations? Explain. How, specifically, will you respond to audience reservations?

Reflect and Apply

1. What is the most pressing issue for you at school, at your job, and as a concerned citizen? What kind of claim seems most appropriate for each issue? Explain.

2. Working with the claims you draft for each issue in question one above, sketch out a warrant for each claim. Anticipate problems an audience may have accepting these warrants. Describe these problems.

3. As this chapter explains, good arguments fit various pieces together. Based on the argument you are working on now, which piece comes to mind first? How will you build the rest of the argument after beginning with this piece?

KEEPING IT LOCAL

The narrative that begins this chapter addresses one of many environmental issues before us today. This particular issue, construction of a coal-burning plant, has been the focus of several strong arguments in recent years. These arguments were effective because writers matched claim with purpose. In some cases, writers built problem-based claims because their purpose was to argue that construction should stop. Another writer used a claim of cause to explain the health risks the coal-burning plant would cause, and another opted for a claim of evaluation, because her purpose was to expose an unfair (in her view) assault on the health of everyday people. Arguments become practical when writers know where they stand on issues and the claim and information they want their audiences to accept. In the matter of the coal plant, writers used certain argumentative strategies to dignify and address a matter of great local concern. These individuals believed that many people would suffer from the effects of coal emissions, especially children, the elderly, and people with upper respiratory conditions. Their structured arguments allowed them a voice. At this point, construction of the plant continues—as does the regular back-and-forth between opponents and supporters. Politics and professional agendas being what they are, we know that even the very strongest arguments can sometimes have little effect on an audience. But it is essential that you put your best foot forward when you feel strongly about an issue, even when there is no immediate promise of success. This is precisely what these student writers have done. While construction of the plant has not stopped, their voices are now audible and part of an increasingly important conversation in the community and in classrooms. Their voices are clear because they built complete arguments, arguments that included clear claims and justification for their claims.

● - - - - - - - - - - - ●

In order to go public with a claim and a successful argument that addresses an issue of concern, you must include all the elements essential to a sound argument. What is your preferred method of getting started on this process? Contrast the challenge of building an argument with challenges posed by writing assignments in other classes. What are your observations?

CHAPTER 11

Support an Argument with Fact (*Logos*), Credibility (*Ethos*), and Emotion (*Pathos*)

For the past three semesters you have been on the dean's list at your university. This semester, you have worked particularly diligently, even cutting back hours at work, in order to make the president's list. You are extremely upset and confused, then, when you check your grades and see that you have a "D" in your English course. You did not receive comments on your final essay, so you do not know what happened with that assignment.

You've ranted to your friends and cried to your parents, but you have not yet contacted your professor. She has not been very friendly throughout the semester and you are frankly intimidated by her. Instead, you filed an arbitration request, and a meeting has been set for you, your professor, and the arbitration committee. Meanwhile, you gather all of your graded essays, along with your professor's comments, copies of the current essay, and your professor's syllabus. You are hoping that having a moderator between you and your professor will allow you to express your concerns and obtain a grade change.

All Illustrations by iStockphoto.com/A-digit

COMMUNITY

School-Academic

Workplace

Family-Household

Neighborhood

Social-Cultural

Consumer

Concerned Citizen

TOPIC: Grades

ISSUE: Unfair Semester Grade

AUDIENCE: Arbitration Committee

CLAIM: My semester grade in English is unfairly low and needs to be changed.

In Chapter 2, "Explore an Issue that Matters to You," you learned how to focus on the needs and values of your argument's audience. In Chapter 3, "How to Establish Context through Research," you discovered some great sources of material that will support your claim. What do you do with all of that material, though? This chapter helps you to decide what to do with the material you've gathered. What kinds of support should be used at various points in your argument? Given what you know about your audience and the type of claim you are making, you'll now learn how to determine which of three kinds of support (factual, emotional, or personal credibility) best back your claim.

In Chapter 11 you will learn to:

- Identify the types of support that can be used in argument.
- Determine when and where to use each type of support in an argument.

Field-Specific Support

As you probably know, people are not easily convinced of anything: they need different kinds of proof before they buy into an idea. Your first step in gathering support for your claim must be to determine what kind of support will be acceptable to your audience.

When looking for evidence to support your claims, you must first determine what types of evidence are appropriate in your field. Will the support that is acceptable in a biology class be acceptable in a political science class as well? Will the types of evidence you need to support your evaluation of new business sites be different from the types of evidence you would supply to the IRS in a dispute of your taxes?

Figure 11.1 An audience needs a variety of proofs before it can believe an argument. The arguer's task is to filter through the support to find the proofs best suited to an audience.

A science class may value observation, results of experiments, and lab reports. Your English teacher would prefer your own ideas and interpretations of a novel shored up by literary theory. A sociology course may value interviews; a business course, case studies. You may want to call attention to the abusive treatment of women in domestic violence relationships using emotionally charged language. This may be appropriate in a women's studies course; however, it may be inappropriate in your business writing course, for example, in a paper on the costs of domestic violence to the workplace.

It is important to understand your audience, and part of doing so is knowing what type of support it values. For example, if your audience is involved in a particular industry or profession, you can research trade and scholarly journals and read books in the field in order to determine what kinds of evidence the authors use. If you are writing to colleagues about your own field of study, you will improve your chances of supplying the best support for your arguments by asking colleagues, bosses, and professors for guidance.

Find Support for the Physical Sciences

Students in chemistry, biology, physics, engineering, and geology courses look to observation to determine how the world works. Lab reports and literature reviews help these students develop their arguments. Arguments in these courses can use the following as support:

- Results of experiments
- Observation logs

Additional Resources for Writing in the Sciences

Davis, Holly B., Julian F. Tyson, and Jan A. Pechenik. *A Short Guide to Writing About Chemistry*. Longman, 2009. Print.

Gastel, Barbara. *Health Writer's Handbook*. 2nd ed. Wiley-Blackwell, 2004. Print.

"Lab Reports." The Center for Communication Practices at Rensselaer Polytechnic Institute, Troy, New York. Web. http://www.ccp.rpi.edu/resources/lab-reports/

McMillan, Victoria E. *Writing Papers in the Biological Sciences*. 5th ed. Boston: Bedford/St. Martin's, 2012. Print.

"Writing in the Sciences: A Handout." University of North Carolina. Web. http://writingcenter.unc.edu/handouts/sciences/

Find Support for Education, History, and Social and Behavioral Sciences

For writers in education, the emphasis is often on defining educational problems and suggesting solutions. Students of history, anthropology, and sociology examine how people live, in the past and now. Political science students ask questions about the workings of governments. Economics students try to figure out how economies work. Arguments in these courses can use the following as support:

- Statistics
- Interviews
- Surveys
- Artifacts
- Documentaries
- Primary sources such as newspapers, diaries, photographs, bills of sale, deeds, and advertisements
- Audio and visual documentaries

Additional Resources for Writing in the Social Sciences

"Anthropology." University of North Carolina. Web. http://writingcenter.unc.edu/handouts/anthropology/

"History." University of North Carolina. Web. http://writingcenter.unc.edu/handouts/history/

Rosnow, Ralph, and Mimi Rosnow. *Writing Papers in Psychology*. 9th ed. Boston: Cengage, 2011. Print.

"Sociology." University of North Carolina. Web. http://writingcenter.unc. edu/handouts/sociology/

"Writing in Education and Human Development." Lynchburg College. Web. http://www.lynchburg.edu/writing-center/writing-education-and-human-development

Find Sources for the Humanities and the Arts

What counts as support in humanities courses such as literature, art, music, and philosophy? In humanities courses, the emphasis is on interpretation based on close reading, listening, and viewing. Arguments in these courses can use the following as support:

- The actual texts, films, pieces of art or architecture, or pieces of music being studied
- Critical articles published in scholarly journals
- Interviews with authors and performers

Additional Resources for Writing in the Humanities

Barnet, Sylvan. *A Short Guide to Writing about Art*. 10th ed. New York: Longman, 2010. Print.

Barnet, Sylvan, and William E. Cain. *A Short Guide to Writing about Literature*. 12th ed. New York: Longman, 2011. Print.

Bellman, Jonathan. *A Short Guide to Writing about Music*. 2nd ed. New York: Longman, 2006. Print.

Corrigan, Timothy. *Short Guide to Writing about Film*. 8th ed. Longman, 2011. Print.

Seech, Zachary. *Writing Philosophy Papers*. 5th ed. Boston: Cengage, 2009. Print.

---

your turn 11a ▶ **PRACTICE Identifying Field-Specific Support**

What kinds of evidence are acceptable in your field? Make a list of the types of support you can use in your classes or in your job. If you are unsure, ask your professor, your boss, coworkers. You can also ask a librarian to help you find journals in your field. What sources do the authors of the journal articles use to support their arguments?

Vince Bucci/Getty Images for Crest

Figure 11.2 Actor and musician Nick Cannon introduces Crest Whitening Plus Scope Extreme Toothpaste at the launch of www.CrestIQ.com.

Use All Three General Kinds of Support

In general, there are three categories of support that can be used in an argument. *Logos*, *pathos*, and *ethos* are the traditional Greek terms given to these categories. Let's begin with *logos*. **Logos**, or support based on facts, refers to the more traditional types of support that we tend to think of first in our writing. For example, if I am arguing that cell phones should be mandatory in every vehicle sold in America, support in the *logos* category could include statistics about how many lives are saved by 911 calls made from cell phones, how much safer it is for drivers to be able to call AAA or towing services from their car, or the time saved by being able to conduct business while driving.

But there are other ways to persuade a reader who may be skeptical about your cell phone argument. **Ethos** is a term that refers to one's authority or expertise on a topic, one's credibility. If, for instance, you own a cell phone yourself, you are in a better position of authority to discuss the advantages of cell phones than someone who doesn't own one. Think about celebrities who provide testimonials for products and services, as in Figure 11.2. The audience is supposed to be convinced that, if Ellen Degeneres uses Brand Q makeup and looks great, then if they use Brand Q, they will look great too. So does this mean that if you don't own a cell phone or wear Brand Q makeup that you cannot write about these products? Of course not. It simply means that you might not have a lot of authority. Always ensure the sources you use to establish your credibility are good and reliable.

The term **pathos** is used to refer to emotional appeal that comes from support such as stories, illustrations, charts, or photos. In our cell phone example, we could use a story of people stranded on the side of the road who used their cell phones to obtain help for their 90-year-old grandmother who was having a heart attack: see how this works? Be careful, though. A story that sounds unconvincing or seems manipulative may backfire. A judicious use of all three types of support will produce the most convincing argument.

Your strongest essays will include combinations of all three types of support. You also need to be able to identify the types of support used in other people's arguments in order to understand the arguments' strengths and weaknesses. If an argument is too loaded with logical support—that is, the argument has lots of facts and figures, statistics, percentages, charts of numbers, and so on—then it will make very little connection with the audience.

If an argument depends too heavily on stories and anecdotes, especially those designed to arouse anger or pity in an audience, then emotion has been achieved, but understanding of the topic may be lacking. A healthy combination of all three types of support is your goal.

Good examples of arguments or persuasion using multiple types of support are the commercials that seek donations for children in impoverished conditions. A commercial may begin with a credible spokesperson, usually a recognizable celebrity (*ethos*), telling the audience that for X amount of money they can support a child in Bolivia for a year (*logos*). The ultimate purpose of these commercials, however, is to part people from their money. Although the viewer may find the pitch so far interesting, he is unlikely to open his wallet until an emotional push (*pathos*) is applied. This is the part of the commercial where you see images of barefoot children digging through massive garbage piles searching for food to eat or listless children with distended stomachs too weak to brush away hovering flies. It is the photography that hits us and propels us to act. Let's look at each appeal individually to see how each works in action.

Use Support Based on Facts and Research (*Logos*)

Logical support, or *logos*, is defined as support that appeals to the audience's reason: facts, figures, statistics, and scientific data. When most people think of facts, they think of cold, hard, logical science. They think of logic as a way of pursuing the truth. The large number of television programs featuring detectives, both fictional and factual, attest to the public's belief that crimes are best solved in a logical manner. The true-crime television series *Cold Case Files* presents numerous cases that are solved solely on the basis of physical evidence. In court cases, forensic evidence—such as blood spatter patterns, DNA matches, and bullet matches—is a great persuader of juries.

There is no disagreement that logical, physical evidence is extremely important in solving crimes and arguing before juries. Your arguments, though, may rarely take you into court. What are other types of logical evidence that can be used in argument?

Although we can all agree that facts are important in an argument, sometimes it can be difficult to separate fact from opinion.

Facts and Opinions

What exactly is a fact? The question seems nonsensical until you examine it closely. To Aristotle, a scholar of ancient Greece, it was a fact that women had fewer teeth than men. To the men and women of the Middle Ages, it was a fact that the Earth was the center of the universe and the sun and planets revolved around it. Until a few years ago, the chemical composition of water was factually recorded as H_2O; according to a 2003 study, though, the chemical structure of water could well be $H_{1.5}O$.

Figure 11.3 Geocentric model of the universe based on the Ptolemaic system

Figure 11.4 Heliocentric model of the universe based on the Copernican system

A quick Internet search will yield many definitions of the word *fact*. Our favorite is "an indisputable truth." Obviously, this definition is disputable. A fact is only a fact until new facts come to light. Huh? Well, let's look at the "truth" surrounding the structure of the universe in the Middle Ages as an example of how facts change.

CLAIM: A divine being created the Earth.

SUPPORT: The Earth is the center of the universe.

The geocentric theory of the universe developed in ancient Egypt and Greece and was the view held until the sixteenth century. Figure 11.3 shows the Earth at the center of the universe and the moon, sun, and other planets revolving around it.

For people who had neither access to space travel nor to the technology to conjecture otherwise, it was common sense that the Earth (created as it was by a divine being) was at the center of all creation. However, in 1543, Nicolaus Copernicus published *De revolutionibus orbium coelestium*, which argued that the universe was actually heliocentric, or sun-centered (see Figure 11.4). What was once a fact, an indisputable truth, was no longer so.

Facts are facts only until new facts come to light. Particularly in the field of science, facts change continually, based on the technology available. In every field, facts are based on the best efforts of scholars and scientists, but facts are understood to be subject to change. The following are all facts:

- The moon is not a planet.
- Memphis is short five inches of rain for 2013.
- The population of Las Vegas is increasing at a rapid pace.

How the facts are interpreted leads to **opinions**:

- Because Memphis's rainfall is currently five inches below normal, the city is experiencing a drought.

What makes this an opinion? Well, it depends on the definition of the term *drought*. Is a designation of drought only made when the number of inches of rain falls below a certain level? Does it also have to do with how many months of low rainfall have been experienced? Some experts may believe that particular conditions justify the label of "drought." Others may disagree about which conditions should be used to make the determination.

When we supply expert opinions from authorities in a field, we are adding evidence that we cannot adequately supply ourselves. We may have an opinion about the lack of rain, but unless we are meteorologists, our assessment of a drought situation will carry little weight. Expert opinion can help us strengthen our arguments. Because expert opinion is gathered from other sources, such as interviews, articles, lectures, and so forth, it should always be credited to the expert and cited properly, whether you paraphrasing or quoting verbatim (see Chapter 4, "Evaluate and Engage with Your Sources").

So what kinds of facts can we use? All of the items in the following list can be interpreted factually. Keep in mind that the line between types of evidence is blurry. An example or a statistic can be included to spark an emotional response (*pathos*) as well as provide valuable logical information (*logos*).

- Images
  - Charts
  - Graphs
  - Photographs
- Statistics
- Scholarly articles
- Physical laws and theories
- Examples

Graphic images such as charts, tables, and photographs may make a stronger point than the metaphorical thousand words, but they are also the easiest to manipulate to the user's advantage. (See Chapter 12, "Enhance Your Argument with Visuals and Humor," to learn how you can use graphics effectively and ethically to present facts.) But graphics can be useful to visually organize information for readers, particularly information to which readers will need to refer frequently, for example, the chart of the Wechsler Adult Intelligence Scale sub-scores shown in Figure 11.5.

Statistics

Statistics can be useful to your reader. While they can be very convincing, they can also be confusing. When you select your statistics, be sure that your reader understands what point you are making with them. You can

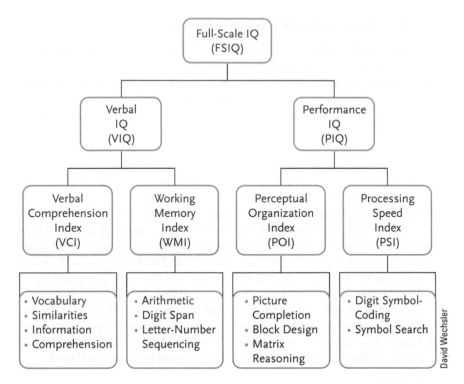

Figure 11.5 The Wechsler Adult Intelligence Scale subscores, an example of an informative graphic

use statistics when you want to compare what happens to one group versus another, as in the following example.

> The National Student Clearinghouse tracks the enrollment of students at 97% of all colleges and universities in the United States. According to data from the Clearinghouse, part-time students who attended four year public colleges and universities were far more likely than full-time students to drop out within six years. Of students who attended part time, 70% had neither graduated nor remained in college after six years. In contrast, 76% of full-time students had graduated after six years, with only 20% dropping out and 4% still enrolled.[1] These statistics support the argument that students who are serious about graduating should strongly consider attending full time.

These are **descriptive statistics**. They answer questions such as, "Who did what where and when?" Statistics used to link cause and effect or to make conclusions about a group larger than the group the original research considered are called **inferential statistics**.

---

[1] Shapiro, Doug, and Afet Dundar. "Completing College: A State-Level View of Student Attainment Rates." *National Student Clearinghouse Research Center*. February 2013.

- According to one study, students who do not take their college placement tests and the classes recommended by those tests fail to complete a degree 35 percent of the time.

Two useful books for learning how to use statistics are *Introduction to the Practice of Statistics*, by David S. Moore and George P. McCabe, and *How to Lie with Statistics*, by Darrell Huff and Irving Geis. The Online Writing Lab at Purdue University offers excellent coverage of writing with statistics as well: http://owl.english.purdue.edu/owl/resource/672/01.

Tips for Understanding and Using Statistics

Some of the problems that come from using statistics arise from an incomplete understanding of what the statistics indicate. If you are going to use statistics in a paper or report, be certain that *you* understand them and their significance, particularly if they come from a study that you did not conduct, which is usually the case for assigned writing. Do your best to verify that the statistics you have provided are accurate and the sources of the information are reliable by asking the questions in the Understand Statistics checklist and in Tips 11a and 11b.

Understand Statistics

- ☐ Who is the provider of your statistics?
    - ☐ Is the source you are using reputable?
    - ☐ Why is the information being gathered by the source (website, journal, etc.)?
    - ☐ Can you trust the information?
    - ☐ Does the researcher explain the methods and conditions of his research?
- ☐ Who is interpreting the data?
    - ☐ Often you will be relying on statistics not only gathered by someone else but also interpreted by someone else. Who is this person?
    - ☐ Is she respected in her field?
    - ☐ Does she supply contact information so that others can contact her to discuss her findings?
    - ☐ Is her work published in credible publications?
    - ☐ Do you feel comfortable using her interpretation of the numbers, or do you see a very different way of reading them?
    - ☐ Are you detecting serious biases?
- ☐ Explain why you are using the statistics. What is your reader to understand about the subject based on the numbers you are providing? Interpret the statistics for the reader.
- ☐ Organize your statistics clearly if your material is lengthy. Graphs and tables are a good way to arrange statistics of the same type

 **tip 11a**

If there is any sort of vagueness or secrecy surrounding the source of your information, it is perhaps not a good source to use.

(time, measurements, people, behaviors, costs, etc.). See Chapter 12, "Enhance Your Argument with Visuals and Humor," for more information on creating graphs and tables.

☐ In accord with most style manuals, do not begin a sentence with a numeral, including percentages.

Incorrect: 30.6% of students who earned a college degree ...

Correct: We found that 30.6% of students who earned a college degree . . .

☐ Don't forget to cite the source of your statistics!

COMMUNITY

School-Academic

Workplace

Family-Household

Neighborhood

Social-Cultural

Consumer

Concerned Citizen

TOPIC: Smoking Risks

ISSUE: Reducing Smoking on College Campuses

AUDIENCE: Student Senate

CLAIM: Because death from lung cancer is greatest in the Southeast, we must make an effort to reduce exposure to smoke by eliminating smoking from all college campuses.

---

tip 11B

Numbers can be very effective in supporting your argument, but your audience has to know that these numbers can be trusted.

Discussion

This is a good issue to support with statistical information. Today's college campuses are often quite diverse, and students of varying ages attend college today. The statistics gathered from charts available through *The Atlas of United States Mortality* found at The National Center for Health Statistics (http://www.cdc.gov/nchs/products/other/atlas/atlas.htm) indicate that the highest death rates for white males aged 40 from lung cancer were found in the Southeast. The rate determined from a study completed in 1992 was 12 percent. This is the kind of startling statistic that could be very persuasive.

Although this author cites a landmark study, the Atlas has not been revised. Would you still use these figures? Why or why not?

Additional Resources for Gathering and Using Statistics

Driscoll, Dana Lynn. "Writing with Statistics." *Purdue Online Writing Lab.* 8 Jan. 2010. Web. http://owl.english.purdue.edu/owl/resource/672/01/

"Finding and Using Health Statistics." *U.S. National Library of Medicine. National Institutes of Health*. 7 Oct. 2012. Web. http://www.nlm.nih. gov/nichsr/usestats/index.htm

U.S. Census Bureau. Web. http://www.census.gov.

Kornblith, Gary J. "Making Sense of Numbers." *History Matters: The U.S. Survey Course on the Web*. July 2002. Web. http://historymatters.gmu. edu/mse/numbers/

Looking for international, national, state, and local statistics? Try FedStats: http://www.fedstats.gov/regional.html

your turn 11b ▶ **PRACTICE Use Statistics**

Examine a set of statistics that you find in an article or on a website by answering the first two question sets in the Understand Statistics checklist. Does the information gathered and interpreted by the researcher or author seem valid based on these questions? If not, why? What is troubling about them?

Scholarly Articles

In Chapter 3, "Develop a Research Plan," you learned how to perform research to find materials that support your claims. In Chapter 4, "Evaluate and Engage with Your Sources," you learned how to document information you have found through your research. The proper use of material from these research sources can go a long way to convince your readers of the strength of your argument. Most of the support you will use in any argument is likely to come from research. Whether you are using questionnaires and surveys; magazine and journal articles; or information from interviews, websites, and documentaries; your goal is to be sure that you are using this information credibly and citing it correctly.

To determine an author's credibility, you can use the Internet to quickly get answers to the questions on the Determine Credibility checklist.

▷ Determine Credibility

- ☐ Is the author attached to an institute of higher learning or a reputable company? Most people, particularly academics, have web pages affiliated with their institutions. Visit the author's page to learn more about him.
- ☐ Is the author published in his field? Are his publications regarded well in his field? Check for reviews of published books. Also, make sure that the journals in which he is publishing have a peer review editing policy. This means that reviewers come from within the field and are usually highly respected and knowledgeable themselves.

☐ Does the author use unprofessional language? Does she belittle her opposition or use an aggressive or sarcastic tone of voice?

☐ Does the author include support that you can verify by further research?

Guidelines for Evaluating Support Based on Fact

- Does it answer all the questions you need it to answer?
- Is the information from a reputable source?
- Does more than one source support your findings?

your turn 11c ▶ PRACTICE Determine Author Credibility

Find two scholarly articles in trade- or field-specific journals. How credible are the journals and the authors? Use the questions in the Guidelines for Evaluating Support Based on Fact to determine if the authors are qualified to write on their subject.

Use Support to Create Credibility (*Ethos*)

There are three things which inspire confidence in the orator's own character—the three, namely, that induce us to believe a thing apart from any proof of it: good sense, good moral character, and goodwill (Aristotle, Rhetoric, Book II, Chapter 1, 1378a: 5–7).

Ethos is the arguer's personality—how he or she is perceived by the audience, specifically in terms of credibility or trustworthiness. Gerry Spence, the famous Wyoming lawyer who is virtually unbeatable in the courtroom, often appears in court wearing cowboy boots and a 10-gallon hat. His tone is down-to-earth, and he plays up his rural persona, or character. He wants his audience, the jury, to associate him with the law and order brought to the Wild West. He gives off an air of being trustworthy and therefore the little guy. This is Spence's character—his *ethos*.

Credibility can be based on one's character. If I am a good person, my argument may be judged to be good as well, even if it has flaws. If I believe what you believe and if I share your values, my argument may be judged as good, even if it is lacking any support. If I am a bad person or if I do not share

Figure 11.6 The speaker achieves professional credibility by engaging her audience with handouts, a PowerPoint presentation, and her professional appearance.

OJO Images Ltd/Jupiter Images

your values, my lack of credibility in your eyes is based on personality, not the support of my argument. Do not underestimate the power of personal credibility. For better or worse, we are judged for our personality as much as for our argumentative strategies.

Although the word *ethos* is related to the word *ethics*, it is not the same thing. It is undeniably important to argue in an ethical manner and not to use one's skill at persuasion for bad ends. *Ethos*, however, is a more general term used to describe the credibility a writer or speaker creates for himself. For example, when I give a lecture on nineteenth-century author Henry James to my American Literature class, my students are convinced of my credibility when they see that I have published articles on James. I have proven that I am worthy of speaking on the subject. If, however, I am teaching a business course and I don't know about TQM (Total Quality Management) or the latest quality control best practices, my students will quickly find all of my lectures on the subject suspect. They will no longer be inclined to consider me an expert.

What about you personally will lend weight to your argument? If you are writing about the dangers of fad diets, for example, what about you will lead your audience to believe your argument? Do you have a history of trying every weight loss gimmick that comes along, or do you have a family member who has that history? Have you lost a great deal of weight by sensible dieting as opposed to following a fad? What about the research you have done on the subject? Have you selected the best arguments? Used the most responsible sources? Arranged your material in such a way that your audience is convinced you know what you are talking about?

Like Gerry Spence, you need to decide how to properly present yourself when you are presenting an argument.

Types of support that create positive credibility:

- **Personal anecdotes.** Do you have a brief personal story that will convince your audience of your connection to the subject of your argument? For example, if you are a believer in cell phone use in cars, perhaps you have an anecdote of a time when a cell phone call saved your or someone else's life.

- **Unbiased consideration of opposing or alternate views.** How you treat any opposing arguments reflects upon your character. Are you negative or sarcastic in discussing alternate views? If so, your tone of voice may damage your credibility with your audience. Being respectful of others' views will help you earn your audience's respect.

- **Strong and careful presentation of support.** If your argument is based on research, be certain that all of your quotations are accurate, that your material is not misrepresented, and that your documentation is clean; sloppy editing and inaccuracies can lead your audience to doubt you and, in turn, your argument.

To increase your credibility, then, you must provide strong evidence retrieved from credible sources, and you must present the evidence without errors in logic or writing, organized in the best way possible.

How you relate to your audience, in writing or speaking, will determine how well your claims and supporting examples are received. If they are well received, you are on your way to persuading your audience. Tone of voice is one way to create a persona readers can relate to and trust. The tone of the writer's voice is related to the point of view being used.

- First person: When a speaker uses *I*, she is relating directly to the audience and discussing the argument as it relates to her.
  - ° Plus: The audience feels that the speaker has authority or background that makes her an expert or someone who can be trusted to speak on the topic.
  - ° Minus: The audience may focus on the speaker more than on the topic of the argument.
- Second person: When a speaker uses *you*, and directly addresses her audience, she forges a connection that is based on a direct sharing of information.
  - ° Plus: The speaker can take on a teacherly or mentoring role.
  - ° Minus: The speaker can take on a lecturing tone of voice, which can be off-putting to an audience.
- Third person: When a speaker uses *they*, she is focusing on the information at hand and not the audience or her own role in the argument.
  - ° Plus: The focus is on the argument and nothing personal or anecdotal.
  - ° Minus: The connection between speaker and audience is weakened by the lack of personal interaction.

Each argument and audience is different, so you will need to do some research to determine which tone of voice is best used in each given situation. In general, academic arguments should be made in the third person with limited personal involvement, unless a professor has authorized first or second person.

Guidelines for Evaluating Support to Establish Credibility

- Does your support make you appear to be an expert on the subject?
- Is all your research well cited and properly formatted?
- Are quotes and paraphrases treated properly?
- If you are using testimonials, do the people who provided them have valid reasons for supporting your ideas?

your turn 11d GET STARTED Establish Your Credibility

Use the "Guidelines for Evaluating Support to Establish Credibility" to review the support you have gathered for your argument.

Use Support to Create Emotion (*Pathos*)

To accomplish your goal of persuading an audience and building the strongest possible argument, use all three types of support. Some writers are often reluctant to use emotion, or *pathos*, in their papers, feeling that to do so is being manipulative or unethical. Other writers use too much emotion, at the cost of providing too little logical support. Aim for balance even as you purposely evoke your audience's emotions. It is also important to know when it would be inappropriate to use emotional appeal. *Pathos* is support that attempts to make a connection with one's audience through anecdotes or graphics that evoke emotion.

The methods you use to evoke an emotional response should be based on your understanding of your audience's values, or what its cultural or historical beliefs are. For example, if you are arguing that children's fashions may be too suggestive and that instituting a school dress code would eliminate this problem, you need to understand what your audience feels about both children's clothing in general and school uniforms in particular.

Before you can select supporting reasons, you need to understand the audience's belief system. What are some of the things parents value in terms of their children?

- Safety
- Cost of clothing
- Comfort
- Individuality
- School performance

COMMUNITY

School-Academic

Workplace

Family-Household

Neighborhood

Social-Cultural

Consumer

Concerned Citizen

TOPIC: Children's Clothing

ISSUE: Children Wearing Suggestive Clothing

AUDIENCE: Parents of School-Age Children

CLAIM: The problem of suggestive clothing worn by school children can be eliminated with the adoption of a school uniform policy.

Discussion

Once you understand what your audience values, it is easier to find reasons that appeal to these values. Then you should determine when and where in your argument an appeal to emotions might work. Yes, parents want their children to be comfortable and they don't want to spend a lot of money on clothing. They may even be somewhat concerned that uniforms or a dress code may stifle creativity and individuality. But of these five values, the two that should stand out as being candidates for emotional support are safety and school performance.

Do you have any statistics about how teenagers perform better when they are not distracted by skimpy skirts or revealing tops? Do you have any scary stories about the dangers to girls wearing suggestive clothing? Statistics that shock and stories that scare are powerful tools in your arsenal of support—as long as you don't overdo it.

Anecdotes

It is often hard for people to connect to big issues until there are individuals to connect with. Individual stories allow an arguer to take an abstract topic and make it concrete and specific. They also help to create common ground with an audience, especially when the audience can identify with, or at least sympathize with the individuals. Persuading an audience is more effective when you can get it on your side.

For example, tax reform is a large, important, yet abstract issue. Making it matter to your audience is easier when you can show how it would affect the lives of ordinary people. On January 24, 2012, when President Obama raised the issue in his State of the Union address, he pointed to Debbie Bosanek, a secretary from Bellevue, Nebraska. She was remarkable for two reasons: one, that she was taxed at a higher rate than her boss, and two, that her boss happened to be Warren Buffett, a billionaire.

Anecdotes, or brief stories, can be used in your argument whenever a good story is needed, but they are particularly well suited to introductions. A good story must have these elements:

- It must be brief. Stories that go on and on will begin to bore the reader. Make it short and to the point, using only those details that are needed to set the scene.

- It must seem real. When a hypothetical story is unrealistic or feels contrived, readers will know that the story has been created to fit the topic.

You can also choose language in telling a story that you know will evoke emotion (sometimes called "loaded language"). Consider this opening from the student argument on fracking that appears in the APA Appendix:

> In Kerns County, California, a cherry orchard is dying. In Washington County, Pennsylvania, a hillside is slipping away. In Shelby County, Texas, a bathtub walks itself down a hallway. In Logan County, West Virginia, a bulldozer plows up the graves of World War II veterans to make a road. In Colorado, a goat gives birth to a head. In Wisconsin, a thousand trucks a day blow by a woman's house, filling it with toxic sand. Her stabling business has been ruined and she fears that her twenty-two month old daughter is at risk.

In addition to using anecdotes, the writer increases the emotion by listing many frightening incidents, and by using colored language designed to register emotionally—words and phrases such as slipping away, ruined, plowing up graves, blowing by a house. The writer also introduces a character most likely to elicit an emotional response: a toddler who is threatened.

Finally, never underestimate the value of humor in establishing an emotional link with your audience. Chapter 12, "Enhance Your Argument with Visuals and Humor," provides more insight into using humor effectively to break the ice with your audience and helping you make sometimes complex or abstract issues more relatable.

Photographs

Photographs go a long way to evoke emotion in an audience. Along with emotion-laden stories, images can produce an effect in your reader that a mere presentation of logical facts cannot. The images here are so familiar that they have become **iconic**. An iconic image is one that represents so much more to the viewer than just the contents of the image itself. It has risen above pictorial representation to become symbolic.

Images such as these can evoke strong emotional responses to your argument. For more information on how to use images in an ethical and appropriate manner, see the material on visual arguments in Chapter 12, "Enhance Your Argument with Visuals and Humor."

Guidelines for Evaluating Support to Evoke Emotion

- Is the emotion you are evoking relevant to the subject?
- Are you being respectful of your audience's ideas and values?
- If you are using hypothetical situations, are they brief and relevant?

Gina Jacobs/Shutterstock.com

Figure 11.7 A memorial in Sandy Hook, Connecticut, commemorates the victims of the school shooting on December 14, 2012.

David Livingston/Getty Images

Figure 11.8 Sgt. 1st Class Charles Shuck and retired military dog Gabe, who completed more than 200 combat missions in Iraq.

your turn 11e ▶ **PRACTICE Determine the Function of Emotion**

- From a daily newspaper, select a story that is not illustrated and that does not include any personal anecdotes. Is the story effective? Why or why not?
- Select a story that seems to need either anecdotes or graphics to elicit emotion. What stories or graphics would you suggest to the author to help him capture the hearts of his readers?

Reflect and Apply

1. What sources are you using to guide your writing strategies for your assignment? Are you writing an argument for biology, sociology, education, or English? The expectations for arguments in each of these areas are unique.

2. How are you ensuring that you have separated fact from opinion— your own and those of your selected research?

3. How are you establishing your credibility? Do you have insider knowledge about this issue? If so, how are you incorporating your own expertise with your research while avoiding personal opinion and bias?

4. Explain why you are or are not using sources that elicit emotions. Is an emotional response from your audience appropriate for the field of your assignment? Why or why not?

5. If it is appropriate to create an emotional response in your audience, how are you ensuring that you are not going so far as to manipulate the audience in an unethical manner?

KEEPING IT LOCAL

IN A RESEARCH PAPER, during a work dispute, in court—these are all places where you will be judged on the evidence you bring to the table. Audiences of your peers, your instructors, and even a jury are not persuaded by only one type of support.

Returning to the example that opened this chapter, consider that your grade change could well hinge on the evidence you have brought to the arbitration meeting. Your facts (e.g., past essay grades, professor syllabus, and policies) combined with your credibility (i.e., your academic standing at the university) and comments made by the professor (e.g., derogatory comments), which serve to provoke anger from the committee, may show that your grade was indeed unfairly evaluated.

Your supporting materials along with your own credibility present a package to your audience, whether they are present to listen to your claim or are reading your argument in print. Think about the package you want to present in order to be successful in your argument.

How are you representing yourself and your claim? Have you gathered all the facts, and are you presenting them clearly in charts or graphs, in a well-organized narrative with properly documented sources? Do you know when it is proper, even necessary, to use emotional support? How are you representing yourself physically and vocally?

CHAPTER 12   Enhance Your Argument
              with Visuals and Humor

CHAPTER 13   Develop and Edit
              Argument Structure and
              Style

PART FOUR

How to Take Ownership of Your Argument: A Style Guide

All Illustrations by iStockphoto.com/A-digit

CHAPTER 12

Enhance Your Argument with Visuals and Humor

After driving past several gas stations searching for a lower price, you realize that you are wasting gas (and money) and pull into the next station. Because last month's hurricane shut down several major pipelines, gas has been scarce and prices are high. You read an article this morning that extolled the virtues of hydraulic fracturing, known as "fracking," and domestic drilling as alternatives to importing oil. A rebuttal by an environmental activist pointed out the dangers to farm animals in areas where fracking has taken place. Is tapping American oil reserves worth long-term dangers to the food we eat?

All Illustrations by iStockphoto.com/A-digit

TOPIC: Environment

ISSUE: Domestic Oil Production

AUDIENCE: U.S. Government

CLAIM: There should be no fracking or drilling for oil in the United States because the risk of major impact on the environment outweighs the minor impact on oil supplies.

In Chapter 12 you will learn how to:

- Identify the strengths and weaknesses of visual arguments.
- Develop your abilities to read visual arguments, including graphs, photographs, and ad campaigns.
- Use visual arguments effectively in your own writing.
- Use humor in surprising ways.

What Are Visual Arguments?

When we think of visual argument, we most often think about advertisements. It's true that this is the form of visual persuasion that we encounter most frequently. But there are many other forms of visual arguments:

- Tattoos
- Hair styles
- Car models
- Viral videos
- Political cartoons
- Fashion
- Art and architecture
- Photographs

All of these forms, and many others, are arguments. They make a claim, and they support that claim by the images they use, their colors, their layout, and the medium in which they appear.

Benjamin Krain/Getty Images

Figure 12.1 An aerial photo captures the devastation in Joplin, Missouri, following a deadly tornado.

Visual imagery can be very powerful. Witness the effects of images of the devastation of a natural disaster (Figure 12.1), the horror of war (Figure 12.2), or the pride felt by a winning team (Figure 12.3).

Popperfoto/Getty Images

Figure 12.2 John Sharpe of Leicester who was a prisoner of War in an internment camp, World War II, September 28, 1945.

Figure 12.3 Team Canada celebrates after winning the men's ice hockey gold medal game between USA and Canada, February 28, 2010, in Vancouver.

 internet activity 12a EVALUATE WEB IMAGES

Visit several news sites on the Internet. How do they use images in their reports? On at least three different websites, identify stories covering the same issue or event . What is different about the way images are used in the three stories? Consider the emotions that are being evoked. Are these emotions appropriate to the news story? How well do the images relate to the storyline?

These sites are the most frequently visited for breaking news:

http://www.cnn.com
http://www.cbsnews.com
http://news.google.com
http://news.yahoo.com
http://www.msnbc.msn.com
http://www.foxnews.com
http://www.time.com/time

http://www.nytimes.com
http://news.bbc.co.uk
http://abcnews.go.com
http://www.reuters.com
http://www.worldnews.com
http://www.cbc.ca/news
http://www.ap.org

Understanding and Using Visual Arguments

You can profitably use visual arguments in your own writing when you want to make an emotional impact that will be heightened by the use of images. Photographs, charts, and graphs can also add credibility to the facts you are

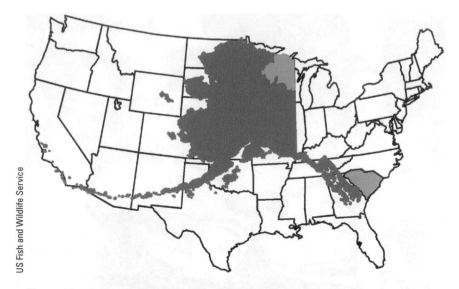

US Fish and Wildlife Service

Figure 12.4 A comparison of the area that is being studied for oil drilling to the state of Alaska specifically and to the United States in general.

using. You will occasionally be asked to provide an argument based totally on visual elements. More often, however, you will be asked to create arguments that include visual elements that bolster your written support. Other times, you will encounter images that make arguments or that are part of arguments that you need to consider critically.

How do we read a visual argument coolly, without allowing what we see to overly affect our emotions? How do we avoid knee-jerk reactions and instead follow up on the story behind the images? It's not easy. Let's take as an example an argument that many people have forwarded over email in recent years, an argument about drilling in the Arctic National Wildlife Refuge, or ANWR. Reading over this type of email message, it's very easy to agree with the arguer's claim that drilling should be allowed. The photographs are quite convincing (see Figures 12.4 and 12.5). Maybe too convincing ...

The anonymous author of the original email (anonymity is tipoff number one—always be skeptical of authors who don't take responsibility for their work) is asking the audience to compare the land that is earmarked for drilling, a small area of the green ANWR region, to the size of the United States. What is being implied? That such a small area is nothing compared with the entire United States. But no one is suggesting that we drill for oil in the entire United States. An either–or fallacy is being set up: either we drill in this one tiny spot or we risk the need to drill everywhere.

Then the author provides another image of Alaska (Figure 12.5) with the exact location of ANWR pinpointed. Again, we're being asked to consider that these 2,000 acres are nothing in comparison to the area that is *not* being drilled.

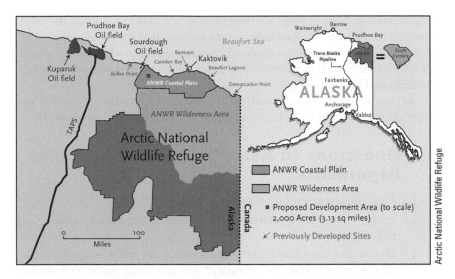

Figure 12.5 Map of the Arctic National Wildlife Refuge.

This very informative map shows the exact location of the drilling and marks the location of other drilling sites. The Kuparuk oil field is the second largest oil field in the United States and is expected to yield 2 billion barrels of oil. It operates on a site that is not part of a wildlife refuge. Although studies indicate that the demands of an oil field would damage the wilderness area of proposed drilling, known as Area 1002, they also indicate that after costs of extracting and producing the oil, between 3.2 billion and 5 billion barrels of oil would reach market. That's a staggering amount. The Kuparuk oil field has been operating since 1981 and is not yet tapped out.

But all of these images, as convincing as they may be in arguing that drilling will not affect the environment, cannot answer the question, "Will the cost and effort required to drill in these areas make us any less dependent on foreign oil?" Some studies indicate that production in the proposed drilling location would not reach its peak until 2030 and would reduce our need for imported oil by only 9 percent.

An argument made by other photographs in the email (see Figure 12.6) is that wildlife would not be affected by the drilling or the facilities needed for production.

Figure 12.6 Caribou along the oil pipeline. Kuparuk Oil Field Arctic, AK.

The animals in these photographs certainly do not look bothered by the facilities. On the other hand, the photos do not tell you that the areas proposed for drilling include the porcupine caribou's calving ground. In addition, the photographs do not include members of American Indian nations whose lives would be disrupted by the drilling.

As convincing as a visual argument can be, you want to make sure that you aren't being convinced by what you see, rather than by your own research.

Questions to Ask While Reading Visual Arguments

- ☐ Does the argument target a specific audience?
- ☐ Is the claim clearly stated in the images, the layout, and/or any included text?
- ☐ Do you detect any bias or stereotypes based on gender, religion, nationality, economic class, or ethnicity? Are you being asked as a reader/viewer to identify with any of these biases?
- ☐ What assumptions does the argument make about either the target audience or the claim itself?
- ☐ Is the argument relying on facts or on emotion to make its claim? Are patriotic or religious icons or symbols used in order to get your attention or to claim affiliation with the reader/viewer?
- ☐ What is not in the image? Are only certain genders, races, or economic backgrounds included?

your turn 12a ➤ **PRACTICE Read Visual Arguments**

Visit any of these sites and "read" the argument that is being made, using the checklist "Questions to Ask While Reading Visual Arguments."

- The White House http://www.whitehouse.gov/photos
- The Marine Corps website—watch the slideshow http://www.marines.mil
- Attica Prison http://www.pbase.com/kjosker/attica_prison&page=1
- Controversial Benetton Ad Campaigns http://www.top10buzz.com/top-ten-controversial-united-colors-of-benetton-ads/
- World War II Army Recruitment Posters (select one) http://www.archives.gov/exhibits/powers_of_persuasion/powers_of_persuasion_home.html

Let's explore an example of how to read and structure a visual argument. For his Natural Resources and Environment course, Alejo decides to research the environmental effects of drilling in Alaska. The question he wants to answer is, "Do the proposed drilling and fracking offer a solution to the oil problem or cause environmental problems that are not worth the risk?" Before developing a claim, he does some research.

Alejo begins his research at the source. At the ANWR website, Alejo watches a video produced by the organization. The video, narrated by a member of the Inuit Nation whose family has always lived in ANWR, provides glimpses of seemingly thriving wildlife alongside photographs of schoolchildren who are benefiting from improvements in the economy that have resulted from oil-related jobs. The site also provides a graph of the number of Alaskans who support the coastal drilling (see Figure 12.7). The writer also cites a 2011 poll of citizens of Karoo, South Africa, where Shell Oil plans to frack. This poll showed that 73% of the population is in favor of gas extraction and that 61% trust Shell.

The images are very persuasive. However, upon further reading, Alejo learns that the small size of the oil field footprint shown in the video cannot be confirmed using other sources. Also, the video does not discuss the possibility of oil spills or what their environmental effects would be. The video also fails to mention the effects that the massive infrastructure construction would have on the porcupine caribou's calving habits.

Alejo also reads several sources that include images of farm animals suffering from the effects of fracking, including animals dying from chemicals released into the air during the oil extraction process. Another video presents fracking as a clean process with very little disruption to the environment—but again, Alejo's further research reveals that the damage from fracking is often invisible. He develops a claim for his project:

As he continues to research his claim and write his own argument, Alejo must simultaneously read the visual arguments he encounters in periodicals and on websites—maps, photographs, videos, charts, and graphs—and consider creating his own.

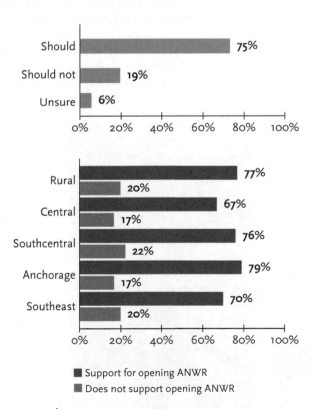

Figure 12.7 Graphs illustrating the percentage of Alaskans supporting drilling in ANWR.

School-Academic
Workplace
Family-Household
Neighborhood
Social-Cultural
Consumer
Concerned Citizen

TOPIC: The Environment
ISSUE: Domestic Oil Production
AUDIENCE: The U.S. Government
CLAIM: There should be no fracking or drilling for oil in the United States because the risk of major impact on the environment outweighs the minor impact on oil supplies.

Reading Photographs and Illustrations

The words used to describe certain events often evoke emotion, but the power of a photograph is unbeatable. This power, unfortunately, can be abused. Images are often used to convince people that something is real when it may not be, as in photos of Bigfoot and the Loch Ness monster (Figures 12.8 and 12.9).

With digital photography, there are no film negatives to examine, and any image can be retouched to look very different from the original. Image-editing

Dale O'Dell/Alamy

Alfred Gescheidt/Photographer€™s Choice/Getty Images

Figure 12.8 A purported sighting of the legendary creature called Bigfoot.

Figure 12.9 A sighting of another legendary animal, the Loch Ness monster.

programs can be used to fabricate images that trick people into believing events unfolded in a particular way.

Photojournalism is a type of news reporting whose goal is to capture the most evocative images of a news event. Some of these images go on to become icons—enduring symbols—that evoke memories of an event, a time period, a crisis, and so forth. Some examples of iconic images are the extremely memorable photograph of United Airlines Flight 175 crashing into the South Tower of the World Trade Center on September 11, 2001 (Figure 12.10), or the photo of Kim Phuc Phan Thi, a child during the Vietnam War, who was photographed running from a napalm bomb.

Photojournalism also can be responsible for changes in society. In 1890, Jacob Riis' *How the Other Half Lives* exposed the poverty of New York City's slum tenements and included evocative images such as the one shown in Figure 12.11. The image of the

AP Photo/Carmen Taylor

Figure 12.10 The horrifying image of *flight* 175 crashing into the World Trade Center, September 11, 2001.

Jacob Riis/Jacob Riis Picture History/Newscom

Figure 12.11 Jacob Riis photograph of Italian immigrants in a yard on Jersey Street in New York City.

Figure 12.12 Student Gunmen at Columbine High School, 1999.

two student gunmen who massacred classmates at Columbine High School in 1999 was a chilling accusation of what can go wrong in our schools (see Figure 12.12).

Images that appear, or do not appear, in public—American monuments and museums, historical places, and so forth—provide interesting arguments about what is accepted, rejected, glorified, or praised. For example, John C. Barans argues that the portraits chosen for inclusion in the National Portrait Gallery in Washington, D.C., comprise an "acceptable" history of the American people.[1]

 Internet Activity 12b **Evaluate Images**

Conduct a search of your favorite Internet sites, whether they are related to shopping, cooking, sports, news, religion, or some other topic. Evaluate the images you find there using the checklist, "Questions to Ask While Reading Visual Arguments" on page 300.

[1]Negotiating the American Identity in the National Portrait Gallery, http://xroads.virginia.edu/~MA98/barans/npg/introframe.htm

Using Photographs and Illustrations in Your Argument

Visual evidence is powerful. Photographs can provide gripping support for an argument. They can show more clearly than words what you are describing. They can be used for both illustration and for manipulation. Your goal obviously is to avoid manipulation. Select your photographs to accomplish what your words may not be able to. We've all seen the "before and after" shots of people who have used a particular diet, piece of exercise equipment, or supplement. The results are often striking and persuasive. You can bet that a reader who sees a photograph of a middle-aged woman who is significantly smaller in her "after" shot is more likely to buy the Fat Blaster Ab Eliminator than a reader who does not see the photograph!

Makeovers have become a staple of contemporary television programming. Programs depicting makeovers of people, houses, and backyards have all become hot, and "before and after" footage is at the heart of the shows. As in the weight-loss example, though, keep in mind that photographs must make a

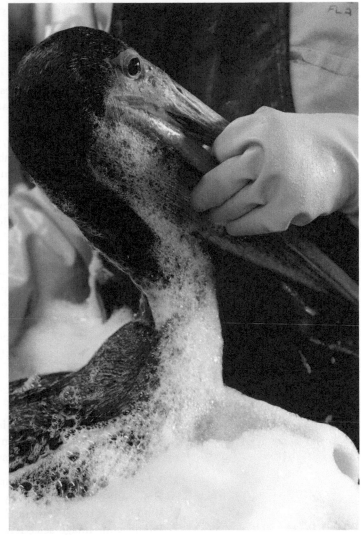

AP Photo/Jack Smith, File

Figure 12.13 A bird soaked in oil from the oil spill caused by the Exxon Valdez, April 1989.

significant impact in order to be persuasive. As mentioned earlier, the line between the types of support (factual vs. persuasive/emotional) is easily crossed. Photos or illustrations of how something works—those in an owner's manual, for example—are clearly factual with no attempt at persuasion. A photograph of the damage created by the BP oil spill can be factual; at the same time, it can also evoke emotion, as in Figure 12.13.

Your sources must always be cited; this holds true with images, not only written information. The following checklist will support your efforts to use and label your images correctly.

▶ Using Photographs and Illustrations

☐ Select the right image for your information. Does the image clearly illustrate the point you are trying to make in the text?

☐ Clearly label the image: what it is and where it was found.

☐ Don't include an image if it does not improve the quality of your argument. You do not want your argument to be cluttered and visually unappealing.

☐ For inclusion in a student paper, permission to use a photograph is generally not needed. For more public purposes, however, you may need to obtain permission. To obtain permission from a publishing house, use the information on the copyright page of the book or consult the publisher's website. When making your request, be sure to include the ISBN (International Standard Book Number; a number publishers use to identify books), which usually appears near the copyright notice or on the back cover of the book.

☐ For permission to use photos and illustrations found in magazines, start with the information found on the credits page or masthead (near the front of the magazine). In some cases, the photographer or artist is not an employee of the publisher, and you may need to obtain permission directly from the photographer or artist. Publishers will often tell you how to contact artists or photographers.

your turn 12b   GET STARTED Use Photographs and Illustrations

Use one of the community topics from Chapter 2, "Explore an Issue that Matters to You," and find images that would support a claim based on your selected topic. Then, answer the following questions:

1. Why did you choose these images?
2. How do the images improve your argument?
3. Who is your target audience?
4. Would your image selection be different if the audience for your claim was different?

Reading Graphs and Charts

Graphs and charts use numbers to illustrate their claims. They can help a reader visualize a claim by showing increases and decreases in anything that can be measured, such as weight loss or presidential approval ratings. Graphs are particularly convincing when the numbers are dramatic. Look at the graph shown in Figure 12.14. It shows the dramatic rise in both global temperatures (the blue and red bars) and carbon dioxide (the black line). Carbon dioxide is considered a common greenhouse gas because it lets sunlight into our atmosphere but traps the heat energy that the sunlight produces. This graph makes it appear that our modern industrial society has produced unprecedented levels of both carbon dioxide and heat: a pretty scary situation.

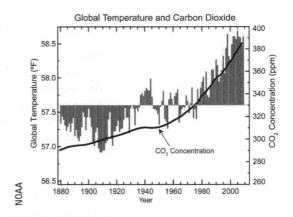

Figure 12.14 A graph showing temperature variation over a 130-year period.

On the other hand, a second graph (Figure 12.15) puts these increases into a much longer timeframe, adding an important context. This graph, like the other one, shows a rise in global temperatures (presented in degrees Celsius, rather than degrees Fahrenheit) and carbon dioxide, but this graph provides a context that makes the current increases look similar to increases that have occurred at other times in the last few hundred thousand years. The recent rise is still significant, but perhaps not as scary because it has happened before. A good student of science would go on to ask, "What about looking at global temperatures for the last few hundred million years?" and "How do the recent increases in carbon dioxide and temperatures compare to the climate, say, when the dinosaurs lived?" If human beings are creating higher levels of carbon dioxide than have ever existed before, the situation truly is scary. A chart showing only the past few decades won't address that important issue.

Graphs can seem difficult to read, and it can also be difficult to tell when their information is misleading. For help, refer to the checklist, "Questions to Ask While Reading Graphs."

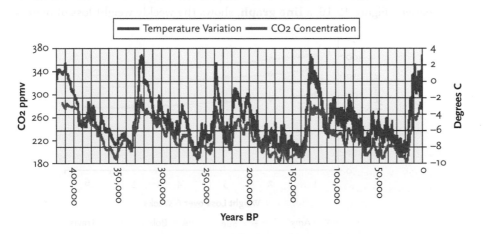

Figure 12.15 A graph showing temperature variation over a longer period of time.

your turn 12c ▶ PRACTICE Reading Graphs

Find a graph in a newspaper or in a news or science magazine that is geared toward the general public. *USA Today* frequently uses graphs as do *Time, Newsweek, US News and World Report, Scientific American,* and *Discover*. Using the questions in the checklist, "Questions to Ask While Reading Graphs," evaluate your selected graph. If there are problems with the graph, what could be done to correct them?

Questions to Ask While Reading Graphs

- ☐ Are all numbers represented and compared the same way: percentages with percentages, numbers with numbers, and so on?
- ☐ Does the *y*-axis start at 0?
- ☐ Are all objects represented in the same scale?
- ☐ Are both the *x*-axis and the *y*-axis labeled, and does the graph have a title?
- ☐ Is the graph understandable without reading the accompanying text?

Using and Creating Graphs in Your Argument

Graphs and tables are an excellent way to condense a large amount of information into a graphic that is easy to read. Any time you are using a lot of numbers in a paragraph, a graphic may be useful to the reader. Graphs can illustrate weight loss, for example, showing more clearly how much two groups of dieters have lost over a period of time, as shown in Figures 12.16 and 12.17, which were created for an essay arguing the effectiveness of two weight-loss programs.

Here we have one way we could compare the weight loss of two "teams" of dieters. Figure 12.16, a **line graph**, shows the weekly weight loss of dieters

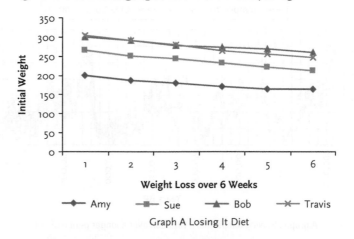

Figure 12.16 A line graph for the Losing It Diet.

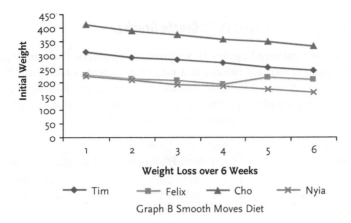

Graph B Smooth Moves Diet

Figure 12.17 A line graph for the Smooth Moves Diet.

on the Losing It diet. Figure 12.17 illustrates the weight loss of dieters on the Smooth Moves diet. As we can see, both groups of dieters lost weight.

But how are these graphs helpful to an argument that one diet is superior to the other? All we can really tell from the two charts is that both teams lost weight. Ultimately, even though these charts are well constructed, labeled properly, and easy to read, they are not useful for comparing the effectiveness of the two diets. A more effective graph for the argument that one diet (Smooth Moves) is superior to the other (Losing It) is the bar graph shown in Figure 12.18.

This graph compares only the total loss for each team, ignoring the weekly ups and downs of individual team members. The **bar graph**, compared with the line graphs, works better to compare the total loss of the two teams—the columns are thicker and have more heft, standing out better and showing the Smooth Moves group's weight loss as more significant than that of the Losing It group.

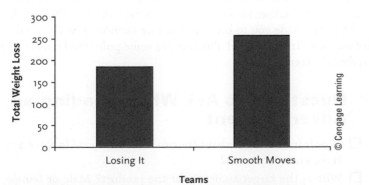

Figure 12.18 A bar graph clearly showing greater weight loss for the Smooth Moves team.

your turn 12d ▸ PRACTICE Create Graphs

You have gathered figures to support an argument that employers are invading workplace privacy at a rate that increases each year. You also note that different kinds of monitoring devices are gaining in popularity among employers. Arrange these figures first in a line graph and then in a bar graph. Which is more effective?

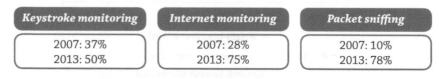

Keystroke monitoring	Internet monitoring	Packet sniffing
2007: 37% 2013: 50%	2007: 28% 2013: 75%	2007: 10% 2013: 78%

Creating Graphs

- ☐ Select the right graph for your information.
- ☐ Use the chart function of your word processing program or your spreadsheet program to try different graph types and to create a clear and uniform graph.
- ☐ Clearly label the components of the graph.
- ☐ Title the graph fully. In the weight-loss example, a title of "Weight Loss" would not give the reader much information about what he was looking at. Be concise, but provide as much information as the reader needs.
- ☐ Ensure that you provide sufficient information so that your reader can interpret the graph without the support of the accompanying text.

Reading Advertisements

For every product imaginable, from widgets to wing-dings, there is an advertising team to promote it with a sustained campaign. Many of these ads don't even use words. Other times, the words are secondary to the visuals. Ads are meant to persuade you to buy a product or service. How this goal is accomplished varies from ad to ad. But here are some points to look for as you read an advertisement.

Questions to Ask While Reading an Advertisement

- ☐ How is information about the product conveyed? Is there any text, or is the entire ad visual?
- ☐ Who is the target audience for the product? Male or female, rich or poor, young or old?

☐ Can you quickly tell what product or service is being advertised?

☐ Is the ad part of a larger campaign?

☐ What strategy is used to sell the product or service? Bandwagon? Celebrity endorsement? Company credibility? Offers to make you rich, thin, beautiful, insert adjective here ___?

☐ Does it appeal primarily with facts, emotions, or credibility?

☐ And, finally, do you believe the claims made in the advertisement?

 Internet Activity 12c Evaluate Advertisements

Do a search on the Internet to find advertisements or, preferably, an entire ad campaign. Use the questions in the checklist, "Questions to Ask While Reading an Advertisement" to evaluate the ad or ad campaign.

PowerPoint Presentations

A student recently lost her brother to a car wreck caused by a driver who was texting while driving. Her insurance agent suggested that, because she wanted to do something to educate others about the dangers of texting, she should create a PowerPoint presentation about her brother's death and the part texting played in the accident. The presentation turned out so well that the police department asked her to present it to driving classes.

PowerPoint presentations are extremely popular, because they can combine visual and written material in a systematic way, using software that is easy to learn. However, although it is fairly easy to create a presentation, it is not easy to create a good presentation. There are many good books available that can teach you how to develop excellent PowerPoint presentations. Here we present our favorite tips for this particular form of visual argument.

Creating PowerPoint Presentations

☐ Select a background design. It is usually best to use the same background for each slide. Avoid designs that are so busy that readers will have difficulty making out the text.

☐ Be consistent with font size and style. Font size should be large enough for an audience to read comfortably. This is 24-point type. This is 32-point type. Play with the font size until it feels right.

☐ Also be consistent with font style. This is Arial. This is Times New Roman. This is very difficult to read. Fancy fonts can be eyesores. TYPING IN ALL CAPS can make your text difficult to read as well.

☐ Turn off the shadow feature that is the default setting for some slide designs.

☐ If you are going to be using several images, you may want to make the file size of each image smaller so that the PowerPoint file is not so big. If your file is too big, others may have difficulty opening it.

☐ Acknowledge all image sources.

☐ Break up text with images, charts, and so forth, and don't cram too much on each slide. If your entire slide is filled with 10-point text that your audience is expected to read, the presentation will not be successful.

☐ Limit the transitions between slides. Just because you can have your words march in and do cartwheels across the slide does not mean you should.

Uses for Humor in Argument

Humor is used in mediation sessions to relieve the stress and anxiety created by a confrontational or argumentative situation. It is employed in police efforts to control crowds and diffuse mob behavior. It is used in courtrooms to make the opponent's case look weak and silly. Many writers and speakers, however, worry that displaying a sense of humor will project a lack of professionalism or make their claims appear less than valid. On the contrary, humor engages your readers. It keeps them interested and allows them to feel that you are a real person, putting forth a real argument. Humor, when correctly used, adds to your ethos as a likeable person with whom your readers can relate and to whom they are willing to listen.

A recent psychological study[2] measured several kinds of motivation for using humor. Three types of humor may be particularly useful in an argument:

1. Self-deprecating humor: With this technique, you poke fun at yourself rather than your rivals. Men tend to use this type of humor more often than women. You wouldn't want to use this to point out serious flaws in your personality, though, because doing so would be detrimental to your argument. You always want to maintain a strong ethos.

2. Other-deprecating humor (or aggressive humor): This kind of humor pokes fun at your opposition. In a playful form of disrespect ("dissing"), it can be seen as just having fun. However, it can also be taken as literal insults and lead to misunderstandings and confrontations. Particularly risky is using aggressive humor in a group of mixed nationalities

---

[2]Martin, R. A. et al. "Individual Differences in Uses of Humor and their Relation to Psychological Well-Being: Development of the Humor Styles Questionnaire." *Journal of Research in Personality* 37 (2003): 48–75.

because humor is often culturally specific. What is perceived as playfulness in one culture may be viewed as an attack in another.

3. Affiliative humor: When you are trying to establish a connection with a group, it is often helpful to find what you and the audience have in common. Do you both share a particular ethnic, religious, or regional background? Do you share an educational experience? If you can identify common ground, you may be able to use humor that outsiders would not understand or appreciate. You may be able to refer to events that only those "in the know" (your group) will understand, allowing you to establish a rapport based on common characteristics or experiences.

Strategies for Using Humor

Anecdotes, or short personal accounts, are one of the most basic techniques used by good writers and speakers. Members of every culture and people of nearly every age value stories, from our preschool bedtime stories, to our love of human-interest stories in the newspaper and stories that come to life on the television or cinema screen. Anecdotes allow the reader to connect with you in a more intimate fashion. When you share in a humorous way an event that members of the audience have possibly experienced, a connection is forged.

Self-effacing humor, or self-deprecation, was explained previously. It is a technique intended to make the writer or speaker appear human and vulnerable—just a regular guy like everyone else. For example, scientists traditionally have had a difficult time connecting with the general public and have difficulties persuading people to see the importance of their research. Stephen Hawking's famous statement, "Black holes ain't so black" is funny. The word *ain't* is humorously incongruous with the idea of a new and sophisticated theory being put forth by the world's most famous living physicist. Hawking attempts to connect with a public who probably understands very little about black holes by asserting that behind the genius IQ lies an ordinary man.

Understatement is a kind of verbal irony. Instead of honestly saying how dramatic something is, the writer underplays it. It often takes a moment for the reader to recognize what is really being said, and that recognition is often humorous. A famous and humorous bit of dialogue from *Monty Python and the Holy Grail* depends on understatement. The Black Knight challenges King Arthur to a fight. "None shall pass," the Black Knight warns. When Arthur chops his arm off, the Knight says, "'Tis but a scratch." Later, with no arms left, he says, "It's just a flesh wound," and when he's nothing but a torso on the ground, he says, "All right, we'll call it a draw."

Understatement in an argument works the same way. Someone in New Orleans after Hurricane Katrina might argue for more funding to rebuild levies, offering that it had been a touch wet and that the old levies had somewhat underperformed. Here the writer is not only using understatement in her argument for more funding, but she is establishing a bond with her fellow

Louisiana readers. Someone outside Louisiana probably couldn't get away with ironic understatement or any humorous comments about the disaster without offending people. Just after Katrina, there was far too much pain for most people to laugh about anything related to the hurricane. Likewise, after 9/11, more than one comedian got into big trouble for trying to make a joke about the attacks. It is easy to see that each of these techniques can have an unintended effect if not used judiciously.

Overstatement (or hyperbole) is the flipside of understatement. It illustrates a point by blowing it up so far that no one can fail to see it. An example of hyperbole, an exaggeration, is comedian Jimmy Kimmel saying "In November, Colorado passed an amendment that legalized the recreational use of marijuana. It's resulted in a surge of 'pot tourism.' People come for the weekend to smoke pot and the next thing they know, it's 30 years later they're still there working in a carbon-neutral coffee shop."

Verbal shorthand can have an effect similar to that of understatement. A great example of this was used in 1978 by the great Wyoming trial lawyer Gerry Spence in a case against *Penthouse Magazine* and its publisher Bob Guccione for libeling former Miss Wyoming Kimberly Jayne Pring. Spence, who typically wore fringed buckskin, referred to Guccione as "the gentleman sitting over there in the velvet pants." That little joke pointed out the situational irony of a slick Brooklyn-born publisher of pornography trying to win the confidence of the good citizens of Cheyenne, when in fact he had very little in common with them and their values.

Never underestimate the power of **visual humor**, either. A good technique to use to deflate an opponent's position is to point out the ironies,

*"I can't remember what we're arguing about, either. Let's keep
yelling, and maybe it will come back to us."*

David Sipress/The New Yorker Collection/www.cartoonbank.com

Figure 12.19 Never underestimate the power of visual humor.

absurdities, and hypocrisies of that position. When a humorous image is used, the results can shout when words can only whisper.

Finding the incongruities in a position or between an opponent and his argument can be an effective way to attack. Whether this technique is used humorously or seriously, it often pays to show the difference between what an opponent says and what he or she does. After all, actions speak louder than words. For instance, in one 2007 Internet investigation (found to be true by several reputable fact-checking sites), environmentalist Al Gore's house was compared unfavorably to President George W. Bush's home. The investigation related the environmentally sound construction of Bush's home and cited the energy-wasting features of Al Gore's.

When others are made fun of **(aggressive humor)**, the targets are often white males. Presumably they are the least vulnerable people in society and thus can be made fun of without much fear of offense. A GEICO car insurance ad campaign even invents a group, cavemen, as a humorous target. The safest thing of all is simply to make fun of oneself—not as a part of a group but as a unique and fallible individual.

Sarcasm is one type of humor that can be viewed as hostile. According to a 2010 study, men tend to be more sarcastic than women.[3] Sarcasm is usually aimed at a particular person, but both sarcasm and irony are reversals of people's expectations. Unlike irony, though, sarcasm is not generally well received in academic writing.

It is good advice to make fun of a situation, the people involved. **Satire** is a way of making fun of society's ills. That is exactly what Jonathan Swift does in "A Modest Proposal," an essay often assigned to college students but not often well understood. In the essay, Swift claims that the solution to Irish poverty is to eat the babies. Saving a people by eating its young is wickedly ironic, but it also serves to show that, by doing nothing, England was in effect doing just that—continuing to prosper at the expense of the Irish, who were "every day dying and rotting by cold and famine, and filth and vermin, as fast as can be reasonably expected." England, he says, "would be glad to eat up our whole nation."

Swift also satirizes the English treatment of the Irish people by referring to the Irish using the language of animal husbandry. He refers to them as "breeders" and mentions "Infant's flesh will be in season throughout the year, but more plentiful in March." It is obvious to most readers that Swift is not criticizing and demeaning the Irish; instead he is supporting them by strongly implying that the English treat them like farm animals. Criticism of others can be okay when it's ironic and is obviously meant to support the criticized group—in this example, the Irish. Direct criticism of the English wasn't likely to draw them into the argument; instead, Swift was trying to shock the English into looking critically at their behavior toward the Irish. The contemporary effect of it wasn't great. Most readers took it as humor

---

[3]Bowles, Andrea, and Albert Katz. "When Sarcasm Stings." *Discourse Process* 48.4 (2011): 215–236.

or a misguided attack. However, because of Swift's wicked wit, the essay has lasted for close to three centuries and has helped to solidify the historical view of Irish mistreatment at the hands of the English.

There are many kinds of humor that can profitably be used in argumentative writing. The few listed here should get you started.

Using Humor in Your Arguments

Geeta is in the same Natural Resources and Environment course as Alejo. She is working on an argument in favor of a vegetarian diet. She has run across figures stating that it takes 2,500 gallons of freshwater to produce one pound of beef. This is because most beef is made by feeding corn to cows, and most of that corn is grown in irrigated fields. Most of that water is lost from the freshwater supplies. In that sense, eating beef is much harder on the water supply than eating vegetables and grains, which are grown and fed directly to us, instead of traveling first through the digestive systems of livestock.

In the course of her research, Geeta discovers that the average American eats 100 pounds of beef per year, and she wants to illustrate how much water the average American uses each day by eating beef. She also wants to show that using water by eating beef is a waste because it is unnecessary for health and nutrition. It's like flushing that water down the toilet. Toilets happen to use 1.6 gallons of water per flush. Here was a place for her to use humor in her argument:

> The average American eats 100 pounds of beef per year, and it takes about 2,500 gallons of fresh water to produce one pound of beef. How much water is that per day? To find out, go home and flush your 1.6 gallons-per-flush toilet. Now flush it again. And again. And five more times. By this point, someone else in your household might have become worried. To throw them off your scent, you should probably groan, and speak softly through the door, asking for the name of a good gastroenterologist. Then flush the toilet 40 more times. But wait, you're not done yet. Push that handle another 200 times. No one in his right mind (or bowels) would ever stand there and waste the water it would take to flush the toilet 248 times, right? But that's just what we're doing every day by eating beef.

That illustration could have been created without the humor, and it would still be effective. It's an amazing statistic to say that by eating beef we use the equivalent of 248 toilet flushes every day. However, the humor may help to win the trust of the audience by sounding less preachy than the information would sound without the humor. It also serves to make the blind wastefulness more concrete, clearly showing the ridiculous excesses of human consumption.

 **Tip 12a**

When Is Humor Appropriate?

There are times when humor has a place in an argument:

- To make a stressful situation seem less stressful.
- To establish an alliance with the audience indicating that "We are all in this together; I am part of your group; I understand your culture, and I demonstrate this via my use of humor that you understand."
- To make oneself appear to be less threatening or appear to be an insider.
- As a way to bridge the distance between disparate groups or views.
- To avoid confrontation.

your turn 12e ▶ **PRACTICE Evaluate Humor In Arguments**

The Onion (http://www.theonion.com) is a news source that publishes satirical stories on current events. Visit the site and evaluate the humor used in one of the articles you find.

1. Based on the guidelines in Tips 12a and 12b, is the humor used appropriately?
2. Does the article use self-deprecating, other-deprecating, or affiliative humor?
3. What techniques does the author use to convey the humor? Anecdotes? Understatement? Visual humor? Sarcasm? Are the techniques effective?

Reflect and Apply

1. How are graphics used in the sources you have found for your argument? Are they persuasive? Are they manipulative? Can they be both at the same time? What are you doing to evaluate the messages presented by the visual arguments in your sources?
2. How are you using graphics in an ethical way, supporting your argument without resorting to manipulation?
3. If you do not use graphics created by others, explain how you are creating your own graphics.
4. Is your topic one for which humor may be used in order to defuse tensions? If so, how are you able to use humor in an appropriate and successful way in your argument?

☞ Tip 12b

When Is Humor Inappropriate?
There are also times when you should not use humor in an argument:

- To belittle another group's values, beliefs, or customs.
- To enforce negative stereotypes.
- To disguise an attack on an opponent's character (just as we would avoid the fallacy of *ad hominem*—see Chapter 5, "Read Critically and Avoid Fallacies").
- To forge an alliance with an audience in order to feel superior over another group.
- To draw attention away from weak support of your claim.
- To play for laughs with off-color jokes or jokes based on sexual innuendoes, body parts, or body functions.

KEEPING IT LOCAL

Gas prices remain volatile, going up and down depending on such vagaries as weather, global conditions, and the economy. Some people fume every time they fill up at the pump, arguing that there is no reason we should have to pay so much for imported oil. Reading and listening to the myriad arguments in newspapers, on news programs, on blogs, and at the water cooler can be overwhelming. It is easy to gravitate toward quick and easy photographs, charts, and graphs that seem to make clear solutions such as, "Drill closer to home."

As we are faced with the growing need to search for new sources of energy, be careful as you evaluate the many solutions proposed by various arguments. Don't be a slave to the lure of visual images without evaluating them for their soundness and determining their credibility and the arguer's reason for using them.

● – – – – – – – – – – – – – – ●

Find images that both support and oppose an argument you are developing. How are the images created to stir your emotions? What techniques are used to sway you? Recognizing the appeal of an argument's graphics can empower you to feel more confident in your reaction to and your assessment of the argument itself.

CHAPTER 13

Develop and Edit Argument Structure and Style

Halfway through the dinner shift at the restaurant where you've worked for the last six years, you peer out into the dining room. Sweat is running under your cap, and you've been cooking like mad. But the dining room is only half full. The owner, Robie, is at the cash register having yet another argument with a customer about the use of an expired coupon. Tonight is the night, you decide. You've got to talk to Robie about the decline in his business. In his efforts to keep costs down, he ends up fighting with his customers and driving them away. If he keeps it up, the place will close and you both will be out of work.

Now the restaurant has closed for the night; everything is cleaned and stored in its proper place. The moment is here, but something holds you back. The speech you've been going over in your head is basically a complaint. You imagine rambling, blaming Robie, and in the end convincing him of nothing except that you don't like him. And that's not true—you've become good friends over the years, even though he's your boss. What you really need is a different approach or format for your message—not a rant or a note, but maybe something more formal, like a presentation. And it needs to be well organized, too, with facts instead of accusations. Maybe you could include statistics from the restaurant industry and some examples—maybe even a case study from someone in Robie's shoes who turned his business around. Although it is late when you get home, now is the time. You begin to lay out your argument.

All Illustrations by iStockphoto.com/A-digit

319

COMMUNITY

School-Academic

Workplace

Family-Household

Neighborhood

Social-Cultural

Consumer

Concerned Citizen

TOPIC: Business

ISSUE: Poor Customer Service Driving Away Customers

AUDIENCE: Your boss, Chef and Restaurateur Robeson Barnes

CLAIM: Getting creative with problem customers can improve customer service and increase sales.

In this textbook you have learned the terms used to discuss argument: *claim, warrant, data, grounds, support,* and *rebuttal.* However, it is rare to use these terms in an actual argument. In writing your claim, you don't say, "My *claim* for this essay is . . ." Nor do you say, "The *warrants* of my argument are . . ." In fact, you generally will not use the first-person pronoun *I* at all. So how do you make sure that your arguments include the language appropriate to argumentative writing? In this section, you will learn how to introduce the various sections of your argument. The three categories of material that you introduce are:

- The argument itself (your claim)
- The support
- The opposition and your rebuttal of the opposition

In Chapter 13 you will learn to:

- Enhance your argument by editing both the argument's structure and its style.
- Improve your argument's structure.
- Enhance your argumentative style.

Consider Your Argument's Claim

Introduce Your Claim

Your introduction, which you will learn more about later in this chapter, has two parts: the hook, which grabs the reader's attention and sets the claim in context, and the claim itself. It is important that your reader know what type of argument you are making from the first paragraph, so the language you use to introduce the claim must provide a roadmap for the reader.

- **Is your claim based on causes or effects?**
  - ° The ~~main cause~~ of acid rain in California is . . .
  - ° Some contributors to the problem of inflation are . . .
  - ° To get to the root (basis) of the problem of welfare fraud, we must consider . . .
  - ° The primary effect of identity theft is . . .
  - ° The outcomes of a peer-based discipline approach are . . .
  - ° An increase in global spending produces . . .
- **Is your claim based on an extended definition?**
  - ° The main point of argument in abortion issues is the *definition* of the term *life*.
  - ° People don't understand global warming because the term has not been *explained* properly.
  - ° To clarify the argument about euthanasia, we must *specify* what is meant by the phrase *quality of life.*
- **Is the claim an evaluation?**
  - ° An *evaluation* of the various solutions to the problem of teenage pregnancy will lead to the most cost-effective method.
  - ° After reviewing the criteria, we can *judge* the most nearly fair labor practices.
  - ° Before suggesting that student achievement has increased, educators should *review* the factors that determine student achievement.
- **Are you proposing a solution to a problem?**
  - ° The *solution* to the problem of overcrowding in schools is . . .
  - ° To *eliminate* childhood obesity, schools should:
    - *Implement*
    - *Enforce*
    - *Provide*
    - *Put into effect*
    - *Stop/end/cease*
    - *Start/begin/initiate*
    - *Use/employ*
    - *Apply*
- **Does your claim argue that something is a fact?** With a claim of fact, concrete, specific language is important but the specific terms used in the discussion will depend on the subject matter.

When your thesis uses specific terminology to cue the reader to expect a specific type of argument, your argument will be more successful. In the case of the restaurant proposal, the claim is that Robie would keep more customers

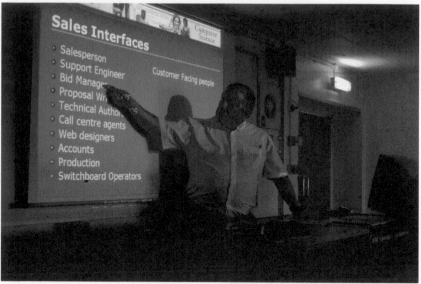

Figure 13.1 Visual presentations can go a long way toward convincing an audience if you are careful to accompany the text with explanations.

if he learned to stop fighting with them. Stating that explicitly might turn Robie off to the argument. It might be better to soft-sell the idea—not hide it exactly but rather imply it. Turn it into a positive. Maybe even save it for the last slide in your PowerPoint presentation. Something like, "Now you can help your customers and grow your business," sounds much better than stating the claim more frankly, such as, "Robie, you need to quit driving your customers out the doors before you have to close them for good." The checklist titled "Edit Your Claim" provides questions to ask while editing your claim.

your turn 13a GET STARTED Edit Your Claim Introduction

Write a claim for a paper you are currently working on so that it uses language that indicates the type of argument you are making: cause–effect, solution, definition, or evaluation. Alternately, use one of the following issues to develop a claim.

- Street improvement
- Degree requirements
- Academic integrity
- Stress
- Sex education
- Diet or food consumption

Edit Your Claim: A Checklist

- ☐ Every claim should answer these questions:
  - ☐ Where do I stand on this issue?
  - ☐ What point of view do I want my audience to accept at the end of my argument?
  - ☐ What is my purpose in delivering this argument?
- ☐ A **claim of cause** should also answer this question:
  - ☐ What, exactly, is the cause–effect relationship I am claiming?
- ☐ A **claim of definition** should also answer these questions:
  - ☐ What is the word or term I intend to define?
  - ☐ What are clear characteristics, examples, and synonyms for the word?
  - ☐ What are specific conditions must my definition meet in order to be accepted by my audience?
- ☐ A **claim of evaluation** should also answer the question:
  - ☐ Have I provided and explained the standards and guidelines I used to make my evaluation?
- ☐ A **problem-based claim** should also answer the questions:
  - ☐ Is it clear what I'm asking my audience to do?
  - ☐ Do my claims propose solutions to problems?
- ☐ A **claim of fact** should also answer the questions:
  - ☐ Precisely what information am I claiming as fact?
  - ☐ Does this claim of fact respond to an issue that can be considered legitimate and arguable?

State Your Claim

Where should your claim be placed in your argument? Should you come right out and state the claim explicitly, or should you be indirect? **Explicit claims** are made obvious by the writer; they are directly stated.

Mark Lange's editorial "Do You Work in Sales? Thank You." directly states its claim in the title, restates it in the subtitle, and restates it several more times throughout the essay:

> Had enough of the recession? Next time somebody pitches you something—whether or not you open your wallet—at least say thanks.

> Because economic growth is a story we tell one another. Transactions are its dialogue. And the authors of both are the master storytellers: salespeople.

> Before you tune out, consider this: Nothing happens until somebody sells someone something. And no matter what the rest of

Lange, Mark. "Do You Work in Sales? Thank You." *Christian Science Monitor* 9 Sept., 2009.

us do all day, our paychecks and prosperity rely on the efforts of salespeople.

And so on. The writer makes his claim obvious because he believes that everyone should act upon it but that currently, not everyone does. He wants to drive his point home.

Implicit claims are implied but not hidden very deeply. They quickly become obvious to the average reader. Implicit claims are common in professional writing, but they are not recommended to students because of the risk of making an unclear claim. Sojourner Truth uses an implicit claim in her speech "Ain't I a Woman?"

> *Well, children, where there is so much racket there must be something out of kilter. I think that 'twixt the negroes of the South and the women at the North, all talking about rights, the white men will be in a fix pretty soon. But what's all this here talking about?*
>
> *That man over there says that women need to be helped into carriages, and lifted over ditches, and to have the best place everywhere. Nobody ever helps me into carriages, or over mud-puddles, or gives me any best place! And ain't I a woman? Look at me! Look at my arm! I have ploughed and planted, and gathered into barns, and no man could head me! And ain't I a woman? I could work as much and eat as much as a man—when I could get it—and bear the lash as well! And ain't I a woman? I have borne thirteen children, and seen most all sold off to slavery, and when I cried out with my mother's grief, none but Jesus heard me! And ain't I a woman?*
>
> *Then they talk about this thing in the head; what's this they call it? [member of audience whispers, "intellect"] That's it, honey. What's that got to do with women's rights or negroes' rights? If my cup won't hold but a pint, and yours holds a quart, wouldn't you be mean not to let me have my little half measure full?*
>
> *Then that little man in black there, he says women can't have as much rights as men, 'cause Christ wasn't a woman! Where did your Christ come from? Where did your Christ come from? From God and a woman! Man had nothing to do with Him.*
>
> *If the first woman God ever made was strong enough to turn the world upside down all alone, these women together ought to be able to turn it back, and get it right side up again! And now they is asking to do it, the men better let them.*
>
> *Obliged to you for hearing me, and now old Sojourner ain't got nothing more to say.*

It isn't until the third paragraph that Sojourner Truth claims that blacks and women ought to be educated, and she only does that with a metaphorical question about measuring cups. Finally in the fourth paragraph, she gives her claim directly, this time by quoting someone who disagrees and using the opposition to give the claim in the negative. Her speech is artful. The audience knew what she stood for: justice and equality for African Americans and women. She didn't need to tell them that; therefore she had some freedom to be artistic and to use rhetorical devices and figures of speech instead of stating her claim explicitly.

Hidden claims are useful when the writer wants the reader to do more of the work. A humorous argument might use irony and never state or even strongly imply the real claim. One example of this is "A Modest Proposal" (1729), in which the explicit claim is that in order to solve the Irish famine, parents should sell their babies as food. Obviously, that's not at all the real claim. Swift is actually arguing that the English and Irish people should step in and work together to solve the problems of poverty and starvation. Swift actually states his true claim toward the end of his essay. Up to that point it remains hidden because until then he is explicitly stating things his country should not do. A good reader understands that Swift isn't really advocating the eating of babies but instead is trying to get people to save the starving and the poor.

> *Therefore let no man talk to me of other expedients: Of taxing our absentees at five shillings a pound: Of using neither cloaths, nor houshold furniture, except what is of our own growth and manufacture: Of utterly rejecting the materials and instruments that promote foreign luxury: Of curing the expensiveness of pride, vanity, idleness, and gaming in our women: Of introducing a vein of parsimony, prudence and temperance: Of learning to love our country, wherein we differ even from Laplanders, and the inhabitants of Topinamboo: Of quitting our animosities and factions, nor acting any longer like the Jews, who were murdering one another at the very moment their city was taken: Of being a little cautious not to sell our country and consciences for nothing: Of teaching landlords to have at least one degree of mercy towards their tenants. Lastly, of putting a spirit of honesty, industry, and skill into our shop-keepers, who, if a resolution could now be taken to buy only our native goods, would immediately unite to cheat and exact upon us in the price, the measure, and the goodness, nor could ever yet be brought to make one fair proposal of just dealing, though often and earnestly invited to it.*

> *Therefore I repeat, let no man talk to me of these and the like expedients, 'till he hath at least some glympse of hope, that there will ever be some hearty and sincere attempt to put them into practice.*

In his essay "On the Decay of the Art of Lying," Mark Twain claims that the art of lying has decayed, that people don't lie nearly so well nowadays, and that the art of lying ought to be restored to its former place of grandeur and perfection. Of course, his hidden claim is that, while we all do lie, we are hypocritical about it and lie to help ourselves and hurt others. In reality, we ought to realize what liars we are and lie only for good, not for evil. Like Swift, Twain can't resist explicitly stating his claim, again toward the end of his argument:

> *Lying is universal—we all do it; we all must do it. Therefore, the wise thing is for us diligently to train ourselves to lie thoughtfully, judiciously; to lie with a good object, and not an evil one; to lie for others' advantage, and not our own; to lie healingly, charitably, humanely, not cruelly, hurtfully, maliciously; to lie gracefully and graciously, not awkwardly and clumsily; to lie firmly, frankly, squarely, with head erect, not haltingly, tortuously, with pusillanimous mien, as being ashamed of our high calling. Then shall we be rid of the rank and pestilent truth that is rotting the land; then shall we be great and good and beautiful, and worthy dwellers in a world where even benign Nature habitually lies, except when she promises execrable weather. Then—But I am but a new and feeble student in this gracious art; I cannot instruct this Club.*

In other arguments, claims may be missing altogether. Stephen Dubner's "What Should Be Done About Standardized Tests? A Freakonomics Quorum," which is readily available online, is really a collection of different opinions by experts. In a way, it has no claim of its own except a set of claims made by other, various experts. Readers get to make a decision and formulate their own claims.

Position Your Claim

A good introduction pulls the reader in and reveals the issue or topic at hand. It may also clearly state the arguer's claim. As a student, the safest thing you can do is to clearly state your claim in your introductory paragraph. However, as you get better at arguing and constructing papers, you will develop the skills to keep your reader in suspense by describing the issue but not your take on that issue. At that time, you can trust your readers to wait.

Your introduction can be short—a paragraph, or perhaps even just a sentence or two—or it can take several paragraphs. The introduction to Richard Louv's book *Last Child in the Woods: Saving Our Children from Nature-Deficit Disorder* is an example of a brief, direct approach to an issue, along with a clear statement of the claim. The initial sentence contains the factual claim that underpins his entire ethical argument:

> *If, when we were young, we tramped through forests of Nebraska cottonwoods, or raised pigeons on a rooftop in Queens, or fished for Ozark bluegills, or felt the swell of a wave that traveled a thousand miles before lifting our boat, then we were bound to the natural world and remain so today. Nature still informs our years—lifts us, carries us.*

Dubner, Stephen J. "What Should Be Done About Standardized Tests? A Freakonomics Quorum." Freakonomics. 20 Dec., 2007.

Pressmaster/Shutterstock.com

Figure 13.2 The best logical support in the world may not keep an audience interested. Using suspense and other strategies will ensure that your audience will stick with you until the end of your argument.

He is saying that because children's experiences of nature permanently bind them to the natural world (the factual claim), we need to make sure children experience nature (the ethical claim). As the introduction continues, we get more of a sense of the ethical argument, of what is at stake for children if we do not introduce them to nature in a meaningful way. Later, he discusses how exposure to nature encourages children to cherish and care for the natural world as they grow into adulthood.

> *For children, nature comes in many forms. A newborn calf; a pet that lives and dies; a worn path through the woods; a fort nested in stinging nettles; a damp, mysterious edge of a vacant lot—whatever shape nature takes, it offers each child an older, larger world separate from parents. Unlike television, nature does not steal time; it amplifies it. Nature offers healing for a child living in a destructive family or neighborhood. It serves as a blank slate upon which a child draws and reinterprets the culture's fantasies. Nature inspires creativity in a child by demanding visualization and the full use of the senses. Given a chance, a child will bring the confusion of the world to the woods, wash it in the creek, turn it over to see what lives on the unseen side of that confusion. Nature can frighten a child, too, and this fright*

Louv, Richard. *Last Child in the Woods: Saving Our Children from Nature-Deficit Disorder.* Chapel Hill, NC: Algonquin Books, 2005.

serves a purpose. In nature, a child finds freedom, fantasy, and privacy: a place distant from the adult world, a separate peace.

Often, the first half of a claim is placed in the opening paragraph and the second half of the claim comes later. However, in Thomas J. Hanson's blog editorial "College Graduation Rates–Statistics Tell a Sad Tale," the first part of the claim is located in the first three paragraphs (as shown in the following excerpt), and the second half of the claim comes much later, starting around paragraph 13.

The results of a first-of-its-kind study recently graced the front pages of the Boston Globe. In "Hub Grads Come Up Short in College," James Vaznis revealed an all too similar refrain regarding college completion rates.

Of the members of the graduating class from Boston high schools for the year 2000 who had gone on to higher education, nearly two-thirds of the class had not earned a college diploma seven years after they had begun collegiate studies.

*The findings were particularly troublesome for a city that has touted its steadily increasing college enrollment rates over the last few years. In simplest terms, **Boston does see more high school graduates enrolled in college than does the nation as a whole, but the college completion rate for those students is actually lower than the national average.***

Hanson is arguing that Boston high school students are completing college degrees at a lower rate than the national average, but that isn't his entire claim. The blogger's whole claim is that this problem is best solved not by the traditional solution of shoring up education from kindergarten through 12th grade, but instead by focusing on the education that colleges themselves provide. We see this later in the essay.

The state of public education has focused on the K-12 system in recent years. *During that time frame, higher education has earned a free pass. In fact, the general consensus from most folks is that America's colleges and universities represent the best of the educational system in our country.*

However, Mark Schneider, the vice president for new educational initiatives at the American Institutes for Research, offers a very contrasting viewpoint. In "The Costs of Failure Factories in American Higher Education," Mark Schneider asks, "If there is virtually universal agreement that American high schools are failing, how do our colleges and universities measure up against such a low benchmark?" Turns out not very well.

Hanson, Thomas J. "College Graduation Rates–Statistics Tell a Sad Tale." Open Education. 20 Nov. 2008.

Hanson says that while the problem is obvious—in fact, that it is "an all too familiar refrain"—the solution is something new. The solution is to examine and improve college education to make it fit student needs better; the rest of the essay goes on to discuss how that might be done. This is really a typical problem–solution essay. The writer merely takes some time to reveal his entire claim.

Another common tactic is to ask a question in the title and let the argument answer it. That way, the reader is hooked in by suspense, at least for awhile. Readers want to read on to find the answer. For other guidelines on writing effective titles, see the section "Supply a Strong Title" later in this chapter.

Still other arguments will hook the reader but leave the claim unstated, perhaps until the conclusion of the argument. Finally, some arguments leave their claim implied throughout, never directly stating it.

How should you introduce your claim to Robie? He is known to be sensitive and to take things personally. That's why he's been arguing with his customers in the first place. Maybe you could start with humor and by agreeing with Robie's views on customer relations. You begin to gather stories of nightmare customers who want something for nothing and take great pleasure in watching retailers dance to meet their needs. Only then will you move to the all important "but." Robie is right, *but* being right isn't always the goal in customer service.

your turn 13b ▶ **GET STARTED Edit Your Claim**

1. How will your argument benefit if you state your claim explicitly?
2. How will your argument benefit if you state your claim only implicitly?
3. Would you ever consider hiding your claim?
4. How could you hide your claim in a way that is still ethical and serves your purposes?

Introduce Your Opposition

As you learned in Chapter 6, "Work Fairly with the Opposition," it is important to present your argument with as little bias as possible. This means respectfully presenting for your reader's consideration opposing or alternate views. (Sometimes there is no view directly opposing your own, yet there are lots of alternative views. For example, you may be arguing that a bullying policy needs to be instituted at your daughter's school. There may be no formal objection to this policy, but there may be differing views regarding how the policy should be implemented.) A clear and objective presentation of the opposition's case is one sign of a strong writer. There are two ways to introduce opposing views in your argument.

- The opposing view is incorrect.
- The opposing view is correct, but . . . (does not completely solve the problem or does not go far enough toward a solution)

The Opposing View Is Incorrect

You may feel that the opposing position is incorrect. You find it mildly inaccurate or wildly wrong. You may be slightly amused by the view, or you may be highly offended. You may find the opposition misleading or downright evil. Regardless of how you feel, the manner in which you present the ideas of others is a mark of your character. A respectful tone of voice and an objective treatment of alternate claims will go a long way to make your argument professional and persuasive. Some structures for introducing an opposing view that you feel is incorrect are:

- No evidence supports X.
- X's example of . . . is incorrect.
- The argument put forth by X is flawed.
- Although X was once a widely held view, recent findings no longer support it.

your turn 13c GET STARTED Edit the Introduction of Incorrect Opposing Views

For your own paper, or for the claim you produced in Your Turn 13a, introduce two opposing views in an objective way.

The Opposing View Is Correct, but . . .

There are times when the opposition is correct; even in these cases, opposition cannot be wished away or ignored. Because it could be construed as unethical or negligent to suppress alternative claims and their support, you must present them. The goal is to present the material objectively and to state clearly why the view either is not actually relevant to the current argument or perhaps why does not go far enough. In the following examples, the italicized words and phrases introduce the opposition and the rebuttal.

- *X is a solution* for several problems *but is not suited* to . . .
- *Although X's* example of . . . may be correct, *it does not apply* to . . .
- The argument put forth by *X has some value, but it has largely been discredited* by . . .
- *X* could be a *good* solution *if* . . .
- It is true that *X is the effect for some* people; *however, for this group* . . .
- *Some of the causes X lists* have been noted. *One of these*, though, *does not* . . .

> **your turn 13d** ▶ **GET STARTED** Edit Your Introduction of Correct Opposing Views
>
> For your own argument, or for the claim you produced in Your Turn 13a, introduce two valid, opposing views. Taking an objective tone, state each view and then rebut it.

Create Strong Introductions

Your introduction is one of the most important sections in your argument. Whether you are producing a report for your boss suggesting a move to a larger site, arguing that your son's high school athletic program needs to set higher grade standards, or writing a research paper for a political science course, your argument needs to include a strong introduction.

The introduction performs two basic functions:

1. It hooks your audience, forcing them to become interested in your topic and to care about its outcome.

2. It provides your audience with your thesis—that is, the claim that you support in the remainder of your argument.

There are many ways to hook your audience. You can tell them a brief story that sets up the claim to come. You can misdirect them, sending them in a direction that is opposite of your true intention. You can set up the conflict explicitly and immediately. The function your introduction absolutely must perform is to get the audience's attention. And you don't have long to do so. Think of how many times you've been in a waiting room somewhere with only a stack of old magazines to entertain you until your name is called. You pick up a copy of *Time* and flip through the pages. You start this article, you start that one. Finally, you settle in to read about the rising crime rate in rural areas. You don't live in a rural area, never even been near a cow. So why did you reject the first two articles but decide to read this one? Probably because the introduction made the subject of rural crime seem interesting. The author provided a hook that drew you in, and you wanted to know more. This is your first job as a writer: make the audience want to learn more. If you don't get their attention from the beginning, all the brilliant reasons and support in the remainder of your argument will never be heard. Let's look at some ways to heighten an audience's interest:

- Anecdote (a brief story)
- Misdirection (fooling the audience for a time)
- Conflict (one thing versus another)
- Suspense (creating anticipation)
- A seeming impossibility (misdirection that generates suspense)

Anecdote

An **anecdote** is a brief story, often a personal memory or experience, that sets the tone for the argument's claim. Anecdotes can be used anywhere in your argument where a good story is needed, but they work especially well to introduce your issue. A good anecdote must have these elements:

- It must be brief. Stories that go on and on will bore the audience. Make your anecdote short and to the point, using only those details that are relevant to your purpose.
- It must seem real. If a hypothetical story is not realistic or feels contrived, an audience can tell.

Marjory Simpson was surprised to see the sheriff's car and ambulance in her neighbor's driveway as she returned from the grocery store. She lifted bags out of her trunk as EMTs wheeled out a gurney covered with a sheet. Moments later, a handcuffed teenager was escorted to the sheriff's cruiser. Jim Stone, the sheriff's deputy, rolled a length of yellow tape around the porch and several trees in the front yard.

Marjory had moved to the small town of Six Acres a year earlier to escape the growing crime rates of Tulsa. This was the second murder in the town since she'd arrived. Maybe she hadn't moved far enough out. It seemed that even in this rural community, crime was on the rise.

How well does this anecdote work as an introduction to the subject of crime in rural areas? First, it is brief, only around 100 words. Second, the story is realistic with no gruesome details thrown in, which might make it seem contrived. A crime scene is described simply, through the eyes of someone who had moved to the country to escape the crime of the big city. Notice, too, the scarcity of details: only a few names, yellow police tape, and bags of groceries—just enough to keep the scene feeling authentic. The claim comes at the end of the paragraph, introducing the issue of rising crime in rural areas, the focus of the argument.

Misdirection

To misdirect an audience is to lead them down one path so that they are temporarily tricked into thinking that the topic or your position is different from the one that is ultimately presented. **Misdirection** gives a bigger punch to the actual claim once it is reached.

A paper I once received from a student began, "Hitler was right." Well, needless to say, that got my attention. Hitler, infamous for being one of the most evil men of all time, was right about something? A nice, polite 18-year-old was agreeing with him? I read further: I was *hooked*, you might say.

"Hitler was right. Our youth are our most important commodity." Okay, I get it. I was led down the path of outrage, tricked just as the author had intended me to be. I was temporarily misdirected from the student's ultimate discussion of the importance of our young people by a quote from Hitler. It worked. The writer had my attention.

Misdirection should have these elements:

- It should lead the audience down an exciting path.
- That path should be false.
- The real situation should be explained quickly so that the audience doesn't feel duped and stop trusting the writer.
- The real situation should also be somewhat interesting.

Arrest rates are skyrocketing. Burglaries are up 25%. Rapes are up 17%. The murder rate has escalated 8% in one decade. Young adults are being incarcerated at a rate that has never been seen. Six Acres, Oklahoma, home to 20,000 inhabitants, is seeing a troubling increase in crime that exhibits no likelihood of slowing.

Initially, the startling statistics lead the audience to believe that the argument is going to be about big-city crime, the likes that are seen in New York or Chicago. The paragraph ends with the seemingly casual mention that it is a small, unknown town experiencing this crime wave. The jolt, and therefore the increased interest level, comes from the unexpected final sentence. The audience wants to know more about these rising levels of rural crime.

Conflict

Use **conflict** when you want to immediately highlight seemingly irreconcilable differences among factions or groups. In argumentative essays, the issue being addressed is often surrounded by conflict. One group wants this, another group wants that. Often, there are many sides an issue. But just as often, there are two groups whose views seem to be lodged at opposite ends of the spectrum. Often the conflict between them seems irresolvable. The introduction is the place to foreground the conflict, establishing the battle lines from the beginning.

Conflict can generate attention and excitement if it has the following elements:

- Two sides the reader cares about—either by liking or disliking at least one side.
- Something at issue that can be decided by a winner and a loser—though it might end up in compromise.
- Some uncertainty as to which side will prevail.

In recent years, many parents have argued that the school districts need to be improved—that is, with the exception of the schools that their own children attend. Surveys indicate that parents with children in magnet programs believe their children's schools are doing fine. They typically fight any changes that school districts want to make in order to improve the school system if those changes threaten the existence or scope of their own schools' programs.

Right away the writer has set up a conflict between parents' concerns about the overall success of their school districts and their concerns that their children's particular schools might be negatively affected by attempts to improve the system. In this case, claims will likely attempt to reconcile the conflict and suggest solutions.

Suspense

Use **suspense** when you want to hold off on presenting the audience with your claim so that you increase anticipation. There are lots of ways of generating suspense, including anecdotes, conflict, misdirection, and seeming impossibilities. But suspense can also be generated by telling only part of a story or leaving out some important piece of information that an audience wants to have. In general, suspense can be created if you:

- Gain the attention of the audience—essentially by promising to reveal something interesting.
- Delay fulfillment of that promise.

It's Friday night, and we are at the Olympics, the Special Olympics, that is. My son is on a relay-race team competing against fourth-graders from all over the school district.

The audience wants to know if the writer's son is going to win. In the remainder of the introduction, this hook, loaded with bait to get the audience's eyes to continue down the page, will need to be followed with a claim. For example, the paragraph can be continued this way:

We want to see his team win, but of course anybody's win is welcome in the Special Olympics, where disabled kids learn that they are not so different from others and can enjoy sports that were once deemed out of their range. Sadly, our anticipation about our son's possible win is small compared to our dread that funds to sponsor the Olympics may be cut. If the government cuts Special Olympics from its budget, this really will be our son's—and other parents', sons', and daughters'—last race.

The hook, and the suspense it generated, has its conclusion in the introduction's final sentence, where the claim is made explicit.

A Seeming Impossibility

One effective type of misdirection is to present an audience with a situation that sounds impossible. Perhaps it sounds too good to be true, too awful to be real, too unlikely to be a mere coincidence, too odd to have been planned. Unlike a standard misdirection, this technique usually involves the audience's understanding that they are purposely being toyed with and kept in suspense, so it isn't necessary to present the real situation as quickly. The solution to the riddle might only come at the very end of a long argument.

Effective misdirection can be created using the following elements:

- Present a highly unlikely claim.
- Resolve the seeming impossibility by explaining the real situation and how it was possible after all.

Perhaps we shouldn't ignore those infomercials for exercise balls, Tai Bo, and diet programs. It seems that looking better not only improves your body but may also save your mind. A new study links overweight, particularly in people who carry extra weight in their midsections, to a higher incidence of Alzheimer's disease.

What seems impossible about this hook is that one's body can size have an effect on the health of one's mind. A normal-weight body, the claim following the hook argues, may be key to avoiding Alzheimer's disease, a disease that attacks the mind. The claim, then is this: to save the mind, mind the body.

Other standard hooks for introductions include the following: using interesting quotations or startling statistics, asking questions that you intend to answer in your argument, and making comparisons, often to show that one side is different in an unanticipated way.

What type of introduction might ease your boss into listening to your argument about his poor customer service? No one wants to face the fact that failure is his or her own fault. You could begin with a few anecdotes of outrageous customer incidents that you have gathered from others. You can show how, in each case, the customer was wrong. Then you can introduce the idea that even wrong customers deserve the best service that can be given. The anecdotes can thus pave the way for Robie to see that he is not alone.

your turn 13e ▶ PRACTICE Edit Your Introductions

Select one of the topics related to the various communities from Chapter 2, "Explore an Issue That Matters to You," and narrow it to a claim. Use three of the following hooks, creating three separate introductions for your claim:

- Anecdote (a brief story)
- Misdirection (fooling the audience for a time)
- Conflict (one thing versus another)

- Suspense (creating anticipation)
- A seeming impossibility (misdirection that generates suspense)

Which approach worked the best? Which seemed the most natural for both the topic and for your writing style?

Write Memorable Conclusions

The conclusion sums up the essay but in a new way. Any piece of writing has to have a conclusion; otherwise, the reader feels cheated. The opening passages of an essay or story make a promise to the reader that what follows will entertain us and/or teach us something. A good conclusion helps to fulfill that promise to the reader. It also offers the reader something memorable to take away from the essay—something to ponder, to come back to later in the day, to argue with.

A good piece of writing will have a really good conclusion—one that doesn't simply repeat the thesis. Nobody wants to read a line that says, "So you see, I told you I would tell you about the dust on television screens, I went ahead and told you about the dust on television screens, and now I am telling you that I told you about the dust on television screens."

The best conclusions do sum up the writing, but they do so by finding a way to reaffirm the claim in some new way. If there is repetition, it is repetition that also includes a difference.

Good conclusions provide a sense of completion and satisfaction, but they can also leave the reader with new questions and with a sense that the topic has life beyond the page, that the issue they've been reading about is not a dead issue.

Good conclusions also give a sense of symmetry and form. They often bring back a theme from the opening by completing an anecdote or showing what has changed or stayed the same. There is even a rare type of conclusion that I call "circling back," which repeats the opening almost word for word, to show the reader how different his or her views are now, after reading, and how much he or she has learned about the topic. In other words, circling back shows readers how far they've come. These four general types of conclusions are very effective:

- Broadening out (A): strengthening
- Broadening out (B): extending
- Opposition
- Circling back

Broadening Out

The most common type of conclusion, by far, is what I call broadening out. It is simply a matter of (A) taking the original claim and showing how it applies more broadly to things beyond the specific topic of the essay, or (B) extending the claim and showing how much deeper it goes or how much more detail is involved. Here are two possible conclusions for the "seeming impossibility" introduction that made the claim that being overweight can lead to Alzheimer's disease. One of the conclusions shows the effects of strengthening; the other shows the effects of extending.

Strengthening

The fact that being overweight can lead to a higher incidence of Alzheimer's disease shouldn't be surprising. If one's body is neglected, the mind is often neglected as well. The switch that controls the gene for Alzheimer's may be kept in the "Off" position with a combination of good physical and mental health. Taking the weight off of the midsection may take the weight off that gene as well, keeping that switch "Off," where it should be.

Extending

The fact that being overweight can lead to a higher incidence of Alzheimer's disease shouldn't be surprising. The link between mind and body has been suggested for years. Many diet books suggest that maintaining a positive outlook can keep the pounds off; self-help books agree that keeping physically fit can lesson feelings of depression. Mind and body work together. Keeping both a healthy mind and a healthy body is a holistic approach to general wellness that other countries, including India and China, have practiced for centuries. Maybe we should take a lesson from them.

In both of these conclusions, the reader is invited to go beyond the basic summary—"there are three factors that connect body weight and Alzheimer's disease"—and to think about how the issues of body and mind can address not only Alzheimer's (strengthening) but also one's holistic health picture (extending).

Opposition

When you use opposition, which is simply the technique of moving from one thing to its opposite, your introduction and conclusion take the theme of the paper in opposite directions. If you start your essay with bitter cold, you could end with comforting warmth. If you start with pollution, you could end with a clean environment, or vice versa. Arguments about problems often end with proposed solutions. Stories about war often begin or end with moments of peace.

In this hook from the misdirection example of an introduction, the author sets up some startling statistics about crime that the reader believes, incorrectly, occur in the city.

> *Arrest rates are skyrocketing. Burglaries are up 25%. Rapes are up 17%. The murder rate has escalated 8% over a decade ago. Young adults are being incarcerated at a rate that has never been seen. Six Acres, Oklahoma, home to 20,000 inhabitants, is seeing a troubling increase in crime that shows no likelihood of slowing.*

The claim, which directly follows this hook, is that these statistics were gathered from rural areas where crime is rising faster than it is in major metropolitan areas. To conclude the argument, the writer can offer a solution to the problem or discuss the good things that still take place in rural areas.

> *Although "big city crimes" that have come to rural areas are decreasing community members' feeling of safety, people in such towns as Six Acres are fighting back. They have organized crime watches in their neighborhoods—even in neighborhoods that are not clearly established.*

In other words, instead of collapsing under the weight of escalating crime and their own fears, residents are fighting back.

Circling Back

The technique of circling back can be very effective. It shows just how far the reader has come in the essay. In one extreme, it can repeat the opening almost word for word, but because the audience has read the body of the essay, audience members realize that the words in the opening mean something quite different than they initially thought. Often, the extent of this change is a measure of how much the reader has learned. It can also be a way of emphasizing a theme of the writing. In the following conclusion, the scene from the "anecdote" introduction is repeated, bringing the reader back to the original scene.

> *As Marjory watched the deputy stringing the yellow crime scene tape like a garland around the neighbor's driveway, she realized that no distance from the city was going to outdistance crime. It had followed her to this rural spot. Perhaps fighting back was going to be the only way to win this race: running wasn't working.*

Now the reader is brought full circle to the essay's beginning. The checklist, "Do's and Don'ts for Creating Successful Conclusions" offers some helpful tips for writing conclusions.

The conclusion for your proposal to Robie is partly written: "here's how your customers can help you grow your business." This will be a strengthening of the argument you have already made. You can sum up the two or three ways of working with customers instead of against them. By accepting all reasonable requests, such as cooking dishes off the menu, accepting expired coupons, and changing the menu to suit customer likes and dislikes, Robie can expect more repeat visits, more money in his pocket, and a secure livelihood for years to come.

Do's and Don'ts for Creating Effective Conclusions

☐ Don't introduce new ideas. The conclusion is the place for winding down, not exploring new avenues.

☐ Don't use clichéd closers, such as "in conclusion" or "to summarize."

☐ Don't simply provide a summary of all your argument's points.

☐ Do use one of the previously described techniques to let the reader know you are finished.

☐ Do be more creative, for example, directing your reader to think about your paper's topic in terms of what may happen in the future.

☐ Do provide a summary of all your paper points. But this time, do so in a different or briefer way, providing a look at the future, a solution, or a final comment.

your turn 13f   PRACTICE Edit Your Conclusions

Use the three hooks you created in Your Turn 13e and create conclusions for them, each using a different choice from the list of conclusion types:

- Broadening out (A): strengthening
- Broadening out (B): extending
- Opposition
- Circling back

Your claim is the most important sentence in your argument. You must be clear about your claim, or your reader will not be. Even if you are clear, you need to verify that your claim—the way you have phrased it in your essay—clearly states what you want it to state.

Edit and Organize Your Argument's Support

With your claim solidified and your audience identified, you are ready to review your support and arrange your argument.

Edit Support

You learned in Chapter 11, "Support an Argument with Fact (Logos), Credibility (Ethos), and Emotion (Pathos)," about the three kinds of support and the value of using as many types of support as you can. Let's look at examples of both successful and unsuccessful support. Use these examples as a guide as you edit your own argument.

Support Based on Facts (Logos)

In his article "Beware the Idea of the Student as a Customer: A Dissenting View," Peter Vaill presents a series of miniature logical arguments. Here is one:

> *Education is clearly a service, not a product, and therefore the heavily units-of-product mode of thinking characteristic of business may not hold in a service endeavor. Many businesses, of course, are learning these difficult lessons as well as higher education.*

This approach is effective as long as the reader agrees with his premises and the way his conclusion follows those premises. With his business professor jargon, he sounds like he knows what he's talking about ("heavily units-of-product mode of thinking"); furthermore, the first idea in the passage is presented as if only an idiot would disagree ("education is clearly a service"). The combined effect is that the reader comes to the same conclusion as the author—that education experts are on the wrong track when they think of education as a product.

With regard to your customer-service proposal with your boss Robie, some of your support should be based on facts—perhaps restaurant-industry case studies and research. For example, one study showed that coupons effectively increase visits from regular customers but not visits from new customers. Another study showed that customer wait time affected profits more than food waste. A case study showed the importance of simplicity in menu design. You doubt that your boss will be swayed by studies like these, but if he asks you a question, you can always pull out this information. He might be impressed by your knowledge and interest in the business.

Support to Generate Credibility (Ethos)

Ethos is about credibility, or social norms. It's about the kinds of things we respect and listen to. Who do we listen to and why? Are they experts on a subject? For example, Dr. Mehmet Oz has created a career for himself as a talk show personality. During his regular appearances on the Oprah Show, he addressed health issues of all kinds.

So, who is Dr. Oz and why do people find him so appealing? First, and most importantly, he is a practicing doctor and directs the Cardiovascular Institute and Complementary Medicine Program at New York-Presbyterian Hospital. Secondly, he has authored or co-authored hundreds of articles on medical issues. The handsome doctor's trim physique also adds credibility to his arguments for healthy eating and exercise. And although Oz's ideas are not accepted by everyone all of the time, he is credible enough to be very influential.

"Beware the Idea of the Student as a Customer: A Dissenting View" by Peter Vaill, University of St. Thomas, Minneapolis-St. Paul, MN, 2000.

To move on, then, who are we as authors and why should anyone listen to our views? What is our ethos? Are we experts in our field, as Oz is in his? Do we make wise choices in the research we do and the support we select for our arguments? Do we make arguments that are consistent with the lifestyle we live and the way in which we present ourselves?

Finally, we have to ask ourselves what will seem credible to Robie? The opinions of other chefs? No, because in his opinion he is the equal of any chef. Research studies? Experts in business? Again, no. Robie is stubborn and egotistical, and he thinks he knows what is best. You decide the best credibility you can offer as support will simply be your caring and concern for his business, along with the knowledge and ideas you bring to the table. He won't be threatened by you, and he just might listen.

Emotion-Based Support (Pathos)

In the article "Are Students the New Indentured Servants?" Jeffrey Williams crafts his argument around an analogy sure to generate emotion: today's college students are like the indentured servants of the American past.

> *For the bound, it meant long hours of hard work, oftentimes abuse, terms sometimes extended by fiat of the landowner, little regulation or legal recourse for laborers, and the onerous physical circumstances of the new world, in which two-thirds died before fulfilling their terms.*

Clearly, most college students will survive to pay off their college loans, but the comparison works on an emotional level. The implication is that the "more than four thousand banks" that profit on the college loan system must not care about what happens to these poor indebted students any more than colonial landowners cared about the welfare of their debt-bound servants.

Good emotional support works because it communicates the high stakes involved in an argument. Reading Williams's piece makes a person want to rescue the poor college students from this system of virtual slavery to wealthy bankers. Good emotional support allows the reader to come to that conclusion, which is far more effective than if Williams had come out and said just that.

Emotional support for your proposal to Robie might come from case studies of failed restaurateurs, presented to show your boss the danger of not changing his ways. Or they might come from success stories, tales of restaurateurs who turned things around just in time. You select the latter, deciding that it is more positive but still shows Robie the dangers of staying stuck.

Williams, Jeffrey J. "Are Students the New Indentured Servants?" AlterNet by | Feb. 5, 2009 your turn 13g GET STARTED **Edit Your Support**

Review the support you've used in your argument. Do you have a combination of logos-, ethos-, and pathos-based support? Does any one type of support dominate? If so, why? If one element is missing, why? Will its exclusion be a problem?

Organize Your Support

You can organize the elements of your argument in many ways. The numbers of the elements below refer to the order of the information. You may use as many paragraphs as you need for each section, although generally one idea to a paragraph is best unless your section has subsections that each need their own paragraphs.

All of these elements tend to be included in effective essays. With regard to the sections of the argument, we recommend that item 1 be followed directly by item 2, and that item 6 be presented last. Items 3–5 can be arranged in any order; decide what works best for your argument.

1. Introduction with Claim
   a. The claim can go anywhere in the introduction, but many writers find that placing it near the end helps lead readers to the essay body.
   b. Beginning the introduction with an attention-grabber like those described in the earlier section, "Create Strong Introductions," works well to draw your readers into your argument.
   c. If you feel the need to justify your warrants, now may be a good time to do so; however, explanation of your warrants can be placed wherever it is needed.
2. Background Information
   If your audience needs a bit of history in order to follow your argument, provide the history right after your introduction. This is also a good place to state why you think the topic is important in the first place, particularly if its importance is in question.
3. Examples Supporting Your Claim
   a. College-length papers usually include between three and five examples supporting their claim. Fewer than three may be kind of skimpy; more than five gets a little long. Base the specific number on the assignment or the needs of the project.
   b. If you feel you must justify your use of these examples, do so as you go.
   c. Opposing Views
   d. Rebuttal of Opposing Views
   e. Conclusion

Three Organization Samples of Body Paragraphs

As you can see, there are many combinations of body paragraphs—just use whatever works best for your particular argument, and make sure all of your bases are covered. Here is an example to support a claim of work discrimination.

Claim: Competent, qualified nurses of color in our hospital are regularly passed over for promotion to better-paying positions.

Let's see how the body elements for this claim can be organized in three different ways. (Note that the number of supporting and opposing examples used here is just for illustration; arguments vary regarding the quantity of support they require.)

Sample Body Arrangement One:

1. Supporting Example One
2. Supporting Example Two
3. Supporting Example Three
4. Opposing View One
5. Rebuttal of Opposing View One
6. Opposing View Two
7. Rebuttal of Opposing View Two

Sample Body Arrangement One:

1. Supporting Example One
2. Research indicates that 45 percent of the nurses in hospitals are African American, Hispanic, or Asian American, yet only 5 percent of hospital administrators are people of color.
3. Supporting Example Two
4. Of the 50 nurses of color who submitted application forms for the six senior positions available at our hospital in 2012, only one was promoted.
5. Supporting Example Three
6. Carla Rivera has been a registered nurse for 25 years and recently received the American Society of Nurses' award for logging 500 hours of community service. She applied for a higher position in her unit and was not even interviewed.
7. Opposing View One
8. Hospital administrators say that the 5 percent of administrators who are people of color is proof that they do promote nurses of various ethnicities.
9. Rebuttal of Opposing View One

10. Upon closer examination, it was found that, of these 5 percent, only two positions had been filled from within.

11. Opposing View Two

12. The hospital also argues that it does not feel that the nurses of color who have submitted applications for higher positions have had the same credentials as their white counterparts.

13. Rebuttal of Opposing View Two

14. There is a wide range of abilities and backgrounds among the nursing staff, and it is generalizing to state that white nurses have better training or education than their African American, Hispanic, and Asian American colleagues.

For this arrangement, the writer chose to present all the supporting evidence for his claim first, and then he tackled the opposing views one by one.

Sample Body Arrangement Two:

1. Supporting Example One

2. Opposing View One

3. Rebuttal of Opposing View One

4. Supporting Example Two

5. Opposing View Two

6. Rebuttal of Opposing View Two

Sample Body Arrangement Two:

1. Supporting Example One

   Research indicates that 45 percent of the nurses in hospitals are African American, Hispanic, or Asian American, yet only 5 percent of hospital administrators are people of color.

2. Opposing View One

   Hospital administrators say that the 5 percent of administrators who are people of color is proof that they do promote nurses of various ethnicities.

3. Rebuttal of Opposing View One

   Upon closer examination, it was found that, of these 5 percent, only two positions had been filled from within.

4. Supporting Example Two

   Carla Rivera has been a registered nurse for 25 years and recently received the American Society of Nurses' award for logging 500 hours of community service. She applied for a higher position in her unit and was not even interviewed.

5. Opposing View Two

   The hospital also argues that it does not feel that the nurses of color who have submitted applications for higher positions have had the same credentials as their white counterparts.

6. Rebuttal of Opposing View Two

   There is a wide range of abilities and backgrounds among the nursing staff, and it is generalizing to state that white nurses have better training or education than their African American, Hispanic, and Asian American colleagues.

In this second example, the writer examines each supporting example and the corresponding opposing view before moving to the next supporting example and its corresponding opposing view.

Sample Body Arrangement Three:

1. Opposing View One
2. Opposing View Two
3. Rebuttal of Opposing Views One and Two
4. Supporting Example One
5. Supporting Example Two

Sample Body Arrangement Three:

1. Opposing View One

   Hospital administrators say that the 5 percent of administrators who are people of color is proof that they do promote nurses of various ethnicities.

2. Opposing View Two

   The hospital also argues that it does not feel that the nurses of color who have submitted applications for higher positions have had the same credentials as their white counterparts.

3. Rebuttal of Opposing Views One and Two

   Upon closer examination, it was found that, of these 5 percent, only two positions had been filled from within. There is a wide range of abilities and backgrounds among the nursing staff, and it is generalizing to state that white nurses have better training or education than their African American, Hispanic, and Asian American colleagues.

4. Supporting Example One

   Research indicates that 45 percent of the nurses in the hospital are African American, Hispanic, or Asian American, yet only 5 percent of hospital administrators are people of color.

5. Supporting Example Two

   Carla Rivera has been a registered nurse for 25 years and recently received the American Society of Nurses' award for logging 500 hours of community service. She applied for a higher position in her unit and was not even interviewed.

In this final example, the writer has opted to address the opposing views first, rebut them, and then concentrate on his supporting examples for the remainder of the essay's body.

When you organize your argument in various ways, you will find that some arrangements work better than others. You may want to start with the opposing sides' arguments and then rebut them so that you can spend the remainder of the essay supporting your claim. Or you may find it more useful to present each of your supporting arguments and the corresponding opposition as you go. By trying different arrangements, you can see what works best for your particular claim and audience.

In your presentation to Robie, your organizational strategy will be based on your desire to win him to your side by first humoring him and then offering him ideas for turning each problem customer into an ally. Unruly families might be happier in the family section, waited upon by Rose, who has four children of her own and can handle just about anything. The too-choosy customer can be satisfied by offering "off-menu" selections with fixed prices designed to reward Robie for his extra efforts. Finally, cheapskate customers might be satisfied by free mini-portions of desserts; Robie hates when desserts go to waste, and once customers taste these unique and sweet creations, some of them will order (and pay for) a full portion.

your turn 13h ▶ **PRACTICE Edit the Arrangement of Your Support**

Develop a claim addressing one of the following topics. Then create three different outlines, each one showing a different organization of body paragraphs, based on one of the preceding examples.

1. Something at work that management seems not to notice
2. Expectations from a teacher in one of your classes

Which organizational strategy works best for your claim and the type of support you are using? Next, label each section to indicate whether it includes support based on facts, support based on emotions, or support based on credibility.

Supply a Strong Title

A really good title will hook the audience. It will probably also reveal the general issue or even the specific topic of the argument. Like introductions, titles build suspense for the audience and draw them into the argument. Types of titles include the following:

- Titles that seem impossible: "Hip-Hop Graffiti Is a Significant American Art Form."
- Titles that represent conflict: "The Kindle's Assault on Academia: Amazon Wants to Corner the Textbook Market: But Don't Think It's Gonna Be Easy"
- Titles that generate suspense, often by leaving the reader wanting to know "how": "Loan Ranger: The Way Americans Pay for College Is a Mess; Here's How to Fix It"
- Titles that mark the beginning of an anecdote, such as the story of a particular family: "A Dad on His Own: A New Baby, a Wife's Death, and . . ."
- Titles that use misdirection: "On the Decay of the Art of Lying"

A less effective but still serviceable title will tell what the issue is, give the specific topic related to that issue, and even present the arguer's claim.

These two titles simply state the claim:

- "Killing the Entrepreneurial Spirit: Government Is Not a Good Investor"
- "Government Initiatives Will Not Reduce Homelessness"

These two titles don't give the claim but do present the issue or topic of the argument:

- "That 'Buy American' Provision"
- "The Potential in Hillary Clinton's Campaign for Women"

A bad title doesn't hook the reader or reveal the issue at hand. Here's a title that does neither:

- "Statement in the Great Trial of 1922"

Don't blame Ghandi for that sub-par title: he didn't write it; he actually gave the statement during a real trial. He had been charged with "bringing or attempting to excite disaffection towards His Majesty's Government established by law in British India."

Titles are sometimes inadvertently misleading:
- "No: Alternatives Are Simply Too Expensive"

Even if we see this title in the context of the environment, a lot of readers might not know the word *alternative* refers to alternative energy sources. That fact isn't mentioned until the sixth paragraph.

- Or titles may have grammatical errors. Here are two examples: "Animal Testing and Their Rights"
- "Is Bank Fees Fair to Customers?"

Before you print out your presentation for Robie, you must work on the title, the first thing he will see. The title should draw him in. What you may be tempted to say is, "Robie, No!" or perhaps, "Quit Killing Customers!" That, however, will only turn him off. Instead, you settle on something innocuous but slightly intriguing: "Three Ways to Fatten the Golden Goose."

your turn 13i ▶ **PRACTICE Edit Your Title to Support Your Claim**

Here are some titles, representing the good, the serviceable, and the unsatisfactory. Can you label which is which? Can you identify the five types of hooks? Can you spot the title that contains its argument's claim and which simply discloses its argument's topic?

1. "Stem Cell Research"
2. "The Consequences of Diesel-Powered Vehicles"
3. "Children Shouldn't Be Tried and Prosecuted as Adults"
4. "Would a Federal Gun Ban Lower Indiana's Crime Rate?"
5. "Space Exploration: Manned or Unmanned?"
6. "Sex Should Be Taught in School"
7. "Thirty-Eight Who Saw Murder Didn't Call Police"
8. "Freedom of the Pulpit"
9. "Student Hits Wall, Leaves"
10. "Gun Control"
11. "Capital Punishment Is Wrong"

Participate Effectively in a Peer Review Session

When you are asked to participate in a peer review session, you are being asked to help a classmate (or work colleague) determine what is working and what is not working in an argument. You are also being asked to listen to feedback about what is and is not working in your own argument. This chapter's guidelines for structure and style can help you identify what is effective and not effective. In this final section, we also provide a flowchart (Figure 13.1) to help you work through the process and make the most of your time as a peer reviewer and as a peer reviewee.

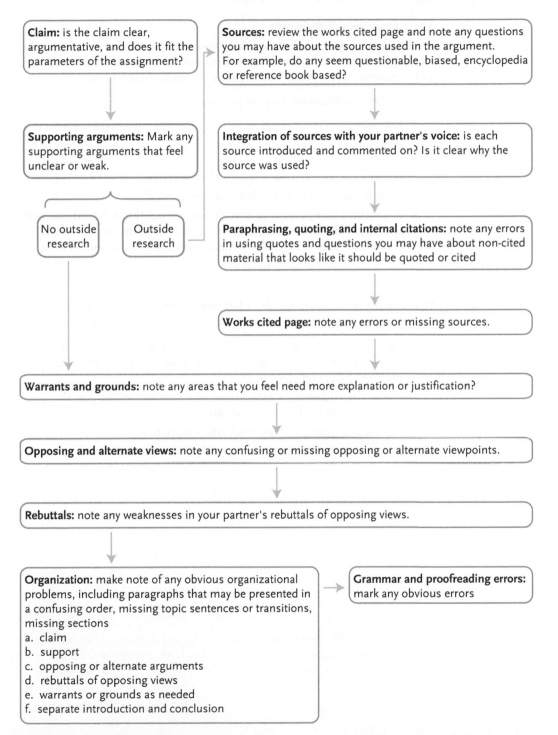

Claim: is the claim clear, argumentative, and does it fit the parameters of the assignment?

Sources: review the works cited page and note any questions you may have about the sources used in the argument. For example, do any seem questionable, biased, encyclopedia or reference book based?

Supporting arguments: Mark any supporting arguments that feel unclear or weak.

Integration of sources with your partner's voice: is each source introduced and commented on? Is it clear why the source was used?

No outside research

Outside research

Paraphrasing, quoting, and internal citations: note any errors in using quotes and questions you may have about non-cited material that looks like it should be quoted or cited

Works cited page: note any errors or missing sources.

Warrants and grounds: note any areas that you feel need more explanation or justification?

Opposing and alternate views: note any confusing or missing opposing or alternate viewpoints.

Rebuttals: note any weaknesses in your partner's rebuttals of opposing views.

Organization: make note of any obvious organizational problems, including paragraphs that may be presented in a confusing order, missing topic sentences or transitions, missing sections
a. claim
b. support
c. opposing or alternate arguments
d. rebuttals of opposing views
e. warrants or grounds as needed
f. separate introduction and conclusion

Grammar and proofreading errors: mark any obvious errors

Figure 13.3 Peer Review Flowchart

Your Role as a Reviewer

Read the assignment carefully, marking areas of concern that your instructor has assigned you to review. If there are no specific review instructions, mark and comment on the issues and concerns shown in Figure 13.3.

In presenting your findings to your partner:

1. Ask your partner to explain anything that does not make sense to you.
2. Although you may have made written comments on many areas of the argument, pick two or three of the most important problems to discuss rather than pointing out a laundry list of errors.
3. Politely point out errors—don't be a know-it-all.
4. Ask if there is anything you haven't pointed out that your critique partner would like to know or, as time permits, if your partner would like you to expound on anything you have marked but have not discussed.

Your Role as a Reviewee

When your partner presents his or her observations (or when your partners present their observations), listen carefully and avoid getting defensive.

1. Take notes. If you do not agree with your reviewer's comments, make note of them anyway. Upon later reflection, you may find that your partner has a good point.
2. Listen for patterns. If more than one reviewer gives you the same advice, you probably want to pay attention.
3. Ask for clarification of any confusing comments.
4. List two or three areas you'd especially like to have clarified.

Reflect and Apply

1. How is your argument's introduction setting the scene for your claim? Explain how your conclusion provides closure for your reader.

2. Explain your reasons for selecting the logical, ethical, and emotional support that you have included. How does each type of support increase your audience's understanding and buy-in? If you have not used all three types of support, explain your decision to leave out one or more types.

3. Review the organization of your argument. Using the Peer Review Flowchart, can you identify any sections that are missing or that need shoring up? Explain how you will address problems.

4. Review your title. Explain how it provides a link to your argument's claim.

KEEPING IT LOCAL

You've done the best you can with your presentation to the restaurant's owner, Robie. His reaction? Better than you had anticipated. Although he doesn't agree that bad customers deserve good service, he is impressed by the amount of work that you did to convince him otherwise. He is willing to consider some of your recommendations. For your part, you are pleased that you will be able to maintain your job while you are still in college.

The success of your proposal came from your willingness to edit every facet of your argument, from the claim and its position to the introduction and corresponding conclusion, the types of support you included, and the arrangement of the ideas on the slides. By taking into account your audience and gearing the argument to his needs and values, you have opened the door to a dialogue in which resolutions can be made and changes set in place.

● – – – – – – – – – – – – – ●

What can you do to ensure that your argument is well-arranged and well-supported? Do you have a friend or classmate you can trust to review your argument and give you good advice? Good arguments are a product of thinking about your own point of view on an issue and then thinking of the best way to present your point of view to others. Are you sure you have done all that you can to persuade your audience?

PART FIVE

An Anthology of Arguments

Anthology 01   School and Academic Community

Anthology 02   Workplace Community

Anthology 03   Family and Household Community

Anthology 04   Neighborhood Community

Anthology 05   Social/Cultural Community

Anthology 06   Consumer Community

All Illustrations by iStockphoto.com/A-digit

Intersections: Contemporary Issues and Arguments

School and Academic Community

About This Reading

Plagiarism, the act of copying or imitating the published work of another writer, is now widespread in our schools and colleges and in journalism. Penalties and policies for this offense vary, but as the author notes at the end, the biggest risk in plagiarizing is the damage it does to one's reputation. This article appeared in *The Christian Science Monitor*.

What Is the Price of Plagiarism?

When someone steals another's words, the penalties can vary widely.
By Karoun Demirjian

If you've kept up with the publishing industry lately, you've heard of Kaavya Viswanathan. The Harvard sophomore got a $500,000 advance from publishing firm Little, Brown, and Co. for her book, "How Opal Mehta Got Kissed, Got Wild, and Got a Life." But her own life took a sour turn after she was accused of copying several passages of her novel either directly or indirectly from books by Megan McCafferty, Sophie Kinsella, Meg Cabot, and Salman Rushdie. It's the most high-profile accusation of plagiarism in a recent spate of scandals that have implicated a variety of figures in a variety of fields.

Last week, Raytheon CEO William Swanson endured public embarrassment and a pay cut when he was outed for copying some of the rules in his book, "Swanson's Unwritten Rules of Management," from Secretary of Defense Donald Rumsfeld, humor columnist Dave Barry, and an obscure World War II-era book by W.J. King. A month ago, researchers from the Brookings Institution in Washington, D.C., unveiled their proof that Russian President Vladimir Putin had copied whole sections of William R. King and David I. Cleland's "Strategic Planning and Policy" in his dissertation. Three years earlier, the newspaper industry had suffered a blow when The New York Times's Jayson Blair was shown to have copied or fabricated dozens of his stories.

Whether in the professional world or the classroom, plagiarism appears to be everywhere. And according to experts, it's on the rise.

"The main reason is the advent of the Internet," says Donald McCabe, a professor at Rutgers University who has studied plagiarism in secondary and higher education for more than a decade. According to his research, 58 percent of high school students admitted to having committed an act of plagiarism in the past year.

© iStockphoto.com/A-digit

"A lot of students in their early education do not get a very good grounding from their instructors about when it's acceptable to use somebody else's material," says Jane Kirtley, who teaches Media Ethics and Law at the University of Minnesota. "There's also a sense among students today that if it's something they can find on the Internet, then by definition, they can use it freely without attributing it to anybody."

The Internet provides plenty of temptations for would-be plagiarists, from essay-writing services to millions of web pages. The easy availability of such resources can cloud judgment and lead to misuse or abuse of information. "On the part of students, there's an eerie logic to justify cheating," says Denise Pope, a lecturer at the School of Education at Stanford University and author. "It's three o'clock in the morning, you're exhausted, you've worked hard . . . rather than getting a zero, you'd take your chances with plagiarism."

The problem is even more pronounced among honors students, who often believe they have the most to lose when it comes to grades, Ms. Pope says. "Students believe their parents would be less upset to find out they cheated if they get the A in the end," she says. "They sort of convince themselves that this is what needs to be done, even if it's wrong."

How wrong plagiarism is perceived to be, though, often depends on the immediate consequences. At Evanston Township High School near Chicago, students receive a copy of the school's plagiarism policy at the beginning of each school year. "If they plagiarize a whole paper, they get an F for the semester. If it's just a major portion, they get an F for the quarter," says Janet Irons, an aide in the English department. All the school's teachers are trained to use Internet plagiarism-detection services like Turnitin.com, which scans papers for similar passages online.

Professor McCabe says that even in high schools without such a protracted policy, F's or suspensions are often standard punishments for plagiarism. But almost half of the teachers he interviewed say they've observed cheating but have not reported it. "It often comes down to 'he said, she said' proof, and that isn't really enough," he explains.

In New Haven, Conn., the Executive Committee at Yale University hears about 35 cases of academic dishonesty per year, according to Jill Cutler, assistant dean and secretary of the committee. Yet the problem is greater than that figure lets on. "There are lots of professors who read a paper, know something is wrong, and decide not to take it up," she says. "Sometimes people think of it as a 'teachable moment.' But it's a lot of work [to make an accusation of plagiarism], and you don't always find sources to prove it happened."

The average punishment for students found guilty of cheating at Yale is a two-semester suspension, Ms. Cutler says. The average punishment is the same at Ms. Viswanathan's institution, Harvard, where the plagiarism policy is outlined in a one-hour lecture during freshman orientation.

But consequences at other campuses vary. Aaron Albert, a freshman who works in the academic dean's office at Washington and Lee University in Lexington, Va., doesn't pause when recalling his school's plagiarism policy. "There's only one punishment for plagiarism here . . . If you're accused and convicted of plagiarism, you're dismissed permanently from the school,"

© iStockphoto.com/A-digit

he says, "People know—if you're gonna plagiarize, you're taking your academic career in your own hands."

At Haverford College in Pennsylvania, which also has an honor code, penalties are recommended by a student Honor Council and can range from suspension or failing grades to more inventive sanctions, such as a public apology or composing an essay about plagiarism. Such remedies and consequences are based on ideals of education and restorative justice, says Joe Tolliver, Haverford's dean of students. "The process is about helping [the student] see the mistake they made and be reinstated into the community," he says.

That type of early recognition can be important, since cheating can have serious financial and even criminal consequences in other areas of life.

"In an academic context, it's really about shame," says Corynne McSherry, an intellectual property attorney in San Francisco and author of "Who Owns Academic Work? Battling for Control of Intellectual Property." "You might be kicked out of your department, or if you're a student, you might get a failing grade. With copyright, you could be taken to court and have to pay damages."

Though plagiarism is not itself a legal offense, many aspects of the act can be construed as copyright infringement, says Glynn Lunney, a law professor at Tulane University. Because anything written is automatically protected by the Copyright Act of 1976, copiers can always be liable for the harm suffered by a person whose work was copied, he says. If an author has a registered copyright, copiers can be liable for legal fees and damages, which range from $750 to $30,000 per work copied. Those fines can rise to $150,000 if the copying is particularly egregious and willfully done.

"Copyright infringement for moneymaking work happens all the time," Mr. Lunney says, adding that the rule is the same whether it's a case like Viswanathan's or Napster's music file-sharing. "That's what all copyright cases are about—it's always in the moneymaking context."

Still, copyright infringement only occurs when one has copied a substantial amount of another's work, says Rochelle Dreyfuss, a law professor at New York University.

"There's a lot that is not copyrightable, like broad concepts," she says. "Similarly, taking facts is also not taking anything that's not copyrightable. And sometimes, if something's written in a very factual, very stripped-down way, the words might not even be copyrightable."

Copying may also lead to fraud charges—which can carry criminal penalties. "Most publishing contracts have a clause where the purported author of the work promises it's their work," says Lunney. If not, the case can go to a district, or even a federal, attorney.

Yet even in cases that do not reach the courtroom, penalties can be enormous. "Whatever legal remedies are available, at the end of the day, the author's reputation is at stake—and that can be very hard professionally," Lunney says.

Analyze This Reading

1. In paragraph four, the writer refers to Professor McCabe's claim that the main reason for the rise in plagiarism is the Internet. Why is McCabe qualified to make this claim?

2. What are the temptations for plagiarizing when gathering research from the Internet?
3. Describe some of the punishments for plagiarizing imposed by colleges and high schools.
4. How does the writer connect plagiarism to the Copyright Act of 1976?

Respond To This Reading

1. What is the plagiarism policy at your college? Is it a campus-wide policy, or is policy determined by individual instructors? What changes, if any, would you make to this policy?
2. Do you agree that the Internet provides too many temptations for plagiarism? If yes, what kind of classroom instruction can be put in place to counter these temptations?
3. Plagiarism, like other kinds of proven deception, damages an individual's reputation. What values do writers ignore when they plagiarize?
4. Should information providers on the Internet have a seat at the table when the issue of plagiarism is being discussed? Explain.

ABOUT THIS READING

In this reading, the writer offers a critique of business schools that, in his view, regard students as customers. The writer, Dr. Gad Saad, is an associate professor of marketing at the John Molson School of Business at Concordia University. He writes a regular blog for *Psychology Today*, "Homo Consumericus: The Nature and Nurture of Consumption." The following reading is a post from that blog.

I'll Have Large Fries, a Hamburger, a Diet Coke, and an MBA. Hold the Pickles.

The Student-as-Customer Metaphor Is Poor Educational Policy
By Gad Saad

Business schools provide a rigorous and stimulating educational experience. Typical curricula contain a broad range of courses ranging from the highly quantitative to the "softer" courses, and from the largely theoretical to the mundanely practical. Notwithstanding the value of a classic business school education, not all is rosy within today's business schools. In my opinion, the greatest threat to the integrity of business education is the "students as customers" metaphor, which is now firmly rooted within the ethos of the business school halls. This leads to a broad range of problems, a few of which I highlight below:

1. Twenty years ago, the typical MBA program took two years of full-time studies to complete, with students taking five or six courses per term (for four terms). Severe competition for students between business schools has led to a positional arms race of an ever-decreasing number of required credits to obtain an MBA. Most programs now offer a one-year accelerated program, which is meant to reflect the "fast pace new

market realities." Call me a purist but I do not see the pedagogic logic that would yield a reduction by half of the number of credits required for a degree from those required less than twenty years ago. Does this mean that twenty years ago, the students simply needed more material to learn but today's students are inherently more knowledgeable and hence require less training? Or perhaps today's students are inherently more intelligent as compared to the "slower" generation of students from twenty years ago? Of course, it is neither of these two cases. The operative force here is the manner by which administrators view prospective students. If they are "customers" then they should indeed be allowed to dictate the "product" that is offered to them. Not surprisingly then, "customers" end up favoring curricula and programs that are shorter in length (i.e., path of least resistance). I believe that the pursuit of knowledge and the enrichment of minds involve more than the commodification of "marketable" degrees.

2. Once admitted into business schools, "customers" are socialized into the "customer is always right" and "customer is king" mindset. Hence, they are likely to complain if they obtain poor grades as this might hinder their chances of landing an interview with Procter & Gamble; they complain if evaluative exercises are scheduled in a manner that conflicts with their work schedules; they complain if the posted office hours conflict with their day jobs (apparently professors should hold office hours in such a way that not a single MBA student is inconvenienced by the posted office hours). This is part and parcel of the mass customization movement that first appeared in the 1980s. Tailor your product offerings in such a manner that it caters to the idiosyncratic needs of each "customer." Finally, at one prestigious business school that I taught at, MBA students had complained that end-of-term teaching evaluations were insufficient as the feedback that they were providing to their professors could only be actionable for future groups of students (i.e., the current crop of students would not benefit from their own insightful feedback). With that in mind, the school in question implemented teaching evaluations both at the end of the term (as usual) as well as halfway through the semester. A group of class representatives would make their way to the professors' offices to provide them with face-to-face constructive feedback: "Professor Saad, you clearly know your material. On the other hand, you should make greater effort to incorporate company examples when discussing multivariate statistical techniques. That said we are very happy with you. Good job. Keep up the good work." In the politically correct world that we live in, it is apparently democratic and liberating both for professors and students to engage in extensive evaluative judgments of one another. "Traditional" modes of pedagogy wherein professors are assumed to have an inherent greater knowledge to impart to students are apparently outmoded elitism.

3. This third and final point is truer of American business schools as compared to their Canadian counterparts. Business school students are construed as sources of future revenue streams (via alumni donations), [and] as such it becomes imperative that students are pampered in outlandish ways. Executive MBA students are particularly known for

imposing extraordinary expectations regarding their "service providers" (euphemism for professors in the parlance of MBA students). For example, "service providers" are expected to attend all EMBA social functions. Incidentally, at some business schools, "service providers" are expected to call up prospective students to advise them that they are very much looking forward to having them enroll in the program. Apparently, this augments the prospective students' sense of self and in turn increases the likelihood that they will enroll in the program. It is perhaps not too far off into the future when professors will be expected to help students with their household chores. "Joe. I am done grading your paper. You'll be happy to know that I have given you the grade that you've instructed me to give you namely[,] an A+. I have also finished the dishes, and your shirts are ironed for tomorrow's class. Will you need me for anything else tonight, or may I go home now?"

I should mention that the great majority of MBA students with whom I have interacted over the years have been nothing less than honest, hard working, and delightful individuals. I am critiquing here the "student as customer" metaphor, and not the MBA student population. "Market realities" should not continue to dilute the purity of the educational process.

Ciao for now.

Analyze This Reading

1. To what does the writer attribute reduced course requirements in business programs today?
2. What does the writer mean, in point 1 and beyond, when he refers to shorter business programs as the "commodification of 'marketable' degrees"?
3. How is the writer using the terms "politically correct" and "outmoded elitism" in point 2? Regarding the term "politically correct," define this term and trace the origins of its current use.
4. Describe the important qualifier in the final paragraph of this reading. Is it necessary? Explain.
5. Where does the writer's claim appear? Is it effectively positioned? Explain.

Respond To This Reading

1. Does the writer's concern with "students as customers" have merit; that is, is this approach to thinking of college students in business programs as customers a reality today? Does this approach apply to students not enrolled in business programs? Explain.
2. Identify passages in this reading where the writer uses sarcasm. Explain why this helps or hinders his argument.
3. What does the writer mean in the final paragraph when he refers to the "purity of the educational process"? How does this contrast with the writer's notion of the "commodification of 'marketable' degrees?"

ABOUT THIS READING

While this argument is aimed at teachers, the writer's ideas about grading will resonate with many students. These ideas look at teachers' grading policies through
categories of accuracy, fairness, and effectiveness. Douglas B. Reeves is chairman
of the Leadership and Learning Center, a consulting firm in Englewood, Colorado,
and author of more than 20 books on leadership and education. This article was
published in *The Chronicle of Higher Education*.

Remaking the Grade, from A to D

By Douglas B. Reeves

Try the following experiment at your next faculty meeting. First ask, "What
is the difference between those students who earn A's and B's and those
students who earn D's and F's?"

You will hear a litany of responses including work ethic, organization,
high-school preparation, and class attendance.

Next ask your colleagues to calculate the final grade for a student whose
10 assignments during the semester had received the following marks: C, C,
MA (missing assignment), D, C, B, MA, MA, B, A. Then calculate the distribution of the final grades.

I've done that experiment with more than 10,000 faculty members
around the world and, every time, bar none, the results include final grades
that include F, D, C, B, and A. It turns out that the difference between the student who earns A's and B's and the one who earns D's and F's is not necessarily a matter of work ethic, organization, high-school preparation, or class
attendance. The difference is the professor's grading policy.

Now change the scene from the faculty meeting to a crisp fall day in the
football stadium. As the afternoon shadows fall on the goal posts, a pass
is thrown to a receiver who lunges for the ball and tumbles into the end
zone. One official signals a touchdown, the second official signals an incomplete pass, and the third official scratches his head in bewilderment. Faculty
members, students, alumni, and trustees rise as one, complaining bitterly
of the unfairness and incompetence of athletics officials who seem unable
to view the same student performance and make a consistent judgment.

Professorial prerogatives notwithstanding, we ought to have a standard
for grading policies that at least rises to the basics we expect of officials on
the athletics field: accuracy, fairness, and effectiveness. Professors are typically granted wide latitude to establish and enforce grading policies within
certain boundaries. It is not acceptable for faculty members to make mathematical errors in grading or routinely award grades that reflect gender
or racial bias. But many grading policies often fall short of the three basic
standards:

Accuracy. The first great assault on accuracy is the use of the zero on a
100-point scale. If the grade of A represents a score of 90–100, B is 80–89,
C is 70–79, and D is 60–69, then the interval between each letter grade, A to
B to C to D, is 10 Points. But if a student fails to submit an assignment and

receives a zero, then the interval from D to zero is 60 points, a sixfold penalty compared with the other grading intervals.

Let us stipulate that work receiving a D is wretched, and that the failure of a student to submit work at all is abysmal. The use of the zero, however, requires us to defend the proposition that abysmal is six times as bad as wretched. Students who fail to turn in work deserve a punishment that fits the crime; perhaps they should be required to do the work, suffer constraints on their free time, or be denied Facebook and Frisbee privileges. But should they lose an entire semester of credit, which can be the ultimate impact of receiving zeros for missing assignments, because of an irrational and mathematically incorrect grading policy? Even Dante's worst offenders were consigned to the ninth—not the 54th—circle of hell. Poets, it seems, understand interval data better than professors in the hard sciences do.

partially disagree

The use of the arithmetic mean, or average, to calculate final grades—often the consequence of computerized grading technologies—is another offense against accuracy in grading. I have reviewed math standards in more than 100 countries and noticed that most students understand early that the average is not necessarily the best way to represent a data set. They understand alternative representations, including the mode, median, and weighted averages, to name a few. They learn that politicians and marketers, among others, will use averages in taxes, employment, and income to mislead voters and consumers. But a decade later, as 19- and 20-year-olds, they are sitting in college classes in which grading policies worship at the altar of mathematical accuracy—engineering, statistics, French literature, educational psychology (the similarities in grading policies can be eerie)—and the use of the average is pervasive.

I've taught graduate statistics courses in which mathematicians are seated next to nurses, teachers, marketers, and biologists. My task was not to evaluate where they started but where they finished. For some of them, multivariate analysis was a recent memory, while for others, high-school algebra was a distant and painful one. The mathematicians soared at the start of class but were challenged a month or two later; their colleagues struggled to remember the basics of algebra at first, but reached their "*Now I get it*" moments during the final days of the class. They argued quite persuasively that the professor should not use the average of their scores to calculate their final grade, but rather should consider their proficiency at the end of the term. I worried, however, that the same graduate students and instructors who argued against the average in that class would return to their own students and, within a few hours, casually apply the average to calculate final grades.

agree.

Fairness. While I would not automatically extrapolate my research findings to other settings, the results are sufficiently alarming to invite introspection. I have found that faculty members sometimes conflate quiet compliance with proficiency. That sends the message to students—female students in particular—that the path to success is acquiescence rather than achievement.

My observation comes first from a simple analysis of the membership of the National Honor Society. In the high school where I volunteer, the gender balance of the student body is equal. Yet the ratio of women to men in the

National Honor Society in this high school is eight to one. I have checked hundreds of coeducational institutions since that observation and found all of them to have a female-to-male advantage. A gender imbalance is also found in the college-matriculation rate of women to men: 58 percent to 42 percent, respectively. I've lost enough debates with women to stipulate that it may be true that they are smarter than men, but I doubt that they are eight times as smart. Some other factor is at work here, and it may be the societal value that elevates behavioral submission over academic performance.

I also analyzed the results of students who received A and B grades but failed external examinations in literacy and math. Those students were disproportionately female and self-identified as ethnic minorities. A cynic might label this the "bless her heart" effect, as in, "She really isn't very proficient, but bless her heart, she showed up every day, participated in class, and didn't give me any trouble."

That may not apply to your student body, but I would ask only that you find out if the dropout and failure rates of your students are equally distributed by gender and ethnicity. If not, it is at least possible that students were lured into the challenge of your institution based upon rewards for quiet compliance, and that then they were punished for not having the skills required for college-level work. Conversely, some minority male students may have never reached the front door of your institution because, as high-school students, they were not rewarded for academic proficiency but punished for abrasive behavior that was unrelated to academic performance.

The most perplexing part of unfair grading policies is that they are rarely intentional. I know of no college or school system that has an affirmative-action policy to secure more bigots and sexists on the faculty. On the contrary, the "bless her heart" effect (pronoun very deliberate) stems not from malice but from compassion.

Effectiveness. Finally, we should consider whether the impact of grading policies has led to improved student performance. A basic question that faculty members must ask is, "Were my students last semester more engaged, responsive, and successful than students in previous years?" If the answer is "yes," then present grading policies are fine. I am astonished, however, at the number of professors who complain loudly that students are disrespectful, inattentive, disengaged, and unresponsive— and yet who wish to pursue the same grading policies they have used for a decade or more.

Fortunately, the solution to the quandary of effective grading practices is close at hand. On the athletics field, I've never seen a coach with a grade book and red pencil, yet I have witnessed many a coach who provides feedback designed to improve performance. Similarly, I've noticed, while watching the conductor of the collegiate orchestra or chorale lead a rehearsal, how infrequently quizzes and tests are administered and how rarely grades are awarded. Instead, the conductor frequently provides feedback for the singular purpose of improving student performance.

The Class of 2013 grew up playing video games and received feedback that was immediate, specific, and brutal-they won or else died at the end of each game. For them, the purpose of feedback is not to calculate an average or score a final exam, but to inform them about how they can improve on their next attempt to rule the universe.

Imagine a class in any other subject, from science to classics, conducted in the same way. The students wail, "Does it *count*?" and the professor responds, "I'm just giving you feedback to improve your performance—try to do better next time" I have never heard students thank their Nintendo machine for its insightful feedback, but I have observed many of them respond more attentively to those machines than to their professors.

Now is the time to make modest but important improvements in grading policy. Without leave of administrators or permission from grading-system programmers, professors can stop the use of the zero. They can suspend the use of the average. They can override the deterministic mentality that drives so many grading systems and provide regular feedback designed to help students actually learn. They can, in brief, be accurate, fair, and effective. It is no more than our students demand of athletics contests and video games. As teachers, we should do no less.

Analyze This Reading

1. What point does the writer make when comparing teachers to athletic officials?
2. In the section on "Accuracy," why does the writer consider the grade of zero to be "irrational and mathematically incorrect"? Describe the problem with using the average of test scores to determine a final grade. With what should this average be replaced?
3. In the section on "Fairness," what concern does the writer have with "behavioral submission and academic performance"? What dangers are associated with this concern?
4. Describe the writer's position on feedback in the "Effectiveness" section.
5. Identify the writer's claim and warrant.

Respond To This Reading

1. Does the writer describe realistic concerns with the grading policies of some teachers? Explain.
2. In your career as a student, describe grading issues you have encountered.
3. In your view, what constitutes fair, competent grading? How would you support your view?

ABOUT THIS READING

Now common in the United States, for-profit colleges are a contentious issue in higher education circles, as critics question the credibility of these colleges while proponents point to their efficiency and cost effectiveness. Michael J. Seiden recently retired as president of Western International University, a for-profit college focusing on business and technology programs. This argument appeared in *The Chronicle of Higher Education*.

[handwritten margin notes: Logos / Ethos / Pathos / if they prove worthy! / dysfunctional society?! / but do they have the skills required to hold up to that degree]

For-Profit Colleges Deserve Some Respect

By Michael J. Seiden

Enrollment in for-profit colleges, while still a relatively small share of the higher-education market, has grown more than tenfold over the past decade. For-profit education companies are now in high demand among venture capitalists and investment bankers, and the industry is one of the rare ones that is faring well in this economy. But while some for-profit education institutions have achieved a certain level of credibility within academe, many education traditionalists still view them with disdain.

I have worked for 25 years as a faculty member, curriculum developer, and administrator for Regis University, the University of Phoenix, and Western International University. As I prepare to retire and reflect on my experiences, it is clear to me that for-profit education has its strengths and weaknesses. It has also had its share of criticism, both fair and unfair.

The key criticisms of the industry concern its:

Aggressive marketing and a lack of admissions criteria. Some for-profit institutions have been sanctioned in the past for overly aggressive marketing and enrollment tactics. In addition, they have been criticized for marketing to any and all potential students, regardless of their ability to handle college-level work. Certainly, if for-profit institutions had more-selective admissions policies, more academically accomplished students would apply.

But it can be argued that everyone deserves an opportunity to receive a quality education. Many people, for any number of reasons, drop out of college, fail to achieve the required grades, or don't go on to college after high school. After years of working, they often achieve a level of commitment and maturity that was previously lacking. Through their work experience they obtain knowledge and skills that are often more relevant than good SAT scores. For-profit institutions, with their relatively open admissions requirements and flexible course scheduling, have been in the forefront of providing those people with renewed opportunities to gain a meaningful college degree.

Large number of student dropouts. While open admission provides an opportunity for many students to further their education, it also creates situations where students who are unprepared or uncommitted to obtaining a traditional education start programs, incur costs, and drop out within the first few courses. That creates excessive student debt, higher default rates on student loans, and financial drains on the institution.

Based on anecdotal and personal experience, evaluations of data, and interviews with students, I classify incoming students into three categories: green, yellow, and red. The green students are those who have the ability and commitment to earn their degrees; they usually constitute about half of the potential new student population. The yellow students are those with a somewhat lower level of commitment and ability; they make up about 25 percent of the potential population. Those students can be identified through testing and salvaged through remedial work. Red students are those who are aggressively recruited even after indicating that they have no real commitment to attaining a college education. Those students should be eliminated from the recruitment process. They use up financial and human resources that could be spent more effectively on the other students.

It has also been my experience that a major reason that students drop out of nontraditional programs is lack of support from employers, families, or others. Retention can be significantly improved if an institution provides not only academic but also lifestyle support for its students.

a lack of such support for any program is incentive to drop out

Nontraditional classroom environments. Traditionalists often frown on for-profit colleges' use of adjunct faculty members. Much of the concern stems from the distinction between a research and a teaching institution. Many full-time faculty members at research universities analyze and develop new methods and theories, while adjunct faculty members teach current practices and rarely break new ground in their fields.

But that is not necessarily inappropriate for career-minded students. Combining faculty members who are generally employed in jobs outside the university with students in similar situations more often creates an exciting learning environment. All participants learn from each other, theory is blended with practice, and ideas are readily challenged.

For example, a student has at times introduced me to a new concept in my field that I have been able to explore and transfer to my own work situation. In many other instances, I have explained a concept to a student and then watched him or her actually put it into practice in the workplace—eventually describing the results to the rest of the class.

agree.

The faculty members at for-profit institutions are often as excited by the education process as those whom they are teaching. In my experience, they actively serve as mentors to students, help develop the curriculum, and participate in academic governance.

Business orientation. Years ago, at one of our institution's comprehensive evaluation meetings, a traditional university professor railed against the use of business terms in describing students and other aspects of the university. "We're academics," she said, "and we know what's best academically." Another team member, the dean of a state university's business school, interjected, "Wait a minute. My state's taxpayers are our customers, and if we don't provide programs and curriculum that will support our students' career needs, we won't be fulfilling our mission."

I must agree with the latter. For-profit universities view their students as customers, and to attract and retain those customers, degree programs and curricula must be market-driven. Students are motivated to earn their degrees because they aspire to upward mobility in their careers. Therefore, while containing the general-education components that traditional institutions and accrediting agencies view as essential, the curricula at most for-profit colleges and universities consist of courses that students' employers demand.

education becomes a commodity. → Students = customers → caters to them

Granted, for-profits' drive for revenue and profitability, and fear of not attracting or losing students, can certainly lead some managers to pressure faculty and staff members to offer a "user friendly" approach to academics: dumbing down the curriculum, inflating grades, and the like. Some for-profit managers may fear that academic rigor will negatively affect enrollment and retention—which will ultimately mean lower revenue. But much anecdotal

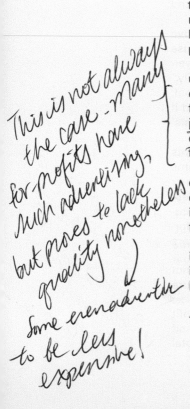

evidence suggests that successful students appreciate academic rigor, and that reducing the difficulty of the course work appeals primarily to those students who will probably not complete their degrees under any circumstances. The best for-profit institutions try to offer academic quality and also achieve financial success through a "creative tension"—a cooperative balancing act between all aspects of the organization.

While traditional universities must hold up their reputation, and must also come to this balance

Based on my experience, I can cite several other positive aspects of for-profit education institutions that should also be considered. First, innovation has been their hallmark, and they have often led the way—from the early days when accelerated courses and evening classes attracted adult learners who weren't being served effectively by traditional education to the explosion of distance learning through online courses. The development of the online library, with many sources for research available to the student or faculty members without having to leave their homes, has significantly increased access to education. The education establishment criticized such innovations in the early days. Today many of the same traditional institutions are modeling their programs on for-profits' programs. For-profit universities have also focused on quality assurance, recognizing that their credibility with respect to academic quality would always be in question within the higher-education establishment, especially as they have become significant competitors for traditional institutions. Standardizing curricula, textbook selection, and course plans has provided not only consistency in course delivery but also a high level of support for adjunct faculty members in their preparation of courses.

only the select few

Further, because faculty members have direct impact on students and, therefore, the success of the institution, extensive training programs are a requirement for the adjunct faculty. Student evaluations of faculty members, as well as staff and peer reviews, are administered regularly and are part of most institutions' continuous improvement efforts.

agree

Finally, because the for-profit institutions are in competition with public universities and community colleges that charge lower tuition, they must offer students something more. Outstanding service, flexible schedules that fit the students' lifestyles, strong faculty members who combine theory with practical experience and who know how to teach, as well as quality, market-driven programs, are what lure students to the for-profit university—even if the tuition is more expensive.

This is not always the case—many for-profits have much advertising, but proves to lack quality nonetheless (some even advertise to be less expensive!)

In reality, all institutions strive to have their revenues exceed their expenses. Sound institutions use the money to enhance the educational experience of the students. Regardless of the nature of a higher-education institution—private or public, research or career-oriented, for-profit or not-for-profit—its quality will be determined by its management.

There have unquestionably been abuses in some for-profit education institutions, but the same can be said about private and public traditional institutions as well. Perhaps it's time to evaluate institutions on their own merits, rather than classify them by stereotypical categories.

Analyze This Reading

1. In the first half of this reading, the writer identifies the pros and cons of four issues associated with for-profit colleges. Summarize the pros and cons for each issue.

2. While the writer defends the merits of for-profit colleges, especially during the second half of this reading, he does bring in an important qualifier in the final paragraph. What is this qualifier? Explain why you regard it as effective or ineffective.
3. If the claim is the last sentence in this argument, explain what kind of claim it is—fact, definition, cause, problem-based, or evaluation.

Respond To This Reading

1. Regarding the four issues that begin this reading, and based on your experience as a college student, do you agree with the writer's assessments of each issue? Why or why not?
2. In defending for-profit colleges and their approaches to students, the writer makes use of conventional business terms—*marketing, customer, innovation,* and *quality assurance.* Now-regular use of these terms in colleges suggests a merger between the worlds of business and academics. Is such a merger normal and natural today, or should the language peculiar to each world be separated?
3. Identify the warrant in this argument. Explain how the values that underlie the warrant are similar to or different from a warrant in an argument arguing against for-profit colleges.

ABOUT THIS READING

This article appeared in *The Nation*, the oldest regularly published weekly news magazine in the U.S. A devoted champion of sustainable food systems, Anna Lappé is a leader in the Real Food Media Project and a founding principal of The Small Planet Institute. Her most recent book is *Diet for a Hot Planet: The Climate Crisis at the End of Your Fork and What You Can Do About It* (2010).

Cafeteria Consciousness

By Anna Lappé

It was a little after midnight, long after the official conference had ended and the 500-plus attendees of the 2007 Food and Society annual get-together had turned in for the night. Tim Galarneau of the California Student Sustainability Coalition; Anim Steel from the Food Project, a Boston-based food and farming nonprofit; David Schwartz from Brown University; and a few other young people were still talking. Hunched over a table in an empty meeting room at the Grand Traverse Resort in Traverse City, Michigan, the group had already been together for hours, continuing a conversation that had been going on for more than a year.

What was keeping them up so late? They were comparing notes. Each was witnessing a burgeoning student movement on college campuses to bring sustainably and fairly raised food into dining halls. From coast to coast, a similar energy and enthusiasm seemed to be bubbling up. Galarneau was seeing it in the massive effort to transform university food across California's esteemed public university system. Schwartz was seeing it back in Providence at Brown, where students were getting increasingly vocal about finding sustainable food. And Steel, a leader in the food-justice movement, had a frontline view from the Food Project's youth-run farm in Boston. From their unique perspectives, both sensed that students were hankering to speak up more loudly for sustainable food; they just needed an effective way to do so. Out of this ongoing conversation, the group would launch the Real Food Challenge.

The concept is simple, really. Students, some who pay as much as $100,000, or more, for four years at a private college, should have a say in what grub their schools serve—and that food should reflect shared values of fairness and sustainability. The Real Food Challenge provides an organizing tool to empower students to persuade their schools to make the move. Schools that join the challenge pledge to shift at least 20 percent of school food to "real food"—sustainably raised, grown with fairness, and from local and regional farms—by 2020.

In addition to this concrete goal, the Challenge also offers schools and student organizers a support network, resources for finding sources of real food, organizer training and a "real food calculator." The calculator provides campuses with a mechanism for quantifying real food, for determining the percentage of real food they currently serve and assessing improvement over time.

The excitement about the Real Food Challenge, Galarneau said, is partly that it taps into students' energy to address the global warming impact of their campuses. One strategy of student environmental activists has been to focus on persuading their schools to reduce their global warming impact through rethinking institutional energy use and turning to renewable energy sources. One of the most successful campus-based efforts to date is the Campus Climate Challenge. The initiative has helped young people in colleges and high schools across the United States and Canada organize to campaign for—and win—100 percent clean-energy policies at their schools.

The Campus Climate Challenge served as inspiration for the Real Food Challenge founders, who were interested in channeling student excitement in a new direction. "There was a lot of momentum around climate change on campuses. Al Gore had swept onto the scene," said Galarneau. "But the activism lacked a connection with the food system." And yet the global food system, from seed to plate to landfill, is responsible for as much as one-third of all greenhouse-gas emissions, largely because it is the single greatest force behind deforestation and soil degradation, both of which release carbon dioxide into the atmosphere. Indeed, livestock production alone is responsible for 18 percent of the world's emissions, more than those produced by all transportation—every SUV, steamer ship and jet plane combined.

"Many young people are realizing that the food system is a key contributor to global warming. They know that we've got to talk about food if we're going to advance a broader sustainability agenda," Galarneau noted.

It would take another year and a half of conversations like the one back in that stuffy meeting room before the Real Food Challenge was officially launched in September 2008. But within a month, the original crew had hard proof that their hunch had been right.

The Challenge launched with eleven pilot schools. Organizers hoped several hundred more would soon join. "During one of our conference calls that first month, we checked to see how many campuses had come on board. We had hoped for maybe 200," said Galarneau. "We already had 230. That's when we knew we'd hit a nerve. People were biting."

By the end of that first year, 329 campuses had joined the network, from Brown University to City College of New York to DeAnza Community College in San Mateo, California. The determined young people who lead the Challenge expect that in another year that number could grow to 1,000, about a quarter of all the two- and four-year colleges and universities in the country. To put the potential impact in context, US colleges and universities currently spend more than $4 billion annually on school food. (Roughly half of school food is contracted out to food-service companies; the rest is managed by the schools themselves.) If it's successful, and the participating schools shift 20 percent of their purchases, the Real Food Challenge will have helped to move nearly $1 billion of food purchases toward sustainability by 2020.

"We're talking about shaking up the system," said Galarneau, "and young people like that."

Connecting the overarching mission of the Real Food Challenge—increasing the amount of fairly and sustainably raised local foods on campuses—to the effort to combat climate change is a complex challenge. First and foremost, there's the problem of quantifying the impact. Unlike getting data on campus energy use—emissions are relatively easy to measure and are usually the direct result of action (or inaction)—getting data on food is difficult. Campuses rarely know the full life story of the food they purchase. In part that's because food- related emissions most ly occur during production, processing and distribution—long before the food shows up in the cafeteria. Plus, even for the "direct" emissions—energy used in dining halls, food waste ending up in landfills—schools often don't have systems in place yet for accurate measurement.

But a data gap doesn't have to mean an action gap. The Real Food Challenge stresses that there are guiding principles for planet-friendly choices schools can make, including cutting back on meat and dairy, reducing waste and packaging, and choosing more sustainably raised and local foods, for instance.

It was not long before the Real Food Challenge piqued the interest of food-service companies. In that initial launch month, said Galarneau, they were contacted by Aramark, Sodexo and Bon Appétit—some of the biggest players in college food service. "They were calling to say they wanted to partner with the Challenge," he said. But Galarneau and the other organizers were wary of official corporate partnerships, concerned that companies would just be latching on to the initiative without actually changing their practices. They'd already seen food-service companies pay lip service to sustainability in their contracts without embracing broad change in the dining halls. As we talked, Galarneau described a 135-page food-service contract he was reviewing, hunting for language that would provide the company loopholes to skirt sustainability. "The devil is in the details," he said.

(On its own, Bon Appétit, which serves 80 million meals a year at campus and corporate facilities, has launched a lowcarbon diet initiative, reducing food waste, promoting composting, educating guests about their food choices and cutting back on beef purchases by 33 percent systemwide between 2007 and 2009.)

Organizers of the Real Food Challenge say their primary focus is on building student engagement. Because food-service directors typically don't have time to make the needed changes, schools need students to help make it happen. Plus, as Steel says, "no matter how committed many of these companies say they are, they can only go as far as students push them."

The Challenge, while popular among students on participating campuses, still faces many hurdles, including getting the ear of administrators facing one of the worst economic downturns in generations. But as the organizers like to point out, many of the climate-friendly prin ciples actually help schools save money. Students at Stanford, for example, borrowed the Love Food, Hate Waste campaign from the United Kingdom to develop a way for people on campus to compost their waste easily. Erin Gaines, former sustainable-foods coordinator at Stanford Dining and Hospitality, and an active member of the Real Food Challenge, told me about their success. In 2007, thanks to the campaign, the school composted 1.2 million pounds of food from campus dining halls and cafes. That's 1.2 million pounds that would have gone into a landfill. Instead, the scraps were taken to a local composting facility, and half of the compost was returned to the school to be used on its gardens and grounds.

Galarneau offered an example from the University of California system. In response to student campaigning, the Santa Cruz campus decided to go "trayless" to address the pile-on phenomenon: students grabbing more food than their stomachs can hold. No trays means less washing. The school has already calculated a savings of more than 1 million gallons of water a year. And no trays means less food waste. Since the policy was introduced, the campus has seen food waste decline by one-third, and it is committed to diverting the remaining waste to compost. "The mantra is 'upcycling,'" said Galarneau, "reducing waste before it becomes waste and then reintegrating waste, through composting, so that it never becomes waste." This one step has helped reduce energy consumption (less dishwater to heat) and emissions (all that food kept out of landfills), saving the school money, which in turn leaves more resources to invest in sustainable food choices.

Galarneau cited an observation economists have made: that once a consumer trend reaches 20 percent of a market, it can become an unstoppable force. What the young people in the Challenge are doing, says Galarneau, is "testing that theory with a push toward purchases that value justice and sustainability." When I talked with Katrina Norbom, a Real Food Challenge member at the University of North Florida, she said, "No matter what, it comes down to the students. If we can create enough support, we can make it happen."

This determination is making an impact well beyond the campus. Alumni of the Real Food Challenge are heading into communities where they're using their passion and organizing skills to expand the market for real food across the country. When I asked Galarneau and Steel for examples, they rattled off a bunch: Sue DeBlieck from Iowa State University is running a farm-to-school project in Maine; Sam Lipschultz, a 2009 Sarah Lawrence graduate, is starting a youth-run farmers' market in one of Brooklyn's poorest neighborhoods; and UC Irvine's Hai Vo, who had been consulting with other youth-empowerment projects after college, just sent in his applications for programs in farm apprenticeship.

The organizers know that shifting 20 percent of school food to "real food" by 2020 is ambitious; but their vision is even bolder—and broader— than that. Currently less than 2 percent of food on most campuses is "real." Nationwide, the figure isn't much different. As Steel said, "If we can't make this shift happen on a campus, how can we expect it to happen elsewhere? And if we *can* do it on campuses, then we can start asking, Why can't we do it everywhere?"

Analyze This Reading

1. What is The Real Food Challenge? What is The Campus Climate Challenge? How did they begin?
2. What is involved in connecting The Real Food Challenge to climate change?
3. What strategies have student organizers of The Real Food Challenge used to address concerns of college administrators, especially economic concerns?
4. The writer regularly quotes student organizers in this article, and this strategy is a way to humanize what otherwise might appear as an abstract issue, one removed from everyday life. Can you humanize, that is, make more personal, the argument you're currently building by bringing in quotations from people in the thick of the issue you're addressing? Explain.

Respond To This Reading

1. What efforts, if any, has your campus made to rely more on locally-grown food?
2. While many Americans are attracted to the idea of sustainably raised food grown on local and regional farms, old food-buying habits seem to win out more often than not. What would motivate you to change your food-buying habits and commit to sustainable food?
3. What claim would you be prepared to defend if you were assigned to argue on the issue of campus food?

ABOUT THIS READING

In this argument, Professor Jeffrey J. Williams alludes to the economic arrangement of indentured servitude in early America as a way to focus on the realities of loan repayment that many students face today. This argument first appeared in *Dissent*, a quarterly magazine devoted to arguing against conformity in American political and intellectual life and for the promise that a democratic society holds.

Are Students the New Indentured Servants?

College student-loan debt has revived the spirit of indenture for a sizable proportion of contemporary Americans.

By Jeffrey J. Williams

When we think of the founding of the early colonies, we usually think of the journey to freedom, in particular of the Puritans fleeing religious persecution to settle the Massachusetts Bay Colony. But it was not so for a majority of the first Europeans who emigrated to these shores. "Between one-half and two-thirds of all white immigrants to the British colonies arrived under indenture," according to the economic historian David W. Galenson, a total of three hundred thousand to four hundred thousand people. Indenture was not an isolated practice but a dominant aspect of labor and life in early America.

Rather than Plymouth, Jamestown was a more typical example of colonial settlement, founded in 1607 as a mercantile venture under the auspices of the Virginia Company, a prototype of "joint-stock" corporations and venture capitalism. The first colonists fared badly because, coming primarily from gentry, they had little practical skill at farming and were ravaged by starvation and disease. In 1620, the Virginia Company shifted to a policy of indentured servitude to draw labor fit to work the tobacco colonies. Indenture had been a common practice in England, but its terms were relatively short, typically a year, and closely regulated by law. The innovation of the Virginia Company was to extend the practice of indenture to America, but at a much higher obligation, of four to seven years, because of the added cost of transit, and also because of the added cost of the brokerage system that arose around it. In England, contracts of indenture were directly between the landowner and servant, whereas now merchants or brokers in England's ports signed prospective workers, then sold the contracts to shippers or to colonial landowners upon the servants' arrival in America, who in turn could re-sell the contracts.

By about 1660, planters "increasingly found African slaves a less expensive source of labor," as Galenson puts it. An economically minded historian like Galenson argues that the system of indenture was rational, free, and fair—one had a free choice to enter into the arrangement, some of those indentured eventually prospered, and it was only rational that the terms be high because of the cost of transit—but most other historians, from Edmund S. Morgan to Marcus Rediker, agree that indentured servitude was an exploitive system of labor, in many instances a form of bondage akin to slavery. For the bound, it meant long hours of hard work, oftentimes abuse, terms sometimes extended by fiat of the landowner, little regulation or legal recourse for laborers, and the onerous physical circumstances of the new world, in which two-thirds died before fulfilling their terms.

College student-loan debt has revived the spirit of indenture for a sizable proportion of contemporary Americans. It is not a minor threshold that young people entering adult society and work, or those returning to college seeking enhanced credentials, might pass through easily. Because of its unprecedented and escalating amounts, it is a major constraint that looms over the lives of those so contracted, binding individuals for a significant part of their future work lives. Although it has more varied application, less direct effects, and less severe conditions than colonial indenture did (some have less and some greater debt, some attain better incomes) and it does not bind one to a particular job, student debt permeates everyday experience with concern over the monthly chit and encumbers job and life choices. It also takes a page from indenture in the extensive brokerage system it has bred, from which more than four thousand banks take profit. At core, student debt is a labor issue, as colonial indenture was, subsisting off the desire of those less privileged to gain better opportunities and enforcing a control on their future labor. One of the goals of the planners of the modern U.S. university system after the Second World War was to displace what they saw as an aristocracy that had become entrenched at elite schools; instead they promoted equal opportunity in order to build America through its best talent. The rising tide of student debt reinforces rather than dissolves the discriminations of class, counteracting the meritocracy. Finally, I believe that the current system of college debt violates the spirit of American freedom in leading those less privileged to bind their futures.

In a previous essay, "Debt Education," in the summer 2006 issue of *Dissent*, I detailed the basic facts and figures of student-loan debt, pointed out how it rewrites the social contract from a public entitlement to education to a privatized service, and teased out how it teaches less than humanistic lessons, about education as a consumer good, about higher education as job training rather than intellectual exploration, and about civil society as a commercial market rather than a polis. I also promoted some solutions, notably the U.S. Labor Party's proposal for FreeHigherEd and fortified forms of public service linked with college. Here, I look more seriously at the analogy to indenture. While it might not be as direct or extreme a constraint as indentured servitude, student debt constrains a great many of Americans. It represents a turn in American thought and hope to permit such a constraint on those attempting to gain a franchise in the adult or work world. I also want to promote a relatively little known proposal for relieving some of the most inequitable terms of student debt, "Income Contingent Loans."

Indentured servitude seems a strange and distant historical practice, like debtors' prison. But there are many ways that college student-loan debt revises for the twenty-first century some of its ethos and features:

- **PREVALENCE** Student-loan debt is now a prevalent mode of financing higher education, applying to two-thirds of those who attend. If upward of 70 percent of Americans attend college at some point, it applies to half the rising population. Like indenture through the seventeenth century, it has become a common experience of those settling the new technological world of twenty-first-century America, in which we are continually told that we need college degrees to compete globally.

- **AMOUNTS** Student debt has morphed from relatively small amounts to substantial ones, loosely paralleling the large debt entailed by colonial transport. The average federal loan debt of a graduating senior in 2004 (the most recent year for which statistics are available) was $19,200. Given that tuitions have nearly doubled in the last decade and grants have barely risen, and that debt more than doubled from 1994, when it was $9,000, not to mention from 1984, when it was $2,000, one can assume that the totals will continue to climb. Also consider that, as happens with averages, many people have significantly more than the median—23 percent of borrowers attending private and 14 percent attending public universities have over $30,000 in undergraduate loans. Added to federal loans are charge cards, estimated at $2,169 per student in 2004, quite often used for necessities; private loans, which have quintupled in number since 1996, when 1 percent of students took them, to 5 percent in 2004, and which have risen in total to $17.3 billion in 2005, a disturbingly large portion in addition to the $68.6 billion for federal loans; and, for over 60 percent of those continuing their educations, graduate-student debt, which more than doubled in the past decade, to a 2004 median of about $28,000 for those with master's degrees, $45,000 for doctorates, and $68,000 for professional degrees.

- **LENGTH OF TERM** Student debt is a long-term commitment—fifteen years for standard Stafford guaranteed federal loans. With consolidation or refinancing, the length of term frequently extends to thirty years—in other words, for many returning students or graduate students, until retirement age. It is not a transitory bond, say, of a year for those indentured in England or of early student debtors who might have owed $2,000. To be sure, it is not as concentrated as colonial indenture, but it is lengthier and weighs down a student debtor's future.

- **TRANSPORT TO WORK** Student indebted-ness is premised on the idea of transport to a job—the figurative transport over the higher seas of education to attain the shores of credentials deemed necessary for a middle class job. The cost of transport is borne by the laborer, so an individual has to pay for the opportunity to work. Some businesses alleviate debt as a recruiting benefit, but unfortunately they are still relatively few. (Another factor is the precipitous rise in student work hours, as Marc Bousquet's stunning indictment, *How the University Works*, recounts. According to recent statistics, students at public universities work an average of twenty-five hours a week, which tends to lower grades and impede graduation rates. Servitude, for many current students, begins on ship.)

- **PERSONAL CONTRACTS** "Indenture" designates a practice of making contracts before signatures were common (they were torn, the tear analogous to the unique shape of a person's bite, and each party held half, so they could be verified by their match); student debt reinstitutes a system of contracts that bind a rising majority of Americans. Like indenture, the debt is secured not by property, as most loans such as those for cars or houses are, but by the person, obligating his or her future labor. Student-loan debt "financializes" the person, in the phrase of Randy Martin, who diagnoses this strategy as a central one of contemporary venture capital, displacing risk to individuals rather than employers or society. It was also a strategy of colonial indenture.

- **LIMITED RECOURSE** Contracts for federal student loans stipulate severe penalties and are virtually unbreakable, forgiven only in death, not bankruptcy, and enforced by severe measures, such as garnishee and other legal sanctions, with little recourse. (In one recent case, the Social Security payment to a person on disability was garnisheed.) In England, indenture was regulated by law, and servants had recourse in court; one of the pernicious aspects of colonial indenture was that there was little recourse in the new colonies.

- **CLASS** Student debt applies to those with less family wealth, like indenture reinforcing class differences. That this would be a practice in imperial Britain, before modern democracy and where classes were rigidly set, is not entirely surprising; it is more disturbing in the United States, where we ostensibly eschew the determining force of class. The one-third without student debt face much different futures, and are more likely to pursue graduate and professional degrees (three-quarters of those receiving doctorates in 2004 had no undergraduate debt, and, according to a 2002 Nellie Mae survey, 40 percent of those not pursuing graduate school attributed their choice to debt). Student debt is digging a class moat in present-day America.

- **YOUTH** Student debt incorporates primarily younger people, as indenture did. One of the more troubling aspects of student debt is that often it is the first step down a slope of debt and difficulties. Tamara Draut, in her exposé *Strapped: Why America's 20- and 30-Somethings Can't Get Ahead*, shows how it inaugurates a series of strained conditions, compounded by shrinking job prospects, escalating charge card debt, and historically higher housing payments, whether rent or mortgage, resulting in lessened chances for having a family and establishing a secure and comfortable life. The American Dream, and specifically the post-Second World War dream of equal opportunity opened by higher education, has been curtailed for many of the rising generation.

- **BROKERS** Student debt fuels a financial services system that trades in and profits from contracts of indebted individuals, like the Liverpool merchants, sea captains, and planters trading in contracts of indenture. The lender pays the fare to the college, and thereafter the contracts are circulated among Sallie Mae, Nellie Mae, Citigroup, and four thousand other banks. This system makes a futures market of people and garners immense profit from them. The federally guaranteed student loan program was originally a nonprofit corporation, Sallie Mae, but in 2004 Sallie Mae became a private, for-profit corporation, reporting record profits in its first three years.

- **STATE POLICY** The British crown gave authority to the Virginia Company; the U.S. government authorizes current lending enterprises and, even more lucratively for banks, underwrites their risk in guaranteeing the loans (the Virginia Company received no such largesse and went bankrupt). In the past few years, federal aid has funneled more to loans rather than any other form of aid (52 percent of all federal aid, whereas grants account for 42 percent).

My point in adducing this bill of particulars is not to claim an exact historical correspondence between indentured servitude and student indebtedness. But, as I think these particulars show, it is not just a fanciful analogy either. The shock of the comparison is that it has any resonance at all, and that we permit, through policy and practice, the conscription of those

376 PART FIVE An Anthology of Arguments

seeking the opportunity of education, especially the young, into a significant bond on their future labor and life. While indenture was more direct and severe, it was the product of a rigidly classed, semi-feudal world; student debt is more flexible, varied in application, and amorphous in effects, a product of the postmodern world, but it revives the spirit of indenture in promulgating class privilege and class subservience. What is most troubling is that it represents a shift in basic political principle. It turns away from the democratic impetus of modern American society. The 1947 Report of the President's Commission on Education, which ushered in the vast expansion of our colleges and universities, emphasized (in bold italics) that "free and universal access to education must be a major goal in American education." Otherwise, the commission warned, "If the ladder of educational opportunity rises high at the doors of some youth and scarcely rises at the doors of others, while at the same time formal education is made a prerequisite to occupational and social advance, then education may become the means, not of eliminating race and class distinctions, but of deepening them." Their goal was not only an abstract one of equality, but also to strengthen the United States, and, by all accounts, American society prospered. Current student debt weakens America, wasting the resource of those impeded from pursuing degrees who otherwise would make excellent doctors or professors or engineers, as well as creating a culture of debt and constraint.

The counterarguments for the rightness of student-loan debt are similar to the counterarguments for the benefits of indenture. One holds that it is a question of supply and demand—a lot of people want higher education, thus driving up the price. This doesn't hold water, because the demand for higher education in the years following the Second World War through 1970 was proportionately the highest of any time, as student enrollments doubled and tripled, but the supply was cheap and largely state funded. The difference between then and now is that higher education was much more substantially funded through public sources, both state and federal; now the expense has been privatized, transferred to students and their families.

Galenson argues that with indenture, "long terms did not imply exploitation" because they were only fitting for the high cost of transport; that more productive servants, or those placed in undesirable areas, could lessen their terms; and that some servants went on to prosper. He does not mention the rate of death, the many cases of abuse, the draconian extension of contracts by unethical planters, nor simply what term would be an appropriate maximum for any person in a free society to be bound, even if they agreed to the bondage. Galenson also ignores the underlying political question: Is it appropriate that people, especially those entering the adult world, might take on such a long-term commitment of constraint? Can people make a rational choice for a term they might not realistically imagine? Even if one doesn't question the principle of indenture, what is an appropriate cap for its amounts and term? In the case of student debt, although it might be a legal choice, it is doubtful whether it is always a rational choice for those who have no knowledge of adult life. One of the more haunting responses to the 2002 Nellie Mae survey was that 54 percent said that they would have borrowed less if they had to do it again, up from 31 percent ten years before. One can only imagine that this informed judgment will climb as debt continues to rise.

Student-loan debt is justified in terms similar to Galenson's by some current economists. Because college graduates have made, according to some statistics, $1,000,000 more over the course of their careers than non-college graduates, one prominent argument holds that it is rational and right that they accumulate substantial debt to start their careers. However, while it is true that many graduates make statistically high salaries, the problem is that those results vary a great deal: some accrue debt but don't graduate; some graduate but, with degrees in the humanities or education, for instance, they are unlikely to make a high salary; more and more students have difficulty finding a professional or high-paying job; and the rates have been declining, so a college degree is no longer the guaranteed ticket to wealth that it once was. An economic balance sheet also ignores the fundamental question of the ethics of requiring debt of those who desire higher education and the fairness of its distribution to those less privileged.

In the past year, there has been more attention to the problem of student-loan debt, but most of the solutions, such as the recent interest rate adjustment for current graduates (so the rates didn't rise when the prime rate increased) or laws forbidding graft to college loan officers, are stopgaps that do not affect the structure and basic terms of the system. The system needs wholesale change. I believe that the best solution is "FreeHigherEd," put forth by the Labor Party (see Adolph Reed's article, "A G.I. Bill for Everybody," in *Dissent*, Fall 2001). It proposes that the federal government pay tuition for all qualified students at public universities, which would cost around fifty billion dollars a year and which could be paid simply by repealing a portion of the Bush tax cuts or shifting a small portion of the military budget. It would actually jettison a substantial layer of current bureaucracy—of the branches of the federal loan program, of the vast web of banking, and of college financial aid offices—thereby saving a great deal. Like free, universal health care, free higher education should be the goal, and it's not impracticable.

The next best solution, I believe, is "Income Contingent Loans." Income Contingent Loans, as their name implies, stipulate an adjustable rate of payment according to income. They were first adopted in Australia in 1989, the invention of the educational policy expert Bruce Chapman, and have since been adopted in the United Kingdom. They are currently supported by The Project on Student Debt. Such loans represent a pragmatic compromise between free tuition and the current debtor system. They provide a safety net for those with the most debt but least resources and they stipulate a reasonable scale of payment for those doing better.

One of the most pernicious aspects of the current structure of student-loan debt is that it puts a particular burden on those who have lower incomes, especially at the beginning of their careers, because the repayment schedule is fixed (there are very limited terms of forbearance, capping at four years). For instance, an elementary school teacher with a salary of $23,900 (the 2005 median) who has a debt of $40,000 after her four years at a private college would have to pay about 15 percent or more of her salary, before taxes. After taxes it might be closer to 25 percent, which would make ordinary living expenses difficult. Income Contingent Loans stipulate a minimum threshold below which one does not have to pay—$23,242 in Australia in 2002. Income Contingent Loans protect those most at risk.

They also have other safeguards and measures of fairness. Beyond the minimum threshold, they stipulate a sliding scale, in Australia beginning at 3 percent and rising to a cap of 8 percent, so that if the teacher got a raise to $30,000 she might have to pay 4 percent. In the United Kingdom, the cap is 6 percent. Rates adjust over the long term, so that if a graduate starts with a low salary but eventually makes a sizable income, then it seems fitting that he pay a higher rate. If you graduate from Carnegie Mellon, where I teach, and get a job in engineering for $80,000 a year, it does not seem an inordinate burden to pay $4,800 a year. But it does seem unreasonable to have to pay $400 a month when you make $18,000 a year.

The real shift is that Income Contingent Loans obligate someone's actual salary. They absorb some of the risk, in a sense, of those who do not attain high salaries, but they also have a certain fairness: they are a kind of tax levied on the actual economic value of a degree, rather than the imagined value. One counterargument is that this is unfair—as with income taxes, those who make more pay at a higher rate. But I would argue that the current system is unfair and unbalanced, insofar as some people derive more benefit from a college degree. For instance, at Carnegie Mellon, the value of a computer science degree is far higher than one in English, so those in computer science should have to pay proportionately more. The Australian system adjusts for degrees in fields such as the humanities.

One practical problem of Income Contingent Loans is collection. In the United Kingdom, collection is administered through income tax. Although this would require a new line or work sheet on our yearly tax report, it would rid us of payment books and complicated refinancing plans and greatly reduce the many layers of financial aid offices, the federal loan system, and the brokers of banking, saving substantially more paperwork as well as money than the system we now have. Banks will lobby that this is inefficient, but the tax system works: it's already in place; and the current system, with its multiple brokers, is hardly more efficient. The specter of socialism would probably be invoked, but the present system is already socialized, insofar as the federal government guarantees the loans—with banks rather than students gaining a good deal of the benefit. Income Contingent Loans would shift the benefit more fully to students.

The College Student Relief Act of 2007 institutes an "Income-Based Repayment Option" on the model of Income Contingent Loans. This is a feint in the right direction, but a muddled one. It mandates qualifying for economic hardship through a labyrinthine process and relies on an overly complicated formula, of the amount of your adjusted gross income exceeding 100 percent of the poverty line, then capping payments at 20 percent of that, which often results in a still substantial payment. (Based on the 2006 poverty line of $10,488 for a single person, our elementary school teacher would have to pay 20 percent of $13,412, or $220.17 a month; in the other systems, she would have to pay little or nothing until she made more.) Such adjustments could lead more qualified students to go into teaching. The advantage of the Australian and British models is that they apply to everyone—you do not have to file yet another set of forms to find out if you qualify, nor can you be rejected—and payments are based on a fixed and clear scale. The Relief Act shows admirable concern for the problem, for instance cutting interest rates from 6.12 percent in 2007 to 3.4 percent in 2011 (much to the displeasure of the banking lobby), but, as with the health care system, adds another codicil to an already far-flung and confusing web of regulations. The Australian and British systems work and are standardized and simple, with one plan for all.

Although it seems as if it crept up on us, student-loan indebtedness is not an accident but a policy. It is a bad policy, corrupting the goals of higher education. The world we inhabit is a good one if you are in the fortunate third without debt, but not nearly so good if you live under its weight. Student debt produces inequality and overtaxes our talent for short-term, private gain. As a policy, we can and should change it.

Analyze This Reading

1. Describe the system of indentured servitude that existed in early America. Why is it considered by most historians to be an "exploitive system of labor, in many instances a form of bondage akin to slavery"?
2. What connection does the writer make between indentured servitude and present-day college student-loan debt?
3. What points does the writer make in his references to the 1947 Report of the President's Commission on Education?
4. What are the counterarguments, or rebuttals, to the writer's position? How does he answer them? Explain how the writer's position is strengthened or weakened by including these counterarguments.
5. What solutions to college student-loan debt does the writer offer? Which solution does he prefer and why?
6. Analyze this reading in terms of the seven parts of Toulmin-based argument. Where do the claim and warrant appear? Is the writer convincing in the support he brings to his argument? Explain. Describe any weaknesses you find in this argument.

Respond To This Reading

1. Has the writer gone too far in comparing the practice of indentured servitude with the hardships students face today repaying loans? Explain.
2. How are you paying for your college education? If you have taken out loans, explain how some of the writer's points are similar to your situation.
3. Evaluate the writer's preferred solution to college student-loan debt.
4. What changes would you argue for regarding the cost of a college education today? How would you justify these changes?

Workplace Community

ABOUT THIS READING

At the University of Maryland, Gar Alperovitz is Professor of Political Economy and a founding principal of the Democracy Collaborative. Among Alperovitz's research interests are community-based economics in an era of globalization and political change that includes peace as a goal. His books include *America Beyond Capitalism: Reclaiming Our Wealth, Our Liberty, and Our Democracy* (2004) and, with Lew Daly, *Unjust Deserts: How the Rich are Taking Our Common Inheritance and Why We Should Take it Back* (2008). Keane Bhatt authors the blog "Manufacturing Contempt," where the writer analyzes how American media representations are "shaped by money, power, and ideology." This article appeared in *Truthout*, a daily newsletter that, in its own words, "works to broaden and diversify the political discussion by introducing independent voices and focusing on undercovered issues and unconventional thinking."

Employee-Owned Businesses Ignored by Mainstream Media

A bold new threat to the economic status quo brings on a press blackout.

By Gar Alperovitz and Keane Bhatt

Social pain, anger at ecological degradation and the inability of traditional politics to address deep economic failings has fueled an extraordinary amount of practical on-the-ground institutional experimentation and innovation by activists, economists and socially minded business leaders in communities around the country.

A vast democratized "new economy" is slowly emerging throughout the United States. The general public, however, knows almost nothing about it because the American press simply does not cover the developing institutions and strategies.

For instance, a sample assessment of coverage between January and November of 2012 by the most widely circulated newspaper in the United States, the *Wall Street Journal,* found ten times more references to caviar than to employee-owned firms, a growing sector of the economy that involves more than $800 billion in assets and 10 million employee-owners— around three million more individuals than are members of unions in the private sector.

Worker ownership—the most common form of which involves ESOPs, or Employee Stock Ownership Plans—was mentioned in a mere five articles. By contrast, over 60 articles referred to equestrian activities like horse racing, and golf clubs appeared in 132 pieces over the same period.

Although 2012 was designated by the United Nations as the International Year of the Cooperative—an institution that now has more than one billion members worldwide—the *Journal's* coverage was similarly thin. More

© iStockphoto.com/A-digit

than 120 million Americans are members of cooperatives and cooperative credit unions, 30 million more people than are owners of mutual funds. The *Journal*, however, devoted some 700 articles to mutual funds between January and October and only 183 to cooperatives. Of these the majority were concerned with high-end New York real estate, with headlines like "Pricey Co-ops Find Buyers."

The vast number of cooperative businesses on Main Streets across the country were discussed in just 70 articles and a mere 14 gave co-op businesses more than passing mention. Together, the articles only narrowly outnumbered the 13 *Journal* pieces that mentioned the Dom Perignon brand of champagne over the same time frame, and were eclipsed by the 40 *Journal* entries that refer to the French delicacy *foie gras.*

Another democratized economic institution is the not-for-profit Community Development Corporation (CDC), roughly 4,500 of which operate in all 50 states and the District of Columbia. Such neighborhood corporations create tens of thousands of units of affordable housing and millions of square feet of commercial and industrial space a year. The *Journal* ran no articles mentioning CDCs in 2012 and only 43 over the past 28 years—less than two a year. Meanwhile, the word *château* appeared in 30 times as many articles, and luxury apartments received 300 times as much coverage over the same period.

Not surprisingly, the growing "new economy movement" championing democratization of the economy has itself received even less coverage, despite growing citizen involvement on many levels. Over the past year, major national, state and other conferences focusing on worker-owned companies, cooperatives, public banking, nonprofit and public land trusts, and neighborhood corporations were oversubscribed, reflecting the growing interest in these forms. The *Journal*, however, gave scant coverage to the movement.

Thousands of other creative projects—from green businesses to new forms of combined community-worker efforts—are also underway across the country but receive little coverage. A number are self-consciously understood as attempts to develop working prototypes in state and local "laboratories of democracy" that may be applied at regional and national scale when the right political moment occurs. In Cleveland, Ohio, for instance, a complex of sophisticated worker-owned firms has been developing in desperately poor, predominantly black neighborhoods. The model is partially structured along lines of the Mondragón Corporation, a vibrant network of worker-owned cooperatives in northern Spain with more than 80,000 members and billions of dollars in annual revenue.

Since 2010 legislation to set up public banks along the lines of the long-established Bank of North Dakota has been proposed in twenty states. Several cities—including Los Angeles and Kansas City—have passed "responsible banking" ordinances that require banks to reveal their impact on the community and/or require city officials to do business only with banks that are responsive to community needs. But municipally led responsible banking initiatives appear to have received no attention in the *Journal*, whereas the newspaper published seven articles this year discussing President Obama's birth certificate.

The limited nature of the coverage can also be seen in particular cases. Recreational Equipment, Inc. (REI) is a highly successful consumer co-op with $1.8 billion in sales for 2011, allowing it to share $165 million of its profits with its 4.7 million active members and 11,000 employees. Organic Valley, a Wisconsin-based cooperative dairy, generated more than $700 million in revenue for nearly 1,700 farmer-owners. From January through October 2012, the Journal referred (briefly) to REI in just three articles; Organic Valley rated just one mention. In combination, REI and Organic Valley appear in the *Journal* only as often as the Cavalier King Charles spaniel, a breed of dog that turned up in four entries in the *Journal*'s pages this year.

Further perspective on the coverage is offered in the way in which "hot topics" are presented, and others of greater economic significance played down. Co-ops in the U.S. generate over $500 billion in annual revenues. The global market for smartphones is estimated by Bloomberg Industries at $219 billion—less than half as large. Furthermore, there are 20 million more co-op members than smartphone users in the United States. The *Journal*, however, published over 1,000 print articles that included the terms "smartphone" or "smartphones" from January through October this year—more than five articles for each piece mentioning co-ops (many of which, as noted, were about upscale Manhattan apartments.)

The print coverage of the *Journal* was analyzed by the Democracy Collaborative of the University of Maryland through the online database ProQuest. Although the assessment focused on the *Journal*, the nation's preeminent source of news for economic and business affairs, a preliminary review suggests that other national media outlets devote a similarly miniscule proportion of space to the exploding "new economy" sector. This highlights the need for greater media exposure regarding important developments toward a more democratic, sustainable and community-based economy.

Analyze This Reading

1. What is the "new economy" and, according to the writers, why don't more Americans know about it?
2. Why might the writers have focused their research solely on *The Wall Street Journal*? What does their research reveal about this publication?
3. The writers bring in extensive factual support for their claim, especially in the form of specific examples. In fact, little if any emotional or ethical support appears in this article. With this strategy in mind, does emphasizing only one kind of support weaken this argument? Explain.

Respond To This Reading

1. What new economy institutions exist in your community? What cooperatives do you belong to?
2. What does the idea of bringing democracy and worker ownership into the workplace look like to you? How does it contrast or overlap with conditions in your present workplace?

ABOUT THIS READING

David L. Hudson, Jr., teaches classes in First Amendment law at Vanderbilt University Law School and at the Nashville School of Law. He has authored a number of books focusing on student speech, including, *Let the Students Speak: A History of the Fight for Free Expression in American Schools* (2011). Hudson also writes regularly for the *ABA Journal: Law News Now*, a publication of the American Bar Association, a professional organization devoted to "defending liberty and delivering justice as the national representative of the legal profession." The following article was published in that journal.

Site Unseen: Schools, Bosses Barred from Eyeing Students', Workers' Social Media

By David L. Hudson, Jr.

See if this sounds familiar: School officials learn that a student may have inappropriate material on a social media site. The officials—ostensibly concerned about bullying and other possible ramifications at school—call the student into the office, force him or her to reveal the password, log on to the site and show the pupil the questionable online content.

Nor are public schools alone. Many universities require students to let officials access their social media, and in some cases impel students to install spying software. Some colleges force their student-athletes to consent to the monitoring of their Facebook, Myspace and Twitter accounts by signing a social media policy. "There are multiple incidents around the country where schools are invading the social media privacy rights of K-12 students," says Bethesda, Md., attorney Bradley Shear, who has written extensively on social media and students.

"But," Shear continues, "it is an epidemic in the colleges. When did it become legal for public universities to be able to require their students to download spying software onto their personal iPhones or social media accounts to monitor pass-word-protected digital content?"

Workplaces, too, are leaning on employees to reveal online info. In 2010, Maryland prison guard Robert Collins said that his employer forced him to reveal his Facebook data to screen for gang ties. The Department of Public Safety and Correctional Services suspended the practice after the American Civil Liberties Union of Maryland filed a complaint on Collins' behalf, claiming the practice violated his personal privacy.

But this year several states have sought to block personal passwords from inquiring principals and bosses.

Legislators Respond

In Delaware in July, Gov. Jack Markell signed into law the Higher Education Privacy Act, which prohibits university officials from forcing students to disclose digitally protected information. According to the statute: "An academic institution shall not request or require that a student or applicant disclose any password or other related account information in order to gain access to the student's or applicant's social networking site profile or account by way of an electronic communication device."

The law also prohibits public and private universities from requiring or requesting "that a student or applicant log on to a social networking site, email account, or any other Internet site or application ... in the presence of an agent of the institution so as to provide the institution access."

For good measure, the law further prohibits university officials from monitoring or tracking a student or applicant's personal electronic communication device.

"I introduced the legislation to protect our students' First and Fourth Amendment rights," says Delaware state Rep. Darryl M. Scott. "If a student is required to disclose their postings, as part of the college application process, would they write and share their thoughts freely? My concern was that they would not."

Scott adds that "as the legislation was under consideration, I spoke with several students who agreed that the intent of the legislation was good and needed. I also spoke with five of the six higher-education institutions, both private and public, and they ... also agreed."

"The Delaware measure is a piece of legislation that protects both schools and students," says Shear, who has worked with several state legislatures to craft the legislation. "Students need to be protected along with the schools."

"Do schools really want to be the social media police?" Shear asks. "Can you imagine if schools have a duty to monitor all of their students' online postings? They could be sued for negligent monitoring or failing to act."

The Delaware legislation also provides for a health and safety exception that gives school public safety officials the ability to monitor student social media when they have a "reasonable, articulable suspicion of criminal activity," or conduct an "investigation, inquiry or determination conducted pursuant to an academic institution's threat assessment policy or protocol."

Scott wanted the Delaware law to protect K-12 students as well, but colleagues were concerned that the bill would protect bullies. That provision was removed and will be reintroduced next session.

Reining In Employers

Minneapolis attorney Wallace G. Hilke, who represents a secondary school student claiming school officials violated her First Amendment rights by demanding her digital password, says the law will prohibit school officials from being able to avoid liability by claiming qualified immunity, a defense against civil rights suits available to government officials when they do not violate clearly established constitutional or statutory law.

"Legislation prohibiting school officials from forcing students to disclose passwords is a good idea because it would completely eliminate the qualified immunity defense, as there would be clearly established statutory authority," Hilke says.

California is following suit. In August, the state Senate approved legislation that would prohibit colleges and universities from formally requesting or demanding that students provide their social media user names and passwords.

"California is set to end this unacceptable invasion of personal privacy," said state Sen. Leland Yee, author of the bill, in a statement. "The practice of employers or colleges demanding social media passwords is entirely unnecessary and completely unrelated to someone's performance or abilities.

"These social media outlets are often for the purpose of individuals to share private information—including age, marital status, religion, sexual orientation and personal photos—with their friends and family," Yee added. "This information is illegal for employers and colleges to use in making employment and admission decisions and has absolutely no bearing on a person's ability to do their job or be successful in the classroom."

The California Assembly also passed a similar bill that would designate anything marked as private on social media accounts as being beyond employers' limits.

Meanwhile, Maryland and Illinois passed similar legislation this year protecting employees from bosses' demands to see personal digital sites. Maryland Gov. Martin O'Malley signed the User Name and Password Privacy Protection and Exclusions Act in May. The Illinois Right to Privacy in the Workplace Act was signed by Gov. Pat Quinn in August.

The Maryland Chamber of Commerce opposed the bill, telling the *Washington Post's* Capital Business blog that employers "have a myriad of legitimate interests in knowing what their employees or applicants have posted about themselves," such as making sure employees are not posting trade secrets or negative comments about customers, using illegal drugs or engaging in other inappropriate behavior.

But a representative for the business group said the chamber will move forward helping employers comply with the new law.

"The law is the law," spokesman Will Burns told Capital Business. "At this point, our goal is to ensure that all businesses know about it so they can adjust any policies that may be contrary to it."

Meanwhile, two U.S. senators—Charles Schumer of New York and Richard Blumenthal of Connecticut—have asked the Department of Justice and the Equal Employment Opportunity Commission to investigate whether such password requirements violate federal law.

"Ultimately, both free speech and privacy interests are at stake when public school officials demand that students reveal their passwords for their social media networks," says free-speech expert Clay Calvert, director of the Marion B. Brechner First Amendment Project at the University of Florida. "It's an Orwellian overreach by school officials—an effort to stretch their jurisdiction and authority over student expression far beyond the confines of campus and into the private homes where social media speech is created."

"I believe such legislation will eventually become the norm, because public policy and case law has indicated that requiring access to password-protected digital content may be against the law," Shear says. "However, since there isn't a federal law or on-point Supreme Court decision, new laws are needed to clarify the legal landscape."

Analyze This Reading

1. The writer is a First Amendment scholar. Why would he be interested in college officials monitoring students' online behavior?
2. Describe the Higher Education Privacy Act. To what does it respond?
3. What argument does the Maryland business community offer in its opposition to the User Name and Password Privacy Protection and Exclusions Act?
4. What kind of support does the writer draw on to establish his credibility in this writing?

Respond To This Reading

1. What is your college's policy regarding access to student social media passwords? Describe your reaction to this policy.
2. The computer software industry makes it easy to monitor students' online activity. In fact, surveillance software is a growing market attracting eager investors. In your sense of things—your college and workplace worlds and the larger world in general—what conditions support this new market?

ABOUT THIS READING

Recently the U.S. Supreme Court ruled in favor of providing constitutional protections to corporations. Many view this as a threat to democracy, as the decision opens the door to unlimited corporate spending in political campaigns among other issues. The following argument appeared in *Synthesis/Regeneration*, a magazine of green social thought. The authors are members of the Women's International League for Peace and Freedom.

Abolish Corporate Personhood (Thinking Politically)

By Jan Edwards and Molly Morgan

Colonies, constitutions and corporations

The history of the United States could be told as the story of who is, and who is not, a person under law. Women, poor people, slaves, and even corporations had long been considered persons for purposes of following the law. This is because early laws were written "No person shall . . ." Corporate lawyers had tried to avoid these laws by claiming corporations were not persons and therefore not required to follow the law. So it was decided that for purposes of following the law, corporations were persons. This allowed corporations to sue and be sued in court among other things. But corporations were not persons with rights in the law, and neither were women, slaves, indentured servants, or poor people. We know some of the ongoing story of human beings' struggle to gain the rights of persons under law, but how did corporations gain these rights?

To understand the phenomenon of corporate personhood, we start by looking at the foundation of US law, the Constitution of the United States of America. This document was written by 55 gentlemen cleverly described by one historian as "the well-bred, the well-fed, the well-read, and the well-wed." Many of them wrote and spoke at length about the inability of the common people to be self-governing.

The word "democracy" appears nowhere in the Constitution. The Constitution only mentions two entities: We the People and the government. We delegate some of our power to the government in order to perform tasks we want government to do. In a representative democracy, this system should work just fine.

The problem is that the phrase "We the People" is not defined in the Constitution. In 1787, in order to be considered one of "We the People" and have rights in the Constitution, you had to be an adult male with white skin and a certain amount of property. This narrowed "We the People" down to about 10% of the population. Those who owned property, including human property, were very clear that this was rule by the minority.

So here was the first definition of who gets to be a person in the United States. Ninety percent of the people, including all the immigrants, indentured servants, slaves, minors, Native Americans, women, and people who did not own property (the poor), were, legally, not "persons."

Without using the words "slave" or "slavery," the Constitution ensures that even if slaves get to free soil, their status as property remains the same. This is just one of the clauses defining property in the Constitution. It also defines contracts, labor, commerce, money, copyright, and war as the province of the federal government. So the Constitution, the foundation of all US law, was not written to protect people—it was written to protect property. The Constitution does contain some protection for people in Section 9, but the Bill of Rights is the concentration of rights for We the People.

Constitutional fallacies

Most people believe that the Constitution, specifically the Bill of Rights, guarantees our rights to freedom of speech, religion, and press, to peaceably assemble, and so forth. People of all political stripes say this. But the truth is, it does no such thing. Almost all of our constitutional protections are expressed as the absence of a negative rather than the presence of a positive. So the First Amendment, for example, does not say, "All citizens are guaranteed the right to free speech"; it only says, "Congress shall make no law . . . abridging the freedom of speech . . ." The First Amendment just restricts the government from specific encroachments; it doesn't guarantee anything. This was not a concern for the people because they had strong bills of rights in their state constitutions, and at that time, the states had more power than the federal government.

If those rights were actually guaranteed in the Constitution, people could, for example, take the Bill of Rights into the workplace. Anyone who thinks workers have free speech while they are on corporate property should ask the workers or talk to a union organizer. Because corporations are property, and because the Constitution protects property rights above all, most people have to abandon the Bill of Rights in order to make a living.

Another word that does not appear in the Constitution is "corporation." The reason is that the writers of the Constitution had zero interest in using for-profit corporations to run their new government. In colonial times, corporations were tools of the King's oppression, chartered for the purpose of exploiting the so-called "New World" and shoveling wealth back into Europe. The rich formed joint-stock corporations to distribute the enormous risk of colonizing the Americas and gave them names like the Hudson Bay Company, the British East India Company, and the Massachusetts Bay Colony. Because they were so far from their sovereign, the agents for these corporations had a lot of autonomy to do their work. They could pass laws, levy taxes, and even raise armies to manage and control property and commerce. They were not popular with the colonists.

So the writers of the Constitution left control of corporations to state legislatures (10th Amendment), where they would get the closest supervision by the people. Early corporate charters were very explicit about what a corporation could do, how, for how long, with whom, where, and when. Corporations could not own stock in other corporations, and they were prohibited from any part of the political process. Individual stockholders were held personally liable for any harms done in the name of the corporation, and most charters only lasted for 10 or 15 years. Most importantly, in order to receive the profit-making privileges the shareholders sought, their corporations had to represent a clear benefit for the public good, such as building a road, canal, or bridge. When corporations violated any of these terms, their charters were frequently revoked by the state legislatures.

That sounds nothing like the corporations of today. So what happened in the last two centuries? As time passed and memories of royal oppression faded, the wealthy people increasingly started eyeing corporations as a convenient way to shield their personal fortunes. They could sniff the winds of change and see that their minority rule through property ownership was under serious threat of being diluted. States gradually started loosening property requirements for voting, so more and more white men could participate in the political process. Women were publicly agitating for the right to vote. In 1865 the 13th Amendment was ratified, freeing the slaves. Three years later, the 14th Amendment provided citizenship rights to all persons born or naturalized in the United States, and two years after that, the 15th Amendment provided voting rights to black males. Change was afoot, and so the ruling class responded.

During and after the Civil War there was a rapid increase in both the number and size of corporations. This form of business was starting to become a more important way of holding and protecting property and power. Increasingly through their corporations, the wealthy started influencing legislators, bribing public officials, and employing lawyers to write new laws and file court cases challenging the existing laws that restricted corporate behavior. Bit by bit, decade by decade, state legislatures increased corporate charter length while they decreased corporate liability and reduced citizen authority over corporate structure, governance, production, and labor.

But minority rulers were only going to be able to go only so far with this strategy. Because corporations are a creation of the government, chartered by the state legislatures, they still fell on the government side of the constitutional line with duties accountable to the people. If minority rule by property was going to be accomplished through corporations, they had to become entitled to rights instead, which required them to cross the line and become persons under the law. Their tool to do this was the 14th Amendment, which was ratified in 1868. From then it took the ruling class less than 20 years to shift corporations from the duty side of the line, where they are accountable to the people, to the rights side, where they get protection from government abuse.

The 14th Amendment, in addition to saying that now all persons born or naturalized in the US are citizens, says that no state shall "deprive any person of life, liberty, or property, without the due process of law; nor deny to any person . . . the equal protection of the laws." The phrase about not depriving any person of life, liberty, or property without the due process of the law is exactly the same wording as the Fifth Amendment, which protects people from that kind of abuse by the federal government. With the ratification of the 14th Amendment, the states could no longer abuse people in that way either. These are important rights. They are written in a short, straightforward manner. After the Civil War and all the agony over slavery, the people in the states that ratified the 13th, 14th, and 15th Amendments were clear that they were about righting the wrong of slavery.

That clarity, however, did not stop the railroad barons and their attorneys in the 1870s and 80s. As mentioned before, those who wanted to maintain minority rule were losing their grip. There was real danger of democracy creeping into the body politic. Until the Civil War, slavery was essential to maintaining the entire economic system that kept wealth and power in the hands of the few—not just in the South, but in the North as well. It was the legalization of a lie—that one human being can own another. Slavery was at the core of a whole system of oppression that benefitted the few, which included the subjugation of women, genocide of the indigenous population, and exploitation of immigrants and the poor.

Now that the slavery lie could no longer be used to maintain minority rule, they needed a new lie, and they used the 14th Amendment to create it. Because these rights to due process and equal protection were so valuable, the definition of the word "person" in the 14th Amendment became the focus of hundreds of legal battles for the next 20 years. The question was: who gets to be a person protected by the 14th Amendment?

In the courts

The watershed moment came in 1886 when the Supreme Court ruled on a case called Santa Clara County v. Southern Pacific Railroad. The case itself was not about corporate personhood, although many before it had been, and the Court had ruled that corporations were not persons under the 14th Amendment. Santa Clara, like many railroad cases, was about taxes. Before the Court delivered its decision, the following statement is attributed to Chief Justice Waite:

> The court does not wish to hear argument on the question whether the provision in the 14th Amendment to the Constitution, which forbids a State to deny to any person within its jurisdiction the equal protection of the laws, applies to these corporations. We are all of the opinion that it does.

The statement appeared in the header of the case in the published version, and the Court made its ruling on other grounds. How this statement appeared in the header of the case is a matter of some mystery and competing theories, but because it was later cited as precedent, corporate personhood became the accepted legal doctrine of the land.

What was it in the 14th Amendment that was so valuable to corporate lawyers and managers? Why did they pursue it so aggressively? At the time, as is still true today, corporations were chartered by state governments, and the 14th Amendment reads "No state shall . . . ." If the word "person" in the 14th Amendment included corporations, then no state shall deny to corporations due process or equal protection of the laws. This allowed corporate lawyers to allege discrimination whenever a state law was enacted to curtail corporations.

This was also the beginning of federal regulatory agencies, so because corporations were now persons under the 14th Amendment, it would be discriminatory not to give them the same rights under federal laws. With the granting of the 5th Amendment right to Due Process (Noble v. Union River Logging, 1893), corporate lawyers could challenge, and the Supreme Court could find grounds to overturn, democratically legislated laws that originated at the federal as well as state levels.

Once corporations had jumped the constitutional line from the "government" side to the "people" side, their lawyers proceeded to pursue the Bill of Rights through more Supreme Court cases. As mentioned above, in 1893 they were assured 5th Amendment protection of due process. In 1906 they were granted 4th Amendment search and seizure protection (Hale v. Henkel). In 1922 they were acknowledged as being protected under the "takings" clause of the 5th Amendment (Pennsylvania Coal Co. v. Mahon), and a regulatory law was deemed to be a "takings."

In 1947 they started getting First Amendment protections (Taft-Hartley Act). In 1976, the Supreme Court determined that money spent for political purposes is equal to exercising free speech, and since "corporate persons" have First Amendment rights, they can basically contribute as much money as they want to political parties and candidates (Buckley v. Valeo).

Every time "corporate persons" acquire one of these protections under the Bill of Rights, it gives them a whole new way of exploiting the legal system in order to maintain minority rule through corporate power. Since 1886, every time people have won new rights, like the Civil Rights Act, corporations are eligible for it too.

Knowing the enemy

It is important to remember what a corporation is to understand the implications of corporate personhood for democracy. A corporation is not a real thing; it's a legal fiction, an abstraction. A corporation can live forever. It can change its identity in a day. If it's found guilty of a crime, it cannot go to prison.

Corporations are whatever those who have the power to define want them to be to maintain minority rule through corporations. As long as superhuman "corporate persons" have rights under the law, the vast majority of people have little or no effective voice in our political arena, which is why we see abolishing corporate personhood as so important to ending corporate rule and building a more democratic society.

Today the work of corporatists is to take this system global. Having acquired the ability to govern in the United States, the corporation is the ideal instrument to gain control of the rest of the world. The concepts, laws, and techniques perfected by the ruling minority here are now being forced down the throats of people everywhere.

First, a complicit ruling elite is co-opted, installed, or propped up by the US military and the government. Then, just as slavery and immigrant status once kept wages nonexistent or at poverty levels, now sweatshops, maquiladoras, and the prison-industrial complex provide ultra-cheap labor with little or no regulation. Just as sharecropping and the company store once kept people trapped in permanently subservient production roles, now the International Monetary Fund and World Bank's structural adjustment programs keep entire countries in permanent debt, the world's poorest people forced to feed interest payments to the world's richest while their own families go hungry.

A world without corporations

What would change if corporations did not have personhood? The first and main effect would be that a barrier would be removed that is preventing democratic change, just as the abolition of slavery tore down an insurmountable legal block, making it possible to pass laws to provide full rights to the newly freed slaves. After corporate personhood is abolished, new legislation will be possible. Here are a few examples.

If "corporate persons" no longer had First Amendment right of free speech, we could prohibit all corporate political activity, such as lobbying and contributions to political candidates and parties. If "corporate persons" were not protected against search without a warrant under the Fourth Amendment, then corporate managers could not turn OSHA (Office of Safety and Health Administration) and the EPA (Environmental Protection Agency) inspectors away if they make surprise, unscheduled searches. If "corporate persons" were not protected against discrimination under the 14th Amendment, corporations like Wal-Mart could not force themselves into communities that do not want them.

So what can we do to abolish corporate personhood? Within our current legal system there are two possibilities: the Supreme Court could change its mind on corporations having rights in the Constitution, or, we can pass an amendment to the Constitution. Either scenario seems daunting, yet it is even more difficult than that. Every state now has laws and language in their state constitutions conceding these rights to corporations. So corporate personhood must be abolished on a state as well as a national level.

The good news is that almost anything we do towards abolishing corporate personhood helps the issue progress on one of these levels. If a city passes a non-binding resolution, declaring their area a "Corporate Personhood Free Zone," that is a step toward passing a constitutional amendment at their state and eventually at the national level. If a town passes an ordinance legally denying corporations rights as persons, they may provoke a crisis of jurisdiction that could lead to a court case. We think both paths should be followed. It was, however, undemocratic for the Supreme Court to grant personhood to corporations, and it would be just as undemocratic for this to be decided that way again. An amendment is the democratic way to correct this judicial usurpation of the people's sovereignty.

We see that corporate personhood was wrongly given. It was given, not by We the People, but by nine Supreme Court judges. We further see that corporate personhood is a bad thing, because it was the pivotal achievement that allowed an artificial entity to obtain the rights of people, thus relegating us to subhuman status. Finally, because of the way corporate personhood has enabled corporations to govern us, we see that it is so bad, we must eradicate it.

Slavery is the legal fiction that a person is property. Corporate personhood is the legal fiction that property is a person. Like abolishing slavery, the work of eradicating corporate personhood takes us to the deepest questions of what it means to be human. If we are to live in a democracy, what does it mean to be sovereign? The hardest part of eliminating corporate personhood is believing that We the People have the sovereign right to do this. It comes down to us being clear about who's in charge.

Analyze This Reading

1. How do the writers interpret the phrase "We the People" in the Constitution?
2. Describe the status of corporations prior to the American Revolution.
3. What points do the writers make regarding the 14th Amendment and corporations?
4. What is the significance of the 1886 Supreme Court case Santa Clara County v. Southern Pacific Railroad? What is the significance of the 1976 Supreme Court determination?
5. According to the writers, what threats to everyday people do corporations pose?
6. The writers conclude with ideas of what our country would become when corporate personhood is disallowed and with suggestions for what can be done to begin this work. Describe these ideas and suggestions.
7. The writers reach far back into American history to establish context for the issue of corporate personhood. With broad, public issues like this one, why are extensive historical references important? And, have you ever experienced a change in your position on an issue before and after conducting research on it? Explain.

Respond To This Reading

1. What is your reaction to the Supreme Court's recent ruling granting "person" status to corporations?
2. While the writers' position on corporate personhood is clear, they do not make room in their argument for opposing views. Does this affect the argument and its credibility? Explain.
3. In some countries, political campaigns are conducted with public financing only, that is, without the support of corporate donations. How, specifically, would political campaigning in the United States be altered with such a system?

4. With attention to terms like *corporate personhood, democracy, We the People*, and *sovereign right*, what issues occur to you after reading this argument? On what single issue are you motivated to argue?

ABOUT THIS READING

This analysis appeared in the daily newsletter *Truthout*. Rinaldo Brutoco is President of the World Business Academy and co-author of two books on energy and climate change: *Profiles in Power* (1997) and *Freedom from Mid-East Oil* (2007). Sam Yau is a recognized business strategist who has worked across numerous industries. He is Director of the Board of Trustees of the Esalen Institute, a "center for exploring and realizing human potential through experience, education, and research."

The Current Business Paradigm is Toxic to Business and Society. Here's How We Change It.

By Rinaldo Brutoco and Sam Yau

The current business paradigm can be summed up in its four flawed principles:

- The business of business is business
- A business exists to maximize value for its shareholders
- Short-term profits are maximized even at the expense of a company's long-term financial health
- Compliance can be equated with business ethics

Current paradigm: the business of business is business

Business being the most pragmatic of all social organizational forms, it historically has focused narrowly on its economic activity without being distracted by the demands of political affiliations, societal and communal needs, environmental concerns, individual aspirations or civic pursuits, except for those which have been legislated or decreed by regulatory agencies, or the occasional token donation to a cultural charity such as the opera.

The principle that "the business of business is business" is derived from the belief that a business can best serve its societal purpose by focusing on doing what it does best—the efficient production and distribution of goods and services.

Current paradigm: a business exists to maximize value for its shareholders

"The social responsibility of business is to increase its profits," said Milton Friedman (The New York Times Magazine, 13 September 1970). "So the question is, do corporate executives, provided they stay within the law, have responsibilities in their business activities other than to make as much money for their stockholders as possible? And my answer to that is, no they do not."

Focusing on maximizing short-term profit allows an unambiguous bottom-line measurement of, and reward for, the company's and business executives' success on a quarter-to-quarter, year-to-year basis. The singular and seemingly objective measurement of profits creates a common language and benchmark for company analyses and makes it possible to communicate a "snapshot" of the monetary financial health of companies to the investing public.

This provides a significant tool, although by no means the only tool, to create a stock market that provides valuation, liquidity, investment opportunities and wealth creation for participants in the economy. And, in fact, rising short term quarterly profits will actually consistently raise the market capitalization of a given business, which in turn leads to a greater value of the shares held by shareholders.

This is the linkage that is often relied upon in using the term "maximizing shareholder value." There are other methods used to maximize shareholder value (e.g., layoffs to reduce payroll, splitting companies up so that shares will achieve a higher multiple separated than they enjoy when combined—such as Abbott Laboratories' decision to split in two), but each of these has the same intended result: yield higher quarterly profits and achieve a higher price earnings ratio on those quarterly profits.

Even if one accepts the questionable assumption that the stock market is a good arbiter of a company's value—by looking primarily at its quarter to quarter earnings—to accept Milton Friedman's dictum, one would need to make the further logical leap that only by taking care of "business" are executives adhering to the basic purpose of the corporate entity (i.e., maximizing shareholder value in the abstract, detached from the broader societal framework within which the corporation exists).

It is quite clear to the present authors that Milton Friedman's dictum is operating as the current business paradigm. Although it lacks depth, contextual relevance, and historical perspective, the vast majority of business executives and most of Wall Street (excluding the large, growing, and more profitable funds that operate in the socially responsible investment arena) actually believe the mantra that business exists to maximize shareholder value. For better or worse, it is the current paradigm.

Current paradigm: short-term profits are maximized even at the expense of a company's long-term financial health

Many institutional stockholders erroneously focus on short-term stock price performance and exert significant pressure on management to increase short-term profits at the cost of long-term financial health. Focusing on quarterly financial reporting requirements, many companies have adopted an orientation of maximizing short-term financial performance instead of seeking long-term growth and sustainable earnings. This puts a company's future at risk. Financially, short-termism is a systemwide problem, co-created by corporate managers, boards, investment bankers, institutional investors, and government.

For a corporation to conduct itself so as to maximize short-term profits and in the process destroy itself, as Enron and many others have done, definitely is not the way to maximize shareholder value. Every farmer knows that you can vastly improve this year's grain sales if you sell your seed corn, but that means you won't even be in the business of growing corn the next season.

The best way to ensure long-term growth in profits is to maintain a maximally effective balance between all the corporate stakeholders such that today's short-term profits reflected in the snapshot financials are based on underlying relationships that will permit profits and net assets to continue to grow over time for the benefits of all stakeholders.

Current paradigm: equating compliance with business ethics

The ethical foundation of the current economic and business system is based on the limited view that ethical obligations arise out of social mandates as expressed by current laws and regulations. Because the human mind is so ingenious, corporations have never failed to find legal loopholes to game any system; they therefore can commit legal actions that are unjust to employees and damaging to the society and environment. And, all too often, corporate executives actually take illegal actions in the expectation they will "get away with it," which all too often they do. As new social issues and new technologies arise, they are usually ahead of what legislators can understand and resolve through appropriate legislation.

A good example of this phenomenon is the AIG financial products called credit default swaps, which were too complicated for most to understand and remained unregulated even as they were identified as the major contributor to the recent collapse of the U.S. financial system.

A better system of ethics, meaning a system more productive and therefore more conducive to making profits, is one based on what one believes one "ought" to do based upon one's heightened sense of a moral compass.

The question for corporate executives is not, "What can we get away with?" The question must be, "Given our power in society, what ought we to do to solve these enormous challenges consistent with our ongoing requirement to accumulate appropriate levels of surplus called 'profits' as we do it?" Failing to do what we ought to do, whether or not it is required by a statute or government regulation, should be seen as an ethical failure; such a failure by any company is a predictor that its profits ultimately will decline.

The only social aspects that the current system can value, capture and measure are those that can be immediately quantified in transitory monetary terms (i.e., reflected as positive on the quarter-to-quarter profit statement). Businesses, being the most dynamic and powerful economic engines, must also be evaluated in their contributions to the societies and communities in which they operate. There simply is no choice but to look at the bigger picture since failure to do so would be like rearranging deck chairs on the Titanic rather than addressing the crisis that is at hand.

The current system in the Western industrialized societies can measure economic contributions, but fails miserably in accounting for the damage and cost to society of the so-called "externalities" that are ignored when profits are made by destroying the public commons without taking into account the cost to society of that destruction in computing the true "profit" earned.

All such externalities must be costed out so that they can be taken into consideration when making economic decisions. A great example where society did this recently on an international level was the adoption of standards governing acid rain.

Fortunately, the acid created by one oil company's refineries in one country fell on that company's and other companies' refineries in other countries, thereby demonstrating the essential truth that a "cost" is a "cost" even if you can escape, for the time being, having to pay it. We are not far from realizing in the business community, as has already been almost universally acknowledged in the scientific community, that the "costs" of climate change will extract a devastating price from all sectors of society, including business.

Once the business community realizes this, and accepts forever more that "there is no free lunch," it will begin to lead the reconstruction of the environment. Fortunately, the companies who understand the symbiosis that occurs when they work with natural systems rather than ignoring or fighting them will profit most from the looming environmental disasters.

It is also time for the business community to realize that a loss of moral bearing, fed by insatiable greed, can lead to highly dangerous business conditions. For example, when business leaders lose their moral bearing, this system provides an ideal vehicle for creating personal wealth through highly inappropriate means: (1) pressuring the board for outsized stock grants, (2) manipulating accounting results, (3) manipulating stock option dates and the company stock price, and (4) taking incalculable or disproportionate risks. All these executive manipulations are often disguised as actions necessary to maximize shareholder value.

Executives hire expensive corporate lawyers to advise them so they can play on the edge of accounting rules and SEC regulations. While playing on the slippery slope of legal gamesmanship, many executives did slip downward into outright frauds, resulting in serious damages to company reputation, stock price collapse, and often bankruptcy of the company and jail time for the executives. Billions and billions of value evaporated overnight, thousands of jobs were lost, and the value of pensions earned over hardworking years was wiped out without a trace. And in the process, through the stock market's crash, much of the paper wealth that those same executives were creating was wiped out—along with the savings of the butcher, the baker and the candlestick maker.

Consequence of current paradigm: reckless short-term pursuit of profits for shareholders at the expense of all other stakeholders

The continuing narrowing of business perspective over the last half century cumulated in the single-minded pursuit of profit maximization by corporations, often at the expense of all other stakeholders, which include employees, suppliers, the community, and protection of the public commons. Compounding this problem is the relentless pressure by the investment community for short-term, quarter-to-quarter returns, driving many companies to focus on short-term financial results instead of building long-term market position and value for all stakeholders. Adding to all these factors is the belief that business can legitimately equate legal compliance with business ethics. The combination of these factors underlies many of the problems of the business world today.

Such problems unfold in many different ways. On the more obvious level, unsafe products for customers, legal exploitation of employees, harsh tactics with suppliers, total disregard of community interests, pollution of the environment, and dangerous financial manipulations are only some of the examples resulting from the relentless drive toward profits for shareholders at the expense of other constituents.

On a more disguised level, executive compensation tied to shareholder value as reflected in the stock market actually provides a powerful incentive for executives to maximize profits in the short term to maximize their own wealth. Since profitable revenue growth is perceived to be the most powerful engine for creating shareholder value and executive wealth, many executives develop an insatiable appetite for growth. Growth for the sake of growth is the ideology of a cancer cell. So it is no surprise that growth for the sake of growth has led to many overpaid mergers and acquisitions, often justified by unrealistic assumptions of financial or strategic synergies. Failed mergers and acquisitions have been a top destroyer of shareholder value. The prospect of enormous wealth for top executives has often induced them to take reckless risks that led to company collapse—or even the collapse an entire industry, like the financial industry in 2008.

More shareholder value has been destroyed in the pursuit of profits in the name of shareholder value maximization than for any other reason. In fact, shareholder maximization not only failed to occur in the run-up to the Great Recession from 2008 to 2009, but shareholder value was destroyed on a massive scale while societal costs were created that will be borne by the next several generations.

For a business to survive and prosper, it must provide a return to shareholders that is comparable to similar companies in the market. Shareholder value is created as the result of management providing superior goods and services in the market it serves.

Creating shareholder value is neither the purpose of a company's existence, nor a company strategy.

Consequence of current paradigm: under-realization of the human potential

Lack of a larger purpose beyond profit maximization naturally has resulted in a failure of understanding of the humanistic aspect of business. You can trace the origin of such a blind spot to the scientific revolution that started in the 17th century and gave birth to the Modern Era. Scientists introduced a vigorous empirical method to investigate the physical world. This scientific method allowed an evidence-based search for knowledge of physical phenomena that for the first time was free from the church's absolute decrees about nature. This great accomplishment in human history propelled both the Renaissance and the Industrial Revolution in the West followed by the Technological Revolution that continues until the present.

Unfortunately, as science achieved its great heights in its ability to understand the natural world and increase the standard of living for humanity, it began to confuse its methodology with claims to truths in all areas of human endeavor. The belief that empirical methods are the only means of knowing in all aspects of human endeavor is sometimes called scientism.

An accompanying belief from scientism is that all human experiences, including our subjective experiences of thoughts and feelings, can be understood and reduced to biochemical interactions in our body. The interest in the study of psychology probing the inner depths of the human psyche declined and gave way to behavioral studies in which humans are assumed to behave according to rewards or punishments, pleasures or pain. In this view, our mind and emotions are merely the results of the neuron interactions in our brain. For centuries, science did not place a great deal of value in first-person subjective experiences. What science could not objectively measure and quantify, it dismissed as non-existent.

Under such influence, business education in the U.S. became science-envy. As part of the trend in specialization, business education was separated from moral philosophy and political economy and new independent business schools were created to pursue their own paths outside the larger philosophical, ethical, political and social context explored during a liberal arts education. Over the years, business schools continued to narrow their focus and become increasingly quantitative and analytical instead of contextual and humanistic.

There are a number of severe consequences. First, business ignores the rich interior of the individuals working in corporations—their aspirations, the power of their intention and vision, their need for a community, their need to belong, and their search for meaning and purpose in their work life.

The current business paradigm recognizes expertise and experience, the need for economic rewards, and the need for recognition of accomplishments and creativity. It gives only limited recognition to interior dimensions because they are difficult to ascertain and therefore considered largely irrelevant.

Instead, business focuses on observable behaviors and concerns itself only with results and outputs that can be objectively measured and that relate directly to revenue or cost. As a result, it has taken a long time for business to begin to recognize that each of us is a whole person—body, emotions, mind, and spirit—and to recognize how we desire to relate to others in a deeper and more meaningful way. Business wants us to bring body and mind to our jobs but does not understand how our emotional and spiritual yearning affects us in our work and personal life.

Only in the last decade, business started to wake up to the role of emotional intelligence, after the publication of the book bearing the same title by Daniel Goleman. The fact that emotional intelligence had been part of our normal human capabilities for eons and that we had lived it with family and friends, but it took someone to write about it to get the attention of the business world is quite revealing about how far our business culture has fragmented our life and reduced our wholeness in our work life. At the same time, we've seen a culture arise in Silicon Valley that has begun to highly value the whole person, that asks how good employees and colleagues feel about coming to work, how they can be creatively stimulated, and how they can be shown appreciation. The Silicon Valley companies most famous for this culture, such as Google and Apple, are the legends of our current business landscape. This illustrates how the companies that first recognize our inherent interconnection with the natural world will be the most profitable in the decades ahead, just as those companies that first recognized the intrinsic wholeness of humans have been far more successful in tapping into human creativity, with profits that show it. Spirituality is the sense of inner stirrings, the search for a deeper self-knowledge, the quest for meaning as a result of becoming part of something bigger than the self, and an opening to the infinite. The longing is often expressed in the care for our fellow human beings, communities, and the environment, as well as in some forms of transcendental divinity.

Under the current paradigm, individual spirituality and values are considered distracting and undesirable in the workplace. And yet such spirituality has the biggest untapped potential for motivation and inspiration in the workplace that business has yet to understand. Business has not grasped the full potential for intentionality, passion, ingenuity, and creativity in its employees.

Most business leaders and executives are decent, hard working and moral individuals. But when they enter into business, they seemingly enter into a game with its unique, unhealthy paradigm, value sets, mantras, cultural mores, and idiosyncratic rules. We play by the rules and we play to win.

Unfortunately, in playing to win, other far more important value sets are discarded or ignored. That blindness, or lack of a sense of stewardship for what we are entrusted with, can become a set of blinders that causes great environmental and human damage that ultimately also compromises profits and real, long-term shareholder value.

It is long past time for business as an institution and individual business people to see the incredible opportunity that exists for rich human relationships in the workplace at every level of the hierarchy, and the potential each individual has to enhance their contribution to their fellow humans and to the planet itself.

Consequence of current paradigm: loss of trust

As a result of the current business paradigm, over the years there has been a steady decline in the public trust of corporations. In a 2009 survey, when respondents in the U.S. were asked about trust in business in general, only 38% said they have faith in business to do what is right, a 20% plunge since the year before. Moreover, only 17% of the respondents in 2009 said they trust information from a company's CEO. Both the 17% and the 38% numbers represent lower levels of trust than those measured in the wakes of Enron, the dot-com bust, and Sept. 11, 2001.

Unfortunately, if the same survey were taken today it would likely reveal an even lower level of trust as a result of the public's perception that business takes care of itself and does so at the expense of other sectors of society. There could be no greater testament to this complete lack of trust in business than the growing Occupy Wall Street movement which continues to grow and expand to cities around the U.S. and throughout the world.

This decline in trust also is playing out in people's everyday lives. More than three-fourths (77%) of survey respondents in 2009 said they refuse to buy products or services from a company they distrust, and 72% said they have badmouthed a distrusted company to a friend or colleague.

It has been a couple of catastrophic years for business, well beyond the evident destruction in shareholder value and the need for emergency government funding during the financial meltdown in 2008 and subsequent recession.

The financial sector drives instead of supports the real economy— the tail is wagging the dog

Our financial system is supposed to support the real economy of goods and services. However in the last 30 years, the unhealthy situation has developed that the real economy has suffered from excesses in the financial sector. These include disproportionate risks in leverage; the creation and worldwide distribution of huge amount of unregulated derivatives which were little more than gambling chips; the use of public-subsidized, low-cost credit for high-risk proprietary trading; and fraudulent underwriting of mortgage loans. Such excesses cumulated in the financial meltdown in 2008 and the subsequent recession of a depth unseen since the Great Depression.

Enormous wealth was transferred from the real economy to the financial sector. In 2007, the year before the bankruptcy of Lehman Brothers, the financial sector's profits accounted for an astonishing 40% of the entire economy. Yes, the tail is wagging the dog. How else to explain that the "best and the brightest" in the financial community continually fall for an earnings story that derives from fatally flawed assumptions that end in financial chaos and often financial panic?

None of the "best and the brightest" in the financial community foresaw the near collapse of the global financial system in 2008 even though many of us outside Wall Street did and warned our associates to abandon the financial markets before the crash occurred. What were we seeing that the brilliant, extraordinarily over-compensated managers and analysts on the Street missed? Simple, we were looking at the fundamental instability and weakness in the financial system that was built on a securitization of paper that was tantamount to printing currency on a printing press with no thought of the value of the goods backing the printed paper.

Watching the creation of $750 trillion in derivatives when the entire global GNP of all countries on earth was only $60 trillion per year was another indication of a system wildly out of control in pursuit of inflated profits built on worthless paper rather than on real economic growth. The economic carnage that followed was the quintessential opposite of maximizing shareholder value, but pursuit of that single-minded goal while wearing blinders is precisely what created the debacle.

The history of the capital markets system over the last 250 years has been characterized by boom and bust cycles. There are many reasons for this, and some such cycles even take names from their perceived cause, such as an "Inventory Cycle." Other cycles are perceived to be precipitated by other directly causative mechanisms but they all have one thing in common: greed.

When someone gets greedy, they get carried away. When a whole bunch of people get greedy, it leads to marketplace excesses that ultimately cause a "bust" which then needs to work itself through the system until a new balance can be restored from which renewed growth can occur. Those various cycles normally occur with a somewhat predictable periodicity as long as one has enough data and one is able to isolate the other factors that might simultaneously be at work.

Most modern economics departments at every decent institution of higher learning study such cycles, and a great body of knowledge has been accumulated and published about them. Those cycles, however, are not at the core of what is currently ailing the global economy.

Something much more fundamental and destructive is at work. Hence, when a television or newspaper commentator blithely "reports" that "all recessions end and this one too will end in time," the reporter is doing the public a great disservice. Even if the reporter is oblivious, the business community should itself become more aware of the unprecedented situation we are facing today.

It is enlightened self-interest for the business community to begin to realize two critical realities at work simultaneously at this point in human history:

(1) business is the most powerful institution on the planet and if it doesn't ensure long term sustainability of the economy and of human civilization itself, human civilization will experience the worst period of chaos and destruction in human history; and (2) because business is the most powerful institution on the planet, it not only singlehandedly has the opportunity to alter the extremely negative future pattern that is evolving, it has the absolute responsibility to do so. The good news is that by rising to the larger mission covered in this article, the business community will in fact create a period of economic prosperity that will dwarf all other boom times.

Why is there any special urgency now for sustainable thinking?

The high probability of climate change having already passed the tipping point ensures a spiraling cycle of devastating environmental phenomena, including droughts punctuated by floods, decreasing food supplies, devastating storms with greater intensity and frequency (especially tornadoes), and a massive shortfall of adequate potable water supplies at the highest elevations (i.e., all glaciers on earth, particularly the Himalayan High Plateau which feeds the great rivers of China and India) as well as in ground water reserves globally. On both counts human civilization is out of time.

That in turn means that corporate profits are in for a prolonged diminution over many, many years. The only way to ensure sustainable shareholder value increases is to address both threats and resolve them. Only business as an institution has the resources and training to do so. There is no other option.

What is the larger purpose of business?

It is to recognize that every human being on the planet has the right to have eight essential needs met: (1) adequate water, (2) adequate food, (3) adequate medical care, (4) adequate shelter, (5) adequate education without regard to gender, (6) adequate clothing, (7) air suitable for humans to breathe, and (8) a society free from violence, rape, torture, and war.

Some believe that achieving these goals is not possible. They are wrong. In fact, with business setting these goals for itself, business as an institution will unleash more wealth per capita by many magnitudes over every era that has preceded this one in history. In a word, creating these solutions will ensure sustainable business profits earned in totally appropriate ways.

The delightful thing about all of this is that ensuring these freedoms for all humans not only will ennoble all of those who labor to achieve these goals, but will also create undreamed of profits for generations to come indefinitely into the future. This is because, as noted above, greed begets ever larger and more destructive cycles of boom and bust. Actually acting sustainably toward all corporate stakeholders creates the opposite—a permanent wave of prosperity based upon abundance thinking rather than scarcity consciousness.

At a time when business profits are moving along at all-time highs in several industries, and the S&P 500 are churning out high profits as a group, the stock market has been extremely volatile and producing lackluster returns for investors.

The stock market today is beginning to reflect what the market sees as dysfunctional and what profits will be one and two years or more into the future. Why? Because the profits of all companies in the western democracies are in jeopardy as their middle classes are devastated and as their political institutions prove they are incapable of dealing with normal everyday challenges, let alone the challenges posed by climate change and our financial system.

How business can create the Second Renaissance – the Eight Human Rights and a healthy planet

A change in the way business perceives its role in society matched with a mentality for sustainability will yield the greatest economic opportunity in human history. Think about it. If you were a Florentine living in the early 1700's, you had an opportunity to realize the extraordinary wealth that was about to be created as a result of the end of the Dark Ages and the beginning of the Renaissance.

Stop and reflect for a moment on the shear brutish nature of life in the Dark Ages, and the flowering that occurred as the Renaissance began, bringing an explosion of wealth initially amongst the merchant classes and ultimately among western society as a whole.

The wealth that was created resulted from a change in mentality. It resulted from a collective change of mind. It all started with a single book: On the Revolution of Heavenly Spheres, by Copernicus. He observed, despite being forced to recant while secretly arranging a posthumous publication of his book, that the earth is not at the center of the universe.

From that humble beginning, humans began to question. In less than 150 years from the publication of Copernicus' mind-changing book, human society saw: the beginnings of the scientific method which began to explain how the physical world really worked and which began to take the place of myth, legend, superstition, and "blind faith"; the Protestant Reformation that cracked the centralized control of the Catholic Church right down the middle and ended its dominance as the unchallenged organizer and controller of western civilization; the beginnings of the first European university at

Bologna, Italy; the flowering of global commerce; the explosion of the arts; and, the beginning of the Renaissance. All that happened within 150 years from a global mind change brought on by one book.

A similar global mind change awaits us. In the Second Renaissance, we value the subjective experience of every human being and return the human to the center of our world, but in harmony with the planet and all its other living inhabitants.

Reconstructing the planet and providing the Eight Human Rights will create an explosion of wealth like the one when the Dark Ages gave way to the Renaissance. Only, this time, the explosion in wealth will be many times greater.

Believing as we do in the next Renaissance, which will be characterized by providing the Eight Human Rights and global reconstruction of natural systems, it is a time of great optimism. We can do it. In fact, we have no other choice. The Two Global Drivers—climate change and our unhealthy financial system which still has a vast pool of unregulated financial derivatives—must be addressed without further delay as each day of delay will yield a cost far greater than humans would be willing to pay if they understood the reality.

Can the Two Global Drivers ultimately be defeated? Yes, if we begin at once. We are capable of it, although we are doing nothing at the moment to address them. In fact, our fossil fuel-based planetary energy system is literally adding fuel to the fire every day in the form of increased CO_2 and methane emissions.

At the same time, we are optimistic that human society can, and must, confront these challenges. And, being people of science and commerce, we believe that no challenge exists on planet earth that cannot be solved with the existing technology and resources at our disposal. All that is missing is the collective will to do so.

It is our hope that the business community will face these enormous challenges, perceive its enormous power to alter the outcome, become aware of the profits which will be lost and the far greater ones that will be gained by providing the will and "can do" attitude to tackle our human dilemmas. To do less would be beneath us as a species. To do less would be profoundly unsustainable as an economic proposition.

Analyze This Reading

1. According to the writers, how has Milton Friedman influenced current conceptions of American business?
2. Describe the dangers of short-termism. What antidote do the writers endorse?
3. Explain the ethical position that the writers recommend for corporate executives. How does this position contrast with how most executives behave?
4. The writers state that, "Growth for the sake of growth is the ideology of the cancer cell." What does this statement mean in the context of business relations? How do the writers support this statement?
5. How has scientism influenced current attitudes to business? How do the writers evaluate this influence?

6. How do the writers contrast boom and bust cycles with a business approach centered in sustainability?

Respond To This Reading

1. In your view how would a sustainable economy differ from the kind of economy we live in now, one driven by short-term profits?
2. The writers refer to Daniel Goleman's book, *Emotional Intelligence: Why It Can Matter More than IQ* (2005). Given today's business paradigm, is it realistic to think that our emotional intelligence can become part of a new business model? Explain.

ABOUT THIS READING

Stress, as the writer explains, is not easy to define, but its effects on the workplace are substantial. Ken Macqueen is Vancouver bureau chief for *Maclean's, CA*, a weekly Canadian current affairs magazine. This report appeared in the October 15, 2007, issue.

Dealing with the Stressed: Workplace Stress Costs the Economy More Than $30 Billion a Year, and Yet Nobody Knows What It Is or How to Deal with It

By Ken Macqueen, with Martin Patriquin and John Intini

Life is hard. You work in a "fabric-covered box," as Dilbert puts it. Some troll in the IT department monitors your every keystroke. Lunch is a greasy slab of pizza al desko, eaten under heavy email fire. Your eyesight is shot, you're going to flab, you've vowed to make this just a 50-hour week because your spouse—toiling in another cubicle across town—needs every night and the weekend to meet her ridiculous deadline. It's 4:59 p.m., and if you're late again the daycare's gonna dump the kid on the street and call Children's Aid. Grab the cell. Grab the BlackBerry. You just know the boss is going to tug your electronic leash if he sees you leaving this early. Yeah, yeah, life is hard.

It's, you know, stressful. Whatever that means.

Stress is part of an explosion in workplace mental health issues now costing the Canadian economy an estimated $33 billion a year in lost productivity, as well as billions more in medical costs. It's become a political priority for Prime Minister Stephen Harper, who recently announced a new Mental Health Commission of Canada. With almost one million Canadians suffering from a mental health disorder, "it's now the fastest-growing category of disability insurance claims in Canada," Harper said. The cause is unclear. "Some blame the hectic pace of modern life, the trend to smaller and fragmented families, often separated by great distances, or the mass migration from small stable communities to huge, impersonal cities," he said. If there was a false note in his speech, it was his optimistic view of society's comprehension of the issue. "We now understand," he said, "that mental illness is not a supernatural phenomenon, or a character flaw."

Well, maybe. Such understanding is hardly universal in the workplace, where, as Harper noted, "stress or worse" exacts a heavy toll. It's as likely that stress-related maladies will be viewed with a combination of cynicism, incomprehension, and a skepticism bordering on hostility. To critics—a field that includes many employers, some academics, and coworkers resentful at picking up the slack—stress is the new whiplash, except bigger, more expensive, harder to define, and even more difficult to prove. Or to disprove.

"Stress," says U.S. author and workplace counsellor Scott Sheperd, "is probably the most overused and misused word in the English language—with the possible exception of love." It means everything and nothing. It is, he argues in Attacking the Stress Myth, "The Great Excuse." Look at the numbers: stress leaves are off the charts and some of the zombies who do show up accomplish little more than draining the company coffee pot.

The cause of this growing hit on productivity is indeed a mystery. Did the world get harder, or did people get softer? Or are employers stuck with an addled labour force of their own creation? It's not as if today's children will be sent to work in the mines. Women aren't struggling to raise six kids, while mourning several more who died in infancy. Men aren't spending 12 hours a day plowing fields behind a mule, or sweating over some mechanical monster of the Industrial Revolution, waiting for an arm or a leg to be dragged into its innards. No, odds are you've got indoor work, no heavy lifting, a 40-hour week (in theory), holiday time, and a big-screen TV waiting at home. How hard can life be?

Well, one person's dream job can be another's nightmare.

Nights, weekends, Janie Toivanen, an employee on the Burnaby campus of video game giant ElectronicArts (Canada) Ltd., gave her all to her job. She was part of the team producing EA's wildly popular NHL game series. EA prides itself on being a work-hard/play-hard kind of place. The complex looks like a workers' paradise, complete with a sand-covered beach volleyball court, an artificial turf soccer pitch, a full-on fitness centre, massage, yoga classes and a steam room. There's a gourmet cafeteria, and an employee concierge service to look after such mundanities as dry cleaning and car washing. In exchange, EA expects a huge degree of worker commitment.

Toivanen, an employee since 1996, earned strong performance ratings in her early years, regular bonuses and stock options. She rose through the ranks, often using what downtime she had to catch up on her sleep. "Ms. Toivanen's career was her life" says a decision last year by the British Columbia Human Rights Tribunal. But life caught up with her. By 2002, at age 47, she was carrying a heavy load, and looming deadlines preyed on her mind and ruined her sleep. Dealings with coworkers were strained, questions from supervisors were met with tears or anger.

She resisted her doctor's urging to take stress leave, fearing it would hurt her career. Finally, on the edge of a breakdown in September 2002, she handed her doctor's note to a supervisor and requested leave, only to be told EA had already decided to fire her. Big mistake. The failure to investigate her deteriorating condition or to accommodate her medical condition violated the provincial human rights code, the tribunal concluded. "She thought that EA was a company that prided itself on looking after employees," it said.

"Instead of investing any time and energy in bringing her back, healthy, to her workplace, it fired her." She spiralled into depression and was placed on long-term disability by her former employer's insurer. At the time of the ruling in 2006 she was still on paid disability. The tribunal ordered EA to pay almost $150,000 in costs, severance, stock option losses and damages, "for injury to her dignity, feelings and self-respect."

Employers neglect the work environment at their peril, warns Bill Wilkerson, a former insurance company president and now CEO of the Global Business and Economic Roundtable on Addiction and Mental Health. "Chronic job stress has emerged in what you might call epidemic terms," he says. He co-founded the group 10 years ago, as private insurers grew alarmed at the runaway impact of mental health issues.

The first indicator was the spiralling costs of prescription drugs for maladies that were "imprecise in their nature," says Wilkerson, who also now serves as chairman of the workplace advisory board of the Canadian Mental Health Commission. Depression, insomnia, hypertension were all part of the mix. "As a business guy I was focused on how we tackled these as costs" he says. After a decade immersed in the science, Wilkerson has no doubt stress is a trigger for mental health issues, and such physical ailments as hypertension and heart attack. But there remains, he concedes, skepticism in boardrooms and corner offices. "We have to talk tough love to business leaders all the time," he says. "Our job isn't to make a case for business, it's to make a business case for mental health."

Still, the skepticism remains. In the case of politicians, for example, some think stress leave is just an excuse to escape political problems. Consider some examples: veteran NDP MP Svend Robinson walked into a public auction in 2004 and stole an expensive ring. Days later, he turned himself in, held a tearful news conference and embarked on stress leave. He was subsequently diagnosed with a bipolar disorder. A year later, Conservative Gurmant Grewal, then an MP from Surrey, B.C., took stress leave after being embroiled in a scandal over secretly recording conversations with senior Liberal officials, among other bizarre incidents. "One of the things that makes me pretty cynical is when I hear a politician or a CEO who's gotten into trouble leave to spend more time with his family, or to take stress leave," says stress researcher Donna Lero of the University of Guelph.

Even when companies think they have clear evidence of malingering, they may find the courts decide otherwise. James Symington, a Halifax police officer and aspiring actor, left work June 11, 2001, citing an elbow injury. He was found fit for duty; instead, he booked off on stress leave. Months later, still on leave, Symington took his service dog to New York to help search for bodies after the terror attacks of Sept. 11. He also worked acting gigs. Symington was fired in early 2005, while still on leave, after the force said he wouldn't co-operate with attempts to get him back to work. This August, the Nova Scotia Court of Appeal cleared the way for Symington to sue the police for malicious prosecution for conducting a fraud investigation into his alleged misuse of stress leave. He's also suing his union, claiming it failed to protect him from a hostile work environment.

Understandably, many employers have become highly skeptical of complaints about excessive stress, and they vent their frustration to people like employment law specialist Howard Levitt, a Toronto-based lawyer for Lang Michener. He says stress issues have mushroomed during his 28 years in the field. "It's become for most employers the single biggest bugaboo in terms of workplace law issues" he says. Companies are "infuriated" by doctors who recommend stress leaves "without any real substantiation." For one thing, the family doctor isn't diagnosing the problem behind the alleged stress. Nor does the doctor know if there are other jobs in the workplace the patient is still capable of doing. The end result, ironically, is a more stressful workplace. "It's a bad motivation for other employees who see these employees getting away with it, and then have to work harder to pick up the slack," says Levitt. "So, often they say, 'Why shouldn't I participate in this scam?' And everybody works a little less hard."

A vocal minority of academics and others share a view that stress is a bogus concept. British author and former Fulbright Scholar Angela Patmore took on the "stress industry" in her 2006 book, The Truth About Stress. She doesn't buy that life in Britain is more stressful than it was, for instance, during the war years or the disease-ridden Victorian era. "The concept of mitigating stress is bollocks," she told Maclean's. "Everywhere in the West we see this message, 'you will drop dead, you will go mad, avoid negative emotions, avoid emotional situations.' None of our ancestors would have understood a word of this." She has an ally in Bob Briner, an occupational psychologist teaching at London University's Birkbeck College. He considers stress a meaningless concept; one that is creating a generation of "emotional hypochondriacs." As he writes, "One of the main explanations for the popularity of stress is that people like simple catch-all ways of 'explaining' why bad things happen, particularly illness."

Whether you believe stress is a real condition with debilitating effects, or the product of a generation of weak-minded workers, this much is indisputable: the costs are real, and spectacular. "Today, our estimate is that mental health conditions—with stress a risk factor—clearly cost the economy $33 billion per annum in lost industrial output," says Wilkerson. Those losses, he adds, "are excessively higher than the cost of health care associated with treating these conditions."

But one of the central problems with treating the apparent stress epidemic is that it remains exceptionally difficult to cure a problem that can't be easily defined. If you ask experts for a definition of stress, you often get a pause and then something like this: it is a highly individualistic, multifaceted response to a set of circumstances that place a demand on physical or mental energy. There is "distress," a negative response to disturbing circumstances. And there is "eustress," so-called good stress. Eustress might come on the day you marry the love of your life. Distress might come on the day the love of your life marries someone else. Stress is a kind of personal weather system, ever changing, its components unique to the individual. It may consist of overwork and job insecurity, combined with colicky children and a sickly mother. It may be an unrealistic deadline, vague expectations and hostile co-workers. It may be the thing that gets you up in the morning, the challenge that makes work bearable, the risk of failure that makes success sweeter. Stress is bad. Stress is good. Stress is a mess. It is also a constantly moving target.

"Is stress quantitatively growing, I don't know" says Shannon Wagner, a clinical psychologist and a specialist in workplace stress research at the University of Northern British Columbia. "What we do know is it is qualitatively changing." Jobs may not be as physically laborious as they were but they're more relentless, she says. "A lot of people now are identifying techno-stress and the 24/7 workday, which we didn't have even 10 or 15 years ago, this feeling of being constantly plugged in, of checking email 500 times a day."

There is ample evidence that people are working longer and harder, skimping on holidays, and paying a price. The work-life balance is out of whack, says Donna Lero, who holds the Jarislowsky Chair in Families and Work at the University of Guelph. She says the stresses today's families face are different, and come from all directions. Workdays are longer, and for most families, including three-quarters of those with children, both parents work. "What used to be three people's work is being done by two, with nobody home when the child is sick," she says. Families are smaller, but they're also scattered. The sandwich generation is often simultaneously handling both child and elder care. "At a time when employers and certainly individuals are voicing concerns about work-family conflict, we're seeing things go in the opposite direction we'd like them to."

Consider the impact on the federal public service. A newly released Treasury Board study of remuneration for some 351,000 public servants notes that disability claims for its two main insurance plans have more than doubled between 1990 and 2002. "Much of the increase" the report concludes, "resulted from growth in cases relating to depression and anxiety." In fact, more than 44 per cent of all new public service disability claims were for depression and anxiety—up from less than 24 per cent a decade earlier. Stress and mental health issues are now the leading reason for long-term disability claims, ahead of cancer. The problem seems to be especially acute in Quebec, where civil servants are off the job an average of 14 days a year, an increase of 33 per cent since 2001, according to a recent report.

Nationally, an estimated 35 million workdays are lost to mental conditions among our 10 million workers. A six-year-old Health Canada report estimates the annual cost of just depression and distress at $14.4 billion: $6.3 billion in treatment and $8.1 billion in lost productivity. And all that only measures the number of people who actually miss time at work. Just as serious may be "presenteeism"—the phenomenon of stressed-out workers who show up to work anyway and accomplish little. It's estimated to cost Canadian employers $22 billion a year. "It's the silent scourge of productivity," says Paul Hemp, who wrote a definitive article on the subject for *The Harvard Business Review* in 2004. A U.S. study of 29,000 adults calculated the total cost of presenteeism at more than US$150 billion.

So what is an enlightened, conscientious employer to do? That's a quandary: in some cases, a generous benefits plan actually increases the likelihood of workers booking off. A study on sick leave published last year by Statistics Canada found unionized workers with disability insurance are far more likely to take extended leaves. The recent federal public service pay study uncovered an interesting fact: prison guards, dockyard workers, heating plant operators and hospital service groups consistently used the most sick leave per capita during the 13-year period under examination. It's understandable that those in "difficult environments like penitentiaries or dockyards" would make more claims, the study notes. But their consistent use of leave over the years "suggests that cultural and management factors may also play a role in the level of demand for sick leave" Translation: some workers take stress leave simply because they can.

It seems the key is to strike a difficult balance between compassion and coddling. It's not easy, but for those who get it right, the results are dramatic. For example, the Vancouver City Savings Credit Union-Vancity has been repeatedly ranked among Maclean's Top 100 employers, in part because of an ingrained employee assistance program and management training in spotting employee problems before they reach a crisis.

Few jobs are as stressful as front-line tellers, especially in Vancouver, with an average 237 bank robberies a year, about the highest rate in Canada. Ann Leckie, Vancity's director of human resources, concedes "one of the greatest negative situations we can face is robbery." Vancity set out in the mid-1980s to limit the personal and financial fallout by contracting Daniel Stone & Associates Inc., its employee assistance provider, to design a robbery recovery program. Branch employees who wish to gather after a robbery can meet with Stone, a clinical counsellor, and others of his staff. Those who wish can have one-on-one sessions later. All have access to a 24-hour help line. Managers keep watch for delayed signs of stress: absenteeism, increased mistakes or mood swings. These workers are urged to seek help.

If it all seems too touchy-feely, consider the results. In B.C., the average post-robbery absence per branch—as paid out by the Workers Compensation Board—is 62 days. "In Vancity [in 2005] 17 of our 19 robberies had no days absent," says Leckie. The other two robberies had an average absence of two days. Leckie does a quick calculation: "That's 1,054 days not lost," she says. "There's a big financial incentive to doing it right."

Doing it right means building mutual trust and respect between employer and employee. It means heading off problems in advance and believing in those employees who need help. "The sense that there are non-sick people obtaining benefits fraudulently is an urban myth," Leckie says. The Vancity program is much copied, but rarely duplicated. "I have seen the program fail," she says. "In a cynical organization you get comments like, 'Well, the only time I get to talk to anyone important is when I have a gun to my head.'"

Sometimes the gun is real, more often it's a metaphor. Maybe bad stress is exactly that: a robbery. It steals joy and purpose and health; and it takes from the bottom line. In that sense it is real, no matter how it is defined, or how cynically it is viewed.

Analyze This Reading

1. Why is Canadian Prime Minister Harper concerned about stress in the workplace?
2. What changes in today's workplace tend to legitimize stress, especially for the "sandwich generation"?
3. The writer brings in statistical information regarding Canada's federal public service employees as well as information regarding Canada's national workforce. Describe this information. How does it contribute to the problem of defining "stress"?

4. The writer suggests that employers must find a "balance between compassion and coddling" if they want to rein in stress leave and then goes on to validate the Vancity approach. Describe this approach.
5. This report includes a mix of facts, statistics, the testimony of experts, and references to actual people. What are the advantages to such a mix?

Respond To This Reading

1. As the writer notes, employers, academics, politicians, and professionals all struggle to define "stress." How do you define this term? How does it affect you at work?
2. Evaluate the practicality of the Vancity approach to stress at work. Would you recommend it for your current workplace? Why or why not?
3. Many understand stress in cultural terms—as a response to the way we live, to what we value, and to the pressures we face as workers. As an individual, what changes, if any, would you argue for regarding the values that produce stress in your life?

ABOUT THIS READING

Rich Meneghello, the author of this reading, is a partner at the Portland, Oregon, office of Fisher & Phillips LLP, a law firm that represents the interests of management. The solution to workplace dating that Meneghello outlines below is crafted so as to steer management and ownership clear of any potential lawsuits that may occur due to love relationships among employees. This reading appeared in *The Daily Journal of Commerce*, a newspaper reporting on the building and construction market in Portland, Oregon.

Solutions at Work: When Love Enters the Workplace

By Rich Meneghello

Problem: A recent survey revealed that approximately 40 percent of U.S. workers have dated a fellow employee, and that another 40 percent would consider doing so. Inevitably, most workplace relationships end. Some end badly, and many of those result in lawsuits involving claims of coercion or retaliation, despite the fact that most of these relationships are completely consensual at the outset. And it's not just the jilted lover who could be your company's next adversary in court. A few years ago a group of California employees uninvolved in a workplace romance succeeded in establishing hostile work environment discrimination based upon favoritism bestowed on those who were romantically linked with a supervisor. This theory of liability will undoubtedly be tested in other states. In response to litigation arising from workplace relationships, many businesses have implemented nonfraternization policies designed to prohibit or discourage workplace relationships. But these "no dating" policies have had limited effect. According to the same survey, 84 percent of U.S. workers either have no idea whether their employer has such a policy or believe it has chosen not to institute one. Clearly, most employers are doing a poor job of making their expectations known to employees on these issues. Additionally, many employers recognize that it is neither possible nor desirable to ban all workplace relationships. First, employers generally prefer not to chaperone employees. Second, most employees consider employer monitoring of personal relationships an invasion of privacy. Finally, and probably most important, outright dating bans simply don't work. Since most workers spend at least one-third of each day in the office, it is hardly surprising that personal relationships will develop. Solution: In response to the limited effectiveness of these policies, many companies have developed Employee Relationship Acknowledgements, otherwise known as "love contracts," in which employees in a relationship make certain disclosures to the employer. A love contract, when properly implemented, can serve as a powerful deterrent to future litigation. With this in mind, any company considering the use of love contracts should be aware of the following:

Essential elements

Although the precise language will vary, an effective love contract should contain the following disclosures:

- the relationship is consensual and not based on intimidation, threat, coercion or harassment;
- the employees have received, read, understood, and agree to abide by the company's policy against harassment and discrimination;
- the employees agree to act appropriately in the workplace and avoid any behavior that is offensive to others;
- the employees agree not to let their relationship affect their work, or the work of their coworkers;
- neither employee will bestow upon the other any favoritism or preferential treatment;
- either employee may end the relationship at any time, and no retaliation of any kind will result;
- the contact information for the person in the HR department [responsible for handling disputes will be made available] (should either employee feel the relationship is affecting his/her work); and
- the employees have had sufficient time to read the document and ask questions before executing it of their own free will.

What if it's a "contract"? Whether the document is an enforceable contract doesn't matter, and is almost beside the point. The real strength of a love contract lies in the nature of the acknowledgements made. It shows that the employer took affirmative steps to maintain a workplace free from sexual harassment and retaliation, and it serves as powerful evidence that, at least at the time of execution, the relationship was consensual. Finally, it reaffirms that both employees are aware of the existence of a policy prohibiting sexual harassment, discrimination, retaliation, and their obligation to abide by it.

Can it prevent litigation? As with many other steps an employer can take, a love contract can be a strong deterrent to employee claims, but it will not prevent all future litigation arising out of a workplace relationship. What it does do is lay the groundwork for a solid defense should a lawsuit develop. For example, aggrieved employees can still claim they suffered retaliation after a breakup, but a love contract confirming that the relationship began consensually can help support a defense that the perceived post-relationship retaliation was based on personal animosity rather than gender-based discrimination.

Considerations before utilizing love contracts

Although not a concern in Oregon, companies with operations out of state should confirm whether privacy laws of that jurisdiction prohibit or limit employer monitoring of workplace relationships. You should also consider how the idea of a love contract will be presented to a couple, and decide in advance what you will do if one of the participants denies the relationship or refuses to sign the document. Finally, since there is no one way of developing an effective love contract, you should consult experienced labor and employment counsel to draft the appropriate language that meets the particular needs and objectives of your property. Love contracts, when properly implemented and appropriately drafted, will reduce the likelihood of litigation arising from workplace relationships. In the event of litigation, an effective love contract will help lessen the chances of misunderstandings or even lawsuits, and bolster a company's defenses in the event one is filed.

Analyze This Reading

1. Why is workplace dating an issue? Why would employers be motivated to have a policy in place?
2. What prevents employers from banning all workplace relationships?
3. The writer claims that a love contract can provide "solid defense" for an employer should a lawsuit arise from a workplace relationship. What does this mean?
4. In your view, at what kind of audience is this argument aimed? Explain.

Respond To This Reading

1. This solution to workplace dating is written from the perspective of management. In your view, does workplace dating need a solution? If you feel that it does, how might you craft a solution from the perspective of employees?
2. Explain whether the "essential elements" of a love contract outlined above are fair or unfair.
3. Are there important features of workplace dating not covered in the writer's solution? If yes, what are they?
4. In addition to the issue of workplace dating, what other issues concern you in your current job? On which of these issues are you motivated to argue?

ABOUT THIS READING

The U.S. Congress continues to struggle with comprehensive immigration reform legislation, especially with regard to border security and pathways to citizenship. In this reading, the writer highlights some of the costs of delaying this legislation. The writer is a coordinator for Interfaith Worker Justice, a national network based in Chicago that mobilizes faith communities to improve conditions for low-wage workers. This article appeared in *Commonweal*, an independent journal of opinion edited and managed by lay Catholics.

I'm Not Dangerous

By Danny Postel

The past six months have seen three of the largest workplace immigration raids in U.S. history. In May [2008], the rural Iowa town of Postville was convulsed when 900 Immigration and Customs Enforcement (ICE) agents stormed a kosher meatpacking plant and arrested 389 workers. In August, ICE agents descended on an electrical equipment factory near Laurel, Mississippi, detaining nearly 600 workers. And in October, the scene was repeated in Greenville, South Carolina, where 330 workers were swept up at a chicken-processing plant.

The humanitarian costs of the raids, according to a statement issued by the U.S. Conference of Catholic Bishops Committee on Migration, were "immeasurable and unacceptable in a civilized society." Children were separated from their parents for days. Those arrested were not immediately afforded the rights of due process. And local communities were, in the words of John C. Wester, bishop of Salt Lake City and chairman of the Committee on Migration, "disrupted and dislocated." These raids, he said, "strike immigrant communities unexpectedly, leaving the affected immigrant families to cope in the aftermath. Husbands are separated from their wives, and children are separated from their parents. Many families never recover; others never reunite."

The bishop called on the Department of Homeland Security, of which ICE is an agency, on President George W. Bush, and on then-candidates John McCain and Barack Obama to "reexamine the use of worksite enforcement raids" as an immigration-enforcement tool. He noted that immigrants "who are working to survive and support their families should not be treated like criminals."

Having visited Laurel after the ICE crackdown, I must report that is exactly how the workers there have been treated and made to feel. The majority of the immigrant workers caught up in the raid were taken immediately to a holding facility in Louisiana. ICE released a number of women, some of them pregnant, on "humanitarian" grounds. But many of them were shackled with ankle bands equipped with electronic monitoring devices. Several expressed their humiliation and shame—not to speak of their physical discomfort—at having been branded this way. For days, one of them told me, she avoided going out in public or to the grocery store. "It makes me look like a criminal, like a dangerous person," she lamented. "I'm not dangerous."

This woman told me she had come to the United States out of sheer desperation. She said she was unable to feed her children in her home village in Mexico. Now, with deportation imminent and no means to pay her bills, she and her coworkers were facing a further harrowing fate.

Immigration raids, even large, media-covered ones, are selective and symbolic in nature. They are orchestrated to send a political message that the government is willing and able to enforce the law. But why penalize the least among us—hardworking people who earn very little and endure some of the harshest conditions in the American workplace? The Postville and Laurel plants both have long histories of taking advantage of their workers. Iowa's attorney general recently filed charges against the Postville meatpacking plant for more than nine thousand labor violations. In July, religious and labor leaders joined more than a thousand marchers in the town to show solidarity with those seized in the ICE raid.

Indeed, religious communities have been playing a pivotal role in the aftermath of these raids. Catholic parishes have been safe havens for families scrambling to feed their children amid the turmoil. Immaculate Conception Church in Laurel and Sacred Heart Catholic Church in Hattiesburg worked virtually round-the-clock to feed and provide for the affected families.

To remedy what the U.S. bishops call "the failure of a seriously flawed immigration system," they "urge our elected and appointed officials to turn away from enforcement-only methods and direct their energy toward the adoption of comprehensive immigration reform legislation." That is now up to the new administration and to Congress.

Analyze This Reading

1. In paragraphs two and four, the writer follows factual information about the largest immigration raids in U. S. history with emotional examples. Describe these examples and analyze them in terms of how they might affect readers of *Commonweal*.
2. On what grounds does the writer question the government's ability to enforce current immigration law?
3. The next-to-last paragraph honors religious communities for providing "safe havens" for families affected by ICE raids. Contrast the values of these communities with the values of the government agency ICE.
4. While the writer is not specific in the final paragraph as to the kind of reform legislation he favors, can you infer the kinds of changes he has in mind? Explain.

Respond To This Reading

1. Many immigrants travel to the United States for jobs and better living conditions. Indeed, numerous states are home to tens of thousands of working illegal immigrants. In the context of the immigration debate, what should the role be of those who employ illegal workers?

2. With special attention to employment and citizenship, describe the kinds of legislative reform you would argue for. What kind of claim would work best with your argument?

3. Should illegal immigrants and their children be allowed to enroll in publicly funded colleges and universities in the United States? Explain.

ABOUT THIS READING

Unlike many other treatments of this issue, the writer frames the wage gap between women and men in the workplace in terms of choice and not discrimination. When she wrote this argument, Denise Venable was a research assistant for the National Center for Policy Analysis, "a public policy research organization that promotes private alternatives to government regulation." This reading appeared in *Opposing Viewpoints: Social Justice*.

Women Do Not Earn Less Than Men Due to Gender Discrimination

By Denise Venable

Tuesday, April 16, 2002, is Equal Pay Day—the day on which many organizations protest wage discrimination between men and women. According to the U.S. Bureau of Labor Statistics, the median income for all women is about three-quarters that of men, although the results vary significantly among demographic groups. Feminist organizations and some politicians point to these statistics as evidence of the United States as a patriarchal society that discriminates against women. But a closer examination leads to a different conclusion.

The Good News. When women behave in the workplace as men do, the wage gap between them is small. June O'Neill, former director of the Congressional Budget Office, found that among people ages 27 to 33 who have never had a child, women's earnings approach 98 percent of men's. Women who hold positions and have skills and experience similar to those of men face wage disparities of less than 10 percent, and many are within a couple of points. Claims of unequal pay almost always involve comparing apples and oranges.

Lifestyle Choices. Women make different choices, and those choices affect how they work. Women often place more importance on their relationships—caring for children, parents, spouses, etc.—than on their careers. A study by the Center for Policy Alternatives and Lifetime television found that 71 percent of women prefer jobs with more flexibility and benefits than jobs with higher wages, and nearly 85 percent of women offered flexible work arrangements by their employers have taken advantage of this opportunity.

Entry and Exit from the Job Market. Women are more likely to enter and leave the workforce to raise children, take care of elderly parents or move with their families. Working mothers are nearly twice as likely to take time off to care for their children as are working fathers in dual-earner couples. Yet time out of the workforce is an enormous obstacle to building an attractive resume and working up the corporate ladder. Women 25 years of age and over have been with their current employer 4.4 years, on average, compared to 5.0 years for men. Data from the National Longitudinal Survey reveal that women between the ages of 18 and 34 have been out of the labor force 27 percent of the time, in contrast to 11 percent for men. Women ages 45 to 54 who have recently re-entered the workforce after a five- or 10-year break are competing against men who have had 20 years of continuous experience.

Part-Time Work. Women are also more likely to work part-time. In 2000, one-quarter of all women employees worked part-time, compared to less than 10 percent of men. Nearly 85 percent of those who worked part-time did so for non-economic reasons; e.g., to spend more time with the family or to further their education. In general, married women would prefer part-time work at a rate of 5 to 1 over married men.

While part-time work usually increases flexibility, the part-time worker loses out on promotions and pay increases. Part-time work also tends to mean lower hourly pay. Shorter labor stints and part-time work contribute to the probability of working for the minimum wage. Nearly two-thirds of minimum wage earners are women.

However, women's wages hold up quite well to men's wages when comparing specific job categories. Among adults working between one and 34 hours a week, women's earnings are 115 percent of men's. Among part-time workers who have never married, and who thus confront fewer outside factors likely to affect earnings, women earn slightly more than men. These statistics suggest that skill level, tenure and working hours—not gender—determine wages.

Occupational Choices. Beyond work behavior, women gravitate to sectors of the economy that compensate workers at lower levels. While women hold 53 percent of all professional jobs in the United States, they hold only 28 percent of jobs in professions averaging $40,000 or more in annual compensation. For example, fewer women have chosen to enter such technical fields as computer sciences, math and science teaching, medicine, law and engineering. In 1998, women earned only 26.7 percent of computer science degrees.

Closing the Gap. Despite all these factors, the gap between men and women's wages has been closing . . . . Over the last 20 years women's earnings have jumped at least 12 percentage points relative to men's earnings, closing the wage differential at every level of education. A change in women's work expectations also has tended to close the gap. Until the 1970s, a minority of women expected to work after marriage. Today, almost 75 percent of young women expect to be working at age 35.

Changing work expectations are an apparent cause of women's increased focus on education, and the enrollment of women in higher education has grown much faster than that of men. Women were awarded more than 50 percent of associate's, bachelor's and master's degrees in the 1990s. Women currently earn more than 40 percent of Ph.D.s, medical and law degrees.

The narrowing of the gender wage gap approximately one percentage point a year since 1980 is particularly significant, since during the 1980s and '90s the overall wage level rose little and the wage inequality between skilled and unskilled workers grew. Without enhanced skills, women's wages likely would have fallen further behind men's. However, market pressures have helped to generate corrective mechanisms, and as the costs of denying employment to women mounted, prejudices were set aside.

Conclusion. Women's work-life patterns and their occupational preferences are significant factors in determining wages. Rather than being "funneled" into low-wage, low-prestige and part-time positions, women often choose these occupations because of the flexibility they offer. After adjusting for these factors, scholars find that the difference between men's and women's earnings is very narrow.

Those who still cite women's 76 cents for every male dollar as evidence of sexism fail to take into account the underlying role of personal choice. The "wage gap" is not so much about employers discriminating against women as about women making discriminating choices in the labor market.

Analyze This Reading

1. How does the writer's position on the wage gap differ from the positions of feminists and some politicians on this issue?
2. What reasons does the writer use with her claim? How does the writer support these reasons?
3. According to the writer, is the gender wage gap narrowing or widening? What information does she use to support her view?

Respond To This Reading

1. Do you agree with the writer's position that the wage gender gap is due largely to choices women make? Explain.
2. The writer is thorough in this short argument with the logical support she brings to each reason. In your view, is the writer's reliance on facts and statistics appropriate for the claim she makes? Would including a few personal examples of women and the wage gap add to or detract from her argument? Explain.
3. In your experience in the workforce, does a wage gap based on gender exist? If yes, how do you explain it?
4. In addition to the issue discussed in this reading, have you experienced in the workplace other gender-related issues? If yes, what single issue might motivate you to build an argument?

Family and Household Community

ABOUT THIS READING

Writer Mary Eberstadt is a research fellow at the Hoover Institution and a consulting editor to *Policy Review*. A prolific writer, Eberstadt's books include *The Loser Letters: A Comic Tale of Life, Death, and Atheism* (2010) and *Home-Alone America: The Hidden Toll of Day Care, Behavioral Drugs and Other Parent Substitutes* (2004). This reading first appeared in *Policy Review*, a bimonthly journal that examines issues related to government, politics, economics, and the role of the United States in the world.

Eminem Is Right: The Primal Scream of Teenage Music

By Mary Eberstadt

What is the overall influence of this deafening, foul, and often vicious-sounding stuff on children and teenagers? This is a genuinely important question, and serious studies and articles, some concerned particularly with current music's possible link to violence, have lately been devoted to it. In 2000, the American Academy of Pediatrics, the American Medical Association, the American Psychological Association, and the American Academy of Child & Adolescent Psychiatry all weighed in against contemporary lyrics and other forms of violent entertainment before Congress with a first-ever "Joint Statement on the Impact of Entertainment Violence on Children."

What Today's Music Says About Today's Teens

Nonetheless, this is not my focus here. Instead, I would like to turn that logic about influence upside down and ask this question: What is it about today's music, violent and disgusting though it may be, that resonates with so many American kids?

As the reader can see, this is a very different way of inquiring about the relationship between today's teenagers and their music. The first question asks what the music does to adolescents; the second asks what it tells us about them. To answer that second question is necessarily to enter the roiling emotional waters in which that music is created and consumed—in other words, actually to listen to some of it and read the lyrics.

As it turns out, such an exercise yields a fascinating and little understood fact about today's adolescent scene. If yesterday's rock was the music of abandon, today's is that of abandonment. The odd truth about contemporary teenage music—the characteristic that most separates it from what has gone before—is its compulsive insistence on the damage wrought by broken homes, family dysfunction, checked-out parents, and (especially) absent fathers. Papa Roach, Everclear, Blink-182, Good Charlotte, Eddie Vedder and Pearl Jam, Kurt Cobain and Nirvana, Tupac Shakur, Snoop Doggy Dogg [currently known as Snoop Dogg], Eminem—these and other singers and bands, all of them award-winning top-40 performers who either are or were among the most popular icons in America, have their own generational answer to what ails the modern teenager. Surprising though it may be to some, that answer is: dysfunctional childhood. Moreover, and just as interesting, many bands and singers explicitly link the most deplored themes in music today—suicide, misogyny, and drugs—with that lack of a quasi-normal, intact-home personal past.

To put this perhaps unexpected point more broadly, during the same years in which progressive-minded and politically correct adults have been excoriating Ozzie and Harriet [TV characters representing the traditional family] as an artifact of 1950s-style oppression, many millions of American teenagers have enshrined a new generation of music idols whose shared generational signature in song after song is to rage about what not having had a nuclear family has done to them. This is quite a fascinating puzzle of the times. The self-perceived emotional damage scrawled large across contemporary music may not be statistically quantifiable, but it is nonetheless among the most striking of all the unanticipated consequences of our home-alone world. . . .

Where Is Daddy?

Even less recognized than the white music emphasis on broken homes and the rest of the dysfunctional themes is that the popular black-dominated genres, particularly hip-hop/rap, also reflect themes of abandonment, anger, and longing for parents. Interestingly enough, this is true of particular figures whose work is among the most adult deplored.

Once again, when it comes to the deploring part, critics have a point. It is hard to imagine a more unwanted role model (from the parental point of view) than the late Tupac Shakur. A best-selling gangsta rapper who died in a shoot-out in 1996 at age 25 (and the object of a 2003 documentary called *Tupac: Resurrection*), Shakur was a kind of polymath [a person of encyclopedic learning] of criminality. In the words of a *Denver Post* review of the movie, "In a perfect circle of life imitating art originally meant to imitate life, Shakur in 1991 began a string of crimes that he alternately denied and reveled in. He claimed Oakland [California] police beat him up in a jaywalking arrest, later shot two off-duty cops, assaulted a limo driver and video directors, and was shot five times in a robbery." Further, "At the time of his drive-by murder in Las Vegas, he was out on bail pending appeal of his conviction for sexual abuse of a woman who charged him with sodomy in New York."

Perhaps not surprising, Shakur's songs are riddled with just about every unwholesome trend that a nervous parent can name; above all they contain incitements to crime and violence (particularly against the police) and a misogyny so pronounced that his own mother, executive producer of the movie, let stand in the film a statement of protesting C. DeLores Tucker that "African-American women are tired of being called ho's, bitches and sluts by our children."

Growing up fatherless might help to explain why Shakur is an icon not only to many worse-off teenagers from the ghetto, but also to many better-off suburban ones.

Yet Shakur—who never knew his father and whose mother, a long time drug addict, was arrested for possession of crack when he was a child—is provocative in another, quite overlooked way: He is the author of some of the saddest lyrics in the hip-hop/gangsta-rap pantheon, which is saying quite a lot. To sophisticated readers familiar with the observations about the breakup of black families recorded several decades ago in the Moynihan Report [a 1965 Senate report headed by Daniel Patrick Moynihan identifying the legacies of slavery, urbanization, discrimination, and matriarchy as reasons why many black families suffer crises] and elsewhere, the fact that so many young black men grow up without fathers may seem so well established as to defy further comment. But evidently some young black men—Shakur being one—see things differently. In fact, it is hard to find a rapper who does not sooner or later invoke a dead or otherwise long-absent father, typically followed by the hope that he will not become such a man himself. Or there is the flip side of that unintended bow to the nuclear family, which is the hagiography [idealization] in some rappers' lyrics of their mothers.

Rap Songs of Dysfunction

In a song called "Papa'z Song Lyrics," Shakur opens with the narrator imagining his father showing up after a long absence, resulting in an expletive-laden tirade. The song then moves to a lacerating description of growing up fatherless that might help to explain why Shakur is an icon not only to many worse-off teenagers from the ghetto, but also to many better-off suburban ones. Here is a boy who "had to play catch by myself," who prays: "Please send me a pops before puberty."

The themes woven together in this song—anger, bitterness, longing for family, misogyny as the consequence of a world without fathers—make regular appearances in some other rappers' lyrics, too. One is Snoop Doggy Dogg, perhaps the preeminent rapper of the 1990s. Like Shakur and numerous other rappers, his personal details cause many a parent to shudder; since his childhood he has been arrested for a variety of crimes, including cocaine possession (which resulted in three years of jail service), accomplice to murder (for which he was acquitted), and, most recently, marijuana possession. ("It's not my job to stop kids doing the wrong thing, it's their parents' job," he once explained to a reporter.) In a song called "Mama Raised Me," sung with Soulja Slim, Snoop Doggy Dogg offers this explanation of how troubled pasts come to be: "It's probably pop's fault how I ended up/Gangbangin'; crack slangin'; not givin' a f—."

Another black rapper who returned repeatedly to the theme of father abandonment is Jay-Z, also known as Shawn Carter, whose third and breakthrough album, *Hard Knock Life*, sold more than 500,000 copies. He also has a criminal history (he says he had been a cocaine dealer) and a troubled family history, which is reflected in his music. In an interview with MTV.com about his latest album, the reporter explained: "Jay and his father had been estranged until earlier this year. [His father] left the household and his family's life (Jay has an older brother and two sisters) when Shawn was just 12 years old. The separation had served as a major 'block' for Jay over the years. . . . His most vocal tongue lashing toward his dad was on the *Dynasty: Roc la Familia* cut 'Where Have You Been,' where he rapped 'F—you very much/You showed me the worst kind of pain.'"

The fact that child abandonment is also a theme in hip-hop might help explain what otherwise appears as a commercial puzzle—namely, how this particular music moved from the fringes of black entertainment to the very center of the Everyteenager mainstream. There can be no doubt about the current social preeminence of these black- and ghetto-dominated genres in the lives of many better-off adolescents, black and white. As Donna Britt wrote in a *Washington Post* column noting hip-hop's ascendancy, "In modern America, where urban based hip hop culture dominates music, fashion, dance and, increasingly, movies and TV, these kids are trendsetters. What they feel, think and do could soon play out in a middle school—or a Pottery Barn-decorated bedroom—near you."

Eminem: Reasons for Rage

A final example of the rage in contemporary music against irresponsible adults—perhaps the most interesting—is that of genre-crossing bad-boy rap superstar Marshall Mathers or Eminem (sometime stage persona "Slim Shady"). Of all the names guaranteed to send a shudder down the parental spine, his is probably the most effective. In fact, Eminem has single-handedly, if inadvertently, achieved the otherwise ideologically impossible: He is the object of a vehemently disapproving public consensus shared by the National Organization for Women [NOW], the Gay & Lesbian Alliance Against Defamation, [conservative politician and writer] William J. Bennett, Lynne Cheney [scholar, author, and wife of former Vice President Dick Cheney], Bill O'Reilly [a conservative news commentator], and a large number of other social conservatives as well as feminists and gay activists. In sum, this rapper—"as harmful to America as any al Qaeda fanatic," in O'Reilly's opinion—unites adult polar opposites as perhaps no other single popular entertainer has done.

There is small need to wonder why. Like other rappers, Eminem mines the shock value and gutter language of rage, casual sex, and violence. Unlike the rest, however, he appears to be a particularly attractive target of opprobrium [contempt] for two distinct reasons. One, he is white and therefore politically easier to attack. (It is interesting to note that black rappers have not been targeted by name anything like Eminem has.) Perhaps even more important, Eminem is one of the largest commercially visible targets for parental wrath. Wildly popular among teenagers these last several years, he is also enormously successful in commercial terms. Winner of numerous Grammys and other music awards and a perpetual nominee for many more, he has also been critically (albeit reluctantly) acclaimed for his acting performance in the autobiographical 2003 movie 8 *Mile*. For all these reasons, he is probably the preeminent rock/rap star of the last several years, one whose singles, albums, and videos routinely top every chart. His 2002 album, *The Eminem Show*, for example, was easily the most successful of the year, selling more than 7.6 million copies.

This remarkable market success, combined with the intense public criticism that his songs have generated, makes the phenomenon of Eminem particularly intriguing. Perhaps more than any other current musical icon, he returns repeatedly to the same themes that fuel other success stories in contemporary music: parental loss, abandonment, abuse, and subsequent child and adolescent anger, dysfunction, and violence (including self-vio-lence). Both in his raunchy lyrics as well as in *8 Mile*, Mathers's own personal story has been parlayed many times over: the absent father, the troubled mother living in a trailer park, the series of unwanted maternal boyfriends, the protective if impotent feelings toward a younger sibling (in the movie, a baby sister; in real life, a younger brother), and the fine line that a poor, ambitious, and unguided young man might walk between catastrophe and success. Mathers plumbs these and related themes with a verbal savagery that leaves most adults aghast.

Eminem's Family Ideal

Yet Eminem also repeatedly centers his songs on the crypto-traditional notion that children need parents and that not having them has made all hell break loose. In the song "8 Mile" from the movie soundtrack, for example, the narrator studies his little sister as she colors one picture after another of an imagined nuclear family, failing to understand that "mommas got a new man." "Wish I could be the daddy that neither one of us had," he comments. Such wistful lyrics juxtapose oddly and regularly with Eminem's violent other lines. Even in one of his most infamous songs, "Cleaning Out My Closet (Mama, I'm Sorry)," what drives the vulgar narrative is the insis-tence on seeing abandonment from a child's point of view. "My faggot father must have had his panties up in a bunch/'Cause he split. I wonder if he even kissed me good-bye."

As with other rappers, the vicious narrative treatment of women in some of Eminem's songs is part of this self-conception as a child victim. Contrary to what critics have intimated, the misogyny in current music does not spring from nowhere; it is often linked to the larger theme of having been abandoned several times—left behind by father, not nurtured by mother, and betrayed again by faithless womankind. One of the most violent and sexually aggressive songs in the last few years is "Kill You" by the popu-lar metal band known as Korn. Its violence is not directed toward just any woman or even toward the narrator's girlfriend; it is instead a song about an abusive stepmother whom the singer imagines going back to rape and murder.

Similarly, Eminem's most shocking lyrics about women are not ran-domly dispersed; they are largely reserved for his mother and ex-wife, and the narrative pose is one of despising them for not being better women—in particular, better mothers. The worst rap directed at his own mother is indeed gut-wrenching: "But how dare you try to take what you didn't help me to get?/You selfish bitch, I hope you f— burn in hell for this shit!" It is no defense of the gutter to observe the obvious: This is not the expression of random misogyny but, rather, of primal rage over alleged maternal abdica-tion and abuse.

Bad Parents Make Bad Teens

Another refrain in these songs runs like this: Today's teenagers are a mess, and the parents who made them that way refuse to get it. In one of Eminem's early hits, for example, a song called "Who Knew," the rapper pointedly takes on his many middle- and upper-middle-class critics to observe the contradiction between their reviling him and the parental inattention that feeds his commercial success. "What about the make-up you allow your 12 year-old daughter to wear?" he taunts.

This same theme of AWOL [absent without leave] parenting is rapped at greater length in another award-nominated 2003 song called "Sing for the Moment," whose lyrics and video would be recognized in an instant by most teenagers in America. That song spells out Eminem's own idea of what connects him to his millions of fans—a connection that parents, in his view, just don't (or is that won't?) understand. It details the case of one more "problem child" created by "His f—dad walkin' out." "Sing for the Moment," like many other songs of Eminem's, is also a popular video. The "visuals" show clearly what the lyrics depict—hordes of disaffected kids, with flashbacks to bad home lives, screaming for the singer who feels their pain. It concludes by rhetorically turning away from the music itself and toward the emotionally desperate teenagers who turn out for this music by the millions. If the demand of all those empty kids wasn't out there, the narrator says pointedly, then rappers wouldn't be supplying it the way they do.

If some parents still don't get it—even as their teenagers elbow up for every new Eminem CD and memorize his lyrics with psalmist devotion—at least some critics observing the music scene have thought to comment on the ironies of all this. In discussing *The Marshall Mathers LP* in 2001 for *Music Box*, a daily online newsletter about music, reviewer John Metzger argued, "Instead of spewing the hate that he is so often criticized of doing, Eminem offers a cautionary tale that speaks to our civilization's growing depravity. Ironically, it's his teenage fans who understand this, and their all-knowing parents that miss the point." Metzger further specified "the utter lack of parenting due to the spendthrift necessity of the two-income family."

That insight raises the overlooked fact that in one important sense Eminem and most of the other entertainers quoted here would agree with many of today's adults about one thing: The kids aren't all right out there after all. Recall, for just one example, [alternative rock artist] Eddie Vedder's rueful observation about what kind of generation would make him or [Vedder's contemporary] Kurt Cobain its leader. Where parents and entertainers disagree is over who exactly bears responsibility for this moral chaos. Many adults want to blame the people who create and market today's music and videos. Entertainers, Eminem most prominently, blame the absent, absentee, and generally inattentive adults whose deprived and furious children (as they see it) have catapulted today's singers to fame. (As he puts the point in one more in-your-face response to parents: "Don't blame me when lil' Eric jumps off of the terrace / You shoulda been watchin him—apparently you ain't parents.")

The spectacle of a foul-mouthed bad-example rock icon instructing the hardworking parents of America in the art of child-rearing is indeed a peculiar one, not to say ridiculous. The single mother who is working frantically because she must and worrying all the while about what her 14-year-old is listening to in the headphones is entitled to a certain fury over lyrics like those. In fact, to read through most rap lyrics is to wonder which adults or political constituencies wouldn't take offense. Even so, the music idols who point the finger away from themselves and toward the emptied-out homes of America are telling a truth that some adults would rather not hear. In this limited sense at least, Eminem is right.

Analyze This Reading

1. According to the writer, what separates today's rock music from that of earlier eras?
2. What insights into rap music does the writer offer in her treatment of gangsta rapper Tupac Shakur? Thematically, what does Shakur have in common with rappers Jay-Z and Snoop Doggy Dog?
3. What explanation does the writer offer for the misogyny present in the lyrics of Eminem and other rappers?
4. According to the writer, what is it about family life that kids understand that parents don't?
5. The writer begins and ends this reading with caustic evaluations of rap music, judging it to be "deafening, foul, and often vicious-sounding stuff" and by referring to a successful rapper as a "foul-mouthed bad-example rock icon." Why might this be risky behavior for a writer? Does the writer move away from this evaluative tone during the body of the argument? Explain.

Respond To This Reading

1. Explain why you agree or disagree with the writer's contention that gangsta rap offers valuable insights into the dynamics of some American families.
2. As the writer notes, many listeners find offensive the lyrics of rap music. Troubleshoot the discomfort of these listeners—is it intended, is it necessary?
3. Imagine that certain leaders in your community—educators, clergy, elected officials, and others—have called for a ban on gangsta rap in certain public places. What would you argue in response to the ban? How would you support your argument?

ABOUT THIS READING

This article appeared in *Maclean's, CA*, a weekly Canadian public affairs magazine. Sue Ferguson is Coordinator of the Journalism Program at Wilfrid Laurier University in Waterloo, Ontario, Canada. At *Maclean's* she served as senior writer and associate editor.

Leaving the Doors Open

Interaction between adoptive and birth families isn't for everyone. But when it works, it can give children a greater sense of being loved.
By Sue Ferguson

Emma Sands was just 2 1/2 weeks old when her father decided that he and her mom needed help. "I was scared about how Carrie was handling the baby—she wasn't herself," says Gary Sands (to protect Emma's privacy, all the names have been changed). He picked up the phone and a social worker soon arrived at his door. Carrie, diagnosed with schizophrenia, was admitted to hospital. Sands, who had spent years in and out of jail for petty crime driven by his drug and alcohol addiction, was left to parent by himself. On his wife's return eight months later, things spiralled out of control once again. "One of her friends introduced me to cocaine," says Sands, "and that was it. I was back in crime—lost my job and ended up going to jail." Emma was sent to live with a foster family and, by her first birthday, the foster parents had applied to adopt her.

Emma turned 12 in February. When Sands, now a youth counsellor and in a new relationship, arrived at her Port Coquitlam, B.C., home for the birthday party with his nine-month-old son, she yelled to friends in the basement, "Wanna meet my baby brother?" The poignancy of that moment wasn't lost on Sands—"I was like, wow," he recalls.

This isn't a story of a birth father reuniting with his child. Outside of a few periods, including a two-month stay in a recovery house, he has seen Emma regularly, taking her to swimming lessons and movies. (Carrie has disappeared from both their lives.) In recent months, Emma, who calls 36-year-old Sands "Daddy Gary," has begun to spend the occasional night at his house. Emma's adoptive parents encouraged the relationship from the beginning—taking her to visit Sands in jail and maintaining contact even when, on parole in the early 1990s, he filed, unsuccessfully, for custody.

Open adoptions of this nature are rare. Traditionally, adoption has been shrouded in secrecy, with every effort made to ensure birth parents and adoptive families never cross paths. But judges, says Adoption Council of Canada chair Sandra Scarth, are increasingly reluctant to sever children's ties to their biological parents, believing that giving kids information about their origins is critical to nurturing a healthy sense of self. For the same reason, private agencies now commonly arrange to have birth parents meet and choose the prospective adopters and keep in touch with their child through letters, photos and, in some cases, visits.

But openness is a scarier proposition for families who opt for public adoption. Parents of permanent wards are often scarred by mental illness and addictions, or have abused or neglected their children. And, unless the law clearly spells out the rights of the various parties (as it does in B.C. and Newfoundland), families who arrange open adoptions are taking a leap of faith. "It's hard to tell potential adopters unequivocally" that the birth family couldn't take the child back into their custody at any time, says Nancy Dale, acting associate executive director of the Children's Aid Society of Toronto. The issue is further complicated in Ontario by a law that prevents the over 6,000 Crown wards with access orders—legal provisions for contact between birth parents and the children taken from them—from getting adopted. "If you have an access order," says Dale, "you grow up in foster care. That's the plan." At least, it is for now. Minister of Children and Youth Services Marie Bountrogianni says the government intends to free kids with access orders for adoption when it's in their best interest and hopes to introduce openness legislation by next year, as part of a wider initiative to boost placement rates.

In the meantime, some families are able to work out ad hoc openness arrangements. Two years ago, Patty and Ken Winer, who live in the southern Ontario town of Arkell and already had biological children Kyra, 13, and Brent, 11, adopted Lisa, now 10, and her brother Joseph, 8. They would happily have also taken brother Alan (a pseudonym), now 14, but because of an access order he remains in foster care. With the help of the local Children's Aid Society, however, Alan regularly visits and phones his siblings. He joined the Winers for 10 days at their cottage in Prince Edward Island last July. He's also served as a go-between, delivering letters and Christmas presents from their birth mother—from whom the children were seized by police three years ago (she's permitted to see Alan six times a year)—to his brother and sister. In time, the Winers say, they'll arrange for Lisa and Joseph to visit her. For now, however, the letter to Lisa—which reads in part "I wish for you a happy home . . . I know I am still learning"—helped alleviate Lisa's feeling of responsibility for her biological mother's well-being, notes adoptive mom Patty. It was "tremendously important" to the girl, she adds.

For Ken Winer, openness is just a matter of common sense. "They will go back and see their mom when they're of legal age," he says. "Why put up a brick wall when it's going to have to then be torn down?" He speaks from experience: both he and his sister were adopted. When his sister later contacted her birth parents, he says, "it just about destroyed our family"—an experience he's not anxious to repeat by searching out his own roots. At the same time, he and Patty insist adoptive parents need to have the last word in arranging the terms of contact. Adopting is "just like when you bring your new baby home from the hospital," says Patty. "You want to hold it for yourself, so you can get adjusted. Then as it gets older, you're OK to let go."

Many adoptive parents fear the birth parents are the ones who won't let go. But, notes Scarth, "people haven't been clamouring to get their children back. In fact, they often fade off into the distance after they're satisfied things are fine with their child." For those, like Gary Sands, who stick around, it's not always easy. In the early days, he says, "I felt like Emma's mine, my personal piece of property." But eventually, "through time and all the heartache," he learned to put her interests ahead of his own. "I'm amazed at myself," says Sands. "I had to be really understanding of the adoptive parents." He even signed an agreement limiting contact to supervised monthly visits if he started to slip into his old ways again.

As for the kids, rather than feeling abandoned, they can gain a sense of being loved and valued by more than one set of parents—a principle behind adoptions within First Nations. Cindy Blackstock, executive director of First Nations Child & Family Caring Society of Canada, recalls the adoption ceremony she attended at Alberta's Yellowhead Tribal Services Agency in 2002. Elders and family members from the children's and the adoptive families' bands were all present. "Watching the community step forward to take care of those five children was the most moving experience in my life," she says. "It was something to be celebrated—nothing to be ashamed of." Were openness readily accepted in public adoptions, she adds, it might help navigate the stormy waters of cross-cultural adoptions. "The children wouldn't have a sense of having to choose."

And, in Emma's case, she hasn't been the only one to benefit. Her adoptive parents, says Gary Sands, "saw me go through a lot of things, show up in messes, crying. They never closed their door on me"—giving a home, in effect, to daughter and father.

Analyze This Reading

1. According to the writer, what is motivating a change in traditional attitudes toward adoption?
2. What is an openness arrangement? What risks does it pose?
3. How does the writer address the fear of some adoptive parents that birth parents may have difficulty letting go of their biological children?
4. The writer includes compelling examples but little research. How does this help or hinder this article?

Respond To This Reading

1. In your view, what conditions should be attached to open adoptions?
2. Were you to write an argument in response to this reading, what would you claim and on what value or principle would you build your argument?

ABOUT THIS READING

Jewel Kilcher is the author of *Chasing Down the Dawn* (2001), a study of her professional life on the road, and a poetry collection, *A Night Without Armor* (1999). She is a successful actress, guitarist, and singer-songwriter, having sold more than 25 million albums. This article appeared in *USA Today Magazine*.

Street Life Is No Life for Children

By Jewel

Coming home after school or a day with friends is something most kids take for granted, but for more than 1,000,000 young people living in this country, there is no place to call home. Youth homelessness is a complex issue that often is overlooked in the U.S.—even as we face a growing crisis of teens and children living alone on the streets. Left to fend for themselves, children as young as 11 years old confront such nightmarish scenarios as human trafficking and drug use, often with little understanding or sympathy from the general public. In June, I testified before the House Ways & Means Committee to support bipartisan resolutions designating November as "National Homeless Youth Awareness Month." Setting November aside in this way should help raise much-needed awareness of the issue, while demonstrating to kids on the streets that Congress is listening, people do want to help, and America cares about their futures.

While youngsters often become homeless due to some kind of family breakdown, there is no one cause. Poverty; lack of affordable housing, access to education, and other resources; unemployment among family members; abuse; and mental health issues all can be contributing factors. The issue of homeless youth is complicated further by misperceptions about children and teens who end up on the streets, as many people immediately jump to easy—but wrong—conclusions. For instance, when walking by a teenage girl sitting on a bench in the middle of a weekday, few might consider whether she is homeless. The easier response is to assume that she probably is just some punk kid who ditched school and is hanging around waiting for her friends. Few onlookers go so far as to consider an even darker reality—such as the fact that this girl might be forced into prostitution to make enough money to put food in her stomach.

This also is a population that is very good at making itself "invisible" to adults—since it is adults who so often have endangered or let these teens down in the past. That boy at your son's high school may seem like a nice, average kid, but he may have no home to return to after the school day; the point is, these girls and boys do not live on the streets or become homeless by choice. The sad truth: many of them feel safer there and, despite what many Americans think, this is not an easily "correctable" condition, land of opportunity or not.

I have a personal understanding of the plight of these young people on the margins, because I experienced homelessness firsthand. When I was 15 years old—I am a native of Utah but was raised in Alaska—I received a vocal scholarship to attend Interlochen Center for the Arts in Michigan. It was a time when, for many reasons, I increasingly felt I no longer could live at home—my parents long ago had divorced—and so the change of scenery was exciting, as was the opportunity to be surrounded by music. However, school breaks—like the upcoming Thanksgiving and Christmas recesses—presented an immediate challenge. Unlike my fellow students, the close of class sessions meant I was on my own. I enjoyed performing solo; so, during one spring break, I jumped on a train heading south and subsequently hitchhiked to Mexico, earning money by singing on street corners. These were my first experiences of life without a safety net, but the harder reality was yet to come. After Interlochen, I moved to San Diego. As a result of a series of unfortunate events and bad breaks, I ended up living in a car. When that car was stolen, along with many of my possessions at the time, I borrowed $1,000 from a friend to buy a van—and that van became home right up until my break into the music industry.

When my story is told in the music press, it can take on a romantic glow, but living in a van was not romantic. I washed my hair in public bathroom sinks. People often would stare at me and make nasty comments. Some would wonder aloud how a "pretty girl" could end up in such a state. Yet, many more simply pretended that I was not there. I was humiliated and embarrassed about my situation and the stigma that was being attached to me. My experience is much like that of other young people fending for themselves, except for the fact that my story has a happy ending. Too many others are not so fortunate. Homeless organizations say that 30% of shelter youth and 70% of street youth are victims of commercial sexual exploitation at a time in their lives when these boys and girls should be finishing up elementary school.

These are just a few of the reasons why I do not believe America's homeless youth population is made up of children who leave home because they want to. Most homeless kids are on the streets because they have been forced by circumstances to believe they are safer alone than in the home they once knew—if that home even exists for them anymore. Others may have reached the end of their economic resources, or those of their family's, and are left trying to climb out of poverty from the disadvantageous position of the streets.

Some researchers estimate that up to 1,600,000 youth experience homelessness each year. Based on the amount of kids turned away from shelters each day, as well as the number of phone calls made to the National Runaway Hotline, those numbers may be even higher. Understand that many homeless kids are running from something, making it difficult to find or count them as part of any single community. What is clear, though, is that life in a shelter or on the streets puts homeless youth at a higher risk for physical and sexual assault, abuse, and physical illness, including HIV/AIDS. Estimates suggest that 5,000 unaccompanied youngsters die each year as a result of assault, illness, or suicide. That is an average of 13 kids dying every day on America's streets.

Anxiety disorders, depression, Post Traumatic Stress Disorder, and suicide all are more common among homeless children. Previous studies of the homeless youth population have shown high rates of parental alcohol or drug abuse. Contrary to many people's misconceptions, however, substance abuse is not a characteristic that defines most youngsters who experience homelessness.

Despite the many challenges faced by homeless kids, there is room for optimism. Statistics show, for instance, that a majority of homeless children make it to school, at least for a period of time. Our education system can become another lifeline for these children in need. If safe shelters, counseling, and adequate support were more available for these kinds of kids and, if we could put increased emphasis on job training programs, there would be greater opportunities for homeless young people to graduate high school and build the skills they need to go on to live healthy and productive lives.

There are a number of organizations that play a critical role in making a positive, long-term difference in the lives of youth in crisis. StandUp For Kids, for example, is a not-for-profit group founded in 1990 by retired Navy officer Richard L. Koca to help rescue homeless and at-risk youth. With its national headquarters in San Diego, the organization is run almost entirely by volunteers, and has established more than 35 outreach programs in 20 states. Its mission is to find, stabilize, and assist homeless and street kids in an effort to improve their lives. YouthNoise, meanwhile, exists in the virtual world—but is equally powerful at inspiring and uniting young people. It runs the first youth-based social network dedicated to social change. Youth homelessness is one of the many critical issues that YouthNoise and its young members tackle, allowing teens to share thoughts on issues and convert ideas to action in their communities.

However, the government and nonprofit sectors cannot do this work alone. It is equally critical that our corporate citizens step up as well. I accepted the role as the first U.S. Ambassador of Virgin Unite, the Virgin Group's charitable arm created by Sir Richard Branson, in order to help one global brand increase its charitable voice and efforts. Through this role, I joined Virgin Mobile USA and The RE*Generation movement in their efforts to raise awareness of youth homelessness—and to support the direct work of programs like StandUp For Kids and YouthNoise.

Finally, the cliché is true—each person can make a difference, particularly this month as we recognize the very first "National Homeless Youth Awareness Month." There are a host of ways to get involved. By volunteering time, donating clothing or money, or simply by spreading the word, each of us can build a better future for children alone on the streets.

Analyze This Reading

1. As an activist for homeless youth, what projects has the writer pursued? What are the goals of each project?
2. What causes and misperceptions of youth homelessness does the writer identify?
3. How do the writer's personal experiences contribute to this reading? What compelling facts and statistics about homeless youth does she include?
4. What "room for optimism" does the writer describe?

Respond To This Reading

1. What is your understanding of homelessness in your community? Does some of the information the writer brings to this reading sound familiar? Are there features of youth homelessness the writer does not mention?
2. Do you share the writer's optimism regarding the challenges of addressing the problem of youth homelessness? What strategies for working with this issue would you add to what the writer mentions?
3. What are the attitudes toward homelessness in your community? Specifically, what are the views of elected leaders, of the business community, of social justice and faith groups, of your friends and family?
4. Were you to argue for a plan to address homeless students at your college, what would you claim? What support would you bring to your claim?

ABOUT THIS READING

This article appeared in *Earth Island Journal*, a quarterly magazine focused on the not-so-obvious connections between the environment and issues of everyday life.

North America: Ecological Breakup

By the Environment News Service

Divorce is a devastating experience. Adults in the midst of a crumbling relationship often become depressed, and children sometimes need psychological counseling to cope with the process. Now, a new study shows that when couples split up, the planet also feels the pain.

A survey by Michigan State University researchers Jianguo Liu and Eunice Yu, published in the Proceedings of the National Academy of Sciences, found that divorced families use up more resources than those that stay together. The reason is simple: When Mommy and Daddy live separately, they take up more space, consuming more energy, water, and land.

"The consequent increases in consumption of water and energy and using more space are being seen everywhere," Liu says. "People have been talking about how to protect the environment and combat climate change, but divorce is an overlooked factor that needs to be considered."

In studying the ecology of marriage and divorce, Liu and Yu examined the US and 11 other countries between 1998 and 2002. They found that if divorced couples were instead living together, there could have been 7.4 million fewer households in those countries. Divorcees required 38 million extra rooms, with concomitant increases for heating and lighting. In the US alone in 2005, divorced households used 73 billion kilowatt-hours of electricity and 627 billion gallons of water that would have been saved had the couple stayed married.

"A married household uses resources more efficiently than a divorced household," Liu says. "This creates a challenging dilemma and requires more creative solutions."

There is at least one solution at hand: The study found that when divorced people got married again, their environmental footprint shrank back to that of consistently married households.

Analyze This Reading

1. What do the writers claim?
2. In their study of the ecology of marriage and divorce, what data did the writers generate?
3. What solution do the writers mention?

Respond To This Reading

1. This treatment of divorce falls outside mainstream perspectives on this topic. In your view, explain why looking at divorce through an ecological lens is or is not a valid perspective.
2. The writers generate a new perspective on divorce by looking at it through an ecological lens. What happens when you view other features of life in your community through an ecological lens, such as public education, dating, health care, sporting events, and heating your home?
3. What single environmental issue motivates you to construct an argument? What will you claim?

ABOUT THIS READING

In his book *Last Child in the Woods: Saving Our Children From Nature-Deficit Disorder*, Richard Louv warns that the health of children is endangered as they spend more time indoors and less time in the natural world. Based on his research, Louv claims that obesity and depression in children are in part due to limited physical activity and too much time alone. His ideas have generated interest in and beyond the United States. This reading is the introduction to *Last Child in the Woods*.

Introduction from Last Child in the Woods

By Richard Louv

One evening when my boys were younger, Matthew, then ten, looked at me from across a restaurant table and said quite seriously, "Dad, how come it was more fun when you were a kid?"

I asked what he meant.

"Well, you're always talking about your woods and tree houses, and how you used to ride that horse down near the swamp."

At first, I thought he was irritated with me. I had, in fact, been telling him what it was like to use string and pieces of liver to catch crawdads in a creek, something I'd be hard-pressed to find a child doing these days. Like many parents, I do tend to romanticize my own childhood—and, I fear, too readily discount my children's experiences of play and adventure. But my son was serious; he felt he had missed out on something important.

He was right. Americans around my age, baby boomers or older, enjoyed a kind of free, natural play that seems, in the era of kid pagers, instant messaging, and Nintendo, like a quaint artifact.

Within the space of a few decades, the way children understand and experience nature has changed radically. The polarity of the relationship has reversed. Today, kids are aware of the global threats to the environment—but their physical contact, their intimacy with nature, is fading. That's exactly the opposite of how it was when I was a child.

As a boy, I was unaware that my woods were ecologically connected with any other forests. Nobody in the 1950s talked about acid rain or holes in the ozone layer or global warming. But I knew my woods and my fields; I knew every bend in the creek and dip in the beaten dirt paths. I wandered those woods even in my dreams. A kid today can likely tell you about the Amazon rain forest—but not about the last time he or she explored the woods in solitude, or lay in a field listening to the wind and watching the clouds move.

This book explores the increasing divide between the young and the natural world, and the environmental, social, psychological, and spiritual implications of that change. It also describes the accumulating research that reveals the necessity of contact with nature for healthy child—and adult—development.

While I pay particular attention to children, my focus is also on those Americans born during the past two to three decades. The shift in our relationship to the natural world is startling, even in settings that one would assume are devoted to nature. Not that long ago, summer camp was a place where you camped, hiked in the woods, learned about plants and animals, or told firelight stories about ghosts or mountain lions. As likely as not today, "summer camp" is a weight-loss camp, or a computer camp. For a new generation, nature is more abstraction than reality. Increasingly, nature is something to watch, to consume, to wear—to ignore. A recent television ad depicts a four-wheel-drive SUV racing along a breathtakingly beautiful mountain stream—while in the backseat two children watch a movie on a flip-down video screen, oblivious to the landscape and water beyond the windows.

A century ago, the historian Frederick Jackson Turner announced that the American frontier had ended. His thesis has been discussed and debated ever since. Today, a similar and more important line is being crossed.

Our society is teaching young people to avoid direct experience in nature. That lesson is delivered in schools, families, even organizations devoted to the outdoors, and codified into the legal and regulatory structures of many of our communities. Our institutions, urban/suburban design, and cultural attitudes unconsciously associate nature with doom—while disassociating the outdoors from joy and solitude. Well meaning public-school systems, media, and parents are effectively scaring children straight out of the woods and fields. In the patent-or-perish environment of higher education, we see the death of natural history as the more hands-on disciplines, such as zoology, give way to more theoretical and remunerative microbiology and genetic engineering. Rapidly advancing technologies are blurring the lines between humans, other animals, and machines. The postmodern notion that reality is only a construct—that we are what we program—suggests limitless human possibilities; but as the young spend less and less of their lives in natural surroundings, their senses narrow, physiologically and psychologically, and this reduces the richness of human experience.

Yet, at the very moment that the bond is breaking between the young and the natural world, a growing body of research links our mental, physical, and spiritual health directly to our association with nature—in positive ways. Several of these studies suggest that thoughtful exposure of youngsters to nature can even be a powerful form of therapy for attention-deficit disorders and other maladies. As one scientist puts it, we can now assume that just as children need good nutrition and adequate sleep, they may very well need contact with nature.

Reducing that deficit—healing the broken bond between our young and nature—is in our self-interest, not only because aesthetics or justice demands it, but also because our mental, physical, and spiritual health depends upon it. The health of the earth is at stake as well. How the young respond to nature, and how they raise their own children, will shape the configurations and conditions of our cities, homes—our daily lives. The following pages explore an alternative path to the future, including some of the most innovative environment-based school programs; a reimagining and redesign of the urban environment—what one theorist calls the coming "zoopolis"; ways of addressing the challenges besetting environmental groups; and ways that faith-based organizations can help reclaim nature as part of the spiritual development of children. Parents, children, grandparents, teachers, scientists, religious leaders, environmentalists, and researchers from across the nation speak in these pages. They recognize the transformation that is occurring. Some of them paint another future, in which children and nature are reunited—and the natural world is more deeply valued and protected.

During the research for this book, I was encouraged to find that many people now of college age—those who belong to the first generation to grow up in a largely de-natured environment—have tasted just enough nature to intuitively understand what they have missed. This yearning is a source of power. These young people resist the rapid slide from the real to the virtual, from the mountains to the Matrix. They do not intend to be the last children in the woods.

My sons may yet experience what author Bill McKibben has called "the end of nature," the final sadness of a world where there is no escaping man. But there is another possibility: not the end of nature, but the rebirth of wonder and even joy. Jackson's obituary for the American frontier was only partly accurate: one frontier did disappear, but a second one followed, in which Americans romanticized, exploited, protected, and destroyed nature. Now that frontier—which existed in the family farm, the woods at the end of the road, the national parks, and in our hearts—is itself disappearing or changing beyond recognition.

But, as before, one relationship with nature can evolve into another. This book is about the end of that earlier time, but it is also about a new frontier—a better way to live with nature.

Analyze This Reading

1. Often, writers choose to begin serious arguments with an anecdote that attempts to draw in readers emotionally. Is the writer's personal anecdote that opens this argument effective? Does it make you want to read on? Explain.

2. Describe the difference the writer identifies between his childhood and his perceptions of childhood today.

3. In paragraph nine, the writer claims that for children today "nature is more abstraction than reality." With what examples does he support this position?

4. In paragraph 10, the writer refers to historian Frederick Jackson Turner's famous thesis that the American frontier ended with Western expansion. Does the writer return to Turner later in the argument to agree or disagree with the historian? And does the writer return to his opening anecdote? In your view, is this circling back to earlier references effective? Explain.

5. In paragraph 11, the writer argues that "Our society is teaching young people to avoid direct experience in nature." Does this statement function as a claim of fact for this argument, or should it be analyzed as a reason supporting another claim?

6. What values does the writer bring to his argument? Do these values contribute to an effective warrant?

Respond To This Reading

1. The term "nature deficit disorder" begins with Richard Louv. While not widely accepted as a legitimate psychological condition, does Louv's term have merit? Do you agree with Louv's contention that our dependence on technology occurs at the expense of children interacting with nature? Explain.
2. With what parts of Louv's argument do you disagree? What parts do you agree with?
3. Identify elements of bias or limited perspective you find in this reading.
4. Louv wants us to think about nature deficit in terms of education, recreation, and health. Are there other issues that occur to you in terms of the younger generation and nature? What would you claim for each issue?

ABOUT THIS READING

Writer Gregory A. Pence is professor of philosophy at the University of Alabama at Birmingham, and in his scholarly work he examines ethical concerns generated by technological innovation in the field of medicine. He has authored *The Elements of Bioethics* (2007), *Cloning After Dolly* (2004), and *Brave New Bioethics* (2003). This reading first appeared in 2004 in *Cloning After Dolly*.

Reproductive Cloning Would Strengthen the American Family

By Gregory A. Pence

A [2003] news release described how a group of professionals approached the World Court, urging it to make reproductive cloning a crime against humanity. Such a move assumes that, regardless of how safe it becomes, reproductive cloning is not wrong because of its lack of safety at present or because the early stage of science now produces too many abnormalities, but because reproductive cloning is intrinsically wrong in itself.

This is not a scientific claim but a philosophical one. Although made by scientists, it lands in that more general realm known as ordinary morality, as do claims about the conduct of physicians who may want to be judged only by the norms internal to medicine but are still judged by norms of truth telling, decency, respect for persons, and fairness that stem from ordinary morality.

Wrong, Regardless of Safety

Several common arguments assert that reproductive cloning is intrinsically wrong, each with a slightly different twist and in different words but all amounting to the same claim—regardless of how safe it becomes or how much good it might create for a particular family, reproductive cloning is essentially wrong. These arguments include the following: reproductive cloning is an evil practice in itself; it inherently destroys the dignity of the child created; it is incompatible with the sanctity of life; it is against the will of God; it inherently dehumanizes children and treats them as commodities; it is evil because one kind of being is used as a resource for another.

A different class of arguments does not claim that reproductive cloning is intrinsically wrong but asserts that it is nevertheless wrong because it *indirectly* leads to bad consequences to the child, the couple, or society. Here reproductive cloning is claimed to be wrong because it is psychologically bad in some way for the cloned child or because the genes of the cloned child may have some hidden abnormality that may not be expressed until adulthood.

Or it is claimed that cloning is harmful to the parents who create a child with strong expectations, or it is wrong to start a practice in society where children are not loved in themselves as God's gifts but treated as commodities designed to bioengineering specifications.

Finally, critics argue that reproductive cloning is indirectly wrong because of its indirect, long-term consequences for society: that it leads to decreased genetic diversity in the human gene pool, that it sends the wrong message to the disabled, and that it will eventually send the wrong message to normals that there is something wrong about them. . . .

Now I want to turn to the more difficult task of making the strongest possible argument, once animal studies make it safe to try, *for* reproductive cloning.

For the sake of conceptual clarity, in the following pages I assume that one day has come when all mammals and especially primates can be routinely and safely originated by cloning with a rate of defects no higher than that found in sexual reproduction in the same species. I assume that studies of cloned human embryos have shown that they can be created in the same way, without any more abnormalities than occur in sexual reproduction. All that assumed, what's the case for allowing safe, human reproductive cloning?

Considering the Importance of Planning Conception

The first argument needs a little background, so let's detour a moment and consider the oft heard claim that an adolescent or adult will be traumatized to learn that he or she was adopted, was created by in vitro fertilization, has an unknown twin, was created by insemination of donor sperm, or was originated by cloning. As I have already argued, these claims are highly speculative and mostly express the projections of critics.

These critics have us imaging a future when cloned children spend hours brooding over the fact that their parents willed their existence and consciously thought about whose genotype they would embody. They envision such children agonizing over whether they will live up to their parents' expectations, traumatized by the fear that they will not and trembling lest they lose their parents' love.

How silly! To see why, we need not go far into the future but merely turn the mirror on ourselves, for there is one question close at hand that is foundational to anyone who was born before 1965: were we really wanted by our parents or were we just accidents? Were we consciously wanted, planned, and deliriously sought after, or were we an unintended-but-foreseeable by-product of having unprotected sex in an age when both contraception and abortion were illegal for all couples, married or not?

First, even if we ask our parents and they swear we were wanted (what would you say to *your* kids?), we will really never know. Second, we don't really care about the answer and probably won't ask our parents, but either way, given all the water under the bridge, the answer is irrelevant.

Nor do we ask our parents whether they really wanted a girl instead of a boy. We don't ask them if they planned to have a child but only years later, once they had their marriage on a better footing or had more money. We don't ask if they thought about adopting instead of conceiving, and if when young they considered a childless lifestyle that involved traveling around the world to exotic locations.

To the extent that children created by cloning are happy, the general happiness in the world increases.

No, we usually don't ask such questions and if we do, our parents are usually a bit uncomfortable (Why are you asking me *that?*). Bonding, affection, and the life of the family have long since carried us beyond such questions, smoothing over unexpected answers. Most of us happily come to believe that our creation was in the stars, just as it should have been.

The Most Wanted Children in Human History

One day children created by cloning will be as indifferent to their origins as we post-1965-born adults are today. So too for their families, bonding, affection, and the life of the family will have long since carried them beyond such questions, smoothing over unexpected problems.

Compare adults created by in vitro fertilization, for whom we now have a 25-year history. As we know, their special origins to them are no big deal: they are just glad to be alive; indeed, many know they are among the most loved children in human history.

Likewise, and to a much greater degree, originating children by safe cloning will spare them any traumas associated with uncertainty about being wanted. With the exception of firstborn sons of childless monarchs of great kingdoms, such children may be the most wanted, most anticipated children in history.

Safe cloning will be intrinsically good for children in giving them a deep, rich sense that their parents sincerely wanted them.

Children created by in vitro fertilization also know they were wanted, but children created by safe cloning have additional assurance because they were wanted not just as generic children but for their general characteristics. Not only will Faith know that Mom and Dad wanted her to exist, but will know that they wanted a girl with a genetic predisposition to strong religious belief. ("Mom and Daddy always wanted a faith-based girl, so the Lord gave them a way to make me. I love them so much and I sure know they love me.")

Safe cloning will be intrinsically good for children in giving them a deep, rich sense that their parents sincerely wanted them, not only as their firstborn child but also as their firstborn child with musical talent. Wrapped in parental reassurance, such children might be more self-confident and self-assured than normal children, who must (if they think about it) be uncertain about why they were created.

Beneath everyone's fears about designer babies and unrealistic parental expectations lies something that is different and good: the idea that children are wanted with a white-hot intensity. That is a very new, unusual idea to most people (except perhaps those who are familiar with clinics for assisted reproduction). We need time to be comfortable with the idea that children need not "just come" but can be intensely wanted. Even when parents don't get everything they want, we will learn that wanting kids intensely is a good thing.

Happier People and a Happier Society

A second argument that reproductive cloning could be in the intrinsic good of children needs a little rope, but not too much. That rope is the assumption that human genetics, proteinomics, and knowledge of functional gene-environment interactions will increasingly reveal not only the causes of bad states, such as depression and hypercholesterolemia, but also of good states, such as being good-natured, generally healthy, and long-lived.

Give me that same assumption here and see if I hang myself. But it's not fair to argue with the assumption that we will come to know which set of genes predisposes people to be happy, healthy, and long-lived. So let's say we do know these genes and how to safely choose them in a child originated by cloning.

Then, ceteris paribus, it would be intrinsically good for the child to have genes that predispose her to being happy, healthy, and long-lived rather than genes that predispose her to being morose and sick, and to die early. Such genes indeed may be *foundational* for a happy life, something that over time we come to see as each child's birthright. One day in the future, getting a healthy gene pack will be like getting fluoride in the water to prevent cavities or getting standard vaccinations against deadly childhood diseases.

Moreover, to the extent that children created by cloning are happy, the general happiness in the world increases. To the extent that their happiness makes their parents, friends, siblings, grandparents, spouses, and their own children happy, their happiness spreads in expanding circles, creating more happiness. All of this is intrinsically good.

Creating Stronger Families

A third kind of argument why reproductive cloning could be an intrinsic good builds on the assumption that creating wanted families is intrinsically good. Make this pro-life, pro-family assumption; if we do so, then safe reproductive cloning will almost certainly be a new kind of tool to use to create such families.

The strongest affirmation of the intrinsic good of reproductive cloning would be if children created by cloning used the same method . . . to create their own children.

Just as insemination of husband's sperm (AIH), anonymous sperm donation (AID), in vitro fertilization (IVF), surrogacy, and ooycte donation were all initially condemned and have now come to be accepted as useful tools in family making, so reproductive cloning one day will be seen the same way. For the one in eleven American couples who are infertile after two years of trying to conceive, how a baby gets created matters very little compared to the fact that the baby has been created.

Another reason why reproductive cloning may come to be seen as intrinsically good and why it should never be taken off the table and treated as a federal crime is that, as environmental toxins and delayed age of attempting first conception rises, citizens of developed societies may one day soon need better tools to aid them in creating children. Canadian sociologists Louise Vandelac and Marie-Helen Bacon of the University of Quebec-Montreal argue that soaring use of environmental pollutants around the world has dramatically decreased fertility in advanced societies. According to these sociologists, increasing breast cancer and endometriosis, as well as declining animal and human sperm counts and potencies, have been "directly associated with the sharp increase in pesticide use and environmental organochlorine chemicals such as polychlorinated biphenyls (PCBs) and hexachlorobenzene (HCB)."

Don't ban reproductive cloning! If we keep polluting our world, as we seem unable to stop doing, we may all be infertile one day and need an asexual way to reproduce humans. (This gives rise to another linkage argument on the other side: clean up the environment or you'll have to accept cloning!)

Cloning as a tool might prevent divorce. Some marriages fall apart owing to a lack of children. In some cases children bind two adults together, getting them over rough times for the sake of the children. This is true for adopted children also; so it is not necessary that the couple created the children themselves.

For some Orthodox Jews and Muslims, being unable to have children is a real curse, in part because the culture and the traditions, to a great extent, revolve around having a family. In such a culture, finding meaning without a family may be difficult. Less commonly, a particular kind of family is highly desired. For example, some marriages may dissolve because only girls are created and no boys. Although feminists argue that cloning should not support sexist choices, isn't it better to have a family based on consenting sexist choices than a divorced single mom or dad? Besides, personal life needs to be cut some space from pervasive moral criticism.

Insurance for Families

Another argument may be called the insurance argument. *Washington* Post columnist Abigail Trafford writes that 70,000 American kids under age 25 die every year, leaving their families devastated. Previous generations of Americans had large families and frequently experienced the death of a child. Now the birthrate has fallen to 2.13 children for every woman, and many women only bear one child. If that child dies, a woman may be past her reproductive age. For example, Katherine Gordon of Great Falls, Montana, whose 17-year-old daughter Emily was killed in a car accident in 1997, wants to clone Emily's genes to create a child. "I know it wouldn't be Emily—it would be her twin sister," she says.

Yes, Trafford agrees, many people find reproductive cloning repugnant, but many medical procedures are more repugnant. We tolerate them to save our lives or, in some cases, to try to create life. In her own case, her maternal grandmother died at age twenty giving birth to her mother, who was raised by her maternal grandparents in Ohio as a late child. Her aunts and uncle treated her as a baby sister and she blended into the family. So life is full of both disasters and surprises, and if we really value families and children, why should we not keep, as insurance, one tool for re-creating both?

Cloned Having Cloned Children

For the next argument for the intrinsic goodness of safe cloning, we should imagine not the forward-looking consent of cloned children (since it's non-sensical to talk of the consent of a being who does not exist about whether he should exist) but the backward-looking endorsement of cloned children. Call this the argument from *presumed consent*.

If cloned children later are told of their unique origins, told about why they were created and why their parents chose a particular genotype, and if such children endorse their method of origination, that would certainly be an argument in favor of this method. If most children created by cloning approve of their unique origins, then we can presume their consent for their origination.

The strongest affirmation of the intrinsic good of reproductive cloning would be if children created by cloning used the same method as adults to create their own children. They would not necessarily or even probably clone their own genotypes, but they might indeed clone someone's. If so, we would have something like rich, deep presumed consent. . . .

The Benefits of Change

Cloning would expand the currently small range of choices about creating children. It would also demystify the process of making children, taking the religious mumbo jumbo out of creation. Consider an analogy: imagine if the only way you could get a car (and this may have been true at one time in some communist countries) was through a lottery from the central allocation authority. If you were a fatalist, you would accept whatever you got, saying, "It's God's will that I drive a Hyundai."

Present conception is a lot like that. Whether you get a child, and what characteristics it has, are determined by other factors, not the parents. Many people now see that as a good thing and think it bad that parents might soon be able to control the kind of kids they have. But that is because everything is new and people fear that parents wouldn't love children chosen for their traits. But just as people once feared that parents wouldn't love their children if the children were planned, so too people will learn that chosen children will be loved more, not less, than those who came unplanned and unchosen.

Because cloning involves a choice about which genotype to reproduce, it would remove the arbitrariness of genetic roulette in sexual reproduction. It would put our growing knowledge of biology and genetics, not religion, behind choices about children. Although religion may be a force for good once children exist, it has generally been a force for evil in blocking scientific ways to overcome infertility or new ways of creating them. Reproductive fatalism is a flawed worldview, asserting that people should accept disease, dysfunction, and infertility. But this is false; all the above are human evils and medicine's enemies.

Reproductive fatalism holds that the status quo is natural and good. Although life now is much better than it was two or three hundred years ago, we know that life now is as good as it gets. To change any more, especially by adopting radical new kinds of biotechnology, is to risk losing everything.

That view is silly. It is almost certainly true that the present state of humanity can be improved in a thousand important ways. No one deserves to be sick, crippled, or barren. No one desires to die from old age or disease. Reproductive fatalists say we don't know enough, are not wise enough, to know when to change. But change in itself is not bad; we should adopt an experimental attitude toward change: judge each change by its consequences. Changes can be reversed if they work out badly (Prohibition, untaxed cigarettes).

Humans Will Be Responsible with Cloning

Nor are the most primitive ways of conceiving children the best ("It was good enough for me"). Having lots of ways to create wanted children is good. Some people will always use the most primitive ways; others will study all available options and choose the methods best for them. For still others, need will drive their choice.

Humans are not, as reproductive fatalists subtly imply, basically bad. When most of us think about it, we really don't believe anymore in Augustine's view of original sin, that human nature is tainted by terrible flaws deep within. No, humans are basically neutral to good. Yes, they are self-interested and possess only limited altruism, but that just proves that humans are neither saints nor perfect. Humans do have the moral ability to judge each case affecting them from experience, compassion, and reasoning, and then to blend many values to get the best answer. This is also true about choices about reproduction.

Similarly, reproductive fatalists and liberals do not want to trust parents to make choices about children, especially traits of children. They see all parents as potential child abusers who need to be monitored by the state. But that view is false to most experience. Most parents are good and want the best for their kids. Hence we can trust most parents without state interference or state regulation to make the best decisions about when and how to create children and how to raise them. . . .

Once the emotion and sensationalism are stripped from the topic of safe, reproductive human cloning, it is surprisingly easy to justify as something intrinsically good for humans. That is because it would be just another tool in our reproductive tool kit for creating families and better humans. And how can those two things not be good?

Analyze This Reading

1. The writer begins with a summary of arguments against reproductive cloning. Does this make the writer seem defensive? Or, given the controversial nature of the issue, is this a practical opening for his argument? Explain.

2. How does the writer counter the argument that children will be "trau-matized" to learn that they were cloned?

3. What reasons does the writer give in his defense of reproductive cloning?

4. What is reproductive fatalism? What point is the writer making when, in the next-to-last paragraph, he lumps together reproductive fatalists and liberals?

Respond To This Reading

1. At the beginning of his argument, the writer criticizes "ordinary moral-ity" and aims to replace it, in the context of reproductive cloning, with another approach to this issue. What is this approach and, in your view, is the writer successful with it?

2. Evaluate the writer's support for his claim. Do you consider it balanced in terms of logical, ethical, and emotional appeals?

3. What is your view of reproductive cloning? On what grounds can you justify your view?

4. Reproductive cloning, one issue generated by advances in medical technology, has been responded to from a range of perspectives— moral, religious, utilitarian, and scientific, among others. Are there other issues in your life and in your community that developments in medical technology have produced? What are they, and is there one that motivates you to argue? Explain.

ABOUT THIS READING

Mugambi Jouet is a contributor to *Huff Post*, or *Huffington Post*, a popular online news site on which this post appeared. Jouet writes about American culture, with particular attention to the impact of religion in American politics, and about international criminal law.

Why Gay Marriage is so Controversial in America

By Mugambi Jouet

Barack Obama's decision to support gay marriage has led to a debate about how it may influence the [2012] presidential election and the future of gay marriage in the United States. But the underlying reasons why gay marriage is so controversial in America are being overlooked. While there is gener-ally no consensus for or against gay marriage in other Western nations, the issue has far more political importance in America, where it is the object of an exceptionally intense debate.

Only a few U.S. states allow gay marriage: Connecticut, Iowa, Massachusetts, New Hampshire, New York, and Vermont. Multiple other states have passed constitutional amendments barring gay marriage, as North Carolina recently did. But the fact that gay marriage is usually illegal in America is not exceptional in the Western world. It is only lawful in Belgium,

Canada, Iceland, the Netherlands, Norway, Portugal, Spain, and Sweden thus far. The *considerable contrasts* one witnesses within the United States are what is remarkable. Several U.S. states are among the world's trailblazing jurisdictions in recognizing gay marriage and gay rights, whereas the leaders of various other states would endorse the criminalization of homosexuality altogether, as is now the case in much of the Third World.

Indeed, after the Supreme Court held in 2003 that consensual sex between men could not be criminalized, many social conservatives were appalled. The Court's 6-3 decision concerned a Texas law that was virtually never enforced. The majority held that the law was unconstitutional because it infringed on fundamental liberty and reflected "stigma" against homosexuals. Justice Antonin Scalia, admired by numerous Republicans as a model judge, wrote a sharp dissent. Scalia posited that the criminalization of gay sex is a legitimate state interest. "Many Americans do not want persons who openly engage in homosexual conduct as partners in its business, as scoutmasters for its children, as teachers in its children's schools, or as boarders in its home," he underlined.

In other words, besides gay marriage, the underlying question of homosexuality is much more controversial in America than in most other Western nations. A 2011 poll of five Western countries found the United States to be the least tolerant on the matter. Sixty percent of Americans felt that homosexuality should be accepted by society, a far lower proportion than the people of Spain (91 percent), Germany (87 percent), France (86 percent), and Britain (81 percent). The views of Republicans mainly accounted for the difference.

Both liberals *and* conservatives in most other Western countries have evolved towards modern norms of tolerance on gay rights. However, a large segment of conservative America has strongly resisted this process. Certainly, conservatives in other Western nations are typically more traditional-minded than its liberal counterparts and many do oppose gay marriage. Still, they are distinctly more tolerant than Republicans. For instance, Nicolas Sarkozy, France's former conservative president, opposed gay marriage but neither he nor his party made the issue a big part of its platform. Meanwhile, in Great Britain, Prime Minister David Cameron and his Conservative Party have *led* efforts to legalize gay marriage.

Moreover, until "Don't Ask, Don't Tell" (DADT) was recently repealed, America stood alone in the West in continuing to ban gays from the military, a policy characteristic of Third World, authoritarian, and Islamist nations. Even though a majority of Republican citizens supported DADT's repeal, only 8 Republican Senators and 15 Republican House Representatives voted to end the discriminatory policy. They notably ignored how DADT's repeal was supported by certain top military figures and a comprehensive Pentagon study. The GOP's stance illustrated how its leaders commonly embrace the religious right's views. After all, it was John McCain, one of the most moderate Republicans of modern times, who led the opposition to DADT's repeal.

Why is conservative America so out of step with the rest of the West when it comes to modern norms of tolerance? One major factor is that conservative America is essentially the only part of the modern Western world where a fundamentalist approach to Christianity is prevalent, as I noted in a prior article. Religious fundamentalists strongly support an ultra-traditional patriarchal family model. That not only explains why women's reproductive rights like abortion and contraception are exceptionally controversial in conservative America, but also why gay rights cause such polemic.

The clash over gay rights is an extension of the conflict between traditional patriarchy and the more egalitarian gender system of modern times. Patriarchy seeks to affirm unambiguous gender roles and obligations. Men are expected to be "masculine" and women to be "feminine." Homosexuality inherently challenges the foundations of traditional patriarchy since men seemingly assume a "feminine" identity and women a "masculine" one. Homosexuality consequently imperils the religious right's conception of the family, which is fundamentally patriarchal. Because religious conservatives also tend to equate sexuality with procreation, at least in principle, they commonly find homosexuality taboo. These are among the reasons why the religious right laments that the recognition of gay marriage amounts to an "assault on the family" or an effort to "destroy society." What may sound like hyperbole is true from the point of view of the patriarchal traditionalist.

The legalization of same-sex marriage further threatens the American religious right's conception of marriage as a sacred institution. Religious conservatives fear that it will be at risk if its definition becomes a mere matter of secular government policy, as noted by Naomi Cahn and June Carbone in *Red Families v. Blue Families*. The "sanctity of marriage" will be further undermined if the institution is open to "profane" homosexual unions. Unlike many American conservatives, liberals tend to regard marriage primarily as an expression of love and commitment, often taking God out of the equation.

The religious factor behind opposition to gay marriage is less present elsewhere in the Western world, where indifference or skepticism towards religion is far more common than in America. Approaches to religion can also differ significantly. Contemporary European Christians, for instance, are rather moderate in its faiths, particularly when compared to American evangelicals. While the Catholic Church condemns homosexuality and same-sex marriage, its influence is nowadays limited in Europe except in a few nations, especially Poland, Italy, and Ireland. Additionally, like numerous American Catholics, European Catholics frequently disregard the Church's teachings on questions like contraception, abortion, and gay rights. In sum, once religious conservatism is absent or moderate, opposition to gay marriage becomes less intense.

Of course, homophobia is not only spurred by religious conservatism. It can equally reflect uneasiness or animosity towards people who are perceived as different, just like racism, sexism or xenophobia. In that regard, homophobia presumably exists in all countries to a lesser or greater extent. Yet, the extraordinary weight of Christian fundamentalism in conservative America exacerbates concerns about sexual morality.

The question of gay rights illustrates the great polarization between contemporary liberal America and conservative America. An international comparison suggests, however, that liberal America is much closer to other Western nations than to conservative America when it comes to embracing modern norms of tolerance.

Analyze This Reading

1. Where does the US rank among other Western countries in terms of its tolerance for gay marriage? How does the writer explain this ranking?
2. The writer contends that "liberals tend to regard marriage primarily as an expression of love and commitment." In contrast, how do conservatives tend to regard marriage?
3. The writer asserts "that liberal America is much closer to other Western nations than to conservative America when it comes to embracing modern norms of tolerance." Does the writer earn the right to make this bold statement; that is, does he bring in enough context to support his contention? Explain.

Respond To This Reading

1. With attention to the final paragraph of this blog post, in your view is there a danger in America lagging behind other Western nations in its tolerance of gay marriage? Explain.
2. The writer frames his treatment of gay marriage in terms of politics and religion, perhaps the contexts in which many Americans engage with this issue. What other frames, apart from politics and religion, are appropriate for thinking about the issue of gay marriage in American life? Identify these frames and describe the insights into this testy issue they can make available.

ABOUT THIS READING

American Dahr Jamail was an unembedded journalist during the 2003 Iraq Invasion, posting reports on his website, *Dahr Jamail's MidEast Dispatches*. He is also a contributing writer to *Al Jazeera*, among other publications, and a contributing writer for *Truthout*, the daily online news site in which this article appears. His books include *Beyond the Green Zone: Dispatches from an Unembedded Journalist in Occupied Iraq* (2007) and *The Will to Resist: Soldiers Who Refuse to Fight in Iraq and Afghanistan* (2009).

A Morally Bankrupt Military: When Soldiers and Their Families Become Expendable

By Dahr Jamail

The military operates through indoctrination. Soldiers are programmed to develop a mindset that resists any acknowledgment of injury and sickness, be it physical or psychological. As a consequence, tens of thousands of soldiers continue to serve, even being deployed to combat zones like Iraq and/ or Afghanistan, despite persistent injuries. According to military records, over 43,000 troops classified as "nondeployable for medical reasons" have been deployed to Iraq and Afghanistan nevertheless.

The recent atrocity at Fort Hood is an example of this. Maj. Nidal Hasan had worked as a counselor at Walter Reed, hearing countless stories of bloodshed, horror and death from dismembered veterans from the occupations of Iraq and Afghanistan. While he had not yet served in Iraq or Afghanistan, the major was overloaded with secondary trauma, coupled with ongoing harassment about his being a Muslim. This, along with other factors, contributed towards Hasan falling into a desperation so deep he was willing to slaughter fellow soldiers, and is indicative of fissures running deep into the crumbling edifice upon which the US military stands.

The case of Pvt. Timothy Rich also demonstrates the disastrous implications of the apathetic attitude of the military toward its own. Not dissimilar from Major Hasan, who clearly would have benefited from treatment for the secondary trauma he was experiencing from his work with psychologically wounded veterans, one of the main factors that forced Private Rich to go absent without leave (AWOL) was the failure of the military to treat his mental issues.

Rich told Truthout, "In my unit, to go to sick call for mental health was looked down upon. Our acting 1st Sergeant believed that we shouldn't have mental issues because we were too 'high speed.' So I was afraid to go because I didn't want to be labeled as a weak soldier."

What followed was more harrowing.

"The other problems arose when I brought my girlfriend down to marry her. My unit believed her to be a problem starter so I was ordered not to marry her, taken to a small finance company by an NCO and forced to draw a loan in order to buy her a plane ticket to return home. They escorted her to the airport and through security to ensure that she left. Once the NCO left she turned around and hitchhiked back to Fort Bragg. Before the unit could discover us, we went to the courthouse and got married. We were then summoned by my Commander, Captain Jones, to his office and reprimanded. He called me a dumb ass soldier and a shit bag for marrying her and told my wife that she was a fool to marry someone as stupid as me. Members of my unit started referring to me as Pvt. Bitch instead of Pvt. Rich. The entire episode caused a lot of strain in our relationship. Unable to cope with all this, I bought two plane tickets and went AWOL with my wife."

Rich was later apprehended when a federal warrant was issued against him. After 11 days in a country jail, he was transported back to Fort Bragg in North Carolina. On August 17, 2008, he was wrongly assigned to Echo Platoon that was part of the 82nd Airborne, whereas his unit was part of the 18th Airborne.

Rich recollects, "I was confused when they assigned me to the 82nd. I was dismissed as a liar when I brought this up with my NCO Sgt Joseph Fulgence and my commander, Captain Thaxton. I ended up spending a year at Echo before being informed that I was never supposed to have been in the 82nd."

At Fort Bragg, he was permitted to seek mental health treatment and was diagnosed with schizophrenia, psychosis, insomnia and a mood disorder. This, however, did not stop his commander from harassing him. His permanent profile from the doctor restricted him from being on duty before 0800 (8 AM) hours, but his commander, Sergeant Fulgence, dismissed the profile as merely a guideline and not a mandatory directive. The soldier was accused of using mental health as a pretext to avoid duty. So, Rich was up every morning for first formation at 0545 (5:45 AM). It wasn't until he refused to take his medication because it made him groggy in the morning that his doctor called his commander and settled the matter. By then, Rich had already been forced to violate his profile for six months.

During this period, his mental health deteriorated rapidly. The combined effect of heavy medication and restrictions on his home visits resulted in his experiencing blackouts that led him to take destructive actions in the barracks. When he was discovered talking about killing the chain of command, he was put on a 24-hour suicide watch that seemed to have served little purpose, because on August 17 he was able to elude his guards and make his way to the roof of his barracks.

"I climbed onto the roof of the building and sat up there thinking about my family and my situation and decided to go ahead and end my suffering by taking a nose dive off the building," Rich explained to Truthout.

His body plummeted through the air, bounced off a tree, and he landed on his back with a cracked spine. The military gave him a back brace, psychotropic drugs and a renewed 24-hour suicide watch, measures as effective in alleviating his pain as his failed suicide attempt.

When Truthout contacted him just days after his failed suicide attempt, a fatigued Rich detailed his hellish year-long plight of awaiting a discharge that never came. "I want to leave here very bad. For four months they have been telling me that I'll get out next week. It got to the point that the NCOs would tell me just to calm me down that I'd be going home the next day. They went as far as to call my wife and requesting her to lie that she was coming to get me the next day. I eventually stopped believing them. I didn't see an end to it, so I figured I'd try and end it myself."

The noncommissioned officers in his barracks thought it was hilarious that Rich had jumped, and he was offered money for an encore that could be videotaped.

At the time he was in a "holdover" unit, comprised mostly of AWOL soldiers who had turned themselves in or had been arrested. Others in his unit had untreated mental health problems like him or were suffering from severe PTSD (post-traumatic stress disorder) from deployments in Iraq and or Afghanistan.

According to Rich, every soldier in his platoon was subjected to abusive treatment of some kind or the other. "It even got to the point when our 1st Sergeant Cisneros told us that if it were up to him we all would all be taken out back and shot, and that we needed to pray to our gods because we were going to pay (for our actions)."

Tim's wife Megan had to bear his never-ending ordeal in equal measure. She witnessed the military's callousness up close. She informed Truthout, "Since February of this year, Tim's unit had been telling him he would be out in two weeks. After two weeks when he asked, they would repeat the same thing. At times he would get excited and start packing his belongings and I would try to figure out how to get him home to Ohio. He would call me crying in relief because he thought we were going to be together again real soon. The military forced me to lie to him too. When he realized they did not mean to release him he grew very destructive during his black out spells. Eventually he simply gave up on coming home."

Megan first realized there was a problem with the way the military was treating her husband when she noticed him doing and saying things that were out of character for him, like apologizing for not being a good husband and father and being openly suicidal. He had also begun to self-medicate with alcohol, an increasing trend among soldiers not receiving adequate mental-health treatment from the military.

She revealed to Truthout, "He had quit for the girls and me but it seems like he could not handle the stress and needed an escape. This caused a huge problem between us and we began to argue about it. He became severely depressed, pulled away from me, and started to do things he normally doesn't do, such as giving away his money and belongings, and telling the recipients that he wouldn't need those things in hell."

She sensed that her husband would be in trouble if he were to stand up for himself, so she began to advocate on his behalf. Her attempts to do so met with fresh abuse from his commanders. The chain of command banned her from the company barracks and had her escorted off post. The couple was commandeered into Sergeant Fulgence's office where they were chastised. The sergeant referred to Megan as "a bad mother" and "a bitch." When Megan attempted to leave the office in protest, the sergeant ordered her to stay and listen to what he had to say.

This was followed by an encounter with the commander of the platoon, Commander Thaxton. The commander in this case ordered Tim to shut up, and threatened him with confinement. He demanded that Megan explain what kind of mother would bring her child to a new location without a place to live. She tried telling him that the AER loan was for her to come to Fort Bragg since they had lost their house after Tim's arrest and loss of job. Although the paperwork for the loan clearly stated that it was for her travel, food and lodging at Fort Bragg, the commander insisted it was for an apartment. When Tim intervened to say that the $785 would not be sufficient to pay rent and bills, especially since he wasn't being paid his wages and his wife couldn't work because of the baby, and according to Tim, both Sergeant Fulgence and Captain Thaxton "had a nice laugh over that" and dismissed the duo, referring to them as "juvenile dumb-asses."

After Tim returned from being AWOL and was brought up on charges, he went through 706 (a psychology board) that declared him mentally incompetent at the time of his being AWOL. It took a painfully long amount of time for the charges to be dismissed without prejudice. The soldier believes that his superiors deliberately refused to do the requisite paperwork for his clearance and subsequent resumption of his pay.

He told Truthout, "Every time I came on base I got arrested even though I was on active duty again. Then my wife and I got an AER loan for her to come down to Fort Bragg. When she got there and my pay continued to be withheld, the AER money ran out and my wife and child had to sleep in the van we owned. When my unit found out they called the Military Police and ordered me to give custody of my daughter to my father." When Tim refused to do that, they punished him by confining him to the barracks and barring his wife from entering the base. To add insult, the chain of command took away his van keys and said that neither he nor Megan was allowed use it.

The nightmare ended when the military finally released Pvt. Timothy Rich, and by default, Megan. He was discharged and "allowed" to enter the ranks of US citizens searching for jobs and health care. Their traumatic journey to that starting point is what distinguishes them from their civilian counterparts.

Rich's advice to anyone thinking of joining the military today: "Don't join. Everything they advertise and tell you about how it's a family friendly army is a lie."

Sgt. Heath Carter suffered a similar fate at the hands of an indifferent military command. Upon return from the invasion of Iraq, he discovered that his daughter Sierra was living in an unsafe environment in Arkansas under the care of his first wife, who had full custody of the child. Heath and his new wife, Teresa, started consulting attorneys in order to secure custody of Sierra, who also suffered from a life-threatening medical condition. Precisely during this time, the military chose to keep changing Carter's duty station from Fort Polk, Louisiana, to Fort Huachuca, Arizona, then to Fort Stewart, Georgia. Not only did these constant transfers make it difficult for Carter to see his daughter, they also reduced his chances of gaining custody of Sierra. Convinced that this was a matter of life and death for his daughter, he requested compassionate reassignment to Fort Leavenworth, Missouri, about two hours from his first wife's home in Arkansas.

His appeals to the military command, the legal department, chaplain and even to his congressman failed, and the military insisted that he remain at Fort Stewart, Georgia. Having run out of all available avenues, in May 2007 he went AWOL from Fort Stewart and headed home to Arkansas where he fought for and won custody of Sierra, and was able to literally save her life by obtaining needed medical care for her.

However, on January 25 of this year, Carter was arrested at his home by the military police, who flew him back to Fort Stewart where he has been awaiting charges for the past eight months. Being a sergeant, he is in a regular unit and not in a holdover, but that does not help his cause. Initially, his commander told him it would take a month and a half for him to be sent home. Several months later, it was decided he would receive a court-martial.

Carter feels frustrated, "Now I have to wait for the court martial. It's taken this long for them to decide. If we had known it would take this long, my family could have moved down here. Every time I ask when I'll have a trial, they say it is only going to be another two weeks. I get the feeling they are lying. They have messed with my pay. They're trying to push me to do something wrong."

His ordeal has forced Carter to reflect on the wars. He admits that, although his original reason for going AWOL was personal and he had otherwise been proud of his missions, he sees things in Iraq differently today. "I don't think there is any reason for us to be there except for oil."

Yet, both Private Rich and Sergeant Carter were offered deployments to Afghanistan amid their struggles. It is soldiers like these that the military will use to fill the ranks of the next "surge" of troops into Afghanistan, which at the time of this writing, appears to be as many as 34,000 troops.

The stage is set for more tragic incidents like the recent massacre at Fort Hood.

Analyze This Reading

1. What does the writer claim in the first paragraph? What context does he provide for his claim?
2. What kinds of support does the writer use? Are the cases of Private Rich and Sergeant effective? Explain.
3. While this text is a report and not an argument, would the report have benefited from attention to the conventional elements of argument, such as a warrant, opposing points of view, and reasons? Explain.

Respond To This Reading

1. What is your understanding of how our military personnel are responded to when they express concern about health and sickness? Does it fall in line with the writer's view? Why or why not?
2. Were you a member of a citizens advisory group charged with monitoring veterans affairs in your community, what regulations would you insist on and what resources in the community would you enlist in support?

Neighborhood Community

ABOUT THIS READING

Leo W. Banks is a writer and historian who has written extensively on Arizona history. He is the author of *Rattlesnake Blues: Dispatches from a Snakebit Territory (2002)*. This article appeared in the *Tucson Weekly*, an alternative newsweekly.

Under Siege

By Leo W. Banks

You couldn't find a better place to have lunch than this cramped, dusty Cochise County cook shack. It has every bit of ambience that Arizona ranch country can offer, including a wood-slat ceiling covered with strips of tin from a dismantled pigpen. In ranching, nothing goes to waste, so when Ruth Evelyn Cowan had the opportunity to collect some scrap from her parents' New Mexico ranch, she grabbed it.

The tin might rattle in the wind and drum in the rain, but those sounds create a symphony for Cowan, who loves this place and this life. She was born into it 57 years ago, and you can see that it suits her down to the mud on her boots. You don't have to listen hard to hear the contentment in her voice when she goes on about her American Brahman cattle—big, silver, hump-backed animals with floppy ears that she talks to as if they were her kids.

But this is Southern Arizona under siege, so there really is only one subject on the agenda, one issue that dominates all others here: the border with Mexico and the invasion of illegals who, every day and every night, rush to fill this yawning vacuum. . . .

You can't name a category of human being—good-hearted or crooked, kind or mean—or a nation, religion or ethnic group that isn't using this border to sneak into America illegally. The numbers boggle the mind. In January [2005] alone, the Border Patrol in the Tucson sector impounded 557 smuggling vehicles, confiscated 34,864 pounds of marijuana and arrested 35,704 illegals, according to agency spokesman Jose Garza.

The important number is one they can't pinpoint with certainty: how many got through. But figure it this way, using the common belief that, conservatively, for every arrest the Border Patrol makes, another two illegals make it through: With almost 500,000 arrests in the Tucson sector [in 2004], that means somewhere in the neighborhood of 1 million illegals broke into the country successfully—an average of almost 3,000 every 24 hours. And arrests for 2005 are up 10 percent, according to Garza.

Fear and Anger

Because of the sheer number of illegals—as well as their desperation, their willingness to destroy property and intimidate, and the always-simmering fear—Cowan and husband, Bob Giles, have sold most of their cattle and are significantly scaling back their ranching operation.

"I feel such relief," says Cowan of the decision she and her husband made. "I'm tired of continually looking over my shoulder. I'd like to be able to get up in the morning and not have the first part of my day spent repairing damage from the night before. I'd like to be able to live on my own ranch, but I don't feel safe there. I want a rattlesnake to be the worst thing I have to worry about. . . .

"I'm not an angry person, but I'm just ticked all the time, and that's not a healthy way to live. We're all so angry here. We're tired of the apathy of people who live elsewhere. What's happening here is everyone's problem, not just ours. We're tired of people who live in another country thumbing their noses at our laws, our culture and our customs, and threatening what we've spent generations building. . . .

"I'm a rich rancher," Cowan says, her tone mocking the very idea. "Well, I guess I *am* rich in a way. I have my husband, my parents, my friends, the ability to work and make a living. As far as cash in my pocket, I don't have that. Financially, I've been devastated. But I feel spiritually, emotionally and physically bankrupt, too. In my lifetime, I've never been where I am today. I don't want to see the damage the illegals have done anymore, I don't want to look at it; I don't want to fix it. That's a whole new me, because I'm 9-foot-tall and bulletproof. The illegals have changed everything."

Caught in the Path of Smugglers

She's right, and it's happening up and down the Arizona-Mexico border. A way of life is being run through a grinder. The way people think, how they go about their days, the way they work, the way they view the government—everything is changing. The smuggling trade has done this, by its sheer vastness, by the corrupting profits it produces.

Four Mexican towns abutting the Arizona border—Cananea, Altar, Naco and Agua Prieta—once quiet, traditional, mostly safe, anchored by a few old families, have become the primary smuggler-staging grounds. Their central plazas bustle with men, women and children who stay in the hotels, eat at the restaurants, buy hats, water bottles, clothes and shoes, and lounge around in public until it's time to hop a cab up to the line.

With them comes a post office wall full of bad guys allied with the movement of people and drugs north—enforcers, cutthroat coyotes, gang bosses, gang soldiers and on and on. Ordinary Mexicans, those not involved in the trade, don't like seeing these people filling their streets, the smugglers or their charges. They view the latter just as many Southern Arizonans do—as invaders.

They're from somewhere else. They dress differently. They look different. Fearful parents in these towns order their kids to stay indoors because they don't want them playing near the strangers. They call them *crosseros,* Spanish for "crossers." Stay away from the crossers, they tell their kids.

Losing Faith in Government

Close to dark, the cabs move out. From the right hilltop vantage point on the Arizona side, you can set up a lawn chair, fire up a cheap cigar and watch the invasion. You see the headlights streaming north, virtual convoys of Ford Crown Vics and beat-up old Mercurys filled to the windows with

soon-to-be illegals. From Cananea—where a legal taxi permit now costs an astonishing $15,000—they follow a dirt road that splits about l0 miles south of the border, one fork leading to the San Rafael Valley, in the mountains above Patagonia; the other to the San Pedro River Valley. In some cases, their feet don't hit the ground until they're literally a quarter-mile from the international fence.

It's an enormous business, and by any measure, a historic migration that is profoundly changing our country. But none of it is happening according to anybody's plan, certainly no American legislative body, and here's the biggest rub—it's a revolution of appetites. Mexico benefits by dumping off its poorest, avoiding the thorny responsibility of taking care of its own people, and it benefits from the cash these laborers send home, which, after oil, now constitutes that government's second-largest income source. But American appetites contribute greatly as well, specifically, our appetite for cheap labor and illicit drugs, which creates this powerful magnet effect, pulling people and dope to the border.

For those living on the line, that might be the worst of it—the recognition that their own people help fuel the daily chaos in which they live. It breeds in good citizens a corrosive cynicism, especially toward government—the same government to which they've been loyal all their lives, and to which they pay taxes and rely on for protection. . . .

Life in a War Zone

We're in Cowan's pickup truck now, driving across a broad stretch of southeast Arizona on an inspection tour of the war zone. The road we're traveling, Davis Road, is a particular menace, a stretch of hot blacktop that connects Highway 80, near Tombstone, with Highway 191 above Douglas.

It doesn't look especially perilous as it rolls over its 23-mile course. But the frequent dips and doglegs can leave drivers blind and at the mercy of smugglers who screech around the turns, sometimes at 100 mph. Cowan has twice been run off this road, and like others in the vicinity, she avoids traveling here at night. But she can't avoid it entirely, because portions of her 17,000-acre spread straddle Davis Road. . . .

Cowan keeps her own gun stashed under the console of her truck as we drive Davis Road, a supremely sane thing to do in a place where automatic-weapons fire from drug runners shatters the night quiet, and the daytime signs of smuggling are everywhere. Just look around: hubcaps hooked to range fences—signals for coyotes or druggies to cross there; cars with Florida and California plates, probably stolen, wheeling up and down the road; cattle gates mangled by smuggler cars. Cowan says every single gate along Davis Road has been smashed at least once.

With her weekend's work as a flight attendant done, Cowan would return to Arizona to run the ranch. Her husband, Bob, now 58, who lives and works in Phoenix running his own company, would drive the 200 miles to Tombstone, work with her on Saturdays and Sundays, then drive the 200 miles back to Phoenix on Sunday night. "It was very hard," Bob Giles says. "I wonder now how the hell I survived it. But we needed the money I sent down there to run the ranch."

But the damage caused by illegals in Cowan's absence kept getting worse, which made going to work a peculiar torture. She knew the odds were good that something bad was happening back on the ranch, but she didn't know what it was, and couldn't do anything about it anyway. "If I'm in Japan, what can I do about a problem in Arizona?" she asks. "All I can do is worry. It got to the point where I stopped calling home."

Illegal immigration became the hell that followed her around the world. There was no escaping it.

The Effects on Personal Property

On work weekends, her routine was to drive to Phoenix, catch a flight to L.A. and begin whatever assignment she had from Northwest. But while parking at the Phoenix airport, she said, she'd sometimes spot vehicles that she'd seen crossing her property the day before. The van or truck would park, and a dozen or more illegals would jump out, then head to the terminals to catch flights all across the country.

Sometimes, Cowan says, they were even on her flight to L.A., and because she speaks fluent Spanish, she was often asked to translate for, quite possibly, the very same individuals who'd just trashed her property.

"So many things have happened; I can't remember the chronology," Cowan says as we drive. "It all blends together."

She points to a pasture out the driver's window. "See, over there, I have a water line they keep cutting. So I rigged a faucet to it so they could drink without letting thousands of gallons drain out. But now they don't turn off the faucet, so the water runs out anyway."

Three north-south smuggling trails cross Cowan's land, and so many illegals walk them that they spooked her cattle, making them wild. Wild cattle don't gain as much weight, and when ranchers go to market, they sell quality and weight. She also followed a specific breeding program, but with her gates constantly left open and fences cut, her herds were becoming mongrelized and more susceptible to disease from neighboring cattle.

The Waste They Leave Behind

Cowan takes pride in how she manages her property, and in the past six years, she's received more than $375,000 in various grants for watershed rehabilitation. But the illegals leave behind piles and piles of human feces, which, after a rain, drain into the gullies and into the water supply.

"Should we test to see whether the feces in the water is from cows or people?" she asks. "In some places on my land, the native grasses have been trampled so heavily they won't grow back in my lifetime, and I'll be blamed."

In October [2004], she had nine at-risk kids out on the ranch picking up the illegals' garbage. They bagged a spectacular 6,080 pounds over five days. Four months later, it was all back again. She once called the EPA [Environmental Protection Agency] to report dumping of trash on state trust land. "Who's doing the dumping?" the bureaucrat asked.

"Illegals."

"Oh," said the bureaucrat. "We don't have a department to deal with that."

A Chilling Warning

One day, Cowan came across a blue Chevy pickup with a camper shell parked off Davis Road. Opposite it, on the other side of the road, there was a man standing near his truck. He pretended to be inspecting a sign that Cowan had put up. It said: "If this were Crawford, Texas, the National Guard would be here." She knew immediately the man was spotting for a coyote. She drove up to him and rolled down the window. He was Anglo, middle-aged, with tattoos along both arms and bright blue eyes.

In a sickeningly sweet voice, he said, "Oh, do you have a problem with illegals around here?"

Right then, the Chevy across the street bolted toward Tombstone. Even though she was pulling a 16-foot stock trailer, Cowan roared off in pursuit, punching 911 on her cell as she went. Tombstone's marshals intercepted the Chevy, finding 19 illegals inside. It was a good outcome, except that the coyotes, listening in on police scanners, heard everything the dispatcher and the deputies said. A few days later, a relative with ties to the sheriff's office delivered a chilling warning to Cowan: The coyotes know who you are, and they know where you are, so watch your back.

No Escaping the Invasion

Night begins to fall over a long day in the war zone. We're on Leslie Canyon Road, north of Douglas. It's two lanes, no traffic, mostly pastureland straddling the blacktop. One of the pastures belongs to Cowan, and there's a red truck parked on the shoulder near her pasture gate, two men standing beside it. They have no reason for being there, and they're acting strange.

Cowan drives a mile past the gate, pulls to the shoulder to wait, and we talk some more. She has remained even-tempered through the day, in the telling of every wrenching episode, and she has tried to keep perspective. She acknowledges that many factors have contributed to the difficulties of ranching in Southern Arizona—everything from the nine-year drought to housing development that has brought dogs that run in packs, killing calves.

But the illegals have been the tipping point. She could survive everything else. She can't survive the invasion. "It just consumes you," she says. "If you're not at a meeting talking about it, you're repairing something they've done, or you're standing on the highway looking at a dead animal, because they left a gate open. You have to decide: Is this more important than my quality of life, my health, my marriage?"

The Emotional Toll

We double back—to check on the mysterious red truck and the two men. They're gone. Then Cowan spots them again, down the pasture road, about a half-mile beyond the gate. The men have cut the lock, closed the gate again and looped the chain back into place. You have to look closely to see it, which is no doubt what they wanted.

Now it starts—the uncertainty, the jangled nerves. Who are these guys? Are they using the pasture for a drug drop? Are these the coyotes out to get even with Cowan?

She gets on her cell and calls the Cochise County sheriff. Then we wait, wondering if this time, she'll have to pull that gun.

It's a rotten feeling. It shouldn't be this way. For the first time all day, Cowan's temper cracks, and under the strain, she cries. She makes a fist. "I feel so violated. I just get wound up so tight I want to scream. It's just goes on and on and on, every day."

This event ends much better than it might have. The men tell sheriff's deputies they're Douglas residents and American citizens out hunting for the afternoon. They claim the lock was already cut when they came along. Cowan wants to press charges, saying she's placed legal notices in three area newspapers, describing the property in English and Spanish and stating that her land is off limits to hunters, and the pasture fence is plastered with "Keep Out" signs.

But on the border, gates mean nothing. Your possessions are up for grabs. Private property means nothing.

Analyze This Reading

1. What does the writer mean when he refers to immigration across the Mexico-Arizona border as a "revolution of appetites"?
2. The writer personalizes ideas about immigration by drawing on the experiences of Ruth Cowan. Refer to some of these experiences, and describe how they help deliver these ideas.
3. To what values, attitudes, and beliefs does the writer appeal? In what ways are these appeals effective or ineffective?
4. While the writer does not include a claim or reasons supporting a claim, he does supply much specific information. Based on this information, what could the writer claim if he wanted to convert this report into an argument?

Respond To This Reading

1. In your view, why is immigration legislation reform taking so long? Why is enforcement of existing legislation so difficult?
2. Like most of us, Ruth Cowan is protective of her neighborhood, even though her 17,000-acre property is unlike what we own or rent. How is immigration affecting your neighborhood and other neighborhoods in your community? How do local media report on this issue? What attitudes about immigration are not reported in local media?
3. Imagine building a middle-ground argument in response to the issue described in this report. What two extreme positions would you identify? What middle ground would you argue for?

ABOUT THIS READING

Raised in New York City, Manissa McCleave Maharawal and Isabelle Nastasia are students in the City University of New York (CUNY) system. Maharawal studies in the anthropology department of the CUNY Graduate Center and is an organizer with the People of Color Caucus, the Free University, and Occupy Wall Street.

Nastasia studies critical pedagogy and intersectionality at Brooklyn College and is an organizer with the Brooklyn College Student Union and with New York Students Rising. This op-ed appeared in *Truthout*.

Why Race Matters After Sandy

By Isabelle Nastasia and Manissa McCleave Maharawal

During the fall of 1962, residents of the Bedford-Stuyvesant neighborhood of Brooklyn saw the trash accumulating on their sidewalks and realized that the city didn't care about them the way it did about others. Their children had to play in stinky garbage while other neighborhoods had trees and parks. They complained to elected officials and the Sanitation Department, but the problem never got better. So, in response, they began organizing weekly garbage clean-ups across Bed-Stuy—a temporary solution—while also working toward a holistic solution to the abundance of garbage and the scarcity of city resources devoted to the area through on-the-ground organizing. For two years residents and members of the Brooklyn chapter of the Congress of Racial Equality (CORE) organized tirelessly for increased garbage collection, asserting over and over again that "taxation without sanitation is tyranny."

For decades, the red-lining of black and brown neighborhoods by real estate agencies, banks and insurance companies has starved these communities of investment and served to geographically marginalize poor people. This history of economic and social marginalization helped ensure that these communities are also the ones hardest hit by disasters such as Hurricane Sandy. The challenge now facing Occupy Sandy and similar grassroots recovery efforts is to build community power around these structural inequalities through an environmental justice framework, while confronting environmental racism head on.

The concept of environmental racism emerged in the 1980s in East Harlem and the South Bronx as residents realized that their neighborhoods were home to waste processing plants that process over half of the city's commercial waste (in the case of the Bronx) and a disproportionate number of polluting bus depots (in the case of Harlem). These facilities were causing frequent illness, high rates of cancer and chronic asthma among children. Environmental racism gives a name to the harmful burden of facilities such as waste transplant stations, bus depots and power plants on communities where people of color tend to live.

This kind of analysis is important for two reasons. Firstly, it articulates that environmental factors are part of broader systematic disenfranchisement. Upper-middle class white neighborhoods are able to keep polluting facilities out while working-class neighborhoods of color get disproportionately saddled with this harmful infrastructure. Secondly, this analysis came from activists living and working in these neighborhoods, standing up against noxious facilities and clamoring for meaningful job opportunities, well-funded public schools, healthy and affordable food, and parks and other community spaces.

After Sandy, people in the affected communities are feeling the effects of this same phenomenon of environmental racism. Speaking to the Associated Press, one Staten Island resident, a Mexican immigrant named Miguel Alaracon Morales, explained, "My son has asthma and now he is worse. The house has this smell of humidity and sea water. It is not safe to live there. I am starting to feel sick, too." As he spoke, he held his two-year-old asthmatic son, Josias. This storm, and all disasters of its type, are not a "great equalizer," as is often claimed; they're actually only a disaster for the 99 percent, and in particular for the poorest and most disenfranchised members of our society.

In New York City's post-Sandy moment there are lessons to be learned from the community-led centers that emerged in New Orleans after Katrina. Our School at Blair Grocery, a community home-school and urban farm—which Isabelle helped to establish and has spent every summer since 2008 working with—is currently the only school that serves high school-aged youth and the only food vendor besides a corner store in the Lower Ninth Ward, whose population is down to 4,000 from over 14,000 before the storm. This independent alternative school confronts structural disenfranchisement by highlighting four main community needs: meaningful employment, healthy and affordable food, education for young people, and community-led public planning. Helping students earn their GEDs and avoid the school-to-prison pipeline, Our School at Blair Grocery works with black youth from the Lower Ninth with the long-term goal of building alternative institutions for the neighborhood that can withstand any crisis: economic, political and environmental.

In working with these youth one learns that they wouldn't articulate their day-to-day activities as "resistance," and they would also never call it "recovery." The students understand that the challenges their neighborhood faces are rooted in a history that goes much further back than Katrina, so their efforts are not merely an attempt to return their community to the status quo before the storm. The teachers and students at the school are working together to build an institution outside of the corporate, top-down model offered to them. This vision allows them to re-envision how they generate and consume energy, as well as how to transform the production, distribution and consumption components of the food system—local visions of energy independence and food sovereignty.

In comparison to Occupy Sandy, "mutual aid" was not a term that was used in the context of New Orleans because it was seen as a contradiction— outsider volunteers aiding residents was not "mutual" or egalitarian, per se. Many of the organizations that put racial justice at the center of their analysis instead endorsed the strategy of "bottom-up" organizing, which prioritizes the needs of poor people of color as those who are most affected by the disaster unveiled by Katrina. The environmental justice movement has always had "bottom-up" organizing at the center of its strategies— mostly because few outside of these communities, who aren't suffering from asthma and high cancer rates, will fight against their root causes. Now in New York City, bottom-up organizing is needed again.

The community-led models of CORE and Our School at Blair Grocery demonstrate how to employ an analysis of environmental racism that takes into account the intersections of race, class, public planning and environmental degradation. Occupy Sandy's slogan "solidarity, not charity" is a starting point, but it doesn't go far enough in pushing allies from outside the most affected areas to understand how to avoid perpetuating the system they benefit from in recovery efforts. If we placed bottom-up organizing alongside mutual aid in our tools of recovery, it would mean organizers and volunteers taking direction from residents—not only to get back on their feet but to transform their communities as they see fit.

In doing, we must also continue to practice direct action and make demands of city government. In 1962, after the city kept ignoring their demands, CORE organizers devised the campaign Operation Clean Sweep. Residents used brooms to sweep up the garbage left by the city on the side of the street, while CORE trucked the garbage to downtown Brooklyn and dumped it on the doorstep of Brooklyn's Borough Hall on September 15, 1962. CORE demanded a "First-Class Bedford-Stuyvesant Community" and "Integration with Better Sanitation." (Yotam Marom also told this story in his most recent article at Waging Nonviolence.)

Occupy Sandy needs to be not just another form of relief, or even recovery, but a force for social change that simultaneously works on a comprehensive strategy for community power. It needs to build infrastructure around housing, healthcare, food and energy sustainability that also make life easier for those most affected by environmental racism on a day-to-day basis. While protest should always be a part of our long-term strategy, we believe that Occupy Sandy must, to some extent, continue moving the solely protest-driven model adopted by Occupy Wall Street to embody movement practices led by communities.

This is already happening. While portrayals of Occupy Sandy in publications like The *New York Times* offer a depoliticized "feel-good relief" model of what is taking place, long-term strategy has been the goal since the beginning of the effort. "We were always thinking long-term," says Michael Premo, an Occupy Sandy organizer with experience in post-Katrina recovery. "Since day one we have been thinking about building a long-term grassroots resistance network that can win shit."

Learning from the organizing of CORE in Bed-Stuy in the 1960s, the environmental justice movement of the 1980s and post-Katrina models of alternative institution-building, we must realize that only through bottom-up, community-led structures can we confront systemic inequity in these neighborhoods. Doing this means taking on issues of privilege and racism, issues that Occupy Wall Street often has had trouble addressing. It means confronting supposed colorblindness and putting a racial justice analysis at the center of the analysis. This needs to happen in orientation trainings for volunteers, in organizing meetings, in our relationship-building with community leaders, in how aid is distributed, and in the physical gutting and rebuilding of people's homes.

We are making the road by walking right now. We have the paths left by past organizing models as reference points, but it is up to us to create the local solutions we need to address the global climate crisis in the midst of a racist society.

Analyze This Reading

1. What do the writers mean by the term "environmental racism?" Identify examples used to define this term.
2. How are activists responding to the devastation of Hurricane Sandy?
3. Discuss the differences the writers highlight between "mutual aid" and "bottom-up organizing" as responses to natural disasters like Katrina and Sandy.

Respond To This Reading

1. Where are landfills and facilities that pollute located in your community? Do their locations follow the pattern described in this reading?
2. CORE and Occupy Sandy in many ways are relief organization that exist outside the sphere of government agencies. What do these organizations offer to communities in trouble that the government does not? As a community member, are you more inclined to support outside-the-mainstream organizers than government relief efforts? Explain.

ABOUT THIS READING

Writer Leyla Kokmen is the program coordinator for the Health Journalism graduate program at the University of Minnesota. She also has worked as a staff reporter for several newspapers, including the *Seattle Times* and the *Denver Post*. This reading appeared in *Utne Reader*, a bimonthly magazine that gathers and reprints articles and essays on new cultural trends.

Environmental Justice for All

By Leyla Kokmen

Manuel Pastor ran bus tours of Los Angeles a few years back. These weren't the typical sojourns to Disneyland or the MGM studios, though; they were expeditions to some of the city's most environmentally blighted neighborhoods—where railways, truck traffic, and refineries converge, and where people live 200 feet from the freeway.

The goal of the "toxic tours," explains Pastor, a professor of geography and of American studies and ethnicity at the University of Southern California (USC), was to let public officials, policy makers, and donors talk to residents in low-income neighborhoods about the environmental hazards they lived with every day and to literally see, smell, and feel the effects.

"It's a pretty effective forum," says Pastor, who directs USC's Program for Environmental and Regional Equity, noting that a lot of the "tourists" were eager to get back on the bus in a hurry. "When you're in these neighborhoods, your lungs hurt."

Modern Environmental Activists

Like the tours, Pastor's research into the economic and social issues facing low-income urban communities highlights the environmental disparities that endure in California and across the United States. As stories about global warming, sustainable energy, and climate change make headlines, the fact that some neighborhoods, particularly low-income and minority communities, are disproportionately toxic and poorly regulated has, until recently, been all but ignored.

A new breed of activists and social scientists are starting to capitalize on the moment. In principle they have much in common with the environmental justice movement, which came of age in the late 1970s and early 1980s, when grassroots groups across the country began protesting the presence of landfills and other environmentally hazardous facilities in predominantly poor and minority neighborhoods.

How do we get the work, wealth, and health benefits of the green economy to the people who most need those benefits?

In practice, though, the new leadership is taking a broader-based, more inclusive approach. Instead of fighting a proposed refinery here or an expanded freeway there, all along trying to establish that systematic racism is at work in corporate America, today's environmental justice movement is focusing on proactive responses to the social ills and economic roadblocks that if removed would clear the way to a greener planet.

The new movement assumes that society as a whole benefits by guaranteeing safe jobs, both blue-collar and white-collar, that pay a living wage. That universal health care would both decrease disease and increase awareness about the quality of everyone's air and water. That better public education and easier access to job training, especially in industries that are emerging to address the global energy crisis, could reduce crime, boost self-esteem, and lead to a homegrown economic boon.

That green rights, green justice, and green equality should be the environmental movement's new watchwords.

"This is the new civil rights of the 21st century," proclaims environmental justice activist Majora Carter.

A lifelong resident of Hunts Point in the South Bronx, Carter is executive director of Sustainable South Bronx, an eight-year-old nonprofit created to advance the environmental and economic future of the community. Under the stewardship of Carter, who received a prestigious MacArthur Fellowship in 2005, the organization has managed a number of projects, including a successful grassroots campaign to stop a planned solid waste facility in Hunts Point that would have processed 40 percent of New York City's garbage.

Her neighborhood endures exhaust from some 60,000 truck trips every week and has four power plants and more than a dozen waste facilities. "It's like a cloud," Carter says. "You deal with that, you're making a dent."

The first hurdle Carter and a dozen staff members had to face was making the environment relevant to poor people and people of color who have long felt disenfranchised from mainstream environmentalism, which tends to focus on important but distinctly nonurban issues, such as preserving

Arctic wildlife or Brazilian rainforest. For those who are struggling to make ends meet, who have to cobble together adequate health care, education, and job prospects, who feel unsafe on their own streets, these grand ideas seem removed from reality.

Expanding the Green Movement

That's why the green rights argument is so powerful: It spans public health, community development, and economic growth to make sure that the green revolution isn't just for those who can afford a Prius. It means cleaning up blighted communities like the South Bronx to prevent potential health problems and to provide amenities like parks to play in, clean trails to walk on, and fresh air to breathe. It also means building green industries into the local mix, to provide healthy jobs for residents in desperate need of a livable wage.

Historically, mainstream environmental organizations have been made up mostly of white staffers and have focused more on the ephemeral concept of the environment rather than on the people who are affected. . . . Today, though, as climate change and gas prices dominate public discourse, the concepts driving the new environmental justice movement are starting to catch on. Just recently, for instance, *New York Times* columnist Thomas Friedman dubbed the promise of public investment in the green economy the "Green New Deal."

Van Jones, whom Friedman celebrated in print last October, is president of the Ella Baker Center for Human Rights in Oakland, California. To help put things in context, Jones briefly sketches the history of environmentalism:

The first wave was conservation, led first by Native Americans who respected and protected the land, then later by Teddy Roosevelt, John Muir, and other Caucasians who sought to preserve green space.

The second wave was regulation, which came in the 1970s and 1980s with the establishment of the Environmental Protection Agency (EPA) and Earth Day. Increased regulation brought a backlash against poor people and people of color, Jones says. White, affluent communities sought to prevent environmental hazards from entering their neighborhoods. This "not-in-my-backyard" [NIMBY] attitude spurred a new crop of largely grassroots environmental justice advocates who charged businesses with unfairly targeting low-income and minority communities. "The big challenge was NIMBY-ism," Jones says, noting that more toxins from power plants and landfills were dumped on people of color.

The third wave of environmentalism, Jones says, is happening today. It's a focus on investing in solutions that lead to "eco-equity." And, he notes, it invokes a central question: "How do we get the work, wealth, and health benefits of the green economy to the people who most need those benefits?"

Poor Communities Suffer Most

There are a number of reasons why so many environmental hazards end up in the poorest communities.

Property values in neighborhoods with environmental hazards tend to be lower, and that's where poor people—and often poor people of color—can afford to buy or rent a home. Additionally, businesses and municipalities often choose to build power plants in or expand freeways through low-income neighborhoods because the land is cheaper and poor residents have less power and are unlikely to have the time or organizational infrastructure to evaluate or fight development.

"Wealthy neighborhoods are able to resist, and low-income communities of color will find their neighborhoods plowed down and [find themselves] living next to a freeway that spews pollutants next to their schools," USC's Manuel Pastor says.

Moreover, regulatory systems, including the EPA and various local and state zoning and environmental regulatory bodies, allow piecemeal development of toxic facilities. Each new chemical facility goes through an individual permit process, which doesn't always take into account the overall picture in the community. The regulatory system isn't equipped to address potentially dangerous cumulative effects.

In a single neighborhood, Pastor says, you might have toxins that come from five different plants that are regulated by five different authorities. Each plant might not be considered dangerous on its own, but if you throw together all the emissions from those static sources and then add in emissions from moving sources, like diesel-powered trucks, "you've created a toxic soup," he says.

In one study of air quality in the nine-county San Francisco Bay Area, Pastor found that race, even more than income, determined who lived in more toxic communities. That 2007 report, "Still Toxic After All These Years: Air Quality and Environmental Justice in the San Francisco Bay Area," published by the Center for Justice, Tolerance & Community at the University of California at Santa Cruz, explored data from the EPA's Toxic Release Inventory, which reports toxic air emissions from large industrial facilities. The researchers examined race, income, and the likelihood of living near such a facility.

More than 40 percent of African American households earning less than $10,000 a year lived within a mile of a toxic facility, compared to 30 percent of Latino households and fewer than 20 percent of white households.

As income rose, the percentages dropped across the board but were still higher among minorities. Just over 20 percent of African American and Latino households making more than $100,000 a year lived within a mile of a toxic facility, compared to just 10 percent of white households.

The same report finds a connection between race and the risk of cancer or respiratory hazards, which are both associated with environmental air toxics, including emissions both from large industrial facilities and from mobile sources. The researchers looked at data from the National Air Toxics Assessment, which includes estimates of such ambient air toxics as diesel particulate matter, benzene, and lead and mercury compounds. The areas with the highest risk for cancer had the highest proportion of African American and Asian residents, the lowest rate of home ownership, and the highest proportion of people in poverty. The same trends existed for areas with the highest risk for respiratory hazards.

According to the report, "There is a general pattern of environmental inequity in the Bay Area: Densely populated communities of color characterized by relatively low wealth and income and a larger share of immigrants disproportionately bear the hazard and risk burden for the region."

The Impact of Racism

Twenty years ago, environmental and social justice activists probably would have presented the disparities outlined in the 2007 report as evidence of corporations deliberately targeting minority communities with hazardous waste. That's what happened in 1987, when the United Church of Christ released findings from a study that showed toxic waste facilities were more likely to be located near minority communities. At the 1991 People of Color Environmental Leadership Summit, leaders called the disproportionate burden both racist and genocidal.

Framing the environmental debate in terms of opportunities will engage the people who need the most help.

In their 2007 book *BreakThrough: From the Death of Environmentalism to the Politics of Possibility*, authors Ted Nordhaus and Michael Shellenberger take issue with this strategy. . . . They argue that some of the research conducted in the name of environmental justice was too narrowly focused and that activists have spent too much time looking for conspiracies of environmental racism and not enough time looking at the multifaceted problems facing poor people and people of color.

"Poor Americans of all races, and poor Americans of color in particular, disproportionately suffer from social ills of every kind," they write. "But toxic waste and air pollution are far from being the most serious threats to their health and well-being. Moreover, the old narratives of intentional discrimination fail to explain or address these disparities. Disproportionate environmental health outcomes can no more be reduced to intentional discrimination than can disproportionate economic and educational outcomes. They are due to a larger and more complex set of historic, economic, and social causes."

Today's environmental justice advocates would no doubt take issue with the finer points of Nordhaus and Shellenberger's criticism—in particular, that institutional racism is a red herring. Activists and researchers are acutely aware that they are facing a multifaceted spectrum of issues, from air pollution to a dire lack of access to regular health care. It's because of that complexity, however, that they are now more geared toward proactively addressing an array of social and political concerns.

"The environmental justice movement grew out of putting out fires in the community and stopping bad things from happening, like a landfill," says Martha Dina Argüello, executive director of Physicians for Social Responsibility-Los Angeles, an organization that connects environmental groups with doctors to promote public health. "The more this work gets done, the more you realize you have to go upstream. We need to stop bad things from happening."

"We can fight pollution and poverty at the same time and with the same solutions and methods," says the Ella Baker Center's Van Jones.

Poor people and people of color have borne all the burden of the polluting industries of today, he says, while getting almost none of the benefit from the shift to the green economy. Jones stresses that he is not an environmental justice activist, but a "social-uplift environmentalist." Instead of concentrating on the presence of pollution and toxins in low-income communities, Jones prefers to focus on building investment in clean, green, healthy industries that can help those communities. Instead of focusing on the burdens, he focuses on empowerment.

Spreading the Message

With that end in mind, the Ella Baker Center's Green-Collar Jobs Campaign plans to launch the Oakland Green Jobs Corps this spring. The initiative, according to program manager Aaron Lehmer, received $250,000 from the city of Oakland and will give people ages 18 to 35 with barriers to employment (contact with the criminal justice system, long-term unemployment) opportunities and paid internships for training in new energy skills like installing solar panels and making buildings more energy efficient.

The concept has gained national attention. It's the cornerstone of the Green Jobs Act of 2007, which authorizes $125 million annually for "green-collar" job training that could prepare 30,000 people a year for jobs in key trades, such as installing solar panels, weatherizing buildings, and maintaining wind farms. The act was signed into law in December as part of the Energy Independence and Security Act.

While Jones takes the conversation to a national level, Majora Carter is focusing on empowerment in one community at a time. Her successes at Sustainable South Bronx include the creation of a 10-week program that offers South Bronx and other New York City residents hands-on training in brownfield remediation and ecological restoration. The organization has also raised $30 million for a bicycle and pedestrian greenway along the South Bronx waterfront that will provide both open space and economic development opportunities.

As a result of those achievements, Carter gets calls from organizations across the country. In December [2007] she traveled to Kansas City, Missouri, to speak to residents, environmentalists, businesses, and students. She mentions exciting work being done by Chicago's Blacks in Green collective, which aims to mobilize the African American community around environmental issues. Naomi Davis, the collective's founder, told Chicago Public Radio in November [2007] that the group plans to develop environmental and economic opportunities—a "green village" with greenways, light re-manufacturing, ecotourism, and energy-efficient affordable housing—in one of Chicago's most blighted areas.

Carter stresses that framing the environmental debate in terms of opportunities will engage the people who need the most help. It's about investing in the green economy, creating jobs, and building spaces that aren't environmentally challenged. It won't be easy, she says. But it's essential to dream big.

"It's about sacrifice," she says, "for something better and bigger than you could have possibly imagined."

Analyze This Reading

1. What are "toxic tours"? How do the tours connect to the environmental justice movement?
2. According to the writer, what is the focus of the new environmental justice movement? Why does environmental justice activist Majora Carter consider this movement the "new civil rights of the 21st century"?
3. How does the environmental movement differ from mainstream environmentalism?
4. How does Van Jones, President Obama's former director of the Environmental Protection Agency, summarize the history of environmentalism in America? Describe the research the writer brings in to support Jones's contention that we are experiencing a third wave of environmentalism. Why does Jones consider himself a "social-uplift environmentalist" rather than an environmental justice activist?

Respond To This Reading

1. The writer refers to activists in the new environmental justice movement as wanting to frame the environmental debate in terms of opportunities instead of arguing that "systematic racism is at work in corporate America." Following through with this idea, do you see opportunities for greening lower income neighborhoods in your community? If yes, what are they?
2. Do you consider yourself either a social-uplift environmentalist or environmental justice activist? If yes, what influences your thinking? What work needs to be pursued in your community?
3. What single issue in your local environment needs attention? Were you to build an argument in response to this issue, what would you claim, and how would you support your claim?

ABOUT THIS READING

Writer Tim Guest, a contributor to *The Guardian* and *Daily Telegraph*, both British newspapers, here looks at the escalating problem of virtual crime spilling over into the real world. This article first appeared in *New Scientist*, a magazine, in the words of its founders, "for all those men and women who are interested in scientific discovery, and in its industrial, commercial and social consequences."

Crime in Virtual Worlds Is Impacting Real Life

By Tim Guest

As murders go, it was an open and shut case. In February last year [2005], Qiu Chengwei, a 41-year-old man from Shanghai, loaned his prized sword, called a dragon sabre, to his 26-year-old friend Zhu Caoyuan. Without telling Qiu, Zhu sold it for 7,200 yuan [$950], pocketing the proceeds. Qiu complained to the police that Zhu had stolen his sword, but they refused to help. So early one morning a month later, Qiu broke into Zhu's house and stabbed him to death.

Qiu confessed to police, and a few months later was sentenced to life imprisonment. But while the murder was quickly solved, the question of whether Zhu was guilty of theft is still [as of 2006] unsettled. In the trial, the court heard that the police refused to help Qiu because in their eyes Zhu hadn't broken any laws—the sword wasn't real. It was a virtual weapon that Qiu's character gave Zhu's in an online fantasy game called Legends of Mir, which has over a million players.

The murder is one of a string of similar cases in which virtual crimes have spilled into the real world. It is a phenomenon that has caught players, games companies and police forces off guard, and they are just beginning to experiment with ways to deal with it. The consensus is to settle disputes and punish bad behaviour inside the game if at all possible. To do this some players have organised virtual mafias to help other players get even, and recently some games companies have begun meting out justice themselves by banishing the evil-doing characters to what is effectively a virtual jail, and even crucifying them.

Lawbreaking Is No Surprise

When you consider the number of people playing these games, it is perhaps not surprising that some break the law. Each week, around 30 million people worldwide abandon reality for imaginary realms with names like EverQuest, EVE Online and World of Warcraft. While there have always been games that encourage "criminal" behaviour as part of the game, there has been a big change recently. What you do in the game can now make real money, and lots of it.

Virtual items began to acquire a real-world value when new players wanted to advance quickly in these games without having to spend hours looking for weapons or gaining magical powers. This created a grey market for rare virtual goods, first on eBay and then on scores of other websites set up to help this trade. Soon, exchange rates between game money and real currencies emerged that have helped line the pockets of thousands of players.

For example, in 2004, in a game called Project Entropia, David Storey of Sydney, Australia, bought a virtual island populated by virtual wild animals for $26,500—not for fun, but for profit. He now charges a tax for virtual hunting rights, and rents virtual beachside property, from which he has already earned $10,000. Earlier this month [May 2006], MindArk, Project Entropia's developer, blurred the boundary between the virtual and the real worlds still further when it launched a cash card players can use at ATMs around the world to withdraw money against their virtual hoards, calculated according to the Project Entropia exchange rate. In 2004 IGE, a virtual item trading website based in Boca Raton, Florida, estimated the global market in virtual goods to be worth around $880 million a year and growing. When this kind of money is involved, it's a fair bet that from time to time virtual crime is going to turn into the real thing.

And games are full of virtual crimes. Mafia men, pimps, extortionists, counterfeiters and assassins populate various virtual worlds, eager to make a fast buck. There's even a terrorist collective in one game hell-bent on bringing about the end of their own online world. Most keep their activities confined to the virtual, but the line is becoming increasingly blurred.

No Laws Against Virtual Crime

Take the tale of Istvaan Shogaatsu—an infamous character in EVE Online, a space piracy game—played by dental technician Tom Czerniawski from Toronto, Canada. Shogaatsu is the CEO of Guiding Hand, a mercenary corporation that destroys other players' characters for profit. Czerniawski describes him as "a cut-throat without morals or mercy."

In May 2005, Czerniawski/Shogaatsu was contacted with an anonymous offer of 1 billion ISK—the Eve currency, worth around . . . [$700] when traded in the real world—for a "Pearl Harbor" style attack on another player's corporation, Ubiqua Seraph. Arenis Xemdal, Guiding Hand's "valentine operative" played by Bojan Momic, also of Toronto, spent four months wooing the head of Ubiqua, known as Mirial, who then hired him. To make Xemdal look good, Shogaatsu staged raids deliberately intended to fail, and four months later Mirial appointed Xemdal as her trusted lieutenant. She handed him the access codes to Ubiqua's warehouses: the key to her virtual safe.

It was time for Shogaatsu and his associates to make their move. A Guiding Hand battleship appeared near Mirial's position. She fled for a nearby space station, but before she could reach safety, Xemdal turned his lasers on her. Across the galaxy, Guiding Hand operatives looted six warehouses. Shogaatsu delivered Mirial's corpse to the client, but kept the stolen property as spoils of war.

The EVE developers, CCP, based in Reykjavik, Iceland, looked fondly on Istvaan's operation—not least because, as the story spread through the Internet, the game gained thousands of new subscribers. But many players were outraged. After the heist, Czerniawski received nine email and telephone death threats. The cash and merchandise stolen by Guiding Hand amounted to 30 billion ISK—about . . . [$20,000]. To Mirial and others connected with the Ubiqua Corporation, the loss felt very real.

The incident shone a bright light on the frontier-style ethos of many games. It had taken Mirial over a year to build up her virtual empire, but she had no recourse: no laws protect her players from virtual losses. Games developers need it to remain that way, as they want to keep their responsibility to a minimum. Gaming would be unsustainable if every unpleasant act became punishable in the real world.

In spite of this, Czerniawski told me he and his Guiding Hand co-conspirators were concerned they might be accused of committing a real-world crime, such as wire fraud, so to avoid this they were careful to keep all contact within the game.

Taking Crime Beyond Virtual Boundaries

What happens when the distinction between actions inside the game and outside it is less clear? For example, is exploiting a bug in a game to make hard cash breaking the rules? In December 2004, Noah Burn, a 24-year-old from Myrtle Beach, South Carolina, did just that in EverQuest II.

In the real world Burn worked as a furniture salesman. So when he got bored of his exploration of the virtual world, he set up a "furniture" store inside the game. His character, a barbarian called Methical, found places to buy desirable virtual goods cheaply and then sold them at a profit. One afternoon he put a chair up for auction—this normally removes the item from the virtual world. Later that day he got a message from someone who had bought the chair, but when he looked over to his virtual showroom, the chair was still there. Sitting at his computer, Burn realised he had stumbled on a gold mine. He quickly sent a message to his friends online: "I think I just duped [duplicated] something." Burn had discovered a bug in the game's code which meant he could "dupe" items at will. Selling real furniture pays well, he says, "but not as well as in EverQuest II."

Along with a friend, Burn set up a production line, copying expensive candelabras that players used to decorate their virtual homes. After a day of trading, they had two virtual platinum pieces—at a time when one platinum piece sold for $300. The next night they duped, Burn says, "until our eyes bled." Bored with candelabras, they switched to a virtual animal called a Halasian Mauler dog, the highest value item they could dupe. In virtual terms, the two were rich. They bought virtual mansions, the best spells and the most expensive horses they could find.

Then they took a step out of the game and began to sell the proceeds of their virtual counterfeiting for dollars. Burn knew he was doing something questionable and every day expected Sony, the owner of EverQuest II, to fix the bug. Two weeks later they were still selling, now at 50 percent of the market rate, just to shift more platinum. They were scammed too: they lost $5,000 when buyers took their items without paying. But they kept on selling. They sold so much virtual currency that prices dropped 60 percent. Burn made so much money that he decided to consult a lawyer to see if he was breaking the law. The lawyer threw up his hands. "He had no idea what I was talking about."

Companies are starting to accept that some sort of policing is necessary. As a rule, the medieval approach prevails—those who break the rules are suspended, or exiled from the virtual world.

Players began to post complaints about the sudden inflation on various web forums. Then three weeks after he discovered the bug, Burn logged on to find it had been fixed. Their spree was at an end. Burn says his little cabal made $100,000 in total, of which he got the lion's share. "It has allowed me to go to Hawaii and Paris, as well as pay off student loans," he says.

Sony banned some of Burn's accounts the next day, but there was no way of working out which items were counterfeit and so no way of penalising him. "It's like the Wild West right now, and we're kind of like these outlaws," Burn says. "I feel like Billy the Kid."

Real Consequences—and Real Protection

Burn may have made real money, but the consequences of his actions were confined to the game world. Others have bridged the gap between the two. Between October and December last year [2005] a group of residents in a game called Second Life—who cannot be named for legal reasons—experimented with attacks on the fabric of the Second Life universe itself. They constructed self-replicating objects which copied themselves over and over until the whole universe became overcrowded and the game's servers crashed. One group even created an object resembling a block of virtual Semtex [a plastic explosive]. Just like a real bomb, when it exploded, the servers running that section of the universe went down, destroying the realm and everything in it.

Linden Lab, which runs Second Life, says the attacks cost the company time and money and were a clear violation of US Code Title 18, section 1030—which outlaws "denial-of-service" attacks. The law says, in effect, that if you knowingly transmit information to a computer involved in communication beyond the boundaries of the state that results in $5,000 or more of damage, you face a hefty fine and up to 10 years' imprisonment. Linden Lab called in the FBI, in what is probably the first criminal investigation of activities that originated inside a virtual world. "These attacks affect the ability of our servers to provide a service for which people are paying us money," says Ginsu Yoon, Linden Lab's counsel.

In Linden Lab's eyes, at least, planting a virtual bomb should be considered a real crime.

It's not only the games companies that say in-game crimes have real consequences. The player who owned Mirial spent a large amount of time and effort amassing her virtual wealth. Its theft and her character's murder was a tangible loss. Cases like these only serve to emphasise that the issue of ingame justice is becoming a serious concern.

To date, the absence of law enforcement inside these games has led to players setting up their own alternatives. Jeremy Chase, a customer service manager and IT specialist based in Sacramento, California, formed the Sim Mafia within the game Sims Online. Players could hire Chase and his virtual employees to perform all the services you might expect from a bona fide crime family.

As the popularity of Sims Online waned, Chase moved his crime family to another game run by Linden Lab, a free-form universe called Second Life, where he renamed himself Marsellus Wallace. Now, for the right amount of virtual currency, Chase's family will "sort out" any problems you have with another Second Life resident. . . . In the real world Chase's mafia activities would pit him against the law. Online, Wallace is well known to Linden Lab and has become a minor celebrity within the game. For now he continues to act with impunity.

Laying Down the Virtual Law

But slowly, things are changing. For many people, online gaming is now a major part of life—a third of Second Life players spend more time in the game than in the real world. So companies are starting to accept that some sort of policing is necessary. As a rule, the medieval approach prevails—those who break the rules are suspended, or exiled from the virtual world. Linden Lab now runs a points system: the more frequently you misbehave and the worse the transgression, the more negative points you get. The higher the rate at which you accrue points, the more severe the punishment. "Violations that target other characters or make Second Life feel unsafe or unwelcoming are dealt with more aggressively," says Linden Lab's Daniel Huebner.

Banishment is a blunt tool, however, as players can simply creep back into the game under another name and identity. And in any case, the issue of punishment per se throws up a tough question for games companies: isn't the point of the virtual worlds to escape the restrictions of the real one?

So Linden Lab is testing an alternative approach of rehabilitating offenders. In January, Second Life resident Nimrod Yaffle reverse engineered some computer code to help him steal another player's virtual property. He was reported and became the first resident to be sent to a new area of the game, The Cornfield—a kind of virtual prison. Every time he logged on all he could do was ride a virtual tractor and watch an educational film about a boy who drifts into a life of crime.

Other games are also trying to keep punishments in tune with their setting. For example, Cynewulf, played by an electrical engineer from Flint, Michigan, is perhaps the only American alive who has some experience of crucifixion. He is a resident of a new game called Roma Victor, which is based in Roman Britain, and a barbarian. In April [2006] he spent seven days nailed to a cross for ruthlessly killing new players as soon as they entered the game.

The punishment had an effect. "It was surprisingly agonising for just being a game," Cynewulf says. "Being jeered at by the Romans while immobilised is not much fun. Particularly since they are all weaklings who deserve to die by my sword."

Acts like Cynewulf's virtual murders can usually be clearly labelled as crimes. But what about more subtle forms of disagreement? What if your neighbour builds a huge tower block that blocks the light to your virtual garden? Who can you turn to? Last year, two law students, known in Second Life as Judge Mason and Judge Churchill, decided to solve this problem by opening the Second Life Superior Court. Residents could take their arguments, large or small, to the in-world courtroom. With reference to the Second Life rules, and their own knowledge of real-world law, the judges would resolve disputes.

Predictably, not all Second Life residents liked the idea. "What a mind-numbingly futile exercise," Tony Walsh wrote on a Second Life bulletin board. "So now we have yet another level of tedious bureaucracy to Second Life." Others wondered whether the court would have any teeth to back up a judgement, or even what would happen if a Linden (a character played by an employee of Linden Lab) was the target of a case. To clarify their non-involvement, Linden Lab requested that the court change its name. It is now the Metaverse Superior Court. With its teeth removed, the court fell into disuse. The idea isn't totally dead: there is one small community in Second Life, called New Altonburg, that successfully polices itself. Linden Lab would like more communities to handle their own disputes, and its wish may not be that far-fetched.

If crime in the online community continues to flourish, expect the laws and regulations of the real world to eventually catch up with residents of Second Life and other virtual worlds. When that happens, you can bet it won't be long before they start wishing for a third life to escape to.

Analyze This Reading

1. The writer uses the term "frontier-style ethos" to refer to the behavior of some virtual game players. Define this term, and summarize some of the examples the writer uses.
2. Describe the law that made possible the first criminal investigation of crime within a virtual world.
3. What kind of policing are some companies using to combat in-game crime?
4. What is the writer implying when he refers to "a third life to escape to" in the final paragraph?
5. Discuss how the writer does or does not effectively acknowledge views different from his own.

Respond To This Reading

1. If you are a virtual game player, what is your view of in-game justice? Is it necessary? Explain.
2. Under what conditions, if any, should justice for virtual crimes carry over into the real world?
3. Some may question the validity of building an argument in response to a game that originates in a virtual environment. Explain why you would or would not argue on this kind of issue.

ABOUT THIS READING

When this argument was published, Philip Mattera was head of the nonprofit organization Corporate Research Project, a center that helps organizations and groups research and analyze companies. This reading first appeared under the title, "The Greenwashing of America," on *TomPaine.com*, a project of the Institute for America's Future.

Greenwashing Remains a Challenge to the Green Building Community

By Philip Mattera

In the business world these days, it appears that just about everything is for sale. Multibillion-dollar deals are commonplace, and even venerable institutions such as the *Wall Street Journal* find themselves put into play. Yet companies are not the only things being acquired. This [2007] may turn out to be the year that big business bought a substantial part of the environmental movement.

That's one way of interpreting the remarkable level of cooperation that is emerging between some prominent environmental groups and some of the world's largest corporations. What was once an arena of fierce antagonism has become a veritable love fest as companies profess to be going green and get lavishly honored for doing so. Earlier this year, for instance, the World Resources Institute gave one of its "Courage to Lead" awards to the chief executive of General Electric [GE].

Every day seems to bring another announcement from a large corporation that it is taking steps to protect the planet. IBM, informally known as Big Blue, launched its Project Big Green to help customers slash their data center energy usage. Newmont Mining Co., the world's largest gold digger, endorsed a shareholder resolution calling for a review of its environmental impact. Home Depot introduced an Eco Options label for thousands of green products. General Motors and oil major ConocoPhillips joined the list of corporate giants that have come out in support of a mandatory ceiling on greenhouse gas emissions. Bank of America said it would invest $20 billion in sustainable projects over the next decade.

Many of the new initiatives are being pursued in direct collaboration with environmental groups. Wal-Mart is working closely with Conservation International on its efforts to cut energy usage and switch to renewable sources of power. McDonald's has teamed up with Greenpeace to discourage deforestation caused by the growth of soybean farming in Brazil. When buyout firms Texas Pacific Group and KKR were negotiating the takeover of utility company TXU [in 2007], they asked Environmental Defense to join the talks so that the deal, which ended up including a rollback of plans for 11 new coal-fired plants, could be assured a green seal of approval.

Observing this trend, *Business Week* detects "a remarkable evolution in the dynamic between corporate executives and activists. Once fractious and antagonistic, it has moved toward accommodation and even mutual dependence."

The question is: who is accommodating whom? Are these developments a sign that environmental campaigns have prevailed and are setting the corporate agenda? Or have enviros been duped into endorsing what may be little more than a new wave of corporate greenwash?

An Epiphany About the Environment?

The first thing to keep in mind is that Corporate America's purported embrace of environmental principles is nothing new. Something very similar happened, for example, in early 1990 around the time of the 20th anniversary of Earth Day. *Fortune* announced then that "trend spotters and forward thinkers agree that the Nineties will be the Earth Decade and that environmentalism will be a movement of massive worldwide force." *Business Week* published a story titled "The Greening of Corporate America."

The magazine cited a slew of large companies that were said to be embarking on significant green initiatives, among them DuPont, General Electric, McDonald's, 3M, Union Carbide and Procter & Gamble. Corporations such as these put on their own Earth Tech environmental technology fair on the National Mall and endorsed Earth Day events and promotions.

A difference between then and now is that there was a lot more skepticism about Corporate America's claim of having had an epiphany about the environment. It was obvious to many that business was trying to undo the damage caused by environmental disasters such as Union Carbide's deadly Bhopal [India] chemical leak, the *Exxon Valdez* oil spill in Alaska and the deterioration of the ozone layer. Activist groups charged that corporations were engaging in a bogus public relations effort which they branded "greenwash." Greenpeace staged a protest at DuPont's Earth Tech exhibit, leading to a number of arrests.

Misgivings about corporate environmentalism grew as it was discovered that many of the claims about green products were misleading, false or irrelevant. Mobil Chemical, for instance, was challenged for calling its new Hefty trash bags biodegradable, since that required extended exposure to light rather than their usual fate of being buried in landfills. Procter & Gamble was taken to task for labeling its Pampers and Luvs disposable diapers "compostable" when only a handful of facilities in the entire country were equipped to do such processing. Various companies bragged that their products in aerosol cans were now safe for the environment when all they had done was comply with a ban on the use of chlorofluorocarbons. Some of the self-proclaimed green producers found themselves being investigated by state attorneys general for false advertising and other offenses against the consumer.

Transforming Corporate Images

The insistence that companies actually substantiate their claims put a damper on the entire green product movement. Yet some companies continued to see advantages in being associated with environmental principles. In one of the more brazen moves, DuPont ran TV ads in the late 1990s depicting sea lions applauding a passing oil tanker (accompanied by Beethoven's "Ode to Joy") to take credit for the fact that its Conoco subsidiary had begun using double hulls in its ships, conveniently failing to mention that it was one of the last oil companies to take that step.

At the same time, some companies began to infiltrate the environmental movement itself by contributing to the more moderate groups and getting spots on their boards. They also joined organizations such as CERES, which encourages green groups and corporations to endorse a common set of principles. By the early 2000s, some companies sought to depict themselves as being not merely in step with the environmental movement but at the forefront of a green transformation. British Petroleum [BP] started publicizing its investments in renewable energy and saying that its initials really stood for Beyond Petroleum—all despite the fact that its operations continued to be dominated by fossil fuels.

This paved the way for General Electric's "ecomagination" p.r. [public relations] blitz, which it pursued even while dragging its feet in the cleanup of PCB contamination in New York's Hudson River. GE was followed by Wal-Mart, which in October 2005 sought to transform its image as a leading cause of pollution-generating sprawl by announcing a program to move toward zero waste and maximum use of renewable energy. In recent months the floodgates have opened, with more and more large companies calling for federal caps on greenhouse gas emissions. In January [2007] ten major corporations—including Alcoa, Caterpillar, DuPont and General Electric— joined with the Natural Resources Defense Council and other enviro groups in forming the U.S. Climate Action Partnership. A few months later, General Motors, arguably one of the companies that has done the most to exacerbate global warming, signed on as well.

A Cause for Celebration or Dismay?

Today the term "greenwash" is rarely uttered, and differences in positions between corporate giants and mainstream environmental groups are increasingly difficult to discern. Everywhere one looks, enviros and executives have locked arms and are marching together to save the planet. Is this a cause for celebration or dismay?

Answering this question begins with the recognition that companies do not all enter the environmental fold in the same way. Here are some of their different paths:

- **Defeat.** Some companies did not embrace green principles on their own—they were forced to do so after being successfully targeted by aggressive environmental campaigns. Home Depot abandoned the sale of lumber harvested in old-growth forests several years ago after being pummeled by groups such as Rainforest Action Network. Responding to similar campaign pressure, Boise Cascade also agreed to stop sourcing from endangered forests and J.P. Morgan Chase agreed to take environmental impacts into account in its international lending activities. Dell started taking computer recycling seriously only after it was pressed to do so by groups such as the Silicon Valley Toxics Coalition.

- **Diversion.** It is apparent that Wal-Mart is using its newfound green consciousness as a means of diverting public attention away from its dismal record in other areas, especially the treatment of workers. In doing so, it hopes to peel environmentalists away from the broad anti-Wal-Mart movement. BP's emphasis on the environment was no doubt made more urgent by the need to repair an image damaged by allegations that a 2005 refinery fire in Texas that killed 15 people was the fault of management. To varying degrees, many other companies that have jumped on the green bandwagon have sins they want the public to forget.

- **Opportunism.** There is so much hype these days about protecting the environment that many companies are going green simply to earn more green. There are some market moves, such as Toyota's push on hybrids, that also appear to have some environmental legitimacy. Yet there are also instances of sheer opportunism, such as the effort by Nuclear Energy Institute to depict nukes as an environmentally desirable alternative to fossil fuels. Not to mention surreal cases such as the decision by Britain's BAE Systems to develop environmentally friendly munitions, including low-toxin rockets and lead-free bullets.

In other words, the suggestion that the new business environmentalism flows simply from a heightened concern for the planet is far from the truth. Corporations always act in their own self-interest and one way or another are always seeking to maximize profits. It used to be that they had to hide that fact. Today they flaunt it, because there is a widespread notion that eco-friendly policies are totally consistent with cutting costs and fattening the bottom line.

When GE's "ecomagination" campaign was launched, CEO Jeffrey Immelt insisted "it's no longer a zero-sum game—things that are good for the environment are also good for business." This was echoed by Wal-Mart CEO Lee Scott, who said in a speech announcing his company's green initiative that "being a good steward of the environment and in our communities, and being an efficient and profitable business, are not mutually exclusive. In fact they are one [and] the same." That's probably because Scott sees environmentalism as merely an extension of the company's legendary penny-pinching, as glorified efficiency measures.

Chevron Wants to Lead

Many environmental activists seem to welcome the notion of a convergence of business interests and green interests, but it all seems too good to be true. If eco-friendly policies are entirely "win-win," then why did corporations resist them for so long? It is hard to believe that the conflict between profit maximization and environmental protection, which characterized the entire history of the ecological movement, has suddenly evaporated.

Either corporations are fooling themselves, in which case they will eventually realize there is no environmental free lunch and renege on their green promises. Or they are fooling us and are perpetrating a massive public relations hoax. A third interpretation is that companies are taking voluntary steps that are genuine but inadequate to solve the problems at hand and are mainly meant to prevent stricter, enforceable regulation.

In any event, it would behoove enviros to be more skeptical of corporate green claims and less eager to jump into bed with business. It certainly makes sense to seek specific concessions from corporations and to offer moderate praise when they comply, but activists should maintain an arm's-length relationship to business and not see themselves as partners. After all, the real purpose of the environmental movement is not simply to make technical adjustments to the way business operates (that's the job of consultants) but rather to push for fundamental and systemic changes.

Moreover, there is a risk that the heightened level of collaboration will undermine the justification for an independent environmental movement. Why pay dues to a green group if its agenda is virtually identical to that of GE and DuPont? Already there are hints that business views itself, not activist groups, as the real green vanguard. Chevron, for instance, has been running a series of environmental ads with the tagline "Will you join us?"

Join them? Wasn't it Chevron and the other oil giants that played a major role in creating global warming? Wasn't it Chevron that used the repressive regime in Nigeria to protect its environmentally destructive operations in the Niger Delta? Wasn't it Chevron's Texaco unit that dumped more than 18 billion gallons of toxic waste in Ecuador? And wasn't it Chevron that was accused of systematically underpaying royalties to the federal government for natural gas extracted from the Gulf of Mexico? That is not the kind of track record that confers the mantle of environmental leadership.

In fact, we shouldn't be joining any company's environmental initiative. Human activists should be leading the effort to clean up the planet, and corporations should be made to follow our lead.

Analyze This Reading

1. The writer begins by citing examples of cooperation between corporations and environmental organizations. With what question does he frame this cooperation?
2. What does the term *greenwash* mean? When and under what circumstances does this term come into use? What examples does the writer refer to in his discussion of *greenwash*?
3. With what information does the writer support his concern about "the suggestion that new business environmentalism flows simply from a heightened concern for the planet"?
4. What advice does the writer have for enviros (environmental activists)?

Respond To This Reading

1. Explain why you agree or disagree with the writer's concluding thought that we should resist joining the environmental initiatives of corporations.
2. What evidence of greenwash is there in your community? How do you evaluate it?
3. Connections between environmental problems and corporate behavior are clear on global, national, and local levels. Identify an issue within this large topic, and stake out a claim and reasons to support it. At whom would you aim your argument? What would you hope to accomplish?

ABOUT THIS READING

Tracie McMillan is a freelance journalist who writes about access to healthy food, especially with regard to poor and middle-income neighborhoods. She has won several national awards for her investigative journalism on this topic, including the James Aronson Award for Social Justice Journalism. This reading appeared on *Salon.com*, an online magazine that focuses on news, entertainment, politics, culture, and technology.

Jicama in the 'Hood

Legislators and local food activists are fighting to get healthy, organic food into the nation's poorest neighborhoods.

By Tracie Mcmillan

Amid a crowd of New York City public high-schoolers, Antonio Mayers, 16, is trying—with modest success—to wrap his head around the idea of freezing a mango pit for later consumption as a popsicle.

"How long you put it in the freezer?"

"Just until it gets, you know, frozen. It's really good," says Michael Welch. Welch is leading Mayers and his tittering cohorts in a cooking class coordinated by EatWise, a New York nutrition and food systems education group. As simple as that mango may seem, for Welch's students—and their counterparts in the many high-density, urban areas around the country that researchers have deemed "food deserts" for their lack of grocery stores— fresh fruit, indeed fresh *anything,* is largely inaccessible. Welch has carefully selected today's dishes with his students in mind, a calculation that has resulted in a menu featuring both local sweet corn and Philadelphia Cream Cheese. "Not all these kids can afford the high-end and organic stuff," explains Welch. "I wanted it to be something they can find in their neighborhood." Continuing his presentation, Welch shows his skeptical students some of the less-familiar ingredients they'll be using: jicama, raw corn sliced from the cob, honey. Much of the produce was grown in local dirt, a particularly relevant fact given the venue: Stone Barns, the Westchester County estate James Beard-recognized chef Dan Barber has transformed into a working sustainable farm, education center and restaurant. The site is just 30 miles from Manhattan, but the combination of fine dining at Blue Hill Stone Barns restaurant and the rolling farm it overlooks are a world away from the concrete grid where Welch's students buy their groceries. Indeed, Stone Barns is to New York foodies what Alice Waters' Edible Schoolyard and Chez Panisse are to food-conscious San Franciscans: an institution committed to wholesome food and local ingredients, set on convincing the next generation to avoid industrial food in its favor. It's a lofty goal, one routinely—and effortlessly—sold to food acolytes, but today Stone Barns is aiming at a different audience.

There is, it appears, something lost in the translation—and the lesson this July Saturday hits a few snags. After Welch's class has scarfed down the results of the recipes they've prepared—the fruit salad and tuna wraps are deemed "slammin!" but the three-bean salad met with skepticism—the group reassembles to offer their opinions.

"What did you like about the food? What do you like to make in the summer?" he asks the crowd.

"Pop tarts!" yells out Stephen Colsn, 14.

Ebony Williams, 18, disagrees. "Toaster strudels!"

"I like those!" says Colsn.

While teens' taste for sugary junk is nothing new, in this case, the kids are motivated by more than just an insatiable sweet tooth. While Colsn says he understands the importance of local food, and that he should eat more vegetables, he's quick to note that it's also easier said than done near his home in Harlem.

"At the Garden of Eden, everything is maintained," he says, referring to an immaculate, upscale grocery a 15-minute walk from his apartment. "But sometimes it costs more money. I just go to the bodega or the corner store."

Colsn might not know it, but he's just expressed one of the most salient critiques of the earnest, though sometimes elitist, slow food movement typified by Barber, Waters and their ilk: For most Americans eating healthfully is not a question of finding locally grown, organic apples. It's a question of finding an edible apple near their homes, period.

The sheer lack of quality food in low-income neighborhoods is bringing some unlikely colleagues to the foodie pioneers' table. Spurred by concerns equal parts public health and fiscal prudence, a burgeoning movement of politicians, lawyers and advocates—and the occasional retail developer or small business owner—is leading a charge to improve access to better food among the nation's poor. In doing so, they are infusing public policy with a notion traditionally considered a luxury: That fresher, higher-quality food is worth some trouble.

In an effort to bring the message home, Rep. Nydia Velazquez, D-N.Y., last week introduced in the House the Bodegas as Catalysts for Healthy Living Act. Velazquez was spurred on by dramatically high rates of obesity and diabetes in her New York district, and her legislation, if enacted, would create a grants program designed to help small stores stock healthier food like fresh produce and low-fat milk, market it aggressively, and supplement their work by partnering with local health groups. The bodega bill marks the first federal effort around issues of structural access, but Pennsylvania has been testing the local waters for a while. In 2004, Gov. Ed Rendell estab-lished a state program to encourage the development of supermarkets in low-income areas found to be lacking them; since its inception, the pro-gram has spawned seven new grocers and helped four existing ones stock healthier options.

These formal legislative efforts represent the beginning of a shift from questions of consumption—prescribing certain foods while proscribing others—to access. As such, they also form the top tier of a vast and uncoor-dinated campaign to get healthy food to the nation's poor neighborhoods. Some efforts garner ridicule, as has an initiative by New York City Council member Joel Rivera to limit the density of fast food restaurants. Other proj-ects focus on raising fresh produce right in the neighborhoods, as did the South Central Urban Farm in Los Angeles until its bulldozing a few months ago. Still others focus on retail. Brooklyn, N.Y., will soon supplement the nationally known Park Slope Food Coop—sometimes derided as a yuppie magnet—with a similar enterprise in East New York, a venture motivated by concerns over that low-income community's high rates of obesity and diabetes.

If using bodegas for health promotion sounds far-fetched, store owners and public health experts are betting they can prove you wrong. Velazquez's bill has backing from the Bodega Association of the United States, and was developed partly in response to recommendations from the New York City health department. What's more, store owners like Christian Diaz, a Bushwick, Brooklyn, bodeguero, are coming around to the cause, eyeing health food and fresh produce as a new market opportunity. When Diaz opened his bodega 18 months ago, he started out stocking mostly whole milk, but soon ramped up his low-fat options.

"I was only bringing in, like, two gallons" of low-fat milk at first, says Diaz. "Now I'm carrying a case and a half. Little by little, people are starting to get more oriented on the low-fat products." What's more, he's eager to start carrying quality fruits and vegetables, a service offered by less than one-third of the neighborhood's bodegas, according to a recent health department study. (The same research also found that eight in 10 of the neighborhood's food stores are bodegas.) Diaz initially explored the idea of stocking fresh fruits and vegetables, and then largely jettisoned it once he researched refrigerator costs. "The reason I put 'market' on the name of the business is I wanted to put in a fruit market," says Diaz. "People do come in and ask for it."

Part of the inspiration for legislation like the bodega bill comes from a small but growing body of research suggesting a link between poor access to food and higher rates of obesity and related conditions like diabetes and heart disease. "You can't choose healthy food if you don't have access to it," says Mari Gallagher, a national expert on local markets and community development who authored a recent report on "food deserts"—areas with no food stores or ones a distance away—in Chicago.

Indeed, for all the ruminations on the perils of the modern food economy—from bestselling author Michael Pollan's disturbing finding in "The Omnivore's Dilemma" that industrial corn so thoroughly dominates the American diet that we are "corn chips with legs," to the widely published statistic from Iowa State University that most food travels 1,500 miles to make it onto American store shelves—a more rudimentary concern has begun to present itself: Proximity to plate. Even when Gallagher's researchers controlled for income and education, rates of obesity rose as the distance to the nearest grocery store increased. "We did find a real relationship between obesity and grocery store placement," she says. There's also reason to believe that better access helps foster better diet. For every additional supermarket in a census tract, for example, fruit and vegetable consumption has been shown to increase by as much as 32 percent, according to a 2001 American Journal of Public Health study.

Food deserts are almost exclusively found in poor, urban areas, where premier retailers—particularly shops like Whole Foods, which have based their business on charging a premium price for premium foods—often fear to tread. Even when large retailers are eyeing an urban locale, nuts-and-bolts concerns such as complex zoning laws, high land prices and few available lots often pose difficulties for companies that are used to dealing with the suburbs. That leaves small-scale corner stores to fill the gap—and residents with fewer food choices and higher grocery bills. Low-income communities have an average of one midsize or large grocery store per 80,000 residents, compared to one for every 25,000 residents in wealthy communities, according to a recent Brookings Institution survey of 10 American cities. The same study also found prices to be higher in small stores; a survey of 132 food items found that over two-thirds were more expensive at small grocers than at supermarkets. And even the simple fact of higher cost may lead to health problems. A Rand Corporation study published last year linked higher prices for produce with greater rates of obesity.

But obesity itself comes with a hefty price tag—yet another reason legislators are joining the food fray. Annual spending on obesity-related health problems in America in 1998 was an estimated $80 billion, according to the journal *Health Affairs*, and likely has risen since. Nor does it appear that it will abate soon; ever since the surgeon general declared an obesity epidemic in 2001, the bad news just keeps coming: Obesity could soon overtake tobacco as the No. 1 killer in the U.S., according to the Centers for Disease Control.

Well before food access was making it onto the legislative roster, getting good food in the 'hood was being tackled by a scrappier set of operatives: the people who lived there. "We were observing local health problems in the community related to diet," says Brahm Ahmadi, co-director of the People's Grocery, a West Oakland, Calif., food justice group. "The initial goal was to create a worker-owned community grocery store and education center."

When Ahmadi and his two co-founders confronted a steep learning curve—none of them had run a business before—they scaled back the retail component to a "mobile market." They bought a milk truck, then outfitted it with a booming sound system, a graffiti paint job and a load of fresh produce; it has since become a community fixture. This year, they're hoping to get a "Soul Box" program off the ground, where they'll hook food stamp recipients into community supported agriculture clubs, groups that partner with a farmer who delivers fresh produce weekly in exchange for payment upfront. Next year, the group hopes to finally open a store.

Though it would be easy to rest on its laurels, the growing organization—it now boasts five full-time positions—is thinking bigger than just one truck and one store. People's Grocery devotees pride themselves on addressing a complex, interconnected set of food-related issues. At the top of the list is advocating and practicing sustainable agriculture and urban farming, with a goal of creating a locally based food system, ideally while generating jobs and stability in their communities.

All of which situates groups like People's Grocery not in opposition to the affluent, consumer-based charge led by Pollan and Waters, but rather as the grass-roots flip side of it. "They've been pioneering quite a bit," Ahmadi says of the food luminaries. "But that hasn't quite trickled down to the challenges of healthy food in West Oakland." Which, he adds, is precisely where groups like his come in. "A lot of our current planning is geared toward a long-term vision of placing people into food companies to bridge that divide," he says, emphasizing that organic companies have traditionally aimed for an up-market consumer.

They may have their work cut out for them. Back at Stone Barns, the cooking class has finished, and the students have reassembled en masse. Animated chatter bubbles through the room—there's a general distaste for the haute cuisine sandwiches dispensed at lunchtime by farm staff, and talk of a McDonald's run back in the city is making the rounds—and then a dozen kids take center stage at the front of the room.

The presenters are summer interns and volunteers with EatWise, the nutrition education group that has brought everyone to Stone Barns today. Joelina Peralta, a feisty 18-year-old from Bushwick with a mane of curls sprouting from a ponytail, starts the group off with a quick go-around about the benefits of eating locally. Everyone seems to grasp that local food is fresher, better for the environment and helps the New York economy— an achievement that would make even the most dyed-in-the-wool foodie swoon. Then Victor Lopez, a diminutive 15-year-old from East New York, sporting bling in both ears, takes over.

"Have any of you heard about a farmers market?" He pauses for effect. "Not too much? That's OK, that's why I'm here." With a magician's show-manship, Victor announces that they will be having a taste test and unveils two paper plates of diced tomato, one from a farmers market, the other a grocery store.

To a trained eye, it's easy to pick out the farm-fresh tomato's bright red, juicy flesh, and cast a disdainful look at the pinkish, mealy option on the other plate. Yet, for most of the kids gathered, this is their first encounter with taking a critical look at food. When the three volunteers come up for a taste, results are mixed. Two choose the farm tomato, to the delight of the EatWise interns—but Cesar Pimentel, a lanky 21-year-old youth program staffer who brought several students with him, shakes his head. "I like that one!" he says. "The grocery store!"

The scene hits home for Joelina, who says she's gone through a metamorphosis since joining EatWise. "They just grew up with that type of food, so they are used to that," she says of her fast-food-loving peers, adding that before she started working with EatWise she was the same. Now, she's trying to eat well, but she's finding it rough going in Bushwick. "I was in the supermarket not too long ago; I was trying to buy some organic stuff and I couldn't find anything at all," she explains. Another time, she stopped at the corner store and picked up some tomatoes, only to find that her palate had begun to outstrip her budget. "It was like, it had no flavor at all," she groans. "It was disgusting."

Analyze This Reading

1. What is a "food desert"? The writer mentions public, private, and legislative responses to food deserts. Describe these responses.
2. What research does the writer include that links food accessibility with obesity and diabetes?
3. According to the writer, how do the People's Grocery and EatWise offer alternatives to more affluent, consumer-based approaches to healthy food?

Respond To This Reading

1. Based on your access to healthy food, is the writer accurate in her contention that, for many Americans, access to healthy food is based on where one lives? Explain.
2. The local food movement, part of the larger movement in America in recent years to move toward sustainability, includes a justice component. Describe this component. Can you connect it to your community and your food-buying habits? Explain.
3. How much control can and should residents of a neighborhood have in the food they buy and consume? On what values do you base your response?
4. Identify a single issue related to your food consumption that motivates you to argue. What kind of claim would best serve your purpose in this argument?

ABOUT THIS READING

A professor of communications at Monmouth University, Eleanor Novek researches the role of communication in racial residential segregation. This reading appeared in *Shelterforce*, a magazine published by the National Housing Institute and devoted to issues in the fields of housing and community development.

You Wouldn't Fit Here

By Eleanor Novek

In *Race in America: The Struggle for Equality*, Patricia J. Williams, a legal scholar, recalls seeing an advertisement for a two-bedroom apartment in Madison, Wisconsin. The landlord agreed to meet her at the address to show the place. Williams, who is African-American, arrived first. "I saw her catch sight of me as I sat on the doorstep. I saw her walk slower and slower, squinting at me as I sat in the sunshine. At ten minutes after three, I was back in my car driving away without having seen the apartment. The woman had explained to me that a 'terrible mistake' had occurred, that the apartment had been rented without her knowledge . . ."

Williams's experience is a common one for people of color in all walks of life. Decades after the passage of federal fair housing laws, housing discrimination and racial segregation are alive and well in the United States. Many communities still operate under a strict "virtual apartheid," and in some parts of the country, racially divided neighborhoods are even more prevalent than they were before civil rights legislation. Extensive regional and national studies have documented that minority home seekers receive less assistance than whites in finding housing that meets their needs and are more likely to be turned down for mortgage loans and home insurance than comparably qualified white applicants. Buyers of all races continue to be steered toward neighborhoods where their own ethnic groups are concentrated.

While many ethnic groups have encountered housing discrimination, no group has experienced the sustained high level of residential segregation that has been imposed on African Americans. Segregation has concentrated African Americans into disadvantaged neighborhoods characterized by higher crime rates, fewer public services, and lower housing values. It has restricted their access to job opportunities, information resources and political influence. Schools in segregated areas are plagued by high dropout rates and severe educational disparities that threaten the life chances of African-American children. Racial residential segregation is a primary cause of urban poverty and inequality in the United States.

Although many forces are responsible for this persistence of racial segregation, the role of communication is often overlooked. Since passage of the Fair Housing Act, polite social interaction is often used to carry the same ugly messages formerly stated directly, with entire conversations conducted as if something other than race is causing the denial of housing. These communication strategies have helped to preserve segregation where the law has tried to dismantle it.

History of Residential Segregation

Scholars track the institutionalization of racial separation to the early 1900s, when large numbers of blacks migrated from the rural South in search of factory jobs. When they tried to settle in the largely white urban areas of the North and the Midwest, they met with exclusion, intimidation and violence.

Whites in some cities boycotted and harassed businesses like boarding houses, hotels, and real estate firms that provided shelter to African Americans. Other whites established suburbs where they used zoning laws and exclusionary deeds to keep out people of color. Responding to these dynamics, real estate agents found it easiest and most profitable to steer home buyers and renters to neighborhoods where people of their own races were already concentrated.

Such steering was soon underscored by federal policies. In the 1930s and '40s, the Federal Housing Administration underwrote mortgages in segregated white neighborhoods, while directing lenders to turn down minority mortgages. Between 1930 and 1960, fewer than 1 percent of all mortgages in the nation were issued to African Americans. In the 1960s, urban renewal plans placed low-income housing projects in minority neighborhoods, concentrating the nation's poorest residents in the same neighborhoods occupied by people of color.

The Federal Fair Housing Act of 1968 outlawed overtly discriminatory market practices like exclusionary deeds, steering and redlining, but it had relatively little effect on established routines among real estate agents and lenders. Over the next two decades, despite increases in income, education and job status for minorities, housing patterns remained segregated. In the 1990s, despite modest changes in newer suburban neighborhoods in the South and West, segregation actually deepened in many cities. Between 1996 and 1998, the U.S. Department of Justice prosecuted more than 80 cases of criminal interference with housing rights, including cross-burnings, shootings and fire-bombings.

Biased Brokers

Such acts of violence are not the primary way that segregation is reinforced in much of the country, however. Real estate sales and rental agents, mortgage lenders and insurers all have significant influence on the choices home buyers make. And despite the Fair Housing Act, race still influences their interactions with their customers.

First, there is direct discrimination. Minority home buyers receive less assistance than whites in finding housing that meets their needs, and are more likely to be turned down or overcharged for home loans and insurance than comparably qualified white applicants. Doug Massey and Nancy Denton describe in *American Apartheid: Segregation and the Making of the Underclass* how racial minority customers are told that the unit they want to see has just been sold or rented, or they are shown only one advertised unit and told that no others are available.

At some real estate offices, Massey and Denton note, minority customers are "told that the selling agents are too busy and to come back later; their phone number may be taken but a return call never made; they may be shown units but offered no assistance in arranging financing; or they may be treated brusquely and discourteously in hopes that they will leave." National studies using matched pairs of testers have documented these actions at real estate firms and mortgage lenders around the country. Many of these abuses originate in the earliest personal interactions between sellers and buyers, or in the first informational materials home buyers confront.

Less directly abusive, but even more clearly perpetuating segregation is the practice of steering, whereby customers are strongly encouraged, both by what they are shown and by "commentary," to buy or rent in single-race neighborhoods where they "fit in." When consumers want to inspect housing in locations where they would be in a racial minority, some real estate agents try to discourage them through conversation. In Bloomington, IN, an agent warned an Asian woman and her white husband away from a house they wanted to buy because it was not in "a mixed neighborhood." And a white woman in Ocean, NJ was assured by an agent that "this is a great neighborhood—there are none of them here." Real estate salespeople often say they know other agents who discuss the racial makeup of neighborhoods with clients, but they refuse to discuss such practices in detail, fearful of backlash from those agents.

Research demonstrates that white buyers typically hear positive comments from agents praising neighborhoods and schools in mostly white areas, but they hear discouraging comments about neighborhood amenities and schools when a neighborhood's population is more than 30 percent black. Black customers tend to hear little commentary—positive or negative—from agents about predominantly black neighborhoods, but they are invariably warned against buying in predominantly white areas because of the possible "trouble" they would face there.

Advertising Exclusivity

Newspaper real estate ads are a key source of information for home seekers, and they often contain discriminatory messages. The Federal Fair Housing Act forbids references to race, color, religion, sex, handicap, familial status or national origin in real estate advertising, but subtler messages of exclusion in photographs or text often get through. In some real estate markets, for example, the models shown in photographic ads for homes and apartment complexes are all white, and very blonde. Some have described neighborhoods "where Wally and the Beaver would feel right at home," or homes built in "the style of Northern Europe," available only to "a select few" or representing "a return to family values."

These tactics have resulted in individual complaints and lawsuits. Some courts have ruled that using only white models in real estate advertisements sends a discriminatory message to other races. In one study, African-American and white respondents viewed groups of real estate ads with white models only and with a mix of black and white models. Typical responses to the all-white ads included: "Because the 'actors' are perceived to be all Europeans, I would question if African Americans would be welcome here," and "From people pictured on posters, this apartment complex is 'for white only.'"

In 1993, in partial settlement of a lawsuit, The *New York Times* began requiring that real estate ads containing photos of people be representative of the racial makeup in the New York metropolitan area. Some advertisers responded by removing all human figures from their ads. In 1994, the publishers of the *Philadelphia Inquirer* and the *Philadelphia Daily News* cautioned advertisers not to use "coded" text in ads, including "such words and phrases as traditional, prestigious, established and private community, which, when used in a certain context, could be interpreted to convey racial exclusivity."

Data Labeling

Internet marketing sites and the practice of computer-assisted target marketing have added a new twist to communication about race and real estate. Many residential sales firms, including brands like Century 21 and Re/MAX, have established consumer web sites to attract customers, offering prospective home buyers information and advice from mortgage rates to moving tips. Some sites furnish "neighborhood profile" services, where consumers can type in the street address or zip code of a home and receive a description of nearby schools, crime rates, and property values. Or they may offer "neighborhood matching," a service that allows relocating buyers to type in the zip codes of their current neighborhoods and find communities in other cities with comparably priced housing.

The demographic information on Internet real estate sites is provided by marketing services such as Lysias, Taconic Data, CACI Marketing Systems and Claritas. These firms combine demographic data from the U.S. Census with consumer spending research and package the information for easy use by commercial clients. Such firms pioneered "cluster marketing" techniques in the 1980s, analyzing the consumer habits of neighborhoods across the U.S. by zip code and then assigning them catchy nicknames like "Affluent Suburbia," "Mid-City Mix," and "Metro Singles."

However, some of these profiles categorize neighborhoods not only by zip code and consumer behavior, but also by ethnic signifiers. For example, a profile offered by CACI Marketing Systems characterized one zip code as having mostly black residents who had not completed high school and "tend to purchase fast food and takeout food from chicken restaurants." Claritas' online "Hispanic Mix" neighborhood profile is decorated with a cartoon image of a brown-skinned mother shopping at a sidewalk market, and describes residents who are pro basketball fans and use money orders to pay their bills.

MicroVision's middle-income "City Ties" cluster (where residents are said to eat at chicken restaurants, smoke menthol cigarettes, and read *Ebony* magazine) is illustrated by a photo of a smiling black family with three children. Its upscale "Metro Singles" cluster (where residents are said to use sunburn remedies and have dental insurance) is illustrated by a blonde white woman reclining alone on a sofa.

In February 1999, the National Association of Realtors took a stand against the use of racial and ethnic demographic information on members' real estate websites, but a number of firms continue the practice. These techniques have recently come under fire from community groups and citizens.

ACORN, a nonprofit fair housing organization, has charged Wells Fargo/ Norwest Mortgage with racial discrimination over the company's Internet real estate site (which has since been taken down). Plaintiffs argued that the website's neighborhood profiles used "overt racial classifications" to discourage people from inspecting or buying homes in predominantly minority areas by exaggerating the desirability of areas deemed white occupied and the drawbacks of areas classified as minority occupied. The plaintiffs also claim the site's neighborhood matching feature steered residents of predominantly minority zip codes to other minority zip codes, and referred residents of predominantly white zip codes to other white zip codes.

The practices described above are common but hard to track, located more often by anecdotal example than by research. Although they are not as dramatic as acts of violence and not as quantifiable as redlining, they play a significant role in the persistence of housing discrimination. Together, they may be as discouraging to the growth of integrated communities as the easier-to-measure practices of discriminatory pricing, mortgage lending and insurance underwriting. However, these habits that support segregation can be broken by a concerted effort to bring them into the light of day. . . .

First, let's talk about what is going on. The absence of public dialogue is one of the conditions that allow racial discrimination to persist. Most individual home buyers see themselves not as change agents but as consumers whose decisions are merely individual choices that have no broader impact. Community organizations and coalitions play a key role in helping to raise public awareness of segregation and the contemporary problems it creates.

Second, community organizations can strengthen their case by partnering with researchers and journalists to more precisely document the scope of residential segregation in their communities. Academic researchers can teach local groups techniques for tracing social patterns and analyzing their impact in a community over time. Journalists can bring the issue of segregation to public attention. Rather than focusing their stories on individual acts of housing bias involving a few people, news organizations need to cover residential segregation as an issue story, highlighting the social processes and outcomes that affect thousands of people. Such efforts can begin to raise broader public support for changes in policy. Publishers and editors should also assess the racially exclusive advertising practices in their own real estate sections and pressure advertisers to change.

Finally, we must call on public officials at local, state and federal levels to address residential segregation through assertive social programs. Models for these already exist, such as the one developed by the Fund for an Open Society in Philadelphia. This plan calls for the creation of neighborhood enterprise zones dedicated to residential integration. It suggests the creation of mortgage subsidies and tax exemptions for homeowners, and recommends that participating localities be made eligible for dedicated funding for new construction and school support. The Fair Share Housing Center in Cherry Hill, NJ works with residents of Mt. Laurel, NJ to develop low-income housing that would allow some of Camden's inner city residents to afford suburban housing. The South Orange/Maplewood Community Coalition on Race is also testing out some of these ideas.

Segregation is a stubborn problem. Although some communication practices have been used to circumvent fair housing and integration, others can help. Let's talk frankly about the racial makeup of our neighborhoods. Let's document and publicize what is going on. Let's define segregation as a social harm rather than as an inconvenient byproduct of individual preferences. And let's come up with alternatives for viable communities with quality of life for all.

Analyze This Reading

1. What is "virtual apartheid"? According to the writer, what have been its effects?
2. Identify the claim in this argument. What kind of claim is it?
3. What factual information does the writer bring to her treatment of the history of residential segregation?
4. How do the strategies of steering, advertising, and data labeling contribute to residential segregation?
5. What methods for breaking the habits of residential segregation does the writer recommend?

Respond To This Reading

1. What is your experience or the experiences of others you know with racial residential segregation? Are some of the strategies described by the writer for maintaining this kind of segregation familiar? Explain.
2. How does this argument fit with your understanding of other forms of racial segregation?
3. Consider building an argument in response to one feature of racial residential segregation, either as it exists in your community or as it exists in general in America. Of the several features described in this argument, which might compel you to argue? What kind of claim would you build your argument around?

ABOUT THIS READING

James Q. Wilson is Ronald Reagan Professor of Public Policy at Pepperdine University. His books include *Moral Judgment* (1997), *The Marriage Problem: How Our Culture Damages Families* (2002), and *Understanding America: The Anatomy of an Exceptional Nation* (2008, ed. with Peter Schuck). This reading appeared in *Commentary*, a monthly magazine that, in its own words, sees itself as "consistently engaged with several large, interrelated questions: the fate of democracy and of democratic ideas in a world threatened by totalitarian ideologies; the state of American and Western security; the future of the Jews, Judaism, and Jewish culture in Israel, the United States, and around the world; and the preservation of high culture in an age of political correctness and the collapse of critical standards."

Bowling with Others

By James Q. Wilson

Ethnic and racial diversity is an important social characteristic in neighborhoods because, in the long run, it promotes connections between different social groups, reducing ethnocentric behavior. According to political scientist Robert D. Putnam, ethnically integrated neighborhoods help solidify social solidarity by helping create new, inclusive social identities. In the short term, however, it is difficult for people to adapt to ethnically diverse surroundings. Studies focusing on the impact of diversity on the social well-being of neighborhoods prove that ethnically diverse neighborhoods currently rate consistently below ethnically homogenous neighborhoods. Mixed ethnic groups reveal a lower level of social trust across different groups, resulting in little or no group unity. Forced integration, such as initiatives helping minorities gain access to communities where they have never lived before, are limited in their ability to promote true ethnic integration. Although the legal system should be used to strike down blatantly racist policies, government mandates forcing diversity into neighborhoods will not be successful until families find common ground on their own, based on similar moral values. These values cross ethnic lines, and can form a strong basis for true integration.

In his celebrated book *Bowling Alone*, the political scientist Robert D. Putnam argued that America, and perhaps the Western world as a whole, has become increasingly disconnected from family, friends, and neighbors. We once bowled in leagues; now we bowl alone. We once flocked to local chapters of the PTA [Parent Teacher Association], the NAACP [National Association for the Advancement of Colored People], or the Veterans of Foreign Wars; now we stay home and watch television. As a result, we have lost our "social capital"—by which Putnam meant both the associations themselves and the trustworthiness and reciprocity they encourage. For if tools (physical capital) and training (human capital) make the modern world possible, social capital is what helps people find jobs and enables neighborhoods and other small groupings of society to solve problems, control crime, and foster a sense of community.

Social Capital and Communities

In *Bowling Alone*, Putnam devised a scale for assessing the condition of organizational life in different American states. He looked to such measures as the density of civic groups, the frequency with which people participate in them, and the degree to which (according to opinion surveys) people trust one another. Controlling for race, income, education, and the like, he demonstrated that the higher a state's level of social capital, the more educated and affluent are its children, the lower the murder rate, the greater the degree of public health, and the smaller the likelihood of tax evasion. Nor is that all. High levels of social capital, Putnam showed, are associated with such civic virtues as greater tolerance toward women and minorities and stronger support for civil liberties. But all of these good things have been seriously jeopardized by the phenomenon he identified as "bowling alone."

After finishing his book, Putnam was approached by various community foundations to measure the levels of social capital within their own cities. To that end he conducted a very large survey: roughly 30,000 Americans, living in 41 different communities ranging downward in size from Los Angeles to Yakima, Washington, and even including rural areas of South Dakota. He published the results this year [2007] in a long essay in the academic journal *Scandinavian Political Studies* on the occasion of his having won Sweden's prestigious Johan Skytte prize.

Putnam's new essay takes an in-depth look not at social capital per se but at how "diversity"—meaning, for this purpose, racial and ethnic differences—affects our lives in society. Such diversity is increasing in this country and many others, if for no other reason than immigration, and so Putnam has tried to find out how it changes the way people feel about their neighbors, the degree of their confidence in local government, their willingness to become engaged in community-wide projects, and their general happiness.

When ethnic groups are mixed there is weaker social trust, less car pooling, and less group cohesion.

The ethnic and racial diversity that Putnam examines is widely assumed to be very good for us. The more time we spend with people different from us, it is said, the more we will like and trust them. Indeed, diversity is supposed to be so good for us that it has become akin to a national mandate in employment and, especially, in admissions to colleges and universities. When the Supreme Court decided the [*University of California v.*] *Bakke* case in 1978, the leading opinion, signed by Justice Lewis Powell, held that although a university was not allowed to use a strict numerical standard to guarantee the admission of a fixed number of minority students, it could certainly "take race into account," on the theory that a racially diverse student body was desirable both for the school and for society at large.

As a result of this and similar court rulings, not only colleges but many other institutions began invoking the term "diversity" as a justification for programs that gave preferences to certain favored minorities (especially blacks and Hispanics). Opponents of these programs on constitutional and civil-liberties grounds were put in the difficult position of appearing to oppose a demonstrated social good. Did not everyone know that our differences make us stronger?

But do they? That is where Putnam's new essay comes in. In the long run, Putnam argues, ethnic and racial diversity in neighborhoods is indeed "an important social asset," because it encourages people to form connections that can reduce unproductive forms of ethnocentrism and increase economic growth. In his words, "successful immigrant societies create new forms of social solidarity and dampen the negative effects of diversity by constructing new, more encompassing identities."

Whatever his beliefs about the positive effects of diversity in the long run, however—not only does he consider it a potentially "important social asset," but he has written that it also confers "many advantages that have little or nothing to do with social capital"—Putnam is a scrupulous and serious scholar (as well as a friend and former colleague at Harvard [University]). In the *short* run, he is frank to acknowledge, his data show not positive effects but rather the opposite. "The more ethnically diverse the people we live around," he writes, "the less we trust them."

Diversity, Putnam concludes on the basis of his findings, makes us "hunker down." Not only do we trust our neighbors less, we have less confidence in local government, a lowered sense of our own political efficacy, fewer close friends, and a smaller likelihood of contributing to charities, cooperating with others, working on a community project, registering to vote—or being happy.

Diversity and improved solidarity have gone hand in hand only in those institutions characterized by enforced authority and discipline.

Of course many of these traits can reflect just the characteristics of the people Putnam happened to interview, rather than some underlying condition. Aware of the possibility, Putnam spent a great deal of time "kicking the tires" of his study by controlling statistically for age, ethnicity, education, income or lack of same, poverty, homeownership, citizenship, and many other possible influences. But the results did not change. No matter how many individual factors were analyzed, every measure of social well-being suffered in ethnically diverse neighborhoods—and improved in ethnically homogeneous ones.

Diversity and Neighborhoods

"Shocking" is the word that one political scientist, Scott Page of the University of Michigan, invoked to describe the extent of the negative social effects revealed by Putnam's data. Whether Putnam was shocked by the results I cannot say. But they should not have been surprising; others have reported the same thing. The scholars Anil Rupasingha, Stephan J. Goetz, and David Frewater, for example, found that social capital across American counties, as measured by the number of voluntary associations for every 10,000 people, goes up with the degree of ethnic homogeneity. Conversely, as others have discovered, when ethnic groups are mixed there is weaker social trust, less car pooling, and less group cohesion. And this has held true for some time: people in Putnam's survey who were born in the 1920s display the same attitudes as those born in the 1970s.

Still, Putnam believes that in the long run ethnic heterogeneity will indeed "create new forms of social solidarity." He offers three reasons. First, the American military, once highly segregated, is today anything but that—and yet, in the Army and the Marines, social solidarity has increased right alongside greater ethnic diversity. Second, churches that were once highly segregated, especially large evangelical ones, have likewise become entirely and peaceably integrated. Third, people who once married only their ethnic kin today marry across ethnic and religious (and, to a lesser degree, racial) lines.

I can offer a fourth example: organized sports. Once, baseball and football teams were made up of only white or only black players; today they, too, are fully integrated. When Jackie Robinson joined the Brooklyn Dodgers in 1947, several teammates objected to playing with him, and many fans heckled him whenever he took the field. Within a few years, however, he and the Dodgers had won a raft of baseball titles, and he was one of the most popular figures in the country. Today such racial and ethnic heckling has virtually disappeared.

Unfortunately, however, the pertinence of the military, religious, or athletic model to life in neighborhoods is very slight. In those three institutions, authority and discipline can break down native hostilities or force them underground. Military leaders proclaim that bigotry will not be tolerated, and they mean it; preachers invoke the word of God to drive home the lesson that prejudice is a sin; sports teams (as with the old Brooklyn Dodgers) point out that anyone who does not want to play with a black or a Jew is free to seek employment elsewhere.

But what authority or discipline can anyone bring to neighborhoods? They are places where people choose to live, out of either opportunity or necessity. Walk the heterogeneous streets of Chicago or Los Angeles and you will learn about organized gangs and other social risks. Nor are these confined to poor areas: Venice, a small neighborhood in Los Angeles where several movie stars live and many homes sell for well over $1 million, is also a place where, in the Oakwood area, the Shoreline Crips and the V-13 gangs operate.

In many a neighborhood, ethnic differences are often seen as threats. If blacks or Hispanics, for whatever reason, are more likely to join gangs or commit crimes, then whites living in a neighborhood with many blacks or Hispanics will tend to feel uneasy. (There are, of course, exceptions: some, especially among the well-educated, prefer diversity even with all its risks.) Even where everyone is equally poor or equally threatened by crime, people exhibit less trust if their neighborhood is ethnically diverse than if it is homogeneous.

Of Putnam's three or four reasons for thinking that ethnic heterogeneity will contribute to social capital in the long run, only one is compelling: people are indeed voluntarily marrying across ethnic lines. But the paradoxical effect of this trend is not to preserve but to blunt ethnic identity, to the point where it may well reduce the perception of how diverse a neighborhood actually is. In any case, the fact remains that diversity and improved solidarity have gone hand in hand only in those institutions characterized by enforced authority and discipline.

Strong families living in neighborhoods made up of families with shared characteristics seem much more likely to bring their members into . . . associational life.

The legal scholar Peter H. Schuck has written an important book on this issue. In *Diversity in America*, he examines three major efforts by judges and government officials to require racial and income diversity in neighborhoods. One of them banned income-discrimination in the sale and rental of housing in New Jersey towns. Another enabled blacks who were eligible for public housing to move into private rental units in the Chicago suburbs. In the third, a federal judge attempted to diversify residential patterns in the city of Yonkers, New York, by ordering the construction of public housing in middle-class neighborhoods selected by him.

Although the Chicago project may have helped minorities to enter communities where they had never lived, the New Jersey and Yonkers initiatives had little effect. As Schuck writes, "Neighborhoods are complex, fragile, organic societies whose dynamics outsiders cannot readily understand, much less control." A court can and should strike down racist public policies, but when it goes beyond this and tries to mandate "diversity," it will sooner or later discover that it "cannot conscript the housing market to do its bidding."

Reducing Segregation

Taking a different approach, Thomas Schelling, a Nobel laureate in economics, has shown in a stimulating essay that neighborhood homogeneity and even segregation may result from small, defensible human choices that cannot themselves be called racist. In fact, such choices can lead to segregation even when the people making them expressly intend the opposite. Suppose, Schelling writes, that blacks and whites alike wish to live in a neighborhood that is (for example) half-white and half-black. If one white family should come to think that other white families prefer a community that is three-fourths white, and may move out for that reason, the first white family is itself likely to move out in search of its own half-white, half-black preference. There is no way to prevent this.

People who celebrate diversity . . . are endorsing only one part of what it means to be a complete human being, neglecting morality.

Schelling's analysis casts a shadow of doubt on Putnam's own policy suggestions for reducing the disadvantages and stimulating the benefits of ethnic heterogeneity. Those suggestions are: investing more heavily in playgrounds, schools, and athletic fields that different groups can enjoy together; extending national aid to local communities; encouraging churches to reach out to new immigrants; and expanding public support for the teaching of English.

The first recommendation is based on the implicit assumption that Schelling is wrong and on the even more dubious assumption that playgrounds, schools, and athletic fields—things Putnam did not measure in his survey—will increase the benefits of diversity even when age, income, and education do not. The second is empty: Putnam does not say what kind of aid will produce the desired effects. If he is thinking of more housing, Schuck has already shown that providing this usually does not increase diversity. If he is thinking of education, in the 1970s federal judges imposed forced busing in an effort to integrate schools; it was an intensely unpopular strategy, both among those whose children were being bused and among those whose neighborhoods were being bused into.

The third proposal, encouraging outreach by churches, might well make a difference, but how do we go about it? Require people to attend an evangelical church? Would Robert Putnam attend? I suspect not. And as for the final recommendation, teaching English at public expense to everyone, it is a very good idea—provided one could break the longstanding attachment of the education establishment to bilingual instruction.

Shared Values Increase Unity

Whether we should actually seek to transform the situation described by Putnam's data is another question. I do not doubt that both diversity and social capital are important, or that many aspects of the latter have declined, though perhaps not so much as Putnam suspects. But as his findings indicate, there is no reason to suppose that the route to the latter runs through the former. In fact, strong families living in neighborhoods made up of families with shared characteristics seem much more likely to bring their members into the associational life Putnam favors. Much as we might value both heterogeneity and social capital, assuming that the one will or should encourage the other may be a form of wishful thinking.

That is because morality and rights arise from different sources. As I tried to show in *The Moral Sense*, morality arises from sympathy among like-minded persons: first the family, then friends and colleagues. Rights, on the other hand, grow from convictions about how we ought to manage relations with people not like us, convictions that are nourished by education, religion, and experience.

People who celebrate diversity (and its parallel, multiculturalism) are endorsing only one part of what it means to be a complete human being, neglecting morality (and its parallel, group and national pride). Just as we cannot be whole persons if we deny the fundamental rights of others, so we cannot be whole persons if we live in ways that discourage decency, cooperation, and charity.

In every society, people must arrange for trade-offs between desirable but mutually inconsistent goals. James Madison [fourth president of the United States], in his famous *Federalist* Number Ten, pointed to just this sort of trade-off when he made the case for a large national government that would ensure the preservation of those individual rights and liberties that are at risk in small communities. When it comes to the competing values of diversity and the formation of social capital, as when it comes to other arrangements in a democracy, balance is all.

Analyze This Reading

1. What is the writer's view of Robert D. Putnam's position on ethnically integrated neighborhoods? What does the writer claim in response to Putnam's position?
2. What is "social capital"? How does it differ from "physical capital" and "human capital"? In what academic discipline do these terms originate?
3. How does the writer view military, religious, and athletic models of integration next to the neighborhood model proposed by Putnam? What separates the first three models from the neighborhood model?
4. How does the writer use the work of Schuck and Shelling to support his claim?

Respond To This Reading

1. In your view, is the writer fair and open-minded in his many references to Putnam? In your answer, explain how the writer's treatment of Putnam strengthens or weakens the argument.
2. The writer concludes his argument with an idea about shared values and unity. Do you agree with the writer's idea? Explain.
3. "Diversity" is a term regularly used in discussions about many institutions in American life—our schools, workplaces, neighborhoods, and places of worship, among others. From your understanding, why is diversity desirable in our institutions, and from what conditions does this desire originate?
4. Describe your own neighborhood in terms of its diversity—ethnic, racial, and economic—and identify issues that connect to your neighborhood's heterogeneity or homogeneity. What would you argue in response to one of these issues?

Social/Cultural Community

ABOUT THIS READING

This reading appeared in the September 11, 2009, edition of the *Christian Science Monitor* and was prepared by the *Monitor's* editorial board.

The Potential in Hillary Clinton's Campaign for Women

No other secretary of State has so focused on women's rights. It's a powerful shift.

By the Christian Science Monitor Editorial Board

When Hillary Rodham Clinton traveled to Africa last month, she visited war-racked eastern Congo to speak out against widespread rape by militias. She choked up after meeting with two rape victims and promised more US help—$17 million for medical treatment and security for victims.

Now she's taking the issue to the United Nations, where the US is leading an effort to shore up a resolution to end sexual violence against civilians during armed conflict. The Security Council passed Resolution 1820 last year, but follow through is sorely lacking.

Women's rights are becoming a signature issue for America's top diplomat. In her official travels, Mrs. Clinton talks with women, meets with female activists, and presses the twin challenges of women's rights and abuse with political leaders. She wants US development aid to focus more on women, and has appointed the first US ambassador for global women's issues.

The Bush administration, too, championed women's rights, especially in Muslim countries such as Afghanistan. But no secretary of State has sought to make women as high a priority as Clinton is attempting. It's a potentially powerful shift. If she can pull it off.

Obstacles abound, including the unruly thicket of US aid programs. But the greatest challenge is the deeply rooted culture in countries that oppress women and girls—often violently and even to the point of enslavement, sexual and otherwise. Honor killings, child brides, female infanticide—all of these accepted customs need to be realized as unacceptable.

As it seeks to promote women's rights, the US faces a paradox: The push could backfire if it comes off as a lecture or is perceived as another modern Western idea that will cause societal upheaval. But Clinton is wisely framing the issue in terms of countries' own interests.

Her pitch: Healthcare for women, especially maternal care, makes for healthier children and families. Schooling for girls contributes to economic progress. Microloans to women pay handsome dividends as women pay them off and invest further in businesses and their families' welfare. (The majority of the world's small-holder farmers are women.)

Some experts also see a link between the oppression of women and the problems of extremism and terrorism.

© iStockphoto.com/A-digit

"It is a very-well-researched fact that women are key to economic progress and social stability," Clinton said in India this summer.

Global aid groups, the World Bank, the US military, and economists agree. "Gender inequality hurts economic growth," reports Goldman Sachs.

Attitudes in male-dominated countries can change once men see the monetary benefits of female empowerment. Writers Nicholas D. Kristof and Sheryl WuDunn give a convincing example of this in their new book, "Half the Sky: Turning Oppression Into Opportunity for Women Worldwide."

They tell of Saima Muhammad, a poverty-stricken wife and mother near Lahore, Pakistan, who suffered daily beatings from her jobless husband. For lack of food, she had to send her daughter to live with an aunt. When her second child, a girl, was born, Saima's husband was urged by his mother to take a second wife so he could father a son.

Then Saima got a loan of $65 through a Pakistani group that lends exclusively to women. She started an embroidery business that now employs 30 families in the neighborhood (including her husband). She paid off her husband's debt (more than $3,000), kept her girls in school, and upgraded her house, adding running water and TV.

The authors write that Saima's husband is now more impressed with girls. They are "just as good as boys," he says.

Of course, women's rights are human rights. They don't need to be justified for any other reason than that. But in many countries, the path to that realization may well begin with economic self-interest, and Clinton is right to recognize this.

Analyze This Reading

1. What obstacles are in the way of Hillary Clinton's efforts to make women's rights a signature issue in her work as secretary of State? How is Clinton framing her approach to women's rights in view of these obstacles?
2. What example of female empowerment is offered by authors Kristof and WuDunn? What kind of change might this example be a model for?

Respond To This Reading

1. In your view, why might economic self-interest be a more practical approach to women's rights than arguing against cultural practices that injure women and girls?
2. The writer presents deeply rooted cultural attitudes toward women in foreign countries as an obstacle that Secretary of State Clinton must work around. Are there similar obstacles in the United States regarding attitudes toward women? What are they? Should these obstacles be worked around rather than confronted directly? Explain.

ABOUT THIS READING

Daniel J. Solove is an expert in privacy law. He is regularly cited in scholarly journals and frequently interviewed by the mainstream media. His 2007 book, *The Future of Reputation: Gossip, Rumor, and Privacy on the Internet*, won the McGannon

Award, an honor given to the "most notable book addressing issues of communication policy published during the previous year." This article appeared in *Salon*, a website covering political news and entertainment.

Why "Security" Keeps Winning Out Over Privacy

By Daniel J. Solove

Far too often, debates about privacy and security begin with privacy proponents pointing to invasive government surveillance, such as GPS tracking, the National Security Agency surveillance program, data mining, and public video camera systems. Security proponents then chime in with a cadre of arguments about how these security measures are essential to law enforcement and national security. When the balancing is done, the security side often wins, and security measures go forward with little to no privacy protections.

But the victory for security is one often achieved unfairly. The debate is being skewed by several flawed pro-security arguments. These arguments improperly tip the scales to the security side of the balance. Let's analyze some of these arguments, the reasons they are flawed, and the pernicious effects they have.

The All-or-Nothing Fallacy

Many people contend that "we must give up some of our privacy in order to be more secure." In polls, people are asked whether the government should conduct surveillance if it will help in catching terrorists. Many people readily say yes.

But this is the wrong question and the wrong way to balance privacy against security. Rarely does protecting privacy involve totally banning a security measure. It's not all or nothing. Instead, protecting privacy typically means that government surveillance must be subjected to judicial oversight and that the government must justify the need to engage in surveillance. Even a search of our homes is permitted if law enforcement officials obtain a warrant and probable cause. We shouldn't ask: "Do you want the government to engage in surveillance?" Instead, we should ask: "Do you want the government to engage in surveillance without a warrant or probable cause?"

We shouldn't be balancing the costs of completely forgoing surveillance against privacy. Instead, the security interest should only be the extent to which oversight and justification will make surveillance less effective. In many cases, privacy protection will not diminish the effectiveness of government security measures all that much. Privacy is losing out in the balance because it is being weighed against completely banning a security measure rather than being balanced against merely making it a little less convenient for the government.

The Deference Argument

Many security proponents argue that courts should defer to the executive branch when it comes to evaluating security measures. In cases where Fourth Amendment rights are pitted against government searches and surveillance, courts often refuse to second-guess the judgment of the government officials. The problem with doing this is that, unless the effectiveness of the security measures is explored, they will win out every time. All the government has to do is mention "terrorism," and whatever it proposes to do in response—whether wise or not—remains unquestioned.

But it is the job of the courts to balance privacy against security, and they can't do this job if they refuse to evaluate whether the security measure is really worth the tradeoff. Deference is an abdication of the court's role in ensuring that the government respects constitutional rights. The deference argument is one that impedes any effective balancing of interests.

The Pendulum Argument

In times of crisis, many security proponents claim that we must swing the pendulum toward greater security. "Don't be alarmed," they say. "In peacetime, the pendulum will swing back to privacy and liberty."

The problem with this argument is that it has things exactly backward. During times of crisis, the temptation to make unnecessary sacrifices of privacy and liberty in the name of security is exceedingly high. History has shown that many curtailments of rights were in vain, such as the Japanese-American internment during World War II and the McCarthy-era hysteria about communists. During times of peace, the need to protect privacy is not as strong because we're less likely to make such needless sacrifices. The greatest need for safeguarding liberty comes during times when we are least inclined to protect it.

The War-Powers Argument

After Sept. 11, the Bush administration authorized the National Security Agency to engage in warrantless wiretapping of the phone calls of Americans. Headquartered in Maryland, the NSA is the world's largest top-secret spy organization. The NSA surveillance program violated the Foreign Intelligence Surveillance Act (FISA), a federal law that required courts to authorize the kind of wiretapping the NSA engaged in. The Bush administration didn't justify its actions on an argument that it was acting legally under FISA. Instead, it argued that the president had the right to break the law because of the "inherent constitutional authority" of the president to wage war.

The war-powers argument is so broad that it fails of its own weight. If the president's power to wage war encompasses breaking any law that stands in the way, then the president has virtually unlimited power. A hallmark feature of our legal system is the rule of law. We repudiated a monarchy in the American Revolution, and we established a nation where laws would rule, not a lone dictator. The problem with the war-powers argument is that it eviscerates the rule of law. The most unfortunate thing is that Congress responded with a mere grumble, nothing with teeth—and not even teeth were bared. The message is now clear—in times of crisis, the rule of law can be ignored with impunity. That's a terrifying precedent.

The Luddite Argument

Government officials love new technology, especially new security technologies like biometric identification and the "naked scanners" at the airport. The security industry lobbies nervous government officials by showing them a dazzling new technology and gets them to buy it. Often, these technologies are not fully mature. Security proponents defend the use of these technologies by arguing that privacy proponents are Luddites who are afraid of new technology. But this argument is grossly unfair.

To see the problems with the Luddite argument, let's look at biometrics. Biometric identification allows people to be identified by their physical characteristics—fingerprint, eye pattern, voice and so on. The technology has a lot of promise, but there is a problem, one I call the "Titanic phenomenon." The Titanic was thought to be unsinkable, so it lacked adequate lifeboats. If biometric data ever got lost, we could be in a Titanic-like situation—people's permanent physical characteristics could be in the hands of criminals, and people could never reclaim their identities. Biometric identification depends on information about people's characteristics being stored in a database. And we hear case after case of businesses and government agencies that suffer data security breaches.

One virtue of our current clunky system of identification is that if data gets leaked, a person can clean up the mess. If your Social Security number is seized by an identity thief, you can get a new one. For sure, it's a hassle, but you can restore your identity. But what happens if your eye pattern gets into the hands of an identity thief? You can't get new eyes. Given the government's existing track record for data security, I'm not sure I'm ready to risk the government having such critical information about me that could cause such lasting and unfixable harm if lost. This isn't Luddism—it's caution. It is heeding the lessons of the Titanic. Security proponents just focus on the benefits of these technologies, but we also must think about what happens if they fail. This doesn't mean not adopting the technologies, but it means we should be cautious.

These are just a few of the flawed arguments that have shaped the privacy/security debate. There are many others, such as the argument made by people who say they have "nothing to hide." We can't have a meaningful balance between privacy and security unless we improve the way we debate the issue. We must confront and weed out the flawed arguments that have been improperly skewing the conversation.

Analyze This Reading

1. Which side of the security vs. privacy issue does the writer favor? Refer to two of the arguments the writer analyzes to support your answer.
2. What examples does the writer pull from our history to debunk the "Pendulum Argument?"

3. Describe the "Titanic phenomenon" and how the writer applies it to his position.

Respond To This Reading

1. The security vs. privacy issue in American life has been debated for centuries. For example, American icon Ben Franklin wrote in 1775 that, "They that can give up essential liberty to obtain a little temporary safety, deserve neither liberty not safety." Where do you stand on this issue? With reference to the five arguments the writer condemns, which arguments do you condone? Which do you reject?
2. In 2011 President Obama signed the *PATRIOT Sunsets Extension Act of 2011,* an act that allows for roving wiretaps, investigating a company's business records, and surveillance of individuals, often referred to as "lone wolves," suspected of terrorist activity not connected to terrorist groups. Do you favor this extension act? Explain.
3. In your view, what is the reasonable balance between privacy and security today?

ABOUT THIS READING

This reading was prepared by The Leadership Conference on Civil Rights Education Fund (LCCREF), part of the Leadership Conference on Civil Rights. LCCREF is focused on education and research; its aim is to generate awareness of the need for national policies that promote civil rights and economic and social justice. This reading appeared on the LCCREF web site.

Wrong Then, Wrong Now: Racial Profiling Before & After September 11, 2001

By LCCREF

Advocates of racial profiling reason that terrorists are most likely to belong to certain racial, ethnic, or religious groups. However, many examples prove that this assumption is false. Not only is racial profiling unhelpful, it actually *hinders* the antiterrorism effort by making it harder for law enforcement officials to investigate truly suspicious individuals. There are also several implementation problems with racial profiling. From a purely practical perspective, it can be impossible to correctly identify a person's race. Also, terrorists will change their techniques if they know officials are looking for people with certain characteristics. And finally, profiling may upset and alienate people who are likely to identify terrorists. For all these reasons, racial profiling is an ineffective antiterrorism tactic.

The assumptions driving terrorism profiling are the same as those behind traditional, street-level profiling—i.e., that a particular crime (here, terrorism) is most likely to be committed by members of a particular racial, ethnic or religious group, and that members of that group are, in general, likely to be involved in that kind of criminal activity. . . . These assumptions are flawed.

First, it is not true that terrorist acts are necessarily perpetrated by Arabs, or that the perpetrator of a terrorist act is likely to be an Arab. While all the men involved in the September 11 hijackings were Arab nationals, Richard Reid, who on December 22, 2001, tried to ignite an explosive device on a trans-Atlantic flight, was a British citizen of Jamaican ancestry. Prior to September 11, the bloodiest act of terrorism on United States soil was perpetrated by [Oklahoma City bomber] Timothy McVeigh. Non-Arabs like John Walker Lindh can be found in the ranks of the Taliban, al Qaeda and other terrorist organizations. At the same time, the overwhelming majority of Arabs, Arab Americans, Muslims, South Asians and Sikhs are law-abiding persons who would never think of engaging in terrorism.

Profiling Hinders the Anti-Terrorism Effort

Focusing on the many Arabs, South Asians, Muslims, and Sikhs who clearly pose no threat to national security detracts from the anti-terrorism effort. First, it diverts precious law enforcement resources away from investigations of individuals—including Arabs and Muslims—who have been linked to terrorist activity by specific and credible evidence. Second, it ignores the possibility that someone who does not fit the profile may be engaged in terrorism, or may be an unwitting accomplice to terrorism.

That race is an ineffective measure of an individual's terrorist intentions was made clear in a memorandum circulated to American law enforcement agents worldwide by a group of senior U.S. law enforcement officials in October 2002. The memorandum, entitled "Assessing Behaviors," emphasized that focusing on the racial characteristics of individuals was a waste of law enforcement resources and might cause law enforcement officials to ignore suspicious behavior, past or present, by someone who did not fit a racial profile. One of the authors of the report noted: "Fundamentally, believing that you can achieve safety by looking at characteristics instead of behaviors is silly. If your goal is preventing attacks . . . you want your eyes and ears looking for pre-attack behaviors, not characteristics."

The memorandum urged investigators to focus on actual behavior involving selection of targets, recruitment and organization of members, acquisition of skills, assessing vulnerabilities of targets, acquiring financing, probing boundaries, communicating with conspirators, using insiders, maintaining secrecy, and acquiring weapons. An emphasis on race, the memorandum noted, distracts from the observance of potentially suspicious behavior. This memorandum answers one of the main arguments of those who support racial profiling in the context of airport searches— i.e., that it is simply logical to focus precious law enforcement resources on Arab men rather than on older women from Minnesota or Swedish au pairs. What U.S. intelligence experts have made clear is that *any* emphasis on personal characteristics, rather than on behavior, misdirects scarce anti-terrorism resources.

This is not to say that law enforcement can never rely on race in fighting terrorism. As in street-level law enforcement, it is permissible to rely on race as part of a suspect-specific description. No one argues, for example, that the police cannot follow up on a specific tip that a group of Arabs is plotting terrorist acts in a particular apartment building by questioning Arabs who live in that building. Assuming the reliability of the source or the specificity of the information, identification of an individual's race carries with it the real potential for uncovering criminal activity.

Profiling, by contrast, is a scattershot device that is so crude as to be virtually useless. It is no coincidence that the questioning of 8,000 young Arab men in late 2001-early 2002 yielded virtually no leads about terrorism—there was no evidence to suggest that any of these men knew anything about terrorism in the first place.

Applying Racial Profiles Is Difficult

Racial profiling is particularly foolish in the anti-terrorism context for three additional reasons. First, even if one accepts the false assumption that terrorists are likely to be Arab or Muslim, the *application* of the profile is fraught with error. . . . Many persons who are neither Arab nor Muslim can get caught up in the terrorism profiling web. Consider these other examples from the airport security context:

- On October 22, 2001, four Hispanic businessmen were escorted off a Delta flight after passengers alerted airline staff that the men appeared to be Middle Eastern.

- On September 26, 2001, a group of six passengers of Indian ethnicity were questioned aboard a United Airlines flight from Los Angeles to Washington, D.C. The men were taken to the back of the plane, where they were first questioned by a pilot and then by FBI and INS [Immigration and Naturalization Service].

- On September 24, 2001, a Canadian woman of Indian origin was removed from her US Airways flight from Toronto to Las Vegas because her last name was similar in pronunciation to the name of one of the September 11 hijackers, Mohammed Atta. She was told that her name was "Middle Eastern" and therefore suspicious.

- A flight bound for New York's LaGuardia Airport was accompanied on its descent by a military plane after a passenger raised suspicions about a group of entertainers from India who were passing notes and changing seats. The group was detained for questioning and released five hours later without being charged. The passengers were not terrorists; they were animated because they were excited about visiting New York.

Thus, the profile of a terrorist as an Arab or Muslim has been applied to individuals who are neither Arab nor Muslim (e.g., Hispanics, Indians, and Sikhs). Profiling of Arabs and Muslims amounts to selective enforcement of the law against anyone with a certain type of "swarthy" foreign-looking appearance even if they do not in fact fit the terrorist profile. The profile is then useless in fighting terrorism, as well as offensive to an ever-broadening category of persons.

Terrorist Organizations Are Adaptable

Second, using racial profiling in the anti-terrorism effort is a classic example of refighting the last war. As noted above, al Qaeda and other terrorist organizations are pan-ethnic: they include Asians, Anglos, and ethnic Europeans.

They are also adaptive, dynamic organizations that will learn how to use non-Arabs such as Richard Reid to carry out terrorist attacks, or to smuggle explosive devices onto planes in the luggage of innocent people. The fact that the September 11 hijackers were Arab means little in predicting who the next terrorists will be. Racial profiling in any case is a crude mechanism; against an enemy like al Qaeda it is virtually useless.

Profiling Alienates Possible Information Sources

Third, and perhaps most important, the use of profiling in the anti-terrorism context, as in the street-crime context, alienates the very people that federal authorities have deemed instrumental in the anti-terrorism fight. Arab, South Asian, and Muslim communities may yield useful information to those fighting terrorism. Arabs and Arab Americans also offer the government an important source of Arabic speakers and translators. The singling out of Arabs, South Asians, Muslims, and Sikhs for investigation regardless of whether any credible evidence links them to terrorism will simply alienate these individuals and compromise the anti-terrorism effort. In particular, to the extent that federal authorities use the anti-terrorism effort as a pretext for detaining or deporting immigration law violators, individuals who might have information that is useful against terrorism may be afraid to come forward. At a minimum, those individuals will choose not to register, thereby defeating the very purpose of the registration program.

The alienation that results from terrorism profiling is compounded by the clumsy and insensitive manner in which it has thus far been carried out. . . . Arabs, South Asians, Muslims, and Sikhs who have tried to cooperate with authorities and to comply with the law have consistently been met by verbal (and sometimes physical) abuse; complete insensitivity to their cultural and religious practices; and a general lack of respect. . . . This treatment has caused many Arabs, South Asians, Muslims, and Sikhs to alter their behavior in order to avoid confrontations with authorities. Khaled Saffuri, a Lebanese man living in Great Falls, Virginia, says he makes sure to shave closely and wear a suit every time he flies; stays silent during flights and makes sure not to go to the bathroom in the middle of the flight; and sometimes avoids flying altogether in favor of long drives to his destinations in order to avoid air travel. In October 2002, Canada even issued a travel advisory warning those of its citizens born in Middle Eastern countries against traveling to the United States because of the hassles they would encounter. One celebrated Canadian, author Rohinton Mistry, who is of Indian descent and neither Arab nor Muslim, cancelled his book tour of the United States because he was "repeatedly and rudely" stopped at each airport along his tour route.

A Track Record of Failure

Recent events have demonstrated the futility of relying on profiles to predict who engages in targeted violence. In the fall of 2002, the Washington, D.C., area was shaken by a series of sniper attacks. Traditional profiles of serial killers assume that they are disaffected White men. Of course, the two men charged with the attacks are Black—an African American Gulf War Veteran,

John Allen Muhammad, and Jamaican-born John Lee Malvo. Their capture was hailed by law enforcement authorities as a triumph of "old fashioned police work" and entailed the investigation of multiple leads, the pursuit of evidence nationwide, and the use of the media and the public to help develop the facts. The investigation showed how reliance on a profile "can have [police] chasing a stereotype while the real culprit slips away."

Profiling has proven to be an inaccurate indicator of other types of targeted violent crimes. Traditional profiles presumed that political assassins were male. But women—Sarah Jane Moore and Lynette "Squeaky" Fromm—carried out assassination attempts on the life of President [Gerald] Ford. And in a situation directly analogous to the one facing Arabs and Muslims today, the 10 individuals found to be spying for Japan during World War II were Caucasian. They clearly did not fit the profile that caused America to order the internment of thousands of Japanese Americans.

Old-Fashioned Methods Are Still Best

The same kind of old-fashioned police work that tracks down serial killers, assassins, and spies will help catch terrorists, not reliance on broad, inaccurate, and confusing racial stereotypes. Federal authorities have also taken many useful steps to improve airport security that pose no threat to civil rights. The use of improved technology to detect explosives, luggage matching protocols, better training of screeners, and reinforcing of cockpit doors, for example, are all prudent measures to enhance airport security. *These* are the types of weapons, along with behavior-based surveillance, that will win the war against terrorism.

Those who support the use of profiling against Arabs, South Asians, Muslims, and Sikhs argue that America must resort to profiling given the stakes. The opposite is in fact true. The stakes are so high that the nation cannot afford to use an anti-terrorism mechanism as deeply flawed as racial profiling.

Analyze This Reading

1. What is the writer's view on racial profiling and terrorism? What distinction in terms of tracking terrorists does the writer make between racial characteristics and behavior?
2. What reasons does the writer provide to argue against applying racial profiles? What examples are used in support of these reasons?
3. What methods does the writer endorse to combat terrorism?

Respond To This Reading

1. The writer is systematic in bringing in support that argues against racial profiling as an effective method of fighting terrorism. Is this support persuasive? Does it support the view that old-fashioned methods are best?
2. Have you observed examples of racial and ethnic profiling in the media, in your community, or in your school? In your view, what fuels this kind of profiling?

3. Identify an example of profiling, and research its origins. What kind of claim would you draft in response to your findings? At what audience would you aim your argument?

ABOUT THIS READING

This short opinion column appeared in the online edition of *The Daily Athenaeum*, a student newspaper at West Virginia University (WVU). "The DA," as it's referred to on campus, is an affiliate of *UWIRE*, a wire service operated by journalists at more than 800 American colleges whose purpose is to make available to member colleges articles from student newspapers. Doug Walp is a Journalism major at WVU, sports writer for The DA, and freelance writer for the Associated Press.

The Importance of Political Awareness in America

By Doug Walp

Politics are toxic.

They're boring, seemingly over-emphasized and certainly over-publicized in the media during any normal year. It's even worse as we creep closer to the 2012 presidential election; even those that manage to consistently abstain from the collective political commentary find themselves being coerced into the conversation.

For these reasons and many more, college-age students often disconnect themselves with the national political issues at hand.

Who can blame them, right?

Despite the obvious need to prioritize academics, college has also always been a time for social expansion among other aspects of maturity. In other words, the latest legislation passed down from our nation's policymakers is usually not the most prominent conflict in our lives.

But what we sometimes fail to realize is that our generation is standing on the precipice of an imminent and monumental political shift in our country. And by taking the initiative to remain proactively politically informed, our generation—along with our modern beliefs and ideals—will soon supplant those of our parents and other generations before us.

It's a critical responsibility, despite the fact that so many young people take it so lightly.

The battle against SOPA (Stop Online Piracy Act) and PIPA (PROTECT IP Act) have brought to light some of our generation's capabilities to stand up against potential political injustices—especially through the means of the Internet—but have also highlighted some of our shortcomings.

For instance, the PIPA bill was introduced to the U.S. Senate last May, but it took nearly a year for public awareness about such a threatening piece of legislation to reach the point where policymakers finally had no choice but to pull the bill while they come up with a less-controversial way of targeting copyright infringement.

It was promising that such attention could be brought to a specific piece of legislation so quickly, where in less-democratic countries it would have almost certainly passed without even the possibility of debate, but regrettable in the sense that it took such a wide-scale campaign to raise awareness about a piece of legislation embedded with countless sacrifices of our basic civil rights entitled by the Constitution.

Despite the fact many are now "basking in the glory of victory" over SOPA and PIPA, the truth is the battle for enforcing copyright infringement is far from over. The only way to ensure we can continue to effectively drive back similarly restrictive legislation is to remain proactively informed and at least somewhat politically involved.

This responsibility applies to older generations as well—before the widespread Jan. 18 blackouts by a multitude of websites (Google, Wikipedia, etc.) caught the attention of the national news, hardly anyone I had talked to over the age of 40 was familiar with either SOPA or PIPA, or how it in anyway affected them.

Too often, our society depends on these major media outlets to keep us up-to-date and informed on critical, developing national news. This is simply a misappropriation of responsibility.

Each voting individual in our society is responsible for gathering their own information about our nation's policies to make informed, independent decisions.

That doesn't mean I'm prescribing you to engage in thorough political discussion on a daily basis or to go scouring through heaps of political legislation looking for that one minor civil injustice someone else might have missed.

It just means that part of our collective responsibility as American citizens is being educated enough on the political process and new laws that are being introduced in order to continue to improve collective social conditions and keep lawmakers in check.

Admittedly, it's easier said than done.

But a concerted effort by a majority of our generation to become more politically aware could literally turn the tide in American politics, beginning to shift policies and bring about a more agreeable status quo for the future.

Analyze This Reading

1. What motive does the writer offer to his peers for staying politically informed? What examples does he deploy to support his position?
2. What does the writer mean when he accuses "major media outlets" of a "misappropriation of responsibility?"

Respond To This Reading

1. The writer twice uses the word "shift," once in paragraph five and again in the final paragraph. While he does not specify how our country is about to shift politically, what is your sense of this shift, if any, that is taking place now in American politics?
2. What issues in your life motivate you to pay attention to politics and/or to speak out in response?

3. On the local level, that is, in the context of decision-making proce-
    dures in your community—by a town council, county commission,
    school board, municipal agency, etc.—what changes would you make
    to encourage your colleagues to participate actively?

ABOUT THIS READING

Michael N. Nagler is president of the Metta Center for Nonviolence Education,
a contributing writer to the online site *New Clear Vision*, and Professor Emeritus
at the University of California, Berkeley. He is the author of *The Search for a
Nonviolent Future* (2001). This article appeared in *Truthout*.

The Cassandra Syndrome

By Michael N. Nagler

Last month, 57 people lost their lives in eight mass shootings across
America. "The killing grounds," Timothy Egan wrote in The *New York Times*
last week [April 8, 2009], "include a nursing home, a center for new immigrants, a child's bedroom. Before that it was a church, a college, a daycare
center." It is hard to argue when he calls this epidemic "the cancer at the
core of our democracy."

It's not that hard to understand why we're experiencing an upsurge in
"senseless violence." More to the point, it isn't all that hard to see what we
can do about it.

This rash of killings was an uptick on a very general trend. That's important, because we don't want to just level out the trend that is already higher
than any country calling itself civilized should put up with: we want it drastically lower. We want the killing to stop. It's not particularly easy to face why
we've been inflicted with all this violence, but we must, because how else
will we find a solution. And in the end, the solution may not be as unpleasant as we think.

As a colleague of mine in Public Health recently declared, "We are
increasing violence by every means possible." He was talking about the
mass media. The enormously high, and increasing, level of violence in the
"entertainment" industry–including the violent emphasis of the nightly
news–makes violence seem normal, unavoidable, sexy and fun–even a
source of meaning. The studies documenting this go back for decades, only
lapsing for a while in the early eighties when scientists began to realize
nobody was listening to them. They could say, as the US Surgeon General's
Scientific Advisory Committee on Television and Social Behavior said in
1972, that the "preponderance of evidence" makes it very clear that television was already making young (and other) people more unfeeling and
aggressive; they could complain about it in PTA meetings (as I have done)
or shout it from the rooftops: neither policymakers nor producers nor us,
the end consumers, paid much attention.

Summing up in 1996, psychologist Madeline Levine wrote, "there is a large, consistent, and damning body of evidence that says that watching a lot of violence makes children aggressive and fearful;" and she adds, tragically, "we are losing our awareness of what it means to be human." Since then we not only did not reduce violent viewing, we "advanced" from passive television to interactive games that, according to preliminary evidence and common sense, dehumanize people more effectively.

What scientists and the public did not know when this research began (and the public still does not) is the striking evidence now available from non-invasive methods to study brain activation, primarily Magnetic Resonance Imaging. It has given physical reality to the observation of all psychologists and anyone who knows a child that we're profoundly imitative creatures. In a conversation I had about the effects of the mass media recently with UCLA neuroscientist Marco Iacoboni, he told me that we humans are so "wired for empathy" that, "If we could stop all the violence for a week, it would never come back." Translating this into practical terms, anyone who could step out of the "exciting" barrage of violent imagery would so reduce his or her artificial provocation to violence that the rest of the problem could, over time, be brought down to very minimal levels. Enough of us doing this and we'd be on our way to living in a nonviolent culture.

Since government is not likely to intervene (it sounds too much like censorship), and the industry itself shows no sign of waking up to its responsibilities, we are left with one recourse, and fortunately it's a good one: if we don't buy, they don't sell. You may think, "Oh, I'm just one person," but that's the point: As writer George Orwell said of a hanging he had to witness back in the bad old colonial days in Burma, "One life less; one world less." Never underestimate the damage that's being done to your mind—or the power of your example once you repair it.

Am I saying that everyone who wants to stop this shameful mayhem should stop watching violent programming, even when it's disguised as news? I am. But I also say something else: let's have more legitimate satisfactions that take us in the opposite direction. Real human contact is the most effective substitute. Of course, actual people can be a pain in the neck (present company excepted), but it's way more fulfilling to talk to your neighbors, have coffee with an old friend or a potential new one, say your piece at a book club, or even have a reasonable argument with someone who disagrees with you than trying to have a passive relationship with pixels on a flat screen.

Gandhi had a famous formula he called the "Seven Social Sins." Wealth Without Work was one of them, I remember, and Science Without Humanity. I think if the Mahatma were physically alive today he would add Entertainment Without Discretion. So let's not turn our scientists into Cassandras, doomed to predict the future with nobody believing them. Let's act, at least individually and in our families, before we become a civilization without a future.

Analyze This Reading

1. According to the writer, how do non-invasive methods used to study brain activity, such as Magnetic Resonance Imaging, offer an explanation for our predisposition to violence?
2. What antidote to violence-watching does the writer offer?
3. In the final paragraph, the writer employs a term from Greek mythology, "Cassandra." What is a Cassandra and how is the writer using the term?

Respond To This Reading

1. In paragraph six, the writer draws on scientific evidence to argue that stepping out of the "barrage of violent imagery" would reduce the levels of violence in our world. Discuss the extent to which you agree or disagree with this contention.
2. Some critics of the writer's argument contend that it's unrealistic to think that we can step outside of our viewing habits, suggesting that we are addicted to various screens these days and are thus unable to distinguish between what we need and what we want. Are you addicted? What would get in the way of reducing or shutting down your viewing habits and the regular intake of violent images?

ABOUT THIS READING

At the time of this writing, writer Valerie White was executive director of the Sexual Freedom Legal Defense and Education Fund. This reading appeared in *The Humanist*, a bimonthly magazine that, in its own words, "applies humanism—a naturalistic and democratic outlook informed by science, inspired by art, and motivated by compassion—to broad areas of social and personal concern."

A Humanist Looks at Polyamory

By Valerie White

There are two words that I apply to myself which, considered together, probably place me in one of the smallest categories of humanity. Those are polyamorous and Humanist. There is no way of knowing what percentage of the population engages in an open, responsible, and respectful multi-partner lifestyle, although it is likely that the number runs quite high and accounts for hundreds of thousands of people in the United States. But let's estimate that it's 2 percent (a number I found bruited about on the Internet), and that Humanists comprise less than 10 percent. That would put me in the class polyamorous Humanist, which comprises 0.2 percent of the general population. Of course, I think there is a correlation: I think it's probable that Humanists are more likely to be polyamorous and that polyamorists are more likely to be Humanist than the rest of the population.

I knew I was polyamorous and I knew I was Humanist before I knew the words.

Raised by atheist parents, I never had any god belief to lose and I've never acquired any, either. Being churchless in the 1950s wasn't an easy thing for a child to cope with, though, and it was with a sigh of homecoming that I discovered Unitarian Universalism [UU] when in college in 1962. I don't remember hearing the word Humanism until the mid 1980s, when my mother, who lived with me then, was a subscriber to the *Humanist*. I joined the American Humanist Association, publisher of the *Humanist*, on my own soon afterward. Ever since then that's what I've called myself.

What Is Polyamory?

I learned the word polyamory a few years later in 1994. . . .

I expect it would be useful for me to define polyamory, which is living by the principle that it is possible to love more than one person at a time without deception or betrayal.

I've known since my late teens that monogamy wasn't natural to me. Judging from the amount of garden variety cheating, swinging, and serial monogamy that goes on in our society, many many other people aren't naturally monogamous, either. I understand there may be people who, after they commit themselves to a partner, never feel a stirring of romantic or erotic interest in anyone else, but I'm not one of them. Heck, even Jimmy Carter admitted to lusting after other women in his heart.

"Well, of course" you say. "You can feel an attraction to someone besides your partner but you don't have to act on it." Maybe. An awful lot of people do act on it, however, and consequently a lot of marriages break up over adultery.

Without polyamory my choices would be:

1. cheat, lie, betray, deceive
2. engage in agreed-upon recreational sex, swapping with other couples
3. eschew committed relationships
4. embrace celibacy
5. chafe in resentful frustration

I find all five of these alternatives unacceptable. I live my life in a relationship in which each of us accepts that the other may have additional loving relationships. I can't imagine living any other way. This lifestyle is predicated upon the assumption espoused by Humanist science fiction writer Robert Heinlein that "love doesn't subtract; it multiplies." It is perhaps most melodically expressed in Humanist Malvina Reynolds' beloved song:

Love is something if you give it away,
Give it away, give it away.
Love is something if you give it away;
You end up having more.
It's just like a magic penny;
Hold it tight, and you won't have any;
Lend and spend it, and you'll have so many
They'll roll all over the floor.

Poly people believe that the deep, mutual love that glows in a longstanding relationship isn't necessarily destroyed by the energy that kindles in a new one.

The Biology of Polyamory

What is the biology of polyamory? Is it hardwired in the genes? Nobody knows. I suspect that many, perhaps most people, have the capacity to love multiple partners. An awful lot of people have had more than one lover. Many other species in the animal kingdom are poly, including humans' close cousins the bonobo chimpanzees. Even supposedly monogamous animals like swans turn out to hatch eggs fathered by multiple males.

In humans, however, is an instinctual drive for multiple partners only hardwired for males? Can it be true that the evolutionary advantage for men is to spread their seed as widely as possible and for women to cleave only to one? I doubt it. Why wouldn't it be evolutionarily advantageous for a woman to have more than one man who was willing to beat off saber-tooth tigers from her and her baby—and have a selection of men to mate with in pursuit of better offspring?

Love Enriches Love

To polyfolk, loving more than one partner comes as naturally as loving more than one child: you don't stop loving your firstborn when your next child comes along. In fact, you may feel that your first love is given new dimension when a new love enriches your life.

But a life of this kind requires honesty, openness, respect, self-confidence, trust, and, above all, communication. It's hard work. It can be painful. But I find it worthwhile. And it is completely congruent with my Humanist values. Doesn't choosing to love more than one person honestly and responsibly derive from these core Humanist principles found in Humanist Manifesto II of 1973?

We affirm that moral values derive their source from human experience. . . .

Happiness and the creative realization of human needs and desires, individually and in shared enjoyment, are continuous themes of humanism. . . . We believe in maximum individual autonomy consonant with social responsibility. . . . While we do not approve of exploitive, denigrating forms of sexual expression, neither do we wish to prohibit, by law or social sanction, sexual behavior between consenting adults. The many varieties of sexual exploration should not in themselves be considered "evil". . . . Short of harming others or compelling them to do likewise, individuals should be permitted to express their sexual proclivities and pursue their lifestyles as they desire. We wish to cultivate the development of a responsible attitude toward sexuality, in which humans are not exploited as sexual objects, and in which intimacy, sensitivity, respect, and honesty in interpersonal relations are encouraged.

Humanist Manifesto III, published in 2003, adds:

Humans are social by nature and find meaning in relationships. Humanists long for and strive toward a world of mutual care and concern, free of cruelty and its consequences, where differences are resolved cooperatively without resorting to violence. The joining of individuality with interdependence enriches our lives, encourages us to enrich the lives of others, and inspires hope of attaining peace, justice, and opportunity for all.

To answer the question that everyone asks: yes, polyamorous people can get jealous. But we know that jealousy is the fear of losing something valued and so, when jealousy arises, all parties rally round to reassure the jealous one. Polyamorous people can also feel "compersion," taking joy from a beloved partner's pleasure with another love.

Forms of Polyamory

There are almost as many ways to practice polyamory as there are polyamorous people. Lots of people have one primary partner and one or more "secondary." Groups of people form an intimate network or a "group marriage." Poly people live in triads and quads and larger assemblies that are similar to the way traditional couples live. Popular mythology to the contrary notwithstanding, it appears there are as many male-female-male triads as the other way around.

A subset of polyamory is polyfidelity, which is just what it sounds like; people practicing polyfidelity are sexually exclusive within their group. Polyamorous people can be heterosexual, bisexual, or homosexual. There are people practicing polyamory who are in their seventies and in their teens. In fact, there is some reason to believe that poly-style multi-partnering is the norm in the younger cohort.

There are almost as many reasons to be polyamorous as there are polyamorous people. Some people are poly simply because they want to have more sex. Some are poly because they want to have less. Some are poly because they love the excitement and energy of new relationships; some because they like the mutuality of group living. Some are poly because they don't find that one person can meet their emotional needs while others are poly because they don't want to be solely responsible for one person's emotional needs.

How did this movement (and it is a movement, with several national organizations, local support groups in most major cities, e-mail lists, matchmaking websites, and even a denominational UU group) get started and how did it get its name? The word polyamorous was coined by Morning Glory Zell in 1990 and is a hybrid of a Greek root meaning "many" and a Latin root meaning "love." Zell said she could have been consistently Latin or Greek and called it omni-amory or polyphilia, but they sounded like diseases.

Fictional Influences

In 1961 American science fiction writer Robert Heinlein wrote a novel entitled *Stranger in a Strange Land.* Its premise is that it's possible to love more than one person at a time: openly, honestly, spiritually, and sexually. While that idea wasn't exactly new (after all, there have been menages a trois in real life, in fiction, and in the movies for a long time), the concept fired the imaginations of lots of people in those years leading up to the 1967 summer of love, and a movement was born. Other novels by Heinlein, such as *The*

Moon Is a Harsh Mistress, Friday, and *Time Enough for Love* are also cited by polyfolk as inspirational.

However, Heinlein and his fans weren't the only ones to be suggesting or advocating new ways of looking at relationships. Robert Rimmer's 1965 novel, *The Harrad Experiment,* and other novels also suggested that loving, committed, and respectful relationships don't have to be sexually exclusive. Rimmer himself lived in a quad for many years with his wife and another couple. I had the honor once of meeting him and his wife; I discovered from talking to him that he valued his role as one of the fathers of the poly movement. When he died recently he was remembered as one of the founders of polyamory. Many people seized on Rimmer's premise and tried to create working multipartner relationships. The 1972 self-help book, *Open Marriage,* by George and Nina O'Neill contributed to the trend, even though many people found it curiously asexual.

In 1983 a study by Philip Blumstein and Pepper Schwartz reported that 15 to 28 percent of married couples in the sample group had "an understanding that allows non-monogamy" but weren't aware that other people were doing the same thing. It took the invention of the Internet to create the current explosive growth of the poly movement, as people who knew they wanted multiple relationships could finally find each other. (If you were to do a Google search on "polyamory" today you would get 75,000 hits.)

More About Love than Sex

Naturally, the thing most people think about when they learn of multipartner relationships is sex. When I was interviewed recently by a British women's magazine, the resulting article was balanced and fair but all the highlighted quotes were about sex. Intercourse is not the primary reason people seek polyamorous relationships. As a friend of mine once remarked, "Polyamory is about more love, not more sex." In fact, poly folk quip that they are too busy communicating and scheduling to have time for sex.

Sometimes it's easier to understand a concept by learning what it is not. Polyamory is not infidelity. Polyamory is not promiscuous, superficial, unthinking, irresponsible sex. Polyamory is not swinging. In my mind swinging is a perfectly responsible choice when neither party is coerced. But when swingers agree that they won't develop loving relationships with the people they swing with, swingers aren't polyamorous. When swingers do develop lasting, loving friendship with their swing partners I would say that what they're doing is indistinguishable from polyamory.

If you look for polyamory on the Internet you'll find that, like Humanism, there have been many attempts to define it. Most of them utilize words like ethical, responsible, honorable, open, honest, intentional, and principled.

I am a Humanist and I am polyamorous. I was both of these things before I had terms for them. I find my Humanism and my polyamory congruent and satisfying and I wouldn't part with either of them.

Analyze This Reading

1. What is "polyamory"? How does the writer view polyamory in evolutionary terms?

2. What is the polyamorist view of sexuality? Of jealousy?
3. What forms does polyamory take? Why do people become polyamorous?
4. In the author's view, why is polyamory more about love than sex?
5. Based on the description *The Humanist* reproduced in the "ABOUT THIS READING" section that precedes this article, what values do you associate with the audience the writer aims to reach in this article?

Respond To This Reading

1. In your view, what keeps polyamory from wider acceptance than the 2 percent of Americans the writer estimates to be polyamorous?
2. The writer concludes by addressing misconceptions about polyamory, rejecting ideas that it is "promiscuous, superficial, unthinking" and that it involves "irresponsible sex." What is your view of polyamory as the writer defines it?
3. What issues do you associate with love relationships involving sex? What would you claim in response to the most important of these issues?

ABOUT THIS READING

Writer Jeff Yang's books include *I Am Jackie Chan: My Life in Action* (with Jackie Chan, 1998) and *Eastern Standard Time: A Guide to Asian Influence in American Culture, from Astro Boy to Zen Buddhism* (1997). With Parry Shen and Keith Chow, he edited *Secret Identities: The Asian American Superhero Anthology* (2009). This reading appeared on Salon.com, an online news magazine.

Killer Reflection

Cho and other Asian shooters were portrayed as "smart but quiet" and "fundamentally foreign." What do these stereotypes reveal, and what do they obscure?

By Jeff Yang

Like everyone else, I first reacted to the news of the April 16 shootings at Virginia Tech with shock—visceral and blinding. Sick with horror, but hungry for information, I went through what has become a ritual exercise whenever tragedy or catastrophe strikes—9/11, the tsunami, Katrina. I turned on the television, sorted through the cascade of conflicting details on competing news sites, and began exchanging rapid-fire e-mail and instant messages with friends of every background, from regions around the world. With each new revelation, we shared our common emotions: grief for the victims and their families; rage at the murderer; bitterness at the ready availability of weapons capable of exacting such a devastating toll.

Then came the word that the killer, this faceless stranger responsible for a crime of historic lethality, was Korean American, and the tenor of the messages changed dramatically. Suddenly, most of it was from Asian American friends and colleagues, with a fresh and unique range of concerns. Some expressed guilt, inexplicable and unwarranted, that a child of our community might be responsible for such mayhem: "As a Korean, I do feel partly guilty and responsible," said CeFaan Kim, an associate producer at NY1 News. "Every person I've spoken to who's Korean, and that's a large number, feels the same way. It's a cultural difference, but the fact that our community shares this feeling is simply fact."

Some expressed reluctant empathy: "Ours is not always a forgiving culture," said Jenny Song. "There's a lot of pressure to make it in the top 5 percent—be it schools, jobs, society, etc.; we tend to have an overall closed culture in which you're either 'in' or 'out,' with very little room for those who are a little different or don't fit in with standard norms. I can't help but wonder if there are certain aspects of our culture that may have compounded his feelings. I can't help feel as though this incident is also a wake-up call for Korean society in many ways."

And others wrote words of fear and alarm, decrying the constant representation of the Asian-born but American-raised perpetrator Seung-Hui Cho as a foreigner, pointing to blog postings attacking Asians as an inscrutable, unassimilable threat from within, and noting unconfirmed reports of backlash—a South Korean flag being burned in Fort Lee, N.J.; a Korean American student in Manhattan threatened by white classmates.

"Most of the perpetrators of mass school killings have been white," said Paul Niwa, a journalism professor at Emerson College. "After those shootings, do you think white people felt guilty that the shooter was white? Do you think white people felt that since the shooter was white, that the shooter would give society a bad impression of whites? A shooter can be white and nobody thinks that race played a part in the crime. But when someone nonwhite commits a crime, this society makes the person's race partially at fault."

Reading these comments, I found myself caught in a dilemma. I want to think that race is not a factor in the toxic mix of rage and psychological disturbance that has occasionally discharged as this kind of violence. And, certainly, in most cases it isn't: Teenage angst is colorblind, and the triggers for crimes like these have included parental abuse, schoolyard persecution, romantic obsession—phenomena that exist beyond culture or ethnicity.

But professor Niwa is right: When race enters the equation—when the perpetrator of a crime of this type is black, like "Beltway Snipers" John Allen Muhammad and his ward Lee Boyd Malvo, or Asian, like Cho—it rises to the surface and stays there, prompting inevitable discussions about whether "black rage" or "immigrant alienation" were somehow to blame; whether in some fundamental fashion, color of skin, shape of eye, or nation of origin lie at the seething, secret heart of such tragedies.

There have been two other widely reported school shooting sprees by Asian perpetrators. One of them, the case of University of Iowa exchange student Gang Lu, even served as the inspiration for Chen Shi-zheng's new film, "Dark Matter," which won the Alfred P. Sloan Prize at this year's Sundance Film Festival. On Nov. 1, 1991, Lu, a promising, Beijing-born physics student, brought a pair of pistols into a department meeting and opened fire, killing five people and paralyzing a sixth, before shooting himself fatally in the head. A *New York Times* article on the film quotes Vanderbilt University physics professor James Dickerson as saying that Asian students are often the victims of "unstated racism" and the preconception that they are smart, hardworking and unlikely to complain. "As a result they wind up as cogs in the research machine and remain isolated from the rest of the community and the culture," says Dickerson. "It's something not widely discussed in the physics community." It then goes on to quote Harvard math professor Shing-Tung Yau on the "high expectation" placed on children by Chinese families. "When they realize that they cannot achieve it, they get very upset," he says. "They also compete among themselves severely."

The other case is that of Wayne Lo, a Taiwanese-born student who moved to Billings, Mont., with his family at the age of 13, then attended Simon's Rock College in Great Barrington, Mass. Accounts of his case—which took place a little over a year after Gang Lu's rampage, on Dec. 14, 1992—carefully use his intelligence (he was accepted at Simon's Rock on the W.E.B. DuBois Minority Scholarship!), his exquisite talent in classical music (he excelled on violin!), and his previous history as a quiet, unassuming individual to counterpoint his bloody rifle attack, which killed two and wounded four others. Here's a typically lyrical quote, from a feature by the New York Times' Anthony DePalma: "Only Mr. Lo knows what led him to turn away from the classical music he once loved and instead embrace the violent, discordant music known as hardcore, and a surly group of students who were equally entranced by it. Only he knows how the same fingers that danced with such agility and emotion over the strings of a violin could, as the police say, have pressed the trigger of a semiautomatic assault rifle, shattering the campus silence and ripping through several lives." As with Lu, news reports also emphasized Lo's foreign birth—sometimes implying, sometimes outright stating that Lo's cultural difference may have led to his sense of isolation, of being disrespected, of social exclusion, and ultimately, to his deadly eruption.

The degree to which these paired memes—"smart but quiet" and "fundamentally foreign"—are repeated in the coverage of these two crimes is striking. In Lo's case, it was enough to prompt attorney Rhoda J. Yen to write a paper titled "Racial Stereotyping of Asians and Asian Americans and Its Effect on Criminal Justice: A Reflection on the Wayne Lo Case" for Boalt School of Law's Asian Law Journal, in which she raises the theory that this racial imagery may have tainted Lo's ability to receive a fair trial.

The reporting around Seung-Hui Cho seems to have followed the same through-line: Right here on Salon, Joe Eaton reported one of Cho's high school classmates calling him "a quiet guy, a really, really quiet guy," but also a "'supersmart' student known for his math skills." Most news reports have also referred to him as a "resident alien," a legally proper but semiotically complex term that seems to emphasize difference—while a "legal permanent resident" sounds like someone who belongs in this nation, an "alien" doesn't even sound like he belongs on this planet. It's a word that seems designed to be followed by "invader"—a phrase whose appropriateness is underscored by the pictures of Cho, scowling and fisting guns at the camera, that now stare out from every news site.

There's no excusing Cho's crimes, or those of Lu and Lo before him. All three were guilty of heinous acts, of ruining and ending lives, and merit no apology for what they did. The point of bringing up all three is not to defend them, but to ask whether media and society have too easily conflated them, bundling their individual cases in a convenient packaging that subtly evokes those hoary, oddly contradictory typecasts of the "model minority" whiz kid and invading "yellow peril."

One contributor to the legal group blog De Novo, who actually attended college with Wayne Lo and was close friends with one of his victims, has gone so far as to draw a direct comparison between Cho and Lo. While acknowledging Rhoda Yen's journal article and disavowing any intent to suggest that race was a primary reason for those two slides into murderous violence, "Dave" nevertheless notes that "across the board, college shooters seem to be males under some pressure for success, academic and/or sexual, which would seem to include many Asian males." Dave then admits that this suggestion itself rests on a "model minority" stereotype. And that's a quandary we often find ourselves in when invoking race here—or really, anywhere: It's challenging to talk about it in a complex and constructive fashion, so it's often tossed out, or put into play via crude and simplistic clichés.

Excluding race from the equation entirely eliminates some very real criteria we might use to better understand why acts like this occur, and how to perhaps prevent them in the future. Parental expectations among Asian Americans, particularly within immigrant families, are indeed great; racism and casual discrimination does exist; social isolation may be more likely if you're in a situation where the people around you mostly don't look like you or share your background.

Perhaps most important, there are wide differences between cultures in how mental illness is perceived, with Asian cultures largely rejecting the concept of psychological disorder as a disease—to the point of refusing treatment, ostracizing sufferers, and even suppressing discussion of the topic. Could this attitude, combined with a lack of culturally sensitive counseling, have resulted in the inner turmoil of Lu, Lo and Cho being overlooked or underplayed? "Asian immigrants are not as liberally educated about mental illness as others in the U.S.; they feel it is something strange, something you shouldn't deal with or discuss," says psychiatrist Dr. Damian Kim, who has practiced clinically for 35 years, and who has written a book on mental health for immigrants that is available in both Korean and English. "For them, seeking treatment is an indication that there's something wrong with you."

But focusing on race, particularly using the lens of stereotype, flattens individuality, and obscures other factors that are more meaningful and important. "Pressure for success, academic and/or sexual" isn't in and of itself a reason for someone to go out and commit mass murder. I know hundreds of young Asian males who experienced that kind of pressure as adolescents, who grew up silent, studious and socially awkward; who were perceived as different, to the point of being excluded or taunted; who had unusual hobbies and obsessions—and who've never shot off anything except their mouths.

I'm one myself. While attending St. Ann's School in Brooklyn, N.Y., back in the mid-'80s, I worked on a student film with my equally weird friends called "Burnout," a horror-comedy that recast our high school as "Sat-An's School," an institution run by a group of diabolical cultists who manipulate a young, misanthropic student to murder his peers and teachers in various silly and bloody ways. We launched the production with the cooperation of faculty and administration, some of whom played themselves. The film was never finished—SATs and parental expectations got in the way.

But I wonder, if I proposed that script as a high schooler today, a quiet Asian American male with few friends and odd interests, would I be automatically dropped into a box marked "potential spree killer"? And if I were tagged with that combination of model minority and yellow peril as a result, if I found myself surrounded by people appalled that a "good, quiet Asian boy" might write a gory slasher flick about a student maniac . . . would that help or hurt?

Analyze This Reading

1. How does the writer respond to the observations of Professor Niwa?
2. According to the writer, how did the media stereotype Seung-Hui Cho and other Asian-born perpetrators? What words and terms does the writer identify as contributing to this stereotyping?
3. How does stereotyping conceal important cultural influences and thus limit more accurate understanding of individuals like Seung-Hui Cho, Gang Lu, and Wayne Lo?'
4. The writer concludes this article with a personal story. Is this movement away from public, objective treatment of the issue into private anecdote effective in terms of engaging the reader? Is this a strategy you can see yourself using in an argument? Explain.

Respond To This Reading

1. Professor Niwa contends that race, and eventual stereotyping, becomes a factor in the media when the perpetrators are not white. Explain why you agree or disagree with this contention. Support your position with examples.
2. What is the danger of racial and ethnic stereotyping? Is it present in your school? What issues exist in your community that warrant discussion about the kind of stereotyping that the writer addresses?
3. Imagine drafting an argument in which you focus on the language of ethnic stereotyping. What terms would you isolate and discuss?

Consumer Community

ABOUT THIS READING

Writer Judith Simmer Brown is professor of religious studies at Naropa University in Colorado and a Buddhist scholar. This reading appeared in *Contemporary Issues Companion: Consumerism*, edited by Uma Kukathas.

A Buddhist Perspective on Consumerism

By Judith Simmer Brown

Western Buddhism must serve the world, not itself. It must become, as the seventh-century Indian master Shantideva wrote, "the doctor and the nurse for all sick beings in the world until everyone is healed; a rain of food and drink, an inexhaustible treasure for those who are poor and destitute." We can only imagine the kinds of suffering our children will encounter. Even now, we see the poor with not enough food and no access to clean drinking water; we see ethnic and religious prejudice that would extinguish those who are different; we see the sick and infirm who have no medicine or care; we see rampant exploitation of the many for the pleasure and comfort of the few; we see the demonization of those who would challenge the reign of wealth, power, and privilege. And we know the twenty-first century will yield burgeoning populations with an ever-decreasing store of resources to nourish them.

Fueling the suffering is the relentless consumerism which pervades our society and the world. Greed drives so many of the damaging systems of our planet. The socially engaged biologist Stephanie Kaza said that in America each of us consumes our body weight each day in materials extracted and processed from farms, mines, rangelands, and forests—120 pounds on the average. Since 1950, consumption of energy, meat, and lumber has doubled; use of plastic has increased five-fold; use of aluminum has increased seventy-fold; and airplane mileage has increased thirty-three-fold per person. We now own twice as many cars as in 1950. And with every bite, every press of the accelerator, every swipe of the credit card in our shopping malls, we leave a larger ecological footprint on the face of the world. We have squeezed our wealth out of the bodies of plantation workers in Thailand, farmers in Ecuador, and factory workers in Malaysia.

The crisis of consumerism is infecting every culture of the world, most of which are now emulating the American lifestyle. David Loy, in *The Religion of the Market*, suggests that consumerism is based on two unexamined tenets or beliefs:

1. growth and enhanced world trade will benefit everyone, and
2. growth will not be constrained by the inherent limits of a finite planet.

The ground of consumerism is ego gratification, its path is an ever-increasing array of wants, and its fruition is expressed in the Cartesian perversion—"I shop, therefore I am." While it recruits new converts through the flood of mass media, it dulls the consumer, making us oblivious to the suffering in which we participate. Shopping is a core activity in sustaining a culture of denial.

With the collapse of communist countries throughout the world, the growth of consumerism is all but unchallenged. As traditional societies modernize, consumerism is the most alluring path. Religious peoples and communities have the power to bring the only remaining challenge to consumerism. And Buddhism has unique insights which can stem the tide of consumptive intoxication.

How do we respond to all the suffering created by consumerism? How will our children respond? It is easy to join the delusion, forgetting whatever Buddhist training we may have had. But when we return to it, we remember—the origin of suffering is our constant craving. We want, therefore we consume; we want, therefore we suffer. As practitioners, we feel this relentless rhythm in our bones. We must, in this generation, wake up to the threat of consumerism, and join with other religious peoples to find a way to break its grip. We must all find a way to become activists in the movement which explores alternatives to consumerism.

As Western Buddhists, we must recognize the threats of consumerism within our practice, and within our embryonic communities and institutions. From a Tibetan Buddhist point of view, consumerism is just the tip of the iceberg. It represents only the outer manifestation of craving and acquisitiveness. Twenty-five years ago, my guru, the Vidyadhara Chogyam Trungpa Rinpoche, wrote one of the first popular Dharma books in America, *Cutting Through Spiritual Materialism*. Its relevance only increases each year. He spoke of three levels of materialism—physical, psychological, spiritual—that rule our existence as expressions of ego-centered activity. Unchallenged, materialism will co-opt our physical lives, our communities, and our very practice.

Physical materialism refers to the neurotic pursuit of pleasure, comfort, and security. This is the outer expression of consumerism. Under this influence, we try to shield ourselves from the daily pain of embodied existence, while accentuating the pleasurable moments. We are driven to create the illusion of a pain-free life, full of choices that make us feel in control. We need 107 choices of yogurt in a supermarket so that we feel like queens of our universe. We go to 24-Plex movie theaters so that we can see whatever film we want, whenever we want. We need faster pain relievers, appliances to take away all inconvenience, and communication devices to foster immediate exchange. All of these create the illusion of complete pleasure at out fingertips, with none of the hassle of pain. When we are ruled by this kind of physical materialism, we identify ourselves by what we have.

But this is just the beginning. On the next level, psychological materialism seeks to control the world through theory, ideology, and intellect. Not only are we trying to physically manipulate the world so that we don't have to experience pain, we do so psychologically as well. We create a theoretical construct that keeps us from having to be threatened, to be wrong, or to be confused. We always put ourselves in control in this way: "As an American I have rights. As a woman, I deserve to be independent from expectations of men in my society. I earn my own salary, I can choose how I want to spend it. As a Buddhist, I understand interdependence."

Psychological materialism interprets whatever is threatening or irritating as an enemy. Then, we control the threat by creating an ideology or religion in which we are victorious, correct, or righteous; we never directly experience the fear and confusion that could arise from facing a genuine threat. This is particularly perilous for the Western Buddhist. In these times, Buddhism has become popular, a commodity which is used by corporations and the media. Being Buddhist has become a status symbol, connoting power, prestige, and money. His Holiness's picture appears on the sets of Hollywood movies and in Apple Computer ads; Hollywood stars are pursued as acquisitions in a kind of Dharmic competition. Everyone wants to add something Buddhist to her resume. Buddhist Studies enrollments at Naropa have doubled in two years, and reporters haunt our hallways and classrooms. Buddhist conferences attract a veritable parade of characters like myself, hawking the "tools" of our trade. Our consumer society is turning Buddhism into a commodity like everything else. The seductions for the Western Buddhist are clear. We are being seduced to use Buddhism to promote our own egos, communities, and agendas in the marketplace.

This still is not the heart of the matter. On the most subtle level, spiritual materialism carries this power struggle into the realm of our own minds, into our own meditation practice. Our consciousness is attempting to remain in control, to maintain a centralized awareness. Through this, ego uses even spirituality to shield itself from fear and insecurity. Our meditation practice can be used to retreat from the ambiguity and intensity of daily encounters; our compassion practices can be used to manipulate the sheer agony of things falling apart. We develop an investment in ourselves as Buddhist practitioners, and in so doing protect ourselves from the directness and intimacy of our own realization. It is important for us to be willing to cultivate the "edge" of our own practice, the edge where panic arises, where threat is our friend, and where our depths are turned inside out.

What happens when we are ruled by the "three levels of materialism"? The Vidyadhara taught that when we are so preoccupied with issues of ego, control, and power we become "afraid of external phenomena, which are our own projections." What this means is that when we take ourselves to be real, existent beings, then we mistake the world around us to be independent and real. And when we do this we invite paranoia, fear, and panic. We are afraid of not being able to control the situation. As Patrul Rinpoche (1808–1887) taught:

Don't prolong the past,
Don't invite the future,
Don't alter your innate wakefulness,
Don't fear appearances.

We must give up the fear of appearances. How can we do this? The only way to cut this pattern of acquisitiveness and control is to guard the naked integrity of our meditation practice. We must be willing to truly "let go" in our practice. When we see our racing minds, our churning emotions and constant plots, we touch the face of the suffering world and we have no choice but to be changed. We must allow our hearts to break with the pain of constant struggle that we experience in ourselves and in the world around us. Then we can become engaged in the world, and dedicate ourselves to a genuine enlightened society in which consumerism has no sway. Craving comes from the speed of our minds, wishing so intensely for what we do not have that we cannot experience what is there, right before us.

How can we, right now, address materialism in our practice and our lives? I would like to suggest a socially engaged practice which could transform our immediate lifestyles and change our relationship with suffering. It is the practice of generosity. No practice flies more directly in the face of American acquisitiveness and individualism. Any of us who have spent time in Asia or with our Asian teachers see the centrality of generosity in Buddhist practice.

According to traditional formulation, our giving begins with material gifts and extends to gifts of fearlessness and Dharma. Generosity is the virtue that produces peace, as the sutras [Buddhist scriptures] say. Generosity is a practice which overcomes our acquisitiveness and self-absorption, and which benefits others. Committing to this practice may produce our greatest legacy for the twenty-first century.

Analyze This Reading

1. What information does the writer use to describe consumerism in the United States? Why does she connect consumerism with suffering?
2. What are the dangers of physical, psychological, and spiritual materialism? What examples does the writer use to describe these dangers?
3. Early in this reading, the writer claims that "Religious peoples and communities have the power to bring the only remaining challenge to consumerism." What role can Buddhism play?

Respond To This Reading

1. Contrast the values associated with consumerism with values the writer endorses in this reading. How would life be different if the writer's values were to take hold?
2. Some contend that consumerism, and its emphasis on acquisitiveness, is the engine that drives our economy and defines our culture. With this in mind, is it realistic to think that a religious perspective—like Buddhism, Christianity, or Judaism—can alter Americans' need to consume?
3. As a consumer, what issues do you have, especially in terms of your consumption of products and services regarded as essential today? What would you claim in response to the most pressing of these issues?

ABOUT THIS READING

This reading appeared in *Opposing Viewpoints: Censorship* (2005), edited by Andrea C. Nakaya. It is an excerpt from the 2004 U.S. Court of Appeals Tenth Circuit decision upholding the constitutionality of the National Do Not Call Registry, where consumers can request that they not receive phone calls from commercial telemarketers. Critics of the registry claim that it restricts the right to free speech guaranteed by the First Amendment. The writer, David Ebel, is a judge for the U.S. Court of Appeals Tenth Circuit.

Telemarketers Should Be Censored

By David Ebel

We hold that the do-not-call registry is a valid commercial speech regulation because it directly advances the government's important interests in safeguarding personal privacy and reducing the danger of telemarketing abuse without burdening an excessive amount of speech. In other words, there is a reasonable fit between do-not-call regulations and the government's reasons for enacting them.

The Registry is Consistent with the First Amendment

Four key aspects of the do-not-call registry convince us that it is consistent with First Amendment requirements. First, the list restricts only core commercial speech, i.e., commercial sales calls. Second, the do-not-call registry targets speech that invades the privacy of the home, a personal sanctuary that enjoys a unique status in our constitutional jurisprudence. Third, the do-not-call registry is an opt-in program that puts the choice of whether or not to restrict commercial calls entirely in the hands of consumers. Fourth, the do-not-call registry materially furthers the government's interests in combating the danger of abusive telemarketing and preventing the invasion of consumer privacy, blocking a significant number of the calls that cause these problems. Under these circumstances, we conclude that the requirements of the First Amendment are satisfied.

A number of additional features of the national do-not-call registry, although not dispositive, further demonstrate that the list is consistent with the First Amendment rights of commercial speakers. The challenged regulations do not hinder any business' ability to contact consumers by other means, such as through direct mailings or other forms of advertising. Moreover, they give consumers a number of different options to avoid calls they do not want to receive. Namely, consumers who wish to restrict some but not all commercial sales calls can do so by using company-specific do-not-call lists or by granting some businesses express permission to call. In addition, the government chose to offer consumers broader options to restrict commercial sales calls than charitable and political calls after finding that commercial calls were more intrusive and posed a greater danger of consumer abuse. The government also had evidence that the less restrictive company-specific do-not-call list did not solve the problems caused by commercial telemarketing, but it had no comparable evidence with respect to charitable and political fundraising.

The national do-not-call registry offers consumers a tool with which they can protect their homes against intrusions that Congress has determined to be particularly invasive. Just as a consumer can avoid door-to-door peddlers by placing a "No Solicitation" sign in his or her front yard, the do-not-call registry lets consumers avoid unwanted sales pitches that invade the home via telephone, if they choose to do so. We are convinced that the First Amendment does not prevent the government from giving consumers this option. . . .

In *Rowan v. United States Post Office Dep't*, the Supreme Court upheld the right of a homeowner to restrict material that could be mailed to his or her house. The Court emphasized the importance of individual privacy, particularly in the context of the home, stating that "the ancient concept that 'a man's home is his castle' into which 'not even the king may enter' has lost none of its vitality." In *Frisby v. Schultz*, the Court again stressed the unique nature of the home and recognized that "the State's interest in protecting the well-being, tranquility, and privacy of the home is certainly of the highest order in a free and civilized society.". . . As the Court held in Frisby: One important aspect of residential privacy is protection of the unwilling listener. . . . [A] special benefit of the privacy all citizens enjoy within their own walls, which the State may legislate to protect, is an ability to avoid intrusions. Thus, we have repeatedly held that individuals are not required to welcome unwanted speech into their own homes and that the government may protect this freedom. Likewise, in *Hill v. Colorado*, the Court called the unwilling listener's interest in avoiding unwanted communication part of the broader right to be let alone that Justice [Louis] Brandeis described as "the right most valued by civilized men.". . .

Protecting Consumers from Deception and Abuse

The telemarketers assert that the do-not-call registry is unconstitutionally underinclusive because it does not apply to charitable and political callers. . . .

The national do-not-call registry is designed to reduce intrusions into personal privacy and the risk of telemarketing fraud and abuse that accompany unwanted telephone solicitation. The registry directly advances those goals. . . .

The FTC [Federal Trade Commission] has found that commercial callers are more likely than non-commercial callers to engage in deceptive and abusive practices. . . . Specifically, the FTC concluded that in charitable and political calls, a significant purpose of the call is to sell a cause, not merely to receive a donation, and that non-commercial callers thus have stronger incentives not to alienate the people they call or to engage in abusive and deceptive practices. ("Because charitable solicitation does more than inform private economic decisions and is not primarily concerned with providing information about the characteristics and costs of goods and services, it is not dealt with as a variety of purely commercial speech.") The speech regulated by the do-not-call list is therefore the speech most likely to cause the problems the government sought to alleviate in enacting that list, further demonstrating that the regulation directly advances the government's interests.

In sum, the do-not-call list directly advances the government's interests reducing intrusions upon consumer privacy and the risk of fraud or abuse by restricting a substantial number (and also a substantial percentage) of the calls that cause these problems. . . .

We hold that the national do-not-call registry is narrowly tailored because it does not over-regulate protected speech; rather, it restricts only calls that are targeted at unwilling recipients. . . . The do-not-call registry prohibits only telemarketing calls aimed at consumers who have affirmatively indicated that they do not want to receive such calls and for whom such calls would constitute an invasion of privacy. . . .

The national do-not-call registry does not itself prohibit any speech. Instead, it merely "permits a citizen to erect a wall. . . that no advertiser may penetrate without his acquiescence." Almost by definition, the do-not-call regulations only block calls that would constitute unwanted intrusions into the privacy of consumers who have signed up for the list. Moreover, it allows consumers who feel susceptible to telephone fraud or abuse to ensure that most commercial callers will not have an opportunity to victimize them. . . .

Least-Restrictive Alternative

The telemarketers argue that it would have been less restrictive to let consumers rely on technological alternatives such as caller ID, call rejection services, and electronic devices designed to block unwanted calls. Each of these alternatives puts the cost of avoiding unwanted telemarketing calls on consumers. Furthermore, as the FCC found, "[a]lthough technology has improved to assist consumers in blocking unwanted calls, it has also evolved in such a way as to assist telemarketers in making greater numbers of calls and even circumventing such blocking technologies." Forcing consumers to compete in a technological arms race with the telemarketing industry is not an equally effective alternative to the do-not-call registry.

In sum, the do-not-call registry is narrowly tailored to restrict only speech that contributes to the problems the government seeks to redress, namely the intrusion into personal privacy and the risk of fraud and abuse caused by telephone calls that consumers do not welcome into their homes. No calls are restricted unless the recipient has affirmatively declared that he or she does not wish to receive them. Moreover, telemarketers still have the ability to contact consumers in other ways, and consumers have a number of different options in determining what telemarketing calls they will receive. Finally, there are not numerous and obvious less-burdensome alternatives that would restrict less speech while accomplishing the government's objectives equally as well. . . .

For the reasons discussed above, the government has asserted substantial interests to be served by the do-not-call registry (privacy and consumer protection), the do-not-call registry will directly advance those interests by banning a substantial amount of unwanted telemarketing calls, and the regulation is narrowly tailored because its opt-in feature ensures that it does not restrict any speech directed at a willing listener. In other words, the do-not-call registry bears a reasonable fit with the purposes the government sought to advance. Therefore, it is consistent with the limits the First Amendment imposes on laws restricting commercial speech.

Analyze This Reading

1. What reasons does the writer give for the court's decision to uphold the creation of the National Do Not Call Registry?
2. What specific support does the writer offer in defense of his position?

3. How does the writer differentiate between commercial telemarketing and solicitation for charities and political fundraising?

Respond To This Reading

1. In your view, does the writer treat the opposition fairly? Explain.
2. Telemarketing, a kind of advertising, is viewed in the court's decision as an invasion of personal privacy. How do you define "personal privacy"? In addition to telemarketing, are there other invasions of personal privacy in American life that need attention? If yes, what are they?
3. As a consumer in general, what issues are before you in terms of advertising, privacy, and choice? What single issue motivates you to argue?

ABOUT THIS READING

The topic of peer-to-peer lending is one feature of microfinance, a movement geared toward making financial services available to people living in poverty and to people who struggle with securing loans from traditional banks. Many note that this movement began with the work of Muhammad Yunus, a Bangladeshi economist who in the 1970s developed a system of microcredit to aid local entrepreneurs. Yunus went on to found the Grameen bank and in 2006 was honored with the Nobel Peace Prize. The following article, by journalist Ray Fisman, appeared on *Slate*, an online magazine devoted to current affairs and culture.

It's Like eBay Meets Match.com: Does Peer-to-Peer Lending Work?

By Ray Fisman

Back in 2007, it took little more than a steady pulse to get a loan, albeit a subprime one, from credit officers eager to push loans out the door. Now that the real estate bubble has gone bust, a steady job and 20 percent down is scarcely enough to persuade banks to lay out for a mortgage, home repairs, or anything else.

To fill this financing gap, an increasing number of borrowers are turning to "peer to peer" networks that connect individual borrowers directly to lenders, cutting out the banking middleman. These networks have now financed nearly a half a billion dollars in lending. This is still a long way from the $931 billion in loans and leases that Bank of America had on its balance sheet in 2008, but it's growing rapidly. Peer-to-peer lenders describe themselves as a solution to many of the banking sector's current weaknesses, from the lack of small-business finance to the evils of payday lending (which now serves as financing of last resort for those shut out of formal banking altogether).

Economists have been studying these peer-to-peer lending programs from the beginning, and their findings are now starting to show up on the Web. They've discovered that while the sites may be useful for some high-risk borrowers—those who stood little chance of attracting loans from traditional banking institutions—these credit markets also result in loan decisions tainted by human frailty and bias. It seems that the middleman—with his credit models and balance-sheet analysis for evaluating prospective borrowers—may provide some value after all.

In the old days, if you wanted to opt out of traditional banking, you'd need friends and family willing and able to finance home improvements or business ideas. Similarly, the only alternatives for safekeeping one's nest egg were trustworthy acquaintances or the proverbial mattress. The peer-to-peer movement argues that Web-based technology may extend this personal banking network into a nationwide community of lenders and borrowers that could obviate the need for conventional banks.

On Prosper, the largest of the peer-to-peer sites, the process is a little like eBay-meets-Match.com. Lenders select from among a catalog of prospective borrowers much as singles "shop" an Internet dating site for potential partners. A typical listing includes a personal narrative making a case for the loan and a picture of the borrower. (These pictures often also include kids, puppies, and other images that might tug on a lender's sympathies.) In addition to this (unverified) information, Prosper lists hard data from borrowers' credit reports, including past delinquencies, credit lines, and ranges for income and credit rating. Once a desirable borrower is identified, lenders place bids specifying how much they're willing to lend to a particular borrower and at what interest rate. So if many lenders perceive that a borrower is a good credit risk, he's likely to get all the money he needs at low rates. High-risk cases will end up paying higher interest rates and may not attract funding at all.

Why might the general public do a better job at evaluating the chances of default than the trained personnel of banking institutions? Most obviously, person-to-person loans aren't burdened with an extra layer of potentially corrupting bureaucracy. We now know that loan officers were motivated to push loans out the door without sufficient concern for risk and default, with their banks quickly packaging and selling off bundles of subprime mortgages in what turned out to be a ruinous game of hot-potato lending. Personal lenders may also better pick up on "soft" characteristics of borrowers—a compelling story or convincing picture—that may be a true indication of likely repayment. Loan officers burdened by institutional rules on borrower collateral or credit history may not have the discretion to act on such information.

Yet there are equally compelling weaknesses to the personal banking model. A quick browse of Prosper or any other peer-to-peer site makes it clear that borrowers trade on emotion. The rational, calculating banker may not be swayed by the photo of three adorable kids (who may not even be the borrower's own kids) designed to influence Prosper lenders. Further, the bank's job doesn't end with borrower selection: Banks also watch over borrowers to make sure they're using the money for productive investments rather than trips to Vegas and put the screws to people with outstanding loans to make sure they get paid back.

Researchers are finding that there is some truth to both views. A team of Harvard and University of Amsterdam economists using detailed data from Prosper—including precise credit scores for all loan applicants—found that

Prosper lenders are in fact quite adept at assessing the creditworthiness of prospective borrowers. Though the site keeps borrowers' credit ratings confidential—they report 40-point ranges rather than actual scores—those with higher ratings nonetheless obtained lower interest rates than those with low ratings. This is partly because borrowers use hard information like repayment history and credit card records, much as a bank officer would. But the researchers also find that a lender's ability to predict credit score is more accurate than could be explained by accounting for the tangible financial data available on Prosper's Web site, implying that they also make (accurate) inferences about credit risk from the pictures and stories posted online. This "soft" information is particularly important for higher-risk borrowers with little financial history to guide lenders' decisions. Overall, the researchers conclude that Prosper's credit market operates quite efficiently and without a bank pocketing a slice of the proceeds.

Yet others have found that there are significant limits to the rationality of personal lending, which is encumbered by many all-too-human prejudices and idiosyncrasies. For example, my colleague Enrichetta Ravina has documented that there is a massive beauty premium—i.e., cheap loans for pretty women—enjoyed by Prosper borrowers, despite the fact that better-looking people are in fact more likely to default on their loans. Economists Devin Pope and Justin Sydnor find that racial discrimination also taints the online loan market—black borrowers are much less likely to obtain funding and more likely to pay higher interest rates relative to otherwise-similar whites looking for financing.

(The researchers also find that loans to black borrowers are more likely to turn delinquent, to some extent validating the higher interest rates they face. However, given the relatively short history of Prosper lending, it's still too early to tell whether these late repayments will translate into higher default rates.)

What does all of this suggest for the future of peer-to-peer lending? Small-scale lenders have shown themselves to be savvy in their lending decisions. They are affected to some extent by human miscalculation and bias, but then again, so are bank loan officers. Employees of big banks are human beings, too, and may be similarly seduced by beauty or vulnerable to racism. Add the entertainment value of finding and following your own loan "investment portfolio," and the peer-to-peer movement seems likely to be more than a passing fad. (Though it's unlikely that individual lenders will ever have the means or sophistication to work out the terms of a million-dollar Park Avenue penthouse mortgage or a billion-dollar loan for Chrysler.)

Yet before we celebrate the end of banking as we know it, it's important to remember that the Web sites connecting borrowers to lenders are middlemen themselves. And this presents an additional layer of risk for those making loans through these sites. In fact, if you visit the Web sites of Prosper, you'll find that it's currently shuttered to new lending, pending regulatory approval from the Securities and Exchange Commission. (Lending Club, another leading site, just completed a similar "quiet period.") Among other things, regulators are concerned with what will happen to lenders' investments if a site goes bankrupt. If, say, Citibank went belly up tomorrow, depositors' savings would be insured up to $250,000 by the FDIC. Not so for those choosing to invest their savings through a peer-to-peer network. There is the possibility lenders may face delayed repayment if they get repaid at all (though both Prosper and Lending Club now have backup plans in case they go under). So once again, it raises the concern of businesses taking risks with other people's money. And given the lessons of the past few years, the SEC is probably wise to make sure this latest round of financial innovation doesn't end up as the financial crisis of the future.

Analyze This Reading

1. What is peer-to-peer lending, why is it becoming more common, how does it work, and what role does Web-based technology play in this kind of lending?
2. The writer brings in research conducted by economists to reveal the potential strengths and weaknesses of peer-to-peer lending. How does this contribute to a fair and objective presentation of this topic?
3. With what advice does the writer conclude this article?

Respond To This Reading

1. Would you consider being a lender or borrower in a peer-to-peer lending network? Explain.
2. In your experience as a borrower, as a holder of credit cards, and/or as a citizen aware of our recent banking crisis, what issues occur to you after reading this article? Which of these issues might motivate you to build an argument?

ABOUT THIS READING

This reading appeared in *New Internationalist*, a monthly magazine, coedited by writer Dinyar Godrej. The magazine, in its own words, exists to "report on the issues of world poverty and inequality; to focus attention on the unjust relationship between the powerful and powerless worldwide; to debate and campaign for the radical changes necessary to meet the basic needs of all; and to bring to life the people, the ideas and the action in the fight for global justice."

The Ad Industry Pins Us Down

By Dinyar Godrej

Buddhism and Hinduism recommend it. A retreat from clamour, a wondrous detachment that allows the material world to float up, like a sloughed-off skin, for one's dispassionate consideration. Whether they offer useful advice on re-engaging after this revelation, I don't know. The first astronauts saw a floating world, too. It provoked suitably joined-up thoughts about its (and our) fragility and essential unity.

But there are other worlds. And the one that elbows itself to the front of our attention's queue painstakingly creates surface and whips up froth. It's the one that the 125 residents of Clark, Texas, signed up to in 2005 when they changed the name of their township to Dish in return for a decade's free cable TV from the DISH Network. Hey, what's in a name except a wacky corporate PR opportunity, right?

The bubbly, dazzling world of which Dish has become an emblem shows little sign of floating up for our inspection. If we inspect it nonetheless, it reveals itself to be firmly riveted down by that old culprit—disproportionate corporate power.

Advertising is a bit of a compulsive liar. In the early days it was quite bare-faced—the beverage giant, Dewar's, claiming in the 1930s that their Scotch whiskey repelled colds and flu; cigarette brands claiming that they soothed the throat and helped asthma. Some of this still goes on. Quack cures are advertised in numerous Majority World countries. The half of all Mexican citizens who are overweight are pummelled daily on TV by products that promise to melt 10 centimetres off the waistline in two hours.

Repeat After Me

Nowadays, regulatory bodies will see off many of the more obviously fraudulent claims.

But advertising is involved in soul fraud instead. If that sounds a bit deep, just stay with me a while.

Advertising today has little to do with introducing a new product or describing an existing one's virtues. It has everything to do with images, dreams and emotions; stuff we are evolutionarily programmed to engage with but which is, almost without exception in the ad biz, fake. Imagine how much attention you would pay if there were just text and no images. When ads for Sprite (owned by Coca-Cola) proclaimed: 'Image is nothing, thirst is everything', they were reassuring people that they were right to be distrustful, while building up images of honesty and straight talk, using professional basketball players to push the product. Sprite jumped several notches up the soft-drink rankings; moolah was minted. Image was everything, even if it was purporting to be an anti-image. Amid the visual clutter, advertising—the chief agent of the mess—has to jump out at us. It must trigger off associations, however tangential, that will keep our attention. Endless repetition through media channels should build up a handy cloud of associations. According to one industry executive: 'In the context of most advertising, particularly passively consumed media like television and cinema, learning is incidental, not deliberate. This is why people tell you they are not influenced by advertising. They are not actively trying to take anything away from the experience, and therefore are not influenced at that time; but the effects will show up later, long after a particular viewing experience is forgotten.'

Much effort is expended upon trying to sink boreholes into the vast iceberg of the subconscious mind, probably because the products being flogged are in reality just variations on the same old same old. A recent buzzword is 'neuromarketing'. Neuroscientists and psychiatrists are searching for the buy-button in the brain. This involves putting subjects into brain-scanning machinery and pitching concepts and images at them to see which ones make the lights flash. In one experiment, subjects were made to blind-taste Pepsi and Coke. Pepsi scored higher in terms of response in the ventral putamen, the part of the brain associated with feelings of reward— i.e., most thought Pepsi tasted better. But when the subjects were informed which drink was Coke before they tried it, their medial prefrontal cortexes lit up. This is an area of the brain believed to control cognition. Most now said they preferred Coke. So just the name had prompted memories and brand nostalgia which influenced the taste of the stuff. One might question the validity of using expensive hospital equipment and highly trained medical professionals to explain choices of fizzy drinks with no nutritional value whatsoever—but that would be to get a bit real.

The good news is that all this dubious effort is just as likely to fail as it is to succeed. If an ad can latch on to the emotion of a winning goal in a football match or the tears and triumphs of *Pop Idol* [the British parent of *American Idol*], then there's a good chance it will do the trick. Much else is trial and error. Focus groups assembled to pretest the vibe are notoriously unreliable as they can be suggestible and become dominated by loudmouths.

Anxieties of Influence

One might well ask: so what? So what if silly money. . . pushes the usual goods/junk, if I can still make an informed choice about what I buy?

Well, maybe. . . . But how would you react if all this were seeping into the very pores of the culture you're part of—and changing it? Mass advertising is about brands with the most money behind them pushing to the top. Smaller companies with less of this fluff-muscle don't always survive.

More perniciously, corporate giants try every trick in the book to control our media channels. Much of the mainstream media exists to sell audiences to advertisers. Newspapers aren't profitable based on sales alone. The missing factor is ad money. It's their lifeblood. Teen magazines (especially those aimed at girls) are little more than catalogues for products—and that's the content. The profile of the chubby hero who saved a life is usually tucked away at the end. Here's what an agency representing Coca-Cola demanded in a letter to magazines: 'We believe that positive and upbeat editorial provides a compatible environment in which to communicate the brand's message. . . . We consider the following subjects to be inappropriate and require that our ads are not placed adjacent to articles discussing the following issues: Hard News; Sex related issues; Drugs (Prescription or Illegal); Medicine (eg chronic illnesses such as cancer, diabetes, AIDS, etc); Health (eg mental or physical conditions); Negative Diet Information (eg bulimia, anorexia, quick weight loss, etc); Food; Political issues; Environmental issues; Articles containing vulgar language; Religion.' So, not much chance of a mention of the intimidation of union workers in Coke's Colombian plant, or of the charges of water pollution in India, then.

If anyone still thought they were watching 'the news' on CNN, anchor Jack Cafferty's on-air views might disabuse them: 'We are not here as a public service. We're here to make money. We sell advertising, and we do it on the premise that people are going to watch. If you don't cover the miners because you want to do a story about a debt crisis in Brazil at the time everybody else is covering the miners, then Citibank calls up and says, 'you know what? We're not renewing the commercial contract.' I mean, it's a business.' In the US, one study found that 40 per cent of the "news" content of a typical newspaper originated in press releases, story memos and suggestions from PR companies.

Hungry for Cool

More subtle is the cultural shift wrought in the media—light, non-political television programming that contributes to a 'buying mood'; magazines filled with little nuggets of 'instant gratification'; serious newspapers that insert lengthy travel and fashion sections for no obvious reason. So much happiness, so unbearable. Advertising consistently portrays 'lifestyles' that are beyond the reach of all but the wealthy. This is somehow viewed as 'apolitical'. Yet charities' ads calling for dropping Southern debt or opposing cruelty to animals often fall foul of regulators or media ad-sales teams for being 'too political'.

As a child I loved the ads before the movie. They were zippy and bright. I found the varied angles they took before the 'Ta-dahhh!' moment when the product was plugged ingenious. I still find the creative energy that goes into them intriguing, but feel tired by their consistently conservative values and know better about the social, economic and environmental issues behind the products they push. I also feel fed up by the sheer volume of the glitzy deluge. Corporate advertisers know this fed up feeling all too well and have responded with marketing moves that look less like traditional advertising but seep more than ever into our lives. The upshot is that everything gets branded, logo-ed or sponsored. Supermarkets that shaft farmers sponsor children's play areas and school computers. Children are employed to hand out freebies to other kids and talk them up 'peer marketing'. Conspicuous charity abounds, trying to make the brand look more benign—for example, Ronald McDonald House offers accommodation to families with sick children. Product placement sneaks into movies, TV shows, computer games and even novels. Our email and cell phones are bombarded. Most websites would collapse without revenue from ads that get ever more lively and mysterious.

With traditional advertising showing diminishing returns, corporations get into all sorts of contortions. The apparel company Diesel ran a multimillion-dollar campaign contrasting clothing ads with scenes of hardship in North Korea; Benetton notoriously used the image of a man dying of AIDS to push its duds. Wow, just feel that edge!

Advertising and the Transformation of Desire

A certain amount of advertising is probably unavoidable—indeed, countries that curb it often flood mental spaces with political propaganda instead. But the worldview the ad biz pushes is so out of touch with real life that it can mess up our heads. Ever wondered where that urge to shop when you're feeling a bit down comes from? Or how our desire for social change or rebellion gets transformed into speed, sex, indulgence and living for the moment? Why is so much of our culture about dictating taste (the tyrannies of 'cool') and transforming it into want? Why are disadvantaged groups (be they dark-skinned, sexual minorities, people with disabilities, you name it) so absent from this trendy world, unless they are being fetishized by niche marketing?

With the deluge comes avoidance. Ungrateful wretches that we are, we try to block out as much as we can. TV advertising is in crisis. Ad guru Lord Saatchi thinks young people nowadays have 'continual partial attention'—the kind of brain that's constantly sifting but records little. His answer is for companies to strive for 'one-word equity' to fit this goldfish attention span—Be™, Live™, Buy™, anyone?

This dizziness is reflected in the philosophical musings of Maurice Lévy, top honcho of advertising giant Publicis: 'Consumers do not want only to be given an astonishingly wide-ranging choice. They want that choice to be renewed at intervals that are always shorter. This is the reason why we have to redefine our very notion of time. What we have to deal with is not only change, but an acceleration of change itself. Not only transformations, but the transformation of transformations: it will be a real challenge to make fidelity out of inconstancy.'

He doesn't stop to ponder how his work is all about creating this blur of inconstancy. Advertising's influence is being implicated in eating, compulsive and attention-deficit disorders. In the Majority World the big brand steamroller is intent on creating Westernized aspirational cultures often at odds with local cultures. If we are to free identity from consumerism, reality checks are our strongest weapon. If struck by an ad, it's useful to measure how much of it is actually telling you something about the product and how much is image. Brands are eager that you identify with them, make them a part of your lives—deny them that privilege. Independent media (like the *NI* [*New Internationalist*] and, yes, this is a shameless plug) can give us all the dirt we need to chuck at corporate ad lies. Thinking before we buy, and buying nothing—especially when irrational urges prompt us to do otherwise—are bound to punch a few holes. The idea of our world and its public spaces as shared commons is becoming increasingly visible. Streets are being reclaimed by 'citizen artists' redrawing ads to reveal their subterfuges, and by social movements gathering to protest government by corporations.

There's quite a bit of ad-industry nervousness as brands come under attack and marketing tactics backfire. Could the industry one day start to tell us things we actually want to know? The distorting mirror will need to shatter first before a floating world comes into view.

Analyze This Reading

1. What examples does the writer bring in to support his contention that advertising is what he terms "soul fraud"?
2. According to the writer, what is the connection between advertising and content in the news media?
3. What tactics does the writer recommend for freeing our identities from consumerism?

Respond To This Reading

1. Toward the end of this reading, the writer refers to advertising executive Maurice Lévy's speculation that consumers demand wide-ranging choices in advertisements they take in and that advertisements occur at shorter intervals. Do you agree that, as consumers, we have expectations for the advertisements we experience? If yes, offer a few examples.

2. Without providing examples, the writer asserts that identity—that is, the way we think about ourselves—is manipulated and transformed by skillful advertising and its appeals. If you agree, mention a few examples of skillfully constructed ads, and identify their appeals.

3. In your view, are American consumers capable of making informed, conscious choices in how they spend their money? Explain.

4. Identify an issue generated by advertising in the news you take in, the products you consume, or the entertainment you pursue. What will you claim, and what specific support will you use?

ABOUT THIS READING

This article appeared in the November 20, 2012 issue of *Permaculture: Inspiration for Sustainable Living*, a publication devoted to the sustainability movement. Mark Boyle is author of *The Moneyless Manifesto* (2012), an endorsement of moneyless living.

Buy Nothing Day 2012 is Approaching. Could You Stop Spending for One Day?

By Mark Boyle

It's a classic scene from *The Simpsons*. A flock of marketing executives sit around a large table in a boardroom; sales, they're told, are down in the third fiscal quarter, and they're the people whose *raison d'être* is to make the graphs head northeasterly again. They break out into discussion, before a cigar-smoking man, with deep furrows of concern in his brow, intervenes. He decides that they need to create a new day, and that it needs to be something "warm and fuzzy". Cut to a new scene, where Homer is unwrapping his "Love Day" present, a talking toy bear called *Sir Loves-a-Lot*, whilst his daughter Lisa fills the rubbish bin full of Love Day wrapping paper.

Born out of the monetary economy's fundamental need to convert freedom into monetised activities, *Buy Something Day* has been sold to us under various, more palatable monikers: Father's Day, Sweetest Day, Valentine's Day, even Boss's Day (a day in North America when—you couldn't make this stuff up—employees thank bosses for being kind and fair). In the US the more sceptical have begun calling these "Hallmark Holidays" (referring to the American greeting card company), cynically suggesting that our honourable and skilled marketeers may be inventing these days merely out of the profit motive, and not for the common good.

How 'Buy Something Day' Became 'Buy Nothing Day'

One of the only "days" invented that hasn't morphed into a *Buy More Meaningless Crap* exercise is international Buy Nothing Day. Initiated in 1992 by the subversive magazine *Adbusters*, it has historically taken place on what is known as Black Friday in the US, the day the Christmas shopping season kicks off there, and on the following day in the UK. Its purpose, on the face of it, is to ask us to take one day off shopping of any sort. The day itself is symbolic—its real purpose is to help us to drastically reconsider our consumption habits on a longer-term basis.

Reducing our consumption, we are told, would be terrible for the rampaging beast known only as *The Economy*. But here is where the sleight of hand takes place. Politicians and economists have been conflating words relating to *economy* with words relating to *finance* for so long that we have come to think that economics is all about money.

Economics V.S. Freeconomics

Economics actually has nothing in particular to do with money; it's about how we meet our needs. The monetary economy is one model out of many, and is a very recent one at that. It's a model that seems intent on converting all our intimate human relationships into services to be bought and sold, whilst reducing the splendour and pageantry of the Earth into imperishable units of account. If we could instead meet our needs locally (or, as a transitional strategy, by utilising the mega-tonnes of stuff we've already produced), along with freeing ourselves from the desire to have bigger, shinier distractions, then why wouldn't we?

This question has become especially potent considering how easy buying nothing has become. As the monetary economy has continued its descent, the gift economy has boomed. Gift circles, guerrilla gardening, swishing (clothes-swapping) evenings, couch-surfing, Freecycling, Freeconomy, open-source ecology and software, freeskilling, book-sharing clubs, forest gardening, scrumping apples to make cider to fuel free street-parties, skipping and squatting, Permaculture design, street freecycling, helpX, WWOOFing and Freeshops make up a fraction of the myriad ways in which you can participate in the gift economy to some degree, all of which lie somewhere on the global-to-local spectrum. And millions of people are now figuring this out for themselves.

Credit must go, in part, to George Osborne, Christine Lagarde, Darth Vader, Angela Merkel and their ilk for their unintended assistance in the popularisation of non-monetary economics. Freeconomy, the alternative economic system I founded in 2007, has recently sky-rocketed in countries such as Greece, Spain, Portugal and Ireland, countries where the national currency has become almost as scarce as an honest politician.

There are now thousands of ways you can de-monetise every aspect of your life, to whatever degree works in your unique circumstances. In doing so, not only will you drastically reduce your ecological footprint, but you'll also rediscover your sense of interdependency with the rest of your local community and the land under your feet, for if money has come to replace relationships, that's exactly what you'll rediscover.

You'll also free yourself up from the financial imperative that forces many of us to do work that is a crime to the human spirit, liberating your hands and minds to do the work that your heart is calling you to do. Combine all these practical solutions with a bit of imagination, and–believe it or not–you could even live completely moneylessly if you so wished. If I have been able to, trust me, anyone could.

How to Take Part in 'Buy Nothing Day'

Given how widespread gift economics is becoming, I ask you to test the waters by joining me in a Buy Nothing Month in 2013. Pick a month, any month. January would be a perfect opportunity for all sorts of good reasons. Create your own rules. Make them realistic enough to be achievable yet challenging enough to be considered an appropriate response to the ecological and social issues we're confronted with.

Some of you may not be prepared to forage from the wilds or the supermarket bins, whilst others will get excited by the adventure of it. A few of you will be up for a completely moneyless month, whilst for others going moneyless in terms of travel or entertainment may be more appropriate. The point of it is to take stock of your consumption habits, and to see what areas of your life you can replace monetary transactions with real relationships. The extent to which you take it is up to you.

The worst that can happen is that you'll save a few quid. The best? You may realise what a little part of you already knows—that there is another way of getting rich than accumulating more material wealth.

Analyze This Reading

1. What is the purpose of Buy Nothing Day?
2. Contrast the gift economy with the monetary economy. What examples does the writer use to explain the gift economy?
3. According to the writer, what are the advantages of a Freeconomy?
4. Among the terms that the writer examines closely are *economy* and *finance*. What can be gained by questioning the use of certain terms in an argument; that is, how can this kind of examination serve an argument's purpose?

Respond To This Reading

1. In your view, how would living without money alter your social relationships?
2. Should you choose to endorse moneyless living and move away from our traditional economy that is built on money, what opportunities would no longer be available to you? What new opportunities might emerge?
3. One reviewer of author Mark Boyle's book, *The Moneyless Manifesto*, writes that Boyle "is a brave man" and that this book "explodes the myth about money and brings the reader nearer to the truth that money is not true wealth." Is Boyle brave? If money is not true wealth, what is?

ABOUT THIS READING

Journalist Andy Kroll is based in Washington, D. C., and is an associate editor at *TomDispatch*, an email publication that makes available articles and opinion from the world press, and is a staff writer at *Mother Jones Magazine,* a nonprofit news organization named after Mary Harris "Mother" Jones, a union organizer and staunch opponent of child labor in the late-nineteenth and early-twentieth centuries and at one time referred to as "the most dangerous woman in America."

How the McEconomy Bombed the American Worker: The Hollowing Out of the Middle Class

By Andy Kroll

Think of it as a parable for these grim economic times. On April 19th, McDonald's launched its first-ever national hiring day, signing up 62,000 new workers at stores throughout the country. For some context, that's more jobs created by one company in a single day than the net job creation of the entire U.S. economy in 2009. And if that boggles the mind, consider how many workers applied to local McDonald's franchises that day and left empty-handed: 938,000 of them. With a 6.2% acceptance rate in its spring hiring blitz, McDonald's was more selective than the Princeton, Stanford, or Yale University admission offices.

It shouldn't be surprising that a million souls flocked to McDonald's hoping for a steady paycheck, when nearly 14 million Americans are out of work and nearly a million more are too discouraged even to look for a job. At this point, it apparently made no difference to them that the fast-food industry pays some of the lowest wages around: on average, $8.89 an hour, or barely half the $15.95 hourly average across all American industries.

On an annual basis, the average fast-food worker takes home $20,800, less than half the national average of $43,400. McDonald's appears to pay even worse, at least with its newest hires. In the press release for its national hiring day, the multibillion-dollar company said it would spend $518 million on the newest round of hires, or $8,354 a head. Hence the *Oxford English Dictionary's* definition of "McJob" as "a low-paying job that requires little skill and provides little opportunity for advancement."

Of course, if you read only the headlines, you might think that the jobs picture was improving. The economy added 1.3 million private-sector jobs between February 2010 and January 2011, and the headline unemployment rate edged downward, from 9.8% to 8.8%, between November of last year and March. It inched upward in April, to 9%, but tempering that increase was the news that the economy added 244,000 jobs last month (not including those 62,000 McJobs), beating economists' expectations.

Under this somewhat sunnier news, however, runs a far darker undercurrent. Yes, jobs are being created, but what kinds of jobs paying what kinds of wages? Can those jobs sustain a modest lifestyle and pay the bills? Or are we living through a McJobs recovery?

The Rise of the McWorker

The evidence points to the latter. According to a recent analysis by the National Employment Law Project (NELP), the biggest growth in private-sector job creation in the past year occurred in positions in the low-wage retail, administrative, and food service sectors of the economy. While 23% of the jobs lost in the Great Recession that followed the economic meltdown of 2008 were "low-wage" (those paying $9–$13 an hour), 49% of new jobs added in the sluggish "recovery" are in those same low-wage industries. On the other end of the spectrum, 40% of the jobs lost paid high wages ($19–$31 an hour), while a mere 14% of new jobs pay similarly high wages.

As a point of comparison, that's much worse than in the recession of 2001 after the high-tech bubble burst. Then, higher wage jobs made up almost a third of all new jobs in the first year after the crisis.

The hardest hit industries in terms of employment now are finance, manufacturing, and especially construction, which was decimated when the housing bubble burst in 2007 and has yet to recover. Meanwhile, NELP found that hiring for temporary administrative and waste-management jobs, health-care jobs, and of course those fast-food restaurants has surged.

Indeed in 2010, one in four jobs added by private employers was a temporary job, which usually provides workers with few benefits and even less job security. It's not surprising that employers would first rely on temporary hires as they regained their footing after a colossal financial crisis. But this time around, companies have taken on temp workers in far greater numbers than after previous downturns. Where 26% of hires in 2010 were temporary, the figure was 11% after the early-1990s recession and only 7% after the downturn of 2001.

As many labor economists have begun to point out, we're witnessing an increasing polarization of the U.S. economy over the past three decades. More and more, we're seeing labor growth largely at opposite ends of the skills-and-wages spectrum—among, that is, the best and the worst kinds of jobs.

At one end of job growth, you have increasing numbers of people flipping burgers, answering telephones, engaged in child care, mopping hallways, and in other low-wage lines of work. At the other end, you have increasing numbers of engineers, doctors, lawyers, and people in high-wage "creative" careers. What's disappearing is the middle, the decent-paying jobs that helped expand the American middle class in the mid-twentieth century and that, if the present lopsided recovery is any indication, are now going the way of typewriters and landline telephones.

Because the shape of the workforce increasingly looks fat on both ends and thin in the middle, economists have begun to speak of "the barbell effect," which for those clinging to a middle-class existence in bad times means a nightmare life. For one thing, the shape of the workforce now hinders America's once vaunted upward mobility. It's the downhill slope that's largely available these days.

The barbell effect has also created staggering levels of income inequality of a sort not known since the decades before the Great Depression. From 1979 to 2007, for the middle class, average household income (after taxes) nudged upward from $44,100 to $55,300; by contrast, for the top 1%, average household income soared from $346,600 in 1979 to nearly $1.3 million in 2007. That is, super-rich families saw their earnings increase 11 times faster than middle-class families.

What's causing this polarization? An obvious culprit is technology. As MIT economist David Autor notes, the tasks of "organizing, storing, retrieving, and manipulating information" that humans once performed are now computerized. And when computers can't handle more basic clerical work, employers ship those jobs overseas where labor is cheaper and benefits nonexistent.

Another factor is education. In today's barbell economy, degrees and diplomas have never mattered more, which means that those with just a high school education increasingly find themselves locked into the low-wage end of the labor market with little hope for better. Worse yet, the pay gap between the well-educated and not-so-educated continues to widen: in 1979, the hourly wage of a typical college graduate was 1.5 times higher than that of a typical high-school graduate; by 2009, it was almost two times higher.

Considering, then, that the percentage of men ages 25 to 34 who have gone to college is actually decreasing, it's not surprising that wage inequality has gotten worse in the U.S. As Autor writes, advanced economies like ours "depend on their best-educated workers to develop and commercialize the innovative ideas that drive economic growth."

The distorting effects of the barbell economy aren't lost on ordinary Americans. In a recent Gallup poll, a majority of people agreed that the country was still in either a depression (29%) or a recession (26%). When sorted out by income, however, those making $75,000 or more a year are, not surprisingly, most likely to believe the economy is in neither a recession nor a depression, but growing. After all, they're the ones most likely to have benefited from a soaring stock market and the return to profitability of both corporate America and Wall Street. In Gallup's middle-income group, by contrast, 55% of respondents claim the economy is in trouble. They're still waiting for their recovery to arrive.

The Slow Fade of Big Labor

The big-picture economic changes described by Autor and others, however, don't tell the entire story. There's a significant political component to the hollowing out of the American labor force and the impoverishment of the middle class: the slow fade of organized labor. Since the 1950s, the clout of unions in the public and private sectors has waned, their membership has dwindled, and their political influence has weakened considerably. Long gone are the days when powerful union bosses—the AFL-CIO's George Meany or the UAW's Walter Reuther—had the ear of just about any president.

As *Mother Jones*' Kevin Drum has written, in the 1960s and 1970s a rift developed between big labor and the Democratic Party. Unions recoiled in disgust at what they perceived to be the "motley collection of shaggy kids, newly assertive women, and goo-goo academics" who had begun to supplant organized labor in the Party. In 1972, the influential AFL-CIO symbolically distanced itself from the Democrats by refusing to endorse their nominee for president, George McGovern.

All the while, big business was mobilizing, banding together to form massive advocacy groups such as the Business Roundtable and shaping the staid U.S. Chamber of Commerce into a ferocious lobbying machine. In the 1980s and 1990s, the Democratic Party drifted rightward and toward an increasingly powerful and financially focused business community, creating the Democratic Leadership Council, an olive branch of sorts to corporate America. "It's not that the working class [had] abandoned Democrats," Drum wrote. "It's just the opposite: The Democratic Party [had] largely abandoned the working class."

The GOP, of course, has a long history of battling organized labor, and nowhere has that been clearer than in the party's recent assault on workers' rights. Swept in by a tide of Republican support in 2010, new GOP majorities in state legislatures from Wisconsin to Tennessee to New Hampshire have introduced bills meant to roll back decades' worth of collective bargaining rights for public-sector unions, the last bastion of organized labor still standing (somewhat) strong.

The political calculus behind the war on public-sector unions is obvious: kneecap them and you knock out a major pillar of support for the Democratic Party. In the 2010 midterm elections, the American Federation of State, County, and Municipal Employees (AFSCME) spent nearly $90 million on TV ads, phone banking, mailings, and other support for Democratic candidates. The anti-union legislation being pushed by Republicans would inflict serious damage on AFSCME and other public-sector unions by making it harder for them to retain members and weakening their clout at the bargaining table.

And as shown by the latest state to join the anti-union fray, it's not just Republicans chipping away at workers' rights anymore. In Massachusetts, a staunchly liberal state, the Democratic-led State Assembly recently voted to curb collective bargaining rights on heath-care benefits for teachers, firefighters, and a host of other public-sector employees.

Bargaining-table clout is crucial for unions, since it directly affects the wages their members take home every month. According to data from the Bureau of Labor Statistics, union workers pocket on average $200 more per week than their non-union counterparts, a 28% percent difference. The benefits of union representation are even greater for women and people of color: women in unions make 34% more than their non-unionized counterparts, and Latino workers nearly 51% more.

In other words, at precisely the moment when middle-class workers need strong bargaining rights so they can fight to preserve a living wage in a barbell economy, unions around the country face the grim prospect of losing those rights.

All of which raises the questions: Is there any way to revive the American middle class and reshape income distribution in our barbell nation? Or will this warped recovery of ours pave the way for an even more warped McEconomy, with the have-nots at one end, the have-it-alls at the other end, and increasingly less of us in between?

Analyze This Reading

1. What is the "barbell effect" that the writer refers to? How do technology and education figure into this effect?
2. According to the writer, why is it important for the GOP to oppose organized labor?
3. The writer brings to this article two portmanteau words—*McEconomy* and *McWorker*—two words that combine into one. For each portmanteau word, no definition is offered. To what extent is this a risky strategy? Were these words immediately understandable to you? Explain.

Respond To This Reading

1. To what extent do you see workers polarized in your community in terms of income and job security?
2. Explain why labor unions are the best way to restore the middle class. Or, if you disagree with this position, discuss other means by which more American workers can achieve a path to higher wages and advancement.
3. How do you relate to the term *career*? What conditions would you change, or keep the same, when you think of this term?

ABOUT THIS READING

In this reading, writer and former editor of the *Paris Review* Oliver Broudy interviews Peter Singer. Singer is the DeCamp Professor of Bioethics at Princeton University and author of *Animal Liberation* (1975), a book many consider to be at the center of the animal rights movement. This interview originally appeared on *Salon.com*, a daily online magazine that focuses on liberal politics.

The Practical Ethicist: "The Way We Eat" Author Peter Singer Explains the Advantage of Wingless Chickens, How Humans Discriminate Against Animals, and the Downside of Buying Locally Grown Food

By Oliver Broudy

Oliver Broudy: *One of the things that distinguishes your new book* [The Way We Eat: Why Our Food Choices Matter] *is all the field research that went into it. What most shocked you, over the course of doing this research?*

Peter Singer: Probably this video I saw of this kosher slaughterhouse, *AgriProcessors.* I guess I had this idea that kosher slaughter is more strictly controlled than normal slaughter, and when you see that video and you see these cattle staggering around with their throats cut, and blood pouring out—by no stretch of the imagination is this just a reflex movement. It goes on and on. And this happens repeatedly, with many different animals.

How are kosher animals supposed to be slaughtered?

They are supposed to be slaughtered with a single blow of a sharp knife across the throat. There's a virtually instant loss of consciousness, because the brain loses blood so quickly. That's the idea, anyway. But when you see this video, it's so far from that, I really did find it quite shocking.

You mention in your book that cows today produce three times as much milk as they did 50 years ago. That's a great advance, isn't it?

It is an advance, but you have to consider how this has been achieved. Fifty years ago, cows were basically fed on grass. They walked around and selected their food themselves, food that we can't eat, chewing it up and producing milk that we *can* eat. Now cows are confined indoors, and a lot of their food supply is grown specifically for them, on land that we could have used to grow food for ourselves. So it's actually less efficient, in that we could have gotten more food from the land if we didn't pass it through the cow.

Most of us have an idealized notion of what an organic farm is like. You visited an organic chicken farm in New Hampshire. Did it meet your expectations?

I have to say that it didn't. I guess I was expecting some access to pasture for the hens. When I got to this place, although it was in a beautiful green valley in New Hampshire, and it was a fine, sunny fall day, there were no hens outside at all. The hens were all in these huge sheds, about 20,000 hens in a single shed, and they were pretty crowded. The floor of the shed was basically a sea of brown hens, and when we asked about access to outdoors, we were shown a small dirt run which at the best of times I don't think the hens would be very interested in. In any case the doors were closed, and when we asked why, we were told that the producer was worried about bird flu. So, yes, it was not really what I expected. It was still a kind of a factory farm production—although undoubtedly it was much better than a caged operation.

How much space are birds allotted in caged operations?

In the U.S., birds have as little as 48 square inches, a six- by eight-inch space. The United Egg Producers' standards are gradually increasing over the next five years. We'll get up to 67 square inches. But that's still not the industry average, and even 67 square inches is just [the size of] a sheet of standard letter paper. In a cage, the birds are unable to stretch their wings. The wingspan of the bird is about 31 inches, so even if you lined one bird up on the diagonal, she wouldn't be able to spread her wings. And there's not just one bird in these cages, there are four or five. The weaker birds are unable to escape from the more aggressive birds. They end up rubbing against the wire and getting pecked, so they lose a lot of feathers, and they can't lay their eggs in the nesting box.

One good thing about this organic farm in New Hampshire is that there was this row of nesting boxes. It's been shown that hens have a strong instinct to lay in this kind of sheltered area. Conrad Lawrence, the science fiction writer and author of *The Council to Save the Planet,* once compared requiring a hen to lay in an open space to asking a human to shit in public. They don't like it.

What if it were possible to genetically engineer a brainless bird, grown strictly for its meat? Do you feel that this would be ethically acceptable?

It would be an ethical improvement on the present system, because it would eliminate the suffering that these birds are feeling. That's the huge plus to me.

What if you could engineer a chicken with no wings, so less space would be required?

I guess that's an improvement too, assuming it doesn't have any residual instincts, like phantom pain. If you could eliminate various other chicken instincts, like its preference for laying eggs in a nest, that would be an improvement too.

It seems to come down to a trade-off between whether the bird has wing space or whether you can fit more birds in your shed, and therefore have to pay less heating costs. How does one go about weighing these alternatives? How does the ethicist put a price on the impulse of a chicken to spread its wings?

We recognize the chicken as another conscious being. It's different from us, but it has a life, and if something is really important for that chicken, if it would work hard to try to get it, and if we can give it without sacrificing something that's really important to us, then we should. If it's a big burden on us, that's surely different, but if it's a question of paying a few more cents for eggs, when we pay just as much if not more for a brand label we like, then we ought to be prepared to pay more for eggs so that the chicken can enjoy its life, and not be frustrated and deprived and miserable.

What constitutes a big burden? Doubtless the chicken farmer would say that building a larger shed or paying a bigger heating bill is a big burden.

It's only a burden to him if it harms his business, and it only harms his business if he can't sell the eggs he produces because other producers who don't follow those standards are selling eggs more cheaply. So, there's two ways around that: Either you have ethically motivated consumers who are prepared to pay a somewhat higher price for humanely certified eggs, or you cut out the unfair competition with regulations. Prohibiting cages, for example. And that's been done already, in Switzerland. And the entire European Union is already saying you can't keep hens as confined as American hens; it's on track to require nesting boxes, and areas to scratch, by 2012. So you can do it, and it doesn't mean that people can no longer afford to eat eggs.

In your book you discuss this in terms of the right of the chicken to express its natural behavior.

I tend not to put it in terms of rights, because philosophically I have doubts about the foundations of rights. But yes, I think these animals have natural behaviors, and generally speaking, their natural behaviors are the ones they have adapted for. And if we prevent them from performing those natural behaviors, we are likely to be frustrating them and making them miserable. So, yes, I think we ought to try to let them perform those natural behaviors.

Could you explain your position on "speciesism," and what this has to do with your call to "expand the circle"?

The argument, in essence, is that we have, over centuries of history, expanded the circle of beings whom we regard as morally significant. If you go back in time you'll find tribes that were essentially only concerned with their own tribal members. If you were a member of another tribe, you could be killed with impunity. When we got beyond that there were still boundaries to our moral sphere, but these were based on nationality, or race, or religious belief. Anyone outside those boundaries didn't count. Slavery is the best example here. If you were not a member of the European race, if you were African, specifically, you could be enslaved. So we got beyond that. We have expanded the circle beyond our own race and we reject as wrongful the idea that something like race or religion or gender can be a basis for claiming another being's interests count less than our own.

So the argument is that this is also an arbitrary stopping place; it's also a form of discrimination, which I call "speciesism," that has parallels with racism. I am not saying it's identical, but in both cases you have this group that has power over the outsiders, and develops an ideology that says, "Those outside our circle don't matter, and therefore we can make use of them for our own convenience."

That is what we have done, and still do, with other species. They're effectively *things*; they're property that we can own, buy and sell. We use them as is convenient and we keep them in ways that suit us best, producing products we want at the cheapest prices. So my argument is simply that this is wrong, this is not justifiable if we want to defend the idea of human equality against those who have a narrower definition. I don't think we can say that somehow we, as humans, are the sole repository of all moral value, and that all beings beyond our species don't matter. I think they do matter, and we need to expand our moral consideration to take that into account.

So you are saying that expanding the circle to include other species is really no different than expanding it to include other races?

Yes, I think it's a constant progression, a broadening of that circle.

But surely there's a significant difference between a Jew, for instance, and a chicken. These are different orders of beings.

Well, of course, there's no argument about that. The question is whether saying that you are not a member of my kind, and that therefore I don't have to give consideration to your interests, is something that was said by the Nazis and the slave traders, and is also something that we are saying to other species. The question is, what is the relevant difference here? There is no doubt that there is a huge difference between human and nonhuman animals. But what we are overlooking is the fact that nonhuman animals are conscious beings, that they can suffer. And we ignore that suffering, just as the Nazis ignored the suffering of the Jews, or the slave traders ignored the suffering of the Africans. I'm not saying that it's the same sort of suffering. I am not saying that factory farming is the same as the Holocaust or the slave trade, but it's clear that there is an immense amount of suffering in it, and just as we think that the Nazis were wrong to ignore the suffering of their victims, so we are wrong to ignore the sufferings of our victims.

But how do you know at what point to stop expanding the circle?

I think it gets gray when you get beyond mammals, and certainly it gets grayer still when you get beyond vertebrates. That's something we don't know enough about yet. We don't understand the way the nervous systems of invertebrates work. . . .

I wanted to list a few factoids that jumped out at me while reading your book, and if you want to comment on them I'd love to hear your thoughts. First, each of the 36 million cattle produced in the United States has eaten 66 pounds of chicken litter?

The chicken industry produces a vast amount of litter that the chickens are living on, which of course gets filled with the chicken excrement, and is cleaned maybe once a year. And then the question is, what [do] you do with it? Well, it's been discovered that cattle will eat it. But the chickens get some slaughterhouse remnants in their feed, and some of that feed they may not eat, so the slaughterhouse remnants may also be in the chicken litter. So that could be a route by which mad-cow disease gets from these prohibited slaughterhouse products into the cattle, through this circuitous route.

Second factoid: 284 gallons of oil go into fattening a 1,250-pound cow for slaughter?

That's a figure from David Pimentel, a Cornell [University] ecologist. The fossil fuel goes into the fertilizer used to fertilize these acres of grain, which are then harvested and processed and transported to the cattle for feed. We get back, at most, 10 percent of the food value of the grain that we put into the cattle. So we are just skimming this concentrated product off the top of a mountain of grain into which all this fossil fuel has gone.

So even if we all started driving Priuses we'd still have these cows to worry about.

Yes. In fact, there's a University of Chicago study that shows that if you switch from driving an American car to driving a Prius, you'll cut your carbon-dioxide emissions by one ton per year. But if you switch from a typical U.S. diet, about 28 percent of which comes from animal sources, to a vegan diet with the same number of calories, you'll cut your carbon-dioxide emissions by nearly 1.5 tons per year.

Third factoid: We have more people in prison in the United States than people whose primary occupation is working on a farm?

Isn't that amazing? Just as an example, when I wrote *Animal Liberation* 30 years ago or so, there were more than 600,000 independent pig farms in the U.S. Now there are only about 60,000. We're still producing just as many pigs, in fact more pigs, but there has been such concentration that we are now producing more pigs with a tenth as many pig farms. The same has happened in dairy and many other areas.

And finally, it turns out that a wood chipper is not the best way to dispose of 10,000 spent hens?

Yes, this also came to mind when you asked me what most shocked me. This was in San Diego County, in California. Neighbors noticed that a local chicken farm was getting rid of hens at the end of their laying period by throwing them by the bucketload down a wood chipper. They complained to the Animal Welfare Department, which investigated, and the chicken farmer told them that this was a recommendation that had been made by their vet, a vet who happens to sit on the Animal Welfare Committee of the American Veterinary Medical Association. The American Veterinary Medical Association, I should say, does not condone throwing hens down a wood chipper, but it is apparently done. We've also had examples of hens being taken off the conveyor belt and simply dumped into a bin, where by piling more hens on top, the hens on the bottom were suffocated. These old hens have no value, that's the problem, and so people have been killing them by whatever means is cheapest and most convenient.

So if you were stuck with 10,000 spent hens, what would you do with them?

I think you have a responsibility. Those hens have been producing eggs for you for a year or 18 months. You have a responsibility to make sure they are killed humanely. And you can do that. You can truck them to a place where there is stunning, or, better still, you can bring stunning equipment to the farm, and you can make sure that every hen is individually stunned with an electric shock and then killed by having its throat cut.

I thought you might suggest a retirement program.

That's an ideal that some people would like to see, but if you have to maintain and feed hens when they are no longer laying eggs, that will significantly increase the cost of the egg, and even the organic farms don't do that.

After reading this interview, some readers might be inspired to change their diets. If you could suggest one thing, what would it be?

Avoid factory farm products. The worst of all the things we talk about in the book is intensive animal agriculture. If you can be vegetarian or vegan that's ideal. If you can buy organic and vegan that's better still, and organic and fair trade and vegan, better still, but if that gets too difficult or too complicated, just ask yourself, "Does this product come from intensive animal agriculture?" If it does, avoid it, and then you will have achieved 80 percent of the good that you would have achieved if you followed every suggestion in the book.

Analyze This Reading

1. What solutions does Singer offer regarding more humane methods of raising chickens? How does he justify his ideas?
2. What definition does Singer offer for the term *speciesism*? How does the idea of suffering inform Singer's thinking on this term?
3. What advice does Singer offer for changing our diets?

Respond To This Reading

1. This interview is not a formal argument, but it does contain support that could be used in an argument. Looking at the factoids discussed in the interview, for example, what sort of claim could the factoids serve? Would their appeals be primarily logical? Explain.
2. Singer urges readers who consume chicken, beef, and pork to recognize the suffering that factory farm–raised animals endure. Are you satisfied with Singer's recommendation that we pay more for animal products so that animals can be raised in better conditions? Can you offer recommendations in addition to or apart from Singer's regarding the factory farming of animals? Explain.
3. Imagine building an argument on an issue related to intensive animal agriculture, or factory farming. On what values and philosophical foundation would your argument rest?

ABOUT THIS READING

The issue discussed in this reading concerns Chinese-made products and their safety and quality. Writer Dali L. Yang earned his Ph.D. in political science from

Princeton University and is now a professor in the Department of Political Science at the University of Chicago. This reading first appeared under the title "Total Recall" in *The National Interest*, a quarterly journal of international affairs and diplomacy.

Outsourcing Compromises the Safety and Quality of Products

By Dali L. Yang

China once languished, a closed economy with several hundred million people living in abject poverty. Today [2008], it is a major engine for world economic growth. It boasts a rising middle class and the world's largest foreign-exchange reserves. There can no longer be talk about global trade without mentioning the dragon [China], and the American consumer would be hard-pressed to live without goods bearing the "Made in China" label.

For the past year [2007–2008], though, that very label has suffered from some serious image problems. Reports of toxic Chinese-made products have mushroomed: toys covered in lead paint, melamine-tainted pet food, defective tires, toothpaste containing diethylene glycol, contaminated fish and more. There is also talk of unlicensed Chinese chemical companies eager to manufacture and supply fake, subpotent or adulterated drug products. To be sure, the bulk of Chinese exports to the United States are made or assembled to American specifications. Nonetheless, the lengthening list of unsafe goods from China also points to the simple fact that, in their quest for lower costs and higher profits, far too many China-based manufacturers are willing to cut corners at the expense of consumer safety.

Economic Growth Breeds Corruption

At their heart, China's real and exaggerated brand-image problems stem from a unique intersection of the American need for instant gratification and China's poisonous witches' brew of a "post-communist personality" with few moral moorings and an unfailing enthusiasm for getting rich. Too often now, the acquisitiveness so palpable in Chinese society knows no scruples, shifts the costs to others, and is married to opportunism and cunning. Of course, there are many businessmen who have made it big by working hard and honestly, but it's the anything-goes mind-set that rests at the root of many undesirable practices in China: from decadence to all manners of fake certificates, fake products, adulterated food and drinks, rampant official corruption and sheer disregard for the rights of workers in sweatshops. For many, socialism with Chinese characteristics has a lot in common with the early stage of capitalism Karl Marx described as primitive accumulation.

This phenomenon finds its roots in the Chinese brand of communism from which it was borne and the reforms from which it was shaped. Begun in the 1970s, the proliferation of unruly manufacturers and exporters in China sprang from an environment where the potential for entrepreneurship among peasants and tradesmen was stifled. Technicians were jailed for moonlighting as consultants, and collective farms were enthralled to the party-state. Private business activities were severely punished or suppressed.

But after years of oppression, the government began to allow market-oriented reforms to modernize China's economy. Within a decade, the forces of enterprise were unleashed, but hand in hand with growth came rampant corruption. Reform making and profit making have often meant getting ahead of official policies and bending and breaking existing laws and regulations.

Along with these market reforms came preferential treatment for those of "the Party." China's leaders (and especially Deng Xiaoping) opened the floodgates, allowing government and party agencies, the armed police and even the People's Liberation Army to supplement their budgets with profits that they generated on their own. Here we see the strange melding of the strong party-state that desired a profit with the willingness to bend the rules: government control and unruly capitalism. By the 1990s, the Chinese mentality was then fully transformed. Though the Tiananmen crackdown of 1989 [a pro-democracy movement of university students that was ended by military force] closed the route to political reforms, the raw energy unleashed in China was instead channeled to the pursuit of material wealth. Mammon [riches, material wealth] became the new religion. Business fever took over.

The amazingly quick turn from the asceticism of the Mao era to the cult of Mammon under the leadership of the same Communist Party has landed China in what author Xiaoying Wang termed "a moral wasteland." Indeed, this is the world of doublespeak, with everybody mouthing the rhetoric of the moment as dictated by the party and yet often doing exactly the opposite of what's prescribed. . . .

Product Safety and Quality

It is fitting that one of the most popular books in today's China, written by Li Zhongwu in 1912, highlights how thick skins and cunning were the ingredients for getting ahead in Chinese history.

The reality of this "personality" can be frightening, leading many manufacturers to search for loopholes to slip through to get a leg up due to the relentless pressure for cheaper products. Their goal is to make some quick money, using deceit if necessary. This was apparently the case for suppliers who provided lead paint to the ill-fated toy makers. Likewise, some Chinese suppliers of wheat gluten deliberately added melamine, an industrial chemical, to artificially boost their product's protein reading and thus grade and price. In this situation, Gresham's Law [which states that bad money drives good money out of circulation] prevails; honest firms find it hard to stay in business by competing on price. Even though a fix is available—manufacturers can lower costs and increase profits by improving the efficiency of production processes—oftentimes they just seek to substitute cheaper components. That can be done without sacrificing quality, but that often doesn't happen.

Yet, even with all this finger pointing, we have to keep in mind that the Chinese can't be blamed for all of the safety problems with products manufactured in-country. According to a Canadian analysis of data on toy recalls over the last twenty years, the majority of the recalls involving millions of toys manufactured in China were caused by design defects, with pri-mary responsibility lying with the toy companies. Indeed, a Mattel execu-tive recently admitted that the "vast majority of those products that were recalled were the result of a design flaw in Mattel's design, not through a manufacturing flaw in China's manufacturers." In such cases, the solution for the resultant safety problems needs to come from the (mostly U.S.) toy companies.

Product-quality and safety cases are generally related to the continuing quest by manufacturers to lower production costs.

Unfortunately, the rest of the product-quality and safety cases are gen-erally related to the continuing quest by manufacturers to lower produc-tion costs in the face of distributors buying at low prices, a rising currency, and rising labor and raw-material costs. But this unbridled drive to profit, with all its market obstacles and ensuing corruption, has not escaped the Chinese government. Almost from the beginning, it was clear some reining-in was needed. So the contemporary history of economic growth and mar-ket expansion is also a history of the modern regulatory state. First steps were put in place—imperfect, but an encouraging start—and all hope for a "morally reformed" China is certainly not lost.

Building the Foundation

No fools they, in the early 1990s, the Chinese leadership took an initial stab at regulation after recognizing the need to build and rebuild the institu-tional infrastructure for a market economy. No modern economy allows the unbridled pursuit of self-interest, especially when that pursuit causes harm to others. In addition to the obvious internal problems, the collapse of communist regimes in the former Soviet Union and Eastern Europe and, later, the downfall of governments in South Korea and Indonesia during the Asian financial crisis spurred Beijing on even more. The Chinese leadership first reconfigured the tax and fiscal system to strengthen the central gov-ernment's fiscal capabilities and then revamped the central banking system to enhance financial supervision and promote financial stability.

Of special significance was the divestiture program undertaken amid the Asian financial crisis. In one bold move, the Chinese leadership got the People's Liberation Army, the armed police, the judiciary as well as a host of other party and state institutions out of the business of doing business. This divestiture helped bring rampant smuggling and related corruption under control and was critical to the development of a level economic playing field.

With the passage of time, China's leaders have also undertaken sev-eral rounds of government streamlining and restructuring to deal with an unruly market and rapidly changing socioeconomic conditions. In China, as in other developed nations, a bureaucratic alphabet soup of bodies has emerged to protect the rights of consumers, investors and workers. The advent of a consumer society and growing public awareness, in particular, have pushed safety and quality to the fore of policymaking. And happily, some of these institutions are becoming effective. . . .

While improved regulatory capability—up-to-date product standards, abilities to monitor, test and punish—is a necessity and can go a long way toward the mitigation of product-quality issues, it is generally less effective when dealing with rogue businesses whose intentions are to evade detection and make a quick buck. Shutting down a toxic plant after a scandal is one thing. Using bureaucracies for effective preventive measures is another.

While China has established various regulatory agencies, enforcement has not been optimal.

Cracks in the Mortar

The Chinese government realized that simply creating an array of institutions was not enough—the bureaucracy must also function well, something especially difficult to achieve in developing societies. From poor interagency cooperation to a lack of resources and sheer logistical difficulties, troubles remained. Herein lies the crux of the problem for regulators and consumers in the United States and elsewhere when it comes to the quality of products imported from abroad. While China has established various regulatory agencies, enforcement has not been optimal. Regulatory authority is now fragmented among a multitude of government agencies—each mindful of its own turf and interests—that often fail to work together, especially at the local levels. . . . Failure among the regulators to coordinate and cooperate with each other is believed to have contributed to the deadly milk-powder scandal that came to light in 2004 [when melamine was added to foods to make them appear to have a higher protein content].

Making matters worse, the interests between central and local authorities often diverge. In particular, lower-level authorities may be more tolerant of counterfeiters and other dishonest businesses in their jurisdictions simply because these businesses generate employment and tax revenue. In the words of a *Business Week* reporting team: "Even if Beijing has the best intentions of fixing problems such as undrinkable water and unbreathable air, it is often thwarted by hundreds of thousands of party officials with vested interests in the current system."

Partly to mitigate such divergence, the Chinese government has in recent years promoted the hierarchical integration of regulatory administrations, especially within the provinces. But, as pessimists argue, "China has built a bureaucratic machine that at times seems almost impervious to reform."

China's sheer scale and vast regional disparities present major challenges, too. While the major cities can deploy more personnel, resources and technology to enhance regulatory supervision, this is far from the case in outlying areas, where many of the small businesses, including counterfeiters, are often located.

Last but certainly not least, corruption has plagued some of the regulatory agencies, both in the headquarters and in the localities. Under Zheng Xiaoyu, the former head of the SFDA [State Food and Drug Administration], and his close associates, some pharmaceutical companies were able to obtain a large number of new drug approvals by submitting fake data and bribe money. Zheng was executed for bribe taking and dereliction of duty in 2007.

A history of Chinese regulatory developments in the reform era is thus one about the struggle to curb regulatory corruption and deal with and overcome various institutional flaws. As China's regulatory agencies contend with internal conflicts and cope with external pressures, are we sure they'll be able to effectively address their product-safety and quality problems? . . .

Chinese officials openly express their annoyance at Western media reports they feel exaggerate the magnitude of China's product-safety problems.

Building Better

Sometimes a strong party-state is a very good thing. The successful corrective measures with respect to aviation safety and antidoping in international sports are undoubtedly encouraging. China is able to comply with international rules and norms. Recognizing that China's reputation was at stake, China's leaders took on serious reforms and tough regulatory actions. Unlike in many other developing countries, China, with its Communist Party, has the capacity to get things done when it matters.

Efforts to overcome corruption and cheating in the wake of opening up the Chinese market solved some problems, but created others. Though Chinese officials openly express their annoyance at Western media reports they feel exaggerate the magnitude of China's product-safety problems, they do realize that the reputation of "Made in China" is imperiled—and they care. As Vice Premier Wu Yi noted, bad press had caused "serious damage to China's national image." The government saw the writing on the wall and has taken a new wave of steps to improve watchdogging.

To help fix the problems plaguing regulatory agencies, like fragmentation and poor policy coordination, the State Council established a leading group on product quality and food safety in 2007. The leading group, headed by Vice Premier Wu Yi, is comprised of representatives from fifteen government agencies. And the Chinese government is putting muscle into policy implementation. Building on its long-standing efforts to improve market order, the Chinese government launched a nationwide campaign in August 2007 to investigate and fight the manufacture and sale of fake or substandard food, medicine and agricultural products. By October, the Chinese government had arrested 774 people in the crackdown. As of late November 2007, authorities had also closed down nearly eight thousand slaughterhouses for operating without licenses or for failing to meet government standards. For toy manufacturers blamed for producing toxic products, the Chinese government has suspended their export licenses—the kiss of death for an export business. Foshan Lee Der Toy Co., one of the first to be blamed for Mattel toys containing lead, was shut down. The owner committed suicide.

But most importantly, the Chinese are upgrading quality standards in all areas, from food to pharmaceuticals. They're taking proactive measures to strengthen the monitoring and supervision of production and supply chains for food and manufactures, including implementing monitoring and inspection programs for wholesale farm-produce markets in all major cities, introducing recall mechanisms for food and more rigorously testing the quality of export products at the border.

In spite of the domestic campaign and crackdown, it is simply impossible for Chinese regulators to achieve full compliance in the domestic market in a short time period. There are hundreds of thousands of firms and families involved in producing food and manufactures. So, the focus of governmental action is, in the words of Wu Yi, "to strengthen the system of supervision and control over product quality, especially relating to *exports.*" This means that, while there will be general improvement, the improvement in the domestic market will likely lag behind that of exports.

The United States and China have reached agreements to strengthen the quality of Chinese exports.

International Expectations

As with aviation-safety regulation and antidoping, the international pressure on China to improve product quality has been accompanied by international assistance. We can hope this collaboration will be as effective. On products ranging from preserved and pet foods and farm-raised fish to certain drugs, medical devices and toys, the United States and China have reached agreements to strengthen the quality of Chinese exports. Whereas previously, authorities would ignore the errant or unlicensed factories until after a product-quality problem had been uncovered, the agreements signed during the Third U.S.-China Strategic [and] Economic Dialogue in December 2007 require Chinese exporters to register with the government and accept inspections to ensure compliance with American standards. This is clearly designed to mitigate counterfeiting and safety problems before the products even leave China.

Western buyers, mindful of the high costs of safety-related recalls, have become more demanding when it comes to quality and safety.

Also as part of the agreements, and as an indication of the growing interdependence between the Chinese and American economies, Beijing has allowed U.S. inspectors to become "embedded" in China to monitor the quality standards of certain Chinese export products, ensuring they meet U.S. quality standards. Stationing U.S. FDA [Food and Drug Administration] personnel abroad helps bridge different regulatory systems. This kind of cooperation is a nascent but significant step toward deep regulatory integration and may also be replicated in other countries. All this highlights the disparity between American and developing-world standards.

Meanwhile, even without the major Chinese government initiatives, the massive recalls would have caused businesses on both sides of the Pacific to modify their behavior. Western buyers, mindful of the high costs of safety-related recalls, have become more demanding when it comes to quality and safety. On the other side, many Chinese manufacturers quickly adopted more rigorous testing and tightened quality standards to keep the orders coming in. Those unable to bear the rising costs and risks have simply exited the market.

It's unlikely that government regulation will be fully effective in the Chinese domestic market, if for no other reason than the sheer number of businesses that need to be regulated. But when it comes to Chinese exports to developed markets, the message is clear: Beijing will ensure products destined for American markets meet U.S. standards. As Wu Yi said, "China will live up to its responsibilities and obligations when it comes to product quality and food safety." Both government initiatives and market forces will point the way. After all, China's reputation is at stake.

Analyze This Reading

1. According to the writer, what is motivating Chinese manufacturers to compromise product safety? What is the "post-communist personality" the writer attributes to Chinese manufacturers?
2. What have been the effects of the Chinese government's efforts to regulate product quality and safety?
3. What agreements were reached during the Third U.S.–China Strategic Economic Dialogue in December 2007?
4. Why is there a disparity between China's regulation of products destined for export and those produced for internal consumption?
5. A clear strength of this writing is the writer's ability to surround his ideas with broad historical context. Point to 2-3 paragraphs where this broad context occurs.

Respond To This Reading

1. Recalls of products made in China, the United States, and other countries occur because quality and safety are compromised. What values, attitudes, and principles are in play when products are recalled with regard to the parties involved—consumers, manufacturers, and governments?
2. As a consumer, what concerns have you experienced with product safety and quality? How have you responded?
3. Imagine that you are presiding over a meeting of local manufacturers and consumer groups who have been convened to discuss product quality and safety in your community. What goals would you articulate at the beginning of the meeting?

Concerned Citizen Community

ABOUT THIS READING

This argument is authored by Harry Binswanger, professor of philosophy at the Ayn Rand Institute. In this reading, the author argues that an open immigration system should replace a quota system and takes on the thorny issues of government infringing on individual rights, immigrants stealing jobs from native workers, and the role of immigrants in creating wealth for a country. It originally appeared in *Capitalism Magazine*.

The United States Should Adopt Open Immigration

By Harry Binswanger

This is a defense of phasing-in open immigration into the United States. Entry into the U.S. should ultimately be free for any foreigner, with the exception of criminals, would-be terrorists, and those carrying infectious diseases. (And note: I am defending freedom of entry and residency, not the automatic granting of U.S. citizenship.)

An end to immigration quotas is demanded by the principle of individual rights. Every individual has rights as an individual, not as a member of this or that nation. One has rights not by virtue of being an American, but by virtue of being human.

One doesn't have to be a resident of any particular country to have a moral entitlement to be secure from governmental coercion against one's life, liberty, and property. In the words of the Declaration of Independence, government is instituted "to secure these rights"—to protect them against their violation by force or fraud.

A foreigner has rights just as much as an American. To be a foreigner is not to be a criminal. Yet our government treats as criminals those foreigners not lucky enough to win the green-card lottery.

Quotas Treat Immigrants as Criminals

Seeking employment in this country is not a criminal act. It coerces no one and violates no one's rights (there is no "right" to be exempt from competition in the labor market, or in any other market).

It is not a criminal act to buy or rent a home here in which to reside. Paying for housing is not a coercive act—whether the buyer is an American or a foreigner. No one's rights are violated when a Mexican, or Canadian, or Senegalese rents an apartment from an American owner and moves into the housing he is paying for. And what about the rights of those American citizens who want to sell or rent their property to the highest bidders? Or the American businesses that want to hire the lowest cost workers? It is morally indefensible for our government to violate their right to do so, just because the person is a foreigner.

Immigration quotas forcibly exclude foreigners who want not to seize but to purchase housing here, who want not to rob Americans but to engage in productive work, raising our standard of living. To forcibly exclude those who seek peacefully to trade value for value with us is a violation of the rights of both parties to such a trade: the rights of the American seller or employer and the rights of the foreign buyer or employee.

Thus, immigration quotas treat both Americans and foreigners as if they were criminals, as if the peaceful exchange of values to mutual benefit were an act of destruction.

The Rights of the Individual Above All

To take an actual example, if I want to invite my Norwegian friend Klaus to live in my home, either as a guest or as a paying tenant, what right does our government have to stop Klaus and me? To be a Norwegian is not to be a criminal. And if some American business wants to hire Klaus, what right does our government have to interfere?

The implicit premise of barring foreigners is: "This is our country, we let in who we want." But who is "we"? The government does not own the country. Jurisdiction is not ownership. Only the owner of land or any item of property can decide the terms of its use or sale. Nor does the majority own the country. This is a country of private property, and housing is private property. So is a job.

American land is not the collective property of some entity called "the U.S. government." Nor is there such thing as collective, social ownership of the land. The claim, "We have the right to decide who is allowed in" means some individuals—those with the most votes—claim the right to prevent other citizens from exercising their rights. But there can be no right to violate the rights of others.

Our constitutional republic respects minority rights. Sixty percent of the population cannot vote to enslave the other 40 percent. Nor can a majority dictate to the owners of private property. Nor can a majority dictate on whom private employers spend their money. Not morally, not in a free society. In a free society, the rights of the individual are held sacrosanct, above any claim of even an overwhelming majority.

The rights of one man end where the rights of his neighbor begin. Only within the limits of his rights is a man free to act on his own judgment. The criminal is the man who deliberately steps outside his rights-protected domain and invades the domain of another, depriving his victim of his exclusive control over his property, or liberty, or life. The criminal, by his own choice, has rejected rights in favor of brute violence. Thus, an immigration policy that excludes criminals is proper.

Likewise, a person with an infectious disease, such as smallpox, threatens with serious physical harm those with whom he comes into proximity. Unlike the criminal, he may not intend to do damage, but the threat of physical harm is clear, present, and objectively demonstrable. To protect the lives of Americans, he may be kept out or quarantined until he is no longer a threat.

But what about the millions of Mexicans, South Americans, Chinese, Canadians, etc. seeking entry who are not criminal and not bearing infectious diseases? By what moral principle can they be excluded? Not on the grounds of majority vote, not on the grounds of protecting any American's rights, not on the grounds of any legitimate authority of the state.

Understanding the Nature of Rights

That's the moral case for phasing out limits on immigration. But some ask: "Is it practical? Wouldn't unlimited immigration—even if phased in over a decade—be disastrous to our economic well-being and create overcrowding? Are we being told to just grit our teeth and surrender our interests in the name of morality?"

This question is invalid on its face. It shows a failure to understand the nature of rights, and of moral principles generally. Rational moral principles reflect a recognition of the basic nature of man, his nature as a specific kind of living organism, having a specific means of survival. Questions of what is practical, what is to one's self-interest, can be answered only in that context. It is neither practical nor to one's interest to attempt to live and act in defiance of one's nature as a human being.

Yet that is the meaning of the moral-practical dichotomy. When one claims, "It is immoral but practical," one is maintaining, "It cripples my nature as a human being, but it is beneficial to me"—which is a contradiction.

Rights, in particular, are not something pulled from the sky or decreed by societal whim. Rights are moral principles, established by reference to the needs inherent in man's nature qua man. "Rights are conditions of existence required by man's nature for his proper survival." ([philosopher and author] Ayn Rand)

Every organism has a basic means of survival; for man, that means is: reason. Man is the rational animal, *homo sapiens*. Rights are moral principles that spell out the terms of social interaction required for a rational being to survive and flourish. Since the reasoning mind cannot function under physical coercion, the basic social requirement of man's survival is: freedom. Rights prescribe freedom by proscribing coercion.

"If man is to live on earth, it is right for him to use his mind, it is right to act on his own free judgment, it is right to work for his values and to keep the product of his work." (Ayn Rand)

Rights reflect the fundamental alternative of voluntary consent or brute force. The reign of force is in no one's interest; the system of voluntary cooperation by mutual consent is the precondition of anyone achieving his actual interests. . . .

Work Is Limitless

One major fear of open immigration is economic: the fear of losing one's job to immigrants. It is asked: "Won't the immigrants take our jobs?" The answer is: "Yes, so we can go on to better, higher-paying jobs."

The fallacy in this protectionist objection lies in the idea that there is only a finite amount of work to be done. The unstated assumption is: "If Americans don't get to do that work, if foreigners do it instead, we Americans will have nothing to do."

But work is the creation of wealth. A job is a role in the production of goods and services—the production of food, of cars, computers, the providing of internet content—all the items that go to make up our standard of living. A country cannot have too much wealth. The need for wealth is limitless, and the work that is to be done is limitless. . . .

Unemployment is not caused by an absence of avenues for the creation of wealth. Unemployment is caused by government interference in the labor market. Even with that interference, the number of jobs goes relentlessly upward, decade after decade. This bears witness to the fact that there's no end to the creation of wealth and thus no end to the useful employment of human intelligence and the physical effort directed by that intelligence. There is always more productive work to be done. If you can give your job to an immigrant, you can get a more valuable job.

What is the effect of a bigger labor pool on wage rates? If the money supply is constant, nominal wage rates fall. But real wage rates rise because total output has gone up. Economists have demonstrated that real wages have to rise as long as the immigrants are self-supporting. If immigrants earn their keep, if they don't consume more than they produce, then they add to total output, which means that prices fall (if the money supply is constant).

And, in fact, rising real wages was the history of our country in the nineteenth century. Before the 1920s, there were no limits on immigration, yet our standard of living rocketed upward. Self-supporting immigrants were an economic benefit not an injury.

The protectionist objection that immigrants take away jobs and harm our standard of living is a solid economic fallacy.

Welfare and Overcrowding Concerns

A popular misconception is that immigrants come here to get welfare. To the extent that is true, immigrants do constitute a burden. But this issue is mooted by the passage, under the [Bill] Clinton Administration, of the Personal Responsibility and Work Opportunity and Reconciliation Act (PRWORA), which makes legal permanent residents ineligible for most forms of welfare for five years. I support this kind of legislation.

Further, if the fear is of non-working immigrants, why is the pending legislation aimed at employers of immigrants?

America is a vastly underpopulated country. Our population density is less than one-third of France's.

Take an extreme example. Suppose a tidal wave of immigrants came here. Suppose that half of the people on the planet moved here. That would mean an unthinkable 11-fold increase in our population—from 300 million to 3.3 billion people. That would make America almost as "densely" populated as today's England (360 people/sq. km. vs. 384 people/sq. km.). In fact, it would make us less densely populated than the state of New Jersey (453 per sq. km.). And these calculations exclude Alaska and Hawaii, and count only land area.

Contrary to widespread beliefs, high population density is a value not a disvalue. High population density intensifies the division of labor, which makes possible a wider variety of jobs and specialized consumer products. For instance, in Manhattan, there is a "doll hospital"—a store specializing in the repair of children's dolls. Such a specialized, niche business requires a high population density in order to have a market. Try finding a doll hospital in Poughkeepsie. In Manhattan, one can find a job as a Pilates Method teacher or as a "Secret Shopper" (two jobs actually listed on Craig's List [www.craigslist.org]). Not in Paducah.

People want to live near other people, in cities. One-seventh of England's population lives in London. If population density is a bad thing, why are Manhattan real-estate prices so high?

The Value of Immigrants

Immigrants are the kind of people who refresh the American spirit. They are ambitious, courageous, and value freedom. They come here, often with no money and not even speaking the language, to seek a better life for themselves and their children.

The vision of American freedom, with its opportunity to prosper by hard work, serves as a magnet drawing the best of the world's people. Immigrants are self-selected for their virtues: their ambitiousness, daring, independence, and pride. They are willing to cast aside the tradition-bound roles assigned to them in their native lands and to re-define themselves as Americans. These are the people America needs in order to keep alive the individualist, hard-working attitude that made America.

Here is a short list of some great immigrants: Alexander Hamilton, Alexander Graham Bell, Andrew Carnegie, most of the top scientists of the Manhattan Project, Igor Sikorsky (the inventor of the helicopter), Ayn Rand.

Open immigration: the benefits are great. The right is unquestionable. So let them come.

Analyze This Reading

1. What does the writer claim, and what qualifiers does he attach to his claim?
2. On what value or principle is the claim based?
3. On what grounds does the writer support his contention that quotas treat immigrants like criminals?
4. In paragraphs 9 through 15, the writer makes a moral case for phasing out limits on immigration. Describe this moral case.
5. What objections, or rebuttals, to his argument does the writer anticipate? How does he counter them?
6. This argument concludes with attention to the value of immigrants. How are immigrants valuable?

Respond To This Reading

1. Do you agree with the writer's position on open immigration? Explain.
2. Issues that fall under the topic of immigration are numerous. What immigration issues are current in your community? Describe a recent conversation you had about immigration.
3. What single immigration issue motivates you to argue? What would you claim, and what kinds of support would you bring to your argument?
4. The writer grounds his argument in values of rights, individuality, and property. What values would motivate you to argue on an immigration issue?

ABOUT THIS READING

This reading appeared in writer James L. Dickerson's book, *Yellow Fever: A Deadly Disease Poised to Kill Again.* Dickerson is a former social worker who has authored numerous books and articles on health issues.

Climate Change Could Cause Disease Resurgence

By James L. Dickerson

A 2002 study conducted by researchers at Princeton University and Cornell University concluded that climate warming is allowing disease-carrying viruses such as yellow fever to invade North America. As a result, the researchers warn that yellow fever and other related diseases could become more common as milder winters allow the seasonal survival of more mosquitoes. A warmer climate also could enable mosquitoes to move into areas once protected by cold weather. "In all the discussion about climate change, this has really been kind of left out," said Drew Harvell, a Cornell University marine ecologist and lead author of the study. "Just a one-or-two-degree change in temperature can lead to disease outbreaks."

An Alarming Increase of Disease

The comprehensive two-year study, developed by the National Center for Ecological Analysis and Synthesis, is the first to look at disease in terms of global warming. Said Harvell: "What is most surprising is the fact that climate sensitive outbreaks are happening with so many different types of pathogens—viruses, bacteria, fungi and parasites—as well as in such a wide range of hosts, including corals, oysters, terrestrial plants, birds and humans." Added coauthor Richard Ostfeld, from the Institute of Ecosystem Studies in Millbrook, New York: "This isn't just a question of coral bleaching for a few marine ecologists, nor just a question of malaria for a few health officials—the number of similar increases in disease incidence is astonishing. We don't want to be alarmist, but we are alarmed." Andrew Dobson, a Princeton epidemiologist associated with the study, says the risk for humans is going up: "The diseases we should be most worried about are the vector [insect] transmitted diseases." Even with small temperature increases, he concludes, natural ecosystems are disrupted in such a way as to create more fertile habitats for infectious diseases such a malaria and yellow fever.

Among those individuals not convinced that global warming will bring diseases such as yellow fever into the United States is the CDC's [Centers for Disease Control and Prevention's] Ned Hayes, which, according to one's point of view, is either comforting or highly disturbing. Hayes thinks that a yellow fever epidemic caused by global warming, as opposed to one caused by terrorists, has little chance of getting a foothold in the United States because of the country's high socioeconomic level and because of the prevalence of window screens and air conditioning. . . .

Not in agreement with Hayes are the researchers who conducted a 1998 study funded by the Climate Policy and Assessment Division of the EPA [Environmental Protection Agency], the National Institute of Public Health, and the Center for Medical, Agricultural, and Veterinary Entomology of the US Department of Agriculture. Using computers to simulate the circulation of the earth's climate, the researchers predicted that rising temperatures will increase the range of a mosquito that transmits the dengue fever virus. All three computer models used by the researchers indicated that dengue's epidemic potential increases with a relatively small temperature rise. At risk are the United States and all other countries around the world that are located in temperate zones, especially those that border on endemic areas where the disease is currently prevalent. "Since inhabitants of these border regions would lack immunity from past exposures, dengue fever transmission among these new populations could be extensive," says Jonathan Patz, lead author for the report and a physician at Johns Hopkins School of Public Health. "Our study makes no claim that climate factors are the most important determinants of dengue fever. However, our computer models illustrate that climate change may have a substantial global impact on the spread of dengue fever."

Global Warming and Mosquitoes

Perhaps the best method of determining the effect of global warming on yellow fever is to examine the effect that warmer temperatures are having on related mosquito-borne diseases such as dengue, malaria, West Nile fever, and encephalitis. If they show signs of increased incidence, then it is only a matter of time before the yellow fever virus makes its reappearance.

Paul R. Epstein, associate director of the Center for Health and the Global Environment at Harvard, feels that those diseases are going to become more prevalent because of the mosquito's sensitivity to meteorological conditions. "Cold can be a friend to humans," he writes, "because it limits mosquitoes to seasons and regions where temperatures stay above certain minimums. Winter freezing kills many eggs, larvae and adults outright . . . within their survivable range of temperatures, mosquitoes proliferate faster and bite more as the air becomes warmer. At the same time, greater heat speeds the rate at which pathogens inside them reproduce and mature. . . . As whole areas heat up, then, mosquitoes could expand into formerly forbidden territories, bringing illness with them."

West Nile Virus

One of the most disturbing developments in recent years has been the arrival of the West Nile virus. In August 1999, tissue samples from a dead crow found in the New York City area and from a horse that died of a central nervous system disease on Long Island, New York, were sent to the National Veterinary Services Laboratories in Ames, Iowa, for identification. Meanwhile, more than two dozen cases of suspicious equine illness were identified in Suffolk and Nassau Counties on Long Island.

By September, the Centers for Disease Control and Prevention was able to identify the infected tissue samples as hosts to West Nile virus, a disease first isolated in 1937 in Africa and the Middle East. It is closely related to St. Louis encephalitis, which is indigenous to the United States and Canada, but, as of August 1999, West Nile virus had never been isolated in tissue samples in North America.

Accompanying the deaths of dozens of horses and thousands of birds in the New York City area was an outbreak of human encephalitis that baffled health officials because it appeared to be a new strain. As the human death toll rose, genetic sequencing studies revealed that humans, birds, and horses were all infected by the same strain of West Nile, one that showed strong similarities to isolates from the Middle East.

Almost right away, the disease, which is spread from animals to humans by mosquitoes, began moving from New York to New Jersey and Connecticut, where 83 cases of West Nile were reported within one year. By 2005 the disease had spread all the way to California, infecting humans in almost every state except Maine, Alaska, and Hawaii. At greatest risk are those people over 50 years of age.

"Yellow fever is transmitted from human to mosquito to human, but with West Nile the reservoir of infection is the birds and possibly some reptiles and you have a different dynamic—humans are sort of incidental," says Dr. Ned Hayes. "You don't get human to human transmission with West Nile. The disease has spread east to west, north to south, going to both Canada and Mexico, but we still don't know what's going to happen in the United States. It is possible it could continue to cause locally intense epidemics in certain parts of the country, and it's also possible it might take a course like St. Louis encephalitis, which flares up after years of dormancy."

Learning from Other Diseases

West Nile is of interest to yellow fever researchers because it demonstrates the speed with which a mosquito-induced disease can spread from state to state within a relatively brief period. Since West Nile can be spread only from animal to human, it is a friendlier disease, epidemically speaking, than yellow fever, which can spread with lightning speed from mosquito to human to mosquito to human. For those concerned about the reemergence of yellow fever in the United States, West Nile's unhindered march across the heartland offers little in the way of comfort.

Malaria is another mosquito-related disease that is raising red flags. Each year the disease kills more than 3,000 people, mostly children. Some scientists predict that, by the end of [the 21st] century, the zone of malaria transmission will increase from one containing 45 percent of the world's population to one containing 60 percent. Malaria has a long history in the United States, but public health measures throughout the country were successful in isolating the disease and restricting it to California by the 1980s. As temperatures have risen since then, the threat has increased the incidence of malaria. In recent years, outbreaks have occurred in Florida, Texas, Georgia, Michigan, New Jersey, New York, and, to the surprise of many, Toronto, Canada.

Similarly, St. Louis encephalitis, a flavivirus related to Japanese encephalitis, has shown gains in recent years, with record spikes in the 1990s, which, incidentally, were the hottest years of this century. In the summer of 1999, New York City experienced an outbreak of encephalitis that killed a number of people. Normally, encephalitis, which causes inflammation of the brain, can effectively be treated, but the survival odds are lessened for those with weakened immune systems or for senior citizens.

At the time of the New York outbreak, Dr. Cathey Falvo, director for International and Public Health at NewYork Medical College, was concerned whether the increased temperatures would allow the disease to survive the winter. Falvo was particularly concerned about the effect that global warming was having on increased incidence of the disease. If global warming continues on its present course, she said, milder winters will result that will not be cold enough to kill the microbes, thus allowing the organisms to still be around when mosquitoes again become active in the spring.

Analyze This Reading

1. What did researchers at Princeton and Cornell find in their study of climate change and disease? Are other researchers the writer refers to in agreement with these findings? Explain.
2. In the writer's view, why are warm temperatures a concern regarding mosquitoes and disease pathogens?
3. In addition to yellow fever, what other diseases does the writer discuss that could become threats in the United States due to warmer temperatures?
4. The writer has limited support of his claim to factual and statistical information and the testimony of experts. Given the issue he's working with, in your view is this a practical strategy, or should the writer have broadened the kinds of support he uses?

Respond To This Reading

1. Discuss why the writer is or is not convincing in the connections he suggests between temperature and disease.
2. In mainstream treatments, climate change and global warming have been discussed chiefly in terms of CO_2 emissions and sea level rise. In addition to the potential for disease outbreak mentioned by the writer, are there other areas of life you believe would be affected?
3. What attitudes to climate change do you encounter in your classes and in your community? What issues within this topic would motivate you to argue?

ABOUT THIS READING

Tom Engelhardt, co-founder of the American Empire Project, runs the Nation Institute's *TomDispatch.com*. He is the author of *The End of Victory Culture*, a history of the Cold War and beyond, as well as a novel, *The Last Days of Publishing*. He also edited *The World According to TomDispatch: America in the New Age of Empire*, an alternative history of the Bush years. This essay appeared in *Truthout*, the publication of an organization that, in its words, "works to broaden and diversify the political discussion by introducing independent voices and focusing on undercovered issues and unconventional thinking." Engelhardt's claim, that the United States is perpetually at war, offers a strong critique of recent presidential administrations.

Is America Hooked on War?

By Tom Engelhardt

State of War

Because the United States does not look like a militarized country, it's hard for Americans to grasp that Washington is a war capital, that the United States is a war state, that it garrisons much of the planet, and that the norm for us is to be at war somewhere at any moment. Similarly, we've become used to the idea that, when various forms of force (or threats of force) don't work, our response, as in Afghanistan, is to recalibrate and apply some alternate version of the same under a new or rebranded name—the hot one now being "counterinsurgency" or COIN—in a marginally different manner. When it comes to war, as well as preparations for war, more is now generally the order of the day.

This wasn't always the case. The early Republic that the most hawkish conservatives love to cite was a land whose leaders looked with suspicion on the very idea of a standing army. They would have viewed our hundreds of global garrisons, our vast network of spies, agents, Special Forces teams, surveillance operatives, interrogators, rent-a-guns, and mercenary corporations, as well as our staggering Pentagon budget and the constant future-war gaming and planning that accompanies it, with genuine horror.

The question is: What kind of country do we actually live in when the so-called U.S. Intelligence Community (IC) lists 16 intelligence services ranging from Air Force Intelligence, the Central Intelligence Agency, and the Defense Intelligence Agency to the National Reconnaissance Office and the National Security Agency? What could "intelligence" mean once spread over 16 sizeable, bureaucratic, often competing outfits with a cumulative 2009 budget estimated at more than $55 billion (a startling percentage of which is controlled by the Pentagon)? What exactly is so intelligent about all that? And why does no one think it even mildly strange or in any way out of the ordinary?

What does it mean when the most military-obsessed administration in our history, which, year after year, submitted ever more bloated Pentagon budgets to Congress, is succeeded by one headed by a president who ran, at least partially, on an antiwar platform, and who has now submitted an even larger Pentagon budget? What does this tell you about Washington and about the viability of non-militarized alternatives to the path George W. Bush took? What does it mean when the new administration, surveying nearly eight years and two wars' worth of disasters, decides to *expand* the U.S. Armed Forces rather than shrink the U.S. global mission?

What kind of a world do we inhabit when, with an official unemployment rate of 9.7 percent and an underemployment rate of 16.8 percent, the American taxpayer is financing the building of a three-story, exceedingly permanent-looking $17 million troop barracks at Bagram Air Base in Afghanistan? This, in turn, is part of a taxpayer-funded $220 million upgrade of the base that includes new "water treatment plants, headquarters buildings, fuel farms, and power generating plants." And what about the U.S. air base built at Balad, north of Baghdad, that now has 15 bus routes, two fire stations, two water treatment plants, two sewage treatment plants, two power plants, a water bottling plant, and the requisite set of fast-food outlets, PXes, and so on, as well as air traffic levels sometimes compared to those at Chicago's O'Hare International?

What kind of American world are we living in when a plan to withdraw most U.S. troops from Iraq involves the removal of more than 1.5 million pieces of equipment? Or in which the possibility of withdrawal leads the Pentagon to issue nearly billion-dollar contracts (new ones!) to increase the number of private security contractors in that country?

What do you make of a world in which the U.S. has robot assassins in the skies over its war zones, 24/7, and the "pilots" who control them from thousands of miles away are ready on a moment's notice to launch missiles—"Hellfire" missiles at that—into Pashtun peasant villages in the wild, mountainous borderlands of Pakistan and Afghanistan? What does it mean when American pilots can be at war "in" Afghanistan, 9 to 5, by remote control, while their bodies remain at a base outside Las Vegas and then can head home past a sign that warns them to drive carefully because this is "the most dangerous part of your day"?

What does it mean when, for our security and future safety, the Pentagon funds the wildest ideas imaginable for developing high-tech weapons systems, many of which sound as if they came straight out of the pages of sci-fi novels? Take, for example, Boeing's advanced coordinated system of hand-held drones, robots, sensors, and other battlefield surveillance equipment slated for seven Army brigades within the next two years at a cost of $2 billion and for the full Army by 2025; or the Next Generation Bomber, an advanced "platform" slated for 2018; or a truly futuristic bomber, "a suborbital semi-spacecraft able to move at hypersonic speed along the edge of the atmosphere," for 2035? What does it mean about our world when those people in our government peering deepest into a blue-skies future are planning ways to send armed "platforms" up into those skies and kill more than a quarter century from now?

And do you ever wonder about this: If such weaponry is being endlessly developed for our safety and security, and that of our children and grandchildren, why is it that one of our most successful businesses involves the sale of the same weaponry to other countries? Few Americans are comfortable thinking about this, which may explain why global-arms-trade pieces don't tend to make it onto the front pages of our newspapers. Recently, the *Times* Pentagon correspondent Thom Shanker, for instance, wrote a piece on the subject which appeared inside the paper on a quiet Labor Day. "Despite Slump, U.S. Role as Top Arms Supplier Grows" was the headline. Perhaps Shanker, too, felt uncomfortable with his subject, because he included the following generic description: "In the highly competitive global arms market, nations vie for both profit and political influence through weapons sales, in particular to developing nations. . . . " The figures he cited from a new congressional study of that "highly competitive" market told a different story: The U.S., with $37.8 billion in arms sales (up $12.4 billion from 2007), controlled 68.4% of the global arms market in 2008. Highly competitively speaking, Italy came "a distant second" with $3.7 billion. In sales to "developing nations," the U.S. inked $29.6 billion in weapons agreements or 70.1 percent of the market. Russia was a vanishingly distant second at $3.3 billion or 7.8 percent of the market. In other words, with 70 percent of the market, the U.S. actually has what, in any other field, would qualify as a monopoly position—in this case, in things that go boom in the night. With the American car industry in a ditch, it seems that this (along with Hollywood films that go boom in the night) is what we now do best, as befits a war, if not warrior, state. Is that an American accomplishment you're comfortable with?

On the day I'm writing this piece, "Names of the Dead," a feature which appears almost daily in my hometown newspaper, records the death of an Army private from DeKalb, Illinois, in Afghanistan. Among the spare facts offered: he was 20 years old, which means he was probably born not long before the First Gulf War was launched in 1990 by President George H.W. Bush. If you include that war, which never really ended—low-level U.S. military actions against Saddam Hussein's regime continued until the invasion of 2003—as well as U.S. actions in the former Yugoslavia and Somalia, not to speak of the steady warfare underway since November 2001, in his short life, there was hardly a moment in which the U.S. wasn't engaged in military operations somewhere on the planet (invariably thousands of miles from home). If that private left a one-year-old baby behind in the States, and you believe the statements of various military officials, that child could pass her tenth birthday before the war in which her father died comes to an end. Given the record of these last years, and the present military talk about being better prepared for "the next war," she could reach 2025, the age when she, too, might join the military without ever spending a warless day. Is that the future you had in mind?

Consider this: War is now the American way, even if peace is what most Americans experience while their proxies fight in distant lands. Any serious alternative to war, which means our "security," is increasingly inconceivable. In Orwellian terms then, war is indeed peace in the United States and peace, war.

American Newspeak

Newspeak, as Orwell imagined it, was an ever more constricted form of English that would, sooner or later, make "all other modes of thought impossible. It was intended," he wrote in an appendix to his novel, "that when Newspeak had been adopted once and for all and Oldspeak forgotten, a heretical thought . . . should be literally unthinkable."

When it comes to war (and peace), we live in a world of American Newspeak in which alternatives to a state of war are not only ever more unacceptable, but ever harder to imagine. If war is now our permanent situation, in good Orwellian fashion it has also been sundered from a set of words that once accompanied it.

It lacks, for instance, "victory." After all, when was the last time the U.S. actually won a war (unless you include our "victories" over small countries incapable of defending themselves like the tiny Caribbean Island of Grenada in 1983 or powerless Panama in 1989)? The smashing "victory" over Saddam Hussein in the First Gulf War only led to a stop-and-start conflict now almost two decades old that has proved a catastrophe. Keep heading backward through the Vietnam and Korean Wars and the last time the U.S. military was truly victorious was in 1945.

But achieving victory no longer seems to matter. War American-style is now conceptually unending, as are preparations for it. When George W. Bush proclaimed a Global War on Terror (aka World War IV), conceived as a "generational struggle" like the Cold War, he caught a certain American reality. In a sense, the ongoing war system can't absorb victory. Any such endpoint might indeed prove to be a kind of defeat.

No longer has war anything to do with the taking of territory either, or even with direct conquest. War is increasingly a state of being, not a process with a beginning, an end, and an actual geography.

Similarly drained of its traditional meaning has been the word "security"—though it has moved from a state of being (secure) to an eternal, immensely profitable process whose endpoint is unachievable. If we ever decided we were either secure enough, or more willing to live without the unreachable idea of total security, the American way of war and the national security state would lose much of their meaning. In other words, in our world, security *is* insecurity.

As for "peace," war's companion and theoretical opposite, though still used in official speeches, it, too, has been emptied of meaning and all but discredited. Appropriately enough, diplomacy, that part of government which classically would have been associated with peace, or at least with the pursuit of the goals of war by other means, has been dwarfed by, subordinated to, or even subsumed by the Pentagon. In recent years, the U.S. military with its vast funds has taken over, or encroached upon, a range of activities that once would have been left to an underfunded State Department, especially humanitarian aid operations, foreign aid, and what's now called nation-building. (On this subject, check out Stephen Glain's recent essay, "The American Leviathan" in the *Nation* magazine.)

Diplomacy itself has been militarized and, like our country, is now hidden behind massive fortifications, and has been placed under Lord-of-the-Flies-style guard. The State Department's embassies are now bunkers and military-style headquarters for the prosecution of war policies; its officials, when enough of them can be found, are now sent out into the provinces in war zones to do "civilian" things.

And peace itself? Simply put, there's no money in it. Of the nearly trillion dollars the U.S. invests in war and war-related activities, nothing goes to peace. No money, no effort, no thought. The very idea that there might be peaceful alternatives to endless war is so discredited that it's left to utopians, bleeding hearts, and feathered doves. As in Orwell's Newspeak, while "peace" remains with us, it's largely been shorn of its possibilities. No longer the opposite of war, it's just a rhetorical flourish embedded, like one of our reporters, in Warspeak.

What a world might be like in which we began not just to withdraw our troops from one war to fight another, but to seriously scale down the American global mission, close those hundreds of bases—recently, there were almost 300 of them, macro to micro, in Iraq alone—and bring our military home is beyond imagining. To discuss such obviously absurd possibilities makes you an apostate to America's true religion and addiction, which is force. However much it might seem that most of us are peaceably watching our TV sets or computer screens or iPhones, we Americans are also—always—marching as to war. We may not all bother to attend the church of our new religion, but we all tithe. We all partake. In this sense, we live peaceably in a state of war.

Analyze This Reading

1. Does the writer answer the question that is the title of this essay? Explain.
2. According to the writer, how might America's early leaders evaluate our military involvement today? What values does the author imply our early leaders had that today's leaders do not have?
3. Paragraphs three through nine begin with rhetorical questions, that is, questions with obvious answers and that are asked to emphasize a point of view. What are the questions that begin these paragraphs, and what obvious answers does the writer intend?
4. In paragraph nine, the writer asserts that Americans are uncomfortable thinking about the sale of American-made weapons to other countries. What is the source of this discomfort?
5. The term "newspeak" appears in paragraphs 12 and 13 and is taken from British writer George Orwell's 1948 novel *1984*, a text in which "newspeak" is part of an imaginary language characterizing a nation built on deception and one that eventually fails. With the terms *victory, security, peace,* and *diplomacy* in mind, how is the writer using the term *American Newspeak* in this essay?

Respond To This Reading

1. Do you agree with the writer's concluding thought that "we live peaceably in a state of war" and that "war is our new religion"? Explain.
2. While this essay includes plenty of logical support in terms of facts and figures, the writer omits any substantial opposition to his argument. How does this omission affect your reading of the essay?
3. Some topics raised in this essay include America's military presence in other countries and its effect on taxpayers, the reality of "robot assassins" (paragraph seven), weapons sales, and the contention that the United States has not won a war since World War II. Are there issues

within these topics, and within other topics related to our military decisions, that might motivate you to argue? Describe these issues, and
draft a claim for each.

4. Focus on a single current issue in the news involving the American
military. Learn about this issue by reviewing to how it is covered by
two or more radio stations, television stations, or online news magazines. Can you apply the term *American Newspeak* to coverage of the
issue in the sources you identify? Explain.

ABOUT THIS READING

This article appeared on *Truthdig*, a news website centered on "digs," or in-depth
investigations of current issues, facilitated by authorities and experts in their
fields. Journalist Chris Hedges has written extensively about war and terrorism;
his books include *War is a Force that Gives Us Meaning* (2002), *Empire of Illusion:
The End of Literacy and the Triumph of Spectacle* (2009), and with cartoonist Joe
Sacco, *Days of Destruction, Days of Revolt* (2012). Hedges writes a weekly column
for *Truthdig* and is an active member of the Green Party of New Jersey.

Corporate Media Obituary of Occupy Premature

*If we build a mass, diverse, nonviolent movement that weakens
the pillars of the power structure, we will win.*

By Chris Hedges

In every conflict, insurgency, uprising and revolution I have covered as a
foreign correspondent, the power elite used periods of dormancy, lulls and
setbacks to write off the opposition. This is why obituaries for the Occupy
movement are in vogue. And this is why the next groundswell of popular
protest—and there will be one—will be labeled as "unexpected," a "shock"
and a "surprise." The television pundits and talking heads, the columnists
and academics who declare the movement dead are as out of touch with
reality now as they were on Sept. 17 when New York City's Zuccotti Park
was occupied. Nothing this movement does will ever be seen by them as a
success. Nothing it does will ever be good enough. Nothing, short of its dis-
solution and the funneling of its energy back into the political system, will
be considered beneficial.

Those who have the largest megaphones in our corporate state serve
the very systems of power we are seeking to topple. They encourage us,
whether on Fox or MSNBC, to debate inanities, trivia, gossip or the personal
narratives of candidates. They seek to channel legitimate outrage and direct
it into the black hole of corporate politics. They spin these silly, useless stories from the "left" or the "right" while ignoring the egregious assault by
corporate power on the citizenry, an assault enabled by the Democrats and
the Republicans. Don't waste time watching or listening. They exist to confuse and demoralize you.

The engine of all protest movements rests, finally, not in the hands of the protesters but the ruling class. If the ruling class responds rationally to the grievances and injustices that drive people into the streets, as it did during the New Deal, if it institutes jobs programs for the poor and the young, a prolongation of unemployment benefits (which hundreds of thousands of Americans have just lost), improved Medicare for all, infrastructure projects, a moratorium on foreclosures and bank repossessions, and a forgiveness of student debt, then a mass movement can be diluted. Under a rational ruling class, one that responds to the demands of the citizenry, the energy in the street can be channeled back into the mainstream. But once the system calcifies as a servant of the interests of the corporate elites, as has happened in the United States, formal political power thwarts justice rather than advances it.

Our dying corporate class, corrupt, engorged on obscene profits and indifferent to human suffering, is the guarantee that the mass movement will expand and flourish. No one knows when. No one knows how. The future movement may not resemble Occupy. It may not even bear the name Occupy. But it will come. I have seen this before. And we should use this time to prepare, to educate ourselves about the best ways to fight back, to learn from our mistakes, as many Occupiers are doing in New York, Washington, D.C., Philadelphia and other cities. There are dark and turbulent days ahead. There are powerful and frightening forces of hate, backed by corporate money, that will seek to hijack public rage and frustration to create a culture of fear. It is not certain we will win. But it is certain this is not over.

"We had a very powerful first six months," Kevin Zeese, one of the original organizers of the Occupy encampment in Freedom Plaza in Washington, D.C., said when I reached him by phone. "We impacted the debate. We impacted policy. We showed people they are not alone. We exposed the unfair economy and our dysfunctional government. We showed people they could have an impact. We showed people they could have power. We let the genie out of the bottle. No one will put it back in."

The physical eradication of the encampments and efforts by the corporate state to disrupt the movement through surveillance, entrapment, intimidation and infiltration have knocked many off balance. That was the intent. But there continue to be important pockets of resistance. These enclaves will provide fertile ground and direction once mass protests return. It is imperative that, no matter how dispirited we may become, we resist being lured into the dead game of electoral politics.

"The recent election in Wisconsin shows why Occupy should stay out of the elections," Zeese said. "Many of the people who organized the Wisconsin occupation of the Capitol building became involved in the recall. First, they spent a lot of time and money collecting more than one million signatures. Second, they got involved in the primary where the Democrats picked someone who was not very supportive of union rights and who lost to [Gov. Scott] Walker just a couple of years ago. Third, the general election effort was corrupted by billionaire dollars. They lost. Occupy got involved in politics. What did they get? What would they have gotten if they won? They would have gotten a weak, corporate Democrat who in a couple of years would be hated. That would have undermined their credibility and demobilized their movement. Now, they have to restart their resistance movement.

"Would it not have been better if those who organized the occupation of the Capitol continued to organize an independent, mass resistance movement?" Zeese asked. "They already had strong organization in Madison, and in Dane County as well as nearby counties. They could have developed a Montreal-like movement of mass protest that stopped the function of government and built people power. Every time Walker pushed something extreme they could have been out in the streets and in the Legislature disrupting it. They could have organized general and targeted strikes. They would have built their strength. And by the time Walker faced re-election he would have been easily defeated.

"Elections are something that Occupy needs to continue to avoid," Zeese said. "The Obama-Romney debate is not a discussion of the concerns of the American people. Obama sometimes uses Occupy language, but he puts forth virtually no job creation, nothing to end the wealth divide and no real tax reform. On tax reform, the Buffett rule—that the secretary should pay the same tax rate as the boss—is totally insufficient. We should be debating whether to go back to the Eisenhower tax rates of 91 percent, the Nixon tax rate of 70 percent or the Reagan tax rate of 50 percent for the top income earners—not whether secretaries and CEOs should be taxed at the same rate!"

The Occupy movement is not finally about occupying. It is, as Zeese points out, about shifting power from the 1 percent to the 99 percent. It is a tactic. And tactics evolve and change. The freedom rides, the sit-ins at segregated lunch counters, the marches in Birmingham and the Montgomery bus boycott were tactics used in the civil rights movement. And just as the civil rights movement often borrowed tactics used by the old Communist Party, which long fought segregation in the South, the Occupy movement, as Zeese points out, draws on earlier protests against global trade agreements and the worldwide protests over the invasion of Iraq. Each was, like the Occupy movement, a global response. And this is a global movement.

We live in a period of history the Canadian philosopher John Ralston Saul calls an interregnum, a period when we are enveloped in what he calls "a vacuum of economic thought," a period when the reigning ideology, although it no longer corresponds to reality, has yet to be replaced with ideas that respond to the crisis engendered by the collapse of globalization. And the formulation of ideas, which are always at first the purview of a small, marginalized minority, is one of the fundamental tasks of the movement. It is as important to think about how we will live and to begin to reconfigure our lives as it is to resist.

Occupy has organized some significant actions, including the May Day protests, the NATO protest in Chicago, an Occupy G8 summit and G-8 protests in Thurmont and Frederick, Md. There are a number of ongoing actions—Occupy Our Homes, Occupy Faith, Occupy the Criminal Justice System, Occupy University, the Occupy Caravan—that protect the embers of revolt. Last week when Jamie Dimon, the CEO of JPMorgan Chase, testified before a U.S. Senate committee, he was confronted by Occupy protesters, including Deborah Harris, who lost her home in a JPMorgan foreclosure. But you will hear little if anything about these actions on cable television or in The Washington Post. Such acts of resistance get covered almost entirely in the alternative media, such as The Occupied Wall Street Journal and the Occupy Page of The Real News.

"Our job is to build pockets of resistance so that when the flash point arrives, people will have a place to go," Zeese said. "Our job is to stand for transformation, shifting power from concentrated wealth to the people. As long as we keep annunciating and fighting for this, whether we are talking about health care, finance, empire, housing, we will succeed.

"We will only accomplish this by becoming a mass movement," he said. "It will not work if we become a fringe movement. Mass movements have to be diverse. If you build a movement around one ethnic group, or one class group, it is easier for the power structure and the police to figure out what we will do next. With diversity you get creativity of tactics. And creativity of tactics is critical to our success. With diversity you bring to the movement different histories, different ideas, different identities, different experiences and different forms of nonviolent tactics.

"The object is to shift people from the power structure to our side, whether it is media, business, youth, labor or police," he went on. "We must break the enforcement structure. In the book 'Why Civil Resistance Works,' a review of resistance efforts over the last 100 years, breaking the enforcement structure, which almost always comes through nonviolent civil disobedience, increases your chances of success by 60 percent. We need to divide the police. This is critical. And only a mass movement that is nonviolent and diverse, that draws on all segments of society, has any hope of achieving this. If we can build that, we can win."

Analyze This Reading

1. In the writer's view, what is the connection between media and the ruling class?
2. What assessment does the writer make of the Occupy movement involving itself in traditional electoral politics? What examples are used to support this assessment?
3. How does the writer make use of philosopher John Ralston Saul and occupier Kevin Zeese? How do the ideas of these thinkers build or detract from the credibility of the writer?

Respond To This Reading

1. Born on September 17, 2011 in Zuccotti Park in New York City's financial center, Occupy Wall Street coined the slogan, "We Are the 99%." What does this slogan mean to you? Does it capture, as many contend, an economic reality in America? Explain.
2. The final paragraphs of this reading attend to a discussion of a diversity of tactics and their importance to a successful Occupy movement. Explain why it is or is not important, in your view, for Americans to be having this kind of discussion.

ABOUT THIS READING

When this reading was published, writer David Kelley was director of the Institute for Objectivist Studies, renamed "The Atlas Society" in 2004, an organization devoted to the principles of Ayn Rand, champion of individualism and capitalism. This reading is excerpted from Kelley's book, *A Life of One's Own: Individual Rights and the Welfare State.*

Private Charity Should Replace Welfare

By David Kelley

Charity is the effort to help those in need. But need varies. Sometimes it is brief but intense, the product of an emergency like a hurricane or fire, and the victims need only temporary support to restore their normal, self-supporting lives. Other people are in need as a result of longer term mental or physical disabilities, and a longer term investment is necessary if they are to realize whatever potential they can. Need can arise from sheer bad luck, from factors truly outside the person's control; emergencies are once again the obvious example. At the other extreme, the straitened circumstances in which some people live are entirely their own doing, the result of abandoning responsibility for their lives. Most cases fall in between the extremes; poverty is the result of bad luck and bad choices in various degrees. As Alexis de Tocqueville observed, "Nothing is so difficult to distinguish as the nuances which separate unmerited misfortune from an adversity produced by vice. How many miseries are simultaneously the result of both these causes!"

For that reason, effective charity requires discrimination among cases and the use of measures adapted to the circumstances of the people one is trying to help. This was a central theme of 19th-century philanthropy. Relief workers in that era, especially in America, generally opposed government charity, like the British Poor Law, because it encouraged idleness, teaching the populace that income was possible without work. "Gratuitous aid," wrote New York charity worker John Griscom, produces a "relaxation of concern on the part of the poor to depend on their own foresight and industry." Many of the settlement houses and missions had "work tests"—men were expected to chop wood, women to sew, before they received meals or lodging—as a way of distinguishing freeloaders from people willing to take responsibility for themselves.

Governments find it extremely difficult to draw such distinctions. They simply provide benefits amounting to an alternative way of life for those at the bottom of the economic ladder, with no regard for merit and little regard for circumstance. Though welfare benefits hardly provide a comfortable existence, and benefit levels in some programs such as Aid to Families with Dependent Children (AFDC) had declined in real terms, the package of benefits in many states was more attractive than entry-level work. . . .

None of this is to say that a life on welfare is attractive. The welfare system is demeaning. It imposes on recipients every roadblock and indignity the bureaucratic mind can conceive. The problem is that both the benefits and the drawbacks fall upon the worthy and the unworthy alike. Government programs are unable to draw the distinctions necessary for effective charity because of four factors inherent in their nature as government programs:

1. If welfare is provided by the government in a modern liberal society, it must be construed as a right; it cannot depend on the personal virtues or vices of recipients or their willingness to take responsibility for themselves.

2. Since the state is the agency of coercion, its actions must be governed by the rule of law. Government bureaucrats cannot be given discretionary power to discriminate among recipients on the basis of personal morality or psychology.

3. As the agency of coercion, the government of a free country must also refrain from intruding into the personal dimensions of life, and this precludes the kind of active involvement often required for effective help.

4. Because government programs are bureaucratic and subject to the political process, they cannot have the flexibility to adapt to change, the spirit of innovation, and the diversity of approaches that private agencies have. . . .

Private agencies, by contrast, increasingly recognize the need to replace automatic help with contracts specifying terms that recipients must meet in order to receive help. This is especially true of shelters for the homeless, which deal with the toughest cases: many of the homeless are substance abusers who have been exploiting both public and private agencies—selling food stamps, getting free meals to conserve cash, and so forth—in order to obtain money for drugs and alcohol. At the Center for the Homeless in South Bend, Indiana, those seeking help must agree to abide by a strict set of rules; to receive any aid beyond the minimum, they must work with a case worker to create a plan for becoming self-sufficient. At Step 13 in Denver, those seeking shelter must agree to take Antabuse (a drug that causes sickness if one consumes alcohol) and submit to drug tests; and they can be expelled for disruptive behavior. Above and beyond the specific rationales for those rules, they convey the message that help is conditional, not an entitlement, and that irresponsibility will have consequences. . . .

To be sure, there are fads in private philanthropy, and there is waste. Some charities spend disproportionate amounts of money on fundraising, using the proceeds of one direct-mail campaign to pay for the next one. But there are published standards on fundraising costs that donors can use to compare the organizations soliciting their money, and the better charities far exceed those standards. Government programs, moreover, do not avoid the problem of a "patchwork of services" attributed to the private sector. Despite the existence of hundreds of government programs, some 40 percent of people living below the poverty line receive no government assistance.

Government programs are subject to the political process. Legislative majorities representing diverse interests and viewpoints must come to agreement before any change is possible. Social service bureaucracies are bound by administrative law, which requires complex rules and procedures for carrying out the legislature's intent. Diversity, flexibility, and innovation are the last things one could hope for under such conditions. As is the case with other enterprises run by government, service is slow and unresponsive to customers, wasteful, bureaucratic, and constantly influenced by political considerations. The problems with AFDC [Aid to Families with Dependent Children], for example, had been clear since the 1960s, and every administration since then had promised reform. But it took 30 years to get the first significant change in the program—the reforms of 1996—and even those are partial.

Private agencies, by contrast, can adapt more quickly to changing circumstances and to feedback about the success or failure of their efforts. They] can adopt new ideas about how to provide aid most effectively without having to go through the federal budget process or being bound by administrative law. Because private agencies are separate and independent, each can go its own way, experimenting with new approaches without putting other agencies at risk; there is no need to find a single nationwide approach. The welfare reforms of 1996 gave states much more latitude to adopt different ways of providing benefits to the poor, and the states have already begun experimenting with some new approaches. But "the laboratory of democracy" provided by 50 states cannot compare with the experience to be gained through hundreds of thousands of private agencies, from local shelters and youth programs to nationwide charities.

In addition to the greater freedom that private agencies enjoy, they have a much greater incentive to look for solutions that work. Government programs are funded by taxes, and failure rarely results in a program's being cut; failure is more often used as an argument that more money is required. But a private agency must raise funds from donors who contribute voluntarily. Its donors are customers who want to see results and can take their money or their volunteer time elsewhere if an organization is not producing results.

In short, a private system of charity has all the advantages of a free market over government planning. It is now common knowledge that government planning does not work in the commercial realm. Why would we expect things to be different in the philanthropic realm?

The Promise of Private Aid

Despite the advantages of private over public programs for helping the poor, many people have expressed misgivings. One common argument among theorists is that charity must be government run because it is what economists call a "public good." If Person A wants to see Person B's poverty or suffering relieved, A can obtain that value if someone else helps B no less than if A helps B himself. This is one of the features of a public good: nonpayers aren't excluded from benefiting. Each of us thus has an incentive not to help the poor, in the expectation that others will help them, and if we all act on that incentive no help will be forthcoming. The only way out of that dilemma is collective provision, to which individuals are forced to contribute.

But it is irresponsible to want help given without any corresponding desire to help. Some people do behave that way, but not everyone; despite the logic of the public-goods argument, many people are moved by the countervailing logic of the old question, What if everyone did that? In 1995;

for example, 68.5 percent of households contributed to charity, giving an average of $1,017. Nearly half the adult population (93 million people) did volunteer work. Volunteers in formal programs gave 15.7 billion hours, or the equivalent of 9.2 million full-time employees, with a value estimated at $201 billion. The poor, moreover, are not an indivisible pool of suffering that must be alleviated as a totality. It is individuals who are poor, and their plight usually makes the strongest claim on family members, neighbors, and others in the community who know them. A great deal of private charity is local in nature. In helping a given person in my community, I may be conferring unintended value on other community members who know or encounter him, but not on an entire society. Those other community members, moreover, are more likely to know me and thus be in a position to exert social pressure on me to contribute.

But will private, voluntary giving be enough? That is the first question raised whenever the proposal to privatize charity is put forward. The large private charities are often the most vehement in opposing cutbacks in government spending—understandably, since most of them receive a major portion of their funding from government contracts. "Private charity is built on the foundation of government welfare," argues an official of Catholic Charities USA, which gets more than half its funds from government. "We can do what we do because Government provides the basic safety net."

Governments at all levels currently spend about $350 billion on means-tested programs. Charitable giving by individuals, foundations, and corporations came to $144 billion in 1995, but only about $12 billion of that was for human services; another $13 billion was for health, a category that includes some services for the poor. Offsetting this huge disparity is the fact that many people give much more in time, as volunteers, than in money. In the category of human services, the value of volunteer time came to about $17 billion in 1995. Americans also spent 4.6 billion hours doing informal volunteer work—caring for an elderly or disabled person, helping a neighbor—with a value of perhaps $50 billion.

Even so, by the most generous estimates, private giving for the relief of poverty is well under 30 percent of government spending. Since it does not come close to matching government expenditures, how could it possibly replace them? But that hardly counts as an argument against privatization, for three major reasons. The first is that government causes a significant amount of the poverty it aims to relievehave. . . . The package of benefits available to poor mothers typically has a higher value than the money they could earn in an entry-level job. A young mother who has grown up in a welfare family and never completed high school or held a job can easily be sidetracked from the working economy by the welfare system. In addition . . . government regulations such as the minimum wage, occupational licensing, and business restrictions keep the otherwise enterprising poor from helping themselves. Without those barriers to self-reliance, and without the subsidies that undermine the incentives for self-reliance, it stands to reason that many fewer people would be welfare dependents.

Second, a good deal of the money government spends on means-tested programs never reaches the poor. John Goodman of the National Center for Policy Analysis and others, for example, estimated that in 1992 the nonwelfare income of poor people was $94 billion short of the income necessary for them all to live at or above the poverty line. That is less than one-third of the money government spent to lift them out of poverty. The rest goes to the welfare bureaucracy, consultants, and others who administer the system. Of course it would not be possible simply to send that $94 billion to the poor without some administration, nor would that money eliminate poverty. Poverty is more often caused and sustained by behavioral problems than by strictly financial ones. Still, it is hard to believe that the advantages of private over public aid would not produce a considerable savings.

Third, by nationalizing the charity industry, the government has displaced private spending on the poor. The $300 billion that government spends is taken from the private economy. Some portion of that sum would otherwise be spent on goods and services that create new entry-level jobs, providing opportunities for the poor. And some portion would be contributed to charities. Sixty years of AFDC and 30 years of the Great Society programs have produced the expectation that government will provide an adequate safety net for the poor, and people have shifted their charitable giving to religion, the arts, and other areas. Although it is not possible to quantify this "crowding out" effect precisely, or to predict the amount of private giving that would be shifted to aid for the poor if welfare were privatized, historical research has provided a few hints.

In a detailed study of Indianapolis in the 1870s and 1880s, when government aid was reduced as part of a nationwide reaction against "outdoor relief," Stephen T. Ziliak found that private contributions increased by approximately the same amount. Figures from the 1930s are also illuminating. From 1930 to 1932, as the Great Depression deepened, both government and private spending on poverty relief increased six-fold. After Roosevelt's election, government spending continued to increase rapidly as new programs were introduced, but private spending declined rapidly as people assumed that responsibility had been shifted to the government.

At the same time, private charitable organizations shifted their efforts from poverty relief to other goals. At the New York Association for Improving the Condition of the Poor (AICP), for example, "Many families formerly cared for by AICP have been turned over completely to public relief departments." Thus it is not surprising that charitable giving today goes predominantly to religion and other objects, with human services receiving a relatively small portion. But there is every reason to believe that the proportions would change if government were not already spending so much in this area.

We do not know with any certainty what the result would be of leaving aid to the poor in private hands. We can't predict what ideas people will come up with to solve the problems they observe. One can certainly find grounds for pessimism. In his study of 19th-century Indianapolis, for example, Ziliak found that replacing government spending with private funds had no effect on the average spell of welfare dependence, nor on the number of people finding jobs and becoming self-supporting. Nevertheless, private agencies can provide aid on a conditional basis rather than as an entitlement, and thus more effectively encourage responsibility. They can draw distinctions on the basis of character and psychology, tailoring the help they provide in ways that the government cannot. They can intervene in the personal lives of recipients in ways that get to the root of problems but would be intrusive violations of freedom if done by government workers. And private agencies can be much more flexible, responsive to changing circumstances, experimental, and diverse than government bureaucracies.

Nor can we predict how much aid would be given in a private system, nor in what forms. Our point of departure, morally speaking, is not the needs of recipients but the generosity of donors. It is the donors who set the terms. Recipients do not own those who support them, and thus do not have a right that must be met, come what may. Those who would privatize poverty relief do not have the burden of showing that all poverty would be dealt with as effectively as it is today by government programs, although . . . that [is] extremely likely. The burden is on those who support government programs to show why they think the poor are *entitled* on altruistic grounds to the aid they are receiving.

Compassion and generosity are virtues, and the charitable help they prompt us to provide the less fortunate is, for most of us, a part of what it means to live in a civilized society. But compassion, generosity, and charity are not the sum of morality, nor even its core; and they are not duties that create entitlements on the part of recipients. The poor do not own the productive, nor are the latter obliged to sacrifice the pursuit of their own happiness in service to the poor. If individuals are truly ends in themselves, then charity is not a duty but a value we choose to pursue. Each of us has the right to choose what weight charity has among the other values in our lives, instead of having the government decide what proportion of our income to take for that end. And each of us has the right to choose the particular people, projects, or causes we wish to support, instead of having government make that decision for us.

Analyze This Reading

1. According to the writer, why are government approaches to charity ineffective?
2. In the author's view, why are private agencies a better approach to poverty? Why do they have a greater incentive to work for solutions? How does he support this view?
3. The writer claims that private charities can replace government welfare programs even though private giving is less than 30 percent of what the government spends. What reasons and support does the writer bring to this claim?

Respond To This Reading

1. The writer concludes with a discussion of poverty in terms of duties and rights. For you, is contributing to poverty relief a right or a duty? Explain.
2. Via your local newspaper archives and government data available online, access information about services to the poor and homeless in your community in terms of both government and charitable sources. What approach to poverty relief dominates? What would you change, if anything?

3. In your own experience as a donor, do you favor charities that attend to local populations, or do you favor broader, international charities, or both? Explain.

ABOUT THIS READING

Writer Paul Roberts is author of *The End of Oil* (2004) and contributes articles on environmental and economic issues to *Harper's Magazine*. This reading appeared in *Opposing Viewpoints: Energy Alternatives*, edited by Barbara Passero.

Over a Barrel

Of the alternative fuels and gadgets that are technically viable today, many simply cannot compete with fossil fuels or existing technologies.

By Paul Roberts

As encouraging as all this new energy awareness is, actually weaning the United States from fossil fuels is far easier said than done. To begin with, our current energy infrastructure—the pipelines and refineries, the power plants and grids, the gasoline stations, and, of course, the cars, trucks, planes, and ships—is a massive, sprawling asset that took more than a century to build and is worth some $1 trillion. Replacing that hydrocarbon monster with "clean" technologies and fuels before our current energy problems escalate into catastrophes will likely be the most complex and expensive challenge this country has ever faced.

And just as we've tended to underplay the flaws in our hydrocarbon energy system, we've also held far too rosy a notion of the various energy alternatives that are supposed to replace oil. In fact, to the extent that most politicians even discuss alternative energy, it tends to be in the rhetoric of American Can-Doism, a triumphant vision in which the same blend of technological prowess, entrepreneurial spirit, and market forces that helped us build an atom bomb, put a man on the moon, and produce the TV dinner and the microchip can now be counted on to yield a similar miracle in energy. Thus we find ourselves imagining a future powered by solar cells, bio-diesel, wind farms, tidal power, cold fusion, and, of course, hydrogen fuel cells, all currently being created in busy research labs and brought to us by a Free Market that is responding naturally, efficiently, and inexorably to the rising price of oil.

Yet the hard truth is that this hyper-optimistic dream is plagued by a variety of potentially killer flaws. First, many of these new technologies are nowhere near ready for prime time and exist mainly in the conceptual stage, if that. Second, of the alternative fuels and gadgets that are technically viable today, many simply cannot compete with fossil fuels or existing technologies. Third, while the market is indeed a marvelous mechanism for bringing innovation to life, the modern economy doesn't even recognize that the current energy system needs replacing. You and I may know that hydrocarbons cost us dearly, in terms of smog, climate change, corruption, and instability, not to mention the billions spent defending the Middle East. But because these "external" costs aren't included in the price of a gallon of gasoline, the market sees no reason to find something other than oil, gas, or coal.

Limitations of Hydrogen and Natural Gas

In late July 2004, financial analysts from across North America joined a conference call with Dennis Campbell, the embattled president of a shrinking Canadian company called Ballard Power Systems. Just a few years before, Ballard had been the toast of energy investors and the acknowledged leader in the campaign to move beyond oil. Its main product, a compact hydrogen fuel cell that could power a car, was widely hailed as the breakthrough that would smash the century-long reign of the gasoline-powered internal combustion engine. In early 2000, Ballard shares were trading for $120, allowing the company to raise a near-record $340.7 million in financing and touching off a wave of expectations that a fuel-cell revolution was imminent.

Since then, however, as fuel cells have been hobbled by technical problems, Ballard has seen its share value plummet to $8, as energy investors have all but abandoned hydrogen in favor of the latest energy darling, the gas-electric hybrid. During the conference call, Campbell insisted that hybrids were only a temporary fix, and that fuel cells remained the only long-term solution to problems like climate change and declining energy supplies. He was, however, forced to acknowledge that consumers and businesses alike were "discouraged by the long wait and the uncertain timelines" for fuel cells and had been "seduced by the lure of an easier solution to the energy and environmental challenges that we face."

In many respects, Ballard is the perfect cautionary tale for the entire roster of alternative fuels and energy technologies, which, for all their huge promise, are, upon closer inspection, plagued by problems. For example, many energy experts see natural gas as the most logical interim step in eventually weaning ourselves from oil. Natural gas emits less carbon dioxide and pollutants than does oil (and certainly coal); it can be used in everything from cars to power plants; it's also easily refined into hydrogen—all of which make it the perfect "bridge" fuel between the current oil-based economy and something new. But even as demand for gas grows in the United States, domestic production is in decline, meaning we'll have to import an increasing volume via pipelines from Canada or through liquefied natural gas terminals in port cities. Even assuming we overcome the political hurdles, simply building this costly new infrastructure will take years, and, once completed, will leave us dependent on many of the same countries that now control the oil business. (The biggest gas reserves are in the Middle East and Russia.)

Above all, gas doesn't solve the climate problem; it merely slows the rate at which we emit carbon dioxide [CO_2]. According to the United Nations Intergovernmental Panel on Climate Change, in order to cut CO_2 emissions fast enough to actually prevent catastrophic warming, we eventually need to produce most of our energy with carbon-free technology. And we're a long way from "most." Today, hydrocarbons own the energy market—40 percent of our energy comes from oil, 23 percent each from gas and coal. Nuclear provides around 8 percent, while renewable, carbon-free energy accounts for barely 5 percent of our total energy supply. Of that "good" energy, nearly 90 percent comes from hydroelectric dams, which are so expensive and environmentally nasty that their future role is extremely limited. The rest comes mainly from "biomass" usually plants and crop waste that are either refined into fuels, like ethanol, or burned to make steam.

Limitations of Solar and Wind

And what about solar and wind? As it turns out, the two most famous alternative energy technologies together generate less than half a percent of the planet's energy. Here's a depressing fact: The entire output of every solar photovoltaic (PV) cell currently installed worldwide—about 2,000 megawatts total—is less than the output of just two conventional, coal-fired power plants.

Why do alternatives own such a puny share of the market? According to conventional wisdom, Big Oil and Big Coal use their massive economic power to corrupt Big Government, which then hands out massive subsidies and tax breaks for oil and coal, giving hydrocarbons an unbeatable advantage over alternatives. In truth, much of the fault lies with the new energy technologies themselves, which simply cannot yet compete effectively with fossil fuels.

Consider the saga of the solar cell. Despite decades of research and development, solar power still costs more than electricity generated from a gas- or coal-fired power plant. And although PV cell costs will continue to fall, there remains the problem of "intermittency"—solar only works when the sun is shining, whereas a conventional power plant can crank out power 24 hours a day, 365 days a year. (Wind presents a similar problem.) To use solar and wind, utilities must have backup power, probably coal- or gas-fired plants.

Eventually, utilities will solve the intermittency problem—probably with superfast "smart" power grids that can connect wind or solar farms built across the nation, or even the hemisphere, effectively getting power from wherever the sun is shining or the wind is blowing and delivering it to customers. But the very scale of this solution illustrates an even more serious weakness for wind and other renewables: They lack the "power density" of the fossil fuels they seek to replace. Coal, for example, packs a great deal of stored energy in a relatively small volume. As a result, a coal-fired plant requires only a few hundred acres of space, yet can supply electricity for 200,000 homes. By contrast, to generate equal power from wind, which is far less power-dense, you'd need a wind farm of more than 200 square miles in size. Given that by 2030, almost 60 percent of the global population is expected to live in cities of 1 million or more, meeting our power needs with wind, solar, or other renewables will be challenging indeed. "Supplying those buildings from locally generated renewable energies is either impractical or impossible," says Vaclav Smil, an expert in energy economies at the University of Manitoba. The "power-density mismatch is simply too large."

The most dramatic example of the mismatch between fossil fuels and their would-be competitors, however, can be found in the fuel cell. For decades, hydrogen proponents have argued that fuel cells, which turn hydrogen and oxygen into electricity while emitting only water vapor, are the key to the next energy economy. Like a battery that never needs charging, fuel cells can power office buildings, laptops, and especially cars, where they are roughly three times as efficient as a traditional internal combustion engine. And because you can make hydrogen by running electric current through water, advocates envisioned a global system in which power from solar, wind, and other renewables would be turned into hydrogen.

This compelling vision helps explain why the "hydrogen economy" was so touted during the 1990s, and why companies like Ballard Power Systems could partner with giants like DaimlerChrysler and Ford, igniting a fuel-cell mania that dazzled investors and policymakers alike. Indeed, in his 2003 State of the Union address, President [George W.] Bush vowed that, within 20 years, fuel cells would "make our air significantly cleaner, and our country much less dependent on foreign sources of oil."

In truth, even as the president was promising better living through hydrogen, the reality of a hydrogen economy was moving farther and farther away. While the basic technology remains promising, making hydrogen turns out to be far more difficult than advertised. The easiest and by far cheapest method—splitting natural gas into carbon and hydrogen—is hampered by domestic shortages of natural gas. And while it is possible to extract hydrogen from water using renewably generated electricity, that concept suffers from the power-density problem. Studies by Jim MacKenzie, a veteran energy analyst with the World Resources Institute, show that a solar-powered hydrogen economy in the United States would require at least 160,000 square miles of photovoltaic panels—an area slightly larger than the state of California—and would increase national water consumption by 10 percent. "We could do it," MacKenzie told me [in 2003]. "But it would be expensive."

But hydrogen's biggest problem is the fuel cell itself, which, despite decades of research, is still too expensive and unreliable to compete with the internal combustion engine. As of [2003], the best fuel cells were still 10 times as costly as an equivalently powered gasoline engine. Hydrogen advocates argue that once fuel cells can be mass-produced, costs will drop dramatically. Yet while that's true, it's also true that gasoline engines will also improve over time—in fact, they already have. With the gasoline-electric hybrid, for example, the internal combustion engine has, in a stroke, doubled its fuel economy and halved its emissions—but without forcing consumers to use a complicated new technology or fuel. Barring some technological breakthrough that dramatically lowers costs or improves performance, the fuel cell may remain one step behind the gasoline engine for a long time, further delaying the moment it can begin displacing its hydrocarbon rival.

Constraints of the Market Economy

This, then, is the central dilemma facing the architects of the next energy economy. Left to themselves, markets will indeed move us to new energy technologies, but these technologies may not be the ones we ultimately want or need. For example, while the hybrid does cut emissions and fuel use, as Ballard's Campbell testily points out, hybrids "still require fossil fuel" and thus can only be an interim solution. To be sure, interim solutions are essential, but if we concentrate only on half-measures, long-term technologies may not become economically viable fast enough to stave off an implosion of our energy system—be it from runaway climate change in 2015 or the collapse of the Saudi government in 2005.

Thus a true energy revolution—one that begins moving away from fossil fuels entirely—can't succeed or even get started until we can somehow induce the market to "see" the true costs of energy, and, specifically, just how environmentally and politically expensive "cheap" fossil fuels really are.

Analyze This Reading

1. How does the writer support his contention that the "modern economy doesn't even recognize that the current energy system needs replacing"?
2. On what grounds does the writer claim that hydrogen and natural gas are not practical energy alternatives to oil and coal?
3. How do the terms *power density* and *hydrogen economy* function in the writer's argument?

Respond To This Reading

1. Explain why you agree or disagree with the writer's assertion that our current economy cannot accommodate the expense and delays associated with alternatives to fossil fuels.
2. It is common knowledge that Germany leads the world in alternative energy production. Conduct some research and determine why this is so. What is it that Germany is doing that the United States is not? Do your research findings confirm or call into question Roberts's argument?
3. Consider drafting an argument that calls for a local structure—a government agency, a school, an office building, or an apartment building—to have its electricity supplied by alternative energy sources. What support would you bring in? What values would form your warrant?

ABOUT THIS READING

Matthew Rothschild is editor of *The Progressive* and author of *You Have No Rights: Stories of America in an Age of Repression* (2007). This reading appeared in *The Progressive*, a news magazine with a liberal perspective on politics and culture.

Nationalize the Banks

By Matthew Rothschild

The financial crisis has shown that banks have little regard for public interest and are simply concerned with saving their private shareholders. Because of this, the government bailout money has remained locked up in the banks and has not induced the private owners to begin lending again. To rectify this problem, the government should have bought the banks outright and converted them to public institutions, guaranteeing that they would start lending out money in order to speed an overall economic recovery.

One Treasury official after another is doing somersaults on a wire to distract us from the obvious: We need to nationalize many of the banks, not save them as private entities.

The banks got us into this financial mess in the first place by making unwise home loans and by speculating in unregulated credit-default swaps tied to those loans. They have taken the entire world economy down with them. They don't deserve to be bailed out.

If our government really believed in free enterprise, these banks would be out of business right now.

Instead, first the [George W.] Bush Administration and now the [Barack] Obama Administration have decided to act like an iron lung for the banks, pumping hundreds of billions of dollars into them to keep them alive.

There is no reason to do that.

And it would have been cheaper to buy them outright.

The Banks Have Already Been Bought

"The day we gave Citigroup their second infusion we could have bought them for the same $20 billion," says economist Dean Baker. "On top of that, we guaranteed $300 billion of assets. We could have bought Citigroup several times over."

Still, the banks aren't solvent. Baker estimates that the losses on most of their balance sheets outweigh their capital. This is a recipe for indefinite bailouts.

If we're the major shareholders, as we now are with Citigroup and Bank of America, we ought to have a major say [in how banks are run].

Nobel Prize-winner in economics Joseph Stiglitz also sees the irrationality of leaving the banks in private hands.

"In effect, the American taxpayers are the major provider of finance to the banks," he wrote on CNN's website. "In some cases, the value of our equity injection, guarantees, and other forms of assistance dwarfs the value of the 'private' sector's equity contribution. Yet we have no voice in how the banks are run."

We don't have a voice because the Bush Administration tied no strings to the $350 billion. But if we're the major shareholders, as we now are with Citigroup (taxpayers hold a 7.8 percent stake) and Bank of America (6 percent), we ought to have a major say. And if we're going to throw more money at them, why not just purchase the banks themselves? If we want companies to receive loans, why not get rid of the middleman, and have the government lend directly to businesses and to homeowners?

Hoarding the Cash

The banks have not done what the government told us they were supposed to do when it lavished the first $350 billion on them. They didn't start lending more. "The last thing in their mind was to restart lending," wrote Stiglitz. And even today, they have a strong incentive to sit on their cash.

"There is still no assurance of a resumption of lending," Stiglitz explains. "Having been burned once, many bankers are staying away from the fire. . . . Many a bank may decide that the better strategy is a conservative one: Hoard one's cash, wait until things settle down, hope that you are among the few surviving banks, and then start lending. Of course, if all the banks reason so, the recession will be longer and deeper than it otherwise would be."

So, since lending is vital to the economy, and since the private banks won't lend, let's buy up some insolvent banks so we can get the lending going ourselves. The private sector has proven that it can't or won't do the job. The public sector must step in. Put a different way, if we want companies to receive loans, why not get rid of the middleman, and have the government lend directly to businesses and to homeowners?

"For the moment, there's no choice," says Robert Pollin, professor of economics at the University of Massachusetts-Amherst. "Relative to a year ago, lending in the U.S. economy is down an astonishing 90 percent. The government needs to take over the banks now, and force them to start lending." (Pollin wants the government to sell the banks back into private hands, later on, with stringent regulations.)

We're shelling out gobs of public money for these [banks] . . . but we're not running these companies in the public interest.

Private Companies Do Not Operate for Public Interest

Truly nationalized banks, run by the government for the people, would help out the economy as a whole. As Stiglitz put it, under private ownership, there's a "huge gap between private rewards and social returns." Under public ownership, "the incentives of the banks can be aligned better with those of the country. And it is in the national interest that prudent lending be restarted."

We could reap other social returns from nationalization, as well. "If the banks were nationalized, the government could declare a moratorium on foreclosures for the properties it controls, and move to restructure mortgages—perhaps at subsidized rates—for homeowners," writes Joshua Holland of AlterNet.

As it is right now, we're getting some of the vices of nationalization without all the virtues. We're shelling out gobs of public money for these companies—in many cases, more money than the companies are actually worth—but we're not running these companies in the public interest. We're allowing the companies to remain in private hands, for private purposes.

"We have a financial system that is run by private shareholders, managed by private institutions, and we'd like to do our best to preserve that system," said Treasury Secretary Timothy Geithner.

Why is that the job of the Obama Administration?

I thought its job was to make the economy work for the American public. And keeping the banks in private hands isn't getting the job done. Throwing hundreds of billions of dollars, over and over, to keep these banks on life support makes no sense.

Unless you want to ensure that the shareholders get artificially inflated returns and the executives get to keep their jobs.

Or unless you are too snug in your ideological straitjacket to even consider the most rational way to proceed.

Fears about Nationalization

And that's the problem today. The word "nationalization" shuts off the debate. Never mind that Britain, facing the same crisis we are, just nationalized the Bank of Scotland. Never mind that [President] Ronald Reagan himself considered such an option during a global banking crisis in the early 1980s.

"When a bank is insolvent, the regulators put it into receivership," says James Galbraith, professor of government at the LBJ [Lyndon Baines Johnson] School of Public Affairs of the University of Texas at Austin. "The Reagan Administration had a plan to do it with all the big banks in 1982 and 1983, if a single large Latin American country had defaulted. Let me repeat that: the Reagan Administration."

But the Obama Administration is not considering receivership, much less genuine nationalization in the interests of the majority of Americans. Cluttered with worshippers of the private sector, skittish about being tagged "leftist," and beset by obdurate Republicans, the Obama Administration has blocked off the path to true nationalization. Instead, it is opting for gimmicky proposals to take some bad debts off the books—all in service of those "private shareholders" that Geithner so adores.

Granted, nationalization over the long haul is a risky business, too, which is why Pollin resists it.

"We would have every reason to expect a wide range of failures and misjudgments, including 'crony capitalism'—privileged back-room dealings with selected non-financial firms," Pollin writes in *Boston Review*.

Pollin is also worried about the political fallout. "The failures of the nationalized system could be the very thing—perhaps the only thing—that could shift the target of public outrage over the collapse of the financial system off Wall Street and onto the U.S. government," he wrote.

While these are certainly legitimate concerns, we've seen what the private sector does—not only when left to its own devices but also when bailed out by hundreds of billions of our funds.

Yes, if it took over some of the banks, the government would have to carefully design a system to prevent corruption. And yes, there would be bumps along the road.

But we've had enough bumps on the road marked "private."

If we're going to be shelling out the money, we might as well run the store.

Analyze This Reading

1. According to the writer, to whom is it unfair to leave banks in private hands? How does he support this idea?
2. What is the writer's view of the "middleman" in the banking crisis?
3. How does the writer use the economists in his argument? Are they all in agreement about nationalizing banks? Explain.

Respond To This Reading

1. What effects do you see in your life and in your community as a result of the banking crisis? Do you agree with the writer that banks should be nationalized so as to stimulate lending? Explain.

2. As a concerned citizen, what local parties would you involve in discussion about lending in your community? Would you make this a public or private discussion? Explain.

3. Identify a single issue connected to banks in your community—lending practices, altered fees, or executive pay, for example, to name a few—and draft a claim in response to this issue. How would you respond to those opposed to your claim?

ABOUT THIS READING

This article appeared in *Harvard Magazine*, a publication produced for Harvard University graduates. Alexander Keyssar is Professor of History and Social Policy at the John F. Kennedy School of Government at Harvard University. His best known book is *The Right to Vote: The Contested History of Democracy in the United States*, published in 2000 and revised and updated in 2009. He is a frequent contributor to popular publications on topics of politics and American history.

Voter Suppression Returns

By Alexander Keyssar

THE 2012 election campaign—for Congress as well as the presidency—promises to be bitterly fought, even nasty. Leaders of both major parties, and their core constituents, believe that the stakes are exceptionally high; neither party has much trust in the goodwill or good intentions of the other; and, thanks in part to the Supreme Court, money will be flowing in torrents, some of it from undisclosed sources and much of it available for negative campaigning.

This also promises to be a close election—which is why a great deal of attention is being paid to an array of recently passed, and pending, state laws that could prevent hundreds of thousands, perhaps millions, of eligible voters from casting ballots. Several states, including Florida (once again, a battleground), have effectively closed down registration drives by organizations like the League of Women Voters, which have traditionally helped to register new voters; some states are shortening early-voting periods or prohibiting voting on the Sunday before election day; several are insisting that registrants provide documentary proof of their citizenship. Most importantly—and most visibly—roughly two dozen states have significantly tightened their identification rules for voting since 2003, and the pace of change has accelerated rapidly in the last two years. Ten states have now passed laws demanding that voters possess a current government-issued photo ID, and several others have enacted measures slightly less strict. A few more may take similar steps before November—although legal challenges could keep some of the laws from taking effect.

The new ID laws have almost invariably been sponsored—and promoted—by Republicans, who claim that they are needed to prevent fraud.

(In five states, Democratic governors vetoed ID laws passed by Republican legislatures.) Often working from a template provided by the conservative American Legislative Exchange Council (ALEC), Republican state legislators have insisted that the threat of election fraud is compelling and widespread; in December 2011, the Republican National Lawyers Association (RNLA) buttressed that claim by publishing a list of reported election crimes during the last 12 years. Republicans have also maintained that a photo ID requirement is not particularly burdensome in an era when such documents are routinely needed to board an airplane or enter an office building. Public opinion polls indicate that these arguments sound reasonable to the American people, a majority of whom support the concept of photo ID requirements. The Supreme Court has taken a similar view, although it left open the possibility of reconsidering that verdict if new evidence were to emerge.

Critics of these laws (myself included) have doubted both their necessity and their ability to keep elections honest. The only type of fraud that a strict photo ID rule would actually prevent is voter impersonation fraud (I go to the polls pretending to be you), and, in fact, voter impersonation fraud is exceedingly rare. In Indiana, where the Republican-dominated legislature passed one of the first new ID laws in 2005 (on a straight party-line vote), there had been *no* known instances of voter impersonation in the state's history. In Texas, a strict ID law was enacted last year, although the 2008 and 2010 elections gave rise to only five formal complaints about voter impersonation (out of 13 million votes cast). "There are more UFO and Bigfoot sightings than documented cases of voter impersonation," quipped one Texas Democrat. Close inspection of the RNLA's inventory of election fraud, moreover, has found it to be flawed and misleading; most election experts believe that the greatest threat to election integrity comes from absentee ballots—a threat that would not be addressed by the current laws.

As importantly, the burdens placed on prospective voters by these ID requirements are not trivial. Men and women who already possess driver's licenses or passports, of course, will be unaffected. (So too will those in Texas who have permits to carry concealed weapons—since those permits meet the ID requirement.) But citizens who lack such documents will now be obliged to assemble various other pieces of paper (birth certificates, naturalization forms, proof of residence, etc.) and make their way (presumably without a car) to a government office that can issue an official photo ID. Who are these men and women? Studies indicate that they are disproportionately young or elderly, poor, black, and Hispanic; demographically, they are more likely than not to vote Democratic. (In states covered by the Voting Rights Act, such as Texas and South Carolina, the photo ID laws are being challenged by the Department of Justice on the grounds that they disproportionately affect minorities.) The number of people potentially affected is considerable: the Texas secretary of state, for example, estimates that at least 600,000 already registered voters do not possess the documents to cast ballots in November. New York University's respected Brennan Center for Justice has estimated that a total of more than five million people may lack the requisite identification documents in states that have passed new ID laws.

How many people will actually be prevented from casting ballots by these laws in November? What impact will these laws have on participation?

The straightforward answer is that none of us (scholars, commentators, politicians) really know—because the laws are recent and measuring their impact is difficult. (We should know more after November, since several studies will be conducted during this election.) The number is unlikely to be huge, particularly since various pro-voting-rights groups (as well as the Democratic party) will work hard to help people get their ID documents. But it could certainly be large enough to affect the outcome of close races for Congress and even for the presidency.

Whether they have a decisive impact on the election or not, the ID laws—as well as other measures designed to inhibit voting—are disturbing, particularly when located against the backdrop of our extended history of conflict over the right to vote and its exercise. Although the United States has long prided itself on being a paragon of democracy, we did not possess anything even approximating universal adult suffrage until the late 1960s—even though universal suffrage is commonly regarded as an essential ingredient of democracy. It took many decades of mobilization and struggle for voting rights in all states to be extended to African Americans, women, Native Americans, and those who lacked property; at different historical moments, some states (suffrage requirements were largely a matter of state law) also excluded "paupers," the illiterate, the non-English speaking, and those whose jobs made them too transient to meet long residency requirements.

Moreover, our history has not been one of steady and inexorable progress toward a more inclusive polity. In the very long run, to be sure, we have become more democratic, but there have been numerous moments in our past when the pendulum swung in the opposite direction: men and women who were enfranchised found themselves losing that right. This happened to African Americans in several northern states before the Civil War and in all southern states in the late nineteenth century. It also happened to women in New Jersey in the early 1800s, to men who became "paupers" because of economic downturns, to citizens who could not pay poll taxes (or pass literacy tests), and to prison inmates in Massachusetts in 2000, just 12 years ago. Suffrage rights have contracted as well as expanded.

In addition to this mottled pattern of enfranchisement and disfranchisement, our nation has also witnessed periodic episodes of "voter suppression"—a label frequently invoked by critics to characterize the current wave of photo ID requirements. "Voter suppression" differs conceptually from outright disfranchisement because it does not involve *formally* disqualifying entire groups of people from the polls; instead, policies or acts of "suppression" seek to prevent, or deter, eligible citizens from exercising their right to vote. Historically, voter suppression seems to arise when organized political forces aim to restrain the political participation of particular groups but cannot, politically or constitutionally, disfranchise them outright. This occurred, of course, in the post-Reconstruction South when white Democratic "redeemers" utilized a variety of techniques (ranging from violence to complex ballot arrangements to poll taxes to orally administered "understanding" tests) to circumvent the Fifteenth Amendment and keep blacks from voting. (Eventually, the suppression of the black vote in the South shaded into, and became, disfranchisement through clever legal innovations such as the all-white Democratic primary.) The phrase "vote suppression" was first widely used in the United States in the 1880s.

Legal efforts to place obstacles in the path of legitimate voters also recurred in the North between the Civil War and World War I, targeted primarily at the immigrant workers who were flooding into the country. California and New Jersey, for example, began to require that immigrants present their original, sealed naturalization papers at the polls; various states limited the hours that polling places or registration offices were open (at a time when the 10-hour work day was common), while simultaneously requiring annual registration in large cities but not in towns. In New York, in 1908, authorities sought to winnow out Jewish voters—many of whom were socialists—by designating Saturdays and Yom Kippur as registration days. Such measures were commonly justified as necessary to prevent fraud.

The recent wave of ID laws (and their cousins) bears a close resemblance to past episodes of voter suppression, particularly those of the late-nineteenth and early-twentieth centuries. The laws seem tailored less to guarantee the integrity of elections than to achieve a partisan purpose; the targeted constituencies—those directly affected by the laws—tend, once again, to be the poor, the less advantaged, or members of minority groups. It may not be a coincidence that the phrase "voter suppression"—like "vote suppression" in the 1880s—has become a prominent part of our political vocabulary during an era of large-scale immigration and in the wake of a dramatic extension of voting rights to African Americans.

This is not to say—the point is important—that there is anything intrinsically wrong with a system of election administration that requires voters to present some type of ID card or photo ID at the polls. Many countries demand that voters present their national identification cards (or special voting cards) when they show up to cast their ballots. Preventing election fraud is a legitimate state function, and, as Rhode Island's independent governor, Lincoln Chafee, recently observed while signing a new ID measure into law, asking for identification can be "a reasonable request to ensure the accuracy and integrity of our elections." Requiring voters to present an ID need not be suppressive or discriminatory.

The devil is in the details—as is always true with laws that tap the tension between election integrity and access to the ballot box. Like many critics of the recent legislation, I could welcome a photo ID requirement—*if* it were made clear that it was the responsibility of the state (rather than of private citizens) to insure that every eligible man and woman possessed such documentation. Imagine, for example, a system in which any voter who arrived at the polls without an official ID could apply for one at the polling place (it could be mailed out in subsequent weeks) and then was permitted to cast a provisional ballot (which would be counted if she proved to be eligible). In time, everyone would become equipped with an appropriate ID, and meanwhile no one would be denied the opportunity to vote. (Rhode Island's new law contains some of these elements.) Such a system would be costly, particularly at the outset, but the expense would be the price of keeping elections democratic while addressing the concerns of those worried about fraud. The state, in effect, would accept responsibility for solving the access problem that its anti-fraud measure had engendered.

Alas, that does not seem to be what the sponsors of the current measures have in mind. In 2008, for example, Indiana's state government simply tossed the access problem into the laps of individual citizens, leading to a widely publicized episode in which elderly nuns who had been voting for decades arrived at the polls but were not permitted to vote because they lacked driver's licenses. Other states have adopted the same posture: it is up to potential voters to figure out how to navigate around the new obstacle that the state has placed in their path. As a consequence, some of those voters—perhaps thousands, perhaps hundreds of thousands—will end up being unable to cast ballots in a very important election. Whatever the numbers turn out to be, the laws themselves are unworthy of a modern, sophisticated nation that identifies itself as democratic. They are not effective policy instruments; they chip away at the core democratic value of inclusiveness; and they resonate with the worst, rather than the best, of our political traditions.

Analyze This Reading

1. Describe procedures some states have in place to make voting difficult. Who sponsors these procedures and under what rationale?
2. What do critics of voter ID laws claim? What evidence do they bring to their claim?
3. According to the writer, how do today's efforts to suppress voting resemble suppression efforts during earlier periods of American history?
4. Under what conditions would the writer favor voter ID requirements?

Respond To This Reading

1. What argument would you make to ensure that any new voter registration laws encouraged rather than limited voting?
2. Some opponents of the present wave of voter ID legislation contend that Super PACs—that is, large Political Action Committees with no limits on spending—are behind this movement. To what extent does this kind of spending energize or deflate American democracy?

Classic American Arguments

ABOUT THIS READING

After voting illegally in the 1872 presidential election, writer Susan B. Anthony (1820–1906) was tried and fined $100. This reading is the text of Anthony's 1873 speech in which she responds to her arrest.

On Women's Right to Vote

By SUSAN B. ANTHONY

Friends and Fellow Citizens: I stand before you tonight under indictment for the alleged crime of having voted at the last presidential election, without having a lawful right to vote. It shall be my work this evening to prove to you that in thus voting, I not only committed no crime, but, instead, simply exercised my citizen's rights, guaranteed to me and all United States citizens by the National Constitution, beyond the power of any State to deny.

The preamble of the Federal Constitution says:
We, the people of the United States, in order to form a more perfect union, establish justice, insure domestic tranquility, provide for the common defense, promote the general welfare, and secure the blessings of liberty to ourselves and our posterity, do ordain and establish this Constitution for the United States of America.

It was we, the people; not we, the white male citizens; nor yet we, the male citizens; but we, the whole people, who formed the Union. And we formed it, not to give the blessings of liberty, but to secure them; not to the half of ourselves and the half of our posterity, but to the whole - people—women as well as men. And it is a downright mockery to talk to women of their enjoyment of the blessings of liberty while they are denied the use of the only means of securing them provided by this democratic-republican government—the ballot.

For any State to make sex a qualification that must ever result in the disfranchisement of one entire half of the people is to pass a bill of attainder, or an ex post facto law, and is therefore a violation of the supreme law of the land. By it the blessings of liberty are for ever withheld from women and their female posterity. To them this government has no just powers derived from the consent of the governed. To them this government is not a democracy. It is not a republic. It is an odious aristocracy; a hateful oligarchy of sex; the most hateful aristocracy ever established on the face of the globe; an oligarchy of wealth, where the right govern the poor. An oligarchy of learning, where the educated govern the ignorant, or even an oligarchy of race, where the Saxon rules the African, might be endured; but this oligarchy of sex, which makes father, brothers, husband, sons, the oligarchs over the mother and sisters, the wife and daughters of every household—which ordains all men sovereigns, all women subjects, carries dissension, discord and rebellion into every home of the nation.

© iStockphoto.com/A-digit

Webster, Worcester and Bouvier all define a citizen to be a person in the United States, entitled to vote and hold office.

The only question left to be settled now is: Are women persons? And I hardly believe any of our opponents will have the hardihood to say they are not. Being persons, then, women are citizens; and no State has a right to make any law, or to enforce any old law, that shall abridge their privileges or immunities. Hence, every discrimination against women in the constitutions and laws of the several States is today null and void, precisely as in every one against Negroes.

From: http://www.nationalcenter.org/AnthonySuffrage.html

Analyze This Reading

1. Where does the writer's claim appear? What kind of claim is it?
2. To what values does the writer appeal?
3. What is an "oligarchy"? How does the writer use this term in her argument?
4. What alliance does the writer create in her final paragraph?

Respond To This Reading

1. While this speech was delivered in the nineteenth century, do ideas in the speech resonate with life in the twenty-first century? Explain.
2. What single issue in your life would allow you to confidently refer to the Constitution in an argument? What kind of claim would best suit your purpose?

ABOUT THIS READING

Writer Mary Antin (1881–1949) immigrated to the United States in 1894 from Russia. She is the author of *From Plotzk to Boston* (1899); her autobiography, *The Promised Land* (1912); and *They Who Knock at Our Gates: A Complete Gospel of Immigration* (1914). This reading is excerpted from *They Who Knock at Our Gates;* the title is taken from a question Antin addresses early in the book.

Have We Any Right to Regulate Immigration?

By MARY ANTIN

And these words, which I command thee this day, shall be in thine heart: and thou shalt teach them diligently unto thy children. . . . And thou shalt write them upon the posts of thy house, and on thy gates.

DEUT. VI, 6, 7, 9.

If I ask an American what is the fundamental American law, and he does not answer me promptly, "That which is contained in the Declaration of Independence," I put him down for a poor citizen. He who is ignorant of the law is likely to disobey it. And there cannot be two minds about the position of the Declaration among our documents of state. What the Mosaic Law is to the Jews, the Declaration is to the American people. It affords us a start-ing-point in history and defines our mission among the nations. Without it, we should not differ greatly from other nations who have achieved a con-stitutional form of government and various democratic institutions. What marks us out from other advanced nations is the origin of our liberties in one supreme act of political innovation, prompted by a conscious sense of the dignity of manhood. In other countries advances have been made by favor of hereditary rulers and aristocratic parliaments, each successive reform being grudgingly handed down to the people from above. Not so in America. At one bold stroke we shattered the monarchical tradition, and installed the people in the seats of government, substituting the gospel of the sovereignty of the masses for the superstition of the divine right of kings.

And even more notable than the boldness of the act was the dignity with which it was entered upon. In terms befitting a philosophical discourse, we gave notice to the world that what we were about to do, we would do in the name of humanity, in the conviction that as justice is the end of government so should manhood be its source.

It is this insistence on the philosophic sanction of our revolt that gives the sublime touch to our political performance. Up to the moment of our declaration of independence, our struggle with our English rulers did not differ from other popular struggles against despotic governments. Again and again we respectfully petitioned for redress of specific grievances, as the governed, from time immemorial, have petitioned their governors. But one day we abandoned our suit for petty damages, and instituted a suit for the recovery of our entire human heritage of freedom; and by basing our claim on the fundamental principles of the brotherhood of man and the sovereignty of the masses, we assumed the championship of the oppressed against their oppressors, wherever found.

It was thus, by sinking our particular quarrel with George of England in the universal quarrel of humanity with injustice, that we emerged a distinct nation, with a unique mission in the world. And we revealed ourselves to the world in the Declaration of Independence, even as the Israelites revealed themselves in the Law of Moses. From the Declaration flows our race con-sciousness, our sense of what is and what is not American. Our laws, our policies, the successive steps of our progress—all must conform to the spirit of the Declaration of Independence, the source of our national being.

The American confession of faith, therefore, is a recital of the doctrines of liberty and equality. A faithful American is one who understands these doctrines and applies them in his life.

It should be easy to pick out the true Americans—the spiritual heirs of the founders of our Republic—by this simple test of loyalty to the principles of the Declaration. To such a test we are put, both as a nation and as individu-als, every time we are asked to define our attitude on immigration. Having set up a government on a declaration of the rights of man, it should be our first business to reaffirm that declaration every time we meet a case involv-ing human rights. Now every immigrant who emerges from the steerage presents such a case. For the alien, whatever ethnic or geographic label he carries, in a primary classification of the creatures of the earth, falls in the human family. The fundamental fact of his humanity established, we need only rehearse the articles of our political faith to know what to do with the immigrant. It is written in our basic law that he is entitled to life, liberty, and the pursuit of happiness. There is nothing left for us to do but to open wide our gates and set him on his way to happiness.

That is what we did for a while, when our simple law was fresh in our minds, and the habit of applying it instinctive. Then there arose a fashion of spelling immigration with a capital initial, which so confused the national eye that we began to see a PROBLEM where formerly we had seen a familiar phenomenon of American life; and as a problem requires skillful handling, we called an army of experts in consultation, and the din of their elaborate discussions has filled our ears ever since.

The effect on the nation has been disastrous. In a matter involving our faith as Americans, we have ceased to consult our fundamental law, and have suffered ourselves to be guided by the conflicting reports of commissions and committees, anthropologists, economists, and statisticians, policymongers, calamity-howlers, and self-announced prophets. Matters irrelevant to the interests of liberty have taken the first place in the discussion; lobbyists, not patriots, have had the last word. Our American sensibility has become dulled, so that sometimes the cries of the oppressed have not reached our ears unless carried by formal deputations. In a department of government which brings us into daily touch with the nations of the world, we have failed to live up to our national gospel and have not been aware of our backsliding.

What have the experts and statisticians done so to pervert our minds? They have filled volumes with facts and figures, comparing the immigrants of to-day with the immigrants of other days, classifying them as to race, nationality, and culture, tabulating their occupations, analyzing their savings, probing their motives, prophesying their ultimate destiny. But what is there in all this that bears on the right of free men to choose their place of residence? Granted that Sicilians are not Scotchmen, how does that affect the right of a Sicilian to travel in pursuit of happiness? Strip the alien down to his anatomy, you still find a *man*, a creature made in the image of God; and concerning such a one we have definite instructions from the founders of the Republic. And what purpose was served by the bloody tide of the Civil War if it did not wash away the last lingering doubts as to the brotherhood of men of different races?

There is no impropriety in gathering together a mass of scientific and sociological data concerning the newcomers, as long as we understand that the knowledge so gained is merely the technical answer to a number of technical questions. Where we have gone wrong is in applying the testimony of our experts to the moral side of the question. By all means register the cephalic index of the alien,—the anthropologist will make something of it at his leisure,—but do not let it determine his right to life, liberty, and the pursuit of happiness.

I do not ask that we remove all restrictions and let the flood of immigration sweep in unchecked. I do ask that such restrictions as we impose shall accord with the loftiest interpretation of our duty as Americans. Now our first duty is to live up to the gospel of liberty, through the political practices devised by our forefathers and modified by their successors, as democratic ideas developed. But political practices require a territory wherein to operate — democracy must have standing-room — so it becomes our next duty to guard our frontiers. For that purpose we maintain two forms of defense: the barbaric devices of army and navy, to ward off hostile mass invasions; and the humane devices of the immigration service, to regulate the influx of peaceable individuals.

We have plenty of examples to copy in our military defenses, but when it comes to the civil branch of our national guard, we dare not borrow foreign models. What our neighbors are doing in the matter of regulating immigration may or may not be right for us. Other nations may be guided chiefly by economic considerations, while we are under spiritual bonds to give first consideration to the moral principles involved. For this, our peculiar American problem, we must seek a characteristically American solution.

What terms of entry may we impose on the immigrant without infringing on his inalienable rights, as defined in our national charter? Just such as we would impose on our own citizens if they proposed to move about the country in companies numbering thousands, with their families and portable belongings. And what would these conditions be? They would be such as are required by public safety, public health, public order. Whatever limits to our personal liberty we are ourselves willing to endure for the sake of the public welfare, we have a right to impose on the stranger from abroad; these, and no others.

Has, then, the newest arrival the same rights as the established citizen? According to the Declaration, yes; the same right to live, to move, to try his luck. More than this he does not claim at the gate of entrance; with less than this we are not authorized to put him off. We do not question the right of an individual foreigner to enter our country on any peaceable errand; why, then, question the rights of a shipload of foreigners? Lumping a thousand men together under the title of immigrants does not deprive them of their humanity and the rights inherent in humanity; or can it be demonstrated that the sum of the rights of a million men is less than the rights of one individual?

The Declaration of Independence, like the Ten Commandments, must be taken literally and applied universally. What would have been the civilizing power of the Mosaic Code if the Children of Israel had repudiated it after a few generations? As little virtue is there in the Declaration of Independence if we limit its operation to any geographical sphere or historical period or material situation. How do we belittle the works of our Fathers when we talk as though they wrought for their contemporaries only! It was no great matter to shake off the rule of an absent tyrant, if that is all that the War of the Revolution did. So much had been done many times over, long before the first tree fell under the axe of a New England settler. Emmaus[1] was fought before Yorktown,[2] and Thermopylæ[3] before Emmaus. It is only as we dwell

---

1. Village near Jerusalem, site of a successful battle fought by the Jewish Maccabees against their Greek occupiers in 164 BCE.
2. The British surrender at Yorktown, Virginia, in 1781 ended the major fighting of the American Revolution.
3. Site of a famous mountain pass battle of the Greeks against the Persian conqueror Xerxes in 480 BCE.

on the words of Jefferson and Franklin that the deeds of Washington shine out among the deeds of heroes. In the chronicles of the Jews, Moses has a far higher place than the Maccaban brothers. And notice that Moses owes his immortality to the unbroken succession of generations who were willing to rule their lives by the Law that fell from his lips. The glory of the Jews is not that they received the Law, but that they kept the Law. The glory of the American people must be that the vision vouchsafed to their fathers they in their turn hold up undimmed to the eyes of successive generations.

To maintain our own independence is only to hug that vision to our own bosoms. If we sincerely believe in the elevating power of liberty, we should hasten to extend the reign of liberty over all mankind. The disciples of Jesus did not sit down in Jerusalem and congratulate each other on having found the Saviour. They scattered over the world to spread the tidings far and wide. We Americans, disciples of the goddess Liberty are saved the trouble of carrying our gospel to the nations, because the nations come to us.

Analyze This Reading

1. According to the writer, what principles in *The Declaration of Independence* make the United States a distinct nation? How does the writer apply these principles to the issue of immigration?
2. According to the writer, what groups are to blame for making immigration an issue in the United States? What do these groups do? What moral line do they cross?
3. What obligation do the American people bear regarding immigrants, according to the writer?
4. How do references to Christian and Judaic law serve the writer's purpose? Why might such references be acceptable to her audience at the time she was writing?

Respond To This Reading

1. What events since the publication of this reading would make the writer's view on immigration more or less acceptable to a present-day audience?
2. In the context of immigration today, do you agree with the writer's assertion that Americans have an obligation? Explain.
3. While the writer treats immigration singly and in general terms, what issue within this big topic concerns you? What kind of argument would you work with to serve your purpose?

ABOUT THIS READING

This reading, submitted under the pseudonym "Publius," first appeared on November 14, 1787, in the *Independent Journal*, a semi-weekly newspaper and journal that featured essays, opinion, and various notices and announcements and that published the 85 essays and articles known as the *Federalist Papers*, that collectively argued for the ratification of the *United States Constitution*.

The Federalist No. 6

Concerning Dangers from Dissensions Between the States

By ALEXANDER HAMILTON

To the People of the State of New York:

The three last numbers of this paper have been dedicated to an enumeration of the dangers to which we should be exposed, in a state of disunion, from the arms and arts of foreign nations. I shall now proceed to delineate dangers of a different and, perhaps, still more alarming kind—those which will in all probability flow from dissensions between the States themselves, and from domestic factions and convulsions. These have been already in some instances slightly anticipated; but they deserve a more particular and more full investigation.

A man must be far gone in Utopian speculations who can seriously doubt that, if these States should either be wholly disunited, or only united in partial confederacies, the subdivisions into which they might be thrown would have frequent and violent contests with each other. To presume a want of motives for such contests as an argument against their existence, would be to forget that men are ambitious, vindictive, and rapacious. To look for a continuation of harmony between a number of independent, unconnected sovereignties in the same neighborhood, would be to disregard the uniform course of human events, and to set at defiance the accumulated experience of ages.

The causes of hostility among nations are innumerable. There are some which have a general and almost constant operation upon the collective bodies of society. Of this description are the love of power or the desire of pre-eminence and dominion—the jealousy of power, or the desire of equality and safety. There are others which have a more circumscribed though an equally operative influence within their spheres. Such are the rivalships and competitions of commerce between commercial nations. And there are others, not less numerous than either of the former, which take their origin entirely in private passions; in the attachments, enmities, interests, hopes, and fears of leading individuals in the communities of which they are members. Men of this class, whether the favorites of a king or of a people, have in too many instances abused the confidence they possessed; and assuming the pretext of some public motive, have not scrupled to sacrifice the national tranquillity to personal advantage or personal gratification.

The celebrated Pericles, in compliance with the resentment of a prostitute,[1] at the expense of much of the blood and treasure of his countrymen, attacked, vanquished, and destroyed the city of the *Samnians.* The same man, stimulated by private pique against the *Megarensians,*[2] another nation of Greece, or to avoid a prosecution with which he was threatened as an accomplice of a supposed theft of the statuary Phidias,[3] or to get rid of the accusations prepared to be brought against him for dissipating the

---

1. Aspasia, *vide* Plutarch's *Life of Pericles.*
2. *Ibid.*
3. *Ibid.*

funds of the state in the purchase of popularity,[4] or from a combination of all these causes, was the primitive author of that famous and fatal war, distinguished in the Grecian annals by the name of the *Peloponnesian* war; which, after various vicissitudes, intermissions, and renewals, terminated in the ruin of the Athenian commonwealth.

The ambitious cardinal, who was prime minister to Henry VIII., permitting his vanity to aspire to the triple crown,[5] entertained hopes of succeeding in the acquisition of that splendid prize by the influence of the Emperor Charles V. To secure the favor and interest of this enterprising and powerful monarch, he precipitated England into a war with France, contrary to the plainest dictates of policy, and at the hazard of the safety and independence, as well of the kingdom over which he presided by his counsels, as of Europe in general. For if there ever was a sovereign who bid fair to realize the project of universal monarchy, it was the Emperor Charles V., of whose intrigues Wolsey was at once the instrument and the dupe.

The influence which the bigotry of one female,[6] the petulance of another,[7] and the cabals of a third,[8] had in the contemporary policy, ferments, and pacifications, of a considerable part of Europe, are topics that have been too often descanted upon not to be generally known.

To multiply examples of the agency of personal considerations in the production of great national events, either foreign or domestic, according to their direction, would be an unnecessary waste of time. Those who have but a superficial acquaintance with the sources from which they are to be drawn, will themselves recollect a variety of instances; and those who have a tolerable knowledge of human nature will not stand in need of such lights to form their opinion either of the reality or extent of that agency. Perhaps, however, a reference, tending to illustrate the general principle, may with propriety be made to a case which has lately happened among ourselves. If Shays had not been a *desperate debtor*, it is much to be doubted whether Massachusetts would have been plunged into a civil war.

But notwithstanding the concurring testimony of experience, in this particular, there are still to be found visionary or designing men, who stand ready to advocate the paradox of perpetual peace between the States, though dismembered and alienated from each other. The genius of republics (say they) is pacific; the spirit of commerce has a tendency to soften the manners of men, and to extinguish those inflammable humors which have so often kindled into wars. Commercial republics, like ours, will never be disposed to waste themselves in ruinous contentions with each other. They will be governed by mutual interest, and will cultivate a spirit of mutual amity and concord.

Is it not (we may ask these projectors in politics) the true interest of all nations to cultivate the same benevolent and philosophic spirit? If this be their true interest, have they in fact pursued it? Has it not, on the contrary,

---

4. *Ibid.* Phidias was supposed to have stolen some public gold, with the connivance of Pericles, for the embellishment of the statue of Minerva.
5. Worn by the popes.
6. Madame de Maintenon.
7. Duchess of Marlborough.
8. Madame de Pompadour.

invariably been found that momentary passions, and immediate interest, have a more active and imperious control over human conduct than general or remote considerations of policy, utility or justice? Have republics in practice been less addicted to war than monarchies? Are not the former administered by *men* as well as the latter? Are there not aversions, predilections, rivalships, and desires of unjust acquisitions, that affect nations as well as kings? Are not popular assemblies frequently subject to the impulses of rage, resentment, jealousy, avarice, and of other irregular and violent propensities? Is it not well known that their determinations are often governed by a few individuals in whom they place confidence, and are, of course, liable to be tinctured by the passions and views of those individuals? Has commerce hitherto done anything more than change the objects of war? Is not the love of wealth as domineering and enterprising a passion as that of power or glory? Have there not been as many wars founded upon commercial motives since that has become the prevailing system of nations, as were before occasioned by the cupidity of territory or dominion? Has not the spirit of commerce, in many instances, administered new incentives to the appetite, both for the one and for the other? Let experience, the least fallible guide of human opinions, be appealed to for an answer to these inquiries.

Sparta, Athens, Rome, and Carthage were all republics; two of them, Athens and Carthage, of the commercial kind. Yet were they as often engaged in wars, offensive and defensive, as the neighboring monarchies of the same times. Sparta was little better than a well-regulated camp; and Rome was never sated of carnage and conquest.

Carthage, though a commercial republic, was the aggressor in the very war that ended in her destruction. Hannibal had carried her arms into the heart of Italy and to the gates of Rome, before Scipio, in turn, gave him an overthrow in the territories of Carthage, and made a conquest of the commonwealth.

Venice, in later times, figured more than once in wars of ambition, till, becoming an object to the other Italian states, Pope Julius II. found means to accomplish that formidable league,[9] which gave a deadly blow to the power and pride of this haughty republic.

The provinces of Holland, till they were overwhelmed in debts and taxes, took a leading and conspicuous part in the wars of Europe. They had furious contests with England for the dominion of the sea, and were among the most persevering and most implacable of the opponents of Louis XIV.

In the government of Britain the representatives of the people compose one branch of the national legislature. Commerce has been for ages the predominant pursuit of that country. Few nations, nevertheless, have been more frequently engaged in war; and the wars in which that kingdom has been engaged have, in numerous instances, proceeded from the people.

There have been, if I may so express it, almost as many popular as royal wars. The cries of the nation and the importunities of their representatives have, upon various occasions, dragged their monarchs into war, or

---

9. The League of Cambray, comprehending the Emperor, the King of France, the King of Aragon, and most of the Italian princes and states.

continued them in it, contrary to their inclinations, and sometimes contrary to the real interests of the State. In that memorable struggle for superiority between the rival houses of *Austria* and *Bourbon*, which so long kept Europe in a flame, it is well known that the antipathies of the English against the French, seconding the ambition, or rather the avarice, of a favorite leader,[10] protracted the war beyond the limits marked out by sound policy, and for a considerable time in opposition to the views of the court.

The wars of these two last-mentioned nations have in a great measure grown out of commercial considerations,—the desire of supplanting and the fear of being supplanted, either in particular branches of traffic or in the general advantages of trade and navigation, and sometimes even the more culpable desire of sharing in the commerce of other nations without their consent.

The last war but between Britain and Spain sprang from the attempts of the British merchants to prosecute an illicit trade with the Spanish main. These unjustifiable practices on their part produced severity on the part of the Spaniards toward the subjects of Great Britain which were not more justifiable, because they exceeded the bounds of a just retaliation and were chargeable with inhumanity and cruelty. Many of the English who were taken on the Spanish coast were sent to dig in the mines of Potosi; and by the usual progress of a spirit of resentment, the innocent were, after a while, confounded with the guilty in indiscriminate punishment. The complaints of the merchants kindled a violent flame throughout the nation, which soon after broke out in the House of Commons, and was communicated from that body to the ministry. Letters of reprisal were granted, and a war ensued, which in its consequences overthrew all the alliances that but twenty years before had been formed with sanguine expectations of the most beneficial fruits.

From this summary of what has taken place in other countries, whose situations have borne the nearest resemblance to our own, what reason can we have to confide in those reveries which would seduce us into an expectation of peace and cordiality between the members of the present confederacy, in a state of separation? Have we not already seen enough of the fallacy and extravagance of those idle theories which have amused us with promises of an exemption from the imperfections, weaknesses and evils incident to society in every shape? Is it not time to awake from the deceitful dream of a golden age, and to adopt as a practical maxim for the direction of our political conduct that we, as well as the other inhabitants of the globe, are yet remote from the happy empire of perfect wisdom and perfect virtue?

Let the point of extreme depression to which our national dignity and credit have sunk, let the inconveniences felt everywhere from a lax and ill administration of government, let the revolt of a part of the State of North Carolina, the late menacing disturbances in Pennsylvania, and the actual insurrections and rebellions in Massachusetts, declare—!

So far is the general sense of mankind from corresponding with the tenets of those who endeavor to lull asleep our apprehensions of discord

10. The Duke of Marlborough.

and hostility between the States, in the event of disunion, that it has from long observation of the progress of society become a sort of axiom in politics, that vicinity or nearness of situation, constitutes nations natural enemies. An intelligent writer expresses himself on this subject to this effect: "NEIGHBORING NATIONS (says he) are naturally enemies of each other unless their common weakness forces them to league in a CONFEDERATE REPUBLIC, and their constitution prevents the differences that neighborhood occasions, extinguishing that secret jealousy which disposes all states to aggrandize themselves at the expense of their neighbors."[11] This passage, at the same time, points out the EVIL and suggests the REMEDY.

Publius

Analyze This Reading

1. In what context are the Federalist Papers written and published?
2. The writer compares states with nations. How does this strategy serve his argument?
3. What examples does the writer use to announce the dangers of separate nations and states?
4. What is the "EVIL" and what is the "REMEDY" the writer refers to in his conclusion?
5. Publius, as noted in the introduction to this reading, is a pseudonym for a writer. Conduct some research and identify this writer. Why might the writer have adopted a pseudonym, and why might the writer have chosen Publius as a pseudonym?

Respond To This Reading

1. Many contend that the issue to which the writer is responding is still present today, more than 200 years after the publication of this reading. What present-day issues would confirm this contention?
2. Identify a local issue that pits a state and the federal government against one another. What claim would you argue in response to this issue?

ABOUT THIS READING

Thomas Jefferson (1743–1826), third president of the United States, is the principal author of the five-person committee charged with preparing the Declaration of Independence, a declaration that would separate America from British economic and political rule. The Declaration was submitted to the Second Continental Congress and approved on July 4, 1776—but not without substantial changes, one of which included deletion of Jefferson's insistence that the institution of slavery be abolished.

---

11. Vide Principes des Negociations par l'Abbé de Mably.

In Congress, July 4, 1776

The Unanimous Declaration of the Thirteen United States of America

By THOMAS JEFFERSON

When in the Course of human events it becomes necessary for one people to dissolve the political bands which have connected them with another and to assume among the powers of the earth, the separate and equal station to which the Laws of Nature and of Nature's God entitle them, a decent respect to the opinions of mankind requires that they should declare the causes which impel them to the separation.

We hold these truths to be self-evident, that all men are created equal, that they are endowed by their Creator with certain unalienable Rights, that among these are Life, Liberty and the pursuit of Happiness.—That to secure these rights, Governments are instituted among Men, deriving their just powers from the consent of the governed,—That whenever any Form of Government becomes destructive of these ends, it is the Right of the People to alter or to abolish it, and to institute new Government, laying its foundation on such principles and organizing its powers in such form, as to them shall seem most likely to effect their Safety and Happiness. Prudence, indeed, will dictate that Governments long established should not be changed for light and transient causes; and accordingly all experience hath shewn that mankind are more disposed to suffer, while evils are sufferable than to right themselves by abolishing the forms to which they are accustomed. But when a long train of abuses and usurpations, pursuing invariably the same Object evinces a design to reduce them under absolute Despotism, it is their right, it is their duty, to throw off such Government, and to provide new Guards for their future security.—Such has been the patient sufferance of these Colonies; and such is now the necessity which constrains them to alter their former Systems of Government. The history of the present King of Great Britain is a history of repeated injuries and usurpations, all having in direct object the establishment of an absolute Tyranny over these States. To prove this, let Facts be submitted to a candid world.

He has refused his Assent to Laws, the most wholesome and necessary for the public good.

He has forbidden his Governors to pass Laws of immediate and pressing importance, unless suspended in their operation till his Assent should be obtained; and when so suspended, he has utterly neglected to attend to them.

He has refused to pass other Laws for the accommodation of large districts of people, unless those people would relinquish the right of Representation in the Legislature, a right inestimable to them and formidable to tyrants only.

He has called together legislative bodies at places unusual, uncomfortable, and distant from the depository of their Public Records, for the sole purpose of fatiguing them into compliance with his measures.

He has dissolved Representative Houses repeatedly, for opposing with manly firmness his invasions on the rights of the people.

He has refused for a long time, after such dissolutions, to cause others to be elected, whereby the Legislative Powers, incapable of Annihilation, have returned to the People at large for their exercise; the State remaining in the mean time exposed to all the dangers of invasion from without, and convulsions within.

He has endeavoured to prevent the population of these States; for that purpose obstructing the Laws for Naturalization of Foreigners; refusing to pass others to encourage their migrations hither, and raising the conditions of new Appropriations of Lands.

He has obstructed the Administration of Justice by refusing his Assent to Laws for establishing Judiciary Powers.

He has made Judges dependent on his Will alone for the tenure of their offices, and the amount and payment of their salaries.

He has erected a multitude of New Offices, and sent hither swarms of Officers to harass our people and eat out their substance.

He has kept among us, in times of peace, Standing Armies without the Consent of our legislatures.

He has affected to render the Military independent of and superior to the Civil Power.

He has combined with others to subject us to a jurisdiction foreign to our constitution, and unacknowledged by our laws; giving his Assent to their Acts of pretended Legislation:

For quartering large bodies of armed troops among us:

For protecting them, by a mock Trial from punishment for any Murders which they should commit on the Inhabitants of these States:

For cutting off our Trade with all parts of the world:

For imposing Taxes on us without our Consent:

For depriving us in many cases, of the benefit of Trial by Jury:

For transporting us beyond Seas to be tried for pretended offences:

For abolishing the free System of English Laws in a neighbouring Province, establishing therein an Arbitrary government, and enlarging its Boundaries so as to render it at once an example and fit instrument for introducing the same absolute rule into these Colonies:

For taking away our Charters, abolishing our most valuable Laws and altering fundamentally the Forms of our Governments:

For suspending our own Legislatures, and declaring themselves invested with power to legislate for us in all cases whatsoever.

He has abdicated Government here, by declaring us out of his Protection and waging War against us.

He has plundered our seas, ravaged our coasts, burnt our towns, and destroyed the lives of our people.

He is at this time transporting large Armies of foreign Mercenaries to compleat the works of death, desolation, and tyranny, already begun with circumstances of Cruelty & Perfidy scarcely paralleled in the most barbarous ages, and totally unworthy the Head of a civilized nation.

He has constrained our fellow Citizens taken Captive on the high Seas to bear Arms against their Country, to become the executioners of their friends and Brethren, or to fall themselves by their Hands.

He has excited domestic insurrections amongst us, and has endeavoured to bring on the inhabitants of our frontiers, the merciless Indian Savages whose known rule of warfare, is an undistinguished destruction of all ages, sexes and conditions.

In every stage of these Oppressions We have Petitioned for Redress in the most humble terms: Our repeated Petitions have been answered only by repeated injury. A Prince, whose character is thus marked by every act which may define a Tyrant, is unfit to be the ruler of a free people.

Nor have We been wanting in attentions to our British brethren. We have warned them from time to time of attempts by their legislature to extend an unwarrantable jurisdiction over us. We have reminded them of the circumstances of our emigration and settlement here. We have appealed to their native justice and magnanimity, and we have conjured them by the ties of our common kindred to disavow these usurpations, which would inevitably interrupt our connections and correspondence. They too have been deaf to the voice of justice and of consanguinity. We must, therefore, acquiesce in the necessity, which denounces our Separation, and hold them, as we hold the rest of mankind, Enemies in War, in Peace Friends.

We, therefore, the Representatives of the united States of America, in General Congress, Assembled, appealing to the Supreme Judge of the world for the rectitude of our intentions, do, in the Name, and by Authority of the good People of these Colonies, solemnly publish and declare, That these united Colonies are, and of Right ought to be Free and Independent States, that they are Absolved from all Allegiance to the British Crown, and that all political connection between them and the State of Great Britain, is and ought to be totally dissolved; and that as Free and Independent States, they have full Power to levy War, conclude Peace, contract Alliances, establish Commerce, and to do all other Acts and Things which Independent States may of right do.—And for the support of this Declaration, with a firm reliance on the protection of Divine Providence, we mutually pledge to each other our Lives, our Fortunes, and our sacred Honor.

Analyze This Reading

1. In what historical context is this argument produced?
2. What kind of claim does the writer use? What is his warrant? At what audience is this argument aimed?
3. Based on the three kinds of support discussed in Chapter 11, what kind of support does the writer use to defend his claim? Does one kind of support dominate? Explain?
4. What, exactly, does the writer declare?

Respond To This Reading

1. The writer is accusatory and damning in his tone, a strategy that is often counterproductive in an argument. Is it counterproductive in this argument? Explain.

2. Given the context in which we live today—political, social, economic, environmental—are there declarations you are prepared to argue for? If yes, what is the most pressing? What would you claim, on what values would you ground your claim, and what support would you bring to your argument?

ABOUT THIS READING

Writer H. L. Mencken (1880–1956) was a journalist, editor, and literary critic for *The Baltimore Sun*. Mencken made frequent use of satire in his steady critique of American life. This reading appeared in Mencken's 1926 book, *Prejudices: Fifth Series*.

The Penalty of Death

By H. L. MENCKEN

Of the arguments against capital punishment that issue from uplifters, two are commonly heard most often, to wit:

1. That hanging a man (or frying him or gassing him) is a dreadful business, degrading to those who have to do it and revolting to those who have to witness it.
2. That it is useless, for it does not deter others from the same crime.

The first of these arguments, it seems to me, is plainly too weak to need serious refutation. All it says, in brief, is that the work of the hangman is unpleasant. Granted. But suppose it is? It may be quite necessary to society for all that. There are, indeed, many other jobs that are unpleasant, and yet no one thinks of abolishing them—that of the plumber, that of the soldier, that of the garbageman, that of the priest hearing confessions, that of the sand-hog, and so on. Moreover, what evidence is there that any actual hangman complains of his work? I have heard none. On the contrary, I have known many who delighted in their ancient art, and practiced it proudly.

In the second argument of the abolitionists there is rather more force, but even here, I believe, the ground under them is shaky. Their fundamental error consists in assuming that the whole aim of punishing criminals is to deter other (potential) criminals—that we hang or electrocute A simply in order to so alarm B that he will not kill C. This, I believe, is an assumption which confuses a part with the whole. Deterrence, obviously, is one of the aims of punishment, but it is surely not the only one. On the contrary, there are at least half a dozen, and some are probably quite as important. At least one of them, practically considered, is *more* important. Commonly, it is described as revenge, but revenge is really not the word for it. I borrow a better term from the late Aristotle: *katharsis*. *Katharsis*, so used, means a salubrious discharge of emotions, a healthy letting off of steam. A schoolboy, disliking his teacher, deposits a tack upon the pedagogical chair; the teacher jumps and the boy laughs. This is *katharsis*. What I contend is that one of the prime objects of all judicial punishments is to afford the same grateful relief (*a*) to the immediate victims of the criminal punished, and (*b*) to the general body of moral and timorous men.

These persons, and particularly the first group, are concerned only indirectly with deterring other criminals. The thing they crave primarily is the satisfaction of seeing the criminal actually before them suffer as he made them suffer. What they want is the peace of mind that goes with the feeling that accounts are squared. Until they get that satisfaction they are in a state of emotional tension, and hence unhappy. The instant they get it they are comfortable. I do not argue that this yearning is noble; I simply argue that it is almost universal among human beings. In the face of injuries that are unimportant and can be borne without damage it may yield to higher impulses; that is to say, it may yield to what is called Christian charity. But when the injury is serious Christianity is adjourned, and even saints reach for their sidearms. It is plainly asking too much of human nature to expect it to conquer so natural an impulse. A keeps a store and has a bookkeeper, B. B steals $700, employs it in playing at dice or bingo, and is cleaned out. What is A to do? Let B go? If he does so he will be unable to sleep at night. The sense of injury, of injustice, of frustration will haunt him like pruritus. So he turns B over to the police, and they hustle B to prison. Thereafter A can sleep. More, he has pleasant dreams. He pictures B chained to the wall of a dungeon a hundred feet underground, devoured by rats and scorpions. It is so agreeable that it makes him forget his $700. He has got his *katharsis*.

The same thing precisely takes place on a larger scale when there is a crime which destroys a whole community's sense of security. Every law-abiding citizen feels menaced and frustrated until the criminals have been struck down—until the communal capacity to get even with them, and more than even, has been dramatically demonstrated. Here, manifestly, the business of deterring others is no more than an afterthought. The main thing is to destroy the concrete scoundrels whose act has alarmed everyone, and thus made everyone unhappy. Until they are brought to book that unhappiness continues; when the law has been executed upon them there is a sigh of relief. In other words, there is *katharsis*.

I know of no public demand for the death penalty for ordinary crimes, even for ordinary homicides. Its infliction would shock all men of normal decency of feeling. But for crimes involving the deliberate and inexcusable taking of human life, by men openly defiant of all civilized order—for such crimes it seems, to nine men out of ten, a just and proper punishment. Any lesser penalty leaves them feeling that the criminal has got the better of society—that he is free to add insult to injury by laughing. That feeling can be dissipated only by a recourse to *katharsis*, the invention of the aforesaid Aristotle. It is more effectively and economically achieved, as human nature now is, by wafting the criminal to realms of bliss.

The real objection to capital punishment doesn't lie against the actual extermination of the condemned, but against our brutal American habit of putting it off so long. After all, every one of us must die soon or late, and a murderer, it must be assumed, is one who makes that sad fact the cornerstone of his metaphysic. But it is one thing to die, and quite another thing to lie for long months and even years under the shadow of death. No sane man would choose such a finish. All of us, despite the Prayer Book, long for a swift and unexpected end. Unhappily, a murderer, under the irrational American system, is tortured for what, to him, must seem a whole series of eternities. For months on end he sits in prison while his lawyers carry on their idiotic buffoonery with writs, injunctions, mandamuses, and appeals. In order to get his money (or that of his friends) they have to feed him with hope. Now and then, by the imbecility of a judge or some trick of juridic science, they actually justify it. But let us say that, his money all gone, they finally throw up their hands. Their client is now ready for the rope or the chair. But he must still wait for months before it fetches him.

That wait, I believe, is horribly cruel. I have seen more than one man sitting in the death-house, and I don't want to see any more. Worse, it is wholly useless. Why should he wait at all? Why not hang him the day after the last court dissipates his last hope? Why torture him as not even cannibals would torture their victims? The common answer is that he must have time to make his peace with God. But how long does that take? It may be accomplished, I believe, in two hours quite as comfortably as in two years. There are, indeed, no temporal limitations upon God. He could forgive a whole herd of murderers in a millionth of a second. More, it has been done.

Analyze This Reading

1. How does the writer evaluate the two most common attitudes toward capital punishment? What elements of humor does the writer use in his evaluations?
2. What use does the writer make of Aristotle's term *katharsis*? Is the writer sympathetic with those who demand it? Explain.
3. What does the writer claim regarding the death penalty? What kind of claim is it?

Respond To This Reading

1. Given the grave and serious nature of this issue, is the writer's extensive use of humor effective? Explain.
2. With reference to the four kinds of argument discussed in Chapters 8–9, what kind of argument is this? Explain why it is effective or ineffective.

ABOUT THIS READING

Writer Judith Sargent Murray (1751–1820) argued forcefully for equal opportunities for women in the years during and after the American Revolution. She hoped to persuade her readers that the new nation's spirit of independence and self-determination should be extended to women. This reading is part one of Murray's argument, "On the Equality of the Sexes." This reading first appeared in the Boston-based *The Massachusetts Magazine, or, Monthly Museum Concerning the Literature, History, Politics, Arts, Manners, Amusements of the Age* in March 1790.

On the Equality of the Sexes

By JUDITH SARGENT MURRAY

To the Editors of the Massachusetts Magazine, Gentlemen,

The following ESSAY *is yielded to the patronage of Candour.—If it hath been anticipated, the testimony of many respectable persons, who saw it in manuscripts as early as the year* 1779, *can obviate the imputation of plagiarism.*

Is it upon mature consideration we adopt the idea, that nature is thus partial in her distributions? Is it indeed a fact, that she hath yielded to one half of the human species so unquestionable a mental superiority? I know that to both sexes elevated understandings, and the reverse, are common. But, suffer me to ask, in what the minds of females are so notoriously deficient, or unequal. May not the intellectual powers be ranged under these four heads—imagination, reason, memory and judgment. The province of imagination hath long since been surrendered to us, and we have been crowned and undoubted sovereigns of the regions of fancy. Invention is perhaps the most arduous effort of the mind; this branch of imagination hath been particularly ceded to us, and we have been time out of mind invested with that creative faculty. Observe the variety of fashions (here I bar the contemptuous smile) which distinguish and adorn the female world: how continually are they changing, insomuch that they almost render the wise man's assertion problematical, and we are ready to say, *there is something new under the sun.* Now what a playfulness, what an exuberance of fancy, what strength of inventive imagination, doth this continual variation discover? Again, it hath been observed, that if the turpitude of the conduct of our sex, hath been ever so enormous, so extremely ready are we, that the very first thought presents us with an apology, so plausible, as to produce our actions even in an amiable light. Another instance of our creative powers, is our talent for slander; how ingenious are we at inventive scandal? what a formidable story can we in a moment fabricate merely from the force of a prolifick imagination? how many reputations, in the fertile brain of a female, have been utterly despoiled? how industrious are we at improving a hint? suspicion how easily do we convert into conviction, and conviction, embellished by the power of eloquence, stalks abroad to the surprise and confusion of unsuspecting innocence. Perhaps it will be asked if I furnish these facts as instances of excellency in our sex. Certainly not; but as proofs of a creative faculty, of a lively imagination. Assuredly great activity of mind is thereby discovered, and was this activity properly directed, what beneficial effects would follow. Is the needle and kitchen sufficient to employ the operations of a soul thus organized? I should conceive not, Nay, it is a truth that those very departments leave the intelligent principle vacant, and at liberty for speculation. Are we deficient in reason? we can only reason from what we know, and if an opportunity of acquiring knowledge hath been denied us, the inferiority of our sex cannot fairly be deduced from thence. Memory, I believe, will be allowed us in common, since everyone's experience must testify, that a loquacious old woman is as frequently met with, as a communicative man; their subjects are alike drawn from the fund of other times, and the transactions of their youth, or of maturer life, entertain, or perhaps fatigue you, in the evening of their lives.

"But our judgment is not so strong—we do not distinguish so well."—Yet it may be questioned, from what doth this superiority, in this determining faculty of the soul, proceed. May we not trace its source in the difference of education, and continued advantages? Will it be said that the judgment of a male of two years old, is more sage than that of a female's of the same age? I believe the reverse is generally observed to be true. But from that period what partiality! how is the one exalted, and the other depressed, by the contrary modes of education which are adopted! the one is taught to aspire, and the other is early confined and limitted. As their years increase, the sister must be wholly domesticated, while the brother is led by the hand through all the flowery paths of science. Grant that their minds are by nature equal, yet who shall wonder at the *apparent* superiority, if indeed custom becomes *second nature*; nay if it taketh place of nature, and that it doth the experience of each day will evince. At length arrived at womanhood, the uncultivated fair one feels a void, which the employments allotted her are by no means capable of filling. What can she do? to books she may not apply; or if she doth, *to those only of the novel kind,* lest she merit the appellation of a *learned lady;* and what ideas have been affixed to this term, the observation of many can testify. Fashion, scandal, and sometimes what is still more reprehensible, are then called in to her relief; and who can say to what lengths the liberties she takes may proceed. Meantimes she herself is most unhappy; she feels the want of a cultivated mind. Is she single, she in vain seeks to fill up time from sexual employments or amusements. Is she united to a person whose soul nature made equal to her own, education hath set him so far above her, that in those entertainments which are productive of such rational felicity, she is not qualified to accompany him. She experiences a mortifying consciousness of inferiority, which embitters every enjoyment. Doth the person to whom her adverse fate hath consigned her, possess a mind incapable of improvement, she is equally wretched, in being so closely connected with an individual whom she cannot but despise. Now, was she permitted the same instructors as her brother, (with an eye however to their particular departments) for the employment of a rational mind an ample field would be opened. In astronomy she might catch a glimpse of the immensity of the Deity, and thence she would form amazing conceptions of the august and supreme Intelligence. In geography she would admire Jehovah in the midst of his benevolence; thus adapting this globe to the various wants and amusements of its inhabitants. In natural philosophy she would adore the infinite majesty of heaven, clothed in condescension; and as she traversed the reptile world, she would hail the goodness of a creating God. A mind, thus filled, would have little room for the trifles with which our sex are, with too much justice, accused of amusing themselves, and they would thus be rendered fit companions for those, who should one day wear them as their crown. Fashions, in their variety, would then give place to conjectures, which might perhaps conduce to the improvements of the literary world; and there would be no leisure for slander or detraction. Reputation would not then be blasted, but serious speculations would occupy the lively imaginations of the sex. Unnecessary visits would only be indulged by way of relaxation, or to answer the demands of consanguinity and friendship. Females would become discreet, their judgments would be invigorated, and their partners for life being circumspectly chosen, an unhappy Hymen would then be as rare, as is now the reverse.

Will it be urged that those acquirements would supersede our domestick duties. I answer that every requisite in female economy is easily attained; and, with truth I can add, that when once attained, they require no further *mental attention.* Nay, while we are pursuing the needle, or the superintendency of the family, I repeat, that our minds are at full liberty for reflection; that imagination may exert itself in full vigor; and that if a just foundation is early laid, our ideas will then be worthy of rational beings. If we were industrious we might easily find time to arrange them upon paper, or should avocations press too hard for such an indulgence, the hours allotted for conversation would at least become more refined and rational. Should it still be vociferated, "Your domestick employments are sufficient"—I would calmly ask, is it reasonable, that a candidate for immortality, for the joys of heaven, an intelligent being, who is to spend an eternity in contemplating the works of the Deity, should at present be so degraded, as to be allowed no other ideas, than those which are suggested by the mechanism of a pudding, or the sewing the seams of a garment? Pity that all such censurers of female improvement do not go one step further, and deny their future existence; to be consistent they surely ought.

Yes, ye lordly, ye haughty sex, our souls are by nature *equal* to yours; the same breath of God animates, enlivens, and invigorates us; and that we are not fallen lower than yourselves, let those witness who have greatly towered above the various discouragements by which they have been so heavily oppressed; and though I am unacquainted with the list of celebrated characters on either side, yet from the observations I have made in the contracted circle in which I have moved, I dare confidently believe, that from the commencement of time to the present day, there hath been as many females, as males, who, by the *mere force of natural powers,* have merited the crown of applause; who, *thus unassisted,* have seized the wreath of fame. I know there are who assert, that as the animal power of the one sex are superiour, of course their mental faculties also must be stronger; thus attributing strength of mind to the transient organization of this earth born tenement. But if this reasoning is just, man must be content to yield the palm to many of the brute creation, since by not a few of his brethren of the field, he is far surpassed in bodily strength. Moreover, was this argument admitted, it would prove too much, for occular demonstration evinceth, that there are many robust masculine ladies, and effeminate gentlemen. Yet I fancy that [18th century British poet] Mr. Pope, though clogged with an enervated body, and distinguished by a diminutive stature, could nevertheless lay claim to greatness of soul; and perhaps there are many other instances which might be adduced to combat so unphilosophical an opinion. Do we not often see, that when the clay built tabernacle is well nigh dissolved, when it is just ready to mingle with the parent soil, the immortal inhabitant aspires to, and even attaineth heights the most sublime, and which were before wholly unexplored. Besides, were we to grant that animal strength proved any thing, taking into consideration the accustomed impartiality of nature, we should be induced to imagine, that she had invested the female mind with superiour strength as an equivalent for the bodily powers of man. But waving this however palpable advantage, for *equality only,* we wish to contend.

Analyze This Reading

1. Why might the writer open her argument with a reference to plagiarism?
2. Describe the tone the writer uses in her treatment of women's "inventive imagination" and the uses to which it is put.
3. According to the writer, why is a woman's ability to judge presumably inferior to a man's? To what does she trace this difference? What examples does she bring in to explore this question?
4. What is the writer's position on women's "domestick duties"?
5. What does the writer claim? What kind of claim is it?
6. How do the language and structure of this reading serve the writer's purpose?

Respond To This Reading

1. With regard to the writer's principal concern, how have conditions changed in the more than 200 years since this argument was published?
2. The writer contends that women are systematically held back—by institutions, assumptions, and prescribed roles. Are there examples in your life when you have similarly been held back? If yes, what are they? Which is of most concern to you, and what would you want individuals in positions of power to know were you to argue on this concern?

ABOUT THIS READING

Writer Leo Szilard (1898–1964) was a Hungarian-born physicist who, with Enrico Fermi, patented the design for a nuclear reactor in 1939. Szilard later became wary of the devastation nuclear warfare could cause and, on July 17, 1945, with 69 cosigners at the Manhattan Project "Metallurgical Laboratory" in Chicago, petitioned the president of the United States.

A Petition to the President of the United States

By LEO SZILARD AND COSIGNERS

Discoveries of which the people of the United States are not aware may affect the welfare of this nation in the near future. The liberation of atomic power which has been achieved places atomic bombs in the hands of the Army. It places in your hands, as Commander-in-Chief, the fateful decision whether or not to sanction the use of such bombs in the present phase of the war against Japan.

We, the undersigned scientists, have been working in the field of atomic power. Until recently, we have had to fear that the United States might be attacked by atomic bombs during this war and that her only defense might lie in a counterattack by the same means. Today, with the defeat of Germany, this danger is averted and we feel impelled to say what follows:

The war has to be brought speedily to a successful conclusion and attacks by atomic bombs may very well be an effective method of warfare. We feel, however, that such attacks on Japan could not be justified, at least not unless the terms which will be imposed after the war on Japan were made public in detail and Japan were given an opportunity to surrender.

If such public announcement gave assurance to the Japanese that they could look forward to a life devoted to peaceful pursuits in their homeland and if Japan still refused to surrender our nation might then, in certain circumstances, find itself forced to resort to the use of atomic bombs. Such a step, however, ought not to be made at any time without seriously considering the moral responsibilities which are involved.

The development of atomic power will provide the nations with new means of destruction. The atomic bombs at our disposal represent only the first step in this direction, and there is almost no limit to the destructive power which will become available in the course of their future development. Thus a nation which sets the precedent of using these newly liberated forces of nature for purposes of destruction may have to bear the responsibility of opening the door to an era of devastation on an unimaginable scale.

If after this war a situation is allowed to develop in the world which permits rival powers to be in uncontrolled possession of these new means of destruction, the cities of the United States as well as the cities of other nations will be in continuous danger of sudden annihilation. All the resources of the United States, moral and material, may have to be mobilized to prevent the advent of such a world situation. Its prevention is at present the solemn responsibility of the United States—singled out by virtue of her lead in the field of atomic power.

The added material strength which this lead gives to the United States brings with it the obligation of restraint and if we were to violate this obligation our moral position would be weakened in the eyes of the world and in our own eyes. It would then be more difficult for us to live up to our responsibility of bringing the unloosened forces of destruction under control.

In view of the foregoing, we, the undersigned, respectfully petition: first, that you exercise your power as Commander-in-Chief, to rule that the United States shall not resort to the use of atomic bombs in this war unless the terms which will be imposed upon Japan have been made public in detail and Japan knowing these terms has refused to surrender; second, that in such an event the question whether or not to use atomic bombs be decided by you in light of the considerations presented in this petition as well as all the other moral responsibilities which are involved.

Analyze This Reading

1. In what context do Szilard and the cosigners petition the president?
2. What important qualifier appears in Szilard's claim? Describe the warrant that supports this claim.
3. What moral appeal is made to the target audience in this argument?

Respond To This Reading

1. Although no statistics or figures appear in this argument, the writers include substantial support. What kind of support do they use? Refer to a few examples.
2. What issues today might call for an argument similar to this petition, that is, where an argument is delivered using general rather than specific kinds of support?

ABOUT THIS READING

Isabella Baumfree changed her name to Sojourner Truth (1797–1883) in 1843 and proceeded to distinguish herself as an abolitionist and women's rights advocate. Truth delivered this speech in December 1851 at the Ohio Women's Rights Convention in Akron. The speech was transcribed in 1863 by Frances Dana Barker Gage, an organizer of the convention, and may contain inaccuracies. For example, it is generally believed that Truth had 5 children, not 13, as reported by Gage, and that the convention was relatively calm and orderly and not disruptive and characterized by mob behavior, as Gage later reported.

Ain't I a Woman?

By SOJOURNER TRUTH

Well, children, where there is so much racket there must be something out of kilter. I think that 'twixt the negroes of the South and the women at the North, all talking about rights, the white men will be in a fix pretty soon. But what's all this here talking about?

That man over there says that women need to be helped into carriages, and lifted over ditches, and to have the best place everywhere. Nobody ever helps me into carriages, or over mud-puddles, or gives me any best place! And ain't I a woman? Look at me! Look at my arm! I have ploughed and planted, and gathered into barns, and no man could head me! And ain't I a woman? I could work as much and eat as much as a man—when I could get it—and bear the lash as well! And ain't I a woman? I have borne thirteen children, and seen most all sold off to slavery, and when I cried out with my mother's grief, none but Jesus heard me! And ain't I a woman?

Then they talk about this thing in the head; what's this they call it? [member of audience whispers, "intellect"] That's it, honey. What's that got to do with women's rights or negroes' rights? If my cup won't hold but a pint, and yours holds a quart, wouldn't you be mean not to let me have my little half measure full?

Then that little man in black there, he says women can't have as much rights as men, 'cause Christ wasn't a woman! Where did your Christ come from? Where did your Christ come from? From God and a woman! Man had nothing to do with Him.

If the first woman God ever made was strong enough to turn the world upside down all alone, these women together ought to be able to turn it back, and get it right side up again! And now they is asking to do it, the men better let them.

Obliged to you for hearing me, and now old Sojourner ain't got nothing more to say.

Analyze This Reading

1. In the speaker's view, what is "out of kilter"? What parties are involved?
2. What credibility does the speaker bring to her speech?
3. How does the "cup" metaphor function? What commentary on men and religion does the speaker offer?
4. Unlike most authors of significant arguments and speeches in American history, Truth lacked the ability to read and write, training that was forbidden under law during the period of slavery. Given her audience—nearly all white, educated, middle-class women—what values does Truth touch that made her speech successful?

Respond To This Reading

1. Are Truth's attitudes about gender, race, and religion applicable today? Explain.
2. Some literary critics view Truth as a figure bridging issues of race and gender. Identify public figures, or trends, or movements today that bridge issues across different areas of life, such as the environment, class, the law, race and ethnicity, gender, and spirituality. What single figure, trend, or movement embodies a bridge issue that might motivate you to argue? What areas are bridged, and what would you claim?

ABOUT THIS READING

A controversial figure today for his views on racial accommodation, writer Booker T. Washington (1856–1915) was an influential voice for many African-Americans during the late nineteenth and early twentieth centuries. Washington was Tuskegee Institute's inaugural principal, and his popular autobiography, *Up from Slavery* (1901), was required reading for many American students of earlier generations. This reading is the text of Washington's speech at the Cotton States and International Exposition in Atlanta in 1895, delivered before a largely white audience, some of whom were businessmen.

Atlanta Compromise Address

By BOOKER T. WASHINGTON

Mr. President and Gentlemen of the Board of Directors and Citizens:

One-third of the population of the South is of the Negro race. No enterprise seeking the material, civil, or moral welfare of this section can disregard this element of our population and reach the highest success. I but convey to you, Mr. President and Directors, the sentiment of the masses of my race when I say that in no way have the value and manhood of the American Negro been more fittingly and generously recognized than by the managers of this magnificent Exposition at every stage of its progress. It is a recognition that will do more to cement the friendship of the two races than any occurrence since the dawn of our freedom.

Not only this, but the opportunity here afforded will awaken among us a new era of industrial progress. Ignorant and inexperienced, it is not strange that in the first years of our new life we began at the top instead of at the bottom; that a seat in Congress or the state legislature was more sought than real estate or industrial skill; that the political convention or stump speaking had more attractions than starting a dairy farm or truck garden.

A ship lost at sea for many days suddenly sighted a friendly vessel. From the mast of the unfortunate vessel was seen a signal, "Water, water; we die of thirst!" The answer from the friendly vessel at once came back, "Cast down your bucket where you are." A second time the signal, "Water, water; send us water!" ran up from the distressed vessel, and was answered, "Cast down your bucket where you are." And a third and fourth signal for water was answered, "Cast down your bucket where you are." The captain of the distressed vessel, at last heeding the injunction, cast down his bucket, and it came up full of fresh, sparkling water from the mouth of the Amazon River. To those of my race who depend on bettering their condition in a foreign land or who underestimate the importance of cultivating friendly relations with the Southern white man, who is their next-door neighbor, I would say: "Cast down your bucket where you are"—cast it down in making friends in every manly way of the people of all races by whom we are surrounded.

Cast it down in agriculture, mechanics, in commerce, in domestic service, and in the professions. And in this connection it is well to bear in mind that whatever other sins the South may be called to bear, when it comes to business, pure and simple, it is in the South that the Negro is given a man's chance in the commercial world, and in nothing is this Exposition more eloquent than in emphasizing this chance. Our greatest danger is that in the great leap from slavery to freedom we may overlook the fact that the masses of us are to live by the productions of our hands, and fail to keep in mind that we shall prosper in proportion as we learn to dignify and glorify common labour, and put brains and skill into the common occupations of life; shall prosper in proportion as we learn to draw the line between the superficial and the substantial, the ornamental gewgaws of life and the useful. No race can prosper till it learns that there is as much dignity in tilling a field as in writing a poem. It is at the bottom of life we must begin, and not at the top. Nor should we permit our grievances to overshadow our opportunities.

To those of the white race who look to the incoming of those of foreign birth and strange tongue and habits for the prosperity of the South, were I permitted I would repeat what I say to my own race, "Cast down your bucket where you are." Cast it down among the eight millions of Negroes whose habits you know, whose fidelity and love you have tested in days when to have proved treacherous meant the ruin of your firesides. Cast down your bucket among these people who have, without strikes and labour wars, tilled your fields, cleared your forests, builded your railroads and cities, and brought forth treasures from the bowels of the earth, and helped make possible this magnificent representation of the progress of the South. Casting down your bucket among my people, helping and encouraging them as you are doing on these grounds, and to education of head, hand, and heart, you will find that they will buy your surplus land, make blossom the waste places in your fields, and run your factories. While doing this, you can be sure in the future, as in the past, that you and your families will be surrounded by the most patient, faithful, law-abiding, and unresentful people that the world has seen.

As we have proved our loyalty to you in the past, in nursing your children, watching by the sick-bed of your mothers and fathers, and often following them with tear-dimmed eyes to their graves, so in the future, in our humble way, we shall stand by you with a devotion that no foreigner can approach, ready to lay down our lives, if need be, in defense of yours, interlacing our industrial, commercial, civil, and religious life with yours in a way that shall make the interests of both races one. In all things that are purely social we can be as separate as the fingers, yet one as the hand in all things essential to mutual progress.

There is no defense or security for any of us except in the highest intelligence and development of all. If anywhere there are efforts tending to curtail the fullest growth of the Negro, let these efforts be turned into stimulating, encouraging, and making him the most useful and intelligent citizen. Effort or means so invested will pay a thousand per cent interest. These efforts will be twice blessed—"blessing him that gives and him that takes."

There is no escape through law of man or God from the inevitable:

The laws of changeless justice bind
Oppressor with oppressed;
And close as sin and suffering joined
We march to fate abreast.

Nearly sixteen millions of hands will aid you in pulling the load upward, or they will pull against you the load downward. We shall constitute one-third and more of the ignorance and crime of the South, or one-third its intelligence and progress; we shall contribute one-third to the business and industrial prosperity of the South, or we shall prove a veritable body of death, stagnating, depressing, retarding every effort to advance the body politic.

Gentlemen of the Exposition, as we present to you our humble effort at an exhibition of our progress, you must not expect overmuch. Starting thirty years ago with ownership here and there in a few quilts and pumpkins and chickens (gathered from miscellaneous sources), remember the path that has led from these to the inventions and production of agricultural implements, buggies, steam-engines, newspapers, books, statuary, carving, paintings, the management of drug stores and banks, has not been trodden without contact with thorns and thistles. While we take pride in what we exhibit as a result of our independent efforts, we do not for a moment forget that our part in this exhibition would fall far short of your expectations but for the constant help that has come to our educational life, not only from the Southern states, but especially from Northern philanthropists, who have made their gifts a constant stream of blessing and encouragement.

The wisest among my race understand that the agitation of questions of social equality is the extremest folly, and that progress in the enjoyment of all the privileges that will come to us must be the result of severe and constant struggle rather than of artificial forcing. No race that has anything to contribute to the markets of the world is long in any degree ostracized. It is important and right that all privileges of the law be ours, but it is vastly more important that we be prepared for the exercise of these privileges. The opportunity to earn a dollar in a factory just now is worth infinitely more than the opportunity to spend a dollar in an opera-house.

In conclusion, may I repeat that nothing in thirty years has given us more hope and encouragement, and drawn us so near to you of the white race, as this opportunity offered by the Exposition; and here bending, as it were, over the altar that represents the results of the struggles of your race and mine, both starting practically empty-handed three decades ago, I pledge that in your effort to work out the great and intricate problem which God has laid at the doors of the South, you shall have at all times the patient, sympathetic help of my race; only let this be constantly in mind, that, while from representations in these buildings of the product of field, of forest, of mine, of factory, letters, and art, much good will come, yet far above and beyond material benefits will be that higher good, that, let us pray God, will come, in a blotting out of sectional differences and racial animosities and suspicions, in a determination to administer absolute justice, in a willing obedience among all classes to the mandates of law. This, this, coupled with our material prosperity, will bring into our beloved South a new heaven and a new earth.

Analyze This Reading

1. What does the writer claim? What kind of claim is it?
2. Describe the "lost ship" metaphor. What purpose does it serve in the writer's argument?
3. What assurances does the writer offer his audience? Why might these assurances be necessary?
4. What audience values does the writer appeal to? What tone does the writer use with his audience?

Respond To This Reading

1. More than a century after Washington delivered the "Atlanta Compromise Address," many literary critics and historians offer harsh criticism of the speaker's willingness to accommodate the concerns of white businessmen at the expense, in the view of some of these critics, of the progress of African-Americans. For example, some identify statements in the address such as "It is at the bottom of life we must begin, and not at the top" as examples of this kind of accommodation. Given the time in which Washington delivered this address, in your view are these critics justified in their commentaries?

2. Some critics of American culture theorize that today we are closer to a colorblind society—that is, that one's color, race, and ethnicity are no longer barriers to opportunity and advancement. What issues in the field of American race relations matter to you? What issue would move you to forge an argument in response?

PART SIX

MLA and APA Documentation Systems

APPENDIX A MLA Documentation and the List of Works Cited

APPENDIX B APA Documentation and the Reference List

MLA Documentation and the List of Works Cited

One of the most important (and possibly tedious) aspects of writing research reports of any type is the documentation. You must supply publication information for every source you use in your writing. This information must appear in a standardized format or style sheet dictated by your company or instructor.

- In the humanities (including fine arts and literature), the most common format is MLA style—that of the Modern Language Association.
- Fields such as sociology, anthropology, education, psychology, and business often require writers to document sources in APA style—that of the American Psychological Association.
- The Council of Science Editors' manual (CSE) is used for the natural sciences, such as biology and geology.

All of these style sheets are similar in *what* information you should provide for a source, but vary in *how* that information is presented. For example, see how a book is cited for MLA, APA, and CSE side by side:

MLA	APA	CSE
Willoquet-Maricondi, Paula. *Framing the World: Explorations in Ecocriticism and Film*. Charlottesville: U of Virginia P, 2010. Print.	Willoquet-Maricondi, P. (2010). *Framing the world: Explorations in ecocriticism and film*. Charlottesville, VA: University of Virginia Press.	1. Willoquet-Maricondi P. Framing the world: explorations in ecocriticism and film. Charlottesville: University of Virginia Press; 2010. 480 p.

The complete guides to MLA and APA can be found on the Internet at a variety of sources. The most reliable source for either style manual is The Online Writing Lab at Purdue University:

(MLA) http://owl.english.purdue.edu/owl/section/2/11/
(APA) http://owl.english.purdue.edu/owl/resource/560/01/

MLA Information

Title Page

A paper using MLA format does not need a separate title page. A header with your last name and the page number, flush right, should appear on each page, including the first. Also on the first page of the essay, your name, the instructor's name, the course number, and the date should be typed flush left, double-spaced, in the upper left corner. The title should be centered horizontally on the page. See the Annotated MLA Research Paper at the end of this chapter for details.

In-Text Citation

Whether you quote, paraphrase, or use someone else's ideas in your essay, you have to do two things: (1) acknowledge within your essay that the material comes from a source and (2) include that source on your works cited page.

There are many ways to cite sources within the body of an argument, a method called *parenthetical citation*. Passages from Hal's essay demonstrate the various ways.

> North Carolina State Senator Austin Allran believes that the government would save millions of dollars now currently lost to state and federal employees playing Solitaire on their office computers if the games were removed from employees' computers (Johnsson).

In this passage, Hal refers to Senator Allran's beliefs about the wastefulness of employees playing computer games. Because that material was found in Patrik Johnsson's article, Hal has to let the reader know that. In this example, he introduces the statement about Allran and then includes the name Johnsson in what is called a *parenthetical citation*. In parenthesis, before the period, is included the author's name as it appears on the works cited page: (Johnsson). If there had been a page number to include as with PDF copies or print copies of books and articles, that number would be included after the author's name, for example (Smith 23).

> Patrik Johnsson notes that the suggested removal of games like Solitaire from worker's computers "goes straight to the issue of distractions from long days at the office and, more fundamentally, how much of their employees' time and concentration employers can reasonably expect to own."

If the author of the source is already included in the sentence, then there is no need to include his name again in a parenthetical. In this example, the quote is introduced with the inclusion of Patrik Johnsson's name. Johnsson is the author so Hal did not need to include his name in the citation. As above, if there were a page number to include, that page number alone would appear in the parenthetical citation (23).

The information in the citation should always appear in the same way it does on the works cited page. Sources with no designated authors can be a bit more challenging.

Here are two samples drawn from a web page. In the first, the web page where the information was found is mentioned in the sentence. There is no need for a parenthetical citation.

> In a recent article, "Workplace Privacy," is listed the most frequent types of workplace monitoring, which include phone monitoring and video surveillance.

In sample two, the web page is not mentioned so a parenthetical is necessary. Remember that the information in the citation should appear as it does on the works cited page. In this example, there is no author so the source begins with the title of the web page—that title is what should be found in the citation. Website URLs are never included in the citation.

> Two of the most frequent types of workplace monitoring include phone monitoring and video surveillance ("Workplace Privacy").

"Workplace Privacy." *EPIC*. Electronic Privacy Information Center, 25 July 2006. Web. 21 May 2013.

General Tips for Writing Works-Cited Pages

A list of **works cited** includes all the sources you have used in your researched essay, the sources from which you have actually cited. If you consulted a source, but didn't cite from it, the source does not belong on your works-cited page.

- Alphabetize sources by authors' last names. If a source does not have a named author, alphabetize by the first word of the title that follows "The" or "A." Do not replace the author's name with the word *anonymous*.
- If there are two or three authors, reverse the first author's name for alphabetizing purposes, but leave the other name(s) in normal order.
  - Davis, John, and Troy Simpson.
- If there are more than three authors, list the first name and add et al., which means "and others."
  - Jamieson, Sandra, et al.
- Titles of articles, essays in books, songs, television episodes, short poems, and short stories are in quotation marks: "Title."
- Titles of magazines or journals, books, CDs, movies, works of art, television shows, long poems, plays, and novels are italicized: *Title*.
- MLA no longer requires the inclusion of URLs. If your instructor wishes you to include URLs, enclose them in angle brackets < > and end with a period.
- If no page numbers are included in the publication information, use n. pag.

Formatting Issues

It is tempting to use online citation machines to format your works cited for you. Is this such a good idea? Yes and No.

Citation Machines and Database Citations: To Use or Not to Use

There are several websites that can help you in creating citations, such as Son of Citation Machine http://citationmachine.net/index2.php and EasyBib http://www.easybib.com/. Students use these with some success. In our experience they are time-consuming and you must still tinker with format. For example, after filling in the provided form at a citation machine site, a formatted citation is returned, but if the citation is longer than two lines, it will still need to be put in hanging indent in your document, and you will also need to change the underlining to italics. Fairly clumsy. The sites also do not have the ability to provide citations for all types of sources, particularly the more complex ones.

Using the Hanging Indent Function

It can be time-consuming, and sometimes frustrating, to individually format each of your entries in your works cited. It is better to format the page once. Follow these instructions to use a hanging indent, which is required by the MLA and makes it easier for readers to see the break between each entry. Your entries will look like this:

Miller, G. Tyler, and Scott Spoolman. *Environmental Science*. 14th ed. Boston: Cengage, 2012. Print.

MLA Documentation: Books

Remember that you find the publication information for a book on its copyright page. The publication information should appear in this order in your citation, and you should use the punctuation as shown:

Single Author

Author's Last Name, First Name. *Title*. City: Publisher, Publication Date. Medium. (Medium, either Print or Web, refers to whether the book is in print or electronic format)

Wilber, Tom. *Under the Surface: Fracking, Fortunes, and the Fate of the Marcellus Shale*. Ithaca: Cornell UP, 2012. Print.

By Two or More Authors

Deffeyes, Kenneth S. and Stephen E. Deffeyes. Nanoscale: Visualizing an Invisible World. Cambridge: MIT Press, 2009. Print.

Two or More Books by the Same Author

Arrange in alphabetical order by title of sources.

Deffeyes, Kenneth S. *Hubbert's Peak: The Impending World Oil Shortage*. Princeton: Princeton UP, 2009. Print
---. When Oil Peaked. New York: Hill and Wang, 2010. Print.

Book by a Corporate Author

Corporate authors include groups of individuals, such as those of an agency or a committee.

Lifetime Learning, Inc. *Learning Principles of the Lifetime Library*. Minneapolis: Lifetime Learning. 2006. Print.

Book with No Author

Some books may not have authors. Alphabetize these by title. The following example would be alphabetized under "E" for Epic, not "A" for anonymous or "T" for The. "Trans." indicates a translator.

The Epic of Gilgamesh. Trans. Stephen Mitchell. New York: Simon, 2006. Print.

A Translation

Citations for books originally published in another language and translated into English should include both the author's name and the translator.

Eco, Umberto. *Inventing the New*. Trans. Richard Dixon. Boston: Houghton Mifflin, 2012. Print.

Republished Book

Older books, such as classic works of literature, philosophy, or history, are often reprinted without changes. Include the original publication date along with the copyright date for the current publication.

Austen, Jane. *Pride and Prejudice*. 1813. Cambridge: Worth, 2006. Print.

An Edition of a Book

Books of essays or articles often have an editor. An editor is the person who compiled the book. There are also editions of a book, which means that a subsequent release of the book may have new material. It is important to include all of this information so that your reader can find the correct source you used.

A Subsequent Edition

A book that has been revised or updated is called a *subsequent edition*. It is important to let your reader know which edition of a book you are citing as the material and page numbers will be different. Cite the book as you normally would, but add the number of the edition after the title.

Nelson, Vaughn. *Wind Energy: Renewable Energy and the Environment.* 2nd ed. Boca Raton: CRC, 2013. Print.

Editions may also appear as "Rev. ed.," which means "revised edition."

The Bhagavad Gita. Trans. Juan Mascaró. Ed. Simon Brodbeck. Rev. ed. New York: Penguin, 2003. Print.

A Work Prepared by an Editor

An edition of a book, particularly one that no longer is under copyright protection, is often compiled with notes by an editor. Cite the book as you normally would, but add the editor after the title.

Radcliffe, Ann. *The Mysteries of Udolpho.* Ed. Bonamy Dobrée. Oxford: Oxford UP, 1980. Print.

An Anthology

An anthology is a collection of works, either of one individual or of many different individuals. An editor compiles the works and often adds notes or an introduction. The abbreviation ed. indicates that the name listed is an editor, not an author.

McKibben, Bill, ed. *The Global Warming Reader: A Century of Writing.* New York: Penguin, 2012. Print.

A Work in an Anthology

If you are citing a work included in an anthology, list the work and its author first in the citation and then the anthology information.

Essay Author's Last Name, First Name. "Title of Essay." *Title of Anthology.* Editor(s) of the anthology. City: Publisher, Publication Date. Medium.

Keeling, Dave. "The Keeling Curve." *The Global Warming Reader: A Century of Writing.* Ed. Bill McKibben. New York: Penguin, 2012. 45–46. Print.

If you are citing several works from one anthology, it is not necessary to include all of the publication information each time. If you include complete information for the full anthology (the McKibben entry in the example below), you can refer readers to that entry rather than repeat the information. For the two essays below (Keeling and Oreskes), only the author's name, the title of the essay, the editor's last name, and the page numbers are included.

Keeling, Anne. "The Keeling Curve." McKibben 45–46.
McKibben, Bill, ed. *The Global Warming Reader: A Century of Writing.* New York: Penguin, 2012. Print.
Oreskes, Naomi. "The Scientific Consensus on Climate Change." McKibben 75–80.

A Book Available Online (An Etext)

Many books are available to be read online, either through a library service or through sites such as Project Gutenberg.

Author's Last Name, First Name. *Title.* Original Publication date if older. *Source of Access to the Book.* Web. Date you accessed the book.

Muir, John. *Travels in Alaska.* 1915. *Project Gutenberg.* Web. 27 Apr. 2013.

A Multivolume Work

Some books are published in volumes. The volumes can be individually titled or differentiated only by the volume number. In the first example below, the citation is referring to the entire five volume set. The second example refers to only one volume of the set.

Pausanias. *Description of Greece.* Trans. W. H. S. Jones. 5 vols. Cambridge: Loeb-Harvard UP, 1918. Print.
Pausanias. *Description of Greece.* Trans. W. H. S. Jones. vol. 1. Cambridge: Loeb-Harvard UP, 1918. Print.

If the volume you are using has its own title, cite the book without referring to the other volumes as if it were an independent publication. In the following example, only one volume of Campbell's 4-volume set of books entitled *The Masks of God* is being cited. Each of the four volumes has its own title.

Campbell, Joseph. *Creative Mythology.* New York: Penguin, 1968. Print.

A Book in a Series

A book title that is part of a series should include the series information as well.

Author's Last Name, First Name. *Title.* City: Publisher, Publication Date. Medium. Title of Series Volume Number if applicable.

Sanders, Ronald L. *The Ethics of Species.* Cambridge: Cambridge UP, 2012. Print. Cambridge Applied Ethics.

An Introduction, a Preface, a Foreword, or an Afterword

Dawkins, Richard. Introduction. *The Origins of Species* and the *Voyage of the Beagle.* By Charles Darwin. New York: Knopf, 2003. ix–xxx. Print.

Poems or Short Stories

Poems and short stories can be found in collections of the author's work, or in anthologies of works including many other authors. The first example is a citation for Komunyakaa's poem published in a volume of the poet's work. The second example is for the same poem published in an anthology edited by others.

Komunyakaa, Yusef. "Sunday Afternoons." *Pleasure Dome: New and Collected Poems.*
    Middletown: Wesleyan UP, 2001. 227. Print.
Komunyakaa, Yusef. "Sunday Afternoons." *The Norton Anthology of African American
    Literature.* 2nd ed. Ed. Henry Louis Gates, Jr. and Nellie Y. McKay. New York:
    Norton, 2004. 2531. Print.

Sacred Texts

There are many versions of scriptural works. Provide the title of the work, the editor of that version, any translation information, and the publication information. Alphabetize by the title of the work. NOTE: Do not alphabetize using "The" or "A."

The Bhagavad Gita. Trans. Juan Mascaró. Ed. Simon Brodbeck. Rev. ed. New York:
    Penguin, 2003. Print.
The Koran. Ed. N. J. Dawood. Rev. ed. New York: Penguin, 2004. Print.
The New English Bible. Ed. Samuel Sandmel. New York: Oxford UP, 1976. Print.

Government Documents

Governments publish a wide variety of documents. These sources are covered in the Primary Sources section in Chapter 3, "Develop a Research Plan."

Documentation: Articles

Documentation gets a little trickier when articles are involved. The publication information can be found in different places and can get confusing. The information you are looking for is author, title of article, title of journal, volume number and issue, year published, page numbers. The publication information is usually at either the top or the bottom of the page.

An Article in a Scholarly Journal

If you have read an article in a print medium, then you should follow this format.

Author's Last Name, First Name. "Title of Article." *Title of Journal* Volume. Issue
    (Year): pages. Print.

Tufekci, Zeynep. "Can You See Me Now? Audience and Disclosure Regulation in
    Online Social Network Sites." *Bulletin of Science, Technology & Society* 28.1 (2008):
    20–36. Print.

Article in a Database

Most college and university libraries (and many public libraries) subscribe to databases of articles that you can read on the computer screen. More and more frequently you will access articles this way. The only difference in documentation is the addition of that database information and the date you accessed the material.

> Author's Last Name, First Name. "Title of Article." *Title of Journal* Volume. Issue (Year): pages. Title of Database. Web. Date you accessed the article.

If page numbers are unavailable, use n. pag (no pagination).

> Weinhold, Bob. "The Future Of Fracking." *Environmental Health Perspectives* 120.7 (2012): A272–A279. *Academic Search Complete*. Web. 27 Apr. 2013.

Articles Found on the Internet

Another way you can access journal articles is through the Internet. Some journal articles can be found online through sites such as Highbeam, Questia, or FindArticles.com. Note that sometimes these articles do not include original volume and issue number or page numbers. Include this information if it is available.

> McBroom, Matthew, Todd Thomas, and Yanli Zhang. "Soil Erosion and Surface Water Quality Impacts of Natural Gas Development in East Texas, USA." *Water* 4.4 (2012): 944–58. Web.

Article in a Magazine

The only difference in citations between journal articles and magazine articles is in the way that issues are dated. Journals usually have a volume and issue number; magazines generally don't, but have a weekly or monthly date instead. The first example is of a monthly magazine, the second is a weekly.

> Author's Last Name, First Name. "Title of Article." *Title of Magazine* Month Year: page numbers. Medium.

> Mooney, Chris. "The Truth about Fracking." *Scientific American* Nov. 2011: 80–85. Print.

> Royte, Elizabeth. "What The Frack Is In Our Food?" *Nation* 17 Dec. 2012: 11–18. *Academic Search Complete*. Web. 27 Apr. 2013.

If you find these articles in a database or on an Internet site, include that information in the same way you do for a journal article.

An Article in a Web Magazine

> Author's Last Name, First Name. "Title of Article." *Title of Online Publication*. Date of Publication. Web. Date of Access.

> Levy, Stephen. "Eric Schmidt and Jared Cohen on What's Next for the World." *Wired*. 26 Apr. 2013. Web. 27 Apr. 2013.

Article in a Newspaper

- Most newspapers have the title of the city as part of its name. If not, add the city name in square brackets [ ] after the title. For example, *The Times-Picayune* [New Orleans].
- Some papers also have different editions, particularly the larger ones such as *The New York Times*. Identify the edition following the date.
- Most articles in a newspaper are not continuous. An article may begin on page one, but then continue on page three. The way to indicate this is to use the +. This tells the reader that the article continues and the reader can follow the continuations by reading the "continues on page #" note at the end of the article segments.
- Also, in a print edition, refer to the section of the paper where the article can be found (A, B, 1, 2, etc.)
- If you access the article through a database, include the name of the database and the date of access.
- For documenting historical newspapers, refer to the Primary Sources section in Chapter 3, "Develop a Research Plan."

Author's Last Name, First Name. "Title of Article." *Title of Newspaper* [City, if not given in title] Date, Edition: page numbers. Medium. Date accessed (if online).

Schwartzel, Erich. "Survey: Pa. Residents Give Cautious Support for Gas Drilling." *Pittsburgh Post-Gazette* 15 May 2013: n. pag. *Newspaper Source Plus*. Web. 16 May 2013.

A Review (of a book, play, film)

To cite a review, include the abbreviation "Rev. of" plus information about the performance that is being cited before giving the periodical information, as shown in following basic format:

Review Author. "Title of Review (if there is one)." Rev. of Book, Performance, or Film Title, by Author/Director/Artist. Title of Periodical day month year: page. Medium.

Coppens, Julie York. "A Cloned Classic? Not Guilty." Rev. of *Twelve Angry Men,* dir. Allen Moyers. *Charlotte Leisure Time* 23 May 2008: 15. Print.

Editorials and Letters to the Editor

To cite a letter to the editor or an editorial, include the word editorial after the title or letter after the author.

"Time for UNC System to Fix the Problem." Editorial. *Winston-Salem Journal* 5 June 2013: A16. Print.
Kneidel, Sally. Letter. *Charlotte Observer.* Charlotte Observer, 13 May 2013. Web. 16 May 2013.

Documentation: Internet-only Sources

In general, your citation for an Internet source should look like this:

Author of Web Page. "Title of Web Page." *Title of Website*. Sponsor of Website, Date
Site was Posted. Web. Date You Accessed the Site.

Remember that if your search engine directs you to a particular *web page*, you must backtrack to determine the name of the *website* that hosts that page if that information is not on the web page. You should look for any author of the site, the web page title, the date posted if provided, and the date you accessed the site.

An Entire Website

Include the website name, the date the site was posted (or last updated), and the date you accessed the material. "n.d." means that no date is provided.

Library of Congress. Library of Congress, n.d. Web. 3 May 2013.

A Page on a Website

More frequently you will cite particular pages from a website. You should provide all the necessary information that will direct your reader to that page, including the author of the page (if known), the title of the page, the title of the website itself, and the dates the page was posted and accessed.

If the search engine directs you to a page and it is not immediately clear what website is hosting that page, you can try deleting everything after a slash in the URL and then keep shortening the URL by increments until you come to the host site.

"What Is Fracking?" *EnergyfromShale.org*. Energy from Shale. 2012. Web. 10 May
2013.

For an academic department home page:

Harvard Graduate School of Arts and Sciences. Home page. *Harvard*. Harvard U, n.d.
Web. 3 May 2013.

For a course home page:

Instructor name. "Title of Course." *Name of School*. Sponsor of site. Date of the
course. Web. Date You Accessed the Site.

Khalil, Yehia. "Introduction to Green Energy." *Yale*. Yale U, Summer 2013. Web. 10
May 2013.

E-mails

Milton, Suzanne. "Re TALTP." Message to the author. 23 May 2013.
    E-mail.

Blog and Discussion Board Postings

Some forums will only include screen names for authors. Blogs may not have authors.

Author's Last Name, First Name (if available). "Title of Web Log Entry." *Title of Website*. Organizational Sponsor if available. Date of Publication. Web. Date Accessed.

"Big Issues: Energy—How to Regulate Fracking." *WSJ Blogs: Marketbeat*. Wall Street Journal, 26 Mar. 2013. Web. 10 May 2013.

Citing Comments Posted to a Web Log

When citing a comment to a web log, include the author's name (or screen name it that is the only name available), and the designation Web Log Comment. If there is a title for the comment, use that in place of "Web Log Comment."

MCM. Web Log Comment. *WSJ Blogs: Marketbeat*. Wall Street Journal, 28 Mar. 2013. Web. 10 May 2013.

Documentation: Interviews

A Personal Interview

Listed by the name of the person you have interviewed.

Yarington, Earl. Personal Interview. 21 May 2008.

A Published Interview

Begin with the name of the person interviewed and include the name of the interviewer.

Zach Galifianakis. "A Comedic Actor Takes a Dark Turn." Interview by Terry Gross. *Fresh Air*. Natl. Public Radio. WHYY, Philadelphia. 29 Sept. 2010. Radio.

Stevens 1

Hal Stevens

Professor Daniels

BUS 321

24 May 2013

Using Work Computers for Personal Business is Not a Problem

A familiar scene plays out in offices everywhere. An employee sitting in his cubicle has just finished a project, grabbed a cup of coffee, and is taking a 15-minute break. He pulls up the Ohio State Buckeyes web site to scout next season's potential recruits. Then he plays a game or two of computer Solitaire. A quick check on his personal email account to see if the birthday present he ordered for his wife has been shipped from Sears yet. Break over, the employee returns to his next project. A week later, he is surprised and angered to be called to his supervisor's office and subjected to a reprimand. The subject? Misusing the company's computers. What employees regard as private computer use during personal time turns out to be not so private after all.

In the above scenario, the company has installed new computer surveillance software, which now monitors employees' every keystroke, visits to online sites, and emails—personal or work-related. Is this an invasion of privacy? Is it legal? The answer is a complicated "yes" and "no." Certain kinds of situations are covered by the topic of privacy, others by the legality of the surveillance performed and whether employees are notified of company monitoring policies. Mostly, though, business owners are able to monitor employee computer use at will. Although it is reasonable that companies expect their employees to use company computers for company activity, it is also understandable and desirable that employees have privacy rights at work in regards to their computer usage.

Stevens 2

France Bélanger and Robert E. Crossler, researchers in the field of information privacy and security, find that little existing research focuses on the issue of electronic privacy of personal information in the workplace. They cite a Pew Internet Project survey, however, that indicates 85% of adults find it of the utmost importance to protect their personal information (1017).

The Electronic Privacy Information Center (EPIC) is a clearinghouse that gathers information on workplace privacy. A recent article, "Workplace Privacy," lists the most frequent types of workplace monitoring:

- Phone monitoring
- Video surveillance
- ID tags that can monitor an employee's location (including GPS monitors that can track employees on the road)
- Keystroke loggers
- Email and Internet usage

In an interview I conducted with Gary Hopkins, CEO of Farm Fresh, an Organic Foods wholesale, he indicates that most of his employees do not like their work habits being subjected to monitoring, but there is little that they can do to prevent it. Hopkins says keeping workers on notice with email and Internet monitoring has increased productivity 22% in the last year alone.

Currently there are few laws that cover the ever-changing technology of electronic communications, as Nancy Flynn, author of the *e-Policy Handbook*, explains:

> In the United States and many third-world countries, workers have very few privacy protections in law. There are few situations where an employee has a due process right to access, inspect, or challenge information collected or held by the employer. There are a patchwork of state and federal laws that

This paragraph gives background material on the subject of electronic monitoring practices. Some background is usually needed to explain the situation that has led to the controversy about an issue.

Introduction of a long quote that is set off 10 spaces from the margin. If the author had not been introduced before the quotation (as is the case here), the citation would appear at the end of the quote, AFTER the period.

Complete Annotated MLA Research Paper

grant employees limited rights. For instance, under federal law, private-sector employees cannot be required to submit to a polygraph examination. However, there are no general protections of workplace privacy except where an employer acts tortuously—where the employer violates the employee's reasonable expectation of privacy.

One law that would seem to be on the side of employees' privacy is the 1986 United States Electronic Privacy Act (ECPA), which "prohibits reading or disclosure of the contents of any electronic communication not intended for the reader" (Teel 6). One important exemption from this act, however, is an employer who owns a company's email system. Several court cases have also sided with employers.

Lothar Determann and Robert Sprague's article comparing advances in European workplace privacy with the lacks in American privacy, points out that in the United States, people have a constitutional expectation of privacy in general, but a low expectation of privacy in the workplace (1022).

Determann and Sprague also explain that employer monitoring has been able to extend its scope to scan emails for viruses and spam and other links that may be harmful to the employees' computers in particular, but to the company network in general. In scanning for harmful activity, workers' log-ons, emails, screen activity, web site visits, among other types of information can be accessed (982). Uncomfortable for employees, though, are the monitoring possibilities that extend beyond company security to track Internet access, electronic chats and online sessions, and remote viewing that may not be work-related. Another concern is that with GPS and wireless features, employees who work from home can be monitored as well (982).

Stevens 4

For example, in *Smyth vs. The Pillsbury Company* (1994), Michael Smyth was fired from his job for sending "inappropriate and unprofessional" comments from his home computer using Pillsbury's email system. The comments to his supervisor "contained threats to 'kill the backstabbing bastards' and referred to the planned Holiday party as the 'Jim Jones Koolaid affair.'" Smyth argued that he had a "reasonable expectation of privacy" in sending emails, regardless of content, because Pillsbury's policies on emails was that they would not be monitored or read. The Pennsylvania District Court ruled in favor of the employer saying, "the company's interest in preventing inappropriate and unprofessional comments or even illegal activity over its e-mail system outweighs any privacy interest the employee may have in those comments."

In addition to problems associated with sending email, there are also concerns about employees spending their work time surfing the Internet or playing computer games. North Carolina State Senator Austin Allran, for example, believes that the government would save millions of dollars now currently lost to state and federal employees playing Solitaire on their office computers if the games were removed from employees' computers (Johnsson).

New York City mayor Michael Bloomberg even fired an employee when he saw an in-progress game on the employee's computer. The employee admitted to occasionally playing a game to take a break from exhausting work, but Bloomberg believes that no time should be spent playing computer games during work time ("Employee Monitoring"). Patrik Johnsson notes that the suggested removal of games like Solitaire from worker's computers "goes straight to the issue of distractions from long days at the office and, more fundamentally, how much of their employees' time and concentration employers can reasonably expect to own."

This example is long enough that it warrants its own paragraph. Resist the temptation to cram as much as you can in one paragraph just because it is all on the same topic.

A topic sentence introducing support.

Complete Annotated MLA Research Paper

Stevens 5

Some proponents of leaving the games on workers' computers argue that they actually increase employee productivity by providing an outlet for stress relief ("Employee Monitoring"). So although many employees who spend a lot of time staring at computer screens feel that taking a break with a computer game rejuvenates them, employers see the time spent "rejuvenating" as wasteful.

Another topic sentence introducing support. Notice that the items of support seem to be presented in increasingly important order.

But a far more serious problem is employees using the company's Internet connection to access inappropriate web sites. Some employees will visit sites at work that they may not want those they live with to know about, for example pornographic sites, or ones that deal with alternative lifestyles, violence, or drugs.

A total of 304 companies participated in the 2007 Electronic Monitoring and Surveillance Survey sponsored by both the American Management Association and the ePolicy Institute. Here are the results of several of the questions about company Internet usage:

- 83% of the respondents said that their organization has a written policy governing the personal use of the Internet.
- 16% of employers record phone conversations; 84% notify employees that their phone conversations are monitored, but only 73% notify employees that their voicemails are also monitored.
- 65% of companies use software to block inappropriate sites (social networking, pornographic, and entertainments sites top the list).

The survey also indicates that although companies have policies regarding electronic privacy, employees rarely read or otherwise pay attention to the policies.

Stevens 6

Most employees would likely agree that visiting certain sites or spending a *significant* amount of time surfing the Internet for non job-related information canbe a problem. But what about smaller increments of time that might act as productive breaks? If any email system provided by an employer is subject to monitoring, how much privacy are employees really allowed at work?

Employers assert that they have a right to know what their employees are doing on company time, particularly with company computers and email systems. Companies worry about loss of productivity. Nancy Flynn notes that employer termination for email and web misuse is increasing: employer terminations for email violations, ranging from violation of company policies and excessive personal use, rose from 14% in 2001 to 28% in 2007 (182). But for employees who spend enormous numbers of hours at work, using email is one of the best ways to take care of personal business that cannot be done after work, such as making doctors' appointments.

Companies also worry about employees giving competitors access to trade secrets and about charges of allowing a hostile work environment if harassing emails are sent from an office computer (Dell and Kullen). Courts mostly side with companies, although occasionally a defendant wins. In *United States vs. Slanina*, the Fifth Circuit Court of Appeals found that because the company by whom Slanina was employed did not have a posted policy about computer usage or Internet monitoring, he "had a reasonable expectation of privacy in his office computer" (Cassily and Draper).

It is the issue of reasonable expectations of privacy which poses the largest stumbling block for a solution to workplace privacy issues. What seems

An item of qualification. Employees do realize that surfing while working can be a waste of time, but they may question the need for oversight of all activity.

Items of opposition. What are some opposing views? How can they be addressed?

Complete Annotated MLA Research Paper

Stevens 7

reasonable to a boss may not seem reasonable to employees. In 1993, Congress passed the Privacy for Consumers and Workers Act. This piece of legislation doesn't ban electronic monitoring, but states that employees must be given notice that they are subject to monitoring in the workplace (Rich). But how does this work for telecommuting employees? Some of the privacy issues that have not been resolved in the area of monitoring employees who work from home are

- the difficulty of the employer to monitor an employee's work at home without crossing over into the employee's private life,
- the inability to determine when an employee is on "duty,"
- and the inability to differentiate between an employee using the computer and another family member. ("Workplace Privacy")

As technology advances, new issues involving the rights of employees to maintain privacy of their electronic lives (email, Internet usage, etc.) will become more tangled. How far can an employer go in scrutinizing their employee's emails? Addressing employees' reasonable expectations of privacy and notifying them of workplace policies are practices already in place for many businesses, but there is no law forcing private businesses to follow these guidelines. The Fourth Amendment guarantees the right of citizens to be safe from unreasonable searches of their "persons, houses, papers and effects" by the government. However, the Internet was not even a faint glimmer of possibility in 18th century America. Should we add an amendment to the Bill of Rights covering electronic privacy? Maybe that is coming.

Hal's conclusion rounds out the discussion, adding interesting material for the reader to think about without offering new items of support or changes of direction.

Stevens 8

Works Cited

American Management Association. "2007 Electronic Monitoring
& Surveillance Survey: Many Companies Monitoring, Recording,
Videotaping—and Firing—Employees." *AMA*. American
Management Association, 2008. Web. 21 May 2013.

Bélanger, France, and Robert E. Crossler. "Privacy in The Digital
Age: A Review of Information Privacy Research in Information
Systems." *MIS Quarterly* 35.4 (2011): 1017-A36. *Business Source
Premier*. Web. 21 May 2013.

Casilly, Lisa H., and Clare H. Draper. *Workplace Privacy: A Guide for
Attorneys and HR Professionals*. Boston: Pike and Fischer, 2004.
Print.

Dell, Kristina, and Lisa Takeuchi Kullen. "Snooping Bosses." *Time*
11 Sept. 2006: 62–64. *EBSCOhost*. Web. 21 May 2013.

Determann, Lothar, and Robert Sprague. "Intrusive Monitoring:
Employee Privacy Expectations Are Reasonable in Europe,
Destroyed in the United States." *Berkeley Technology Law Journal*
26 (2011): 979–1036. Web. 21 May 2013.

"Employee Monitoring: Is There Privacy in the Workplace?" *Privacy
Rights Clearinghouse*. Privacy Rights Clearinghouse, Feb. 2006.
Web. 21 May 2013.

Flynn, Nancy. *e-Policy Handbook*. 2nd ed. New York: AMACOM,
2009.

Hopkins, Gary. Personal Interview. 13 May 2013.

Johnsson, Patrik. "Is That a Spreadsheet on Your Screen or
Solitaire?" *CSMonitor.com*. The Christian Science Monitor, 18
Mar. 2005. Web. 30 Mar., 2013.

Rich, Lloyd L. "Right to Privacy in the Information Age." *Publishing
Law Center*. Publishing Law Center,1995. Web. 21 May 2013.

Complete Annotated MLA Research Paper

Stevens 9

"Smyth vs. The Pillsbury Company (1994)." *Privacy in Cyberspace*.
Harvard Law School, n.d. Web. 30 May 2013.

Teel, Linda M. "Confidentiality and Electronic Mail: Issue of
Privacy." *Delta Kappa Gamma Bulletin* 72.4 (2006): 5-8.
EBSCOhost. Web. 21 May 2013.

"Workplace Privacy." *EPIC*. Electronic Privacy Information Center,
25 July 2006. Web. 21 May 2013.

APPENDIX B

APA Documentation and the Reference List

APA Title Page and Abstract

Title Page

A paper written in APA format should have a separate title page. This title page should have the title of the paper, the author's name, and the school's name. A header, with the text flush to the left and typed in all caps, should be included which will look like this:

Running Head: SHORTENED TITLE OF THE PAPER

On all of the remaining pages of the paper, a running head should be typed as:

SHORTENED TITLE OF YOUR PAPER

Your title should be typed, double spaced, in regular title format and centered in the upper half of the title page. Titles should be no more than 12 words long and may take two lines if necessary.

Below the title should appear your name and then below that the school.

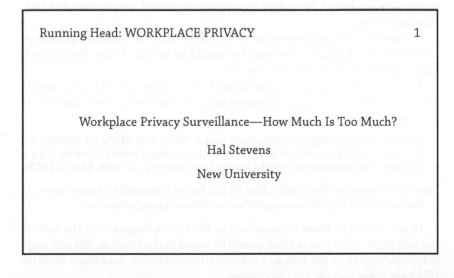

Running Head: WORKPLACE PRIVACY   1

Workplace Privacy Surveillance—How Much Is Too Much?

Hal Stevens

New University

Abstract

The abstract, a summary of your paper, should highlight the key points of your argument. If you are required to supply an abstract, it should be typed on its own page and follow the title page. Your abstract should be no more than one double-spaced paragraph, between 150 and 250 words. The word *abstract* (not in italics) should be typed and centered at the top of the page.

In-Text Documentation

Whether you quote, paraphrase, or use someone else's ideas in your essay, you have to do two things: (1) acknowledge within your essay that the material comes from a source and (2) include that source on your References page.

There are many ways to cite sources within the body of an argument. We will use passages reproduced in this chapter, from an essay by Sabine Ford, to demonstrate the various ways.

> Howarth and Ingraffea (2011) frighten readers by citing the toxicity of fracking fluid additives, many of which are carcinogens, and which are not only secret, but exempt from the Safe Drinking Water Act.

In this passage, Sabine introduces source material from an article written by Howarth and Ingraffea and includes the authors' names as she does so. After their names, she places the year the referenced article was published (2011). Since their names are mentioned in the text, she does not need to include a parenthetical citation.

> Certainly there is a concern that the enormous quantity of water used during fracking poses a risk to water supplies in drought-prone areas like the Eagle Ford Shale in Texas (Allen, 2013).

In this second example, the author's name is not mentioned in the text, so Sabine has to include a citation with the author's name and the year the source was published. Note that the sentence's period comes after the citation, not before.

If there had been a page number to include as with PDF copies or print copies of books and articles, that number would be included after the author's name, for example: (Smith, 2013, p. 23).

The information in the citation should always appear in the same way it does on the References page. Sources with no designated authors can be a bit more challenging.

> With oil prices largely unchanged since 2011, and likely to remain so through 2015, and natural gas prices at their lowest levels in more than a decade, the future looks bright (Short-term energy outlook, May 7, 2013).

Short-term energy outlook. (2013, May 7). *U.S. Energy Information Administration.* Retrieved from http://www.eia.gov/forecasts/steo/report/prices.cfm

In this example, there is no author so the source begins with the title of the web page—that title is what should be found in the citation. The web page is not mentioned in the text so a parenthetical citation is necessary. Website URLs are never included in the citation.

Tips for Writing a Reference List

A **Reference List** is a list of all the sources you have used in your researched essay, the sources from which you have actually cited. If you consulted a source, but didn't cite from it, the source does not belong on your reference list.

- To type your reference list, turn on your hanging indent feature so that all sources will be indented properly without having to use the tab/indent function. Go to Format, Paragraph, and select Indent, hanging.
- Alphabetize sources by authors' last names. If a source does not have a named author, alphabetize by the first word of the article that follows "The" or "A."
- Titles of magazine or journals, books, CDs, movies, works of art, television shows, long poems, plays, and novels are italicized: *Title.*
- Titles of articles, essays in books, songs, television episodes, short poems, and short stories are neither italicized nor in quotation marks.
- For authors' names, include last names and initials. Regardless of the number of authors, reverse all authors' names.
  - Davis, J., & Simpson, T.
- If there are seven or fewer authors, list all names.
- If there are eight or more authors, list the first six names, and three ellipsis points, and add the final name.
  - Davis, J., Collins, P., Gray, L., Clements, H., Simpson, T., Bosch, H., . . . Hunter, B.

APA Documentation: Books

Remember that you find the publication information for a book on its copyright page. Follow the models below for the proper order and marks of punctuation.

Single Author

Author's Last Name, First Initial. (Publication Year). *Title.* City, State: Publisher.

NOTE: In the title, the first word of the title and the first word after any colon should be capitalized, as should any proper nouns.

Wilber, T. (2012). *Under the surface: Fracking, fortunes, and the fate of the Marcellus Shale.* Ithaca, NY: Cornell University Press.

By Two to Seven Authors

List all authors' names, up to seven.

Deffeyes, K., & Deffeyes, S. E. (2009). *Nanoscale: Visualizing an invisible world.* Cambridge, MA: MIT Press.

NOTE: The ampersand (&) is used instead of the word "and." Both authors' names are kept in reverse order.

More than Seven Authors

Scientific articles often are written by a team of contributors, sometimes more than seven. In these instances, you should list the first six authors as above. Replace the remaining authors (up to the last one) with ellipses (. . .). Then list the final author.

Zou, M-Q., Zhang, X-F., Qi, X-H., Ma, H-L., Dong, Y., Liu, C-W., . . . & Wang, H. (2009). Rapid authentication of olive oil adulteration by Raman Spectrometry. *J. Agric. Food Chem.*, 57(14), 6001–6006. doi.: 10.1021/jf900217s

Two or More Books by the Same Author

Include the author's name in each entry and arrange by publication date (earliest to latest).

Deffeyes, K. S. (2009). *Hubbert's Peak: The impending world oil shortage*. Princeton, NJ: Princeton University Press.
Deffeyes, K. S. (2010). *When oil peaked*. New York, NY: Hill and Wang.

Book by a Corporate Author

Corporate authors include groups of individuals, such as those of an agency or a committee. If the publisher is the same as the author, use "Author" in the publisher position.

Lifetime Learning, Inc. (2003). *Learning principles of the Lifetime Library*. Minneapolis, MN: Author.

Book with No Author

Some books may not have authors. Alphabetize these by title. The following example would be alphabetized under "E" for Epic, not "A" for anonymous nor "T" for The.

The Epic of Gilgamesh. (2006). (S. Mitchell, Trans.). New York, NY: Simon and Schuster.

A Translation

Citations for books originally published in another language and translated into English should include both the author's name and that of the translator.

Eco, Umberto. (2012*). Inventing the new*. (R. Dixon, Trans.). Boston, MA: Houghton Mifflin.

Republished Book

Older books, such as classic works of literature, philosophy, or history, are often reprinted without changes. Include the original publication date along with the copyright date for the current publication.

Austen, J. (2006). *Pride and Prejudice*. Cambridge, UK: Worth Press. (Original work published 1813)

An Edition of a Book

Books of essays or articles often have an editor. An editor is the person who compiled the book. There are also editions of a book, which means that a subsequent release of the book may have new material. It is important to include all of this information so that your reader can find the correct source you used.

A Subsequent Edition

A book that has been revised or updated is called a *subsequent edition*. It is important to let your reader know which edition of a book you are citing as the material and page numbers will be different. Cite the book as you normally would, but add the number of the edition after the title.

Nelson, V. (2013). *Wind energy: Renewable energy and the environment*. (2nd ed.). Boca Raton, FL: CRC Press.

Editions may also appear as "Rev. ed.," which means "revised edition."

A Work Prepared by an Editor

An edition of a book, particularly one that no longer is under copyright protection, is often compiled with notes by an editor. Cite the book as you normally would, but add the editor after the title.

Radcliffe, A. (1980). *The mysteries of Udolpho*. B. Dobrée (Ed.). Oxford, England: Oxford University Press. (Original work published in 1794).

An Anthology

An anthology is a collection of works, either of one individual or of many different individuals. An editor compiles the works and often adds notes or an introduction. The abbreviation Ed. indicates that the name listed is an editor, not author.

McKibben, B. (Ed.). (2012). *The global warming reader: A century of writing*. New York, NY: Penguin.

A Work in an Anthology or Edited Book

If you are citing a work included in an anthology, list the work and its author first in the citation and then the anthology information.

Author's Last Name, First Initial. (Publication year). Title of essay. In Editor(s) of the anthology, *Title of anthology* (page numbers). City, State: Publisher.

Keeling, D. (2012). The Keeling Curve. In B. McKibben (Ed.), *The global warming reader: A century of writing* (pp. 45–46). New York, NY: Penguin.

A Book Available Online (An E-text)

Many books are available to be read online, either through a library service or through sites such as Project Gutenberg (<http://www.gutenberg.org>). If a DOI is assigned, use it in place of the URL. (See p. 648 for information on using a DOI.)

Author's Last Name, First Initial. (Original Publication Date). *Title*. Retrieved from URL.

Muir, J. (1915). *Travels in Alaska*. Retrieved from http://www.gutenberg.org/
　　ebooks/7345

A Multivolume Work

Some books are published in volumes. The volumes can be individually titled
or differentiated only by the volume number. In the first example below, the
citation is referring to the entire five-volume set. The second example refers
to only one volume of the set.

Pausanias. (1918). *Description of Greece*. (W. H. S. Jones, Trans.). (Vols. 1–5).
　　Cambridge, MA: Loeb-Harvard University Press.
Pausanias. (1918). *Description of Greece* (Vol. I.). (W. H. S. Jones, Trans.). (Vols. 1–5).
　　Cambridge, MA: Loeb-Harvard University Press.

A Book in a Series

A book title that is part of a series should include the series information as well.

Landon, B. (1997). *Science fiction after 1900: From the steam man to the stars*. In
　　studies in literary themes and genres: Vol. 12. New York, NY: Twayne.

An Introduction, a Preface, a Foreword, or an Afterword

Dawkins, R. (2003). Introduction. In C. Darwin, *The origins of species* and the *Voyage
　　of the Beagle* (pp. ix–xxx). New York, NY: Knopf. (Original work published 1859).

Sacred Texts

References to the sacred texts are cited in-text only, as their sections are usually standardized across editions. In the parenthetical citation, identify the
title, version, and section.

Documentation: Articles

Documentation gets a little trickier when articles are involved. In Chapter 3,
"Develop a Research Plan," you learned how to find articles in computer databases, and what publication information you need to cite articles properly.
The publication information can be found in different places and can get confusing. The information you are looking for is author, title of article, title of
journal, volume number and issue, year published, page numbers. The publication information is usually at either the top of the bottom of the article.

An Article in a Scholarly Journal

Journals can be paginated one of two ways. (1) They can be paginated continuously. If, for example, there are four issues of a journal a year, the first
issue maybe begin with page 1 and end on page 200. Issue two then would
begin with page 201 and continue to page 400. (2) Journals can be paginated
by issue. Each issue will begin with page one.

　　Particularly for journal articles, it's important to note that the APA recommends including something called a DOI (Digital Object Identifier) when
available. A DOI is a publisher-assigned string of numbers that identifies an
article. It provides a more stable way of identifying an article than a URL does
and can be used for print and online sources. DOIs are generally located on

the first page of a journal with the copyright information or in the database overview page for an article.

Continuous Pagination:

Author(s). (Publication Year). Title of article. *Title of Journal, Volume number,* Page numbers.

Allen, T. A. (2013). The south Texas drought and the future of groundwater use for hydraulic fracturing in the Eagle Ford Shale. *St. Mary's Law Journal, 44,* 487–527.

Pagination by Issue:

Author(s). (Publication Year). Title of article. *Title of Journal, Volume number* (issue number), Page numbers.

Glassman, J. K. (2013). Betting on the gas boom. *Kiplinger's Personal Finance, 67*(6), 20–22.

NOTE: The italics of the journal title extends to the volume number, but not the issue and page numbers.

Journal Article Found on the Internet or on a Database

Another way you can access journal articles is through the Internet. Some journal articles can be found online through sites such as Highbeam, Questia, or FindArticles.com. If no DOI is included, include the URL. You do not need to include the name of the database.

McBroom, M., Thomas, T., & Zhang, Y. (2012). Soil erosion and surface water quality impacts of natural gas development in east Texas, USA. *Water, 4,* 944–958. doi:10.3390/w4040944

Howarth, R. W., Ingraffea, A., & Engelder. (2011, September 15). Natural gas: Should fracking stop? *Nature 477,* 271–275. Retrieved from http://www.nature.com/nature/journal/v477/n7364/abs/477271a.html

Article in a Magazine

Author's Last Name, First Initial. (Date including month and day, if available). Title of article. *Title of Magazine, Volume*(issue), Page numbers.

Mooney, C. (2011, November). The truth about fracking. *Scientific American 305*(5), 80–85.

Magazine Article Found on the Internet

Royte, E. (2012, December 17). What the frack is in our food? *Nation 295*(25). Retrieved from http://www.thenation.com

Article in a Newspaper

Some general tips to follow for citing newspapers are

- Alphabetize articles with no author by first word of title, excluding A or The.
- You must use p. or pp. for page numbers in citing newspapers. For a single page, use p., for example, p. B2.

- If an article appears on discontinuous pages, list all appearances, for example, pp. B2, B4 or pp. C1, C3–C4.
- Refer to the section of the paper where the article can be found (A, B, 1, 2, etc.).

Author's Last Name, First Initial. (Date, including Month and Day). Title of article. *Title of Newspaper*, page numbers.

Murawski, J. (2013, 17 May). Wake Co. nuclear plant shut down. *Charlotte Observer*, pp. B1, B3.

Newspaper Article Found on the Internet

NC fracking rule pulled as Halliburton objects. (2013, May 3). *Winston-Salem Journal*. Retrieved from http://www.journalnow.com

A Review (of a book, play, film)

To cite a review, include the abbreviation "Rev. of" plus information about the performance that is being cited before giving the periodical information, as shown in following basic format:

A Review That Includes Its Own Title:

Coppens, J. Y. (2008, May 23). A cloned classic? Not guilty. [Review of the play *Twelve angry men*, Dir. A. Moyers]. *Charlotte Leisure Time*, 15.

An Untitled Review:

Buchanan, M. S. (2013). [Rev. of the book *Ecology and the environment: The mechanisms, marring, and maintenance of nature*, by R. J. Berry]. *Science & Christian Belief, 25*(1), 89–91.

Editorials and Letters to the Editor

To cite a letter to the editor or an editorial, include the words *editorial* or *letter to the editor* after the title.

Kneidel, S. (2013, May 16). Duke Energy could take lead on CO2, but doesn't plan to [Letter to the editor]. *Charlotte Observer*. Retrieved from http://www.charlotteobserver.com

A Government Publication

Cite the author of the publication if the author is identified. Otherwise start with the name of the government agency and any subdivision that served as the corporate author. For congressional documents, be sure to include the number of the congress and the session when the hearing was held or resolution passed. (GPO is the abbr. for the Government Printing Office.)

Brantley, S. R., McGimsey, R. G., & Neal, Christina A. (2009). *The Alaska Volcano Observatory: Expanded monitoring of volcanoes yields results* (U.S. Geological Survey Fact Sheet 2004–3084, v. 1.1). Retrieved from http://pubs.usgs.gov/fs/2004/3084/

United States. Cong. Senate. (2007). *Notification to enter into a free trade agreement with the Republic of Korea.* 110th Cong. 1st sess. Washington, DC: Government Printing Office.

A Pamphlet or Brochure

University of Wisconsin, Eau Claire. (2007). *College alcohol inventory* [Brochure]. Eau Claire, WI.

Dissertations

Dissertations and master's theses may be used as sources whether published or not.

Chen, S. (2000). *Mothers and daughters in Morrison, Tan, Marshall, and Kincaid.* (Doctoral dissertation). *Dissertation Abstracts International, 61,* 2289A.

Hicks, D. E. (2012). *Imaging and imagining the future: Rhetorical visions of environmental discourse in "gasland".* (Doctoral dissertation). Available from ProQuest Dissertations and Theses database. (UMI No. 3508002).

Documentation: Internet-only Sources

In Chapter Three, "Develop a Research Plan," you learned how to gather documentation information from a web page or website. You should look for any author of the site, the website title, the date posted if provided, and the site's home page address—its URL. There is not always an author for a web page or site. Sometimes there is no original posting date. Always provide whatever information you can find about the site.

A Page on a Web Site

Author of Web Page. (Date of Publication). Title of page. *Title of web site.* Retrieved from the site's URL.

Browder, C. (2011, November 10). Fracking brings risk, reward to Pennsylvania; could NC be next? *WRAL.* Retrieved from http://www.wral.com/news/local/

If no author is named, place the page name in the author position.

What is fracking? (2012). *Energy from shale.* Retrieved from http://www.energyfromshale.org/

E-mails

You do not include e-mails or personal interviews in your References list. They are referenced parenthetically in the body of your argument.

(G. Shearin, personal communication, January 4, 2010).

Blog and Discussion Board Postings

WSJ Staff. (2013, March 26). Big issues: Energy—How to regulate fracking [Web log post]. Retrieved from http://blogs.wsj.com/marketbeat/2013/03/26/big-issues-energy-how-to-regulate-fracking/

Ford 1

This sample paper does not include an APA-Style title page. For information on creating a title page, see page 643.

APA requires double-spacing for papers you submit.

Sabine L. Ford

Professor X

ECO 321

January 21, 2013

Frack(tur)ing the Environment: The Dangers of Fracking

In Kerns County, California, a cherry orchard slowly dies. In Washington County, Pennsylvania, a hillside newly trenched for a pipeline slips toward the creek below. In Wysox, Pennsylvania, water from a faucet bursts into flame. In Shelby County, Texas, a bathtub walks itself down a hallway during an earthquake. In Logan County, West Virginia, a bulldozer plows up the graves of World War II veterans to make a road. In Colorado, a goat gives birth to a head. In Wisconsin, a thousand trucks a day blow by the house of a woman with a 22-month-old daughter, filling the house with toxic sand. What do these incidents have in common? They represent a few out of more than a thousand individual stories of people harmed by fracking (Pennsylvania Alliance for Clean Water and Air, 2013). If these and other stories can be believed, damage caused by fracking is both real and commonplace. The question is whether or not that harm outweighs the benefits. If managed properly, it won't. Some have felt the benefits of fracking. In Wysox, Pennsylvania, a man adds 40 rooms onto his Riverstone Inn (Browder, 2011). In Williamsport, a carwash business booms, and the owner buys a hot dog truck and sends it out to feed hungry workers. In Celina, Texas, the population has grown from 200 to 3,000 (Stories from shale, 2012). Across Pennsylvania, farmers reinvest, buying tractors and planting orchards (Schaefer, 2012).

FRACK(TUR)ING THE ENVIRONMENT   Ford 2

So, as all of these examples indicate, fracking may be a health and ecological disaster, putting the lives and livelihoods of ordinary Americans at peril. Or, fracking may be a boon to individuals and the nation, reducing the use of dirty coal, while driving down energy prices and turning the U.S. into a net energy exporter. With fracking, the harm will be mitigated by careful and vigilant management.

First, what is fracking? According to EnergyFromShale.org, an industry website, high pressure liquids are pumped into rock formations to fracture them, releasing otherwise unrecoverable oil and gas deposits (How Hydraulic Fracturing Works, 2012). The largest of all such deposits in the U.S. is the Marcellus Shale, which stretches northeast from Kentucky to Canada.

First, is fracking a necessary means of meeting our energy needs? According to a 2012 report by the International Energy Agency, the U.S. is set to become the world's leading producer of oil by 2017 (2012b). In a separate 2012 report, the International Energy Agency noted that coal demand is rising in all countries but the U.S., which means that at least in this country, we are moving from relatively dirty coal to cleaner burning oil and natural gas (2012a). With oil prices largely unchanged since 2011, and likely to remain so through 2015, and natural gas prices at their lowest levels in more than a decade, the future looks bright (U.S. Energy Information Administration, 2013).

Colorful examples aside, the fears of fracking opponents appear to be valid. Harmful effects that fracking opponents have listed include water contamination, air pollution, environmental degradation, noise, silica dust, cancer, industrial and highway accidents, and even earthquakes. Howarth, Ingraffea, and Engelder

(2011) frighten readers by citing the toxicity of fracking fluid additives, many of which are carcinogens, and which are not only secret, but exempt from the Safe Drinking Water Act. They also cite the lack of scientific study of environmental dangers, the greater carbon footprint of shale gas relative to conventionally produced natural gas, coal, or diesel oil, and past cases of water supply contamination by leaks and spills of fracking return fluids where deep wells for storage are not readily available. To these they add uncertainties of price and supply, and the crowding out of greener energy technologies as producers rush to take up fracking. In their judgment, "the gas should remain safely in the shale, while society uses energy more efficiently and develops renewable energy sources more aggressively" (Howarth et al. 2011).

In the counterpoint to this view, Howarth et al. (2011) also emphasize that hydraulic fracturing already happens in nature, that many of the chemicals used are harmless and found in household products, and that the industry is able to manage the real dangers of contamination from fracking return fluids. Water supplies are abundant in some fracking areas, such as the largest—the Marcellus Shale play—and methane, while a potent greenhouse gas, is neither poisonous nor long-lasting. It degrades quickly, and therefore does less long term harm than carbon dioxide. In this view, with "hydraulic fracturing, as in many cases, fear levels exceed the evidence" (Howarth et al.).

As with most complex issues, there is more than one side. With fracking, the problems are real, but equally real are the benefits, in terms of economic growth, jobs, revitalization of towns and cities, the stability and abundance of energy, the amount of carbon dioxide and other greenhouse gases emitted through energy production, and a reduction in the mercury, acid rain, and smog produced by coal-fired power plants.

There are concerns, however, about the impact on food safety. Many incidents of fracking harm have involved damage to livestock. As Royte (2012) points out, while people may not eat the animals killed by fracking, they very well might eat those animals harmed by it. Once again though, these local incidents are highlighted while other, perhaps broader and more pervasive threats to our food supply go unmentioned. Cooked red meat itself is a carcinogen, and farm animals have often been contaminated by other industrial processes unrelated to fracking. People could be eating animals exposed to all kinds of air, water, and feed contamination.

Certainly there is a concern that the enormous quantity of water used during fracking poses a risk to water supplies in drought-prone areas like the Eagle Ford Shale in Texas (Allen, 2013). In 2011, agriculture used about 75% of water consumed annually in this country; fracking used roughly .3%, less than golf courses at .5% (Jenkins, 2013). Even so, in places where water is scarce, fracking's five million gallons of fresh water consumed per well may drain aquifers and tip the critical balance of supply and demand. In the Eagle Ford Shale play, there has been no difference reported by drillers in groundwater levels, but that doesn't mean that levels won't drop in the future, especially as demand rises with development, and drought conditions worsen, possibly as a result of global warming (Allen, 2013).

Water use in dry areas is not a trivial concern. In the Barnett Shale play it has accounted for 9% of the water used in Dallas, far more than the overall use rate (McBroom, Thomas, & Zhang, 2012).

Complete APA-Style Research Paper

FRACK(TUR)ING THE ENVIRONMENT   Ford 5

In addition, a study performed in that same area showed that soil erosion and water quality increased as a result of drill pad construction. However, it also showed that when a buffer was used, the effects of both were significantly reduced. That supports the idea that damage that happens locally can be managed or prevented by actions taken locally. It supports the conclusion that the dangers of fracking are real but may be manageable.

On the other hand, Mooney (2011) points out that fracking wells, while usually contained if cementing is done properly, "could connect with preexisting fissures or old wells," through which the new well could contaminate ground water. These accidental connections have occurred multiple times, have taken place unexpectedly, and over a distance of more than 2,000 feet. While this will undoubtedly happen, technology is helping to solve many of the other problems inherent in fracking (Brainard, 2013). Membranes can be used to filter out contaminants from the flowback. A gel made from liquefied gas can take the place of water, increasing production without dissolving natural contaminants into the fluid. Surplus methane, ordinarily vented into the atmosphere or flared—that is burned to produce carbon dioxide—could be captured and converted into fuel or fed to genetically engineered microbes to produce ethanol, eliminating the need to use food crops such as corn. And new generation of turbines is making power generation from natural gas significantly more efficient.

It is probably safe to say that no industrial process on such a grand scale will ever be completely safe for workers or the environment. Accidents will happen and the environment will be negatively affected. The question is, do the benefits outweigh the damage? So far, critics have not presented evidence that any of the

FRACK(TUR)ING THE ENVIRONMENT   Ford 6

problems are unsolvable, while proponents have cited many fixes and successful preventative measures. Uncertainties do surround fracking, as they do the entire energy industry, but with careful management, the many benefits can be made to outweigh the risks.

FRACK(TUR)ING THE ENVIRONMENT   Ford 7

References

Allen, T. A. (2013). The south Texas drought and the future of groundwater use for hydraulic fracturing in the Eagle Ford Shale. *St. Mary's Law Journal, 44,* 487–527.

Brainard, C. (2013, June). The future of energy: Oil and gas. *Popular Science.* Retrieved from http://www.popsci.com

Browder, C. (2011, November 10). Fracking brings risk, reward to Pennsylvania; could NC be next? *WRAL.* Retrieved from http://www.wral.com/news/local/

How Hydraulic Fracturing Works. (2012). *Energy from shale.* Retrieved from http://www.energyfromshale.org/

Howarth, R. W., Ingraffea, A., & Engelder, T. (2011, September 15). Natural gas: Should fracking stop? *Nature 477,* 271–275. doi:10.1038/477271a

International Energy Agency. (2012a). Medium-term coal market report 2012 factsheet: Only shale gas stops coal demand growth. *IEA.* Retrieved from http://www.iea.org/newsroomandevents/

International Energy Agency (2012b). North America leads shift in global energy balance, IEA says in latest World Energy Outlook. *IEA.* Retrieved from http://www.iea.org/newsroomandevents/

Jenkins, J. (2013). Energy facts: How much water does fracking for shale gas consume? *The Energy Collective.* Retrieved from http://theenergycollective.com

McBroom, M., Thomas, T., & Zhang, Y. (2012). Soil erosion and surface water quality impacts of natural gas development in east Texas, USA. *Water 4,* 944–958. doi:10.3390/w4040944

FRACK(TUR)ING THE ENVIRONMENT   Ford 8

Pennsylvania Alliance for Clean Water and Air. (2013, March 12).
    List of the harmed [Web log post]. Retrieved from http://
    pennsylvaniaallianceforcleanwaterandair.wordpress.com/
    the-list/

Royte, E. (2012, December 17). What the frack is in our food?
    Nation 295(25), 11–18.

Schaefer, K. (2012, September 18). The stakes get higher in the
    fracking debate [Web log post]. Retrieved from http://seek-
    ingalpha.com/instablog/365869-oil-and-gas-investments-
    bulletin/1081001-the-stakes-get-higher-in-the-fracking-debate

Stories from shale: Lorain, Ohio. (2012). *Energy from shale*.
    Retrieved from http://www.energyfromshale.org/

U.S. Energy Information Administration. (2013, May 7).
    Short-term energy outlook. *EIA*. Retrieved from http://www.eia.
    gov/forecasts/steo/report/prices.cfm

Complete APA-Style Research Paper

GLOSSARY

absolute terms   Terms that suggest overgeneralization, for example "all" or "everyone."

abstract   An abstract is a paragraph-long overview of an argument, essay, or article. It should summarize the writer's claim or thesis and refer to a few important points of support.

ad hominem   This fallacy attempts to mislead an audience by attacking an opponent's character, credibility, or authority instead of focusing on the opponent's argument.

ad misericordiam   This kind of appeal attempts to persuade through pity.

aggressive humor   A type of humor that attacks others and is used to encourage readers of an argument to laugh at or ridicule the opposition.

analogy   To argue by analogy refers to seeking similarities in the way similar situations have been addressed.

anecdote(s)   Anecdotes, a kind of support, are real-life episodes drawn from the life of the arguer, or others, that allow a writer to connect on a personal level with readers.

APA   This refers to a style guide for formatting essays and articles developed by the American Psychological Association that is typically used in the fields of social science, business, and education.

attributive phrases or statements   These are short phrases used to introduce quotations and their authors.

backing   Backing is support for a warrant. It elaborates, often through examples, on the values present in a warrant.

bandwagon fallacy   This kind of fallacy claims that something must be true because everyone, presumably, believes it to be true.

bar graph   A kind of logical support, a bar graph is a chart that uses bars to represent data.

bias   Bias refers to the particular viewpoint or slant that an author or a publication leans toward. A writer with a biased point of view often ignores objective fact and risks losing credibility with an audience.

biased language   Includes language that is strongly leaning to a particular direction with no regard for other points of view.

bibliography file   In the course of preparing an argument, a writer builds a bibliography file to maintain a record of all sources that may be used in an argument. For each source, such a file would include publication information, point of access, and notes.

blanket statements   This dangerous fallacy involves a statement that makes an overly general or absolute claim or reason and leaves the arguer vulnerable to attack.

Boolean search   This refers to a method for looking for information with search engines and in databases that combine search terms, or keywords, with the operators AND, OR, and NOT.

broadening out   This is a technique often used near the end of an argument where the arguer extends a claim to demonstrate how it can be applied, or broadened, to issues beyond the focus of a single argument.

causes   Reasons behind why something occurs; backward-looking.

circling back   This refers to a technique of the writer emphasizing, in a conclusion, a claim by referring, or circling back, to the introduction where the claim is first stated.

circular argument   Instead of providing support for a claim, the arguer simply restates a claim in this kind of fallacy.

claim   A claim is the arguer's position on an issue and the center of an argument. It alerts an audience to an argument's purpose and what the arguer wants an audience to accept or consider.

claim of cause   This kind of claim argues that one thing or event causes another event or chain of events.

claim of definition   This kind of claim defines a key word or term in an issue and then brings in reasons and specific support to justify the definition.

claim of evaluation   A judgment or evaluation is made in this kind of claim, as the arguer claims that something is practical or impractical, ethical or unethical, fair or unfair, healthy or unhealthy, worth our time or not worth our time, wasteful or beneficial, etc.

claim of fact   A claim of fact argues that something is a fact—an event or series of events, a trend, an attitude, or a part of history—that may not be considered a fact by everyone.

common ground   Common ground can be created between an arguer, the opposition, and audience when the arguer is careful to recognize shared values and beliefs.

community   The category of "community" is a convenient way to recognize where issues occur in our lives—at school, in the workplace, with family, in the neighborhood, in social-cultural contexts, as a consumer, and as a concerned citizen.

comparisons   Building a comparison in an argument between an idea you're working with and a similar set of circumstances in the past can clarify for readers a claim, reason, or point of support.

conclusion   A conclusion typically is the final paragraph or two in an argument in which the arguer can remind readers of the claim, point out the need for further research, or urge readers to act in response to the issue at hand.

conflict   This is a type of "hook," or way to engage readers, in the introduction that sets up conflicting ideas the writer will resolve in an argument.

consequences (or effects)   This kind of support is used to argue that something has happened or will happen based on past causes or circumstances.

context   The set of circumstances or facts, past and present, that surround a particular event, situation, or issue.

credible   In an argument this term refers to the reputation of the arguer based on his ability to bring in credible research and to prove to an audience that he is qualified to argue on the issue he's working with.

critical reading   Critical reading involves marking terms that are unknown, questioning a text, and investigating the claims made by the other among other scholarly tasks.

database   A database is a collection of scholarly essays, articles, or other information that can be accessed electronically and then searched. For the purpose of building an argument, academic databases, such as those housed by a college or university, are essential.

deep web   This term refers to material on the Internet that is not searchable by conventional search engines and requires more precise searching, often through web sites and private collections.

definition   There are seven kinds of definitions appropriate for academic writing and argument building—scientific, metaphoric, example, riddle, function, irony, and negation. They may be combined to accommodate the arguer's purpose.

definitional equivalence   This occurs when two things—ideas, theories, points of view, etc.—are defined as being the same, whether or not they are the same.

descriptive statistics   This term describes data in terms of who assembled it and in what conditions.

documentation   This is the process of citing the sources used in an argument in both the body of the argument and the end-of-argument reference pages, such as the Works Cited page.

domain extension   The ending element in a web address, or URL (universal resource locator), that indicates the general origin of the site is known as the domain extension. For example "gov" indicates that the site originates within a government-sponsored agency or department; "edu" for sites within an educational setting; "org" for an organization; and "com" reveals that the site is produced within a commercial or business setting.

double standard   A fallacy in which a standard is applied differently to different groups of people.

easy generalizations   A fallacy type that provides shallow generalizations based on stereotypes or inadequate research.

ebooks   Electronic versions of books.

equivocation   When contradictory claims appear in an argument, the arguer has committed a fallacy of equivocation. This kind of fallacy occurs when a word or term has two meanings and the writer intentionally uses the double meaning to deceive or mislead readers.

ethos   This is a Greek term that refers to the credibility of an arguer based on his ability to demonstrate authority or expertise in an argument.

evaluation   Evaluation is an argument strategy that is used when attempting to convince an audience that one thing is better, more efficient, or more feasible than another.

expert opinion   A writer includes expert opinion in an argument when sources include interviews, articles and essays, and lectures by professors, scholars, or recognized experts in a field. This kind of support adds to an arguer's credibility.

explicit claims   Claims that are directly stated by the arguer.

exploratory essay   An essay that allows a writer to explore an issue based on the writer's knowledge of the issue and what research needs to be pursued to build a competent argument is known as an exploratory essay.

facts   Facts are a kind of logical support and include statements and specific information about an issue that generally are regarded as true.

fallacies   Sometimes referred to as logical fallacies, errors in logic, or pseudoproofs, fallacies in an argument, whether accidental or deliberate, are misleading or deceptive statements that draw attention away from the problems in an argument's claim or support. A fallacy does not stand up to investigation based in sound logic or objective fact.

fallacies of choice   This is a category of fallacies that argues readers have limited choices when such limits do not exist.

fallacies of emotion   This is a category of fallacies that relies heavily on emotional appeals at the expense of other types of support, such as logical and ethical.

fallacies of inconsistency   These are fallacies that refer to assertions in an argument that treat ideas and information differently when they should be treated the same. Also refers to ideas and information treated as the same that should be treated differently.

fallacies of support   This category of fallacies makes connections and conclusions that are misleading and cannot be confirmed.

false analogy   A false analogy claims that situations or ideas are comparable when they are not.

false authority   This involves the endorsement of a position by a person not qualified to make the endorsement. While the person may have authority and expertise in another field, the writer incorrectly assumes that an endorsement based on reputation only is appropriate in an argument.

false clue   *See* red herring.

false dilemma/either–or   A fallacy that suggests only two options can occur for any situation.

false testimonial   Similar to a false authority fallacy, a false testimonial involves the endorsement of a position by a person not qualified to make the endorsement.

field-specific support   This refers to support generally regarded as acceptable in a specific field of study.

finding the incongruities in a position   Pointing out the difference between what an opponent says and what she does.

FLOI method   Examining the external elements of a text (table of contents, preface, chapter organization, index, etc.) in addition to the text itself, is a critical reading strategy known as the FLOI method.

glocal   This term refers to a writer making a connection in an argument between local and global contexts.

hasty generalization   This fallacy occurs when an arguer inaccurately generalizes based on a single case or example.

hidden claims   This is used when an arguer chooses to leave a claim unstated, or hidden, and instead wants readers to determine the claim on their own.

HTML document   A file formatted in HTML does not appear as a print document would, missing page numbers, page breaks, and sometimes images or other formatting.

humor   Used in argumentative writing to relieve stress and anxiety created by a confrontational situation.

iconic   This refers to an image or object that represents substantially more to the viewer or reader than the contents of the image or object itself.

implicit claims   Claims that an arguer implies but does not state directly.

inferential statistics   Statistics used to draw conclusions about a group of data by linking cause and effect are referred to as inferential statistics.

information overload   Situation that occurs when we are faced with too many sources of information.

introduction   An introduction begins an argument; it is the opening paragraph or paragraphs. In addition to engaging information designed to hook the reader, often a claim and sometimes a warrant appear in an introduction.

issue   An issue is a specific problem or dispute that remains unsettled that occurs within a larger topic and within a precise context, or set of conditions.

jargon   This is specialized language—words, terms, and concepts—originating in a specific field or discipline.

kairos or timeliness   In the context of argument, the Greek term *kairos* means delivering an argument at the optimal time, that is, at a time when there is genuine local or academic interest in an issue.

line graph   This graph uses points connected by line segments to show how something changes over time.

local voices   Local knowledge that makes an argument more focused and immediate.

logos   This is support based on verifiable information, such as facts, statistics, and scientific and scholarly evidence.

material equivalence   This fallacy erroneously claims that erroneously claims that two unequal things, such as facts or ideas, are equal or balanced.

microhistory   An argument based on a microhistory interprets primary documents so as to argue against overly general treatments of a historical period and to establish a layer of history generally overlooked.

Middle Ground argument   This approach to an issue involves arguing for a practical middle position between two extreme positions.

misdirection Meant to add suspense in an introduction to an argument, this is a kind of hook that intentionally misleads readers.

MLA style An academic paper formatting guide designed and updated by the Modern Language Association; It is used primarily in the humanities—composition, literature, languages, philosophy, and the arts.

moral equivalence This fallacy involves the mistake of balancing two unequal facts, ideas, or points of view against each other *morally*, as if they are equally bad or good.

moving from boring to interesting This prewriting technique is a way for an arguer to make a personal connection with an issue and thus enliven an argument.

newsreaders These are programs that gather and read items from Internet sources, such as discussion groups and RSS (Really Simple Syndication) feeds.

non sequitur This fallacy refers to a statement in an argument that is illogical; that is, a statement that does not connect logically to the statement preceding it.

Occam's Razor A guideline in philosophy and science, Occam's Razor argues that choosing the simpler of two ideas or theories is best. The guideline originates with William of Ockham (1285–1349), a British theologian and philosopher.

opinions Typically, this refers to a personal belief or attitude not based on research or verifiable information.

opposition This term has two meanings in the context of argument. First, it refers to points of view different from an arguer's. Second, it is a kind of conclusion that moves readers in a direction opposite from that in the introduction.

overstatement (hyperbole) This technique exaggerates, or overstates, so as to draw attention to an idea in an argument.

paraphrasing In an argument, paraphrased material occurs when an arguer puts in his own words the ideas of another writer and then acknowledges the source of the borrowed material.

parenthetical citations This is source information, typically author last name and page or paragraph number, placed in parentheses in the body of a text. This information follows quotations or paraphrased information in an argument.

pathos This kind of support appeals to readers' emotions. It can be achieved by using powerful examples, personal experience, and compelling factual information.

PDF document A file format that provides an image of the document that can be viewed as if it is a print document.

plagiarism The use of published material produced by someone else as if it is the writer's; this includes a range of infractions extending from the accidental omission of a citation to passing off an entire essay as one's own.

post hoc, ergo propter hoc Also known as "false cause," this fallacy mistakenly draws a conclusion based on the chronological order in which events occur and ignores other factors that might offer a more accurate explanation.

precedence Refers to the way a situation has been handled in the past.

prewriting This term refers to techniques and strategies used to organize, arrange, and think through ideas for an argument prior to the formal process of drafting an argument.

primary cause This refers to the cause in an argument that results in an immediate effect.

primary materials *see* primary sources

primary sources In terms of argument, primary sources or documents refer to material gathered from the past—letters, journals, photographs, music, artifacts, etc.—that an arguer interprets in support of a claim.

problem-based claims This kind of claim argues for a precise solution to a problem or issue.

qualifier(s) Qualifiers are used primarily to make claims and reasons more believable. Qualifiers move an arguer away from making overly general or blanket statements.

quoting Quoting is using a source word for word rather than paraphrasing the source.

reasons Reasons help organize an argument. They announce the purposes of some paragraphs, link directly to claim, and are followed by specific support.

rebuttal Vital to successful arguments, rebuttals are points of view on an issue different from the point of view of an arguer. Fair, accurate presentation of rebuttals build an arguer's credibility. Rebuttals often are immediately countered by the arguer.

red herring This is a fallacy that diverts attention away from the issue at hand, often by using false or misleading information.

reference list A list of all sources used in an APA format research argument.

reservations This is a statement that recognizes concerns, or reservations, an audience may hold about a warrant in an argument.

Rogerian argument This approach to argument is aimed at building common ground between an arguer and those holding differing points of view on an issue. Highlighting the strengths of other views is a cornerstone of Rogerian argument.

RSS feed (Really Simple Syndication) These are formats used to publish frequently updated content—such as news, material from blogs, video, and audio—to which Internet users can subscribe.

sarcasm This is a kind of humor that uses irony to ridicule an opponent's position on an issue.

satire In an argument, satire is a form of humor that aims to expose and then ridicule a point of view. Ridicule is often accompanied by a corrective to an opposing view.

scare tactics Common in advertising and politics, this fallacy uses emotionally charged language and dramatic examples to frighten and persuade readers. Use of this fallacy typically is part of an agenda—political or economic—among others.

search engines Vehicles for finding material on the World Wide Web, a search engine crawls the Internet for sites that match keywords used in a search.

search string These are keywords or phrases used to find information when using a search engine. Varying search terms can produce more comprehensive results.

secondary causes Sometimes called peripheral causes, secondary causes are contributing factors to an effect in an argument.

secondary sources Sources that analyze or explain some aspect of your topic. *See* primary sources.

seeming impossibility This technique appears in an introduction to an argument and works as a hook for readers, setting up a problem without an apparent solution.

self-effacing humor This is the use of humor to poke fun at an arguer rather than at the arguer's opponents.

slippery slope (or staircase) This kind of fallacy presumes that one event will set off a series of succeeding events without providing sufficient explanation.

straw man argument This fallacy is based on incorrect information, whether the intention is to deliberately misrepresent an opponent's claims or because the facts being used are plainly incorrect.

summary A synopsis of the original source.

support Evidence and information used to defend a claim is known as support. Kinds of support include logical (*logos*), ethical (*ethos*), and emotional (*pathos*).

surface web In the context of Internet searching, this term refers to information gathered using conventional, non-specific search engines, such as Google, Bing, Dogpile, and Ask.com among others.

suspense Is used to heighten the tension for a reader as to what the claim will actually be.

target audience This is the group or individual at whom an argument is aimed; it is the group or individual the arguer intends to persuade so as to accept a position on an issue.

testimonials A type of fallacy in which an unqualified person endorses a product or stance.

thesis This statement, often appearing early in a piece of writing, is needed to focus the reader and to identify the writer's main idea or purpose. A thesis may or may not offer a point of view or position.

topic A topic is a category—such as local politics, transportation, neighborhood security, race relations, or family planning—that contains numerous issues within it. Specific issues and arguments originate in topics.

Toulmin-based argument This approach to argument is named after Stephen Toulmin (1922–2009), a British philosopher and educator. Toulmin's approach to argument has been adapted as a practical complement to ethics in daily life.

understatement This is a kind of verbal irony that minimizes, or understates, the seriousness of an issue.

visual argument A visual argument delivers a claim on an issue visually—through a photograph, video, cartoon, illustration, etc. Support and a warrant often are included to enhance the claim.

visual humor This argumentative strategy typically uses visual images to point out the irony and hypocrisy in an opponent's position.

warrant This essential feature of argument refers to a deeply-held value, belief or principle that an arguer shares with an audience or opponent.

works cited (page) A feature of MLA documentation, this is the last page in a written argument using research and lists alphabetically sources used in the argument.

INDEX

ABC News, 62
"Abolish Corporate Personhood (Thinking Politically)" (Edwards & Morgan), 386–393
Absolute terms, 115
Abstracts, 86
"A Buddhist Perspective on Consumerism" (Brown), 520–523
Academic community, topics related to, 23–24
Academic Info, 59
Ad hominem fallacies, 124
"The Ad Industry Pins Us Down" (Godrej), 530–535
Ad Misericordiam, 126
Advertisements, 310–311
  purpose of, 174
Advocacy, 145–146
Affiliative humor, 313. *See also* Humor
Aggregators. *See* Newsreaders
Aggressive humor, 312–313, 315. *See also* Humor
"Ain't I a Woman?" (Truth), 615–616
Alperovitz, Gar, 380–382
American Memory Project, LOC, 72
American Psychological Association (APA), 107, 622. *See also* APA documentation
Analogical exploration, 177–178
Analogy, 131
  example of, 178
  explanation of, 169
Anecdotes, 288–289
  to create positive credibility, 285
  humorous, 313
  in introductions, 332
Anthologies
  APA documentation style for, 648

MLA documentation style for, 627–628
Anthony, Susan B., 593–594
Antin, Mary, 594–598
APA documentation, 108. *See also* Documentation
  abstract, 644
  for articles, 649–652
  for books, 646–649
  Internet-only sources, 652–660
  in-text documentation, 645
  reference list, 646
  title page, 644
"Are Students the New Indentured Servants?" (Williams), 341, 371–379
Arguments. *See also* Visual arguments
  about what matters to you, 7–10
  appropriate use of, 6–7
  audience for, 10–11, 40
  based on microhistory, 19, 206, 226–236
  break down, causes of, 15–16
  circular, 119–120
  constructing, to fit purpose, 189
  establishing local context for issue, 11–13
  explanation of, 3, 22
  fallacies in. *See* Fallacies
  humor in, 312–317
  mapping, for target audience, 41–45
  matching with purpose, 16–19, 36
  middle-ground. *See* Middle-ground argument
  opposing views. *See* Opposing views
  parts of, 240, 241
  prompts to get started with, 47–49
  research for. *See* Research

Rogerian. *See* Rogerian argument
  straw man, 122–123
  support functions in, 37–45
  timing of, 46–47
  Toulmin-based. *See* Toulmin-based argument
  types of, 17
  usefulness, 3
  using humor in, 316
Argument strategies
  claims evaluation, 181–183
  comparisons as, 164–168
  definitions as, 158–164
  examining causes/consequences as, 164–168
  exploratory essay as, writing, 183–185
  proposing solutions as, 170–181
Aristotle, 15, 32, 37, 277
Articles
  APA documentation style for, 649–652
  MLA documentation style for, 629–631
Arts, support for, 275
Ask.com, 57
The Associated Press, 63
"Atlanta Compromise Address" (Washington), 616–620
Attributive phrases or statements, 93
Attributive words, 93
Audience
  choice of, 42–43
  defining, 32–33
  determining backing needed to appeal to, 264–265
  emotions of. *See* Emotional appeals
  identification of, 10–11
  interview, 268

poorly defined, and argument
    break down, 15–16
responding to reservations of,
    267–268
target. *See* Target audience
usage to construct warrant,
    260–263
values, 260–261

Backing, 45
    in middle-ground argument, 212
    in Rogerian argument, 223–224
    specific, 265–266
    to support warrant, 263–267
    in Toulmin-based argument, 190,
        192, 195, 197
Bandwagon fallacy, 126
Banks, Leo W., 451–456
Bar graph, 309
BBC News, 63, 72
Behavioral sciences, support for,
    274–275
"Beware the Idea of the Student as a
    Customer: A Dissenting View"
    (Vaill), 340
Bhatt, Keane, 380–382
Bias, 86
    inconsistent treatment and, 130
    in summaries, 146–148
Biased language, explanation of, 146
Bibliography file, 60, 87
Bing, 57
Binswanger, Harry, 555–559
Blanket statements, 115
Blogs, 73
Body paragraphs
    organization samples of, 343–346
    reasons in, 255–257
    sample of, 255–257
Books
    APA documentation for, 646–649
    critical reading, 90–91
    MLA documentation for, 626–629
    searches for, 75–78
Boolean search operators, 61
"Bowling with Others" (Wilson),
    488–495
Boyle, Mark, 535–537
Bradbury, Ray, 30–31
Brainstorming, 29–30
*Brewer's Dictionary of Phrase and
    Fable*, 54
Broadening out conclusion, 336–337
Broudy, Oliver, 542–547

Brown, Judith Simmer, 520–523
Brutoco, Rinaldo, 393–404
Bush, George W., 315
"Buy Nothing Day 2012 Is
    Approaching. Could You Stop
    Spending for One Day?" (Boyle),
    535–537

"Cafeteria Consciousness" (Lappé),
    367–371
"The Cassandra Syndrome" (Nagler),
    508–510
The Catalog of U.S. Government
    Publications, 69
Causes
    argument based on, 164–168
    explanation of, 164
    primary, 165
CBS News, 62
Census Bureau, 69
Charts
    reading methods, 306–308
    used in arguments, 308–310
Circling back technique, 338
Circular argument, 119–120
Claim of cause, 44, 251–252
Claim of definition, 43, 246–248
Claim of evaluation, 44, 249–251
Claim of fact, 44, 243, 244–246
Claims
    appropriate, finding, 244
    checklist for, 323
    choice of, 40–41, 43
    connecting with purpose, 243
    developing, 34–36
    effectiveness of, 241
    evaluation, 181–183
    explanation of, 34, 241–242
    explicit, 323
    false, argument built on, 122–123
    functions of, 241–243
    hidden, 325–326
    implicit, 324–325
    introduction, 320–322
    justification, with warrant, 44, 259
    in microhistories, 232
    position, methods to, 326–329
    reasons to support, 44, 252–254
    state, methods to, 323–326
    support for, 44–45
    in Toulmin-based argument,
        189, 191
    types of, 43–44, 244–252. *See also
        specific types*

Classic American arguments
    "Ain't I a Woman?" (Truth),
        615–616
    "Atlanta Compromise Address"
        (Washington), 616–620
    "Federalist No. 6: Concerning
        Dangers from Dissensions
        Between the States"
        (Hamilton), 598–603
    "Have We Any Right to Regulate
        Immigration?" (Antin),
        594–598
    "In Congress, July 4, 1776: *The
        Unanimous Declaration of
        the Thirteen United States of
        America*" (Jefferson),
        603–607
    "On the Equality of the Sexes"
        (Murray), 609–613
    "On Women's Right to Vote"
        (Anthony), 593–594
    "The Penalty of Death" (Mencken),
        607–609
    "A Petition to the President of
        the United States" (Szilard &
        Consigners), 613–615
"Climate Change Could Cause Disease
    Resurgence" (Dickerson),
    560–563
Clustering. *See* Mapping/clustering
CNN, 62, 72
Columbia Encyclopedia, 54
.com, 59
Common ground
    explanation of, 217
    in Rogerian argument, 217,
        219–220
Communication, solutions, 179–180
Community
    explanation of, 23
    types of, 23–26. *See also specific
        types*
Comparisons
    examples of, 169–170
    explanation of, 168
Complete Planet, 60
Concerned citizen community
    readings
    "Climate Change Could Cause
        Disease Resurgence"
        (Dickerson), 560–563
    "Corporate Media Obituary of
        Occupy Premature" (Hedges),
        569–572

"Is America Hooked on War?"
(Engelhardt), 563–569
"Nationalize the Banks"
(Rothschild), 583–587
"Over a Barrel" (Roberts),
579–583
"Private Charity Should Replace
Welfare" (Kelley), 573–579
"The United States Should
Adopt Open Immigration"
(Binswanger), 555–559
"Voter Suppression Returns"
(Keyssar), 587–591
Concerned citizens topics, 26
Conclusion
broadening out, 336–337
circling back in, 338
function of, 336
guidelines, 339
opposition in, 337–338
Conflict, 333–334
Consequences
argument based on, 164–168
explanation of, 164
Consumer community
"A Buddhist Perspective on
Consumerism" (Brown),
520–523
"The Ad Industry Pins Us Down"
(Godrej), 530–535
"Buy Nothing Day 2012 Is
Approaching. Could You
Stop Spending for One Day?"
(Boyle), 535–537
"How the McEconomy Bombed
the American Worker: The
Hollowing Out of the Middle
Class" (Kroll), 538–542
"It's Like eBay Meets Match.com:
Does Peer-to-Peer Lending
Work?" (Fisman), 527–530
"Outsourcing Compromises
the Safety and Quality of
Products" (Yang), 547–554
"The Practical Ethicist: 'The Way
We Eat' Author Peter Singer
Explains the Advantage of
Wingless Chickens, How
Humans Discriminate Against
Animals, and the Downside of
Buying Locally Grown Food"
(Broudy), 542–547
"Telemarketers Should Be
Censored" (Ebel), 523–527

Consumer-oriented society topics,
25–26
Context, issue
global, 13–14
local, establishing, 11–13
"Corporate Media Obituary of Occupy
Premature" (Hedges), 569–572
Council of Science Editors (CSE),
107, 622
Creative exploration, 175–176
Creative thinking, 171
Credibility. *See also* Ethos
based on personality, 284–285
evaluation of, 82–83
explanation of, 37
support to create, 37–38, 284–286,
340–341
"Crime in Virtual Worlds Is Impacting
Real Life" (Guest), 466–472
Critical reading
to detect fallacies, 112
explanation of, 112
material on Internet, 82–83
research materials, 85–86
Critical thinking exploration, 176
Cultural community topics, 25
"The Current Business Paradigm is
Toxic to Business and Society.
Here's How We Change It."
(Brutoco & Yau), 393–404

Databases
access in deep web, 64–65
in deep web, 59
explanation of, 64
formats, 65–66
in libraries, 64–68
printing or saving articles on, 68
tutorials for use of, 65
"Dealing with the Stressed: Workplace
Stress Costs the Economy
More Than $30 Billion a Year,
and Yet Nobody Knows What
It Is or How to Deal with It"
(MacQueen, Patriquin, & Intini),
404–410
Debt: The First 5,000 Years
(Graeber), 5
Deep web
accessing databases on, 64–65
search engines to access, 59–61
Definitional equivalence, 129–130
Definitions
claims of, 43, 246–248

by example, 162
explanation of, 158
by function, 163
guidelines to use, 158–160
with irony, 163
metaphorical, 161–162
by negating, 164
with riddles, 162
scientific, 161
types of, 160–164
Demirjian, Karoun, 354–357
Descriptive statistics, 280
Dickerson, James L., 560–563
Digital History, 73
Direct quotations, 96–98
Documentation. *See also* MLA
documentation
formats, 107–108, 622
on notes, 84–85
of paraphrases, 101–105
of summaries, 100–101
for works-cited page, 624
Dogmatism, inconsistent treatment
and, 130
Donne, John, 11
Double standard, 128
Dubner, Stephen, 326

Easy generalizations, explanation
of, 139
Ebel, David, 523–527
ebooks, 77
EBSCOhost, 64, 65
Edison, Thomas, 171
.edu, 59
Education, support for, 274–275
Edwards, Jan, 386–393
Either-or thinking, 116–117
Elbow, Peter, 30
Electronic Communications Privacy
Act, 55
"Eminem Is Right: The Primal Scream
of Teenage Music" (Eberstadt),
418–424
Emotion
editing support based on, 341
fallacies of, 124–127
support to create, 287–290
Emotional appeals, 15
support based on, 38
"Employee-Owned Businesses
Ignored by Mainstream Media"
(Alperovitz & Bhatt), 380–382

Encyclopedias, 55
Engelhardt, Tom, 563–569
"Environmental Justice for All" (Kokmen), 460–466
Equivalence
    definitional, 129–130
    material, 129
    moral, 129
Equivocation, 130–131
ERIC, 64
E-texts
    APA documentation style for, 648–649
    MLA documentation style for, 628
Ethical appeals, 15
Ethical issues, 173
Ethos. *See also* Credibility
    example of, 277
    explanation of, 37, 276
    use of support to create, 37–38, 284–287, 340–341
Example, define by, 162
Expertise, valuing, 145–146
Expert opinions, 279
Explicit claims, 323
Exploration
    creative, 175–176
    critical thinking, 176
    historical, 173–174
    metaphorical/analogical, 177–178
    process, 174–175
Exploratory essays
    checklist, 184
    elements of, 183
    explanation of, 183
    sample, 184

Face the Nation, 73
Facts. *See also* Logos
    editing support based on, 340
    explanation of, 277–279
    graphic images as, 279
    statistics as, 279–283
    support based on, 37
Fallacies
    and argument break down, 16
    categories of, 113. *See also specific categories*
    defining, 111–112
    detection of, 111–112
    explanation of, 16, 111
Fallacies of choice
    blanket statements as, 115
    explanation of, 114–115

false dilemma/either-or thinking as, 116–117
    Occam's razor as, 116
    signs of, 118
    slippery slope as, 117–119
Fallacies of emotion
    ad hominem as, 124
    ad misericordiam as, 126
    bandwagon as, 126
    explanation of, 124
    scare tactics as, 126–127
    signs of, 127
    testimonials and false authority as, 125
Fallacies of inconsistency
    definitional equivalence as, 129–130
    equivocation as, 130–131
    explanation of, 128
    false analogy as, 131
    inconsistent treatment as, 130
    material equivalence as, 129
    moral equivalence as, 129
    signs of, 132
Fallacies of support
    circular argument as, 119–120
    explanation of, 119
    hasty generalization, 120
    nonsequitur, red herring and false clue as, 121–122
    pot hoc, ergo propter hoc as, 120–121
    straw man as, 122–123
False analogy, 131
False authority, 125
False clue, 121–122
False dilemmas, 116–117
Families, topics related to, 24
Family and household community readings
    "Eminem Is Right: The Primal Scream of Teenage Music" (Eberstadt), 418–424
    "Introduction" (Louv), 432–435
    "Leaving the Doors Open" (Ferguson), 424–427
    "A Morally Bankrupt Military: When Soldiers and Their Families Become Expendable" (Jamail), 445–450
    "North America: Ecological Breakup" (Liu & Yu), 430–431

"Reproductive Cloning Would Strengthen the American Family" (Pence), 435–442
    "Street Life Is No Life for Children" (Kilcher), 427–430
    "Why Gay Marriage is so Controversial in America" (Jouet), 442–445
Faulty causality, 120–121
"Federalist No. 6: Concerning Dangers from Dissensions Between the States" (Hamilton), 598–603
FedStats, 70
Ferguson, Sue, 424–427
Field-specific support
    for education, history, social and behavioral sciences, 274–275
    explanation of, 272–273
    for humanities and arts, 275
Find Articles, 60
First Measured Century, 70
Fisman, Ray, 527–530
FLOI method, 90–91
"For-Profit Colleges Deserve Some Respect" (Seiden), 363–367
Frank, Thomas, 4
FreeDocumentaries.org, 72
Freedom from Mid-East Oil (Brutoco), 393–404
Freewriting, 30
Functional definitions, 163
Funk & Wagnall's New World Encyclopedia, 55

Geis, Irving, 281
Generalizations, 139–140
Global context
    connecting local context and, 13–14
Glocal, 14, 15
Godrej, Dinyar, 530–535
Gonzalez, Linda, 142–143
Google, 53, 57, 59, 63, 73, 78
Google Books, 77
Google News, 62
.gov, 59
Government documents
    web sites for, 70–71
Graeber, David, 5
Graphic images, use of, 279
Graphs
    bar, 309
    line, 308–309

reading methods, 306–308
used in arguments, 279, 308–310
"Greenwashing Remains a Challenge to the Green Building Community" (Mattera), 472–477
Guest, Tim, 466–472
Guzman, James, 144–145

Hamilton, Alexander, 598–603
Hanging indent feature, 625
Hanson, Thomas J., 328–329
Hasty generalization, 120
"Have We Any Right to Regulate Immigration?" (Antin), 594–598
Hawking, Stephen, 313
Hawthorne, Nathaniel, 87–88
Hedges, Chris, 569–572
Hidden claims, 325–326
Historical exploration, 173–174
History, types of support for, 274–275
Households topics, 24
"How the McEconomy Bombed the American Worker: The Hollowing Out of the Middle Class" (Kroll), 538–542
How the Other Half Lives (Riis), 303
How to Lie with Statistics (Huff & Geis), 281
HTML documents
explanation of, 65, 67–68
Hudson, David L., Jr., 383–386
Huff, Darrell, 281
"A Humanist Looks at Polyamory" (White), 510–515
Humanities, support for, 275
Humor
affiliative, 313
aggressive, 312–313, 315
appropriateness of, 316
function of, 312
inappropriateness of, 317
other-deprecating, 312–313
sarcasm, 315
self-deprecating, 312, 313
strategies for using, 313–316
using in arguments, 316
visual, 314–315

Iconic image, 289
"I'll Have Large Fries, a Hamburger, a Diet Coke, and an MBA. Hold the Pickles" (Saad), 357–359

Illustrations. *See also* Visual arguments
reading methods, 302–306
used in arguments, 305–306
Images. *See also* Visual arguments
web sites to access, 73
"I'm Not Dangerous" (Postel), 413–415
Implicit claims, 324–325
"The Importance of Political Awareness in America" (Walp), 506–508
"In Congress, July 4, 1776: *The Unanimous Declaration of the Thirteen United States of America*" (Jefferson), 603–607
Inconsistent treatment, 130
Inferential statistics, 280
Infomine, 59
Infoplease Almanac, 54
Information overload, 112
Institute for Social Research, 70
.int, 59
Internet. *See also* Web sites
APA documentation style for material found on, 652–660
critically reading material on, 82–83
encyclopedia, 55
evaluation checklist, 83
finding books on, 77–78
government sites on, 70–71
MLA documentation style for material found on, 632–633
research materials on, 53–54
Internet Sacred Text Archive, 77
Interviews, MLA documentation for, 633
Intini, John, 404–410
"Introduction" (Louv), 432–435
Introductions
anecdotes in, 332
conflict in, 333–334
functions of, 331
misdirection in, 332–333
presenting *Seem*ing impossibility in, 335
strong, creating, 331–335
suspense in, 334
Introduction to the Practice of Statistics (Moore & McCabe), 281
Intute, 60
Invention. *See* Pre-Thinking methods
Invisible web. *See* Deep web

Irony, 163
"Is America Hooked on War?" (Engelhardt), 563–569
Issues
affecting communities, 23–26
choice of, 42
establish local context for, 11–13
matters to you, 7–10, 23–26
pre-thinking methods. *See* Pre-thinking methods
within topics, 27–29
"It's Like eBay Meets Match.com: Does Peer-to-Peer Lending Work?" (Fisman), 527–530

Jamail, Dahr, 445–450
Jargon, 86
Jefferson, Thomas, 603–607
"Jicama in the "Hood" (McMillan), 477–482
Jouet, Mugambi, 442–445
Journals, 85–86
Justification, 44

Kairo, 46–47. *See also* Timeliness
Kelley, David, 573–579
Keyssar, Alexander, 587–591
Keyword searches
methods for, 61–62
for podcasts, 73
Kilcher, Jewel, 427–430
"Killer Reflection" (Yang), 515–519
Kimmel, Jimmy, 314
King, Martin Luther, Jr., 218, 224–226
Kokmen, Leyla, 460–466
Kroll, Andy, 538–542

Lambert, Brittney, 143–144
Lappé, Anna, 367–371
Last Child in the Woods: Saving Our Children from Nature-Deficit Disorder (Louv), 326–328
Leadership Conference on Civil Rights Education Fund (LCCREF), 501–506
"Leaving the Doors Open" (Ferguson), 424–427
Librarians' Internet Index (LII), 60
Libraries
databases in, 64–68
research materials in, 53–54
searching for books in, 75–77
Library catalogues, 75–76

Library of Congress (LOC), 69
American Memory Project, 72
LibrarySpot.com, 59
Line graph, 308–309. *See also* Graphs
Liu, Jianguo, 431
Loaded language, 288
Local context
establishing, 11–13
global context and, connecting, 13–14
Local voices, 140–141
Logical appeals
lacking, and argument break down, 15
Logos. *See also* Facts
editing support based on, 340
example of, 277
explanation of, 37, 276
Louv, Richard, 326–328, 432–435

Macqueen, Ken, 404–410
Magazines, 85, 86
ManyBooks.net, 77
Mapping/clustering, 30
argument, example of, 41–45
argument based on microhistory, 231–233
example of, 31
of middle-ground argument, 209–212
of Rogerian argument, 221–224
of Toulmin-based argument, 194–198
Material equivalence, 129
Mattera, Philip, 472–477
McCabe, George P., 281
McCleave Maharawal, Manissa, 456–460
Mcmillan, Tracie, 477–482
Mediation, 218
Mencken, H. L., 607–609
Meneghello, Rich, 410–412
Metaphor, example of, 177
Metaphorical definitions, 161–162
Metaphorical exploration, 177–178
Microhistory
arguments based on, 19, 206, 226–236
focus of, 226–227
local histories and, 227–229
mapping, 231–233
primary materials for, 229–230
sample of, 233–236
scope of, 226–227

subjects and materials for, 230–231
Middle-ground argument, 206, 207–216
explanation of, 17–18, 207
local models of, identification, 214
mapping, 209–212
possibilities of, recognizing, 208–209
practicality of, 207–208
student-authored, 214–216
summaries in, 207–208
Toulmin-based argument *vs.*, 207
.mil, 59
Misdirection
explanation of, 332–333
impossible situations as, 335
MLA documentation. *See also* Documentation
for articles, 629–631
for books, 626–629
explanation of, 107, 108
format for papers using, 623–624
Internet-only sources, 632–633
for interviews, 633
quoted material in original source, 98–99
for works cited page, 624
Modern Language Association (MLA), 107, 622. *See also* MLA documentation
"A Modest Proposal" (Swift), 325
Monopoly, 199
Moore, David S., 281
Moral equivalence, 129
"A Morally Bankrupt Military: When Soldiers and Their Families Become Expendable" (Jamail), 445–450
Morgan, Molly, 386–393
Movies Found Online, 72
Multimedia sources, 72–75
Multivolume works
APA documentation style for, 649
MLA documentation style for, 628
Murray, Judith Sargent, 609–613

Nagler, Michael N., 508–510
Nastasia, Isabelle, 456–460
National Archives, 72
National Criminal Justice Reference Service, 69
National Geographic Photography, 73

"Nationalize the Banks" (Rothschild), 583–587
National Opinion Research Center, 69
National Public Radio, 63
Negation, defining by, 164
Neighborhood community readings
"Bowling with Others" (Wilson), 488–495
"Crime in Virtual Worlds Is Impacting Real Life" (Guest), 466–472
"Environmental Justice for All" (Kokmen), 460–466
"Greenwashing Remains a Challenge to the Green Building Community" (Mattera), 472–477
"Jicama in the "Hood" (McMillan), 477–482
"Under Siege" (Banks), 451–456
"Why Race Matters After Sandy" (Nastasia & McCleave Maharawal), 456–460
"You Wouldn't Fit Here" (Novek), 483–488
Neighborhoods topics, 25
.net, 59
Newspapers
APA documentation style for articles in, 650–651
critically reading, 86
MLA documentation style for articles in, 631
Newsreaders, 64
The New York Public Library Digital Gallery, 73
The New York Times, 63
Non sequitur, 121–122
"North America: Ecological Breakup" (Liu & Yu), 430–431
Note taking, 84–85
and books critical reading, 90–91
and primary source evaluation, 91–92
Novek, Eleanor, 483–488
NPR, video archives, 72

Occam's razor, 116
"On the Decay of the Art of Lying" (Twain), 325–326
"On the Equality of the Sexes" (Murray), 609–613

"On Women's Right to Vote"
    (Anthony), 593–594
Opinions, 279
Opposing Viewpoints Database, 77
Opposing views, 45, 136–153
    and arguments break down, 16
    avoiding bias when summarizing,
        146–148
    avoiding generalizations when
        presenting, 139–140
    common ground, identification of,
        148–151
    in conclusions, 337–338
    correct, 330–331
    explanation of, 137
    incorrect, 330
    introduction, 329–330
    and local voices, 140–141
    and overlapping, 148–151
    overview of, 138–139
    responding to, 151–152
    in Rogerian argument, 217–219
    summarizing opponents' voices,
        141–145
    unbiased consideration of, 285
    value expertise in presenting,
        145–146
.org, 59
Other-deprecating humor, 312–313.
    See also Humor
"Outsourcing Compromises the
    Safety and Quality of Products"
    (Yang), 547–554
"Over a Barrel" (Roberts), 579–583
Overlap, 148–151
Oversimplification, 139
Overstatement, 314

Paragraphs, body, 255–257
Paraphrases
    documentation for, 101–105
    explanation of, 102
    and plagiarism, 102, 104
    second attempt at, 104
Parenthetical citation, 623
Pathos. See also Emotion
    example of, 277
    explanation of, 37, 276
    support to create, 287–290
Patriquin, Martin, 404–410
PBS, video archives, 72
PDF document, 65, 66
Peer review session
    flowchart of, 349

participation in, 348–350
"The Penalty of Death" (Mencken),
    607–609
Pence, Gregory A., 435–442
Periodical articles
    critically reading, 85–86
    evaluation of, 90
Persuasive writing
    lacking, and argument break
        down, 15
"A Petition to the President of
    the United States" (Szilard &
    Cosigners), 613–615
Pew Global Attitudes Project, 70
Photographs. See also Visual
    arguments
    to evoke emotion, 289–290
    reading methods, 302–306
    used in arguments, 279, 305–306
Photojournalism, 303–304
Physical sciences, support for,
    273–274
Plagiarism
    explanation of, 84
    guidelines to avoid, 105–107
    paraphrasing and, 102, 104
Podcast Alley, 73
Podcast Bunker, 73
Policy claim, 248
Population Reference Bureau, 70
Postel, Danny, 413–415
Post hoc fallacy, 120–121
Pot hoc, ergo propter hoc, 120–121
PowerPoint presentations, 311–312
"The Practical Ethicist: 'The Way
    We Eat' Author Peter Singer
    Explains the Advantage of
    Wingless Chickens, How
    Humans Discriminate Against
    Animals, and the Downside of
    Buying Locally Grown Food"
    (Broudy), 542–547
Precedence, explanation of, 169
Prejudice, inconsistent treatment
    and, 130
Pre-thinking methods
    brainstorming, 29–30
    freewriting, 30
    mapping, 30
Pre-writing. See Pre-thinking
    methods
"The Price of Admission" (Frank), 4
Primary causes, 165
Primary material, 229–230

Primary sources. See also Source
    materials
    evaluation of, 69, 91–92
    explanation of, 68
    government, 70–72
    multimedia, 72–75
    types of, 68–69
"Private Charity Should Replace
    Welfare" (Kelley), 573–579
Problem-based claims, 248–249
Problems
    ethical considerations related
        to, 173
    preparation and persistence to
        explore, 171–172
    understanding actual, 172
Process exploration, 174–175
Profiles in Power (Brutoco),
    393–404
Project Gutenberg, 77
Proposal claim, 248
Public Agenda Online, 69
Public memory, 227
Pulitzer Prize, 73
Purpose
    arguments matching with,
        16–19, 36
    connecting claim with, 243
    construct argument to fit, 189

Qualifiers, 34–36
    functions of, 45, 257–259
    in middle-ground argument, 212
    in Toulmin-based argument, 190,
        193, 195, 197
Quick Facts (U.S. Census Bureau), 54
Quotations, 102
    altered, 99–100
    direct, 96–98
    explanation of, 95
    guidelines for using, 95–96
    quoting materials from original
        source, 98–99

Rael, Patrick, 69
Reading, Writing, and Researching
    for History: A Guide for College
    Students (Rael), 69
Readings
    classic American arguments,
        593–620
    concerned citizen community,
        555–591
    consumer community, 520–554

family and household community readings, 418–450

neighborhood community, 451–495

school and academic community, 354–379

social/cultural community, 496–519

workplace community, 380–417

Reading strategies
for longer articles, 86–89
for material on Internet, 82–83
for research materials, 85–90

Reasons
body paragraphs around, building, 255–257
in middle-ground argument, 210–212
in Rogerian argument, 221–223
to support claim, 44, 252–254
in Toulmin-based argument, 190, 191, 194–195, 196

Rebuttals
and arguments break down, 16
functions of, 45
in Toulmin-based argument, 190, 192–193, 195, 197, 207

Red herring, 121–122

Reeves, Douglas B., 360–363

RefDesk.com, 54

Reference list, tips for writing, 646

Reference works, 54–56

"Remaking the Grade, from A to D" (Reeves), 360–363

"Reproductive Cloning Would Strengthen the American Family" (Pence), 435–442

Research
for arguments, 43
books for, 75–78
keyword queries for, 61–62
library databases for, 64–68
news sources to receive updates for, 62–64
overview of, 53
primary sources for, 68–75
topic overviews for, 54–55

Reservations, 45
audience, 267–268

Reuters, 62

Reviews
APA documentation style for, 651
MLA documentation style for, 631

Riddles, 162

Riis, Jacob, 303

Roberts, Paul, 579–583

Rogerian argument, 206, 217–226
common ground in, 217, 219–220
explanation of, 18–19, 217
mapping, 221–224
opposing views in, 217–219
sample, 224–226

Rogers, Carl, 217–218

Root-Bernstein, Michèle, 171

Root-Bernstein, Robert, 171

Rothschild, Matthew, 583–587

RSS feeds
explanation of, 64
usage, and updates for research, 62–64

Saad, Gad, 357–359

Sacred texts
APA documentation style for, 649
MLA documentation style for, 629

Sarcasm, 315

Satire, 315

Scare tactics, 126–127

The Scarlet Letter (Hawthorne), 87–88

School, topics related to, 23–24

School and academic community readings
"Are Students the New Indentured Servants?" (Williams), 341, 371–379
"Cafeteria Consciousness" (Lappé), 367–371
"For-Profit Colleges Deserve Some Respect" (Seiden), 363–367
"I'll Have Large Fries, a Hamburger, a Diet Coke, and an MBA. Hold the Pickles" (Saad), 357–359
"Remaking the Grade, from A to D" (Reeves), 360–363
"What Is the Price of Plagiarism?" (Demirjian), 354–357

Scientific definitions, 161

Scirus, 60

Search engines, 53
to access deep web, 59–61
to access surface web, 57–59
explanation of, 57
to find Internet sources, 57–61
news, 62–63

Searches
Internet, 57–61
terms, gathering, 56

Search strings, 61–62

Secondary causes
examples using, 166–168
explanation of, 166

Secondary sources. See also Source materials
explanation of, 68
types of, 69

Seiden, Michael J., 363–367

Self-deprecating humor, 312, 313. See also Humor

Shared values, identification of, 148–151

"Site UnSeen: Schools, Bosses Barred from Eyeing Students,' Workers' Social Media" (Hudson), 383–386

Slate Magazine, 63

Slippery slope argument, 117–119

The Smithsonian Institute, 73

Smyth v. Pillsbury, 55

Social community topics, 25

Social/cultural community readings
"The Cassandra Syndrome" (Nagler), 508–510
"A Humanist Looks at Polyamory" (White), 510–515
"The Importance of Political Awareness in America" (Walp), 506–508
"Killer Reflection" (Yang), 515–519
"The Potential in Hillary Clinton's Campaign for Women" (Christian Science Monitor Editorial Board), 496–497
"Why 'Security' Keeps Winning Out Over Privacy" (Solove), 497–501
"Wrong Then, Wrong Now: Racial Profiling Before & After September 11, 2001" (LCCREF), 501–506

Social sciences, support for, 274–275

Solove, Daniel J., 497–501

Solutions
communication, 179–180
creative exploration to find, 175–176
critical thinking to find, 176
ethical considerations to find, 173
evaluation, 180
historical exploration to find, 173–174
implementation of, 179

metaphorical/analogical exploration to find, 177–178
preparation and persistence to find, 171–172
process exploration to find, 174–175
proposing, exploratory steps, 170–181
selection of, 178–179
understanding problem to find, 172
"Solutions at Work: When Love Enters the Workplace" (Meneghello), 410–412
Source attribution, 92
Source materials
avoiding plagiarism, 105–107
comment on, 92–95
critically reading, 82–83, 85–90
documentation of, 84–85, 107–108
evaluation of, 81–90
method to summarize, 100–101
paraphrasing and citing paraphrases from, 101–105
quoting and citing quotations from, 95–100
taking notes from. *See* Notes taking
Sparks of Genius (Root-Bernstein), 171
Spence, Gerry, 284, 285, 314
Staircase argument, 117–119
Statistics
descriptive, 280
as facts, 279–283
functions of, 279–280
guidelines for using, 281–282
inferential, 280
Straw man arguments, 122–123
"Street Life Is No Life for Children" (Kilcher), 427–430
Summaries
bias in, 146–148
guidelines for, 100–101
in middle-ground argument, 207–208
of opponents' points of view, 141–145
Support. *See also specific types*
backing, 45
based on facts and research, 277–283
categories of, 276–277. *See also* Ethos; Logos; Pathos
for claims, 44–45

claims, reasons to, 252–254
to create credibility, 37–38, 284–287. *See also* Ethos
to create emotion, 287–290. *See also* Pathos
editing, 340–342
for education, 274–275
evaluation guidelines, 286
factual, 37
field-specific, 272–275
functions, in argument, 37–45
lack of balance in, 15
in microhistories, 231
in middle-ground argument, 212
organizing, 342–346
presentation of, 285
in Toulmin-based argument, 189–190, 191–192, 195, 196
warrant as bridge between claim and, 261–263
Surface web, search engines to access, 57–59
Surfwax, 60
Survey Research, The Writing Center at Colorado State University, 69
Suspense, 334
Swift, Jonathan, 325
Syllogism, 189
Szilard, Leo, 613–615

Target audience
argument mapping for, example of, 41–45
explanation of, 32–33
poorly defined, and argument break down, 15–16
working with, 38–45
"Telemarketers Should Be Censored" (Ebel), 523–527
Testimonials, 125
"The Potential in Hillary Clinton's Campaign for Women" (Christian Science Monitor Editorial Board), 496–497
Thesis, uses of, 321–322
Thomas, at Library of Congress, 71
Timeliness, 46–47. *See also Kairo*
Titles
strong, importance of, 347–348
Topics
choosing issues within, 27–29
explanation of, 27
finding overview material on, 54–55

of interest to specific communities, 23–26
Topix, 63
Toulmin, Stephen, 189
Toulmin-based argument, 187–202, 206
explanation of, 17
mapping, 194–198
student-authored, 198–201
terms of, 189–194. *See also* Backing; Claims; Qualifiers; Reasons; Rebuttals; Support; Warrant
vs. middle-ground argument, 207
Truth, Sojourner, 615–616
Truveo, 72
Twain, Mark, 325–326

"Under Siege" (Banks), 451–456
Understatement, 313–314
"The United States Should Adopt Open Immigration" (Binswanger), 555–559
URL, 57, 58–59
U.S. Census Bureau, 69
U.S. Library of Congress, 69
U.S. National Archives, 72
U.S. Vital Record Information, 70
The U.S. National Archives website, 71
USA Government, 71

Vaill, Peter, 340
Values
audience, 260–261
identification of shared, 148–151
Venable, Denise, 415–417
Visual arguments
advertisements as, 310–311
forms of, 295–297
graphs and charts as, 306–310
photographs and illustrations as, 302–306
PowerPoint presentations as, 311–312
understanding, 297–300
using, 297–300
Visual humor, 314–315. *See also* Humor
"Voter Suppression Returns" (Keyssar), 587–591

The Wall Street Journal, 63
Walp, Doug, 506–508

Warrant
  audience objections to, 267–268
  construction, audience and,
    260–263
  justifying claims by use of, 44, 259
  in middle-ground argument, 212
  in Toulmin-based argument, 190,
    192, 195, 196
  use of backing to support, 263–267
Washington, Booker T., 616–620
Web sites. *See also* Internet
  for multimedia resources, 72–75
  for primary research, 69–70
Wechsler Adult Intelligence Scale, 280
"What Is the Price of Plagiarism?"
    (Demirjian), 354–357
"What Should Be Done About
    Standardized Tests? A
    Freakonomics Quorum"
    (Dubner), 326
White, Valerie, 510–515
The White House website, 71
"Why Gay Marriage is so
    Controversial in America"
    (Jouet), 442–445
"Why Race Matters After Sandy"
    (Nastasia & McCleave
    Maharawal), 456–460
"Why 'Security' Keeps Winning Out
    Over Privacy" (Solove), 497–501
Wikipedia, 55, 78
Williams, Jeffrey J., 341, 371–379
Wilson, James Q., 488–495

"Women Do Not Earn Less Than Men
    Due to Gender Discrimination"
    (Venable), 415–417
Words
  absolute, 115
  attributive, 93
Workplace
  example related to, 40
  topics related to, 24
Workplace community readings
  "Abolish Corporate Personhood
    (Thinking Politically)"
    (Edwards & Morgan),
    386–393
  "The Current Business Paradigm Is
    Toxic to Business and Society.
    Here's How We Change It."
    (Brutoco & Yau), 393–404
  "Dealing with the Stressed:
    Workplace Stress Costs
    the Economy More Than
    $30 Billion a Year, and Yet
    Nobody Knows What It
    Is or How to Deal with It"
    (MacQueen, Patriquin, &
    Intini), 404–410
  "Employee-Owned Businesses
    Ignored by Mainstream
    Media" (Alperovitz & Bhatt),
    380–382
  "I'm Not Dangerous" (Postel),
    413–415

  "Site UnSeen: Schools, Bosses
    Barred from Eyeing Students',
    Workers' Social Media"
    (Hudson), 383–386
  "Solutions at Work: When Love
    Enters the Workplace"
    (Meneghello), 410–412
  "Women Do Not Earn Less
    Than Men Due to Gender
    Discrimination" (Venable),
    415–417
Works Cited page
  explanation of, 96
  guidelines for, 624
World Factbook (CIA), 54
Writing Without Teachers (Elbow), 30
"Wrong Then, Wrong Now: Racial
    Profiling Before & After
    September 11, 2001" (LCCREF),
    501–506

Yahoo!, 57, 59, 63
Yang, Dali L., 547–554
Yang, Jeff, 515–519
Yau, Sam, 393–404
"You Wouldn't Fit Here" (Novek),
    483–488
Yu, Eunice, 431